AA Command

Also available from Methuen
in the series *Monuments of War* by Colin Dobinson

Fields of Deception: Britain's bombing decoys of World War II

AA
Command

Britain's anti-aircraft defences
of World War II

Colin Dobinson

Methuen

Published by Methuen 2001

1 3 5 7 9 10 8 6 4 2

This edition published in Great Britain in 2001 by
Methuen Publishing Ltd
215 Vauxhall Bridge Rd, London SW1V 1EJ

Methuen Publishing Ltd Reg. No. 3543167

A CIP catalogue record for this book
is available from the British Library

ISBN 0 413 76540 7

Typeset in by SX Composing DTP, Rayleigh, Essex

Printed and bound in Great Britain by
St Edmundsbury Press Ltd, Bury St Edmunds, Suffolk

Contents

Appendices

Foreword

This is the second in a series of books arising from English Heritage's assessment of Second World War military remains. Since the 1970s, and especially over the past decade, public concern for the future of these sites and structures has grown significantly. English Heritage is proud to have led the way in developing our knowledge of them and securing protection for a selection of the most important.

The *Monuments of War* series will cover all of the major monument classes from this period, beginning with four books on defences against aerial bombing. In addition to this study of anti-aircraft artillery, bombing decoys – built to deceive the enemy and detract from intended targets – were the subject of *Fields of Deception*, published in 2000. Radar will be the third title in the series, and civil defence the fourth. These books offer much new material, and a novel approach, setting the evolution of Britain's twentieth-century fortifications in their historical context but also – often for the first time – exploring in depth their design and developing geography.

The studies originate in work commissioned by English Heritage's Monuments Protection Programme, a national review of England's archaeological resources, started in 1986 and due for completion around 2010. Central to English Heritage's statutory duties are the promotion of public enjoyment and understanding of the historic environment, and its appropriate and adequate protection. In the case of Second World War remains, our work has involved a three-stage process: first, extensive original research to establish what was built, where, when and why; second, protecting a sample of surviving sites, selected on the basis of their rarity, typicality and survival quality; and third, disseminating the results of this work to a wide audience. This last is arguably the most important element, since continuing public sympathy is an essential prerequisite to assure the long-term future of our monuments of war.

Sir Neil Cossons
Chairman, English Heritage

Preface

THE MONUMENTS OF WAR

This book has two complementary aims: first to present a new study of Britain's anti-aircraft artillery defences on the 'Home Front' during the Second World War, and secondly to demonstrate the rationale for preserving a selection of wartime AA batteries as historical monuments. The first of those is unremarkable in itself. Though much has been written about the domestic air campaigns of World War II, no detailed history of AA defence from 1939 to 1945 has yet appeared. Britain's wartime air defences were a complex and interdependent system, but while we can read a great deal about fighters, much about radar and – recently – even some words on the role of decoy targets,[1] too little has been written about the work of Anti-Aircraft Command. A corrective is overdue.

The second aim, however, may provoke some surprise – especially since it is not a mere subsidiary interest, but supplies the motivating force behind both this book and the series to which it belongs. As Sir Neil Cossons explains in the Foreword, the *Monuments of War* series is sponsored by English Heritage's Monuments Protection Programme (MPP): a long-term project designed to increase understanding and awareness of England's archaeological heritage, a by-product of which is a growing number of ancient and historical sites protected by statute. That brief, naturally, embraces a diverse range of familiar places: prehistoric, Roman and medieval remains, as well as the monuments of industry and others of recent centuries. But in the early 1990s MPP extended its scope to twentieth-century military sites, building upon an active interest in these places previously expressed by several independent research groups, and in response to a degree of public pressure to 'save' specific examples which periodically came under threat.

In this English Heritage was not alone. The belief that wartime remains merit protection is common to all four heritage agencies in the United Kingdom responsible for such matters; colleagues at Cadw in Wales, Historic Scotland and the Department of the Environment (Northern Ireland) share a strong community of purpose. In England, MPP advises government on the selection of sites for preservation under the Ancient Monuments and Archaeological Areas Act, a process known commonly as scheduling. Scheduling is not undertaken lightly, nor is it comprehensive. Instead it must be carefully justified, first by demonstrating the 'national importance' of sites recommended for protection, and second by assessing the site's future management needs. Determining national importance requires secure knowledge rooted in academic research, and to identify the physical characteristics of specific types of sites, and their patterning across the landscape, likewise demands study of a range of sources, historical and archaeological. Before we can begin to weigh the importance of any given class of wartime site we need to understand what was built, where, and why.

Approaching these questions for twentieth-century military sites produced some surprises. The historiography of the Second World War reaches back half a century, fifty years in which the war in most of its aspects has been narrated in thousands of books, billions of words. But despite a recent growth of interest in warfare as an exploiter of land, surprisingly little has been written about the evolving designs and patterning of Second World War fortifications. Histories of Britain's war on the home front naturally discuss the aggregate functions of these places in campaigns – radar's role in the Battle of Britain, anti-aircraft gunnery in the Blitz, and so on – but study of defence sites as *places* has generally been overlooked. There is a huge gap in our knowledge of Britain's wartime defence geography – where, exactly, were the AA batteries? How many were built? How did their patterning change over time, and why? Likewise little had been written about the structural characteristics of defence sites – how were AA batteries designed? How did their fabric evolve in the light of developing operational experience and technical change? Important as these questions surely are, the reader will search in vain for answers in most mainstream writing on the Second World War.

For this there are good reasons, many of them rooted in the practicalities of research. It is surprisingly difficult to compile definitive gazetteers of defence sites in many categories, at least at a level accurate enough to allow meaningful maps to be drawn and the positions revisited on the ground today. For some types of site the exercise is discouraged by sheer weight of numbers – air raid shelters, for example, can be counted in the hundreds of thousands – but a larger obstacle lies in the nature of the sources. During the Second World War the locations of defence sites in most categories were routinely recorded in official documents by grid references, taken to six figures and accurate to 100 metres. These records have generally survived.[2] Information on that scale is perfectly good for our purposes, but its handling is hampered by three problems. First, the records are often scattered. Few types of site had their positions committed to national 'master' lists, but instead were logged in the records of their occupying units, by the formations to which those were answerable, and by regional headquarters. Often a great many documents must be mined to fill out the national picture. These sources are not always easy to identify, nor were they compiled to a consistent format, and most refer only to a point-in-time: reconstructing change in the pattern multiplies the sources to be consulted many times over. Third, this research yields grid references which, frustratingly, are cartographically obsolete. Since wartime Ordnance Survey maps for England, Scotland and Wales used a different projection and grid from their modern equivalents,[3] the discovered grid references must be 'converted' to be compatible with current maps. For various technical reasons this cannot, at present, be reliably achieved by automated means. Each reference must be transformed manually, by direct comparison between the wartime and the modern map.

So the work necessary to reconstruct Britain's defence geography is prodigious – but, for many categories, it is now complete. English Heritage has sponsored this study within England, and more recently cover has been extended to the remainder of the UK in a companion project sponsored by Cadw, the Royal Commission on the Ancient and Historical Monuments of Scotland and DoE (Northern Ireland).[4] In result, for the first time, we now have a near-comprehensive national map of sites in many categories, and at least broad understanding of how and why that map changed over time. In common with most of its companion volumes, this book concludes with a gazetteer showing site locations by modern six-figure grid references. Though originally compiled to serve the needs of heritage management, the benefits of these data to more traditional historical study need hardly be laboured. Britain's wartime landscape has been rediscovered, its tactical maps redrawn.

A second strand of this work is a study of sites as places. Recovering the principles which shaped their design and fabric over time is, in many ways, simpler than building distribution maps, for sources are numerous and usually near to hand. Military manuals take us part of the way, though these need to be read in conjunction with the stream of orders issuing from headquarters modifying scriptural authority in the light of evolving battle experience. More formally-constructed defence works (permanent anti-aircraft batteries among them) conformed to designs issued by central drawing offices within the service ministries, which for army sites was the Directorate of Fortifications and Works at the War Office. DFW's original design drawings, where discoverable, offer the surest guide to the functions and chronology of site layouts and buildings. In common with all sources bearing upon fabric, these can be verified against the evidence of surviving structures on the ground.

These two strands of research – the study of location, and of form – allow us to get a grip upon the character of defence sites, to answer the 'what' and 'where' questions necessary to inform preservation decisions. The 'why' question, in the forms 'why were these sites built?' and 'why are they important?', brings us back to the issue of national significance. For anti-aircraft batteries, as we shall see, that rests upon many considerations: their value in defeating the Luftwaffe; their testimony to the evolving strategy, tactics and science of air defence artillery; and their position in the social and cultural context of twentieth-century conflict. The approach taken in this volume, in common with the *Monuments of War* series in general, is to explore the evolving pattern of sites as part of the weave of wartime history, which in our case means the history of AA Command.

This is not the first account of AA Command's war. That distinction rests with the spirited memoir published in 1949 by General Sir Frederick Pile,[5] its General Officer Commanding-in-Chief from 1939 to 1945, which in turn drew heavily upon his own official *Dispatch* on operations and several unpublished historical studies drafted within the War Office and Cabinet Office.[6] Though published over twenty years ago, Ian Hogg's wider-ranging book *Anti-Aircraft* remains indispensable, likewise two more recent studies by Brigadier N W Routledge in the *History of the Royal Regiment of Artillery* series.[7] Other recent writings include memoirs and histories devoted to the role of ATS women soldiers in Britain's AA defence – a theme which brings wartime experience directly to bear on a pressing contemporary question.[8] None of these studies, however, was intended to explore the issues of structures and defence geography which form a continuous theme here, and nor do many (except Pile's, obliquely) draw much upon the mass of primary AA Command records to be found in the Public Record Office and elsewhere – sources which are too often overlooked in research on the larger history of domestic air campaigns, notably the Battle of Britain and the Blitz.

In those campaigns, as in others, AA Command's war was predominantly a war of compromise: a war against the Luftwaffe in counterpoint to another against an abiding deficit in weapons, manpower, amenities and equipment. That unhappy state of affairs was a legacy from the inter-war period, and to understand how it came about our account begins not in 1939, but much earlier, in the formative era of air defence thinking in the years around 1910. It was in this period that a central question emerged: if the bombers came, would guns or other flying machines prove the better means of persuading them to cease? The issue recurred in one form or another for the next thirty years. During the First World War a barrack-room joke held that of the three most useless things in the world, one was the anti-aircraft gun. By 1918 that jibe had not entirely lost its force, and in an inter-war climate in which the bomber deterrent took primacy over more literally 'defensive' forms of armament, Britain's relative under-investment in fighters was surpassed only by its neglect of AA artillery. The account of the years from 1910 to 1939 in what follows is largely a study of policy and its origin in developing expertise, rather than sites or structures; but exploring that policy is critical to understanding why Britain's AA defences entered the Second World War in the form that they did.

In that war, the subject of the book's central section, AA Command fought three big battles and a series of lesser campaigns. In two of them – the day fighting of summer 1940 and the night attacks of the following winter – it was unprepared. The Battle of Britain was not the gunners' finest hour. 'Their main contribution came later,' wrote Churchill, and left it at that.[9] But by 'later' Churchill did not mean the Blitz of 1940–41, which found AA Command struggling to keep pace. It was during the Blitz that the legacy of the thirties really began to tell. Inadequate stocks of guns were stretched drum-tight over a nation of cities, as first London was bombed and then Coventry, Birmingham, Liverpool, Manchester, Portsmouth, Southampton – it is a long list. But in its last great battle, against the flying bombs in 1944–45, AA Command was ready as never before, and triumphed despite eventually being forced into tactical situations undreamt of before the first V1s began to fall. Though it is not neglected here, the story of AA Command's battle against the flying bomb – Operation *Diver* – will be told in much greater detail in a later volume in this series. The *Diver* operation was a small war in its own right, producing a separate pattern of sites and structures and a landscape legacy all of its own.

It is right that this story and its legacy should be more widely known. AA Command was the only branch of the British army based at home to be in action continuously throughout the war: in the five and a half years from September 1939 to May 1945 there were very few nights and days on which an AA gun was not firing at something, somewhere. Its soldiers in their hundreds of thousands occupied sites from the Shetlands to Cornwall, from East Anglia to Ulster. If we include every searchlight position, every heavy and light gun battery, every anti-aircraft rocket site, the number of places where AA troops were stationed would number tens of thousands; the gazetteer of heavy AA batteries given here alone reaches almost 1200. Everyone in wartime Britain knew an AA site. Some still remember them. A few, remarkably, survive intact. What follows is an attempt to show what they were, what they did, and why their future matters as much as their past. To borrow AA Command's own title for this book is meant as a tribute, however much its author may fear an impertinence.

This book is the work of one author but, in many ways, of six people. Naomi Tummons and Geoff Harrison acted successively as research assistants for the original project from which the

Monuments of War series stems, from 1995 to 1997 handling the cartographic work on English site locations which appears in Appendix IV. Neil Redfern extended this work to the remainder of the United Kingdom in 1997–98, both by processing data and by undertaking a large body of original research.[10] Follow-on work to investigate site survival was undertaken by Michael J Anderton, then of English Heritage's Aerial Survey Team at the NMR, Swindon (as described in Chapter 12); in doing so Mike identified most of the aerial photographs which appear in these pages. I owe a particular debt to Allan T Adams of English Heritage, illustrator to the *Monuments of War* series, for the excellence of draftsmanship which adds so much to the book's exposition.

Research among primary sources was undertaken largely at the Public Record Office, Kew, and in secondary materials at the Cambridge University Library, to both of whose staff I owe thanks. Further assistance was given by the Royal Engineers' Institute, the Royal Artillery Institute, and the Imperial War Museum. Within English Heritage the project was overseen for the Monuments Protection Programme by Dr John Schofield, while Jeremy Lake represented the interests of the Listing Team. For their support throughout I also owe debts to Dr Geoffrey Wainwright (formerly Chief Archaeologist), Graham Fairclough (head of MPP) and Val Horsler (Publications Branch). I am additionally most grateful to Sir Neil Cossons, Chairman of English Heritage, for contributing the Foreword. Others who assisted in various ways were Carol Pyrah and Fred Nash, together with Max Eilenberg, Eleanor Rees and Nicky Pearce at Methuen. To the Imperial War Museum, the National Monuments Record, Mr D S Holmes and Roger Thomas I offer thanks for permission to reproduce the plates. Lastly, I join with English Heritage in expressing warm thanks to the Royal Commission on the Ancient and Historical Monuments of Scotland, Cadw (Welsh Historic Monuments) and DoE (Northern Ireland) for authority to publish the results of the research which, under their sponsorship, extended the geographical scope of this study to the remainder of the United Kingdom.

Colin Dobinson
North Yorkshire
July 2001

List of figures

List of plates

List of Abbreviations

AA	Anti-aircraft
AADC	Anti-aircraft defence command
AAMG	Anti-aircraft machine-gun
ADGB	Air Defence(s) of Great Britain
ADRDE	Air Defence Research and Development Establishment
AFZ	Aircraft Fighting Zone
AI	Airborne interception (radar)
AORG	Army Operational Research Group
ARP	Air Raid Precautions
ATS	Auxiliary Territorial Service
AWAS	Air Warfare Analysis Section
BEF	British Expeditionary Force
BHQ	Battery headquarters
CA	Coast Artillery
CAS	Chief of the Air Staff
CH	Chain home (radar)
CHL	Chain home low (radar)
CID	Committee of Imperial Defence
CRE	Commanding Royal Engineer
DFW	Director(ate) of Fortifications and Works
DoE	Department of the Environment
EAM	Equipment ammunition magazine
E/F	Elevation-finding (attachment)
ETOUSA	European Theatre of Operations United States Army
FA	Fixed Azimuth (system)
GCI	Ground controlled interception (radar)
GDA	Gun Defended Area
GHQ	General Headquarters
GL	Gun-laying (radar)
GOC	General Officer Commanding
GOR	Gun operations room
GPO	General Post Office *or* gun position officer
HAA	Heavy anti-aircraft (artillery)
HE	High explosive
HMB	Height meaning board
HMS	His Majesty's Ship
HP	Horsepower
IAZ	Inner Artillery Zone
ICI	Imperial Chemical Industries
IFF	Identification friend or foe

JIC	Joint Intelligence Committee
LAA	Light anti-aircraft (artillery)
LADA	London Air Defence Area
LMG	Light machine-gun
MAP	Ministry of Aircraft Production
MOWP	Ministry of Works and Planning
MPP	Monuments Protection Programme
NAAFI	Navy, Army and Air Force Institute
NAD	Northern Air Defences
NCO	Non-commissioned officer
NMR	National Monuments Record
OAZ	Outer Artillery Zone
ORG	Operational Research Group
OSDEF	Orkney and Shetland Defences
PPI	Plan position indicator
pdr	pounder (as in 12pdr)
QF	Quick-firing
RA	Royal Artillery
RAE	Royal Aircraft Establishment
RAF	Royal Air Force
RAOC	Royal Army Ordnance Corps
RE	Royal Engineers
RFC	Royal Flying Corps
RGA	Royal Garrison Artillery
RNAS	Royal Naval Air Service
RNVR	Royal Naval Volunteer Reserve
ROC	Royal Observer Corps
RUSI	Royal United Services Institute (for Defence Studies)
SAGW	Surface-to-air guided weapon
SAP	Semi-automatic plotter
SHAEF	Supreme Headquarters Allied Expeditionary Force
SIS	Secret Intelligence Service
SLC	Searchlight control (radar)
TA	Territorial Army
TF	Territorial Force
TI	Target indicator
UP	Unrotated projectile
VIE	Visual identification instruments
USAAF	United States Army Air Force
VP	Vital (later Vulnerable) Point
WRVS	Women's Royal Voluntary Service
ZAA	Rocket anti-aircraft (artillery)

PART I

Preludes

CHAPTER 1

Dark arts

1909 – 1918

One Thursday afternoon early in November 1909 an audience of soldiers and lay people gathered at Woolwich to hear the latest in the Royal Artillery Institution's programme of lectures. Rising to introduce their speaker, the chairman of the proceedings, Major-General H E Belfield, was struck by the size of the audience before him – the largest, as he told them, that he had ever seen in that room. The draw for such a large crowd was already an established figure on the military lecture circuit. Neat, alert, genial, and in his mid forties, the Royal Engineer colonel who mounted the podium on that Thursday afternoon was one of Britain's leading pioneers in the science of manned flight. John Capper was his name: an acquaintance of the Wright brothers, colleague of Samuel Cody, and since May 1906 head of the RE Balloon School at South Farnborough. As Capper ordered his papers and called for the first lantern slide, the audience settled to hear his latest dispatch on 'the military aspect of dirigible balloons and aeroplanes'.[1]

Ranged before Capper on that afternoon were many officers whose professional interests were already turning towards this exciting dimension of military affairs. Few of those needed reminding of the extraordinary progress in recent years. In itself, military flying was not new. Reconnaissance balloons had been used over the battlefield since the late eighteenth century, entering service with the British army in the 1870s, when the RE's balloon establishment had come together briefly at Woolwich before moving in turn to Chatham, Aldershot and then, in 1905, to nearby Farnborough. But by 1909 captive balloons were an obsolescent technology, cast to the sidelines by advances in navigable balloons – airships – whose viability had been demonstrated by French engineers in the closing decades of the nineteenth century and hardened in the first years of the twentieth by the Germans, and notably by Count Zeppelin. By that time, too, the world had the aeroplane – or rather America had the Wrights, who had first flown in 1903, and France was home to a variety of colourful characters, among whom one Santos Dumont had been the first man in Europe to fly a heavier than air machine, in 1906. In the three years following, Germany and France had consolidated their lead in Europe's aviation race. By 1909 the latest Zeppelins could carry twelve people at 35 miles per hour, reaching 6000 feet and commanding a range of 700 miles and an endurance of about eighteen hours. Performance of this distinction meant that the airship, for a time, appeared the more promising vehicle for manned flight, but public demonstrations by the Wrights in France during 1908 and Louis Blériot's dramatic Channel crossing in July of that year showed that the aeroplane, too, was coming of age. And in all of this, despite the advocacy of pressure groups and influential men – notably the press baron Lord Northcliffe – Britain lagged far behind. Britain's first military airship, the little *Nulli Secundus*, made her maiden flight from the broad plain of Farnborough Common as late as autumn 1907. A year or so later British Army Aeroplane Number One lifted from the same turf, with the American Samuel Cody at the controls (such as they were), covering a short track before crashing into a clump of trees. With these achievements behind them Britain's military fliers could at least claim to have entered the aviation race, but the technical contrast between British and German airships could not have been greater. The *Nulli Secundus* was a tiny, non-rigid vessel – unlike the Zeppelins, which were 'rigids', with a self-supporting internal framework – and in this sense was not much more than an elongated balloon with an engine.

Along with Cody, Colonel Capper was a prime mover in these tentative experiments at Farnborough; and Capper, naturally, was a key expert witness to the committee of inquiry on aerial navigation which Britain's Committee of Imperial Defence (CID) set up in November 1908, just a year before his Woolwich lecture, under the chairmanship of Lord Esher. The Aerial Navigation Committee met regularly in the CID's rooms in Whitehall, quizzed a legion of experts, and at the end of January 1909 delivered an unusually bulky and thorough report.[2] The Esher report, however, was hardly the spur to new developments which many of its readers had wished. In the year during which H G Wells published *War in the Air* – the most famous exemplar of an Edwardian literary genre foretelling doom from the skies – the Esher Committee's official futurology was in some respects no less fanciful. Esher's committee thought the future of aviation belonged to the airship, and recommended that continuing British research should be supported by a modest vote of public funds. On the potential of the aeroplane, this group of (mostly) clever and worldly men found itself unable to agree 'whether great improvements may be expected in the immediate future' or if 'the limit of practical utility may have already been nearly attained.' That last judgement could not have been more wrong, and the resulting suspension of official aeroplane research at Farnborough, albeit temporarily, was perhaps the inquiry's most baleful outcome. But easily overlooked in the body of the report was a shrewd aside: the aeroplane, advised Esher, would be 'peculiarly difficult to destroy while in flight'.[3]

In that single sentence the Esher Committee anticipated one of the defining constants of twentieth-century warfare. Ten months on, Capper's talk at Woolwich in November 1909 affirmed that view; and the fact that Capper was led to discuss methods of *destroying* airships and aeroplanes, rather than simply making and flying them, was very much a symptom of the time. By 1909 Britain had been seized by what some historians have characterised as an 'airship panic' – a widespread feeling, fuelled by a large body of futuristic novels[4], and given focus by the expansion of the German air fleet and the web of international tensions which, five years hence, would unleash the First World War. Speaking on his aeronautical work at Chatham in 1908, Capper had covered the specifically military applications of airships merely in a few concluding remarks.[5] Less than a year later his Woolwich talk was a disquisition on air wars and air defence.

So on that November afternoon at Woolwich Capper, not for the first time, contributed to a debate with two closely-related themes: first, whether the dirigible airship or the aeroplane was likely to claim primacy in military aviation, and in what role or roles; and second, how hostile aircraft of whatever type could be guarded against. Both issues provoked a plurality of views. By the autumn of 1909 most agreed that airships and aeroplanes alike would revolutionise military reconnaissance. Some consensus, too, attached to the view that airships, with their rising payloads, would emerge as formidable vehicles of bombardment, even if the technicalities of bomb delivery had yet to be worked out. A few commentators also believed that airships acting *en masse* might deliver an invading army, though many were sceptical about this, and rightly so. But on the question of counter-measures there was no consensus, even if the basic options were starting to emerge. Some said that hostile airships and aeroplanes might best be fought off with other aircraft. Others believed that ground-based artillery would claim the greater role. And there were those, already by 1909, who were starting to suspect that only offensive action against the bases of hostile air fleets would secure command of the skies. The relative merits of these three modes of air defence – which emerged as the fighter aircraft, the anti-aircraft gun, and the bomber deterrent – would be debated for decades to come.

That Britain would enter the First World War with a thin and inefficient layout of anti-aircraft guns owed much to the dominance of an emerging 'fighter' lobby in the five years before hostilities were joined. Among this group Capper had the appearance of a senior master. In his Woolwich talk Capper suggested that reconnaissance airships might be of two types: larger vessels gathering strategic intelligence, flying high – at, say, 5000 or 6000 feet – and smaller variants operating lower down to study tactical dispositions. Capper was pessimistic over the value of ground fire against higher-flying vessels, since small-arms would be practically useless and while some specialised guns had been developed to work against balloons, it would be 'impossible', he said, 'to keep batteries of artillery, or even single guns, scattered all over the country with gun crews ready and prepared for instant action, for perhaps weeks together, waiting for the possible advent of an airship, which will only present a target for a very short period of time.'[6] Mobile guns were a stronger possibility, but even these would be hampered by the idiosyncrasies of the road network through which they would have to chase their prey. More could be expected of ground fire against lower-flying airships operating tactically over a battlefield, since many weapons would be on hand to engage, but in general Capper was not enthusiastic over the value of land-based anti-aircraft fire against dirigibles, whether in their reconnaissance or more vaguely-conceived bombing role. Capper's preference, in 1909, was for guns mounted on defending airships, or on aeroplanes – in other words (though the term would not be coined for some years) for fighter aircraft.

If airships were a challenging target, Capper was even more pessimistic over the chances of destroying an aeroplane by fire from the ground. 'It is extraordinarily invulnerable,' he declared. 'The sustaining surfaces may be pierced with many holes without seriously affecting its flight, and some of its main frames may be bruised or even shattered, without involving its destruction, whilst its small size and high rate of travel will render it a very difficult mark to any artillery.'[7] (Difficult indeed: a few months later an artillery officer compared a Blériot machine flying at 4000 feet to 'a midge'.[8]) One compensation was that aeroplanes could not, in 1909, carry much in the way of payload for bombing, though this was cancelled to some extent by their relative cheapness and ease of manufacture, meaning that aeroplanes might be expected in numbers, when airships might operate only in ones and twos. And the aeroplane, as Capper took pains to point out, was a fast-developing technology. The day was not far off when high-flying machines would be available as reliable bomb-droppers and platforms for reconnaissance. The aeroplane, said Capper, 'again must be fought in its own element – the air'.[9]

Despite Capper's pessimism over the value of guns against aerial targets – or possibly as a corrective to it – the RA Institution attempted to stimulate debate in 1910 by inviting further expert contributions. So it came about that in the next two years the challenges posed by the nascent science of anti-aircraft artillery achieved a thorough airing.[10] There were indeed huge technical problems to be overcome. By 1910 the art of shooting at targets in the air was not new in itself. Guns had been swung upward to engage reconnaissance balloons almost as soon as they appeared over a battlefield – the first, reportedly, were a pair of seventeen-pounder howitzers which in June 1794 the Austrians brought to bear on French reconnaissance balloons spying on their movements at Maubeuge[11] – and by the end of the nineteenth century some manufacturers had developed specialised 'balloon guns', notably Krupps in Germany, who produced a pedestal-mounted 25mm rifle riding on a light cart.[12] But weapons such as this were specialised chiefly in the sense of being mobile, and adapted to fire upwards at targets which were practically sitting ducks. The increasingly high-flying and mobile targets offered by airships and aeroplanes were a wholly different proposition from the static gasbags of the nineteenth century, and offered an artillery problem all of their own.

As we might expect it was the Germans, masters of the airship, who developed the first recognisably-modern AA guns. Since producing their balloon gun Krupps had persisted with work on high-angle weapons, and at the Frankfurt Exhibition of 1909 they and the Ehrhardt firm both showed purpose-built mobile guns specifically designed to engage dirigibles and aeroplanes. One attentive visitor to their stands was Colonel F G Stone of the Royal Artillery, who published an article in the same volume of the RA Institution's *Journal* which carried Capper's lecture.[13] In it, Stone illustrated some impressively modernistic-looking ordnance – Krupp's 12pdr high-angle gun for mounting on a motor lorry, the 40pdr on a fixed pedestal for ship-board use, Erhardt's similarly-mounted 5cm balloon gun – none of which had any practical counterparts in Britain. He also revealed that Krupps had developed a special kind of percussion-fuzed ammunition to shoot down an airship.

Stone's discussion of the new German ammunition empha-sised the point that developing purpose-built anti-aircraft artillery involved far more than simply angling a gun toward the sky and aiming it. The basic choice offered by existing technology was between high explosive (HE) ammunition, which relied for its effects upon blast, and shrapnel, which did its work by disgorging numerous small pellets, rather like a shotgun or a volley of rifle fire: used against an airship, HE would pulverise, or so it was thought, and shrapnel would pierce. Either shell could in principle be impact-fuzed – to detonate on contact – or time-fuzed, that is exploded on the basis of elapsed time from firing, and in either case it was also desirable to have some means of tracing the trajectory of the shot visually, to correct aim. No combination of these methods, however, was self-evidently suitable for AA work. By 1910 German experiments had proved that balloon envelopes were surprisingly resilient to small-arms fire, suggesting that airships were unlikely to be much troubled by shrapnel. High-explosive might yield a greater lethal effect – though there were those who doubted this – as well as easing the danger to those on the ground from falling shrapnel, but this type of round needed precise placing and was attended by many risks. This raised the fuzing question, which by itself presented ordnance engineers with an unprecedented problem. Even assuming that an airship could be hit, its skin would offer such slight resistance to the shell that an impact fuze of great sensitivity would be needed to detonate the charge; but a sensitive fuze would be unstable, and prone to exploding in the gun barrel under the sudden stress of firing, with calamitous results for a high-explosive shell. A time fuze would be safer, but brought many technical complexities in sighting and setting. Working on the basis of the elapsed time from leaving the gun, time-fuzed shells were set to detonate at or near their objective. To identify the required fuze-length the gunners needed precise information on the range of the target from their barrels – the range, that is, in point-to-point distance – which with a known shell velocity would yield the time of flight. But this essential information could be discovered only with delicate optical instruments and to complicate matters further the velocity of the shell was affected by several variables, such as variations in air density with height and barometric pressure. And even when these problems were resolved, the shell had to be launched on a trajectory calculated to intercept the target on its passage through the sky; aiming directly at a moving airship or aeroplane would place the explosion merely where the machine had been when the gun was fired. The challenges of refining height and range-finding, and of 'prediction', as it came to be called, would face AA gunners in perpetuity.

German ordnance engineers tried several solutions to these problems and as the twentieth century entered its second decade so too did their counterparts in France, Britain and elsewhere. The Krupps ammunition developed by 1909 relied upon an impact-fuzed shell using an incendiary compound, which erupted into an 'intensely hot flame' which would consume an airship's envelope by fire. This same shell was fitted with a time-fuzed smoke-generating substance, which began to activate as the round neared its target to allow correction of aim.[14] In Britain the problem was studied by the Ordnance Board, which concluded as a basis for experiment that anti-aircraft guns might rely either on a fast-firing, small calibre technology using impact fuzes, or alternatively on bigger weapons using shrapnel or high explosive detonated by a time fuze. The time fuze, in fact, eventually became the mainstay of shell design, though the first high-explosive ammunition was not fired in British AA defence until October 1915, and then, as we shall see, from a French weapon.

Definitive solutions to these problems lay in the future as the first generation of purpose-built AA guns were tested in the years before the First World War. Following the German successes, in 1910 French engineers produced their first balloon gun, an adaptation of their well-tried 75mm artillery piece; later known as the auto-cannon, this very successful weapon would play an important and unexpected role in the defence of London. In Britain Vickers-Maxim produced a 3pdr weapon, whose shell size unfortunately seems to have been unequal to its task.[15] In common with most pre-war designs these weapons were mobile in the sense of being mounted on vehicles, reflecting assumptions about the nature of air attack which were so obvious at the time as to be seldom laboured in print. One assumption was that machines would approach at a pace which, rapid as it may have seemed by the standards of the day, was in reality leisurely enough to leave time for guns to be moved out to meet them. Another was that hostile operations would be sufficiently low in intensity to make dense layouts of fixed AA weapons uneconomic – a point which Capper had made forcefully in his lecture of November 1909. But when it was considered in depth, the choice between mobile and static guns, or a combination of the two, raised a suite of problems all of its own. Prime among those was the selection of targets warranting defence.

Among the many questions debated in lecture theatres and Whitehall offices in the years before the Great War was the range of places which a hostile air power – in effect, Germany – might attack in the event of war. Military installations, naturally, were seen as the most likely candidates, though precisely which categories from the huge panorama of vulnerable points were in question was a moot point. In his Woolwich talk of November 1909 Capper suggested that at night, 'when airships can keep low down' (thinking themselves immune to ground fire):

[. . .] they could be used with deadly effect on transports, and with considerable power of destruction on bridges, dock gates, arsenals, &c, whilst incendiary bombs may play havoc in supply depôts and stores, and airships so used would cause both moral and material distress to camps, bivouacs and horses, and undoubtedly would harass, by the need for constant watchfulness, posts on the lines of communication and at places far away from the field army.[16]

That was a pretty comprehensive list, typical of those advanced by other speakers of the time,[17] and one whose very diversity tended to support Capper's preference for the flexibility offered by aeroplanes and airships, rather than guns. But not all of these places could be protected at once, either by aircraft or guns, and within this enormous range of possibilities – from destroying magazines to frightening the horses – it was clearly necessary to define some order of priority.

The Admiralty was the first government department to do so. On 4 January 1910, just weeks after Capper's Woolwich talk, a select group of officers of the Naval Intelligence Department gathered to discuss the latest developments in foreign airships and to consider what measures were needed, if any, to protect naval targets against them. Early in their deliberations the group articulated the issues concisely.

It is well known [they reported] that Foreign Powers have for a long time been devoting considerable attention to airship construction and that in knowledge and experience of their capabilities they are at present ahead of us. Germany in particular possesses already a powerful squadron of airships

(7 military, 3 private) and in addition, has several under construction (8 military, 7 private). The military airships are manned by a specially organised Balloon Corps whose whole time is devoted to perfecting their manoeuvring power and extending their utility for fighting purposes. Further, the recent tests made with Zeppelins and other German airships of smaller size show that, so far as distance is concerned, under favourable conditions they are quite capable of reaching this country.

It is unnecessary to emphasise the paralysing effect which the destruction of our cordite factories, of which there are only a limited number, and magazines, would have on the action of the Navy especially, if, as is probable, it took place on or before the outbreak of war. Moreover, the majority of such factories etc are in the neighbourhood of London or in more or less exposed positions near the Thames estuary.

Under the circumstances, it is considered that the possibility of overhead attack on vulnerable points [. . .] cannot be neglected and that early steps should be taken to provide some form of defence to meet it. This is all the more important because special forms of guns, projectiles and fuzes will have to be designed for the purpose, experiments abroad having shown that unless the envelope can be destroyed by the explosion of the gas inside it the airship will not be brought rapidly to the ground.[18]

In these officers' view the threat from the airship rested less on its value in dropping bombs than on its capacity to carry light guns firing high-explosive or incendiary projectiles. Airships, they felt, were so unwieldy and difficult to manoeuvre that bomb-dropping on anything but the largest targets – say dockyards – 'at present need hardly be considered'; more worrisome was the effect on a cordite factory or magazine of the detonation of even a small explosive bullet. That was a misjudgement, and so too was their belief – which they shared with Capper – that airships were best met with other airships. But in other respects the naval group got to the point: from now on, the aerial dimension could never be neglected in defending naval magazines and cordite factories, which must be guarded by guns, aeroplanes or airships, and ideally too by structural means, with earth or armour protection for their roofs. A new era of ground defence, no less than of military architecture, was poised to begin.

But it did not do so for a while yet, at least as far as the 'active' defences were concerned. Although the matter was referred to the Home Ports Defence Committee later in the year,[19] this body concluded merely that airship attacks 'should be regarded as *possible* operations of war', and seems to have been reassured by Capper's view that aeroplanes were likely in time to make practical anti-Zeppelin interceptors.[20] At that, the matter was allowed to rest until May 1912, the month in which the Royal Flying Corps was constituted, when the Admiralty was finally able to confirm to the CID that arrangements had been made between themselves and the War Office to equip ships with 3in semi-automatic guns and to provide a 4in weapon for land use. The land allocation of anti-aircraft weapons, however, was not discussed in detail until 6 August, when a meeting was held at the Admiralty to examine AA protection for the naval magazines at Chattenden and Lodge Hill, to the north of Chatham.[21]

Held two years almost to the day before Britain entered the First World War, this conference appears to have been the first occasion when AA guns were discussed in relation to the protection of named places. By that time Britain's first purpose-built AA weapon was in prospect in the shape of the high-angle 3in 20cwt quick-firing (QF) gun, which launched a shrapnel shell to around 17,000 feet. But by December 1912, when it was finally decided to go ahead with protection for Chattenden and Lodge Hill, the first deliveries of 3in weapons were not expected for some months, so the first scheme called for interim measures. The two magazines were temporarily allocated four 6in breech-loading howitzers, for which double-decked timber platforms were constructed at three sites. Manned by 80 NCOs and gunners of the Royal Garrison Artillery, the four guns were not permanently installed, but were simply kept at Chattenden Barracks to be mounted as necessary.[22] The timber platforms – in effect Britain's first AA gunsites – were complete by mid January 1913,[23] and the guns installed by April.[24]

The concrete emplacements for the permanent weapons were built during the early months of 1913, and were subsequently fitted with two 3in 20cwt guns in exchange for the four howitzers. These, then, were the first truly permanent AA positions in Britain; and they marked the debut of a weapon which, almost incredibly, would continue to serve Britain's AA gunners in a modified form until the closing years of the Second World War. It was not done without resistance, for, in a pattern of events which would repeat itself again and again over the next 30 years, the sites for the new guns met vigorous local objections, in this case from the occupant of Lodge Hill House, a surplus Admiralty-owned property recently let for domestic use, who was indignant to find the emplacements appearing practically in his back yard.[25] But officialdom prevailed over the elderly tenant and his invalid wife, the slightly bewildered pioneers of an anti-anti-aircraft lobby. The Admiralty were emollient. After all, officials explained, the guns would fire only on 'special occasions'; that is when Zeppelins attempted to blow the magazines to smithereens.[26]

With Chattenden and Lodge Hill nestling under the umbrella of artillery cover, preparations for special occasions were soon extended. Although the 3in 20cwt was now established as Britain's standard AA weapon, manufacture of these comparatively sophisticated guns was slow; so much so, indeed, that to extend cover elsewhere the War Office began to cast about for alternatives. One such, soon adopted in the absence of anything better, was the 1pdr Maxim pom-pom, which in 1913 was ingeniously adapted for AA use by staff at the Western District School of Gunnery, based at Golden Hill Fort on the Isle of Wight. An AA version of this weapon was improvised by fitting it to the pedestal mounting for a 6pdr QF weapon designed to engage torpedo-boats, and with this marriage sealed the product was set up at New Needles Battery, on the western tip of the island, and tried out successfully against kites towed by a warship.[27] In this way parts of two conventional coast artillery pieces made a tolerably serviceable AA gun.

Together with the new 3in weapons, 1pdr pom-poms of various types made up the total AA armoury by early April 1914, when contemporary records show that seventeen guns of these types were in place and another seven awaited – 24 in all.[28] It is revealing that every one of these weapons protected (or would protect) a military target, and that the majority were given to installations supporting the navy. By April 1914 the only 3in guns in place were the two at Chattenden and Lodge Hill, though two more were scheduled for Waltham Abbey and the oil installations at Purfleet; additionally two 4in guns were loosely earmarked for coast artillery forts at Portsmouth, though their sites had not yet been finally selected and only one seems ever to have been installed. All the remaining guns were 1pdr pom-poms on garrison or travelling carriages. Supplied in ones and twos, most protected dockyards, magazines and oil installations around London and the Thames. Chattenden and Lodge Hill had these guns to supplement their 3in pieces, along with Chatham Dockyard and Purfleet, Port Victoria at Sheerness, Thameshaven and Waltham Abbey, while Woolwich Arsenal would receive them in due course. So too would the Admiralty building in central London, which seems to have been gunned against the danger of a precision attack. Elsewhere, 1pdrs were in place at Portsmouth, and also further afield at the Cleethorpes wireless telegraphy station, the Elswick works on the Tyne, and Vickers' factories at Barrow. All of these guns were manned by the army.

In this same month, April 1914, Colonel Louis Jackson of the Directorate of Fortifications and Works at the War Office gave a lecture at the Royal United Services Institution in Whitehall on 'the defence of localities against aerial attack'. An experienced fortifications engineer, Jackson spoke at length on the means, structural and otherwise, which could be found to protect military targets such as coast batteries, dockyards, ammunition factories, oil reservoirs, arsenals, wireless stations and stores. In doing so he attempted to look ahead to the great strides which might be achieved by aviation over the next three years. By April 1914, when he spoke, Zeppelins were believed to be capable of ranges up to 1000 miles, their endurance measured in days, not hours. Aeroplanes, too, had more than fulfilled the promise of earlier years, and could fly now at 75 miles per hour for many hours at a time. Ceilings for both were now topping 10,000 feet. By 1917, suggested Jackson, there would be bomber aeroplanes, able to discharge high explosive over all the military targets whose protection he had discussed. And there would be another category of target in the coming war, for Zeppelins and aeroplanes alike, found in 'great centres of population'; of these, explained Jackson, 'London is for us the prime object of consideration.'

Jackson was certainly not the first to warn of London's predicament in a future war, though he may have been uniquely

prescient in identifying 1917 as the year in which aeroplanes
would bomb it. The air bombardment of cities was a *leitmotif* of
excited pre-war novelists, and the spectre of explosive raining
upon London became an occasional theme for those who fuelled
the airship panic – the Aerial League, for example, one of several
independent voices urging greater preparedness in military
aviation, certainly implied it in a 1910 pamphlet which saw the
'nerve centres' of Britain as imperilled.[29] Easily reached from
Zeppelin bases in Germany and found via the narrowing ribbon
of the Thames, the capital of the Empire was indeed a supremely
practicable target for attack. But, equally, some comfort over
London's fate could be drawn from international law, for Article
25 of the Land War Convention, which issued from the 1907
Hague Conference, forbade the bombardment of undefended
places 'by any means whatever', a phrase specifically intended to
refer to air raids.[30] There were many in the pre-war years who
looked to this somewhat loosely-worded rubric as a durable
alternative to artillery. As recently as September 1913, General
Delacroix had written an article in Lord Northcliffe's *Daily Mail*
assuring Londoners that all would be well. 'Even admitting that a
Zeppelin were to pass over the English country side,' wrote the
general, 'it is not easy to see what result would be effected, for
even in time of war it would not be permissible to drop explosives
into unfortified towns.'[31] Jackson was sceptical. 'I have no wish to
be an alarmist,' he assured his RUSI audience, 'or to make
anyone's flesh creep, but I am not prepared to accept this dictum,
even from so eminent an authority.' The convention was out of
date, suggested Jackson, and almost naïvely optimistic, since 'war
is a game that governments play to win. [. . .] Can any student of
international law tell us definitely that such a thing as aerial
attack on London is outside the rules,' he asked, 'and, further,
that there exists an authority by which the rules can be enforced?'
Jackson's next words captured the defining moral issues of
twentieth-century air warfare, and the reality of bombardment,
with almost uncanny precision.

> No doubt it would be a very unkind thing, and would give rise to
> many letters in the *Times*, to cause, for instance, an extensive
> conflagration among the houses of peaceful citizens. But how, if

many of the citizens are Territorials, and some of the buildings contain warlike stores? If a flight of aeroplanes passed over the city, each one dropping a dozen incendiary bombs in different places, would not the result be more than the fire brigade could cope with? If a Zeppelin dropped half a ton of guncotton on to the Admiralty and the War Office, as she might do if not interfered with, what would be the result, in disorganisation and discouragement? What would be the result of cutting off the water supply of the East End, or sinking food-ships in the Thames? These things seem incredible to us, who have only known wars on the frontiers. I confess I am reluctant to go the length of my own arguments, but if it is conceded that London is within the range of action of a hostile Zeppelin or two, and a flight of aeroplanes, such action will soon be possible; and this is the age of the 'knock-out blow' in everything. Would any ruler harden his heart to such action? Who can say? The question seems to hinge on the ultimate results to be expected. If it seemed probable that such panic and riot would be caused as to force the Home Government to accept an unfavourable peace, then perhaps it might be done. [. . .].[32]

That was it. That was what was coming. Though the Kaiser only gradually relaxed his early restrictions on bombing the British capital,[33] the threat once realised was never dispelled, and London like other cities entered the front line in a mode of warfare which, increasingly, pitted the bomber against the civilian. Jackson in 1914 was one of the few to see the future quite so clearly.

Another of Jackson's beliefs was that the gun, rather than the aircraft, would be the key weapon of urban air defence. But when Britain entered the Great War on 4 August 1914 London was practically defenceless and most other targets barely less so. Though many of the guns listed for installation in April were in place by the high summer, there was as yet no recognisable organisation for AA work, no agreed procedures for fire-control and nothing in the way of an early-warning system. And, over and above those problems, no arm of the services as they were constituted at the start of the Great War was properly equipped to take charge of air defence in general. On its formation in May 1912, the Royal Flying Corps had been divided into a Military Wing and a Naval Wing, two partly-autonomous branches whose affinities to their parent services had strengthened in the intervening years. The Military Wing's allotted task had always been to support the Expeditionary Force, which it did in August 1914 by promptly decamping to France, leaving only a small training organisation behind. The Naval Wing – by now reformed as the Royal Naval Air Service (RNAS) – had a distinct role in giving air support, rudimentary as it was, to maritime duties, chiefly through reconnaissance and coastguard services. The result was that in the first weeks of the Great War practically the only military aircraft still on British soil belonged to the RNAS, operating from a loose chain of stations up the east coast, which for all warlike purposes became the sole domestic representative of service aviation. So, ill-equipped as it was for the duty now thrust upon it, on 3 September 1914 the RNAS was given charge of air defence. Apart from its practical necessity, the arrangement was justified by an underlying logic which was clearer in 1914 than it might be today – home defence in the early twentieth century was the job of the Fleet, not the army. But little in the RNAS's brief history had prepared it for this role, which would shape the service's evolution until the duty passed to the RFC (the former Military Wing) early in 1916. Possibly the only advantage of this peculiar arrangement was that Britain's air defences came under the charge of the First Lord of the Admiralty, who was Winston Churchill.

One of Churchill's first moves in what he later described as a 'thankless' and 'almost hopeless' task was to summon a report on the availability of guns, a task handled by the Third Sea Lord (Rear Admiral F C T Tudor). Tudor's report, issued on 4 September, pointed to the availability of twelve 3in guns, together with 38 1pdr pom-poms and around 150 3pdr or 6pdr Hotchkiss guns which could be drawn from naval stocks and converted for high-angle use.[34] How to use them was a question. Although Tudor was strongly in favour of a solid gun defence for London itself, Churchill's thinking was to harden defences at military targets, an instinct rooted in the (perhaps surprising) belief that in this matter at least London could claim little primacy over other cities. So, the bulk of the new weapons were assigned to Chatham, Dover and Portsmouth. London had to make do, at least at first, with a more limited arsenal.

London's defences under this regime were planned jointly by four officers. The Admiralty was represented by Tudor, Captain Murray Sueter (the Director of the Naval Air Department) and Rear Admiral Singer (Director of Naval Operations), while the War Office fielded Colonel L C Jackson of DFW – the same Louis Jackson who had spoken at RUSI five months previously.[35] The resulting plan commands especial interest as the first of a long series which would continue to reshape the defences of London, in fact or in prospect, throughout the First World War and the inter-war period. To begin with, Tudor argued that the 'independent defence of isolated buildings or localities' against air raids was 'practically useless'. His preference instead was for a zonal scheme centred on the area from Buckingham Palace eastward to the region of Charing Cross Bridge, which would be covered by three pairs of searchlights designed to support guns at Admiralty Arch, on the roof of the Foreign Office and the Crown Agents' office in Millbank, each of which had a 1pdr pom-pom in place by 7 September. The lights themselves were mounted on the roof of Charing Cross station, at Lambeth Bridge, and at Hyde Park Corner, and manned in rotation by a corps of 120 special constables.[36] In addition, aeroplane defence, of a sort, was to be provided eventually from a ring of airfields established about ten miles out from the central, vulnerable area. In the first instance a flight of machines was organised at Hendon to 'rise and attack' a hostile airship which might venture over London, while the RFC aeroplanes at Brooklands and Farnborough were put on readiness to assist if necessary. Emergency night landing grounds for these aircraft were also arranged and lit in London itself, at Regent's Park, Kensington Gardens, Battersea Park and the Mall, while day counterparts were established at Hainault Farm and Joyce Green. These were the first of a complex array of home defence stations which would evolve over the next four years.[37]

London's AA defences of September 1914 were not, then, especially dense or sophisticated, and had a Zeppelin hove over the city in these lengthening autumn nights better protection would probably have been provided by the lighting restrictions which actually formed a greater part of these early plans. But expansion was not long in coming. On 2 October orders were issued to mount eight or ten more naval guns and searchlights, extending the defended area eastward to the Bank of England, and in the next fortnight a Captive Balloon Section was established to give lookout at Crystal Palace and a watching post was sited on the roof of the Imperial Institute. Fully mounting the new weapons and searchlights took more than a month, and by 13 October the guns had been supplemented only by a 1pdr pom-pom in St James's Street and another at Gresham College (near the Guildhall), while lights operated by the London Fire Brigade were in place on Battersea and Blackfriars Bridges, at the Cherry Garden Pier in Rotherhithe and at Somers Bridge Road.[38] By the third week in November, however, London could call upon thirteen guns and ten searchlights, a weapon strength quadrupled since the start of the war.[39]

In the interim had come two important developments in organisation. At first the shortage of men to operate London's new AA searchlights was met by the special constables, but as the layout continued to grow it became clear that less extempore measures were needed. The result was a specially-formed branch of the Royal Naval Volunteer Reserve, which came together on 9 October as the Anti-Aircraft Corps, RNVR.[40] The second move was more fundamental. By mid October many minds had been pondering the wisdom of the cabinet's (perhaps hasty) decision of early September to give the navy charge of every AA gun, everywhere. So now came second thoughts. On 16 October the Admiralty and War Office agreed that areas where the army usually manned local defences would also be entrusted to the soldiers for AA purposes – these, chiefly, were the defended ports, where the RGA already operated coast artillery guns, often in historic fortifications of some magnificence – while the navy's responsibility would be confined to 'London and other large towns which came under the heading of undefended areas'. The new arrangement still placed a heavy burden on the navy, and in one way brought the division of Britain's AA defences to the brink of absurdity: for now the soldiers protected the navy's anchorages from air attack (as they long had against warships), while the sailors defended London and, before long, other inland centres miles from any sea. The Royal Navy's endearing habit of treating every landlocked base as a kind of honorary ship certainly helped surmount what might be termed the conceptual difficulties of this arrangement (the navy's air defence HQ later opened at Kenwood House in leafy Hampstead eventually became HMS *Kenwood*),[41] but still it was far from ideal.

The oddity of this arrangement deepened still further when AA defences began to spread to other cities, which they did gradually before Zeppelin raids began in January 1915. The first non-metropolitan target to be defended by naval reservists was Sheffield, which on 31 October was allocated two 6pdr guns and a pair of 24in searchlights; at first manned by staff of the armaments works they were there to protect, on 10 December these weapons were handed over to an 80-man detachment from the RNVR.[42] Although the RGA was now strictly responsible for the AA defences at coastal fortresses – at this date chiefly Chatham, Dover and Portsmouth, following the allocations of guns in September – in practice the soldiers were often assisted by RNVR personnel in an arrangement in which strict demarcation between the services mattered less than obtaining the requisite number of men. Thus a small RNVR unit was formed at Dover on 29 October, to operate the AA searchlights while the RGA handled the guns, and naval men found themselves posted to coastal forts at Chatham and Sheerness.[43]

This is how Britain's air defences stood in the depth of winter 1914, when the German raids began. At first these were minor. The first recorded attack by a hostile aeroplane took place on 21 December, when a lone raider dropped a couple of bombs in the sea off Dover Harbour. A similar incident followed on the 24th, when a bomb came to earth near Dover Castle, while a single seaplane caused a stir on Christmas Day 1914 by flying over Sheerness and Erith. This last incursion met tentative opposition from a flight of six defending aircraft, and also from the 3in guns, 6pdrs and pom-poms of the local AA defences, though the guns merely set a depressing precedent for the opening skirmishes of the 1939–45 war by firing on (and missing) the friendly fighters. None of these inaugural raids achieved anything and after Christmas Day 1914 they were suspended for nearly two months. Thereafter, until the war approached its fourth year, aeroplanes appeared in meagre numbers – usually just ones and twos – and limited their attention largely to sporadic raids on coastal targets. Not until May 1917 did Germany send bombing aeroplanes to Britain in any numbers.

The AA challenge of the first three years of war was instead the airship. Between the first Zeppelin raid of January 1915 and the last, three and a half years later, the Germans sent 277 airship sorties to Britain in 54 separate operations; the 202 sorties which got through would kill 557 people, injure many more and cause substantial damage to property, particularly in London.[44] Britain's AA gunners cut their teeth on the airship, which at first proved as difficult to meet as pre-war theorists had supposed. By the spring of 1915 these raids had laid bare most of the fundamental questions – the questions of tactical principle – which had been chewed over before the war and would continue to exercise air defence planners for many years to come. Should guns be mobile, fixed, or perhaps some combination of both? Should defence be conceived on a 'point' basis, with weapons sited at the target itself, or as some kind of linear barrier, or frontier? How did guns best co-operate with aircraft and with searchlights? How best could early warning be arranged, and what repercussions would different systems bring for the pattern of gun deployment? And – not the least of the gunners' problems – how exactly did one shoot down an airship?

Provisional answers to some of these questions were worked out between the first, isolated Zeppelin raid on 19 January 1915 and the main campaign which opened three months later. The first operation from the Germans' point of view was a definite failure. In conditions of mist and drizzle Zeppelins L3 and L4 ventured unsteadily towards targets on the Humber (a third, originally bound for the Thames Estuary, turned back with engine trouble) but were both carried far south by the wind and dropped their bombs respectively on Great Yarmouth and at scattered points across north Norfolk, the bulk of L4's load being discharged on the undefended town of King's Lynn, which the captain believed to be somewhere in the Humber–Tyne region.[45] No damage of any military importance was done, though two towns-people were killed and thirteen injured.[46] Yet in bombing King's Lynn the machines had strayed uncomfortably close to the royal estate at Sandringham, which was undefended and where, as it happened, the King and Queen were due to spend a week at the end of the month. So it came about that an important departure in the tactics of AA defence was prompted directly by a perceived threat to the body of the sovereign. This was the introduction of a truly mobile element to the stock of guns and searchlights.

More than twenty years hence, during the 1939–45 war, the term 'mobile' as applied to an AA gun would refer to its capacity for movement by trailer and deployment anywhere using a self-contained mounting – both in contrast to 'static' guns, which were anchored to concrete. Such guns could be shifted from area to area in about a day to meet the changing emphasis of attack. By the standards of 1915, however, Second World War 'mobile' guns might have been more aptly termed 'moveable' or 'transportable', since the weapons to which the term was applied in the Great War were more truly mobile in the sense of being rushed from place to place in the actual course of a raid, much as the earlier designers of balloon guns had anticipated. The first of these guns were two 13pdrs on high-angle mountings, supplied to meet the Sandringham threat, fixed to motor lorries; two 24in oxy-acetylene searchlights, similarly mounted, accompanied them.[47] These hybrid contraptions were supplied for the close defence of George V when in Norfolk, but before long the idea that lorry-mounted guns might have applications other than this novel praetorian guard began to take hold.

In the climate of early 1915 mobile AA guns appeared to be useful for several reasons. First, just as Capper had predicted in 1909, fixed weapons could not be installed everywhere, so a mobile element to the defence would enable otherwise open areas to be protected to some extent, given adequate warning. Secondly, the guns could provide some advance cover for London by intercepting approaching Zeppelins *en route*. Thirdly, mobile sections would provide useful training for men assigned to the similar units which, from an early stage in the war, had been sent to perform AA duties, as best they could, in France and Belgium.[48] And lastly, they were eminently practical, since the limited experience so far suggested that Zeppelins might habitually present fairly low-flying targets, falling within range of the smaller guns which could be fixed to lorries. These were the considerations which persuaded the Admiralty to approve a mobile element to the general AA defences toward the end of January, when authority was given to form the Eastern Mobile and Southern Mobile sections of the AA Corps.[49]

Between them the two mobile sections covered so vast an area that some difficulty was found in selecting suitable places for their headquarters.[50] Eastern Mobile was first assigned to Chelmsford, though the idea was dropped before the men took up occupancy and under their commander, Major W G Lucas, this section established itself in Primrose House at Newmarket, a property loaned by the Earl of Rosebery, whence they sallied forth on patrols of the east coast towns. At the same time Southern Mobile occupied a headquarters in a house called The Mound at Whitehill, near Caterham. At first the guns used by these units were something of a compromise: with no pom-poms or 6pdrs to hand, their fast vehicles at first sported small, 0.303in Lewis guns and 0.45in machine guns (the latter with some incendiary ammunition), on high-angle mountings, together with a supply of oxy-acetylene searchlights, equipment which in combination might at least deter a few airships, even if few entertained any illusions over its lethality. Mobile AA defence could be exciting work and the two units soon gained reputations to suit their handling of it. Eastern Mobile won a good reputation, and remained in being until September 1916. Southern Mobile, on the other hand, were reportedly 'a fairly piratical lot, with not much discipline', led by an 'extremely erratic officer' blessed with 'a certain amount of brain, and a large amount of self-assurance'.[51] Both of those judgements may have been unwarranted, but whether through indiscipline or – as is sometimes claimed[52] – the less frequent appearance of Zeppelins approaching across the southern coasts, Southern Mobile was disbanded on 15 June 1915 after four months in being. From then on The Mound became a training centre for RNVR AA Corps troops about to be sent abroad.

With the two mobile sections ready to operate, by late spring 1915 a measure of AA defence was in place across the whole of the south-east and East Anglia. High-angle guns – mostly 3in and 6pdrs – defended Portsmouth, Newhaven, Dover, the Thames & Medway fortress and Harwich, while the mobile units acted as infill (at least in theory) for the approach lanes to London between these areas of permanent fortification. London itself still contained only a modest stock of high-angle weapons – five 3in guns, four 6pdrs, six 1pdr pom-poms[53] – though those newly-arrived since the beginning of the year were positioned with great care: the 3in guns on One Tree Hill at Honor Oak and the Clapton Orient football ground, for example, were reportedly sited to intercept the lines of approach from airship bases respectively in Belgium and north Germany.[54] And, by May 1915, high-angle guns for AA work were also continuing to spread outwards to other targets, with allocations made to the defended ports at the Humber, Tyne, Forth, Cromarty, Liverpool and Barrow, as well as Birmingham, which followed London and Sheffield in the list of inland cities with AA defence, and the munitions targets at Stowmarket, Pitsea, Kynoch Town and Chilworth.[55]

None of these defences could give of their best, however, without adequate early-warning arrangements, which were important to the fixed guns and more or less essential if the mobile weapons were to stand any chance of intercepting their targets. In 1915 the role which, a quarter of a century later, would be performed by radar fell largely upon the civil police. At the start of the war it was arranged that officers sighting hostile aircraft within 60 miles of London would telephone reports to the Admiralty and it was on this model that the reporting system progressively expanded. Early in the new year of 1915 the net was extended to East Anglia, Northamptonshire, Oxfordshire, Hampshire and the Isle of Wight, and in April was widened further to embrace the whole of the United Kingdom. By this time the police reporting system – if such an *ad hoc* arrangement can be so called – had also been supplemented by information from practically any governmental or military source suitably placed to give it. Ships, signal stations at defended ports, airfields and AA sites themselves were all feeding reports of hostile aircraft movements to the central Information Bureau of the AA

Section, who would supposedly retransmit digested news back to the air defence aerodromes, gun stations, the War Office, Scotland Yard and the railways. Accounts differ, however, on how successful this system was. Though an official report from April 1915 claimed the central bureau provided a 'very effective centre for the immediate distribution of reliable information to the whole of the AA defences in the South and East of England',[56] that statement seems to reflect either the expectations of the system in its infancy, or else the AA Section's instinct to downplay its own shortcomings. Others remember the network's tendency to generate a muddle of irreconcilable reports, amid 'overlapping and a fearful congestion of the telephone system'.[57] In reality, few of those submitting information were sufficiently expert to do so. Largely untrained policemen peering skyward hardly offered the keenest eyes for the AA defences and even when hostile airships and aeroplanes were correctly identified the system was so slow as to render positional information hopelessly obsolete by the time it arrived (small wonder, when reporters without a telephone had to send warnings by 'priority telegram'). A senior officer familiar with the system of 1915 later wrote that 'none of the information from any source on land came through quickly enough or accurately enough to be of any use to the defence.'[58]

That was a retrospective judgement, but its truth was apparent even as the main phase of Zeppelin raids began to develop in the spring and summer of 1915. Between mid April and mid October 1915 German airships appeared over Britain on nineteen occasions, on all but seven of which just one vessel was involved (though five came over on two raids in August and October). The raids, it is true, were light by the standards of 1940–41, but the raiders escaped largely scot-free and their effects deepened as the summer wore on. The first six operations roamed over East Anglia, Kent and Essex, before London was bombed for the first time on the night of 31 May. Just as they would in the Blitz of 1940, the Germans targeted their first metropolitan raid at the East End, where seven died, 35 were injured and more than £18,000-worth of damage was caused to property.[59] Something like panic ensued, with ugly scenes in east London and attacks on citizens suspected to be of Germanic origin. There was also criticism of the defences, though the issue of a D-Notice forbidding press reports outside the bounds of official communiques muzzled the papers.[60] In fact no London AA gun fired on this occasion and the RNAS aircraft sent up to intercept caught no more than a momentary glimpse of the military airship LZ38, which was the vehicle for much of the raiding in April and May.[61] And, in general, neither the guns nor the fighter aircraft made much impression on LZ38 or any of her sister ships which visited in 1915. Often the guns were in the wrong place – as in Suffolk, on 29 April, when Eastern Mobile scurried out to meet a raider near Bury St Edmunds but arrived 45 minutes late.[62] On other occasions the gunners, no less than the pilots, either failed to see the airships or were incapable of bringing fire anywhere near. One lucky hit was recorded by the AA guns at Cliffe on 9 May, when LZ38 may have sustained some damage, but the vessel was back over Britain again eight days later. By the end of this phase of operations 203 people lay dead and 524 had been injured in places as widely scattered as Jarrow and Kent. Measured in crude mortality these six months of operations achieved less than many single raids in the Blitz of 1940–41, but their promise disturbed. A raid upon Hull on 6 June led to street riots – fears of civil unrest under the rain of bombs became a widespread fear in the 1930s – while more than half a million pounds' worth of damage (at 1915 prices) was caused in the City on 8 September, London's second raid in two nights and the fourth since 31 May. Then the last raid of the series, on 13 October, achieved by far the largest lethal result, killing 71 people and injuring 128. It was clear that worse was to come.

Worse did come, but not for more than three months, and by then the London defences had undergone another reorganisation. On 12 September, in the wake of London's fourth raid, Admiral Sir Percy Scott was given charge of the capital's AA defences, and immediately set about introducing a vehicle-borne element to the metropolitan guns, as well as demanding more and better fixed weapons. London Mobile was the third such unit to be formed in the war (though following the recent disbandment of Southern Mobile, one of only two actually extant). The choice of commander for this new force was both apt and, as things turned out, historically bountiful. Lieutenant-Commander Alfred Rawlinson was probably one of the best-qualified officers for the new post to be found anywhere in the services, thanks to a unique combination of expertise with motor vehicles and AA guns. Before the war Rawlinson, an enthusiast for motor-racing, had sat on the board of a French car manufacturing firm and had most recently served with an RN armoured car squadron in France; he had also helped organise the AA defences of Paris in the winter of 1914–15, becoming deeply involved in problems of fire-control and fuzing, and at the time of his appointment was at work on novel designs for AA weapons, sights and mountings with the needs of London particularly in mind. To complete his strong connections across the Channel, Rawlinson's brother, General Sir Henry, was then commander of the British army in France.

The fortunes of London Mobile are more thoroughly and more vividly recorded for us than those of any other anti-aircraft unit which served in Britain during the Great War, an historical gift which reaches us through the extraordinary memoir which Rawlinson published in 1923.[63] Despite its sober title, *The Air Defence of London 1915–1918* is as much adventure story as history, and fittingly so from a man whose duties were as singular and as energetic as himself.

Rawlinson was summoned on 11 September to meet Scott and Balfour (who succeeded Churchill as First Lord in May 1915) when it was decided that London Mobile would be formed from a nucleus of Rawlinson's earlier armoured car squadron, using AA weapons of the kind Rawlinson had used in his time at Paris. That meant a trip to France, but when the necessary letter of authority from the Admiralty to the French Minister of War did not appear after five days, Scott wrote the note himself and Rawlinson immediately set off, crossed on the night boat to Boulogne, tapped his French connections to the full, and actually returned to London at the wheel of a brand-new 75mm auto-cannon on its lorry mounting 72 hours later – apparently before the official letter asking for the gun had been written.[64] On Rawlinson's return from this mission on 19 September London Mobile had its first weapon.

Though the single gun which Rawlinson and his team now had at their disposal was not generally superior to the 3in 20cwt,[65] it was so in its ability to fire a time-fuzed high-explosive rather than the common shrapnel shell on which gunners in Britain were still forced to rely. How to deploy this unique prize was difficult to decide, but Rawlinson opted to give a general defence to the area around the Bank of England, selecting for his gun position the Artillery Ground at Moorgate Street, whence the weapon would be rushed in a raid from London Mobile's headquarters at the Talbot works in Ladbroke Grove. This it did for the first time in the raid of 13 October, when a break-neck chase across London brought the auto-cannon into place just in time to engage the airship, the first to come under high-explosive fire over the capital. Rawlinson claimed that the shock of this persuaded the Zeppelin commander to jettison his bombs – which fell in the Petticoat Lane area – and head for home.

After the 13 October incident there came another lull. A fleet of nine Zeppelins operated over the Eastern Counties and the Midlands on 31 January, but after that the defenders had to wait until 5 March for another airship raid. In the interim came the first sea-change in Britain's air defence arrangements since the start of the war, and with it the first resolute step towards victory over the airship. On 10 February the Cabinet ruled that the divided control of AA artillery in place since September 1914 would be abolished, and that general responsibility for air defence would be given to the War Office, a transfer given formal effect on the 16th. Many guns and searchlights in naval hands were transferred to the Royal Artillery, while the RFC was set to take charge of the fighter aircraft work. The fighters themselves were reorganised in the same month, when for the first time all machines dedicated to the defence of London were brought together under a single commander and given greater concentration in deployment. Hitherto scattered around airfields in ones and twos, the aircraft were now pulled together into flights based at just three stations near the capital, the first stage in a process which would eventually produce more than a dozen fully-formed home defence fighter squadrons, deployed at bases reaching up the eastern coast of Britain.[66] Neither of these changes yielded an instant effect, but they marked an important step towards the unified air defence system which emerged later in the war.

Wise as the reorganisation was, however, it did have its

disadvantages, one of which was the loss of Sir Percy Scott, who as a naval officer could no longer continue to head the London defences. He had achieved much in his five months. London's guns had risen from just twelve when he arrived in mid September to 50 in mid February 1916, an arsenal accumulated largely by adding 3in 20cwt weapons, 6pdr QFs and, by now, ten guns for London Mobile, which was also Scott's creation. On the date when the War Office took charge London also boasted a single French 75mm cannon on a fixed mount – additional to those in Rawlinson's hands – the first of a consignment of 35 such weapons under order. Nor was this the whole story, since the guns due for delivery when Scott departed exceeded those actually in place by a factor of two. The 98 guns expected to arrive in the capital over the following months were an extraordinarily diverse batch – 3in, 4in, 4.7in, 3pdr, 6pdr, 15pdrs and even a dozen 2.95in Russian weapons, in addition to the 75mm types.[67] Not all of these were delivered and some might have been of dubious value had they been so; but sheer fire-power, by now, counted for more than consistency in the weapons producing it.

Scott's achievements in bolstering London's guns were soon built upon, though the new plans framed in spring 1916 embodied goals more ambitious than could realistically be attained. The War Office's scheme for London,[68] prepared even before the transfer was enacted, called for a double ring of guns encircling Scott's largely central layout, with positions roughly on circles with five and nine-mile radii centring on Charing Cross. Beyond that would lie a ring of searchlights whose main function was to assist fighter aircraft. Since the London scheme alone called for 500 searchlights and 475 AA guns, against a gun total then available nationally of 295 – fewer than a quarter of which were efficient AA types – this was clearly a very long-term plan; the scheme of early 1916, indeed, was the first of many to set extravagant *desiderata* in relation to present realities, a characteristic typifying AA plans until the end of the Second World War. But it also reflected the principle that AA defence, by early 1916, could be conceived in terms of definite scales to yield a specific performance against a known foe. That was a sign of maturity.

To achieve a truly effective AA layout the War Office desperately needed new guns, and in substitute for the rather haphazard mix which Scott had been obliged to order, in the early months of 1916 supplies were found elsewhere. On paper the War Office's receipts of weapons in the long term looked promising enough: by the end of 1915 some 326 guns of 3in type were on order (though some were earmarked for overseas), along with 62 13pdr 9cwts, but to tide them over until these stocks appeared the War Office made use of 12pdr 12cwt guns robbed from coast artillery forts and converted for high-angle fire (34 of these were in place by the middle of the year), together with 18pdr weapons, 90 of which were found as a stop-gap until the new 3in guns arrived. Few expected much from the 18pdr at first, but it remained in service as an AA gun until the end of the war.[69]

The change of personalities in the hand-over between departments put Field Marshal Lord French, C-in-C Home Forces, in charge of AA defence generally, and in French's hands the AA organisation of the country as a whole was also reworked.[70] Their initial framework was built around a two-tiered hierarchy of defended areas, with the major targets classified as *anti-aircraft commands* (a term only coincidentally similar to the AA Command of the Second World War) and lesser areas as *anti-aircraft stations*. The AA commands of 1916 included all the main defended ports – Cromarty, Forth, Tyne, Tees & Hartlepool, Humber, Harwich, Thames & Medway, Dover, Portsmouth, Portland, Plymouth, Milford Haven, Liverpool and Barrow – together with the more important inland cities, initially London (whose AA defences, uniquely, were divided into seven geographical sections), Birmingham, Leeds and Sheffield. There were, altogether, eighteen AA commands at first, each run by an AA Defence Commander, who was either the local garrison commander for a defended port, or a specially-appointed officer for a city. AA stations were much more numerous. Fifty-nine were named in the War Office's initial plan for the scheme, though as some of these embraced adjacent locales, such as Selby and Howden, Nottingham and Chilwell, or Kynochtown, Pitsea and Thameshaven, the number of discrete targets was somewhat larger. No single characteristic qualified a place as an AA station. Some were manufacturing towns, such as Huddersfield, Manchester or Halifax. Others were minor ports, such as Newhaven or Yarmouth. Many were airfields and airship stations – Bacton, Capel, Cranwell, Eastchurch, Farnborough, Pulham; more such sites would be allocated AA guns as 1916 wore on. For operational purposes AA stations were either run by the chief of the local army command (Northern, Eastern, and so on), or were attached to a nearby AA command.

The early-warning system, too, was improved under army control, by the creation of 'observer cordons' at set distances from vulnerable targets. At first manned by soldiers (though soon transferred largely to the police) these were lines of spotting and reporting posts, usually with an outer cordon at 50 miles out – where warnings gave sufficient flying time for fighters to get airborne and reach interception height over the target – and an inner at 30 miles, from which warning was sent to the guns, lights, and the city itself. At the same time the country was divided for reporting purposes into seven 'Warning Controls', shaped to exploit the existing geography of the arterial telephone lines, with the AA defence commander in each acting as the nexus for all raid reports in his region.

It was these improved arrangements which, in the middle months of 1916, finally defeated the airship. Though the effect of these operations would sharpen again, briefly, in the autumn of 1916, a series of attacks in March and April arguably marked the peak of the airship campaign, when four raids (carried out by a total of fifteen vessels) succeeded in killing 101 people and injuring 270 more.[71] In the second, however, on 31 March, raiders were prevented from reaching London by fierce fire coming up from guns in the eastern reaches of the capital. One was hit and, after a further inconclusive engagement by a fighter, finally crashed off the Kent coast. On this same night a second vessel was damaged while approaching over Suffolk, near Stowmarket, though it managed to limp home.[72] It was on this one night that the airship campaign, in retrospect, can be seen to have turned in the defenders' favour. Though 48 people did die in the raid, in which four other vessels participated, thereafter the Zeppelins became more hesitant, London was left alone until 25 April – when the attack was again beaten back – and the Germans' returns began to diminish. Between 3 April and 2 September the airships operated over Britain on thirteen occasions, in a total of 75 sorties. The last operation saw fourteen Zeppelins active, the largest number of any night in the Great War; but in this whole sequence of attacks only 47 people perished on the ground and little damage was done.

The final, brief phase of determined airship raids saw a return to the capital. Eleven vessels operated on the night of 23 September, nine making landfall over England and bombing London and Nottingham, though of the London force one was hit by AA fire and further injured by a fighter before landing practically intact near Colchester; a second was downed by fighter action alone, crashing in flames near Billericay. Two nights later Germany sent over five airships, of which the greater number delivered attacks probably intended for Leeds (but in the event fell upon Sheffield and Bolton), while a single vessel put in an appearance over Portsmouth. Though undamaged by the thick cluster of AA guns which opened fire around the Portsmouth fortress, this machine made no attack. And the 43 people who died under the bombs on this night represented almost the last heavy casualty toll inflicted by airships in the Great War. A raid by seven vessels operating on the night of 1/2 October resulted in just one death on the ground, for the loss of the airship L31, which was downed by a fighter near Potters Bar, while on the afternoon of 27 November another seven-ship force lost two of its number, again to fighters, for little result. At that, until mid March 1917, airship raiding ceased.

The lion's share of the kills in this phase of operations went to the aircraft of the RFC, who by now had honed their night-fighting skills to the point where lumbering airships were becoming easier meat; of the eight German vessels destroyed in this year, five fell to fighters, two to AA guns and the last to the weather.[73] But the experience of 1916 also taught much of the techniques of AA defence, which if it was not yet a science was steadily leaving its infancy behind. The Zeppelin battle proved that AA gunnery, with its searchlight support, could claim a subtler and more diverse range of functions than simply shooting hostile raiders out of the sky. That was just as well, for at this stage of the game the guns seldom actually hit their targets; but the deterrent effect of intense AA fire was palpable, and evident not just to the gunners, but to civilians on the ground, who were reassured by audible evidence of their city fighting back. Searchlight techniques, in the Zeppelin raids of 1916, advanced to the stage where vessels were routinely caught and held in their steady pencil beams – helpful to the guns, of course, but also to the fighters, whose success against the Zeppelin in 1916 owed a great deal to the pilots simply being able to *see* the raiders, as their predecessors of 1915 had not. And even when the lights failed to engage their quarries, their exposure alerted fighter pilots to the presence of a Zeppelin in the area, and in these pre-wireless and pre-radar days also gave welcome beacons by which to steer. All of this was possible because gunners and searchlight crews on the ground could locate the airships by their sound, when fighter pilots, near deafened by the noise of their own engines, could not.

Lights needed to be used cautiously for fear that they might in themselves mark the target for the raider; and in general the accumulating experience of air attack showed that AA guns and searchlights did bring some new problems all of their own. Probably the most disturbing of these was the outfall from blasting a substantial volume of artillery ammunition into the sky over a densely-populated city. What goes up must come down, and this anti-aircraft shells did in alarming numbers. The more AA fire was thrown skyward the more the raiders were deterred and the safer a city became from German bombs; but, equally, the greater became the hazard from falling shells and shrapnel. Plainly, this pheno-menon implied a theoretical crossover point, at which AA fire killed more people than the lethal potential of the bombs which it had deterred. That point was never approached, but on occasions the harm done to those on the ground reached embarrassing proportions – as on the night of 23 September 1916, when the three people killed and thirteen injured by AA shells represented around one-tenth of the casualties from the night's raid.[74] The problem of what Churchill called 'self-bombardment' would worsen later in the war and resurfaced in the much fiercer London Blitz of 1940.[75] But in a world of harsh pragmatism, a few casualties from friendly fire seemed a small price to pay for efficient gun defence.

By autumn 1916 the solidity of that defence was growing, as guns multiplied and more efficient types replaced the stop-gap equipment common in the first year or so of war. In November 1916 London was working toward an authorised layout of 84 AA guns distributed between 48 gunsites, the majority of them two-gun positions, together with 93 searchlights[76] – way below the abstract ideals set out in the spring and lower indeed than the numbers planned by Scott, but effective enough given that the weapons themselves were by now modern purpose-built types, mostly 3in and French 75mm. But in the relative quiet of winter 1916–17, before the first heavy aeroplane raids introduced their radical change to the air defence picture, the apparent defeat of the Zeppelin seemed to justify easing supply. In January 1917 a consignment of 403 guns ordered for AA defence was tapped for Admiralty use, 190 being diverted to ships and London's allocation falling to 64.[77] At first this hardly seemed to matter. On 16 February airship incursions resumed in desultory fashion when a lone vessel strayed over Kent after bombing the French coast, and even a five-vessel raid on 16 March – the first actual attack since November – caused no casualties on the ground but sacrificed L39 to the French defences over Compiègne. Little more was achieved by a further five-vessel incursion on 23 May, when no fewer than 72 fighter aircraft were put in the air to meet the raiders, who did bomb but without great result. By early summer 1917 the Zeppelin force was practically spent.

The defeat of the Zeppelin by the combined prowess of the British fighters, guns and searchlights was not lost on the German high command, who now, finally, committed themselves to the mode of attack which would dominate the last eighteen months of the Great War. As early as autumn 1914 Germany had harboured a plan to attack London with bomber aeroplanes and had formed a unit cloaked by the bizarre title of the Ostend Brieftauben Abteilung (Ostend Carrier Pigeon Squadron) to do the job. That scheme had faltered, however, through the Germans' arrested advance at Ypres in November 1914, a move which blocked the unit's access to airfields around Calais necessary to reach London with their primitive short-range bombers.[78] Since then aeroplanes had visited Britain regularly, but in such meagre numbers as to pose a negligible threat: thus far incursions by hostile machines had been reported on about 30 occasions, activity amounting to perhaps 45 sorties whose thin scatter of bombs were reckoned to have killed 21 people, two-thirds of those in a unique, five-aircraft raid on Kentish targets in March 1916.[79] But in the late afternoon of Friday, 25 May 1917 this pattern was suddenly broken, when an unprecedentedly large formation of sixteen Gotha bombers appeared high in the sky over the Thames Estuary. Originally bound for London, these aircraft were deterred from pressing inland by heavy cloud banks, and instead wheeled over Essex and Kent, where they released their cargoes on Shornmead camp and Folkestone town. Within minutes 94 people were dead and 192 lay injured. Seventy-four RFC fighters were airborne in defence, and seven AA sites opened up along the track of the formation, but none of the raiders was damaged over England (though one was downed near the Belgian coast by the RNAS working from Dunkirk). So ended the Germans' first heavy aeroplane raid of the First World War, which in its minor but vividly effective way marked the debut of strategic bombing.

Over the next two months Germany launched five more raids on this model, never with fewer than sixteen aircraft and on one occasion with 24. Most got through. London reeled under its first Gotha raid on 13 June, when 162 people were killed and 432 injured in an operation which also took a side-swipe at Margate. By 22 July, when sixteen Gothas attacked Harwich (where less experienced AA gunners enthusiastically blasted away at British fighters), the number of dead had risen to 402 and of those hurt to 1030. Eleven fatalities were attributable to British AA fire, which also succeeded in wounding 74, most of whom suffered on just one night (7 July) when the Germans made their second Gotha raid on the capital.[80] Almost trivial from the perspective of 1944 or '45, by the standards of the Great War these were terrible statistics. In eight weeks and just six operations, the new raids had killed four-fifths as many people as the airships had achieved in the whole of the war so far. And for this, just two Gotha sorties of the 108 recorded appeared to have been terminated by the defences.

These facts alone were sufficient to justify an urgent review of Britain's air defence arrangements; and the resulting reorganisation which was formally endorsed by the War Office on 31 July heralded a transformation in the layout and control of AA guns which, in many ways, prefigured the plans of the inter-war period and the defence arrangements of the Second World War. The new departure of July 1917 was the formation of a fully-integrated air defence system for the capital, known as the London Air Defence Area (LADA), which under the command of a single officer now reshaped the entire air defence resources of south-eastern England (Fig 1). The officer chosen to superintend this work was Major-General E B Ashmore, who exchanged the gas-drenched environment of the Western Front for this new command at home. Ashmore had little direct experience of aerial bombing when he took up his post in late July. 'The bombing of the Army fronts', he later recalled, 'had not up to that time amounted to very much, and I am afraid we of the Expeditionary Force were inclined to look on the troubles of London somewhat light-heartedly. The fact that I was exchanging the comparative safety of the Front for the probability of being hanged in the streets of London did not worry me.'[81]

Ashmore's fears for his neck over the next year or so grew from the immense difficulty which the defences found in getting to grips with the new aeroplane raids. For in almost every respect the Gotha represented a sterner quarry than the Zeppelin. Faster, smaller, more manoeuvrable and better able to defend themselves against fighters, the new bombers amply fulfilled Esher's prediction of January 1909 that the aeroplane would prove 'peculiarly difficult to destroy while in flight'.[82] And if that was true of formations working by day, Ashmore realised that it would be more so when the Germans began to send their Gothas by night. All of Ashmore's advice in the first days of his command pointed to the imminence of this eventuality, which actually did materialise within five weeks of LADA being formed. So in remaking London's air defences against the aeroplane, Ashmore was planning for both present dangers and future threats.

Probably the only advantage to the defenders in this new situation was a certain predictability in the bombers' line of approach. The day raids which were penetrating south-eastern England in summer 1917 were the work of the Germans' 3rd Bombing Squadron, operating from airfields around Ghent, in

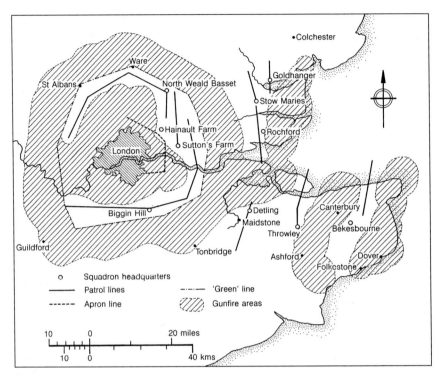

Figure 1 LADA: the developed layout of the London Air Defence Area, 1918. This integrated system of airfields, fighter patrol lines, balloon aprons and gunfire zones was the prototype on which the capital's air defences of later years were built.

Belgium, around 170 miles to the east of London. The main weakness of the aeroplane compared to the airship was its more sharply circumscribed region of action, which restricted the early Gotha formations to more or less direct approach tracks across a swathe of country centring on the Thames Estuary – this in contrast to the Zeppelins, which could cruise widely, approach London from any direction, and loiter when necessary to take stock; the affinity between the Zeppelin and the ship was indeed close. Until July 1917 the AA guns of London and the south-east had been deployed to meet airships operating very much in this way. London's own guns were distributed, by now, in four sub-commands (a rationalisation, implemented in April 1917, of the seven formed early the previous year), whose share of weapons covered the western approaches almost as thickly as the southern, eastern and northern. Of 68 AA guns deployed in London on 1 June 1917, almost all of them on single-gun sites, nineteen were in the Western Sub-Command – since May commanded by Rawlinson, now a lieutenant-colonel[83] – as against 21 in Eastern Sub-Command, eighteen in Northern and ten in Central, which was effectively the historic core of the London layout, still manned by the RNVR.[84] Western Sub-Command, it is true, covered a rather broader front than the others – in fact from Watford anti-clockwise to Bromley; there was no 'Southern Sub-Command' – and was equipped almost exclusively with the French 75mm weapons in which their commander was expert, as against the 3in 20cwt guns used almost exclusively elsewhere; but the point remains that this was essentially an all-round defence. Elsewhere in the south-east – the area which now metamorphosed into LADA – AA defences were in place at Dover (a cluster of eleven guns) and in the Thames & Medway fortress layout, where 32 weapons, two-thirds of them 3in types, were deployed.

This layout, then, was essentially an anti-Zeppelin system, evolved to meet attacks coming at London from any direction. But while defence against the Zeppelin could not yet be wholly dismantled, the more direct lines of approach followed by the Gothas at once enabled Ashmore to think in terms of barriers and more concentrated lines of intercepting fire. His first move was to table the idea of a two-stage artillery defence for the capital, comprising an outer gun barrier and an inner artillery zone, separated by a clear area within which fighters could patrol on set lines unimpeded by friendly fire. Given the Gothas' line of approach, the outer artillery zone was first limited to an area east of the capital, which was armed by redeploying ten guns from the existing London defences, stripping 24 from provincial cities and borrowing a further sixteen from the Admiralty; additionally six mobile batteries were deployed there temporarily.[85] The main purpose of these guns was to break up the formations of incoming bombers, so as to enable the fighters to pick them off singly. To separate guns and fighters the LADA was built around a clear line of demarcation, known as the Green Line, within which aircraft had priority of action, but outside which most of the work was expected to fall to the guns. Within the fighter belt lay the inner artillery zone, the core of the London layout.

In its formative state the LADA system was ready by 12

August, when the Germans launched what would subsequently emerge as their pcnultimate day attack with aeroplanes. The newly-reorganised defences held up well, the fighters on their patrol lines menacing the nine-strong Gotha force sufficiently to prevent any reaching London, though bombs were jettisoned to some effect on Southend and Margate. Six days later the Germans tried again with a much larger force. No fewer than 28 Gothas are believed to have embarked on 18 August, though poor weather foiled them soon after crossing the Belgian coast and the next raid to reach Britain had to wait another four days. The Gothas' final day bombing operation of the Great War, in the mid-morning of 22 August, brought scenes foreshadowing the summer of 1940, as fully 120 fighters were put into the air to cover London – and this against just ten bombers, the remnants of a thirteen-strong force which had been depleted by outbreaks of 'engine trouble' *en route* to Britain. Perhaps these problems were genuine, but frequent technical failures and 'early returns' from sorties would later be widely recognised as typical of campaigns meeting stiffening opposition. Timidity among the German crews would certainly have been justified on this day. One Gotha was downed by an RNAS fighter, while the AA gunners scored their greatest success against aeroplanes of the war so far by shooting down two. A loss rate of 30 per cent could not be sustained and after the raid of 22 August the Germans recognised that a phase in their campaign had been forced to a close. Hereafter their aeroplanes would need greater height, or the cover of darkness.

Although the Zeppelin had been largely defeated in the early summer of 1917, Germany persevered with sporadic airship raids for a further year, with the significant difference that only one, in October 1917, crossed London and their results were generally slight. From the summer of 1917 the Germans were in fact pursuing a definite tactical plan, using aeroplanes against London and the south-east while continuing to pester the Midlands and the north with airship incursions, which apart from any material damage they might cause served to tie down a proportion of the fighters, searchlights and AA guns in the provinces. On 16 June the loss of one airship from the two operating over Suffolk and Kent proved, if proof were still needed, that south-eastern skies had become perilous territory for the Zeppelin; the next two operations, one in August and one in September, roamed Yorkshire, Lincolnshire and Norfolk.

By the summer of 1917 these and other areas fielded an array of AA weapons much developed since the War Office had taken control a year or so before. As the war approached its final year the national layout of gun defences retained the basic hierarchy of AA commands and stations framed in spring 1916, though with much adjustment of groupings and relative strengths. By summer 1917 there were 22 'major' AA formations authorised in Britain – either AA commands for cities or port garrisons with an AA component – comprising all of the eighteen listed in 1916 except Milford Haven (where no AA defences were now authorised), and with the addition of Dundee, Greenock, Aberdeen, Glasgow and Manchester (the last three of which had previously been listed as AA stations). Some of these, however, were major formations only in a technical sense, ranking in the upper tier of the hierarchy only through their status as traditional garrisons. Remote from the usual ambit of the Zeppelins, Portland and Plymouth, for example, fielded just one gun each – Portland's was on the Breakwater Fort, Plymouth's at Stoke – as did Greenock, while Barrow could boast only two (at the Cemetery and Ramsden Dock). The point was that by summer 1917 the realities of German tactics had overtaken the original, somewhat abstract, conception of priorities as the determining factor in the share of guns.

The provincial AA commands mostly used fixed weapons of modern type; the mobile elements, while they continued to exist, occupied a more circumscribed role than they had eighteen months previously. In all, 395 AA guns of all types were listed in the War Office's roster of *Approved Armaments* issued on 1 June 1917 – which gives the approximate position at that date[86] – of which 52 were shared among mobile units and the remaining 343 allocated to fixed AA defences. The mobile units, by now, had been reorganised into a series of numbered batteries, used chiefly for forward coastal deployments; thus 1, 2 and 3 AA Mobile Batteries were based at Eaton Hall in Norwich, 7, 8 and 9 came

under the Humber Garrison and 10, 11 and 12 were based at
Harwich (the missing numbers appear to have been serving abroad,
likewise 13 AA Mobile Battery, which had been formed from
London Mobile in November 1916). These units used 13pdr QF
guns to the exclusion of other types, weapons which were nowhere represented in the fixed defences. The mainstay of the 343
fixed weapons was instead the 3in 20cwt gun, which at 185 pieces
made up more than half the total. Apart from one instructional
piece at Shoeburyness and a cluster of seven at Glasgow, French
75mm weapons were used only by Rawlinson's men in London.
Elsewhere the principal fixed AA gun was the 18pdr QF, of which
90 were approved, mostly allocated to more retired targets where
they were intermixed with 3in, a role also performed by 37 guns
of 12pdr 12cwt type which were on issue in June 1917. The sole
4in Mk IV gun was at Southsea Castle, where it had been since
the summer of 1914.

Although sporadic Zeppelin raids continued to pester the
Midlands and north until the high summer of 1918, changes to
the gun layouts in these areas do not seem to have been great in

Plate 1 First World War anti-aircraft position in the King's Cross area of London, manned by
gunners from the RNVR AA Corps. Some Great War AA sites used timber platforms of this
kind, others were concrete and ground-based.

the last year or so of war and some of those which did occur were the result of knock-on effects from developments in the south. Apart from a biggish but near-disastrous raid on 19 October 1917, which also saw the very last Zeppelin to appear – accidentally – over the capital, the five airship operations between October 1917 and the last on 5 August 1918 brought trivial effects compared to the deepening night offensive against London, which formed the climax of air defence arrangements in the Great War and the model upon which those for the next would be built.

Although Ashmore had every reason to expect night aeroplane raids against London, the range of possible preparations for them in the early autumn of 1917 was circumscribed by the technical limitations of equipment, among other things. 'At that time,' Ashmore later recalled, 'there seemed to be no means of meeting this form of attack;'

> [. . .] for some months it had been carried on by both sides, with impunity, on the Western Front in France. Searchlights were not sufficiently advanced in training or material to pick up and hold an aeroplane, although they could deal pretty well in good weather conditions with the larger, slower moving airship. The lights being unable to illuminate the target, the anti-aircraft guns had nothing to aim at, and could only fire in the direction of the sound. It was necessary to find some new method of employing them until such time as the searchlights improved.[87]

Nor were there many grounds for optimism over the value of fighter aircraft against aeroplanes at night, since few believed that the faster and more agile types best adapted to engaging Gothas – notably Sopwith Camels – were capable of being flown safely in darkness, or of finding their targets when they did so. Pessimism on the first score turned out to be misplaced, thankfully, when in what Ashmore described as 'perhaps the most important event in the history of air defence'[88] three RFC pilots boldly set forth in their Camels to engage the bombers and brought their mounts safely back to earth. But that feat was accomplished in the course of the second night raid, not before; and it is a mark of the desperation which surrounded the approach of this new phase of operations that some bizarre alternatives to conventional defensive technologies were considered. One was a technique in which carborundum powder was blown into the engines of the raiders, in the hope of stalling them (trials, sadly, yielded the opposite effect); another involved sprinkling sulphuric acid on the Gothas from above, an idea which reached no practical test. Yet a third wheeze proposed floodlighting much of southern England to silhouette the German aircraft against the ground, making them easier for the fighters to find. 'It would have been cheaper to move London' was Ashmore's sole comment on that.[89]

The need to confront the night raider on his own terms was confirmed in the first few days of September. Two single-engined aircraft operating against Dover on the night of the 2nd/3rd did little harm, but the next night brought a much heavier raid on targets a step closer to London, bordering the Thames. One hundred and thirty naval ratings died in their sleep at Chatham, when a pair of 100lb bombs hit the drill hall of the naval barracks, and a further 88 were injured. Fluke as this may have been – for no one could claim such accuracy by design for night raids of 1917, or indeed those of 1940 – it meant that the second night incursion by aeroplanes had caused the single most lethal bombing incident of the war. Further bombs from this ten-strong force of Gothas falling on Sheerness produced little result, but then neither did the defences. Scanning the skies on this bright, moonlit night the gunners of Sheerness and Sheppey caught no more than 'fleeting glances' of the aeroplanes which had slaughtered 130 of their comrades and though seven gunsites loosed off rounds in an innovatory 'barrage' pattern no hits were claimed.[90] The one positive outcome of the 3/4 September raid was the discovery that Camels could fly by night, a giant leap in the defensive arts prompted by a 22-year-old veteran named Gilbert Murlis-Green, the acting commander of 44 Squadron at Hainault Farm. Together with Captain C J Q Brand (later Sir Quintus Brand, 'Flossie' to his friends) and Second Lieutenant C C 'Sandy' Banks, Captain Murlis-Green set off in pursuit of the bombers when they were reported over North Foreland. Despite prowling the Thames Estuary for more than an hour, the three Camel pilots saw nothing of the Gothas.[91] But that hardly mattered; the point was that flying a Camel in darkness, and landing one on an improvised flarepath, were both easier than anyone had supposed.

The opportunity to hone these newly discovered skills came just 24 hours later when the Germans, capitalising on a period of good weather, for the first time put Gothas over London at night. The Camels were up again on this occasion, during which the London AA gunners had the chance to develop the technique of barrage fire tried at Chatham the previous night. In all, 37 gunsites fired on 4/5 September,[92] against a raid which turned out to be scattered: Dover and Margate were hit, along with several places in Suffolk and Essex, while only five of the machines reached London. One of the raiders was destroyed, probably by remarkably fine shooting from the AA site at Fort Borstal in the Thames & Medway defences, where Second Lieutenant Charles Kendrew and his men held a Gotha in their searchlight beam for fully seven minutes and seem to have scored a direct hit.[93] But such happy convergences of luck and judgement would prove rare.

Kendrew's achievement aside, the raid of 4/5 September demonstrated that the barrage technique was all the AA gunners really had to rely upon in this new phase of operations. And when the night raids resumed after a lull of twenty days, barrage shooting became the dominant AA gunnery tactic and the main means of meeting the Gothas with artillery in the absence of adequate searchlight guidance. At first the AA barrage was a screen of defensive fire thrown up in front of the advancing formation, at its approximate height. Its purpose was less to destroy aircraft than to deter them by attacking the crews' nerves and by interposing a pattern of AA bursts between the bombers and their objectives. In time, however, elaborate procedures were developed for aiming barrages, initially based upon squares in the horizontal and later identified by code-words which referred to defined portions of the sky above London and its approaches – *Ace of Spades*, *Mary Jane*, *Cold Feet*; these were numerous. As Rawlinson later explained, barrage fire was particularly effective against aeroplanes through the crews' instinct as far as possible to hold formation, combined with one of their machine's innate disadvantages as a bomb-delivery system, compared to the airship, of being unable to loiter or vary its speed to any great extent as tactical conditions required. Once lifted from the turf of its airfield the Gotha, like any aeroplane (until the Harrier), was committed to forward movement within fairly circumscribed parameters of speed; and this meant that opposing gunfire, suitably aimed, could be used to deflect a whole formation from its intended track. In these circumstances geographical barrages came to be used in inventive ways. A common procedure was to open fire on a flank, with shells bursting on an incline across the formation's path; once the bombers swerved away the tactic would be repeated as often as necessary to marshal the aircraft back onto a reciprocal course.[94] No perfect analogy suggests itself, though a trained sheepdog marshalling an agitated flock comes close.

Geographical barrages to be effective demanded reliable information on the height of the approaching formation. By autumn 1917 altitudes by day could be determined with some accuracy by height-finding instruments,[95] but while these techniques may have been equally sound for night use in principle, the sustained searchlight illumination necessary to get some purchase on individual aircraft could seldom be achieved. But then it was realised that if the bombers' height could not be accurately measured, it might instead be *dictated*. This was the main function of the London balloon aprons, a idea of Ashmore's which was tried soon after the 4/5 September raid and adopted in time for the next, on the 24th. The aprons consisted simply of rows of balloons linked by cables from which depended weighted wire streamers. Arrayed across east London, these presented a physical barrier to the bombers and – the real point – forced them to struggle in the narrow vertical band between the top of the apparatus (initially 8000, later 11,000 feet) and their own operational ceiling, which was not much greater. In this way the Gothas, if they were to approach London at all, had to do so at a known height. And it was at that height that the AA shells were fuzed to explode.

Just as the London aprons were distant prototypes of the balloon barrages of the Second World War, so the reorganisation of LADA in September 1917 prefigured the new defensive layout planned for the capital in the mid 1930s. Ashmore's thinking in reordering his resources was to separate fighters and guns, a *desideratum* particularly affecting the zone between the inner artillery layout and the outer barrier away to the east. As things stood in early September this intermediate area still supported a largish population of guns, which were necessarily prohibited from opening up when fighters were about. So, to aid the fighter and make better use of his artillery, Ashmore exchanged these weapons for searchlights – which could guide the RFC pilots in a general way by pointing towards enemy aircraft, if not actually holding them – while the spare guns released by the move, plus some mobile weapons drafted in from elsewhere, were used to push the outer gun barrier further around the north of the capital. A prohibition on British machines working immediately outside the gun line guaranteed that, barring navigational errors, any heard there would be foes.

These measures were well in hand by 24 September, when the Gothas returned to open what would later be known as the Harvest Moon Offensive – the most intensive spate of night aeroplane attacks of the Great War. Raids were attempted on six of the eight nights to 1 October, when the barrage performed reasonably well in keeping the weight of the bombs away from London, though on some occasions its effectiveness seems to have been over-rated through excessive estimates of the number of aircraft trying to attack. The first raid was combined with a Zeppelin foray into the Midlands and north, but neither achieved much. Of the sixteen Gothas which set off for London only three escaped the mechanical trouble and navigational muddles which thwarted their fellows and actually bombed the capital, though others in the force did some damage at Dover and elsewhere and one, for its trouble, was shot down (or perhaps gravely damaged) by the AA guns at Barton's Point.[96] On the next night, again, just three raiders approached London and of these one seems to have been deflected by the barrage coming up in front of him, a phenomenon which was also reported at Dover, where other aircraft trying to attack found similar AA tactics in use.[97] After the 25/26 September raid came a two-day interruption for weather before the largest force of the campaign so far was sent into action on the 28th. In all, 25 Gothas were airborne for London on that night, together with two of the multi-engined Giant machines, debutantes in the offensive against England. Exactly how many of these aircraft approached their target is uncertain (we do know that more than half aborted over the North Sea in the face of worsening weather) but those which did so seem to have lost heart on meeting the outer barrage, which they skirted before turning for home, when as many as three may have fallen to the guns.[98] The next night, 29/30 September, saw seven Gothas dispatched along with three Giants, a number much overestimated by the ground defences at the time – and by Ashmore in his account twelve years later, when he claimed that eighteen or nineteen aircraft attempted to bomb London but all except four were turned away by the barrage, which launched 12,700 shells into the night sky and destroyed at least one Gotha.[99] Deterrence by the guns was clearer on the next night, however, when just six Gothas penetrated the London defences from a force of 25 dispatched (fainter hearts bombed such targets as Chatham, Margate and Dover). The belief that the Germans were doing all in their power to evade the gun barrage may explain the account of the final raid in this series, which suggested that several bombers had climbed to 12–14,000 feet and shut off their engines to run in toward London in a silent glide. Doubts subsequently cast on that interpretation of events are probably justified, but the fact remains that only half of the twelve-strong force which crossed the coast got as far as the capital. Some of the strays may have become lost thanks to the thickening mist which obscured the ground, but equally the barrage probably added to their worries.

If these six nights of raiding did something to vindicate the barrage tactics they also demonstrated some fundamental difficulties in this and any other procedure for engaging aero-planes at night. One was the confusion apt to surround estimates of the number of aircraft operating, which later historians have shown were often lower than Ashmore and his colleagues believed at the time. For immediate purposes in the autumn of 1917 the tendency to over-count – to conflate multiple reports of aircraft movements into a larger total than was justified – was liable to yield false conclusions over the efficacy of the defences. Another problem, more practical and immediately pressing, was the barrage's prodigious consumption of ammunition and guns, whose linings by early October were wearing out faster than they

could be replaced.[100] Both of those problems were solved by the
Ministry of Munitions, who made extra efforts to step up supplies,
but the continuance of barrage techniques which these measures
allowed did nothing to ameliorate a third worry, which was the
ever-rising tally of casualties sustained on the ground from falling
debris – eight died and 64 were injured in the six Harvest Moon
raids. And self-bombardment worsened when Western Sub-
Command's fixed 75mm guns began to use shrapnel shells, which
were more hazardous than high-explosive because the cases fell
intact. The switch came about when the 75mm fixed guns were
installed, chiefly because the French high-explosive ammunition
was not officially sanctioned for British use thanks to fears over
its safety. Ironically, however, by the time of the autumn raids
the British guns were in general using an approved form of high-
explosive shell; so Rawlinson's prized 75mm guns were shifted to
Birmingham and replaced with 3in 20cwt types.

Apart from the final, accidental airship sortie on 19 October,
London was left alone by the German fliers until the end of the
month. Two minor coastal raids on 29/30 and 30/31 October were
followed by a big operation on the next night, when the barrage
seems to have scored a greater success. Twenty-two Gothas operated
and all crossed the English coast, but only eight or ten penetrated
the London defences and those which did so seem to have been
so harassed by gunfire that their bombing was peripheral and
light. And again, on 5/6 December, a force of sixteen aircraft
attacking targets in England managed to reach London with only
six of their number, probably thanks to the barrage which, on this
occasion, also managed to damage at least two of the attackers
sufficiently to bring them to earth in forced landings. Two further
raids before the end of the month, on 18/19 and 22/23 December,
brought respectively the first certain victory of a night-fighter
over a Gotha – fittingly enough scored by Murlis-Green – and a
minor incursion which achieved very little.

By January 1918 Ashmore had some grounds for satisfaction
in the performance of LADA, but none for complacency. The
barrage, it was believed, had done much to protect London – its
primary purpose – though rather little to destroy enemy aircraft
and thus secure the progressive attrition against the enemy's
bomber stocks, personnel and production which fully-successful

air defence requires. The strength of the defences had been steadily growing as the winter deepened.[101] The searchlight density in the aircraft zone had thickened since the first moves in this direction were taken in September, and with building experience and better training their crews were finding the Gothas more often and pinioning them in their beams for longer. At the same time the acknowledged weakness of the standard 60cm searchlight projector was being overcome by introducing a few 150cm types of French manufacture, while orders had been placed for much larger numbers of domestically-produced 120cm lights. Target-finding for the searchlight crews was also, by now, starting to be eased by the introduction of sound-locators, another family of AA instruments which had been developed chiefly by the French. Of the guns themselves, by January 1918 London was relying almost exclusively on the 3in 20cwt, which was generally agreed to be 'the most efficient AA gun in use for Home Defence', leading an order of merit which placed the 18pdr and 13pdr 9cwt second and third; by now all the French 75mm types had gone and apart from 35 weapons of 18pdr type out on London's western gun barrier all the guns in LADA were 3in (hoped-for

Plate 2 Old Lambeth Bridge, London: anti-aircraft searchlights in action.

supplies of more powerful 4in guns came to nothing). Including the weapons at Harwich, Thames & Medway and Dover, two mobile AA brigades and the steadily-encircling outer gun barrier, LADA by mid January 1918 could marshal 233 guns from an authorised total of 249, together with 323 searchlights; there were additionally sixteen naval guns on ships or shore stations acting in support of the general scheme. Eight fully-formed home defence squadrons of the RFC were also operating within the LADA ambit (and two more had been authorised), while the number of balloon aprons had grown to three, with more expected over the following months. In February 1918 a new assessment of German strength for the coming summer suggested that even these impressive totals might not be enough: foretelling a time, not far distant, when the Germans might be able to send 80 aircraft to Britain in a single raid, Lord French argued that AA guns should be increased to 349 (100 extra on the current target), searchlights to 623 (300 more) and that adding 40 aircraft to the fighter fleet, making 264, might be prudent. Partly to ensure no collapse of morale in London, these recommend-ations were approved by the War Cabinet towards the end of February 1918,[102] though the war was over before such a large body of guns and searchlights could be put in place. One new acquisition for the AA defences in the winter of 1917–18, however, was the introduction of 300 Lewis guns, distributed around targets in London and the south-east against the possibility of raids arriving too low for the usual weapons to meet. This batch of 0.303in machine guns was, in effect, the first home defence deployment of what by the Second World War would be termed light anti-aircraft (LAA) artillery. LADA at the start of 1918 was approaching the peak of its strength.

But still it grew, and as the night raids approached their climax on 19 May 1918 Ashmore continued to bolster his might. By the end of April LADA's guns stood at 266, the searchlights at 353, the precious sound-locator devices at 35, and the home defence squadrons at ten.[103] A little later in the spring the Portsmouth AA defences were brought within Ashmore's command, while those guarding the by-now largely untroubled northern cities were reorganised as the Northern Air Defences (NAD). And beyond that, more distant warning of approaching bombers was by now being provided, albeit fitfully, by permanent concrete sound-locators ('acoustic mirrors') positioned on the coast – the vanguard of a defensive technology further developed in the 1920s and early '30s, and only abandoned in 1935 with the first flickerings of radar.[104]

The sound of aeroplanes was much on the gunners' minds early in 1918, as the larger formations of Gothas used in previous months started to be replaced by smaller forces of Giants. Bigger as they were, Giants were little easier to see in the murky vastness of the night sky, but with four (occasionally five) 260 HP Mercedes engines driving pusher and tractor airscrews the audible distinction was unmistakable. Carrying a larger bomb-load and an impressive array of machine-guns, Giants were efficient killing machines, well able to look after themselves in the aerial battlefield over south-eastern England.[105] Though one raid on 28/29 January, the first of the New Year, sent thirteen Gothas and two Giants to England, otherwise until the very last aeroplane raid on 19 May, when 41 machines operated, Giants were used exclusively. Their numbers were indeed small – four on 29/30 January, five on 16/17 February, just one on the next night, six on 7/8 March – and of those sixteen sorties three aircraft failed to deliver their attacks. Nor did they achieve a great deal; just 66 people perished in aeroplane attacks between the end of January and early March, together with sixteen in three raids from navy Zeppelins which roamed the Midlands in March and April. Ashmore believed that the barrage was continuing to do its work, but equally none of the Giants operating on these nights was actually shot down, however many may have been disturbed and deterred. 'We were doing some fending off,' he later recalled, 'but so long as the Germans could count with reasonable certainty on returning home safely, we were doing nothing to put a stop to the raids.'[106] Hope for the future lay in more efficient reporting and control arrangements – especially in the new wireless sets which were beginning to offer continuous ground-to-air communications for the fighters – and in the steadily sharpening skills of the searchlight crews. Though the gun distribution around London was readjusted before mid May 1918, by moving weapons out from the core to the barrier line,[107] by April Ashmore evidently believed he had done everything possible, with current equipment, to raise the standard of the weapons themselves.

So London met the last aeroplane raid of the Great War, on 19/20 May 1918, with the gun and searchlight layout in the condition it had reached at the end of April. This operation was climactic, and not merely in the sense of being final. No fewer than 41 bombers left for England, 38 Gothas returning to the fight along with three Giants to make the biggest German force yet dispatched and one not much smaller than those delivering some of the lesser raids in the Blitz of 1940–41. Not all the members of this 'maximum effort' party made London, but the eighteen Gothas and one Giant which did so in the hour bracketing midnight still made a substantial force by 1918 standards, and were well concentrated in time. Some of the strays had turned back with mechanical trouble, others were lost to the fighters on the way in and some bombed alternative targets, leaving the nineteen-strong London force to face 30,000 rounds of AA ammunition coming up from the barrage, as well as the continuing attentions of fighters on their outbound journeys.[108] And on this night five or six aircraft were destroyed from the 31 which seem to have crossed the coast, a loss rate of almost twenty per cent. Three of those fell to fighters, who managed to intercept the raiders despite their pilots' criticisms of LADA's searchlight performance, and two or three to the AA guns. 'For the defences,' wrote Ashmore, 'this night was a success,' if also admittedly a failure, given the number of aircraft which had penetrated London's defences, killing nearly four dozen of its citizens. But after the raid of 19/20 May London was left alone; and apart from a singularly benign airship sortie over the Norfolk coast on 5 August, the German air offensive against Great Britain was over.

No one knew this, of course, as the tally was counted on the morning of 20 May 1918, and the strength and efficiency of LADA continued to grow for some months yet. Improvements over the summer of 1914 chiefly affected the reporting and control system, which by September had been remade on the ground with an elaborate network of telephone lines, enabling all defence sites of whatever character – gun, searchlight, observer post, airfield – to pass data to a central control, and in the air with wireless control for the defending fighters. By the Armistice, too, the number of guns in LADA had risen to 286 and the searchlights to 387.[109] So the strength of Ashmore's command reached its peak after the threat it was designed to meet was already spent.

With the risk of further raiding dwindling in the summer and early autumn, views on the art of air defence began to assume a retrospective character, as officers and officials whose duty it had been over the previous four years began to reflect on what had been achieved. Some, such as Rawlinson and Ashmore, would commit these thoughts to books after the peace was finally won, while others wrote official minutes and articles in the technical press, as experts would continue to do for much of the inter-war period. The instinct of these men to tell their stories and give their opinions helps us to examine what lessons were learned from the experience of AA gunnery as the Great War ended, seen from a viewpoint close to events.

The central question was that raised by Capper and others before the war began: did guns, or aircraft, offer the best defence against air raids, and especially against the night raider? On this issue the relative performance figures in machines destroyed perhaps throw only a tinted light.[110] During the First World War anti-aircraft guns in Britain are credited with the destruction of two Zeppelins (both in 1916) and nine aeroplanes; fighters by contrast destroyed eight Zeppelins and thirteen aeroplanes, with all the aeroplane casualties (to both arms) falling in the period from May 1917 onwards, when the Gotha raids began. On these figures the AA performance looks poor, especially when set against the five Zeppelins and four aeroplanes whose demise was attributed simply to the weather, and certainly in the latter stages of the war and shortly after it most experts who expressed a view came out in favour of the aeroplane over the gun. Writing in January 1918, in the midst of the night aeroplane raids – so before the full tallies could be made – Lord French remained non-committal: it was 'difficult,' he wrote, 'to determine the ultimate relative value of guns and aeroplanes as weapons of defence [. . .]',[111] though he was confident in his opinion that, at that time, the guns were ahead, thanks largely to their ability to fire at the sound of an invisible target where aircraft could not. But increasingly expert searchlight work, French thought, would be likely to overturn this superiority in time. French was writing in the afterglow of Murlis-Green's first night victory against a Gotha in mid December, and certainly by the end of the war a year later the fighters' popularity was in the ascendant. Rawlinson, a gunner, was trenchant in the pro-fighter view (and sufficiently so to indulge his fondness for eccentric typography in stating it). 'Neither London nor any other district,' he wrote, 'can be successfully defended against air attacks except by means of adequate forces IN THE AIR. [. . .] The defence of any district against AIR attack should not only be carried out *in the air*, but this operation should be undertaken at a considerable distance from the district which it is required to defend.'[112] That is essentially what the fighters of the RFC's 6 Brigade had been doing in the latter years of the First World War, and what the RAF would do in the Second.

Another to share this view was Ashmore, who in drafting a manifesto for the future of British air defence shortly after the Armistice argued that night fighters would 'be the predominant feature' of any future scheme.[113] Ashmore however was careful to stress the necessity for joint action between fighters and guns, a view he based partly on his LADA experience, partly on inferences drawn from events in France, where co-operation was honed to a fine polish in the closing months of the war, and in part, too, on the performance of the French and German defences. But for years afterwards there were those who continued to find in the Great War experience evidence that AA guns, not fighters, were the better bet. Writing as late as the summer of 1940, after the first German air attacks of a new war and – importantly – after H A Jones's volumes in the official history of air power in the Great War had been published, Major Thomas R Philips of the US Army put just this point of view.[114] Philips drew upon Jones's figures to argue that the fighters' contribution to defence had really been a costly failure. In the last fourteen months of the war, said Philips, the number of fighters destroyed in crashes or accidents was double the number of bombers; further, the fighters had to expend enormous efforts in sortie numbers to achieve the small returns they did accomplish; and huge numbers of fighters and expensively-trained pilots were tied up in Britain when they could have been more useful in France. In contrast, argued Philips, AA gunnery sacrificed few trained men and little specialised equipment to enemy action, acted as a powerful deterrent, and in the last fourteen months of the war, against aeroplanes, destroyed more intruders. Philips also drew on the experiences of the Paris defences, where guns predominated, to buttress this vigorously-argued case, likewise the performance of fighters and guns on the Western Front. 'In reality,' argued the major, 'night pursuit failed in Great Britain.'[115]

Some of Philips's case depends upon uncertain figures, notably for the Germans' casualty rate in the night aeroplane raids against LADA, though the margin of error is not so great as to swing the case unequivocally either way. But a central uncertainty lay in assessing the deterrent value of the AA barrage. Ashmore believed it to have been a great success, though H A Jones, in his official history, took a more cautious view, based partly on more accurate – and lower – figures for the number of aircraft operating on specific nights. Whether it really did save London from much greater damage in the Great War remains, of its nature, a difficult question to answer; but the value of 'barrage' anti-aircraft fire would come under question again in the Blitz of 1940–41.

In reaching judgements on the performance of Britain's air defences in the Great War the various commentators were not indulging in a mere academic exercise: their interest, rather, was to draw lessons for future policy. And in this respect it is easy to see how the fighter, in the climate of 1918, seemed to promise more. Fighter defence by the end of the Great War seemed to embody all the essentials to promise steady improvement, as gunnery perhaps did not. By the end of the First World War aviators could look back upon four years of dramatic technical progress in the design of fighter aircraft, in speed, manoeuvrability, reliability, and the capacity to carry weapons and wireless, all of which boded well for the future. Searchlights, too, were greatly improved by the end of the war, and were now widely assisted by sound locators. British gunners, by contrast, had at best the 3in 20cwt weapon introduced in 1913, which even in its ultimate home defence application had done little more than blast prodigious volumes of expensive ammunition into the sky, whence it returned to earth; AA gunnery at the Armistice was a knack, a dark art rather than a science. In 1918 the fighter was a frontier technology, just like the bomber itself, and the one was set to match the other in the technical advances of future years. The wisest judgement on air defence to be drawn from the Great War was not to see fighters and guns as alternatives, but rather to recognise the value of both, acting in concert, as they had in the LADA system. But, when the two technologies were viewed individually, the future potential of fighters seemed to hold the greater promise.

This in essence was the type of thinking which, in the fifteen years following the end of the First World War, would bring about a sharp contrast in technical development between the fighter aircraft and the hardware of AA gunnery, and similarly in the provision made for them in schemes of defence. But as the Great War came to an end, there was also another and still more potent issue to be considered, in a larger debate about the basic role of air power in wars of the future. Six weeks or so before the last aeroplane raid on London a new service had come into being in Britain. Formed on 1 April 1918, the Royal Air Force was born by the fusion of the flying arms of the two older services, the RFC and the RNAS. And the RAF was itself largely a progeny of the Gotha raids. In the summer of 1917, shortly after the first such operations against London, Lloyd George and the Boer General Jan Smuts had embarked upon a study of the air defence issues raised by this new turn of events. The report which arose from this inquiry – in effect the work of Smuts alone – appeared on 17 August 1917 and mapped the future of the aeroplane as an instrument of offensive war. It was, famously, thanks to Smuts' conclusions that an independent air arm was formed seven and a half months later; and thanks to Smuts, too, that the central duty of that new service – its *raison d'être* – came to be defined as attack, not defence, or at least as the one as a means to the other.

An air service [reported Smuts] can be used as an independent means of war operations. Nobody that witnessed the attack on London on 11 July could have any doubt on that point [. . .]. As far as can at present be foreseen there is absolutely no limit to the scale of its future independent war use. And the day may not be far off when aerial operations with their devastation of enemy

lands and destruction of industrial and populous centres on a
vast scale may become the principal operations of war, to which
the older forms of military and naval operations may become
secondary and subordinate.[116]

Given that devastating air bombardment had been predicted
by imaginative writers and military theorists for years before the
start of the Great War, this passage said little that was new –
except that bombing was conceived as an *independent* operation of
war, now envisioned against a background in which its potency
had actually begun to be demonstrated. Smuts' report was
influential. Over-ruling the objections of the two older services,
Lloyd George authorised the formation of an 'Independent Air
Force' in France to begin bomber operations against Germany, as
well as the creation of the RAF itself. When Sir Hugh Trenchard
came back from France to become the first Chief of the Air Staff
(CAS) the die for the next decade was cast. For the next twenty
years AA gunnery would continue to be subordinate to fighter
aircraft in the role of home defence; but defence itself would be
secondary to the burgeoning offensive power of the RAF.

CHAPTER 2

Cold storage

1919 – 1933

In 1929 Ashmore published a book on his experiences with LADA in 1917–18.[1] Largely a retrospect, but also a homily to the politicians of the thirties to preserve the art of *Air Defence*, Ashmore's text of that title commands interest to this day. In his final chapter, the author ruminated upon current trends. By the late 1920s, a decade after the Great War, Ashmore and others of like mind were growing increasingly frustrated by the trend of British air policy. His campaigning book was intended, as much as anything else, as a corrective.

By 1929 the RAF had been in existence for eleven years. In this time British air doctrine had taken its dominant flavour from Trenchard, whose gruffly-stated belief in the deterrent power of the bomber had by now come to symbolise the RAF's view of the world and their place in it. In 1929 Stanley Baldwin's famous assertion that the bomber would 'always get through' lay three years ahead; but what Baldwin said in 1932 was the orthodoxy of the 1920s as much as the thirties. Flowing from the experience of the Gotha raids in 1917–18, the Smuts Report, Britain's own forays into strategic bombing in the last year of war, and the arguments of *post hoc* theorists – among whom the name of the Italian Guido Douhet is probably the best known – by the middle 1920s it was widely held that bomber forces were more or less irresistible instruments of war, answerable only by a response in kind. For Baldwin, in 1932, there was 'no power on earth' which could protect 'the man in the street' from being bombed: fighters, AA guns, searchlights – none of these was much use. Offence was the only defence. Put in crude terms (and shockingly so by the standards of the day) it meant that 'you have to kill more women and children than the enemy if you want to save yourselves.'[2]

At the start of a chapter reviewing a period in which this doctrine held the floor for almost twenty years, it is worth noting that Ashmore rejected it absolutely, in his book and elsewhere. In Ashmore's view, the alumni of what he called the 'bomb-the-other-fellow-is-the-only-way school' missed the lessons of recent history, which should have taught that a sufficiently rigid frame-work of air defence could indeed persuade bomber crews to relent. For Ashmore, too, the bomber doctrine of the inter-war period failed equally on moral and practical grounds. Familiar as we are today with post-1945 debates on the ethics of strategic bombing, it is easy to overlook the intensity of feeling which surrounded the issue long before Guernica, Coventry, Dresden and Hiroshima pushed it to the fore. To Ashmore the prospect that a British government should authorise 'first-strike' bombing was repellent.

> It is not easy [wrote Ashmore] to picture a British Government ordering a great bombing offensive before hostilities have begun; even if such an offensive were only directed against enemy aerodromes. History might be puzzled, might hesitate before deciding that our reason for taking such an action was really defensive, and taken in order to save our capital from destruction. In hypercritical circles one might almost hear the word 'Crime'.[3]

Even without these moral scruples, practical questions remained. At what point would a counter-offensive be launched, and how long would it take to show some effect? 'Weeks, certainly,' thought Ashmore, 'months, perhaps,' in which time London would 'suffer terribly, perhaps intolerably, long before any counter bombing would save her' – assuming that it did. More likely, though, was a slide into carnage. 'To stop the enemy bombing us,' prophesied Ashmore, 'we should attack his aerodromes.'

> Will that make him really sorry? I doubt it. To make him sorry, we must bomb his capital, his industrial areas, in which case our

efforts against his aerodromes must be diminished. We shall then have the edifying spectacle of two nations hammering away at each other's capitals, with no immediate object but mutual destruction.[4]

It was to avoid this gruesome turn of events that Ashmore published his case in 1929 for a heavy reinvestment in strictly *defensive* air armaments at the expense of the bomber deterrent. Later this view would be vindicated, though it is worth noting that, even in 1929, Ashmore may have overstated his case. Though historians in the decades after the Second World War tended to downplay the extent of British investment in air defence during the 1920s and for much of the '30s, their successors have tended to reveal a more complex picture in which interest in the bomber deterrent, though paramount, did not prevent Britain from simultaneously acquiring the best strategic air defences in the world. Writing as recently as 1999, the historian John Ferris has argued that from 1923 to 1934, 'the RAF established an excellent air defence system, which restored the London Air Defence Area's strong foundations and built on it.'[5] As far as the fighter force and air defence intelligence system was concerned, that argument is difficult to dispute. But AA guns and searchlights – which Ferris does not really discuss – were a different matter. If Britain's defence planners put the bomber first in the 1920s and for much of the 1930s, while not neglecting the fighter arm and the ground system necessary to support it, they still allowed AA gunnery to languish almost untended in the lowest echelon of defence priorities. Much of the character of the gun and searchlight panoply with which Britain entered the Second World War resulted from that simple fact.

In making his arguments in 1929 Ashmore was re-fighting a battle which had first been joined in the immediate aftermath of the Great War, when he and others had lobbied vigorously for Britain's complex (and still largely new) system of air defence to be preserved. Ashmore himself fired the opening round, when on 22 November 1918, eleven days after the Armistice, he delivered a paper to Sir William Robertson, C-in-C Home Forces, in which he argued not merely for maintenance of the *status quo* but actually for selective improvements. LADA's balloon aprons should be 'retained', argued Ashmore; the AA artillery should be left 'somewhat as at present', though with modernised guns on LADA's western arm (replacing the 18pdrs) and fewer mounted centrally; searchlight cover should be maintained at the current level, while 6 Brigade's pattern of home defence airfields, control rooms and communications should be left intact. About the only major change Ashmore envisaged was a transfer of executive control of air defence from the War Office to the Air Ministry, which had it been carried through at that time would have given all three service ministries a turn at the job within three years.

As it happens this transfer of control did eventually come, but otherwise Ashmore's proposals yielded little. We might doubt, indeed, whether he ever expected otherwise. Although GHQ Home Forces prepared an after-war AA scheme calling for as many as 2400 Regular and 15,800 part-time Territorial troops, in truth what was missing by autumn 1918 was any identifiable enemy to justify retaining a complex and expensive array of defences; and at the same time governmental instincts for retrenchment were as predictable as the soldiers' vocal and occasionally fractious agitation to return to civilian life. But Ashmore's larger purpose was to secure the technical bedrock of air defence, to prevent the loss of expertise which would surely come if the whole apparatus, redundant as it might seem in the weeks following the Armistice, was simply dismantled. To this others agreed, not least Winston Churchill, who as the responsible minister chaired a conference in February 1919 which affirmed a need to 'keep alive the intricate and specialized art of air defence' and to provide a framework which would allow efficient expansion back to 'war strength'.[6] Three months later a second conference was held to examine what this might mean in practice.[7]

In studying these issues in May 1919 the War Office and the fledgling Air Ministry were working on the assumptions that a proportion of the fixed defences laid down in wartime would be retained for training, and that the AA troops would divide between a core of regulars (who would husband these guns) and a much larger contingent from the Territorial Force (TF). It was assumed further that two or three years' freedom from air raids would give time for this structure to be designed and put in place. But in the light of what happened in the next year, the details of this scheme seem almost naïvely optimistic. In May 1919 the War Office and Air Ministry were expecting the basic organisation of LADA and NAD to remain, with both divided into four AA defence commands within each of which one permanent two-gun AA station and one searchlight site would be retained (four more searchlight sites would also remain near RAF Biggin Hill, where a co-operation squadron would eventually be based). Beyond these, it was proposed that 28 gunsites should be retained with weapons in store – generally three in each AADC – along with 58 search-light positions, to give the troops somewhere to exercise their craft in the training season. Though this skeleton force was based around the four London commands and those elsewhere – with headquarters at Edinburgh, Newcastle, Leeds and Birmingham – the TF recruiting pattern was designed to furnish AA defences in the next war at all the major targets defended in the last.[8]

None of this happened, of course. What killed the scheme was the so-called Ten Year Rule, whose principles had begun to influence thinking by August 1919.[9] Lasting in one form or another until 1932, this stricture posited that no major war would affect home territory for a decade, measured (until the Rule was repealed) from the present moment. In these circumstances the plans of May 1919 were doomed within a few months, and by early autumn some central elements of the air defence structure of 1918 had already gone. The RAF's 6 Brigade was reduced simply to the Home Defence Wing at the end of June,[10] more airfields were abandoned – including the key fighter stations for London at Sutton's Farm (Hornchurch), North Weald and Detling, all of which would later be expensively reacquired – and the AA personnel establishment slashed to just 80 officers and 579 men.[11] At this date the basic skeleton of the AA peace organisation proposed in May still looked like surviving, with the eight AADCs and their attendant training sites simply given to this tiny cadre of caretakers. This was recommended at a third War Office conference, in mid October, when it was agreed that while no 'framework of actual defence is necessary for the present' the proposed AADC headquarters should survive to cater to the Territorial Force, when it was formed, in a national organisation which would include a central AA control centre (probably at Biggin Hill), research establishments and a school on the Isle of

Wight.[12] To all of these details the Army Council pronounced itself in broad agreement, though with the caveat that much would depend upon when Territorial recruiting for AA duties actually began. No one could be sure of this in the climate of winter 1919–20, and a complicating factor newly recognised at this time was that of the eight centres proposed, only three could be formed at existing AA stations: the agreed pattern of property disposals meant that the remaining five would require new sites.[13] In December 1919 the War Office actually went so far as to issue draft plans for these positions – one for a gunsite, one for a searchlight station, one for an RE company headquarters – which are of interest for what they reveal of the trend of AA fabric design in the year or so after the Great War: all were small, utilitarian and hutted, and embodied design principles inherited from wartime permanent gunsites (Fig 2).[14] But none was built. By late February 1920 the climate of retrenchment had deepened to the point where yet another War Office conference concluded that the entire AA organisation could be reduced to a single school for gunnery and searchlight work, provisionally assigned to Andover (though it did allow that AA interests could be represented on a number of committees). Looking ahead, this same conference recognised that a Territorial training organisation for AA work would be necessary and desirable, but for immediate purposes the blunt term 'abolish' was appended to each item in the roster of domestic anti-aircraft infrastructure drawn up less than a year before: the two Air Defence Headquarters (LADA and NAD), the eight AADCs and their RGA companies, the two RE searchlight companies to serve them, and the control centre.[15]

And these conclusions stuck. It was decided in 1920 that the AA establishment for the immediate future would be set at just three AA defence divisions – one Regular, two Territorial – each comprising four AA defence brigades, all to be built up gradually 'as funds allow and the strategical and political situation demand'. During this year the remaining 'wreckage' (so termed) of the wartime AA units was duly gathered together at Aldershot and the Regular brigade was formed in December (with Ashmore in command),[16] though almost a year later this unit was described as 'still practically at cadre strength' – in fact just twenty officers and 100 men were available against an establishment of 30 and 500

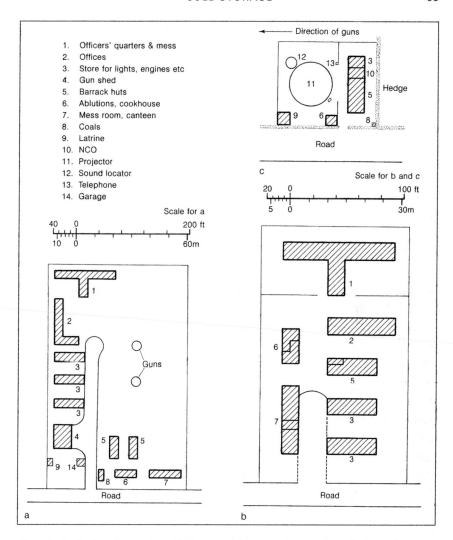

1. Officers' quarters & mess
2. Offices
3. Store for lights, engines etc
4. Gun shed
5. Barrack huts
6. Ablutions, cookhouse
7. Mess room, canteen
8. Coals
9. Latrine
10. NCO
11. Projector
12. Sound locator
13. Telephone
14. Garage

Direction of guns

Hedge

Road

Scale for b and c

20 0 100 ft

5 0 30m

Scale for a

40 0 200 ft

10 0 60m

Guns

Road

Road

a

b

c

Figure 2 Draft plans for AA sites, 1919. No positions were built to these designs, which show (a) an HAA gunsite, (b) a searchlight position and (c) a headquarters, but they do show the trend of structural thinking in the years immediately after the Great War. Permanent HAA sites constructed in the years immediately before the next war obeyed a very different template (see Fig 7).

respectively, a rather top-heavy ratio of chiefs to Indians.[17] Additionally in 1920 a small AA section was formed in the Directorate of Military Operations, and plans were drawn up for the putative Andover school and the Territorial organisation, but that was all.[18] Nothing was done to raise the part-time units in 1920 or 1921, partly because the War Office decided to wait until the disbandment of 21 surplus Territorial infantry battalions released much-needed funds.[19] Just two years after the Armistice the AA organisation of the Great War had practically ceased to exist.

By this time developments of greater moment had begun at the higher levels of defence planning. Despite the strictures of the Ten-Year Rule (which when needs required could prove surprisingly malleable) by 1921 it was clear that home defence policy needed to be underpinned by some guiding principle – by a more sophisticated set of strategic assumptions which would yield targets for personnel and *matériel* and redefine the respective roles of the three fighting services. Yet those assumptions were not at all easy to define. The years around 1920 were a period of flux in defence thinking, as government and the services attempted to assimilate the lessons of the recent past and to anticipate what sometimes seemed a bewildering future. The change was as much technical as strategic. Within the last ten years the aircraft, the submarine and the tank had forced a seismic shift in the nature of warfare. At the same time political and economic factors, in the climate of post-war stringency, were firmly in the ascendant. Politics, too, were in play in relations between the air marshals, the admirals and the generals, and acutely so in the relationship between the *arriviste* Royal Air Force and the older fighting services. There were many in the years following the Great War who questioned the RAF's continued legitimacy as an independent service. In order to survive, Trenchard's fledgling needed a distinct and independent role, different in kind from simple air support to the army and navy. And it was the affirmation of that role, in 1922, which as much as any other factor shaped the fate of anti-aircraft gunnery for much of the inter-war period.

The question of the RAF's continued independence was given early in 1921 to the Standing Defence Sub-Committee of the newly-revived CID, which despite finding itself unable to agree eventually came out in favour of the airmen's claims through a personal report issued by its chairman, Arthur Balfour, in July.

The RAF, argued Balfour, should remain independent, and form the country's main defence against attack from the air; in other spheres of operation the air force would support the army and navy, but in a co-operative rather than subordinate role. These conclusions were duly approved by Cabinet in March 1922. The practical implications of this arrangement, however, were less than clear at that time; and to clarify those Balfour completed a second report, issued on 29 May 1922, in which he made a stalwart case for matching the known air strength of France. It is widely agreed today that Balfour's appraisal of French air power was at least mildly alarmist, if not a little foolish. There was no sign that France harboured hostile intentions toward Great Britain, but with Germany and Russia militarily impotent France's strength did offer a benchmark against which to measure Britain's own.[20] And for other reasons the corollary of Balfour's argument – the expansion of the RAF at home – was not unattractive. For one thing investment in military aviation would stimulate its civil counterpart; and for another the nation which, just four years earlier, had boasted the strongest air force in the world was reluctant to be left behind.

The upshot of Balfour's two reports was a step-change in Britain's air defence planning during 1922. Executive control of the air defence system was transferred from the War Office to the Air Ministry – meaning that thereafter AA defences would be ultimately controlled by an RAF officer – and in August 1922 the Cabinet announced the intention to enlarge the metropolitan air force to 23 squadrons. And it was in the character of that force that the RAF's independent role was most clearly asserted, for despite their avowed function in *defence*, fourteen of the 23 were to be bomber squadrons and only nine would marshal fighters. In this commitment to the bomber arm above the fighter the RAF's inter-war character was set. Trenchard and the disciples of the bomber deterrent had won the day.

For all the shortcomings of the 23-Squadron Scheme (not least the assumption that a French bomber fleet of 300 aircraft could be deterred by a British one of half that number) its ratification in the high summer of 1922 marked the ascent of a philosophy which would continue to shape Britain's air defences until 1937, through many changes of government, staff, strategic conditions and equipment. The commitment to the bomber deterrent as an instrument of defence did not, of course, obviate the need for more literally 'defensive' precautions: there were, after all, to be nine squadrons of home defence fighters, together with AA guns and searchlights in numbers and dispositions to be discussed in a moment. But the belief in the bomber allowed a measure of complacency to undermine active air defence, while at the same time divided control of the personnel and their equipment tended to militate against efficient, integrated planning. From 1922, despite their theoretical unity as a single defensive system under the Air Ministry, the fighter squadrons of the RAF and the gun and searchlight batteries of the army came to be formed, equipped and readied for war too much in isolation from one another, and certainly at widely divergent rates. In fact the 23-Squadron Scheme did not last long as the target for the RAF's metropolitan strength, being replaced by a 52-Squadron Scheme within a year before the whole programme was relaxed in 1925 and then practically frozen before the end of the decade. But throughout this time, whatever the air force was doing, the army was generally languishing in the doldrums.

The 23-Squadron Scheme of August 1922 defined the numerical component of the RAF's contribution to the air defences, but not a great deal more. Another study was necessary to delineate the geography of the scheme and to stipulate the numbers and deployments of guns and searchlights, and this was completed by February 1923 in the authorship of Air Commodore J M Steel and Colonel W H Bartholomew, respectively for the Air Ministry and the War Office. Although the RAF element of this layout was superseded by the 52-Squadron Scheme which emerged only four months later, the geography of the Steel–Bartholomew Plan dictated the basic bone-structure of the air defences in London and the south-east for many years to come (Fig 3). The Plan's debt to LADA is manifest. London itself would be populated by guns designated the Inner Artillery Zone – the IAZ, a style never superseded for the capital's AA layout – bounded to the south and east by an Aircraft Fighting Zone (AFZ) divided into sectors whose reach extended westward into Wiltshire and north as far as RAF Duxford. Each of these letter-coded sectors would be served by a fighter airfield. Further out, a slender Outer

Artillery Zone (OAZ) would serve to break up incoming bomber formations before they reached the fighter aircraft, much as the forward guns of LADA had done in the recent war. Bordering the whole zonal system was a broad swathe of territory designated for forward observer posts, while detached gun layouts would also be provided on the coast for Dover, Portsmouth, the Thames & Medway and Harwich. This was about the limit of the guns thought necessary to foil bombers operating from France in what was essentially a south-eastern scheme.

How many guns were needed? Steel and Bartholomew put the figure at 264, manned by eleven AA brigades (later more fittingly called regiments), with 192 of these given to the IAZ and OAZ and a further 72 to the defended ports. There would additionally be 672 searchlights, distributed widely throughout the layout, serving the defended ports, the two artillery zones and the AFZ.

Figure 3 Air defences planned in Steel–Bartholomew Report, 1923. This integrated system of observer posts, fighter sectors and gunfire zones owed a clear debt to LADA.

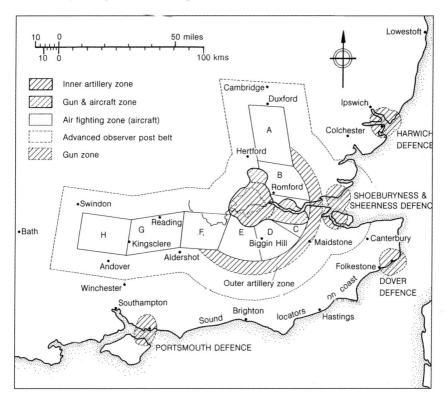

This was the basic plan of the 1920s, though since the newly-authorised increase in the size of the domestic air force to 52 squadrons necessitated amendments, the scheme was re-studied in 1924 by a new committee under Major-General F C Romer, whose report also made recommendations on matters of command and communications. The matter of command took a step forward in January 1925, when on the first of the month a new formation came together at the Air Ministry known as Air Defences of Great Britain (ADGB) to take charge not only of the guns, lights and fighter aircraft, but also the bomber fleet and indeed all aspects of Britain's domestic air defences. With a tiny amendment to its title – Defences becoming 'Defence' – on 1 June 1926 ADGB moved to a new headquarters at Hillingdon House, Uxbridge.

One of the members of the Romer Committee was Ashmore, who in April 1924 had been appointed General Officer Commanding Territorial Army Defence Formations and Inspector General of Anti-Aircraft, titles whose grandiosity rather belied the fact that there were few TA defence formations to command, nor AA units to inspect. One service Ashmore could perform, however, was to study the problem of the observer and raid reporting system required under the new plan, and this he accomplished in a series of experiments in 1924–25. Based closely on the system which had served LADA in 1917–18, the network tested at this time was the genesis of the (Royal) Observer Corps, which was formally constituted in October 1925.[21]

Another requirement of the defence schemes crystallised under Steel–Bartholomew and Romer was longer-range warning of approaching bombers. Britain had lacked much hardware for these purposes in the recent war, but the early forays into acoustic detection using sound-collecting mirrors on the coast had yielded promising results.[22] This comparatively novel technology was kept alive in the immediately post-war years by further experiments with the mirrors installed on the east Kent coast, which continued until at least 1922, and by new work with horizontal acoustic discs, which was undertaken in the early 1920s at Biggin Hill and, from 1923, at a new experimental station at Hythe. From this date until the mid 1930s the Acoustic Research Station at Hythe became the focus of new experiments with a range of sound mirrors, all of them intended to give long-range warning of aircraft approaching over the Channel, from France. They were only superseded, finally, by radar, whose experimental work began in earnest during 1935, and not before plans to extend the system to the Thames Estuary had reached an advanced stage. But throughout the 1920s and the early 1930s it was these huge concrete sculptures on which the long-range early warning for the air defence system, supposedly, would depend.

None of this much affected the gunners, at least not at first. Although the AA units did not long remain at the nadir touched in 1920, five years would pass before much new growth was visible. In 1920–21 the tiny residuum of Regulars continued to exercise at the RGA School at Shoeburyness,[23] though it was frustratingly obvious that the deficit in manpower made 'any but the most elementary of training an impossibility'.[24] Then, very gradually, things began to pick up. Recruiting for the first four Territorial AA units began in 1922, the year in which the 23-Squadron Scheme was approved, when 51 AA Brigade (TA) was formed (the old Territorial Force had become the Territorial Army – the TA – on the previous 1 October), to be followed within the year by the 52nd, 53rd, and 54th.[25] All were based in London. At the same time the AA school was assembled as a stop-gap at Perham Down, near Tidworth on Salisbury Plain. First intended for Andover, alongside the RAF's School of Air Pilotage, by May 1922 the establishment was destined instead for permanent quarters much closer to London at Biggin Hill, where the greater share of a 'large hangar' was released to store the Territorials' 3in guns and a decent collection of brick huts was made available for offices and lecture rooms.[26] It was in these hand-me-downs that the Anti-Aircraft Defence School formally opened for business in November 1922.[27]

It was one thing to form the new Territorial units, quite another to bring them up to strength and ready them for war. In fact no single AA brigade came anywhere near reaching its authorised establishment during the 1920s, despite the modest commitment asked from the volunteers. Understandably enough, perhaps, no one was much attracted to the military reserves in the decade following the Great War, and those men who did nurse an appetite for TA service generally signed up for venerable infantry units with strong local ties and thriving corporate pride. Few recruits were much attracted by AA work, especially when shortages of serviceable equipment meant a training routine dominated by foot drill instead of time on the guns. From 1923 the gunners' annual camps were held at Holme-next-the-Sea in Norfolk, where tented accommodation was set up and the men, in theory, were given live firing practice – two more years would pass before AA artillery gained a permanent training range, which opened in 1925 at Watchet on the Somerset coast.[28] But these practice sessions were hardly the industrious events that the War Office intended. In 1923 the batteries who turned out for annual practice camp stood at about twenty per cent of their theoretical strength, 30 men typically appearing for units supposedly requiring five times that number.[29] In those circumstances little useful work could be done. Even enthusiasts became jaded.

It was in 1925 that the general expansion plan for ADGB enshrined in the 52-Squadron Scheme itself began to slow. Reporting in November, a committee chaired by Lord Birkenhead recommended that growth in the air defences could safely be decelerated to provide the full 52 squadrons for the RAF by 1936, eleven years hence. By 1925 the RAF component of the scheme had in fact made steady headway and almost half of the required squadrons had been formed. In the interim, however, only one new AA unit had come together – 55 AA Brigade, based at Tonbridge in Kent – with the result that the RAF's component had already far outstripped the army's. Britain of course was open to no manifest threat in 1925, and that was just as well; for any hostile bomber approaching during Stanley Baldwin's second premiership would certainly have got through.

In practice the deceleration in the 52-Squadron Scheme was barely sensed by the AA gunners, if only because their own expansion programme was already practically inert. But the middle 1920s did see important progress behind the scenes in a busy round of technical study and experiment on new AA equipment. Although laggardly recruiting for the TA accounted in part for the creaking progress of the gun and searchlight defences, it was also true that the War Office remained hesitant to recruit too freely to a specialism whose hardware and procedures were steadily becoming obsolete. To help close this gap in 1925 the CID set up an Anti-Aircraft Research Sub-Committee, which by the following spring was keeping tabs on a refreshingly diverse range of experiments with guns, ammunition and fire control instruments.[30] Some of this work, by its nature, was inconclusive; but the research programme in these early days included trials with equipment which, often in more advanced variants, would be vital to the AA armoury fifteen years hence (and incidentally conditioned many structural characteristics of wartime gunsites and buildings, as we shall see). One was the Vickers predictor, a clockwork-powered mechanical computer which performed the calculations necessary to determine the bearing, elevation and fuze-length for the guns on the basis of the target's motion through the air, tracked through the gun-layers' optical sights. Resolving the necessary formulae continuously, the device fed data to the guns electrically by cable connections, enabling the crews to lay their weapons in unison (by following a pointer on a dial) under control from the site command post.[31] Tested exhaustively in 1925–26, this hefty black box bristling with levers and dials entered service as the Predictor AA No 1 early in 1927.[32] Other devices under test in 1926–27 included various types of optical heightfinders and rangefinders, including the massive fifteen-foot-long Barr & Stroud heightfinder, another model purchased from the Lavallois company, and modified versions of older types. Early in 1926 the War Office held competitive trials of these instruments at Biggin Hill, only to discover that the operators were so inexperienced as to nullify the whole exercise (though later the Barr & Stroud won the day). And then there were guns, and ammunition. Several dual-purpose AA and coast artillery mountings were under trial or contemplated by early 1926 – including 6pdr and 6in types – none of which produced a serviceable weapon, but more promising was the new 4.7in gun in prospect from Vickers Ltd, which was expected to throw a 50-pound shell to the then prodigious height of 30,000 feet. In the event the 4.7in weapon also languished, but its discussion in the middle and late twenties anticipated the requirement for a fixed heavy AA gun capable of engaging high-flying targets which was eventually met by the 4.5in, the first of which was emplaced eighteen months before the next war.

Encouraging as these technical developments may have been, however, no amount of promised equipment could compensate the AA organisation for a number of near-crippling weaknesses which persisted throughout the late 1920s – problems which ultimately found a public airing, as far as that was possible, in Ashmore's book of 1929. By the time he sat down to write Ashmore had become fully reacquainted with the *minutiae* of Britain's domestic AA defences, since it was in 1926 that he was appointed to command the ground troops manning the guns and searchlights. And throughout these years the barriers to effective training seemed almost insurmountable. Partly this was bad luck. The training season of 1926 was disrupted by the General Strike, an episode which aptly symbolised the larger national malaise at a time when some AA officers were actually buying equipment on the open market from private funds.[33] In this year the TA searchlight units proved far too 'green' to be tested at their positions in the AFZ, so were shuffled off to a training camp while the Regulars of 1 AA Searchlight Battalion stood in for them;[34] the result was some evaluation of the lighted zone, but no realistic training for the men who would actually occupy this region in war.

The need for realism in training became still more acute from the summer of 1927, when the RAF held the first of its full-scale air exercises of the inter-war period.[35] Recommended in an article by Major Oliver Stewart in the *Army Quarterly* for October 1926 and soon officially endorsed,[36] the air exercises would now become a regular, if not an annual, highlight of ADGB's year (no event was held in 1929). Variously configured and often inventive in their imitation of war conditions, the air exercises would always test the aircraft of the RAF and the searchlight crews of the RE much more frequently and realistically than they could the gunners of the RA, who were often left out of the action and sent instead for practice firing at the coastal training camps. Even without the gunners' presence, however, the exercises of the years bracketing 1930 offered some important pointers to their predicament in a future war, as well as advertising the need for air defence in general – findings were widely and excitedly discussed in the press (usually with the conclusion that London had been razed by high explosive and poisoned by gas) and more soberly in the services' 'trade papers', whose correspondents tended towards more measured conclusions. Thus the first exercises, of 1927, in Major Stewart's eyes, 'suddenly and vividly brought back war memories almost in their original clear colours [. . .]'.[37]

Held over five days from 25–29 July, these manoeuvres pitted the bomber forces of 'Eastland' against London, capital of 'Westland', whose very incomplete air defences were deftly explained away by the government already having withdrawn to Manchester, taking most of the guns and searchlights with them. What remained were sufficient lights to illuminate the equivalent of one sector skirting the capital, in which the TA searchlight crews worked with real aircraft for the first time, though on this occasion under the supervision of their Regular counterparts. In practical terms exercises such as this involved the troops and Observer Corps occupying pre-selected 'war' positions with their mobile equipment and going through the motions of intercepting RAF bombers, masquerading as 'hostiles', as realistically as they could – a role-play which was always truer for searchlight men than for gunners, who were denied the climax of live firing to test their expertise. In 1927 these men faced Westland's nine squadrons of bombers – variously Virginias, Horsleys, Fairey Foxes, Hyderabads and DH9s – and supported twelve squadrons of Eastland fighters: the Siskins, Woodcocks, Grebes and Gamecocks of ADGB's Fighting Area.[38]

Whatever their limitations, these evolutions began to yield valuable data from the start. A finding of 1927, generally replicated in later years, was that incoming night bombers could be intercepted in the AFZ under searchlight illumination with relative ease – relative that is to the equivalent procedure during the day, which proved surprisingly difficult in the absence of the AA shell-bursts which had done so much to close patrolling pilots to raiders in the Great War. To Major Stewart, indeed, the indicative role of AA guns was their greatest strength, given that direct hits on an aircraft were probably 'impossible' (though he conceded that as 'open to debate') and deflecting bombers entirely from their goal almost as difficult. Larger questions, too, were raised by the 1927 exercises: about aero-engine design, the value of wireless, and the poor performance of the RAF's fighters against the current generation of bombers, especially the lively, agile Fairey Fox, which left many interceptors embarrassingly outpaced.[39] But, without firing a shot, the AA guns seemed to have proved their worth.

With that point made, however, the gunners were omitted from the exercises in the following years; and in truth there was little point in their taking part, when time could alternatively be spent in live firing at Watchet and Holme. In these circumstances the exercises of 1928 devolved upon the observers, the fliers and the searchlight crews, who despite their worthy contribution in 1927 had been rather thin on the ground. To remedy this during the forthcoming season Air Marshal Salmond at ADGB insisted to the Air Ministry in February 1928 that the coming season's training must connect more firmly with reality by lighting three sectors – C, D and E, to the south-east of London – with the equipment and men who would shoulder this duty in war.[40] In the event all the available searchlight units did take part – the Essex, Kent and Surrey searchlight groups, the 26th and 27th Searchlight Battalions from central London, and the Regulars of 1 AA Searchlight Battalion based at Farnborough – which under the command of Air Vice-Marshal Sir Robert Brooke-Popham worked with twelve squadrons of Westland fighters against Eastland's thirteen bomber units, under Air Vice-Marshal Sir John Steel.[41] And again the defences in general did surprisingly well, the umpires earnestly declaring that just nine of the 57 raids mounted over the whole span of the exercises had evaded the defences entirely, that 151 bombers operating by day had been destroyed, and so on.[42] Some gave these figures more credibility than others and in general the action was, by the standards of 1940, desperately slow; but judged on their own terms this and the previous year's exercises offered reassurance of a sort.

In visualising these proceedings it is important to bear in mind that no fixed infrastructure was provided for the ground defences. The war stations occupied in these manoeuvres were no more than fields identified by grid references in the AA defence schemes. These existed in reams, since the pattern of guns and searchlights had of necessity to be worked out when the overall plan was drawn up. But the proportion actually populated in exercises remained tiny, and even those which were used lacked communications with sector headquarters, or indeed with anywhere else. With no telephone lines installed the searchlight positions, in particular, were unable to report aircraft movements back to their controls – always an important secondary function of searchlight troops – and everyone, so to speak, was rather in the dark.[43] By the end of the decade a specialist committee was overseeing work to link at least some of the sites to the GPO network. Modest as it was, this work marked the first move towards fixing and consolidating the searchlight positions in their war layout.

This limitation hardly mattered in 1929–30, however, since no exercises took place in the first of those years and London was not the focus of events in the second. The air exercises of 1930 instead posited a wholly different scenario in which Britain was divided notionally into two colonial territories, called Red and Blue Colonies, divided by a broken range of imaginary mountains from Surrey to Liverpool. The targets in this battle were less capital cities (though Red's was at Cranwell and Blue's at Old Sarum) than vital war installations, such as a notional port at Catterick, reached by a canal from the North Sea, and important mineral resources in the regions of Hucknall and Bircham Newton. The main difference between this exercise and its predecessors was thus an emphasis upon combat around small, localised points; and chief among these, as the action developed, were airfields.

Though the AA gunners again played no part in these exercises, they were among the most illuminating for the future of AA defences, since the airfield attacks simulated in August 1930 accurately previewed the events of precisely a decade later. Though low-flying airfield attacks were a commonplace of the later stages of the Great War in France, a decade or so later they could be delivered by faster-flying machines – the new Bristol Bulldogs in 1930 – which emphasised their suddenness, sharp destructive power, and near immunity from AA fire. Major Stewart, by now a regular spectator at these events, saw the action first hand. 'The three Red aeroplanes appeared suddenly over the trees,' wrote Stewart, watching the proceedings at a Blue Colony station.

Their coming was totally unexpected, and with the best possible defence organisation it is certain that they would have launched their attack with machine-gun fire or small 20-lb bombs before preparations could have been made by Blue for an adequate reply. And even when the ground defences were in action the converging method of attack caused the three aircraft to present difficult targets and it is by no means certain that they would have been seriously disturbed by machine-gun or ordinary anti-aircraft gun-fire from the ground.[44]

Indeed they would not, and while Stewart was careful to assure his readers that a 'new type of multi-barrelled anti-aircraft gun' was under development to meet tactics such as these, in the event it would be many years before modern, purpose-built light anti-aircraft (LAA) guns were built into the defence plans (the term 'LAA' was not even in currency in 1930). Ten years later, when Göring's young men threw their Messerschmitts and Dorniers into low level attacks on Fighter Command's airfields, there were just 430 such weapons in Britain.[45]

The air exercises of the late 1920s certainly raised awareness of air defence issues among the population at large, but any hopes that public anxieties might yield a flood of new recruits into the TA units were unfounded. In fact the AA units lost men in these years. Early in 1927 the Army Council was obliged to introduce restrictions even on the paltry recruiting then taking place, chiefly for economic (and hence political) reasons in the aftermath of the General Strike.[46] Ashmore was among those who were quick to point out that AA units were the very last who should be subject to restricted 'peace establishments', since these troops, almost uniquely, needed to be at full strength from the first minute of war.[47] But it was no use. The ruling, for a time, limited the batteries in the IAZ to a personnel ceiling sufficient to allow manning of half the guns, but while the moratorium was widely resented it seems to have made little practical difference to units which were already languishing well below war strength. By the end of 1928 the number of AA gun brigades formed remained stuck at five, among which only the four London units contained the three batteries to which they were entitled; 55 AA Brigade at Tonbridge so far consisted of just one sub-unit – 163 AA Battery – making thirteen AA batteries in all. Each of the fully-formed brigades was entitled to a war establishment of 452 gunners, though the ceiling to which they were authorised to recruit was set at just 305 men, with 26 officers in either case. The units' end-of-year returns for 31 December 1928 show that 51 AA Brigade (the most senior in order of formation) was not far from its authorised level, at 22 officers and 290 men, while the other three London brigades were close behind; 163 AA Battery in Kent, on the other hand, had mustered only half of the eight officers and 98 gunners allowed. At this time progress in recruiting to the searchlight battalions and companies was on the whole rather behind that of the artillery, and taken together all the air defence units at the end of 1928 contained 3685 men (including officers) – about 75 per cent of an authorised ceiling of 4965 and rather over half the theoretical establishment. But then, from 1929 onwards, the numbers in every type of unit began to drop. By the end of 1929, 51 AA Brigade's strength had tumbled to 232 men, in a year during which the overall loss of troops topped 500. And the trend continued. Though a few units rallied periodically, chiefly through vigorous local evangelism (whatever the War Office may have believed of its official recruiting campaigns, most initiates to the TA were drawn in by friends), every unit with the exception of the small signals contingent was weaker at the end of 1932 than it had been four years earlier. Among the London gun units 52 AA Brigade lost the better part of a third of its men in these years.[48]

To make matters worse this disturbing trend came at a time when the demands placed upon the AA troops were tending to rise, either in fact or in prospect. In February 1930 a CID sub-committee under the chairmanship of Colonel C G Liddell recommended that the searchlight layout, hitherto confined to the IAZ and Aircraft Fighting Zone, should be pushed outwards to colonise the OAZ as well – a requirement amounting to 120 lights and sound locators and five searchlight companies.[49] Less than a year later the War Office suggested that the commercial ports well to the rear of the defended area might also be given AA guns,[50] to which the Air Staff replied fairly that since 'the provision of adequate forces for the defence zone, and for such ports as Portsmouth which are in front of it, will constitute a commitment beyond the capacity of national defence expenditure for some considerable time [. . .]',[51] this was hardly the moment to think of gunning the Mersey, Humber and Severn. And such proposals were indeed absurd. In this same year (1931) Salmond reckoned that in the event of war just 27 per cent of the guns and 22 per cent of the searchlights already authorised for his command could actually be manned.[52]

The RAF had done better, of course, and despite the progressive slowing of the 52-Squadron Scheme by 1931 four-fifths of the stipulated units had been formed or were actively coming together. Britain's air defences as the thirties opened therefore rested first on the bomber deterrent – Handley-Page Hyderabads, Hinadais and so on – vast, stately biplane bombers unlikely to strike much fear today but formidable enough by the standards of the time. It was this 'bomber first' strategy which Ashmore, of course, condemned in his book of 1929; and this same strategy which Baldwin, serving as Lord President of the Council between his second and third premierships, annunciated so vividly to the Commons and the nation three years later.

Many on the air force side were affronted by what Baldwin had to say on that November day in 1932. To Sir Christopher Bullock, secretary to the Air Ministry, Baldwin's suggestion that the RAF's duties amounted to the competitive slaughter of women and children smeared the air force as a 'barbarian Service';[53] and perhaps this once and future premier had overstepped the mark, victim of what one of his biographers has identified as his 'consuming and sometimes even irrational *idée fixe*' with the bomber.[54] But many gunners believed that Baldwin's outburst would do them some good. Although the claim that the bomber would 'always get through' was tantamount to dismissing the air defences as impotent (and was, incidentally, difficult to reconcile with the evidence of the exercises held since 1927), Major-General Salt, the gunners' current commander, for one believed that recruiting to the TA air defence formations could only benefit from Baldwin's 'man in the street' grasping the danger that he and his family might face.

> [. . .] I have come to the conclusion [wrote Salt in February 1933] that the difficulty in recruiting lies in the apathy of the civil population, and that this apathy is due to the fact that they have

never been educated to realise the very great dangers which threaten them from air-attack. Mr Baldwin's speech in the House of Commons on November 10th 1932 is the only recent occasion I can recall in which the attention of the civil population has been drawn by a public authority to the dangers of air attack on a civil population.[55]

And for Salt, Baldwin's speech brought the whole issue of air defence into the open, where it might now be discussed frankly, unfettered by squeamishness. It also promised Salt a new degree of freedom in his own recruiting campaign.

In going round my units [he continued] I frequently have opportunities of making speeches to assist in this recruiting problem, and at these functions a number of civilians are frequently present. On these occasions, however, I feel that I am not in a position to draw a picture of the horrors of aerial attack, as I do not know whether the policy of the higher authorities is to avoid alarming the civil population. I have, therefore, so far confined myself to pointing out the necessity of air defence units being full up to peace recruiting establishments, owing to their being in all probability the first units of the national forces to be employed in active operations with the enemy. If, however, I could be permitted to point out the dangers which threaten I feel that I could do more useful service.

I request therefore that I may be informed as regards the policy of the Government in this respect.[56]

A fortnight before Salt wrote these words there was a change of chancellor in Germany; and a fortnight later a mysterious fire swept through the Reichstag in Berlin. On the face of things the accession of Adolf Hitler and the rapid consolidation of Nazi power in 1933 might be expected to have galvanised recruiting to Britain's defence services, dissipating the apathy which Salt found among the populace and his own potential recruits. And it is true that recruiting saw a modest resurgence in 1933: although some TA units continued to weaken there were precisely two officers and 105 men more in the AA defence formations at the end of the year than twelve months previously. In Salt's words, however, the gain was 'so small that it will have little effect on the area of the

defences [. . .] which can be manned in case of emergency'. At
the end of the year a draft *Provisional Defence Plan* issued for the
TA air defence formations listed, by grid reference, 28 sites for
guns and 144 for searchlights in the IAZ, 42 gunsites and 156
searchlight positions in the OAZ, and 312 searchlight sites in the
AFZ – 682 separate locations in all.[57] In the event of war, however,
just a small proportion of those could have been manned.

Salt, evidently, was becoming acutely anxious over his deficit
in manpower by the New Year of 1934, and in a plea to the War
Office offered practical suggestions over how it could be overcome. Vigorous publicity was the key. 'Large headlines on the
front pages are necessary to get at likely recruits', he wrote
(adding, revealingly, 'many of whom only read the front pages').
People should be made to understand that 'these units are
maintained for the direct defence of their homes, families and
businesses'; that the work was 'interesting. Only intelligent men
can be accepted and these are the class who would understand
the necessity of providing defence, if only they were educated up
to the dangers which threaten London'; that the ground defences
against air attack had been 'entrusted to the people themselves,
and they should respond to this trust by joining the units provided
for the purpose'; and that the units were 'purely defensive', such
that 'even the most ardent pacifist should feel no compunction in
joining them.'[58]

There were indeed many ardent pacifists in the Britain of
1934, the year in which the national 'Peace Ballot' voted for
disarmament.[59] And two years previously these people and the
population in general had found some grounds for optimism,
thanks to the League of Nations Disarmament Conference at
Geneva which had been in session since February 1932,
struggling through a protracted round of negotiations which the
British delegation had entered with the earnest desire to achieve
worldwide limits on the holdings of military aircraft. But, by early
1934, any hopes that Geneva might avert European air
rearmament were practically spent. Though few of the delegates
at Geneva were prepared to concede everything in pursuit of
peace, German intransigence lay at the root of the talks' collapse.
Thwarted in her demands for 'equality of rights' with other
nations, Germany had withdrawn from the conference table first

in September 1932, a few months before Hitler became chancellor.
A softening of positions by the other delegate brought the Reich
back into the fold when the conference reconvened in February
1933, but despite British restraint in furthering her own air power
expansion during this year – the next year's Air Estimates
published in March 1933 proposed a modest cut in expenditure –
as the year wore on it was clear that the Germans had already
begun to rearm in defiance of Versailles, a move whose
legitimacy France, in particular, would never accept. The
wrangling continued into the summer, before the Germans
finally quit Geneva for the second and last time in October 1933,
protesting at the 'humiliating and dishonourable exactions of the
other Powers.' And with that, the course for the next few years
was set.

CHAPTER 3

Reorientation

1934 – 1939

Although the Geneva conference rumbled on impotently until early 1934, the withdrawal of the German delegation in October 1933 signalled the beginning of a new strategic situation in Europe, and already by November of that year the Defence Requirements Committee (DRC) of the CID had identified Germany as the 'ultimate potential enemy' in a future war.[1] The DRC itself was a progeny of the Geneva impasse. Formed a month after the German secession, the Committee (of service chiefs and senior civil servants) was initially briefed to identify the 'worst deficiencies' in Britain's defences bequeathed by the Ten Year Rule, and among these the incompleteness of ADGB's 52-Squadron Scheme emerged as paramount. The recommendation to complete this programme thus became the main element of the Committee's report, put to Cabinet on 28 February 1934. Acceptance of that argument was not immediate and even in the spring of 1934 there were those in government who pressed for further attempts at arms limitation by negotiation. But these arguments came to nothing and by July the Cabinet had approved the first of the RAF's new round of inter-war Expansion Schemes – subsequently known as Scheme A – which was designed to bring the domestic air force up to a strength of 75 squadrons over the next five years. At the same time the first thoughts on restructuring the geography of the air defences to meet a new German threat were committed to paper.

Issued on 30 July 1934 over the signature of Air Marshal Edgar Ludlow-Hewitt, Deputy Chief of the Air Staff and future head of Bomber Command, the Air Staff paper on reorientation of the air defences offered a concise statement of the new strategic situation poised to develop across the eastern approaches. 'Aircraft operating from the North Sea Coast of Germany,' it advised, 'can now deliver effective attacks on the industrial centres in the neighbourhood of the Tyne and the Tees, the big industrial areas in Lancashire and Western Yorkshire, [and] the industrial centre in the Midlands in and around Birmingham.'[2] None of these areas benefited from the defences advocated by the Steel-Bartholomew and Romer plans of ten years before, whose gun and aircraft fighting zones lay many miles to the south: basically the present, inchoate system was redundant as a defence for the north. At the same time, however, the southern defences remained vital to protect the capital, since bombers flying from captured bases in Holland or Belgium would be 'quite as well placed to deliver effective attacks on London' as those approaching from France. Revealingly, the Air Staff at this stage did not raise the grave possibility that German attacks might be launched from airfields *within* French territory – that spectre had yet to be conjured – but the point remained that the system planned in the mid 1920s needed to be greatly enlarged, and not simply rearranged.

In the Air Staff's view this could be achieved in one of two ways: either by clustering guns and lights around the new targets in a 'discontinuous' system, confining fighter operations largely to the illuminated areas so produced; or alternatively by extending the barrier authorised for the south northwards, with a new limb to the aircraft fighting zone and OAZ and probably with some local AA cover for the main targets. Essentially the choice was between a frontier or an area system. Defence on 'area' lines brought the advantage of simplicity, by avoiding a lengthy extension to the searchlight belt and OAZ and confining the layout to the Tyne–Tees region, Leeds, Manchester, the Midlands (chiefly Birmingham) and the Portsmouth/Southampton area. It would also require marginally fewer searchlights, if rather more guns. Tactically, however, the 'area' scheme brought many anxieties. First among them was the danger that enemy aircraft would simply exploit the gaps between the defended cities, slipping between them to range the country widely, free of searchlight cover, and bombing alternative targets or approaching the gun zones by back routes. Defending only the key cities would also allow the Germans more or less open access to military bases such as Aldershot or Salisbury Plain, and to lesser industrial and communications targets throughout the country: no protection would be possible for Peterborough, for example, or Northampton, Bedford, Swindon, Bristol, and a host of similar places in the middle echelons of strategic importance. Nor would it be wise to confine night-time fighter operations to illuminated skies around the defended areas, which in the industrial areas of Yorkshire and Lancashire would be perpetually shrouded in smog and difficult to protect from suitably-sited airfields. For these specific reasons – but perhaps, too, through an instinctive preference for frontier defences – the Air Staff concluded in July 1934 that a northward extension to the barrier already authorised for the south was a safer bet.

The anatomy of such a system was not difficult to delineate. Air Staff opinion in July 1934 saw 'no effective alternative to [. . .] a continuous defence zone from the Tees, around the Eastward of London to Southampton', the southernmost leg of which would be formed by swinging the original zone running westward further south, to end instead at the Solent. The zone would consist of a uniform, twenty mile deep searchlight area – widened from the fifteen miles currently authorised to allow for increases in aircraft speeds – fronted by a five-mile deep OAZ, though the density of guns and fighters would vary along its length. The strongest gun defences would lie in the zone from Dorking in Surrey to Huntingdon in Cambridgeshire, where weapons would be spaced at one-mile intervals, a density halved between Dorking and Southampton and in the northern stretch from Huntingdon to the Tees. At least sixteen fighter squadrons would command the illuminated area from Huntingdon down to the Solent, with nine disposed in the 200-mile front up to the northern terminal at Middlesbrough. In addition, local AA guns in modest numbers would be provided for the vulnerable cities themselves, and for the largely separate system represented by the defended ports. Altogether, this scheme called for 56 batteries of 3in guns and 84 searchlight companies, with the lion's share of lights (55 companies) absorbed by the AFZ and the largest number of guns (25 batteries) allocated to the OAZ. The London IAZ would claim six companies of lights and twelve AA batteries, much as before.

These ideas were put before the Home Defence Committee on 2 August, when it was decided that the whole problem of air defence planning must be given to an expert sub-committee with a view to issuing a definitive report.[3] Drafting a brief and assembling the group took time, and it was 17 October before the Sub-Committee on the Reorientation of the Air Defence System of Great Britain held its inaugural meeting.[4] Chaired by Air Chief Marshal Sir Robert Brooke-Popham, now the head of ADGB, this select band of nine senior officers gathered at least weekly over the following months in the CID's rooms at 2 Whitehall Gardens, a cul-de-sac off Whitehall. Assembling a new plan for Britain's air defences took just fourteen weeks, although as things turned out this weighty document, signed on 31 January 1935, was only the first of several schemes to issue from the group. Under a succession of chairmen the Reorientation Sub-Committee remained in being until 1939.

The central strategic assumptions given to the committee in autumn 1934 were that the next war would see Britain opposing Germany, with France as an ally, but that Dutch and Belgian airspace might be violated by German aircraft *en route* from their home bases, and perhaps that both countries would be occupied by Germany early in a war. Broadly, then, the war scenario envisioned in 1934 saw air attacks, of uncertain scale and intensity, originating in a eastern arc beginning at a line running south-east from London – roughly along the Franco-Belgian border – and fanning northwards to the Tyne approaches. To meet these, the Brooke-Popham committee was allowed forces set at 'a minimum compatible with an adequate degree of protection', with London as their first priority. Given the need for economy, the committee was asked to formulate a staged plan, aiming first at an 'interim defence' achievable within existing budgets. Anything more ambitious would have to wait, but the committee's terms of reference also required that the defences should furnish 'visible protective measures for the maintenance of public morale'.[5]

The committee's first decision, taken at its inaugural meeting on 17 October, reaffirmed what Baldwin had declared to the

Commons two years previously. Britain's air defences, recorded Brooke-Popham and his colleagues, must be planned on the principle that 'however powerful the air forces of a country may be, they cannot assure complete immunity from hostile air attacks'; and that to meet the raiders which would always get through, 'a proportion of the available air forces must be allocated to Home Defence.'[6] Similarly, in their January 1935 report the committee was careful to stress their adherence to air force orthodoxy in stating that 'the most important function of aircraft is offensive action by bombers, but that a defensive system is also a necessity.'[7] That system, of fighter aircraft, AA guns and searchlights, 'should be limited to the lowest possible minimum' and organised within a sophisticated intelligence framework for raid reporting and control. There was never any doubt that the AA component of this system would continue to be staffed entirely by Territorials; but at the same time the likelihood that air attack would 'synchronise with, or indeed form the commence-ment of, hostilities' required that 'the whole of the defence system [. . .] must be working at its full efficiency in the first hour of war.'[8] In other words the next war might begin, as Colonel Louis Jackson had prophesied of the last, with a knock-out blow.

The essential shape of the system proposed by the Brooke-Popham committee in January 1935 differed little from that sketched by the Air Staff six months previously. The weekly meetings in Whitehall Gardens had seen much debate on the relative merits of discontinuous and continuous gun layouts, the anatomies of searchlight and gun zones, and the requirements for fighter aircraft, most of which led to similar conclusions to those already reached. The committee saw the final system comprising a searchlight belt and OAZ, jointly 26 miles in depth, running from the Solent to the Tees, skirting London and taking in the local defences of Portsmouth–Southampton, the Humber and the Tees (Fig 4). The frontal six miles of this belt would be occupied by the OAZ and the remainder by the lights, while London would retain its IAZ and local defences would be provided for key city targets behind the frontier – Birmingham, Manchester, Sheffield, Leeds – and the defended ports, each of which would evolve into 'gun defended areas' (GDAs), the basic HAA layouts of the coming war (Appendix I). Altogether this system in its mature form demanded

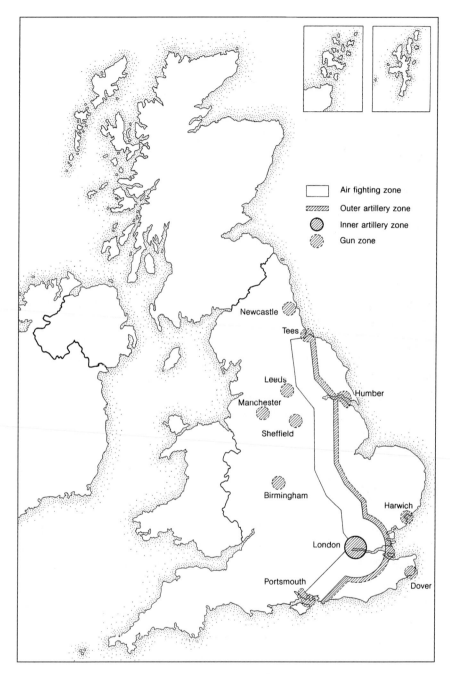

Figure 4 Air defences planned under Reorientation Scheme, 1935, showing the (still schematic) zones for guns, the Outer Artillery Zone – soon to be abandoned – and the searchlight-illuminated Air Fighting Zone. Within two years this plan was supplanted by the Ideal Scheme's new recommended structure (Fig 5).

at least 25 fighter squadrons, together with 57 AA batteries marshalling 456 HAA guns of 3in type (but fewer when modern weapons expected later in the decade began to be supplied) and 90 companies of searchlights: ground defences amounting to 43,500 men and a capital investment of five and a half million pounds.

Maturity, however, would be attained only gradually, via a three-stage programme, the first element of which was scheduled for completion fully five years hence, on 31 March 1940. Completion to Stage Three, and the addition of a Supplementary Stage which the committee thought advisable to close the western approaches to London and bolster local gun defences elsewhere, took the full timetable to a date which, though unspecified, would have comfortably overreached the end of the Second World War. In fact most of the heavy guns for local defence of key targets – the principle upon which AA artillery was actually organised in that war – were scheduled for this remote Supplementary Stage. Beyond that, the committee drew attention to serious deficiencies in guns to meet low-flying aircraft, and also urged that a new committee should be formed to study the application of science to air defence in all its aspects. Particular emphasis was laid on the value of this new body, the heir of the Anti-Aircraft Research Sub-Committee which had last reported in March 1928: 'its composition should be strong', advised Brooke-Popham and his colleagues, 'and it should be able to draw from the best brains obtainable in the country. It should also have wide terms of reference and be endowed, if considered necessary, with special powers for the advancement of its recommendations.' With hindsight these were probably the most influential words in the report, for the body which resulted – the Committee for the Scientific Survey of Air Defence – met first in January 1935 and within a year had brought about the invention of radar.

Only Stage One of this plan hardened into any kind of reality before it was superseded. This phase called for eight gun batteries and six searchlight companies for the IAZ, nine AA batteries for the OAZ (including five for Thames & Medway), and searchlights to cover the belt from Portsmouth to Huntingdon, with the stretch southwards from Godalming restricted to a fifteen-mile depth at first. In all, 36 searchlight companies were needed for this part of the layout. In addition, it was recommended that the Observer Corps should grow to colonise practically the whole country (excepting the northern and south-western fringes), and that the new AA units needed for the second and subsequent stages should be formed and trained within the life of Stage One. Approved by Cabinet on 8 July 1935, for the next year Stage One became the new target at which the AA defences would aim.

This decision was taken in a climate of growing concern at the pace and character of German rearmament. Five weeks after the issue of the Brooke-Popham report Germany admitted what her European neighbours had known for some time, when on 9 March 1935 Göring announced that the Luftwaffe had already reformed in defiance of Versailles. At this news the arms race which would characterise the remainder of the 1930s was joined in earnest, as the British government was forced to embark upon the second of what would become six successive schemes for the expansion of the RAF authorised in peacetime. Approved in May 1935, Expansion Scheme C pushed the RAF's target strength to 3800 aircraft by April 1937 – an objective whose impressive total in numbers rather belied the military value of the force, which was limited by the looming obsolescence of many of the aircraft types ordered. True to contemporary RAF doctrine, Scheme C was designed to produce a deterrent force – 68 of the 93 squadrons authorised were heavy, medium or light bombers – and whatever its weaknesses in *matériel*, it did at least signal the government's continuing commitment to challenge the rise of German air power. But the emphasis upon the bomber arm, which was perpetuated in further schemes authorised over the following three years, reflected the abiding preference for defence by deterrence which, inevitably, tended to sap the impetus to make serious and continuing investment in AA artillery. Over the next two years the disparity between the RAF's offensive strength and Britain's preparedness to meet incoming bombers – with fighters and especially with guns and searchlights – would steadily widen.

The upgrading of the London defences and the extension of AA cover into the new territory proposed by the Brooke-Popham committee inevitably demanded a huge expansion in the numbers of men required for the TA artillery and searchlight units, and a corresponding reassessment of the practicalities of command, organisation, mobilisation procedures, administration and works services. The problem of numbers was solved – or at least addressed – by a much resented policy of converting a selection of Territorial infantry regiments to AA work, a process which began during 1935 with the selection of seventeen such units in the London area and promptly brought recruiting, once again, to a standstill.[9] To wrestle with the remaining logistic problems yet another committee was formed, this one under the chairmanship of Salt's successor, Major-General R D H Tompson.

Where the Brooke-Popham group dealt with matters of higher strategy, it fell to Tompson and his thirteen colleagues to get to grips with the nuts and bolts of reorientation among the Territorial air defence units, and much of the organisational machinery put in place in the four years remaining before war was joined emanated from their deliberations. Tompson's first *Interim Report*, issued on 12 July 1935 and endorsed by the Army Council at the end of the month, was influential chiefly for its proposal that the AA troops should be given their own divisional organisation, reducing the number of authorities with which the gunners had to deal and at the same time providing a tier of command to handle those aspects of their affairs which, at present, were strictly speaking the responsibility of no one.[10] As a result, 15 December 1935 saw the formation of 1 AA Division to cover the AA brigades in London and the south-east, which were in turn shared between four AA groups, for the IAZ, Home Counties, Thames & Medway and East Anglia.[11] No. 1 AA Division was the first of seven equivalent formations to be embodied before war began.

Where Tompson's first report settled administrative questions, its successor ranged more widely. Issued on 6 February 1936, Tompson's second *Interim Report* tackled the very difficult practical problems of how the Territorial gunners and searchlight crews of 1 AA Division could actually be mobilised from peacetime to their war stations, addressing as it did so questions of ordnance services, works and buildings requirements, supply-lines, equipment storage and transport.[12] Elements of the resulting prospectus that the Army Council approved on 12 May 1936 were soon superseded by a CID decision to introduce a static element to the gun layout, which meant that rather less equipment needed to be stored away from the sites where it would be used, but that permanent gunsites would be needed in some numbers. But the basic problem remained: how could a legion of part-time gunners and searchlight operators, together with most of their equipment, be brought to stations which, in principle, needed to be operable on the very outbreak of war? In practical terms the support services available for 1 AA Division had not developed much since the establishment of the TA's London AA brigades in the early 1920s; so, as Tompson and his colleagues were careful to point out, while 1 AA Division now enjoyed an official existence, it totally lacked 'the means of mobilizing or of being maintained in war'.

As things stood early in 1936 the AA units of the TA routinely held a small and usually inadequate proportion of their equipment at their 'peace stations' – the drill halls and other premises where they would meet and as far as possible train in peacetime – but none had yet received its allocation of 'mobilisation equipment', in other words the balance of the quota of guns, lights and ancillary gear which it would need in war. One very good reason for this was that much of the more up-to-date equipment listed for war use had yet to be manufactured; and another was that the units in any case had nowhere to put it. In view of this the War Office's policy at this time was to share out new mobilisation equipment between 1 AA Division itself and the new units due to form in the north to make good the shortfall in gear needed for training. In this way it was expected that all AA units would hold their full quota of training equipment by about 1938. So it was at that point that a stock of genuine mobilisation equipment would begin to accumulate; and it was at that point, too, that stores would be needed to receive it.

One of the most influential recommendations made by the Tompson Committee was that the stores for this mobilisation equipment must lie as near as possible to the war stations where it would actually be used: given the need for rapid deployment, it was no use holding guns and lights in vast ordnance depots such as Woolwich, nor in central storehouses of such size that units would need to draw their equipment in rotation. While it was accepted that cost and other practical considerations would probably necessitate a degree of grouping, the model to be aimed at was the most decentralised pattern of storage possible, in which each unit could realistically draw its full quota of war equipment – including ammunition at a scale of 400 rounds per gun – in twelve hours from stores not more than fifteen miles from any gunsite. Some of the necessary plots or buildings, it was accepted, could probably be found at RAF stations and on existing War Office estate; others, however, would need new sites. Over the next couple of years the acquisition of mobilisation stores on this model became one of the TA air defence formations' main works projects.

Peacetime works services at the gunsites themselves, on the other hand, were altogether less urgent in the climate of early 1936, when all weapons were mobile and the holding of sites arranged by lease rather than purchase. As matters stood when the Tompson Committee made its second report the requirement for sites in 1 AA Division amounted to 120 gun positions and 1056 for searchlights, all of which would need to be furnished when occupied with accommodation for the troops, services such as water and telephone lines, access roads and emplacements for the guns and lights. Yet this was a lighter task than it sounds, since basic earthwork emplacements would be dug by the gunners and searchlight crews themselves, in more or less conformity to type-designs published in their own technical manuals, while the rest of the site fabric could be built up gradually as time allowed; the main thing as always was to get the weapons pointing skyward. In these circumstances the Tompson solution was to appoint a single RE officer to the 1 AA Division staff, who together with a draughtsman and clerk would reconnoitre each site and prepare schedules and plans for the things to be built in war. This is how the works preparations among 1 AA Division's gunsites began in 1936, though by the end of the following year the requirement for bricks and mortar had assumed vastly different proportions.

That dealt with the storage of the guns and the work to be done at their destinations. What of the link between? When the Tompson Committee studied this problem early in 1936 the

Territorial AA units possessed little or no transport of their own, either for the moves from mobilisation stores to sites – which demanded a very large fleet of vehicles for a short time – or for supplies once they were in place, where the requirement was for a smaller, permanent pool. For mobilisation Tompson saw no alternative but to equip each battery permanently with a heavy vehicle of its own – a three-ton, six-wheeled type, complete with towing attachment and winding gear, in exchange for the quasi-mythical 30cwt lorry which each battery was supposed to have in its war establishment but none actually held in peacetime. In addition it was recommended that a further such lorry for each battery should be held in peace by a Royal Army Service Corps detachment, to cart mobilisation equipment and ammunition out to the sites. This, already, came to a weighty and expensive fleet of 192 lorries to be provided for 1 AA Division in peacetime; and to these were added a further 44 smaller vehicles for towing the plethora of trailers carrying the searchlights, sound-locators and generators of the RE troops. Altogether the batteries of the southern division needed 236 vehicles for their peace establishment alone.

The minutiae of lorry supplies and logistics are not the most engaging aspects of Britain's inter-war AA development, no more so the provisions made by the Tompson Committee for weapon maintenance, medical services, signals and a host of smaller niceties necessary to ease the Territorials' passage from peace to war. But their close and purposeful study in the early stages of rearmament makes a revealing contrast with the twenties, when some officers dug deep into their own pockets to furnish their batteries with equipment and, had war come, many of the arrangements settled by the Tompson Committee a decade later would have been lashed together in confusion. For the time being, of course, Tompson's recommendations in 1935–36 were no more than that; despite ready approval by the Army Council few of these objects could be met quickly and a good many required amendment in detail as plans evolved. But the fact that they were studied at all spoke of an emerging realism.

An important set of amendments became necessary soon after Tompson's second report was issued, when on 29 May the Reorientation Committee was invited to examine the implications of deleting the Outer Artillery Zone from the plan. This was a radical proposal. The Brooke-Popham report of January 1935 had allocated 272 weapons to the OAZ, a notional stock whose release enabled some fundamentals of the earlier scheme to be readdressed. After a good deal of complex discussion the Reorientation Committee's new plans were committed to paper issued on 17 June 1936, over the signature of Air Vice-Marshal Philip Joubert de la Ferté, who had succeeded Brooke-Popham as head of ADGB earlier in the year.[13]

In three respects the scheme proposed in the Joubert Report differed markedly from that advanced by Brooke-Popham and his colleagues barely eighteen months before. First, abolishing the OAZ jettisoned the principle of a forward, linear gun layout which had been a feature of every defence scheme since LADA came together in the summer of 1917. Secondly, the proposal that the defences should use a mixture of new 3.7in and 4.5in guns (then under test) signalled a commitment to establish a proportion of the guns on permanent sites, using static weapons in concrete emplacements. Thirdly, the defended ports – currently seen as a disparate scatter of layouts under local fortress commanders – were subsumed within the ADGB system, so drawing all guns and lights into a unified whole. In these respects the June 1936 plan established three fundamental principles which would shape Britain's anti-aircraft defences in the Second World War.

Probably the most radical departure embodied in this plan was the decision to build permanent sites for the heavier guns, which brought long-lasting implications not simply for the tactical principles on which AA defence was organised, but also in practical areas such as land and works costs. The decision was not taken lightly. The committee accepted that a static element to the defence would reduce flexibility in the face of evolving enemy tactics. They were worried, too, that static gunsites might jeopardise the efficiency of units manning them, since gunners continually moving to match the pace of the battle – like their colleagues in field artillery – were thought to remain keener and fitter than those allowed to put down roots at a permanent home.

But the decision of June 1936 was based in sound tactical thinking. Once area layouts were accepted it became clear that each must always contain a minimum number of weapons, and it was this minimum which could safely be met with static guns. And whatever its pitfalls, the arrangement did bring compensating advantages. The 3.7in gun was the largest which could be readily be transported by road and brought in and out of action in a reasonable time, and would be prized for its mobility. But heavier weapons offered better performance – particularly a higher ceiling – which could be exploited to form the hard core of each gun layout, in an arrangement which left room for 3.7s to be added as required.

These were important considerations in the summer of 1936 partly because the proportion of heavy static weapons now envisaged for ADGB was large. The new plan advanced equipment requirements to 608 HAA weapons and 2547 searchlights nationally, organised into 76 AA batteries and 108 searchlight companies (Appendix I). The guns divided between 320 of 3.7in calibre and 288 of the 4.5in or larger type (depending on the final choice) on fixed sites. No 3in guns were included, though in fact modified versions of these weapons would survive for many years yet. Guns were distributed in three categories. Every mobile 3.7in weapon was allocated to a specific town or port, but of the 320 to be supplied less than a third – 96 guns – were inalienably given to their areas, while the remaining 224 were earmarked for a mobile pool. All of these weapons would be kept in drill halls and stores during peacetime. The permanently-emplaced 4.5in guns were designed to be used on two-gun sites, but the committee advised that each of these positions should actually be built for four guns, again to allow flexibility without further structural work.

The distribution of guns between areas was carefully weighed, and in many respects conditioned the layout which was actually in place when war began three years later. Appendix I tabulates the details, but in summary the scheme distributed weapons between six inland areas and eleven ports, among which the 96 guns of the IAZ – half 4.5in, half 3.7in – represented by far the largest share given to any one. Second came the London Docks area, reaching down-river to the Erith–Canvey Island area (but excluding the Thames & Medway fortress, still formally classed as a defended port), where 32 heavy guns and 64 mobile 3.7in types were scheduled. The remaining inland areas – Birmingham, Sheffield, Leeds and Manchester – were each given sixteen 4.5in weapons (or eight sites) and 24 3.7in guns, while the ports were allocated gun strengths reflecting their size and strategic importance. The largest single allocation went to the Tyne, Tees, Sunderland and Middlesbrough, which together shared 32 guns of 4.5in type and the same number of 3.7s, while permanent heavy guns were also earmarked for the Thames & Medway, Portsmouth/ Southampton, Harwich, Dover and Scapa, together with the Forth, Humber and Mersey. Most of these naval and commercial harbours were also allotted 3.7in guns, while these weapons alone were allocated to Plymouth and to Portland, whose sixteen guns might be shared with Milford Haven and also doubled as a reserve for Bristol, which was given no armament of its own. Also undefended in this plan were smaller inland targets such as Bedford, Northampton, Rugby, Leicester, Coventry, Derby and Nottingham, all of which were named as likely beneficiaries from the mobile pool. Similarly, no weapons were allocated to minor ports such as Newhaven or Barrow, though local defence schemes anticipated their supply from the pool and earmarked sites for them.[14] Searchlights in proportion to the guns strengths were provided for all of these areas except Scapa, though by far the largest number of lights – 1848 – was given to the Aircraft Fighting Zone from the Solent to the Tees. The AFZ was also given first call upon the available searchlights, while the planned sequence of building-up personnel and guns ran from the IAZ – ever the senior layout – down through the Thames & Medway fortress and the London Docks area before reaching the ports from Portsmouth to the Forth, and lastly the inland city targets and western harbours, such as Plymouth, Portland and Liverpool. Extending ADGB's domain into the defended ports thus had an important effect upon priorities, tending to promote places such as the Humber or Harwich at the expense of the industrial areas.

As we might expect, this new manifesto for Britain's AA defences was far from being the last to appear before the Second World War. The next general revision, issued only eight months later, introduced some important modifications to planned scales of defence, largely in response to the ever-sharpening estimates of the potency of Hitler's air force, which continued to grow across the North Sea as sub-committees came and went in Whitehall and report succeeded report. But with few exceptions the changes in AA policy to emerge subsequently were chiefly quantitative, or else were refinements on the principles identified in the summer of 1936. Once the report was approved by the CID what we might call the conceptual framework for the wartime HAA defences was in place; next were needed the resources and the political will to clothe it.

In the autumn of 1936 neither of these was exactly abundant. In approving the Joubert Report the CID accepted that the first consignments of 3.7in guns would not be available until 1938/39, when 190 weapons of the 320 required would be supplied from production. Delivery of the first 100 heavy static guns was expected over the same period, though it was still unclear whether these would be the 4.5in type or an equivalent (as matters stood in 1936 the 4.5in had not been fully tested and in fact was approved for issue only in September 1937). The full complement of new guns would not be available until 1940. As a stop-gap work had begun on 'modernising' old stocks of the 3in gun, but no one really believed that these ancient weapons, refurbished or not, would offer much defence against a modern air force.

It was in response to the steadily growing strength of Hitler's Luftwaffe that the Cabinet had approved the latest expansion scheme for the RAF – Scheme F – on 25 February 1936. Like its predecessors, Scheme F laid emphasis upon the bomber arm, which was now set to reach 990 aircraft by 1939, against 420 fighters, and to include a larger proportion of medium and heavy bombers of modern types.[15] There were certainly those at the time who protested the inadequacy of these measures – notably the back-bench MP Winston Churchill, who remained the government's most vociferous critic on this issue throughout the late 1930s – but it remained true that the RAF was at least visibly growing towards definite targets. From many soldiers' point of view the critical failure of air rearmament was the growing disparity between the RAF's expansion as an offensive force and the state of the gun defences, which became proportionally weaker with each successive rise in aircraft numbers. In the summer of 1936 the stock of serviceable AA guns in Britain stood at about 60, and the number of searchlights at 120.[16]

One of those emboldened to speak out on this issue was Hastings Ismay, who in April 1936 had been appointed to the CID secretariat in a newly-created post as deputy to Sir Maurice Hankey, Secretary to the CID.[17] In mid September Ismay submitted a paper to his chief making the difficult claim that War Office was not taking its responsibilities for air defence sufficiently seriously, and that the tenor of planning in this field had been too strongly conditioned by the doctrine of deterrence: exactly the point which Ashmore had made seven years before. Ismay believed firmly that the war to come would begin with a sudden knock-out blow from the air. Aiming for a 'rapid decision' was an established principle of German warfare, argued Ismay, and German sources were already known to be saying that the next war must be short. Moreover, Germany herself was fortifying against attacks of exactly this kind, at least to judge from the intensive civil defence preparations under way in her cities, which far outstripped anything yet contemplated in Britain. And Germany, argued Ismay, judged Britain a relatively easy target.

> In German eyes [wrote Ismay], we are still a nation of shopkeepers, peace-loving and unsuspecting. They probably think, not altogether without reason, that we still nurse the illusion of our insular security, mindful of the fact that no foreign army has landed on British soil for nearly a thousand years, and that the air raids to which we were subjected during the Great War were a nuisance rather than a menace. They know, of course, that we are augmenting and strengthening our regular forces; but so far as they can judge it has not yet penetrated the comprehension of the British people as a whole that the next war will be an affair of whole nations, and consequently, they regard us as the worst organised of all the great Powers for the initial stages of what General Ludendorf calls 'Total War'. The Germans fully appreciate on the other hand, after their experiences of 1914–1918, that the British, if given time, are by far the most formidable of their potential enemies. Their obvious conclusion must be that to fight us at the beginning will be their best, if not their only, chance. In 1914,

this was impossible, since we were virtually inaccessible. To-day they have the means of striking at the very foundations of our existence within a few hours of the declaration of war, or even before it.[18]

In fact this bleak prophecy was disproved by the events of September 1939; but it did appear amply justified in the climate of autumn 1936, and won many adherents as the decade wore on. Although Ismay 'admitted as a general principle that at the present time, the best answer to air attack is counter air attack', this was 'by no means the only answer'. Strong defence was also essential if the threat from the knock-out blow was accepted. In this connection Ismay found the current projections for fighter aircraft numbers 'reassuring', but the War Office's contribution, in the form of AA guns and searchlights was 'anything but satisfactory'. Apart from the three-year delay expected in the supply of modern guns, and the woeful under-provision of light weapons to meet low-flying attack, Ismay was concerned that so vital and immediate a branch of defence as AA gunnery was given to the TA, who could scarcely be expected to achieve peak efficiency in the first hour of war, when he imagined the decisive battle would be fought. And the equipment situation was truly hopeless. Even when all the new guns had been delivered – some time in 1940 – there would be practically no spares, reserves, or capacity for extending the layout beyond the north-east of England. Even the modernised 3in guns would not be available until March 1938, when a mere 360 of these 'makeshifts' were expected. Similarly, only about 500 searchlights were due to be in army hands by April 1937 – less than one-fifth of the minimum required. The full two and a half thousand would be available only in 1938/39. 'The root cause of this state of affairs,' argued Ismay, 'is that the War Office appear [sic] to regard the provision of units for Home Defence as of secondary importance as compared with the provision of the Field Force' – the Expeditionary Force which would go abroad in the early weeks of war. To Ismay's mind all of this was disturbingly reminiscent of the Great War, when the War Office had committed all of the RFC's aircraft to the BEF and, in the first month of hostilities, had been obliged to pass domestic air defence duties to the Admiralty. The underlying problem more than twenty years later was the War Office's instinct to gird itself for land operations abroad, in this case to maintain the integrity of Holland and Belgium, rather than for domestic air defence. But, Ismay argued, the situation of the Low Countries was practically irrelevant to the Luftwaffe's capacity to flatten Britain's cities. Defence, like charity, began at home.

By the autumn of 1936 there was nothing particularly original in what Ismay was saying (nor did he claim otherwise), but his paper captured a mood shared by many in parliament and the services alike. Although the Air Ministry tended to think primarily in terms of the bomber deterrent, over-emphasis upon this far from proven doctrine always looked suspiciously like a panacea justifying lassitude in more direct forms of defence. At the same time the War Office's preoccupation with operations overseas – to many, the army's proper role – fuelled allegations that those in 'high places' were talking, as Basil Liddell Hart put it, of 'money for anti-aircraft home defence as if it were money taken away from the Army'.[19]

The minister to whom these questions devolved was Sir Thomas Inskip, a lawyer and former Attorney General who to the puzzlement of many had recently been appointed by Baldwin as Minister for the Co-ordination of Defence. Inskip was caught in the middle of the competing claims between the offensive and defensive school, which demanded to be weighed not just in purely strategic terms, but also with respect to the continuing policy that air defence planning should aim at the minimum required for adequate security. In these circumstances the minister's next move was bold indeed. On 6 October 1936 he asked for a report to be prepared detailing 'the ideal air defence of the country irrespective of consideration of supply'. At the same time the CID was invited to endorse the assumption, as a basis for planning, that the next war would indeed burst upon the British people with a precipitate knock-out blow. This was the origin of the next major air defence blueprint, known as the 'Ideal Scheme', which would emerge from the Reorientation Committee's deliberations four months later, in February 1937.

On the day that Inskip issued his instructions for work to begin on the Ideal Scheme there appeared the first of many reports issuing from yet another committee charged with investigating a particular aspect of Britain's predicament under air attack. Launched by the CID in March 1936, the work of the Sub-Committee on the Protection of Points of Importance Against Air Attack was intended to address a concern formally voiced in the Brooke-Popham Report of January 1935, but which had been lingering on the sidelines for much longer.[20] This was the prospect of low-flying snap raids on localised targets, of the kind so vividly demonstrated in the 1930 air exercises and now posing a growing threat with the increasing speeds and flexibility of modern military aircraft. The Reorientation Committee's original thoughts on this problem highlighted the vulnerability of industrial and other targets in the Thames area, together with the RAF's airfields, and urged that 'investigations' should be 'pressed forward with the utmost vigour'.[21] Nearly two years later that can hardly be said to have happened, though the Air Ministry had begun to examine the problem as it affected airfields and, with the new committee's work, a start had been made with a general study of the threat posed to industrial and other civil targets. With that work just starting, the Joubert Report of June 1936 had hazarded that about twenty batteries of soldiers would probably have to be formed to handle the LAA guns for low-flying defence, but left the matter there. So the planning which would underpin Britain's provision of light anti-aircraft guns in the war to come had already made a slow start.

An abiding problem in planning defence against low-flying raids was the sheer number and diversity of potential targets open to this form of attack – airfields, certainly, along with dockyards and barracks, but also power stations, railway installations, factories, public utilities, mills, food stores, post offices, telephone exchanges; the list was practically endless. Airfields were an Air Ministry responsibility, but assessment of the vast range of civil targets fell squarely on the shoulders of the Home Office – hence the committee charged with their study was chaired by Wing Commander E J Hodsoll, a retired RAF officer by 1936 serving as Assistant Under-Secretary of State in the Home Office's Air Raid Precautions Department. Hodsoll's committee was not narrowly concerned with allocating AA weapons, but instead worked to draw up a national register of 'Vital Points'

(VPs) warranting protection and recommended what form that protection should take, whether balloon barrages, camouflage, smoke screening or light AA weapons. The number of points justifying gun defences, now and for years to come, was larger than the number of weapons available; but it was Hodsoll's committee which, over the next three years, produced the roster of sites from which those actually protected by LAA at the start of the Second World War were drawn.

A look at the committee's early work in 1936 illustrates its methods and thus the means by which these selections were made. Hodsoll's team divided Britain into seven areas to be visited *seriatim* by inspecting officers, initially Brigadier E H Kelly and Air Commodore I M Bonham-Carter, who began their grand tour on 20 July 1936 in Area No 1 (Northumberland and Durham). In making their inspections the officers were guided by outline rosters of key installations previously compiled by the Home Defence Committee, which were in turn then being revised by that body's Sub-Committee on Sabotage. These lists, while not compiled specifically for the purposes of air defence, at least pointed the officers in the right directions, which in Area No 1 were naturally towards the industrial complexes on the Tyne and Tees. In all, fifteen VPs were identified on Tyneside and ten on the Tees, each of which was classified by lettercode for importance, visibility, vulnerability, warning time available and the likely scale of attack upon it. And of these 25 VPs, three were adjudged needful of AA machine guns – the Dunston power station, the oil depot at Jarrow and, on the Tees, the ICI factory at Billingham.

At the start of their work the Hodsoll committee reckoned that their full national survey could be completed by the autumn of 1938. In the event, of course, assessment of such targets continued uninterrupted in various hands until the end of the Second World War, adapting to newly emerging target groups and categories and shifting strategic priorities; even before war was declared radar stations supplanted every other type of target as the most vital of all vital points, and in summer 1940 were approached in importance by aircraft factories. But one type of target remained a constant anxiety almost throughout: this was the RAF's front-line airfields.

Since the beginning of RAF expansion in the summer of 1934 the Air Ministry had been steadily acquiring a stock of new airfields, to support bomber squadrons in the eastern counties, fighter units near to the aircraft fighting zone, and training functions in the more retired positions of the west and north. More so than their predecessors of the 1920s, these new stations – the first of which opened in 1936 – were planned with an eye to security against air attack, which was achieved chiefly by separating and dispersing their buildings and, increasingly, by plans to scatter their aircraft around the airfield perimeter and to secondary 'satellite' airfields in war. As the Brooke-Popham committee had recognised, however, measures of this kind could provide only partial protection, particularly for stations lying in advance of the OAZ (itself now abandoned) and the searchlight belt, which were strictly speaking defenceless. In studying this question in the summer of 1935 (and reporting in October of that year) the Reorientation Committee judged that high-level bombing of the kind threatening the cities posed little danger to the RAF's airfields, provided that security continued to be won from dispersed layouts and structural measures and night-time 'blackout' could be made complete.[22] But an acute danger stemmed from low-flying attacks delivered by aircraft skimming the treetops, and from dive bombing, either of which could be lethal to the cluster of small, individual targets – technical buildings, barracks, hangars – which airfields offered. For this reason the Reorientation Committee was adamant that active defences should be provided for all RAF stations not adequately safeguarded by their positions. And this in turn raised the question of what kind of weapon was best suited for the close defence of targets open to low-flying attack in general.

In the midst of its work on the Ideal Scheme the Reorientation Committee found time to issue a paper on this subject early in November 1936.[23] In doing so it was reviewing a War Office proposal that the best weapon to equip the LAA units which would soon need to be formed was the twin-barrelled 2pdr pom-pom, the only gun likely to be available offering the necessary rates of traverse and fire to meet both dive-bombers and low-flying aircraft whose speeds, by now, were expected to attain 250 miles per hour. Three hundred of these weapons were ordered, though deliveries were never fully completed since a better alternative would soon be found in the 40mm gun from the Bofors company of Sweden. In the event it was the Bofors, not the 2pdr Vickers, which emerged as Britain's key LAA weapon of the Second World War, but orders for these were not placed until 1938 and at the start of hostilities in September 1939 precious few were available for home defence. As a stop-gap the gunners were allocated a large consignment of Lewis guns on which to train, together with a number of 2pdrs from naval stocks. Three years later the vast majority of LAA weapons in service would still be antiquated Lewis guns.

If suitable weapons for LAA work were still a distant prospect in the winter of 1936–37, raising a corps of men to operate them seemed remoter still. Like their counterparts on HAA guns, the AA machine gun (AAMG) batteries, as they were first known, were formed within the Territorial Army. So much was agreed at a War Office conference on 22 April 1937, when it was also decided that most batteries would need to be raised de novo, rather than through converting existing TA units.[24] This of course added another demand to manpower requirements which, in spring 1937, were still proving very difficult to satisfy. But this problem promised its own solution, since it was believed that many gunners might be recruited from the workforces of the industrial targets themselves – such men, after all, would have a natural interest in their own defence and might be glad to be given the means and the training to do so. As Salt had argued three years previously, all TA soldiers working for ADGB were primarily defending their own cities; in the case of the LAA gunners the association would be more local still.

True as that may have been in principle, by the spring of 1937 recruiting to the Territorial AA brigades remained slow, even if the structure to accept the newcomers was building. The development of the national AA organisation took a step forward on 10 December 1936 when 2 AA Division was formed under Major-General J M R Harrison, who took charge of the Midland and northern AA defences from a headquarters in Derby. In part 2 AA Division's foundation was quickened by events on a much larger stage, since Mussolini's invasion of Abyssinia raised anxieties over British interests in the Mediterranean, the small contingent of Regular AA troops was sent to garrison Malta and, for a time in 1936, there seemed a potential threat to British domestic territory from Italian military adventurism.[25] But early in the following year most of the non-metropolitan AA brigades existed only on paper, in the sense that they had been created practically at the stroke of a pen by converting existing TA units. By May 1937 eighteen Territorial AA brigades had some kind of official existence, but of these seven were still 'in course of conversion', meaning they were yet untrained in their new role, and barely equipped.[26]

Eighteen weeks in the making, the 'Ideal Scheme' commissioned by Inskip in October was issued on 9 February 1937 by Air Chief Marshal Sir Hugh Dowding, who had succeeded Joubert as chairman of the Reorientation Committee in his capacity as AOC Fighter Command, the new formation founded in July 1936 as part of the RAF's restructuring into commands.[27] Inskip's call for an 'ideal' scheme was an incisive and procedurally logical move, since it allowed the air defence planners to think in bold strategic terms, unfettered by the anticipation of logistic or financial constraints. In framing the resulting plan the eight-man Reorientation Committee – among them Major-General Tompson – was for the first time explicitly briefed to assume 'that Germany may attempt a "knock-out" blow from the air, and that this blow would be delivered with the maximum of intensity at the moment of the declaration of war.' (Assuming indeed that this blow did not itself *represent* the declaration.) By early 1937 Germany's capacity to launch a decisive first strike of this kind was widely accepted in principle, if uncertain in detail. '"Ideal" defence must bear some relation to the scale of attack,' counselled Dowding and his colleagues. 'This is an unknown factor where Germany is concerned. We know, however, that she will, almost certainly, possess 1,700 first-line bombers by March 1939, and we have proceeded on the assumption that we may be attacked by that number [. . .].' Haziness in this most crucial piece of intelligence was, of course, central to the lively parliamentary debates which continued to surround the whole issue of air rearmament in the later thirties, a period when Churchill continued to castigate the Baldwin government for under-preparedness in relation to what he believed Hitler's probable strength to be.

The Reorientation Committee's new report was not restricted to considerations of AA gunnery, and as usual this component was reassessed in relation to the whole field of air defence planning, including fighter squadrons and the bomber deterrent, whose primacy the committee continued to affirm. But with the freedom to conjure an 'ideal' world the committee for the first time during the 1930s emphasised the *limitations* of active defence and the need for broader and more connected thinking, encompassing passive and protective measures as much as guns, fighters and lights.

> It is apparent [they reported] that the chances of success, whether by direct or indirect attack, will depend largely on the degree to which the community and its supply system can be protected by passive air defence measures, which include dispersion and an elastic and widely distributed supply system. Adequate dispersion and a suitably elastic supply system, and, above all, the education and training of the general public in air raid precautions are, therefore, just as essential in an 'ideal' defence system as the active defences.
>
> It should be noted that the cost of the equipment for AA units alone for the present ADGB scheme is about £30,000,000, and some 50,000 men will be required to man the defences. While, therefore, each fighter, gun and searchlight added to the defence is theoretically an asset to it, there is a practical limit beyond which such additions are neither feasible nor remunerative in proportion to the effort involved and where that effort can be more economically applied to improving passive measures of defence. Whilst the dispositions and strengths of defending fighter forces and the aircraft zone are, on the whole, independent of passive defence measures, the lay-out of local gun and AAMG defence will be profoundly influenced by the degree to which it has been possible to develop passive air defence measures. It may be cheaper, and equally if not more effective, for instance, to put a vital point underground than to defend it above-ground; or, should it prove possible to provide adequate defence by smoke-screens, guns and lights would be unnecessary.[28]

Given the slow start in civil defence measures made since the Home Office formed its ARP Department in 1935, these were wise and timely reminders, particularly as they appeared just as the first sobering digests of air raid experience in the Spanish Civil War were beginning to circulate through government departments.[29] And in drawing attention to the value of smoke-screens, structural protection and balloon barrages, the committee covered all the defensive measures which were actually in place to greater and lesser degrees when the war began (they omitted only decoys, the first of which were hurriedly improvised in the winter of 1939–40).[30] But whatever ameliorative effects could be wrested from passive techniques, active defence remained the focus of the Committee's inquiry, and here the 'ideal' was for large increases across the board (Appendix I). Practically every-thing in the armoury needed to be at least doubled – fighter squadrons from 21 to 45, searchlights proportionally, LAA guns (2pdrs) from 300 to 600 and HAA weapons from the 608 authorised under the Brooke-Popham Report to a prodigious 1264.

Why such a leap in lights and guns? The answer lies not simply in the growing force of bombers which the defences were planned to meet, but in the rising ranges and speeds of those aircraft – factors which simultaneously opened yet more of the British Isles to air attack while narrowing the opportunity for interception within the existing defence layout. In these circum-stances the Committee saw no alternative but to recommend a substantial expansion in the AFZ, which their plan extended northward to Blyth, broadened to allow greater chance of intercepting faster aircraft, and pushed westwards through an irregular annexe embracing the industrial Midlands and north (Fig 5). Additionally, illuminated areas detached from this much-enlarged continuous zone were proposed for major targets such as Bristol and the Forth–Clyde isthmus, and joining it at Southampton. The rise in AA guns arose chiefly from the need to thicken their concentrations and to extend gun defence to areas previously beyond the Luftwaffe's reach. Under the Ideal Scheme places of the 'highest importance' were now listed for a sixteen-gun density – meaning that a single hostile aircraft could be subjected to simultaneous fire from that number of weapons – falling to a density of four for lesser targets. London and the

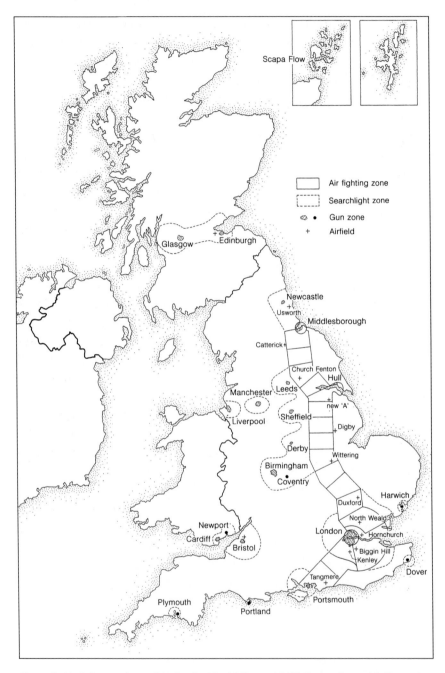

Figure 5 Air defences planned under the Ideal Scheme, 1937. Comparison with Figure 4 shows an extended Air Fighting Zone, more gun defended areas (GDAs) in the north and west and a firmer picture of the airfield layout, thanks to the progressive acquisition of new fighter stations in the mid 1930s. The actual layout of gunsites spawned by this scheme and its later amendments is captured by Figure 9.

Thames & Medway absorbed a weighty proportion of the new hardware which this principle demanded: more than a third of the additional heavy weapons recommended nationally was absorbed by raising the number of these guns from 216 to 448. Increases in density elsewhere were marked. Among the areas listed for defence in the Joubert Report, only Scapa and Dover, with eight guns each, remained untouched by the 'ideal' proposals, while substantial new allocations were made to Glasgow (56 guns), Cardiff and Newport (24 each), which now entered the list of targets for the first time. Among the more remote targets previously allocated guns, the lengthening reach of Göring's air force found its strongest response at Bristol, whose 'ideal' gun defence enjoyed the greatest proportional increase, from sixteen weapons under the old plan to 56 under the new. Of these, typically, 24 weapons would be mobile and 32 fixed. It was a general principle of the 'ideal' recommendations that a large mobile element in the HAA gun stock was essential to keep pace with what was likely to be a fluid air war. To this extent the share of guns between targets was less important than their overall number, and more particularly that the total should include 704 heavy mobiles, a little over half the national arsenal.

Two and a half years later, in the first week of war, the actual number of HAA guns defending Bristol stood at fourteen.[31] The Ideal Scheme was just what its title implied: perfect in the abstract, yet unrealisable in a practical sense, even by the carefully phased programme which Dowding and his colleagues wrote into it. In those circumstances the CID, eventually, handled the scheme in such a way as to distance it one step further from reality, by approving it 'in principle'. Yes, they agreed, this was an ideal system and a useful point of reference for the future; but purposeful planning in the AA field would continue to be governed by the Joubert recommendations of the previous year.

If AA artillery continued to languish as the poor relation of air defence planning as late as spring 1937, the middle years of that decade did see some important technical advances. In many ways the greatest contribution to Britain's wartime AA defences in the 1930s lay in the research and development field which, while it produced little new equipment by the first day of war, laid down a fertile bed of experimental findings and new thinking for the battles to come. The summer of 1937 is a suitable point at which to review these developments, which affected three quite separate technologies: anti-aircraft rockets; radar applied to fire control; and the new generation of heavy guns which began to be delivered to the units in the following year. The first was an old technology, long neglected; the second was vibrantly new; and the third the outcome of a long research programme to find weapons capable of meeting the new generation of bombers which would fight the war to come.

By the mid 1930s rocket research had been dormant in Britain for practically fifteen years. Though solid propellant rockets had made their mark on the battlefield as early as the thirteenth century and enjoyed something of a vogue in the nineteenth, they played little part in the First World War, when their chief use was for signalling. Despite protests from some scientists, Britain ceased experiments in 1919 and for more than a decade the solid-propellant weapon appeared to be obsolete. More was done with liquid-fuelled rockets in the years after the Armistice, first during the 1920s in the United States and by the early 1930s in Germany and the Soviet Union. Germany's first liquid-fuelled rocket flew in 1931, the year in which the Wehrmacht opened its experimental rocketry centre at Kummersdorf, near Berlin, a facility succeeded six years later by the better-known station at Peenemünde on the Baltic coast. The German government's interest in long-distance rockets – which eventually produced the V2 – is often explained as a tactic to circumvent the Treaty of Versailles, since the prohibition on German air power imposed by the post-war settlement could not extend to a technology which, in 1919, did not yet exist. But whatever the Germans' initial motives, it was partly in response to their advances that the British government began to examine rocketry afresh.

Discussions began in December 1934, when Sir Hugh Elles (Master General of the Ordnance) convened a meeting at the War Office to explore the issue in general terms. Basic research in propellants and ballistics made some headway during 1935, but it was not until the following summer that British rocket research was given firm direction. The project launched in July 1936 called for rocket experiments in four areas, among which AA defence was awarded the highest priority, in part to relieve pressure on the manufacturers of conventional guns by substituting a weapon of simple and cheap design. To a great extent the primacy given to AA rocketry retarded progress in the other three fields. Little was done towards building a long-range offensive weapon – a British version of the German V2 – while neither rocket-assisted take-off for aircraft nor air-launched attack rockets were ready for some years. Many came to regret this, particularly since projectiles carried by fighter and fighter-bomber aircraft emerged as the war's most successful branch of rocketry, among other things giving the RAF a lethal anti-tank weapon. But the needs of air defence were paramount in 1936, and developing a ground-launched AA rocket at least seemed the most straightforward of the four tasks when work began.

Guardianship of the rocket project was given to Dr Alwyn Crow, then serving as Director of Ballistic Research at Woolwich, who set up his bench at Fort Halstead in Kent. Staffed by a small team including William Cook, a specialist in ballistics, and Harold Poole, a chemist, Crow's Projectiles Development Establishment began work with a firm and ambitious objective: an explosive rocket of two-inch calibre (or diameter), capable of reaching 15,000 feet in the same time as a 3in anti-aircraft shell, but detonated by a fuze sensitive to the proximity of the target, rather than exploded at a set altitude in the manner of a conventional shell. The proximity fuze, as it was later known, did not reach practical trials until the spring of 1940, but strong headway was made with the missile's propulsion chemistry and basic form in 1937–38, when firing trials were held at Shoeburyness, at Orford Ness in Suffolk and in the western isles of Scotland. The abiding difficulty lay in persuading a thin steel rocket casing to withstand the huge temperatures generated by the solid propellant. The team's first solution was an insulating plastic compound fitted between cordite and case, but this failed dramatically in many test shots, the rocket exploding prematurely or describing a course so wildly erratic that some observers feared for their lives. Close analysis of recovered fragments revealed the problem to lie in the chemical instability of the plastic, which melted in summer

temperatures, broke down when the rocket was fired in cold
conditions, and was attacked by nitro-glycerine in the propellant
when in storage. Crow for a while persevered with alternative
compounds, but eventually redesigned the rocket complete,
using a stronger and heavier casing containing a loose cordite
charge with only a thin skin of insulating material between. This
worked, but it was February 1938 before the new prototype rocket
was ready for trials; and these returned a disappointing performance
compared to that anticipated in 1936.

Rocket testing in Britain's uncertain climate was always
beset by irritating delays, and to defray these at the end of
1938 a sizeable party of scientists and soldiers decamped to
Jamaica. Trials continued there of what by now were known as
'unrotated projectiles' – UPs – under the stewardship of Brigadier
A A S Younger, while Crow remained at home to handle
arrangements for occupying a new test site at Aberporth, on the
south Wales coast near Cardigan. Chosen for its remoteness from
London, Aberporth was formally designated the Projectile
Research Establishment, but no sooner had the station been
commissioned than the impetus of rocket research began to ebb.
Crow's redesigned rockets performed badly in the Jamaican trials,
and in the post-Munich climate materials for weapons manufacture and staff for research were at a premium. Experiments
did continue at Aberporth and, as we shall see, the rocket project
gained a new lease of life in the first year of war. But by 1939
Britain's first innovatory AA weapon of the pre-war decade
seemed to have an uncertain future.

Where the ancient technology of rocketry was only slowly
reshaped to serve the modern art of air defence, the new science
of radar was dedicated to countering the aircraft from its
inception. British experiments with radar, as we have seen, grew
from the recommendations of the Committee for the Scientific
Survey of Air Defence which had first met, under the chairmanship of H T Tizard, Rector of Imperial College, early in 1935.
What followed from that meeting was one of the most significant
and well-known chains of events in the history of science and
warfare. At an early stage in the committee's work contact was
made with R A Watson-Watt, Superintendent of the Radio
Department at the National Physical Laboratory, whose work on

measuring the height of the ionosphere using electromagnetic pulses was soon identified as offering a new means of detecting the approach of aircraft, a function at that date still reliant on the acoustic mirror technology under test since the end of the Great War. Experiments began straight away, first at Orford Ness – where Crow would make his early rocket tests – and from the late summer of 1935 at Bawdsey Manor on the Suffolk coast. The early, and always dominant, work at Bawdsey was directed towards building a general early-warning radar system, the first stations for which were commissioned in 1936 around the Thames Estuary, where they supplanted advanced plans for a new system of acoustic mirrors. By the start of war the primary Home Chain, as it was known, had risen to twenty stations, providing air defence intelligence over a front from the Solent to Scotland.

But general raid warning was only one of the functions of radar which came to be studied at Bawdsey in the second half of the 1930s.[32] Early War Office research was at first directed toward apparatus for coast-artillery fire control – which eventually was achieved – though the burgeoning importance of air defence soon prompted a change of emphasis. Ambitions, at first, were modest enough. From early 1937 the 'Army Cell' at Bawdsey began to develop radar sets to provide short-range early-warning for gun defended areas (GDAs), simply to give the gunners and search-light crews extra time to bring themselves and their equipment to readiness and get it pointing in the general direction of the approaching bombers. Using much the same 'floodlight' principle as the Chain Home equipment, this was comparatively simple to achieve. Before long, however, the army team began to raise the stakes, identifying in radar – or Radio Direction Finding, as it was then known – a potential solution to the problem facing gunners since the Gotha raids of 1917–18, namely how to bring aimed fire to bear on 'unseen' targets at night. In doing so the scientists were entering new areas of research, demanding a stringency in per-formance incomparably greater than that expected from simple early-warning sets. Positional data supplied to the predictor needed accuracy in three dimensions, in other words more or less precise readings of range, azimuth and elevation, the three variables which obsessed radar scientists of the late 1930s. Ideally, too, these data needed to be continuously updated to allow for changes in the target's trajectory; and beyond that, AA fire control radar also required the longest pick-up range possible – in other words high transmitter power and receiver sensitivity – to allow sufficient time to perform the various tasks which would place and explode the shell correctly. Few onlookers expected to see much headway toward these exacting standards for many years, but remarkably the army team managed to refine their equipment, within weeks, to the point where range accuracy stood at about 100 yards over distances up to eight miles. By December 1937 the prototype gun-laying (GL) radars were giving range accuracies of about 25 yards and azimuth errors had dropped below one degree of arc. At the same time means had been found to give the predictor continuously-updated readings in range, though not yet in azimuth or elevation, the first of which relied on spot readings and the second on more sophisticated refinements which would not become available until 1940. The result was that by early 1939, after further tests, the GL Mk I radar could give AA gunners accurate fire-control data in range and very creditable readings on the azimuth of their targets.

The production model of the Mk I consisted of two trailer-mounted cabins with aerials. The transmitter cabin was fixed on its trailer, while the receiver's was rotatable and fitted with demountable aerials for transit and jack-arms for stability in operation. The electronics at the heart of the Mk I were built under contract by Metro-Vickers and Cossor, to whom the War Office supplied the chassis, cabin and trailers for fitting out. The production version of the apparatus could achieve a target pick-up range of about 30,000 yards (seventeen miles) to a tolerance of around 500 yards, and feed accurate and continuous range information to the predictor from the point where the incoming target reached about 14,000 yards (eight miles). Bearing data were obtained by spot readings every half minute or so, and were generally accurate to about one and a half degrees of arc. It was this equipment, the first of many successive variants used during the war, which would enter service in the autumn of 1939.

The third area of technical advance in the 1930s was in gun design.[33] Although AA gunners of the previous decade had continued to rely upon the 3in 20cwt gun of 1913 vintage for training, the rising speeds and altitudes of aircraft generally make it clear that this weapon was becoming increasingly overdue for replacement as the standard AA tool for the 1930s. By 1933 trials had begun with a 4.7in gun, though this proved heavy and cumbersome and was in any case selected largely with the defence of ports for the Admiralty in mind. It was soon replaced, therefore, as a potential standard AA weapon by the 3.7in, whose advantages appeared clear in theory and which reached the stage of more detailed design studies in 1933. The 'modernisation' of the old 3in weapons was undertaken as a stop-gap until further work on the 3.7 could be completed, but at the same time the Admiralty again pressed for a weapon specifically to defend ports, and pointed to their existing commitment to a 4.5in for warships, a gun which seemed to offer great potential for (fixed) land use. Given that a common 4.5in ship-board and land gun would make for economies in ammunition supply, the War Office accepted the Admiralty's idea in principle, with the result that, by 1936, a new generation of heavy AA weapons was in prospect in both the 3.7in (mobile) weapon and the 4.5in static.

At this time mobility was a defining characteristic of the 3.7in gun, and until the autumn of 1937, as we shall see, few had seriously entertained the idea that many would be used with the fixed mounting which the majority actually did employ in the Second World War. In this respect it was conceived as the true successor to the mobile 3in, differing chiefly in its significantly improved ballistic performance. The original specification for the 3.7in called for a travelling weight not exceeding eight tons, a speed on the road of 25mph and a time 'into action' – from arrival at the gun position to the first round being fired – of just fifteen minutes. This was the brief to which detailed working drawings were prepared early in 1934 by both Vickers Armstrong and in-house by the Design Department. Vickers' design was chosen, reaching practical trials in April 1936 and approval for production just one year later. The gun which emerged, the 3.7in Mk I, fired ten rounds of 28lb, time-fuzed high explosive per minute to a practical ceiling of 25,000 feet, substantially more than the 3in 20cwt even in its 'modernised' form (though its weight came in as much heavier than the specification figure of eight tons and, for this reason, many gunners with Field Force units continued to voice a preference for the lighter 3in). Like the GL radar, the 3.7in gun would pass through numerous marks and sub-marks before the end of the war.

The 4.5in naval weapon which was selected for AA use reached its own practical trials rather earlier than the 3.7, in 1936, and after that the work of adaptation was relatively simple. The main job was to provide a single rather than a twin mounting, for which the ship's gun had been intended, and with this complete the design was passed for AA land use in September 1937. Very different in appearance from the 3.7in – not least in the provision of a fully-enclosing frontal shield – the 4.5in was distinguished in performance chiefly by its higher ceiling, which reached 25,000 feet for the early variants and more for subsequent models. Unlike the 3.7in, the 4.5 would always be a static weapon – it could be moved, of course, when absolutely necessary but offered no true 'mobility' – and so always formed the fixed core of the layouts in the areas where it was emplaced.

The War Office's acceptance of the 4.5in gun in September 1937 was the first of a series of events that autumn which, together, marked the long-awaited advance in AA planning between the wars. In May of that year Chamberlain had succeeded Baldwin as leader of the Conservative Party and Prime Minister. It was Chamberlain who ruled, on 8 November, that 'the provision of anti-aircraft defences is to have absolute priority over all other forms of war material'; and further that Inskip should study means of expediting the Ideal Scheme without delay.[34] In the words of one of those closely involved, Chamberlain's ruling 'suddenly, and without prior warning' ushered in 'an electrifying change in the attitude towards home defence'.[35]

How had this electricity been generated? The larger context of Chamberlain's decision lay in the beginnings of doubts over the bomber orthodoxy which had conditioned Britain's defence thinking since the early 1920s. And in practical terms the consequences were largely of Inskip's making. In October 1937 the latest of the RAF's draft expansion schemes – Scheme J, the proposed successor to Scheme F – was put before the ministerial Defence Plans (Policy) Committee, who were asked to approve yet another enlargement of the bomber force at the expense of the fighter arm. Inskip queried it, partly on the basis of cost, but in part too on the grounds of strategic philosophy. In Inskip's view the whole principle of deterrence which had governed Britain's air defence planning for more than fifteen years was simply misguided, at least as a guarantor of security in the actual conditions likely to prevail in the first days of war. Inskip of course was very far from being the first to say this – Ashmore's and Ismay's views, for instance, have been quoted above, likewise those of Basil Liddell Hart – but Inskip was in a uniquely strong position to advance the case against what Ashmore had condemned as the 'bomb-the-other-fellow-is-the-only-way' school (in other words the Air Staff). He did so in these words.

> If Germany is to win she must knock us out within a comparatively short time owing to our superior staying power. If we wish our forces to be sufficient, to deter Germany from going to war, our forces [. . .] must be sufficiently powerful to convince Germany that she cannot deal us an early knock-out blow. In other words, we must be able to confront the Germans with the risks of a long war, which is the one thing they cannot face.
>
> Looking at the matter from this point of view, I cannot take the view that our Air Force must necessarily correspond in numbers and types of aircraft with the German Air Force. I cannot, therefore, persuade myself that the dictum of the Chief of the Air Staff that we must give the enemy as much as he gives us is a sound principle. I do not think that is the proper measure of our strength. The German Air Force, as I have pointed out, must be designed to deliver a knock-out blow within a few weeks of the outbreak of war. The role of our Air Force is not an early knock-out blow – no one has suggested that we can accomplish that – but to prevent the Germans from knocking us out.[36]

What Ismay believed about the relative importance of Bomber and Fighter Commands – which is what this contrast amounted to – applied with equal force to other aspects of the directly defensive armoury, including AA guns on the ground. The state of the whole system as it would stand on 1st January next was summarised in a succinct analysis which Inskip submitted to Chamberlain on 26 October.[37] Despite earlier expectations that the gunners would have 360 converted 3in weapons by March 1938, the latest estimates placed the likely total at only 176 available for home defence on 1 January, to be followed by just 50 more in October and a final consignment of 135 – making 361 in all – a year later. Additionally a smaller number of these weapons was allocated to the Regular AA groups, training schools, and for defences abroad. By 1 January a predictor and heightfinder were expected to be available for each pair of guns, giving 88 sets in all, enough to equip just 22 batteries of the 76 required. Proportionally, the personnel deficit anticipated by the New Year of 1938 was less serious. Despite generally slow recruiting among the Territorial units, Inskip's projections suggested that, collectively, the gun batteries would have reached about 75 per cent of their target strengths of 14,474 officers and men by 1 January, though the searchlight companies would have recruited fewer than half the 34,112 men required for the full scheme. Searchlights were as scarce as guns. In all, 940 were expected by 1 January against the requirement for a little over two and a half thousand, though of these only 500 would actually be distributed to the units for training, with the rest consigned to the mobilisation stores (most of which had yet to be built). There was, after all, little point in issuing equipment which had no men to operate it.

What of the new-generation equipment, of which so much was expected? As matters stood in October 1937 the 4.5in gun was just entering production, while the first deliveries of the mobile 3.7in, whose manufacture had been approved in April were poised to begin. By the New Year just 22 of these weapons were due to be available, together with a few thousand rounds of ammunition, though the first deliveries were committed to the two Regular AA groups rather than the Territorials of ADGB. And even the Regulars were under strength. Established to hold 96 HAA weapons between them, the two AA groups (in twelve-gun batteries) were actually able to operate just half that number thanks to minor deficiencies in manpower among instrument operators and other vital personnel, the effects of which were wholly disproportionate to their magnitude. In the event of a war requiring the Field Force to be sent abroad the Regular AA troops would normally be dispatched in advance to protect the ports where their comrades would land; otherwise, however, they would be available for home defence in one role or another (one option here was to use them to protect the mobilisation stores of their TA counterparts to prevent weapons stocks being destroyed before they could be drawn).[38] But however they were used, with the Regulars' guns added to those of the Territorials Britain on 1 January 1938 could, it was calculated, be defended by two-fifths of the heavy weapons required under the Joubert plan and just one fifth of those deemed necessary for 'Ideal' defence. Practically all of these guns would be obsolescent and there would be no LAA weapons at all. The bottom line was that, under current policies, Britain fielded little AA gun defence worthy of the name.

It was this grave cumulative deficiency which Inskip, in the autumn of 1937, was briefed to remedy. He did so by taking decisions whose ramifications would be felt for years afterwards, not simply in a military or tactical sense, but also in the effect which AA provision made upon Britain's landscape, immediately and historically. In every respect, therefore, the autumn of 1937 was a turning point.

Chamberlain's brief to his minister was to 'prepare a plan for expediting the present programme for the provision of anti-aircraft armament' in a climate in which 'the provision of anti-aircraft defences is to have absolute priority over all other forms of war material.'[39] Inskip was given this task formally on 8 November and by 4 December had finalised the plan. What lay between were many meetings, hurried circulation of drafts and intense discussion, much of it difficult. Although Inskip's name was attached to the plan as responsible minister, the actual details were of course deliberated by many minds, chiefly those of the Reorientation Committee and supernumerary officers co-opted to contribute at this most crucial juncture in the evolution of air defence planning. Ten men worked on the plan within the framework of the Reorientation Committee, among them Ismay and Group Captain R H M S Saundby, whose name would later become prominent through his role as Arthur Harris's deputy at Bomber Command in the latter half of the coming war. Dowding chaired; but one absentee was Major-General Tompson, late commander of 1 AA Division, whose premature death that autumn was widely believed to have been hastened by the strain involved in persuading the War Office to take AA defence seriously. In Liddell Hart's eyes Tompson by late 1937 'seemed to be wearing himself out quicker than he could wear down obstruction'.[40] Cruel it was, then, that the revolution which Tompson had sought for so long broke just too late for him to gather its spoils.

What Inskip and the Reorientation Committee were now embarked upon was largely a study in the art of compromise: simply, to find new ways of hastening the supply of AA guns. Several options were considered.[41] The first and the most influential in the longer term was a proposal to accept a proportion of the existing orders for 3.7in guns on fixed mountings rather than mobile, a contingency which threatened to challenge a central principle of established thinking. A common theme running through all the inter-war AA defence plans, reiterated as recently as the Ideal Scheme of February 1937, was the importance of maintaining the flexibility given by mobile guns, 320 of which were included in the Joubert Report's total of 608 weapons. But thanks to their complex mountings, the mobile 3.7in guns were expensive, took longer to make, and demanded more ancillary equipment than the alternative, which was simply to bolt the weapon to a concrete emplacement. To save time and money, therefore, the committee reluctantly decided to sacrifice mobility to the extent of accepting 120 static 3.7s. Happily, it seemed, these new guns would not need additional permanent sites, since they could temporarily occupy those intended for the 4.5s until these were delivered, and could then be converted back to mobile mountings as the guns were exchanged. It seemed a neat solution: guns would be in place earlier, no new building would be involved, and the 3.7s would eventually become mobile again, restoring the temporary loss in flexibility. But in the event the committee's concession to expediency proved to be the thin end of a very broad wedge. None of the 3.7in statics was ever converted back to a mobile mounting; and in time more and more of these guns came to be accepted, with the result that it was the 3.7in static, not its mobile cousin, which became the mainstay of Britain's HAA arsenal in the Second World War. The long-term consequence which flowed from the committee's decision in Whitehall Gardens on that Tuesday morning in November 1937 was that the war to come would see permanent gunsites built in huge numbers, and that Britain's AA layout for the next ten years would contain an element of fixedness whose proportions no one had previously anticipated and no one ever really wanted.

That was the first compromise. The second up for discussion was whether 4in twin guns from naval reserves or existing Admiralty orders might supplement or replace a proportion of the 3.7s or 4.5s scheduled for AA defence. This was never accepted, partly because further investigation showed that no stocks of such guns actually existed, and in part because no acceleration of gunning could be achieved with a weapon for which no land mounting had ever been designed. The Admiralty did, however, offer Inskip a consignment of about 230 spare 3in guns, and these the minister accepted with thanks. Though no less out of date than their army equivalents, they at least offered the usual panacea of something on which to train.

In Inskip's report it was even suggested that some of the naval guns could be pressed into service as LAA weapons; and when the war began two years later many 3in weapons were indeed used in this role, firing on what were known as Case I sights. But the Inskip plan also included more satisfactory measures to expedite deliveries of purpose-built LAA guns, plans for which still included the 300 twin 2pdrs ordered in late 1936 but had since been supplemented by a further order for 100 guns of 40mm calibre from Bofors. For both, however, the delivery timetable was unacceptably long. Under present arrangements the Bofors consignment was unlikely to be delivered in full until September 1939 and the first not before May 1938, while the shops and plant for manufacturing the 2pdrs at the Nottingham Royal Ordnance Factory and Vickers' works at Openshaw had not even been readied to begin production and no guns would be available before January 1939. To fill this yawning gap the Admiralty, once again, stepped in with spares – specifically 100 2pdr Mk VIIIs direct from production at Crayford, which it was hoped to marry to suitable mountings by the end of 1938. These were reasonable weapons, offering 150 rounds per minute from the twin version and 115 from the single, in contrast to the 120 achievable by the Bofors (though the Swedish gun's 2lb 2oz shell was somewhat larger than the Mk VIII's 1lb 14oz projectile). But even with these weapons in hand the LAA shortage at any date over the next two years would be serious, and only marginally less so after that.

The proposed solutions to these longer-term difficulties were either to request more Bofors guns from Sweden or to make arrangements for their manufacture under licence in Britain. The first option was straightaway ruled out by Messrs Bofors' advice that no spare works capacity existed; the second, however was found to be possible and, in addition, a source for newly-manufactured Bofors guns was found in Poland, whose government had obtained its own manufacture licence from 1935 and had since begun to export their surplus.[42] In this way the shortfall in LAA equipment promised to be met, if still on a uncomfortably long timetable. But to make matters worse in the short term, once the Swedish Bofors began to be delivered their performance so outstripped the domestically-produced 2pdrs that the order for these was cancelled and the Bofors became Britain's main LAA weapon of modern design.

The decision to accept a proportion of 3.7in guns on static mountings was taken just a few weeks after the War Office began to study the land and works requirements for the fixed 4.5in guns scheduled under the Joubert plan, with the result that the winter of 1937–38 brought the first moves toward building permanent gun positions since the latter stages of the First World War. In autumn 1937 the first deliveries of 4.5in weapons were expected as early as the following spring, and while this timetable soon began to slip the need for new positions to accommodate them suddenly appeared rather urgent. So it was that on 4 October 1937 the Director of Military Operations and Intelligence at the War Office circulated a minute advising that 'preliminary reconnaissances' for the sites should begin without further delay.[43]

The building programme which the War Office was now embarked upon would ultimately develop into one of the more extensive and long-lasting military engineering projects of the pre-war and wartime years, as more and more static guns came to be added to the armoury and sites were prepared to receive them. In the beginning, however, the requirements were more closely circumscribed, first by the demand for sites to accommodate 4.5in guns in areas listed for them by the Joubert Report and second by making allowance for the 120 static 3.7s which, in the event, did require sites of their own. In conforming the Joubert scales to the ground, the War Office was not, of course, simply buying land and laying concrete, but adapting tactical principles to the landscape by fitting specifications for cover and fire densities to the real topography of vulnerable areas. It was not easy. In the thinking of 1937–38 guns were sited fairly tightly around their target cities in the expectation that bombing would be reasonably accurate and staged often by day, when self-defending bomber formations would be able to locate their targets with ease. Some guidance to potential positions could be drawn from the existing *Defence Schemes* for London and a few of the defended ports (whose schemes were at that date gradually being revised) but the AA positions written into these handsomely-produced documents were intended for 3in mobile guns, not static 4.5s, whose requirements were very different (the risk of subsidence in mining districts, for example, was acute for such powerful weapons).[44] Revised, interim *Defence Schemes* in any case existed only for a few areas – Thames & Medway, Harwich, Tyne, Newhaven[45] – and offered no guidance for inland cities such as Sheffield, Leeds or Birmingham. A further layer of difficulty was imposed by the vigorous suburban growth of the late 1930s, much of it infill to 1920s ribbon development, which was rapidly colonising the very land where AA batteries needed to be sited. In many cases the War Office found itself pitted against speculative developers in a race to acquire sites in a buoyant open market. And even when these could be found, local objections were often intense and usually successful.[46] Understandably, perhaps, established landowners and proud occupants of new suburban villas no more welcomed AA guns on their doorsteps than did the tenant of Lodge Hill House in 1912. For all these reasons most layouts passed through many drafts before the sites could be juggled into place; and unlike the positions earmarked for mobile guns in the defence schemes of the previous fifteen years, error carried a heavy price. There could be no second thoughts once land was acquired and building begun.

Site-finding began in the autumn of 1937 long before type-designs for gunsites and their components had been drawn up by

the Directorate of Fortifications and Works, who issued their first
blueprints in 1938. At first the siting officers had simply a pair of
templates – one for a four-gun site, the other for a two-gun – and
a list of four-figure grid references defining the kilometre squares
in which each position, ideally, should lie. Reconnaissance seems
to have proceeded in parallel among all the areas listed for static
guns and by spring 1938 most of the layouts, while still liable to
amendment, had achieved some degree of finality, with the original
four-figure squares narrowed to six-figure references (accurate to
100 metres) and the would-be sites allocated provisional names
and numbers. Thus by mid April 1938 reconnaissance in the
London IAZ had identified 30 sites for fixed guns, twelve of which
were earmarked for 4.5in weapons and the remainder temporarily
for 3.7in statics.[47] Though a few of these positions were subsequently
exchanged for alternatives after local and other objections – a site
scheduled for Regent's Park, for example, was relinquished – the
list represented the beginnings of a layout of 64 HAA gunsites
selected in London by the first months of the war. Revealingly,
the distribution of sites bore scant resemblance to that of 1918, or
indeed the pattern of positions selected (but in no sense *built*) for
mobile guns in defence schemes earlier in the 1930s. We know
this because the grid references of the 1938 positions can be set
alongside their earlier equivalents; and what this exercise reveals
is that just two of the 30 sites initially selected for the IAZ
duplicated those on the roster issued in December 1933 (these
were Abbey Wood and Eltham, the first of which was subsequently
dropped), though two more, at Barking Park and Wanstead, were
shifted by only a few hundred yards.[48] A few of the older positions
were re-adopted when the requirement for sites crept upwards
over the next few years, but the near-complete departure from
the phantom layout of the early 1930s emphasises the deep
fracture between London's inter-war defence schemes, based
upon mobile guns, and the static pattern which would serve the
capital in the war to come.

The site reconnaissances completed by the spring of 1938
seem to have covered all the areas, ports and inland cities alike,
which were scheduled for guns under current plans; certainly in
late March the War Office found itself having to act quickly to
acquire 26 plots imminently threatened by competing develop-

ments in 2 AA Division on the Tyne and Tees, and at Manchester, Leeds, Sheffield, Coventry, Birmingham and Derby.[49] The next stage was to develop these places as fully-built gunsites, a huge project which began in 1938 and then merged into a construction programme which continued throughout the Second World War. To do this DFW staff set to work on the first type-design for a fixed emplacement for the 4.5in and 3.7in (static) gun, which was completed in late March 1938 and soon satisfactorily tested on the Shoeburyness range.[50] This standard emplacement was then brought within a general layout plan for a fixed HAA battery (discussed below) and it was to this template that work on the first sites was begun.

With preparations under way on the gunsites 1938 soon became a busy year for anti-aircraft works services all round. Accepting a larger proportion of 'statics' meant that more weapons would be kept on their sites during peacetime than once thought, but storage was still necessary for huge numbers of mobile guns and all the ancillary equipment which Territorials would need to draw when called to their war stations (the timetable for which, moreover, was now being reduced from 48 hours to just twelve).[51] By the time war was declared the national requirement for the mobilisation stores inaugurated by the Tompson committee had risen to 108, buildings together costing more than two million pounds at pre-war prices.[52] In addition, during the last years of peace many Territorial Army centres – successors to the old 'drill halls' – were newly-built for AA units added to the strength of the TA, using both traditionalist neo-Georgian designs and some distinctly modernistic thirties styles.[53] The support infrastructure extended also to nine intermediate ammunition depots and 34 equipment ammunition magazines (EAMs) whence the gunners would replenish their stocks. And beyond these projects, most of which had been in the pipeline for some years, a new works requirement emerged in the spring of 1938 when the War Office decided the time had come to provide additional anti-aircraft practice camps to supplement those which by now existed at Watchet, Manobier, Burrow Head, Weybourne on the north Norfolk coast, and nearby Stiffkey, the first of the LAA camps, which in March 1938 was actively being acquired. A total of six HAA camps was considered necessary at this stage, together with three for light guns,[54] though by the spring of 1939 these requirements had risen to seven and five respectively. Reconnaissance for the first was under way by summer 1938.

The decision to expand the training organisation coincided with the *Anschluss* of March 1938. Hitler's annexation of Austria, the first of several warning signs to flash across Europe in the eighteen months remaining before the violation of Poland, focused public attention upon Britain's air defence preparations in general, and in particular upon the state of the anti-aircraft guns and searchlights. Had Hitler's bombers passed over London rather than Vienna that spring the Luftwaffe would have found Britain protected by just 252 HAA guns and 969 searchlights,[55] assuming that all the AA troops could have been effectively mobilised (a point on which the Munich crisis six months later would cast some doubt). In these circumstances the early summer of 1938 brought the first real opening-up of debate on the state of Britain's air defences, when senior AA officers found themselves pitched into an often uncomfortable role as public advocates for their own cause.

Prominent among the protagonists was Major-General Sir Frederick Pile, Bart, CB, DSO, MC, known to his many friends as Tim. Appointed to command 1 AA Division as Tompson's replacement in the autumn of 1937, General Pile was the officer directly responsible for the defence of London in the year of Munich and in July of 1939 would rise to take command of Britain's entire AA organisation, remaining until three weeks before the end of the Second World War. In many respects (not least the longevity of his command) Pile was an unusual officer: an Irish aristocrat, son of a Protestant Nationalist baronet, whose early upbringing was spent, in his own words, in a political atmosphere which lay 'decidedly to the Left'.[56] Unlike most of his army contemporaries he knew nothing of the English public school. That may or may not have been an advantage, though the somewhat erratic tutoring which resulted – Pile barely received a formal education – almost denied him entry to the army at all.

The stringent academic standards of the Royal Military Academy at Woolwich defeated him entirely at his first attempt, and only intense application at a North London crammer gained his admittance, bottom of his class, as an eighteen-year-old in 1902. Probably that experience reinforced the humility and generosity of spirit for which Pile was widely liked. Passing out of Woolwich with a creditable record two years later, Pile went first as an artillery officer to South Africa and India (which was 'mostly fun') and then to the war in France. Pile wrote little of the Great War in the book which he published in 1949, and nothing at all of the exploits which, by 1918, had brought him mentions in dispatches, the MC and the DSO.

Coming to 1 AA Division only in autumn 1937, Pile was a late arrival on the anti-aircraft scene. He spent much of the 1920s and early '30s in tanks, transferring to the Royal Tank Corps in 1923 and in 1927 rising to command the Experimental Mechanised Force whose manoeuvres on Salisbury Plain prefigured the *Blitzkrieg* techniques later perfected by the Wehrmacht.[57] Pile's time in tanks consolidated his reputation as a 'dangerous' commander, willing to 'chance his arm'.[58] But he was also a progressive, a technician and an earnest enthusiast for tank warfare – a bold position in an era when hidebound cavalrymen were clinging so tenaciously to their mounts that one of Pile's fellow-mechanisers circulated a design for a tank with 'a special attachment for releasing horse manure'.[59] In 1928 Pile became Assistant Director of Mechanisation at the War Office, remaining for four years in which he worked unstintingly on the new light and medium tanks and mechanised artillery on which the British army would depend in the coming war. In 1932 there came an interlude, when Pile found himself posted, somewhat oddly, to command the Canal Infantry Brigade in Egypt; and from there he was delivered to take charge of 1 AA Division (TA).

Pile was thereby pitched into anti-aircraft work at one of the turning points in its inter-war history. This was partly a job, partly a predicament. On the one hand Pile was poised to gather the bounty of Chamberlain's November ruling on equipment; on the other, he inherited a responsibility so onerous – defending London without the tools for the job – that it was generally agreed to have killed his predecessor. And so, like others in the spring of

1938, Pile began to evangelise, to advertise his predicament more widely before suitable audiences. One opportunity came on 12 May 1938, when Pile was guest of honour at a House of Commons dinner hosted by Colonel H L Nathan, MP.

Never intimidated by the London Establishment, Pile used his speech to reveal some disturbing facts. Manpower was building up, he explained, but without sufficient equipment and adequate venues in which to train, progress toward a defence force able to meet attacks on the world's largest and most vulnerable capital remained painfully slow.

> Your city [said Pile] is the best prize in the world. It is the obvious prize for any attack. A short war can only be won against England if it is directed against London [. . .]. The government has decided that the anti-aircraft defences of Great Britain shall devolve on the Territorial Army, and my friends the Territorial colonels round these tables will not misunderstand me if I say that it is a great decision and a very grave decision; because the government have handed over to the Territorial Army what is the most vital defence in this country and they have handed it over to what, one must admit, are part-time soldiers, to soldiers who have got to learn in forty drills and a fortnight's camp, the whole art of anti-aircraft defence. Unlike their brothers who fought so gallantly in the last war they have got no time to make themselves efficient. For them the maximum efficiency must happen at zero hour [. . .].
>
> The success or failure of our firing depends on our training. Our drill halls are designed to accommodate such proportions of our numbers as one would normally expect to parade on one particular night, taking into consideration that they have of the order of forty drills to perform. At times of stress such as we are going through at present, when men enlist in great numbers and when they are very anxious to become trained, they attend every drill they can; they come night after night. Now that in some ways is most estimable, but from the point of view of training it is simply awful because our drill halls are crammed and our equipment has enormous numbers of men round it. We have not got any extra equipment and if we had we could not fit it into the drill halls and our permanent staff instructors are necessarily limited. So that these recruits who come in full of enthusiasm must feel stunned and rather wonder what it is all

about when they find that they are packed into a squad of shall
we say thirty men some distance away from the piece of
equipment which they are supposed to be operating and seeing
very little and getting very little training in the two hours or one
hour of the evening at their disposal.[60]

Pile went on to say that at least another ten thousand men
were needed to defend London adequately, and urged MPs to
do more to promote recruiting in their constituencies and
among local organisations, 'in their local clubs and societies and
even in their Mothers' Meetings. All they had to do was to tell
people from time to time about the 1st Anti-Aircraft Division
and what it was doing.'[61] The vote of thanks to Pile came from
Leslie Hore-Belisha, Secretary of State for War in Chamberlain's
National Government, who of course endorsed everything Pile
had said.

He has given you evidence tonight [said Hore-Belisha] of the
remarkable and unique manner in which Britain is defending
herself against the possibility of aggression. He is not spending this
evening drilling people or even amusing himself. He is spending
the evening – and this is how we are defended – persuading an
important and influential section of the people of London that it
ought to defend itself. What an extraordinary thing – if only some
foreign countries could see what is happening here: the greatest
empire is relying on the eloquence of a general in the British
Army bringing here a map to explain to the citizens of London
why and how they ought to defend themselves. Well! There is no
other country in the world that is in the danger zone of attack that
is proceeding upon that principle, although the principle in this
country is sacred and safe. Under the command of General Pile,
and with the recruits of the calibre that we are getting, I feel quite
satisfied that we shall reach the stage in which we can claim to be
as safe as a people can be.[62]

So the situation was grave, but all would be well. It is worth
quoting these faintly disingenuous words to draw the contrast
with what Pile later had to say about Hore-Belisha's habit of
talking up the condition of Britain's AA defences at a time when
candour would probably have been the wiser course. Only two days

after the dinner Hore-Belisha opened a new AA headquarters at Regent's Park, claiming to the press as he did so that:

> A year ago there was not a single new Anti-Aircraft drill hall nor any old one suitably adapted [. . .]. The searchlight units were then short of searchlights. Every unit now has its quota, and we have a surplus store. The gunner units were then short of guns. Now they all have their 3in guns. These guns, which are the present effective base of our defence, have all been renovated in such as way as to be the equivalent of new guns, and we have manufactured for their use a new and better kind of ammunition to increase their power.[63]

And the future was bright, in Hore-Belisha's account, with the new 3.7s now coming from production at a rate 'well in excess of any estimate that he had ever seen recorded', together with new fire-control instruments, and so on, and so on.[64] Pile was prepared to concede that all of this was probably said for German consumption, but however that may be it certainly wasn't true. There is something distinctly Orwellian in this image of a government minister trumpeting the prodigious success of plans in the face of all the evidence, rather like the state proclaiming the over-fulfilment of the third Five-Year Plan to those starving in the streets. Neither the press nor the gunners were convinced. In that same month the *Daily Express* ran articles highlighting production delays in the new 3.7in gun;[65] and two days after Hore-Belisha's speech at Regent's Park the searching questions in parliament began.

Pile gave several pages of his book to the *cause célèbre* which began in May 1938 and continued into the summer. Briefly, this episode centred around the figure of one Duncan Sandys, a second lieutenant in 51 AA Brigade (TA), Conservative Member of Parliament for Norwood and – more than incidentally – son-in-law to Winston Churchill, whom many suspected of orchestrating the events which followed. Towards the end of May Sandys was among the first to raise questions in the Commons. At the same time he also spoke privately to Hore-Belisha to express concern at the 'grievous shortages' of modern equipment which hampered his own and other units. Hore-Belisha's response seems to have touched the blasé – at any rate he assured Sandys that all would be well, while continuing to make public pronouncements similar to his Regent's Park speech. This complacency, however, whether real or affected, provoked Sandys into a further parliamentary question; and in line with convention, Sandys gave advance written notice of this question to the Secretary of State.

This was the start of the trouble, for Sandys' draft written question embodied evidence that he was in possession of what Pile termed 'more accurate information on the state of anti-aircraft equipment than a mere second lieutenant was entitled to have'.[66] A mere second lieutenant, perhaps; but a Member of Parliament? That was the question which the War Office and eventually the Attorney-General decided they must examine, with a view to establishing whether any contravention of the Official Secrets Act had taken place – and not just on Sandys' part. At an early stage the matter was referred to Pile, whose inquiries soon identified Sandys' source as a brother officer serving in one of the AA brigades. Pile interviewed this officer, and was certainly sympathetic to his plaint that a 'great number of officers thought the Secretary of State was deliberately concealing from the country our position'. They were after all correct to think so. But Hore-Belisha was less accommodating. Disregarding a further letter from Sandys the MP (asking the minister to confirm whether the figures in his possession were true or not), Hore-Belisha began a legal process against Sandys the subaltern. In the meantime Sandys the MP asked his question in the Commons and thus made his figures public.

It was at this point that questions of law and parliamentary procedure took over. At Hore-Belisha's insistence Sandys was interviewed by the Attorney-General, who decided that a court of inquiry must be held. This was duly convened at Horse Guards, but after a good deal of waiting around the officers assembled for it were suddenly told that it was postponed, thanks to Sandys claiming parliamentary privilege, appealing to the Speaker for protection, and making a further Commons statement protesting at his treatment at the Attorney-General's hands. At this point Chamberlain himself formed a committee to investigate the whole matter, which by now had crystallised into the two separate but related questions of parliamentary privilege and official secrecy. All parties involved gave evidence, practically everyone disagreed on what had been said to whom at the various bilateral interviews which had taken place so far and, in Pile's words, 'a really good letting-off of steam occurred.'[67] When the steam cleared Duncan Sandys emerged with his parliamentary privilege upheld. It was a disagreeable incident which, as Pile says rather opaquely, 'did a lot of harm to a great number of people who were quite innocently drawn into a matter of which, in the first instance, they had had no knowledge'.[68] One of these, certainly, was Sandys' original informant, who found himself exiled summarily to the Far East. But Sandys' purpose was served: the point about AA production was made, the public was alerted to the facts, and manufacture stepped up. The incident did its perpetrator no lasting harm. Sandys played a key role in many important air defence and anti-aircraft projects under Pile's command during the war, and crowned his political career as Secretary of State for the Colonies in Macmillan's administration of 1957–63, following appointments at Housing and Local Government, Defence and Aviation.[69] His front-bench career ended in 1964, when he was dropped from the Shadow Cabinet by Edward Heath – another senior Conservative, incidentally, who spent his war in AA Command.[70]

The Sandys case supplied further impetus to AA preparations at a time when the outcome of Chamberlain's November ruling was already beginning to be felt. In April 1938 the CID took a number of decisions designed to enlarge the geography of the air defence system still further – specifically to widen the searchlight-illuminated zone of the AFZ to 40 miles; to reorganise the existing AA formations and raise others as required; and to provide AA guns for RAF airfields outside the limits of the current defensive layout, not simply as a protection against low-flying attack but – in an important departure from existing thinking – to guard additionally against higher-level precision bombing. These decisions were in turn assimilated to a new study produced in mid May, when the Reorientation Committee under Dowding issued another in its ever-lengthening series of reports, this one addressing, in particular, extensions to the AFZ and the use to be made of the 3in guns which would be freed from their current allocations once 3.7in and 4.5in weapons began to be delivered.[71]

In discussing the completed report at a meeting of the Home

Defence Committee on 20 May (when it was approved), Dowding neatly summed up the evolution of the air defence problem since the days before reorientation began. 'Until five years ago,' Dowding explained, 'we were concerned only with the defence of London. The next stage was a defence zone from Southampton to the Tyne which afforded a measure of protection to the areas lying to the west-ward of it. It was now essential to provide protection, directly or indirectly, for as much of the country as possible.'[72] One result was a recommendation to widen the AFZ, ultimately, over much of England, extending it to a depth of 50 miles up the east coast, pushing it outward over the whole of East Anglia and the south-east as far as Bristol and leaving only the south-western peninsula and a band of territory from Bristol up toward Manchester without provision for fighter cover, including continuous layouts of lights (though lights would still accompany the local AA defences of cities in this otherwise dark band). This plan, with its requirement for an additional 44 searchlight companies (4128 lights in all), was commended as representing 'almost finality in what can usefully be done as regards the Aircraft Fighting Zone [. .]',[73] and marked an important step towards extending fighter cover over much of the country. The May recommendations on gun defences dealt almost entirely with the re-allocation of 3in guns to 40 batteries which would be newly formed with 320 weapons released by the substitution of 3.7s and 4.5s. Together with the small increase in 3.7in weapons (up from 320 under the Joubert Report to 352) the new 3in batteries pushed the recommended scale of HAA guns nationally to 960. Despite the Air Ministry's plea that many of the 3in weapons should be diverted to cover aerodromes – twelve bomber stations in the eastern counties and ten (mostly Coastal Command) airfields elsewhere – only six batteries, of 48 guns, were assigned to these targets, to cover the bomber stations with four weapons apiece. (Though even this small allocation was disputed by Pile, who wanted these guns for London and said so in a minority report.) The remaining 282 guns were allotted to existing defended areas, among which London and Thames & Medway were assigned 128, or sixteen batteries. Even with this reinforcement, the Committee agreed that London's artillery defences 'cannot be said to be unduly strong'.[74]

In the wake of the Sandys case and in the climate of growing public concern about the state of the air defences, on 28 June 1938 Hore-Belisha announced the formation of the Anti-Aircraft Corps, a higher-level formation which would take charge of the AA divisions, whose number moreover was now to be increased progressively from two to five. Planning along these lines had in fact been under way for some time when Hore-Belisha made his announcement – the need for a corps organisation had been accepted in principle during the previous December – though the suddenness with which it was now made public appeared to some to have a political flavour. Nonetheless it was widely welcomed by the gunners, for in practical terms the new 1 AA Corps gave them for the first time a superordinate headquarters of their own – shared with Fighter Command at Bentley Priory, Stanmore – wherein a single officer would exercise operational control over a unified anti-aircraft organisation.

This officer was Lieutenant-General Alan Brooke, destined to become one of the most illustrious generals of the Second World War, who had spent much of his previous career in field artillery. Like Pile, his commander of 1 AA Division, Brooke was not exactly overflowing with anti-aircraft expertise when he arrived, nor indeed were most of the other senior appointees installed in the general reshuffle which attended the formation of the Corps. So there was criticism; but in truth the lingering neglect of anti-aircraft provision meant that by 1938 few officers anywhere in the army had risen to senior positions through the specialism of AA itself (those who had won their experience in the previous war were variously out of touch, out of uniform, or dead). In result the Territorial majors and captains running the brigades and batteries of 1938 often commanded deeper specialist expertise than their seniors.

As autumn 1938 approached so did the first major test of that expertise. In August the two existing AA divisions ventured out for a Home Defence Exercise, manning about 800 searchlights around London and elsewhere and, in Pile's 1 AA Division, occupying some 34 gunsites on a skeleton basis. 'We learned a great deal from this exercise,' Pile later reflected, 'about how depressingly bad we were, particularly in the tactical control of our guns.'[75] He might have added that mustering scratch crews for just 34 sites was hardly a monumental achievement either, though considering that the number of HAA weapons in unit hands within 1 AA Division stood at about 100 (mostly 3in types), little more could have been done. Yet this problem of numbers – how many guns were available, and what proportion could be effectively deployed – was about to come under much closer scrutiny as the August exercises drew to a close.

On 8 September Brooke's staff at Bentley Priory sent the War Office a return showing the number of AA guns and searchlights likely to be ready, and their planned dispositions, 'in the event of an emergency arising' in the month from 15 September, a week hence.[76] Though the new 3.7in weapons were now trickling from the factories to the TA units and permanent sites were under construction to receive the big 4.5s, 1 AA Corps armoury a fortnight before the troops were actually called out at the height of the Munich crisis was still hugely dominated by supposedly 'modernised' 3in guns. The figures are worth examining. Within Pile's 1 AA Division there were, to be precise, just 106 HAA guns in unit hands, of which 24 were 3.7s and the remainder 3in; adding weapons which could be scraped together from practice camps and depots, the southern gunners reckoned on being able to find 169 heavy guns in all, of which just 33 would be of modern 3.7in type. LAA stocks were in a far worse state, standing at just 24 guns of 3in type fitted to 'Peerless' lorries, together with eighteen naval 2pdrs. No fewer than 1268 Lewis guns were, however, in the process of being distributed to the units by September 1938, and it was on these old faithfuls which the LAA batteries would continue to rely for some years yet. Additionally, 1 AA Division expected to be able to mobilise 802 searchlights, more than half of which would come from stores. The position in 2 AA Division was worse, the 100 HAA guns available (including just sixteen 3.7s) permitting absurdly thin cover within every defended area – just four 3in weapons at Coventry, for example, eight on the Humber, twelve at Leeds, and so on. This division additionally had eight 3in guns for LAA work, sixteen 2pdrs and 1744 Lewis guns (all but twelve of which were still, somewhat vaguely, 'in course of issue') along with 445 searchlights. That was the Territorial position. In the event of an emergency mobilisation in late September or early October one of the two Regular AA units was assigned to protect Portsmouth,

Southampton, Plymouth and Bristol, between which 35 AA Group were expected to spread 34 HAA guns, 852 LAA weapons (again, mostly Lewis guns) and 69 searchlights. Its companion, 36 AA Group, was assigned to Edinburgh/Rosyth, Glasgow and Scapa with just eighteen HAA guns, 548 LAA (all but four of which were Lewis guns) and ten lights. All of these figures refer, of course, not to the official establishments of the units concerned, nor even in some cases to their actual holding of guns, but the numbers which, in the event of an emergency, it was thought practicable to get out onto the sites and make ready to fire. Nationally, the figures amounted to 341 HAA guns, 4506 LAA (4412 Lewis guns and 94 others) and 1430 sets of searchlight equipment.

The test of these expectations came a fortnight later, when the AA gunners of the TA were actually called out and war stations were occupied in earnest for the first time in twenty years. Ordered at 2.30 in the afternoon of 23 September, the Munich deployment came mid-way between Chamberlain's first visit to Hitler – itself precipitated by the Führer's sabre-rattling speech against Czechoslovakia at the Nuremburg Rally of 12 September – and the four-power conference which was convened at the end of the month, from which emerged the British Prime Minister's 'peace with honour' and the Nazis' partial annexation of Czech territory. The mobilisation of the domestic air defences at the height of this crisis – which for the AA gunners lasted until 14 October – proved a valuable, and sobering, test of the system which had been under development since 1934.

Pile gives an account of events on the rainy Friday afternoon when the gunners received their orders to move.

The men were warned by telegram, telephone, and by personal visits from key-men who had been assembled. The order reached them all over the place – in their homes, offices, places of amusement, everywhere. It was all very amateurish, but it worked. Buses from local LPTB [London Passenger Transport Board] branches joined the other forms of transport. Some, who had their own cars, went round and collected others in the pouring rain without which any such deployment would be incomplete. The bad weather, in fact, added enormously to the difficulties of the men arriving at their isolated gun- and searchlight-sites. The heavy equipment slithered about on the slippery grass, vehicles sank to their axles in mud. Everything that could go wrong seemed to do so in the driving rain, but by the following dawn things seemed somehow to have sorted themselves out. Guns and searchlights were in position, and if they weren't all actually able to operate, that was not [. . .] entirely our fault.[77]

The resulting scatter of occupied gunsites gave some visible reassurance to the population of London, at least, though the military value of the deployment soon came under question. Guns there might be at many sites, along with men to operate them, but would those weapons actually fire if the Luftwaffe droned over the horizon, and if so, would they do much good? In fact the defensive value of the Munich turn-out was much more apparent than real. Many batteries had no predictors, and those which did often discovered them to be faulty; others lacked the dials by which the predictor data was read at the guns or, again, found these vital pieces of equipment inoperative. Flat batteries, missing fuze keys, unfit weapons and frequent mismatching between ammunition and guns added to the troubles, likewise the blank refusal of many civilian storekeepers to depart from working hours negotiated by their trade unions ('lorries were kept waiting for hours at stores and mobilisation centres,' recalled Pile, 'while the storekeepers had their breakfasts and strolled down to their offices.'[78]). Even the relatively primitive AA battery of 1938 was analogous to a complex machine: most of the major components might be there, but a few missing or defective parts reduced the whole interdependent assemblage to so much useless metal. And at many sites even the major components were absent. Very few batteries outside London were able to fasten to their war stations, so the overall strength of 2 AA Division fell short even of the modest expectations of early September. London on the other hand was better served, partly because Pile's division mustered the most practised AA units in the country, some with histories by now reaching back fifteen years. The contrast did not pass unremarked. Allegations in Parliament that provincial layouts had been stripped to fortify the capital were untrue (if only because, as Pile put it, 'you cannot strip what doesn't exist'),[79] likewise suggestions that only 50 guns had actually been deployed nationally. But Pile himself conceded that the number of HAA guns 'ready in all respects for action' was probably no more than 126 – fewer than half the total expected a fortnight before the call-out. The new permanent sites for the 4.5s, reconnoitred a year earlier and by now in varying stages of development, stood all too obviously vacant. In September 1938 not a single 4.5in AA gun had been mounted.

There was a general outcry after Munich, and not simply over the state of the AA defences. (ARP was an even worse shambles, shelters in London and elsewhere consisting of little more than trenches hurriedly dug in parks – the so-called 'Munich trenches' – which generally collapsed over the winter.) But of course the crisis was also a godsend. Territorial recruiting soared and tough questions were asked in Parliament, to which the only responsible answers could be promises to expedite production, delivery and commissioning of the new equipment which, after all, had been awarded top priority almost a year before. Not before time, Hore-Belisha avowed that 'Henceforth we must pay as much attention to our anti-aircraft defences as we have always paid to the maintenance of the Fleet.'

> Every month will find the nation stronger [he continued]. Within two years public opinion on this matter has been changed, a vast organisation has been built up, a great industry has been created, and production has begun. It was at a stage in the process that the emergency arose and the deployment was ordered. The country has a right to know that His Majesty's Government are resolved to see that the legitimate fears at present entertained shall so far as is humanly possible be averted in the shortest possible time.[80]

Much the same impetus was at work at the Air Ministry, where the Air Staff pointed out on 27 October that their projected fighter strength for the summer of 1939 was calculated on the basis that 'the full scale of ground AA defences are provided [sic]. It is absolutely essential therefore that on the 1st August 1939, when we shall still be weak in our Fighter line [. . .] that we should be as strong as possible in our AA ground defences to offset this weakness as far as possible.'[81] At a meeting on 15

December the Reorientation Committee took a hard look at the possibilities open to them in accelerating the AA defences.[82] One outcome was a decision to take firmer hold, urgently, of the sites selected for gun positions to safeguard them against competing claims. Another was to co-ordinate more closely the selection of gunsites with those for searchlights, barrage balloons and shelter trenches. And a third was to make a more definite allocation of available HAA guns between the defended areas then authorised. On this day, 15 December 1938, the number of guns believed to be available stood at 452.

That total was rather less than half the currently approved scale of 960 HAA guns and fractionally over a third of the Ideal scale defined in February 1937, whose quota of 1264 heavy weapons had retained its abstract authority without, so far, being approved as a firm target. And yet, toward the end of January 1939, the War Office argued that the Ideal scale itself 'did not now represent a full insurance against air attack' and pressed for an additional 624 guns beyond the total of 960 already authorised, which would yield a new target of 1584, amounting to the Ideal total of 1264 modern 3.7in and 4.5in plus 320 older 3in guns.[83] It was conceded that the gun totals might be eased downward if a proportion of UP weapons was substituted, but since supply timetables remained uncertain no reliance could be placed on these devices for some time yet. In result, expansion of the HAA defences to the full complement envisaged in the Dowding Report, plus the additional 320 guns requested by the War Office, was approved early in February 1939, two years after the Ideal Scheme's issue and twenty months after the CID had endorsed it 'in principle' (Appendix I). It was not the last increase approved before war was joined, but by itself the decision reduced at a stroke the proportion of the target scale which the AA gun stocks had reached. Seen in these terms, by the spring of 1939 the factories were running as hard as they could merely to stay in the same place.

As these matters were being deliberated in Whitehall the construction programme for the new permanent HAA sites was pressing ahead and the first 4.5in gun was emplaced, amid much fanfare, in February 1939. The sites which had been under development in the major GDAs since reconnaissance began in

Plate 3 Munich: gunners at Paull on the Humber get to grips with the Vickers predictor. Many of these instruments were found to be faulty when unpacked for the crisis.

autumn 1937 were the first permanent AA positions built since the Great War, and conformed to a distinctive design template worked out by DFW in 1938 and applied with a high degree of consistency.[84] The pre-war type-designs for HAA batteries and their components, execution of which continued into the early war period as sites were completed, were only the first in a long series of such plans issuing from the directorate's offices at Romney House in Marsham Street, London SW1. Adaptation and revision of these plans was led by tactical experience, the introduction of new equipment (and the redesign of old), together with developing policy on the troops' domestic accommodation. For all of these reasons newly-built permanent sites – HAA, LAA, rocket and searchlight – established in the ensuing years generally obeyed design principles which speak with greater or lesser clarity of their chronology. That chronology, both nationally and locally, is most reliably determined from study of units' records; but equally, the construction-date and subsequent adaptation of an HAA site surviving today can also to some extent be read from its form.

The pre-war template for a permanent HAA position was framed around the standard emplacement – or 'gunpit' – for the 4.5in or 3.7in (static) gun issued by DFW in March 1938 (Fig 6; Plates 4–5). This was an octagonal, concrete-walled structure, usually banked externally with earth, with two sides formed from massive steel gates to admit the gun for mounting and when necessary for exchange. The weapon was anchored to the concrete floor of the emplacement by a deeply-bedded central holdfast (shown in the inset to Fig 6), designed to take the base-plate common to the 4.5in and static 3.7in. The remaining six sides of the emplacement were occupied by ammunition lockers – structurally integral with the walls – open at either end to permit inspection and withdrawal of the rounds and closed by steel doors. Unlike later gunpit designs, this early example had no integral shelter for the crew, nor any covered space reserved for first-hand maintenance. In time one of the ammunition recesses came to be adapted for this latter role, while shelters adjacent to the emplacements were widely improvised once the sites came to be permanently occupied.

The standard site layout allowed for four of these emplace-ments (Fig 7), since while many positions were initially intended for just two guns allowance was usually made for doubling-up and to prevent the necessity for returning to the position for additional construction. The emplacements were arranged to put the two central guns forward and those to the flanks slightly to the rear (permitting engagements on a flank without firing over the adjacent crew), with the openings in the emplacements set on radial lines centring on the command post. The command post for the battery and the instrument positions lay behind the entire layout, the whole arrangement echoing that used for mobile guns cast in solid form. In the earliest sites all of these were very simple structures. In contrast to the fully-built concrete buildings which would appear after the first year of war, early command posts were not much more than dugouts, chiefly accommodating the telephonists who linked the site to the outside world, while the nearly (open) instrument positions were sometimes shielded by low blast walls and were usually provided, in time, with improvised shelters. The voice, where necessary amplified by a megaphone, was the main means of communication between each of these places and their occupants.

In autumn 1937, when scouting for these sites began, none was expected to have permanent living quarters provided in peacetime: aside from the gunpark, just described, each would require a hut for the caretaker, usually at the point where the access road met the highway, and hutting for storage, the whole enclosed in a surrounding fence. This policy persisted for some time, with the result that few sites were adequately furnished with domestic accommodation when permanent manning began. The provision of accommodation for HAA sites was first considered by the War Office in the summer of 1938, as plans for the pre-war gun layout began to crystallize. Since all AA troops at this date were Territorials, permanent building was generally avoided since the cost involved was uneconomic in relation to the level of use the buildings would be likely to see. Policy settled in October 1938 was to rely upon billeting for permanent sites wherever feasible, and to put troops manning non-permanent guns under canvas. The only fixed structures approved were for static sites where no billets could be requisitioned and existing War Department property was on hand;[85] these would be fully built and minded by caretakers. Prior to the formation of AA Command, the administration of ADGB troops lay with Home Forces commands, who according to a post-war account submitted 'comprehensive schemes' in line with these principles.

The problem of ADGB accommodation was examined again in the general overhaul of defence planning after Munich. By early 1939 it had been decided that relying upon billeting would be unrealistic for many permanent HAA sites, 70 per cent of which were now scheduled for hutting, together with around half of the searchlight positions. The estimates of early 1939 were based upon the assumption that there would be 120 batteries of HAA guns, equating to 240 four-gun positions, each of which would be staffed by 80 men. Assuming that 30 per cent could be billeted, this left 13,440 troops to be accommodated in hutting, or a total of 336 permanent 40-man huts, plus smaller structures for officers. The hutting needs for searchlight detachments were larger, though these sites were expected to rely upon portable 'Weblee' huts, 5370 of which were needed. These estimates were approved in January 1939.

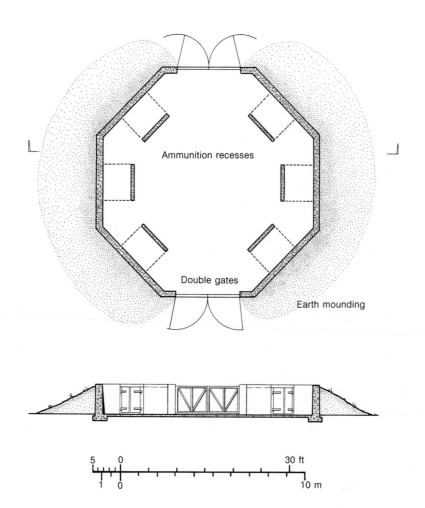

Ammunition recesses

Double gates

Earth mounding

5   0   30 ft

1   0   10 m

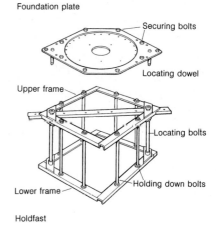

Foundation plate

Securing bolts

Locating dowel

Upper frame

Locating bolts

Holding down bolts

Lower frame

Holdfast

Figure 6 HAA emplacement design (March 1938 pattern) with an inset showing the holdfast assembly which was sunk in the centre. Intended for the 4.5in gun and eventually used for both 4.5s and 3.7s, this was the standard emplacement used on permanent sites of pre-war and early wartime date. A modification based upon early wartime experience is shown in Figure 10.

Plate 4 Slade's Green (ZS1), the most easterly HAA battery in the London IAZ. Though provided with a concrete command post and extensive domestic camp by April 1946, when this photograph was taken, the site's layout of guns shows clear signs of its origin in the late 1930s (compare Fig 7). The same site 48 years later appears as Plate 28.

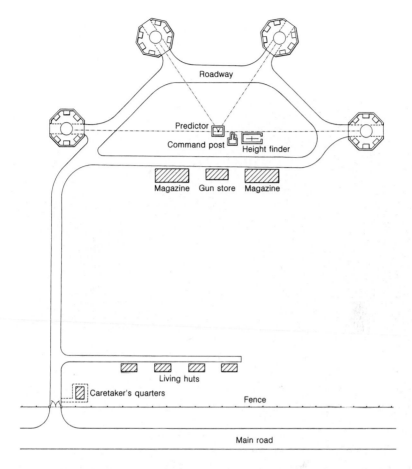

Figure 7 Layout plan for an HAA site, February 1939, using the emplacement type shown in Figure 6. Limited permanent building and reliance on earthwork or sandbagged enclosures for the command post and instruments were chief characteristics of this design, which made little provision for living quarters. This layout was widely used for pre-war and early wartime permanent sites, though individual examples were widely modified later in the war by the addition of concrete command posts, additional emplacements, supplementary buildings, and so on.

In noting the approval of hutting, AA Command's post-war historian adds that 'unfortunately, few people knew how to put them up,'[86] continuing that 'a fine assembly of senior staff officers and representatives of AA Divisions' gathered in the War Office Quadrangle at 11.00 on Monday, 16 January to witness a demonstration arranged by DFW of 'Huts, and their Erection'. Whatever the larger benefits of this event, it was at least timely. On the

Plate 5 A gunpit at Richmond Park (ZS20 in the IAZ) in an early wartime view, with everything neat and tidy and a gleaming 3.7in static. One of London's pre-war permanent gunsites, Richmond Park would later become home to the first mixed HAA battery in Britain.

same day, DFW extended approval to the immediate hutting of all permanent HAA positions except those where billeting was available nearby, further land purchase was needed, or there were objections locally to huts being erected in peacetime, such as on commons and public parks.

On 27 February 1939 the demand for hutting was expanded with the approval of portable huts on all mobile gunsites and searchlight batteries, respectively to the scales of 60 and 70 per cent of the sites in each command.[87] This work, together with the provision of permanent hutting for static sites, was under way in April 1939 when a fresh burden was placed upon materials and labour by the passing of the Militia Act, as a result of which new scales were drawn up to accommodate the first batches of conscript AA soldiers. Much discontent was voiced by Territorials when it was discovered that the approved accommodation scales for these militia camps were more generous than those provided for pre-war volunteers, work on whose sites began to fall behind schedule in some parts of the country owing to the rapidly expanding demands on contractors. Eastern Command seems to have been most advanced, reporting in mid April 1939 that 60 per cent of its static gunsites were now fully hutted and that the remainder would be complete by the end of the month.[88] Contracts for hutting work on Eastern Command's mobile sites were also issued during April, but elsewhere work appears to have been much delayed. As a result, as spring turned to summer, the programme to house the AA troops in many parts of the country was already falling behind.

The final six months before Britain and Germany again found themselves at war were occupied with increasingly anxious attempts to bring the AA defences into readiness for the knock-out blow. The first was a further expansion in personnel. By March 1939 the existing five AA divisions were well established in their headquarters respectively at London, Hucknall, Edinburgh, Chester and Reading, between them parenting 22 AA brigades, many of them re-numbered since the first had been formed in the 1920s.[89] In this month, as Hitler occupied the rest of Czechoslovakia, Hore-Belisha announced large increases in the strength of AA units, together with the intention to raise the number of AA divisions to seven. And to take charge of this newly-expanded structure the existing 1 AA Corps would itself be promoted.

Founded on 1 April 1939, Anti-Aircraft Command inherited as its headquarters the former home of 1 AA Corps, a spacious house called Glenthorn in the grounds of Fighter Command HQ at Stanmore, and also its chief, though Lieutenant-General Alan Brooke would remain for just sixteen weeks more before the baton passed to Sir Frederick Pile. It was a landmark, though one whose prominence looks greater with hindsight than it may have at the time – the formation of AA Command, after all, did not by itself add a single extra gun to Britain's armoury. But like many steps taken in the months after Munich, the command's formation, along with the companion measures announced in the spring, did assert the new seriousness of purpose attaching to anti-aircraft defence in general. And no one foresaw the growth to come. When 1 AA Corps first made house in Glenthorn there was some doubt over whether so large a building was really necessary; within a few years, with Pile's command nationally topping 300,000 personnel, his headquarters had burst its seams, overflowed into a colony of huts among Glenthorn's leafy grounds – the 'Indian village' – and commandeered a second habitation.[90]

The anti-aircraft organisation may have gained a stronger identity with the formation of AA Command, but what it really needed in the spring of 1939 was more men, more guns, and absolute confidence that everything could be mobilised in the event of a snap attack. Despite the loyal work of the Territorials over fifteen difficult years, the Munich muddle was the dominant memory in official minds during the spring of 1939, and the voices which had earlier cautioned that so urgent and vital a duty as AA gunnery should not be given to part-timers were echoing loudly. Practice deployments were planned to sharpen the soldiers and drill their procedures,[91] but when it was judged prudent, in the last week of March, to occupy a proportion of the London defences in the light of the tension surrounding events in Czechoslovakia, it was the Regular AA units, not the Territorials, who found themselves called out. Alerted to this 'emergency' deployment at 6.30 in the evening of 21 March, the two Regular brigades were under orders to move next day to 'sites which would provide an improvised defence against a sudden air attack on London'.[92] Motoring out from Aldershot and Wellington Barracks early the following morning, the two Regular brigades occupied their initial positions with eight 3.7in mobile guns, 61 elderly 3in pieces and – the first time such weapons were deployed in Britain – fourteen pristine Bofors, together with 52 searchlights. After some hurried shuffling next day in search of better sites (and this after a decade and a half of planning for mobile deployments) the Regulars settled down to await the bombers, which never came. It was all rather unnecessary, but the practice was useful and everybody was pleased to find the civil population 'most helpful'.

While this deployment was in hand the planners in Whitehall were looking again at the authorised scales of AA guns for ADGB. Although the HAA establishment had been raised to 1584 guns as recently as February, soon after the War Office began to press for yet another increase, this time with a further 1144 weapons (or rocket projectors, if available) to achieve a 72-gun density over London and the cities of the industrial north and, in result, an HAA total of 2728, more than double the Ideal scale. Nor was that the limit of their proposals, for strengthening the high level cover to such an extent, they argued, would necessitate similar proportional increases in LAA guns to stop the Luftwaffe exploiting the relative weakness in low-level cover which would result. Though not wholly unsympathetic to these ideas, the Air Staff cautioned that so heavy an investment in AA threatened to imbalance the overall air defence system, leading to 'a tortoise policy of protection without a punch'[93] (meaning of course that they would prefer the 30 or 40 million pounds which these additions would cost to be spent on bombers). And yet, perhaps surprisingly, another substantial increase in the target scales for AA was approved, and in May 1939 the long sequence of studies and revisions which had dictated the theoretical AA gun strength since the Steel–Bartholomew Report of 1923 reached its ultimate pre-war edition.

The plans endorsed by the Reorientation Committee in the first week of the month amounted to a watered-down version of the War Office's earlier scheme. Rejecting the view that London and other important centres warranted a 72-gun density – in which any target could be engaged simultaneously by that number of weapons – Dowding and his colleagues nonetheless accepted that the case for substantial increases was justified for key targets within about 40 miles of the east and south coasts as far west as Southampton. This in itself demanded an additional 328 HAA guns, to which the committee added 40 further weapons for Belfast and the naval cordite factory at Holton Heath – two new areas admitted to the roster of GDAs for the first time – and further consignments for a strategic reserve and a mobile pool, which together would hold 336 weapons split equally between them. This brought the total to 704 guns, though since 56 were already allocated to a mobile pool under existing plans the number of new weapons at issue fell to 648. Summed with the previously authorised, this produced a total requirement of 2232 HAA weapons, to be achieved at some time in 1941 – a magic number whose potency would last until August 1940, when it was raised yet again (Appendix I). In addition, a smaller increase was recommended in LAA weapons, to bring the total to 1847 barrels, to be met from a rather smaller number of guns, since some would be twins.[94]

Shortly after these ideas were approved the war came a step closer for the AA troops. The problem of mobilising these men for the knock-out blow had bothered the higher command since the beginnings of rearmament in 1934, and in the end it was solved by pre-empting much of the procedure and manning a proportion of the sites long before war was declared. Thus was born the Couverture – the 'thin covering' of guns – which came into force at the end of May.[95] AA Command's war could fairly be said to have begun with the Couverture. It marked the inception of continuous manning at a proportion of the sites, and since the actual declaration of war in September was something of a non-event as far as the air defences were concerned the everyday lives of many soldiers and officers were affected far more by this precautionary stage than by the real transition to hostilities. The Couverture was a sizeable exercise. Some 288 guns were deployed, in London, Thames & Medway, Dover and Portsmouth,[96] together with 960 searchlights in a 25-mile deep belt from Newcastle to Portsmouth, for the AFZ. Unlike the Munich deployment, many weapons appear to have been emplaced on the new sites developed since autumn 1937, which apart from their other advantages could by now offer reasonable purpose-built accommodation for at least some of the men. And of those there were plenty. One thousand officers and 22,000 Territorial soldiers were called into uniform for the Couverture, to serve on a rota basis in four contingents for a month at a time, half on the gunsites and half at training camp (that at least was the theory, though the Couverture, of course, was superseded before a full cycle of four months had elapsed). Special legislation was necessary to enact this, since the Territorials had in no sense committed themselves to serve on this timetable. Many men were financially straitened by the Couverture, some of their civilian employers were extraordinarily mean, and in general there was much resentment towards the conscript militiamen who were now being drafted into AA Command in numbers and whose treatment was generally kinder than the Territorials', who were long-serving volunteers and, by comparison with the newcomers, technically expert. These feelings of frustration, hardship and grievance were of course an ideal preparation for war.

The Couverture formally lasted until Thursday, 24 August 1939, so was nearing its last month when Pile took over from Brooke on 28 July. It was replaced by a general mobilisation, when key-men went through their carefully planned routine to contact those members of the AA units who were not already at their posts. Gun and searchlight sites were occupied, and the men settled down as well as they could in whatever accommodation the War Office had been able to contrive for them. The day before the mobilisation was ordered Hitler and Stalin had concluded the German-Soviet Treaty of Non-Aggression – the pact which opened the way for Germany's invasion of Poland on Friday, 1 September. Some of the AA units recorded this event baldly in their newly-opened War Diaries, chronicles which would grow vastly over the following six years, as command staff at Stanmore and the gunners and searchlight crews scattered on their sites from Scapa to Cornwall committed the unfolding war to official historical record. Two days later, on the morning of Sunday, 3 September, most of those men were listening to the wireless.

PART II

AA Command

CHAPTER 4

'A merciful respite'

SEPTEMBER 1939 – MAY 1940

A few minutes after Chamberlain finished speaking the rising skirl of air-raid sirens filled the air across London. To Londoners the raid warning of 11.27 on that Sunday morning became one of those rare moments in collective experience which lodge forever in the memory.[1] Most recall where they were and what they were doing when the sirens sounded, and in the main the response was less fear or panic than curiosity: many stood in the open, peering upward to see the long-promised bombers. The gunners of the IAZ were alerted immediately, but as the minutes passed with no enemy aircraft in sight the falsity of the warning began to dawn. In fact the alert was the result of a solitary French aircraft accidentally penetrating the radar cordon and jolting the rather too sensitive air defence system into motion. In the first days of war, indeed, everything was on a hair trigger. The sirens sounded again on the evening of 3 September, and repeatedly in the following days; and on Wednesday 6 September AA Command came into action for the first time by firing on formations over Sheerness and Thameshaven. But that, too, was a mistake. The first aircraft downed by British AA guns in the Second World War was a Bristol Blenheim from 64 Squadron based at RAF Church Fenton.

The Luftwaffe's failure to materialise as expected in these first days of war fostered a sense of relief in AA Command, albeit tempered by the knowledge that the knock-out blow might yet fall at any time. It is certainly true that any sizeable attack in the first days of war, and for many months afterwards, would have

Plate 6 Modern major-general: Sir Frederick Pile, GOC-in-C AA Command, 1939–45.

found the guns thinly spread. On the morning of 3 September just 662 HAA weapons were serviceable and ready to fire in Britain, distributed between 29 GDAs and a scatter of airfields around London.[2] The greater weight lay in the IAZ and the Thames approaches, where nearly two-fifths of the total was concentrated, though in common with those elsewhere the 275 guns in these two areas were dominated by 3in types resurrected from the First World War. Elsewhere the 'thin covering' inherited from the Couverture was practically threadbare. Major cities such as Leeds, Sheffield and Birmingham fielded gun strengths in the low twenties, while Manchester, Coventry and Bristol had barely reached double figures. Only Hull, the Forth, Portsmouth, Southampton and the Tyne could muster around 30 guns apiece.

Light AA was no more plentiful.[3] Of the 156 VPs on AA Command's list on 3 September, only sixteen were wholly without guns, and all of these were in 1 AA Division, where the balloon barrage for London was thought to provide an adequate shield. But apart from a smattering of 2pdrs and some 3in weapons firing on Case I sights, practically all the VPs were defended merely by Lewis guns. Of the new 40mm Bofors there were just 72, the majority distributed between the 20 Chain Home radar stations which were operational – or at least partially so – on this first day of war. Most radar stations had three Bofors, while the balance was scattered around the more sensitive VPs in other categories, the results of the steadily-widening surveys begun in July 1936. The solitary Bofors in 1 AA Division protected the small-arms factory at Enfield, while elsewhere these weapons in ones and twos were given to targets as diverse as Liverpool Docks, the ICI plant at Winnington, the power station at Stourport, the Fawley and Purfleet oil depots, and 'food concerns' in Bristol. The largest number (eight) ringed Dowding's and Pile's joint headquarters at Stanmore. Apart from a few 3in guns working in an HAA role, airfields too were defended chiefly by Lewis guns. As a category of target, however, these had yet to be admitted to AA Command's own roster of VPs and for the first two months of war their guns were crewed by an assortment of local army units.[4] Together with other new targets, adding the RAF's airfields to Pile's responsibilities in October would almost double the number of permanent VPs on AA Command's list in the next few months.

Weak as these defences were, however, with hindsight it is clear that the disposition of AA guns at the start of the Second World War represented a prudent investment of limited capital. Concentrating weapons in the IAZ had been a guiding principle of air defence planning since the Steel–Bartholomew plan of 1923, and though there was no knock-out blow in autumn 1939, when raiding turned to inland cities just a year later London was the first to be hit hard. Similarly, the radar stations which in September 1939 had the best of the light guns were primary targets when the air defence system itself became the object of attack in August 1940. So far, so good, then; and as matters stood in the first days of war, Pile's immediate task was to oversee the deployment of new weapons to redress deficiencies in the national layout. But, inevitably, what might have been a gradual but fairly straightforward expansion towards predefined goals was soon deflected by new circumstances. The actual pattern of Luftwaffe activity in the first weeks of war, coupled with incoming intelligence on what they were likely to do next, soon overturned the theorising of the previous five years.

While the cities and the air defence system remained safe in the autumn of 1939, German forces were far from idle in British territory during these months. Specifically they attacked shipping: first with the U-boat fleet, and soon with a small but efficient force of bombers assigned to maritime duties.[5] The U-boat operations were cruelly effective, and immediately so on 3 September itself, when U-30 sent the liner *Athenia* and 112 of her passengers to the bottom of the Atlantic north-west of Ireland. The soon-introduced convoy system gave some welcome protection, and with few Coastal Command aircraft available for escorts in mid September three aircraft carriers were detailed to operate in Western Approaches – the naval command for the Atlantic seaboard – in order to put some air cover over the vulnerable vessels. But these ships were themselves exposed to grave hazards from U-boats, one of which sank the carrier HMS *Courageous* on 17 September. *Courageous* was one of 41 vessels lost in the first month of war alone.

It was in the midst of these events that Pile suddenly found himself bearing a 'new and very big commitment' to expand AA defences for the Fleet anchorages, the most taxing of several diversions from pre-war plans which now began to exercise the staff at Stanmore. Ports of course had been included in the ADGB system since the Reorientation Committee's paper of June 1936, and the Ideal Scheme of the following February had put the major naval anchorages second only to London in the pick of weapons. Some of these guns were in place in autumn 1939, but the pre-war Admiralty, in fact, had been relaxed about AA cover for the Fleet anchorages, largely because ships at anchor were thought to be self-protecting against air attack.[6] The result was a mixed array of gun strengths among targets of importance to the navy. Portsmouth had 33 guns on 3 September, Southampton and Hull had 30, Rosyth had 29 and the Clyde 22, but Plymouth had just fourteen, Scapa, Invergordon, Portland, Dover and Harwich fielded weapons in single figures and there was no HAA cover at Blyth.[7]

Once the war began, however, the Admiralty began to change its tune. The first anxiety was Scapa, which by September 1939 was in use as a Fleet base additional to Rosyth, and now lay open to attack by bombers operating from north-west Germany. In view of Scapa's use by the Fleet some additional guns had been approved earlier in the year, when in May a further sixteen 3.7in mobiles had been allocated 'in principle', bringing the allocation to 24 (Appendix I). In August Scapa's defences had come under study again, when the CID's Home Defence Committee approved twelve LAA guns for the oil installation at Lyness, along with fighter aircraft cover to be provided on a much longer timetable.[8] These defences, however, had not actually materialised by the outbreak of war, which found Scapa with just eight 4.5s intended to protect the facilities at Lyness when the Fleet itself was at sea and to reinforce the ships' guns when it was not.[9] It was these very limited defences which the Admiralty, rather suddenly, pressed to be vastly increased.

To study requirements a party of officers was dispatched to Scapa on 5 September. Docking alongside HMS *Nelson* in the small hours of Thursday, 7 September, representatives from this eight-man delegation plunged straight into an extempore conference with senior officers in order to settle plans in the time remaining before *Nelson* herself put to sea at first light.[10] The key decisions which would govern the development of Scapa's defences over the next six months were made in these hours. Within the next month, it was decided, Scapa's existing layout of eight 4.5in guns should be supplemented by 24 weapons of 3.7in type, this figure rising ultimately to 96 HAA weapons to give a 30-gun density in all the main approaches to the Flow. Searchlights would be increased to 60 as soon as possible and eventually to 108, while the balloon barrage would also be thickened. Beyond these local measures, the naval representatives also wanted two squadrons of fighters at RAF Wick; together with a range of purely naval defences – notably enhanced anti-submarine measures – these preparations were judged sufficient to remove any necessity for Scapa being evacuated in favour of dispersed anchorages, which would be 'bad for the morale of the fleet, as savouring of scuttling away'. Scapa, in any case, was believed to be 'submarine proof', and in the first days of war many of the alternative anchorages had already been subject to exploratory visits by U-boats.

Within ten days much of the AA element of this 'Q' Plan, as it was code-named, had been approved by the War Office. Pile was told of it formally on 16 September, when the War Office instructed that Scapa's HAA layout should be thickened to 88 guns (trimmed slightly from the 96 first proposed), using 3.7s, and the LAA guns increased to no fewer than 40 2pdrs.[11] The centre of gravity of this vastly transformed GDA would lie around the fleet anchorage in the Flow, but Pile was warned not to neglect Lyness, nor the airfield at Hatston and radar station at Nether Button. The Nether Button area, in fact, was among the first intended recipients of static guns, the initial sixteen of which were allocated on 21 September, when Pile was urged to complete his plans for this vast project without delay.[12] But pending the strengthening of the defences the anchorage was indeed evacuated more or less permanently over the winter of 1939–40.[13]

Buttressing the Scapa guns took time, and in the first fortnight of October the stakes were raised when the Germans took their maritime operations directly to the navy's home ports. Slipping quietly into the supposedly submarine-proof waters of Scapa Flow on 14 October, U-47 managed to sink HMS *Royal Oak* while the battleship lay at anchor a mile offshore. Two days later the AA defences entered the fight. The first German air raid of the Second World War, and the first anti-aircraft engagement against hostile forces, came on Monday, 16 October, when attacks were delivered on shipping in the Forth.[14] Initially this momentous operation looked harmless enough. Hostile aircraft were first plotted around the mouth of the Forth at 09.28 flying high, while further plots made over the next two hours appeared to suggest that coastal reconnaissance was in progress. Spitfires from 602 Squadron of the Royal Auxiliary Air Force at Drem were scrambled to intervene, damaging one Heinkel 111 bomber which they intercepted about a dozen miles off Berwick shortly before 10.30. None of the hostile aircraft plotted during the morning came inland, but at a quarter past two events took a more aggressive turn when Heinkels and Dorniers began to strike courses up the Firth of Forth, weaving through the clouds in an evident attempt to avoid attracting AA fire. In this they failed. The first gunsite to open up was RSG 1 at Dalmeny Park in the Forth GDA,[15] where the crew spotted the intruders for themselves before the gun operations room had received any warning. Hastily exchanging the dummy rounds with which they had been practising drills for live ammunition, the gunners opened fire; and in a direct reversal of the intended procedure, all the neighbouring gunsites immediately joined the battle before the warning which should have alerted them to came through from the gun operations room. One of the raiders was damaged by AA fire in the first seconds of the engagement and then finished off by a Spitfire, and in the next two and a half hours a running battle developed, in which a sequence of about a dozen raiders approached up the Forth, meeting both AA fire and attacks from several fighter squadrons. All followed the same evasive routine when engaged, diving down to low level over the waves where HAA weapons could not easily bear, and launching low-level and dive-bombing attacks on warships at anchor. Many were disturbingly accurate. Seven men died on the tribal class destroyer HMS *Mohawk*, which sustained severe damage to her superstructure from a dive-bombing attack which missed the ship, but managed to put two bombs so close alongside that their detonation on the surface of the water blasted the vessel with splinters. HMS *Southampton*, too, was hit by a bomb which passed straight through the plating of three decks, exited through the hull and exploded underwater, killing just one rating on its way. HMS *Caledonia* and *Edinburgh* emerged from their own attacks more lightly, but for their trouble the Luftwaffe were badly scarred. Fighters accounted for two of their number and AA guns damaged another, while the guns were generally agreed to have done fine work in marking the raiders with shell bursts (despite some of the fighter pilots' bitter complaints that their own Spitfires and Gladiators had been engaged). 'The features of the attack,' recorded a Fighter Command summary, 'were the pertinacity and accuracy of the enemy bombing; the superiority of our own fighters, all of whom were from Auxiliary Squadrons; and the absence of an air raid warning which enabled many Scotsmen to contribute eyewitness accounts to the papers.'[16] They might have added that the guns did well, too; but seldom again would so much be achieved with just 104

rounds of HAA ammunition, which is what the gunners subsequently calculated they had fired.

The raid of 16 October was, for now, an isolated incident. For
the remainder of the month Luftwaffe activity in British skies was
dominated by coastal reconnaissance, especially over the Forth
and the Thames Estuary.[17] Few aircraft penetrated overland, and
while the gunners had the occasional opportunity to open up
they saw little result for their work. For the higher command at
Stanmore the second half of October was occupied with the
deepening problem of satisfying the navy's demand for guns
resulting from the vulnerability of Scapa and the consequent
dispersal of the Fleet elsewhere. As a result of decisions by the
Deputy Chiefs of Staff Committee on 26 October, Rosyth was
promoted to become the 'immediate main operational base' for
the Fleet and the Clyde was designated an 'occasional' anchorage
pending the completion of the Scapa defences, meaning that
more guns would be required at these places simultaneously with
those being arranged for Scapa.[18] Within a few days plans were in
hand to marshal additional guns in the Rosyth/Forth and
Glasgow/Greenock areas,[19] while in early November authority
was given to raise the combined HAA strength at ten ports to no
fewer than 375 guns.[20] Of these, Rosyth, Greenock, Scapa and the
Humber would be the main beneficiaries, between them sharing
287 weapons, including the 88 to be installed at Scapa by June
1940 under the 'Q' Plan, which was now authorised in full.[21]
Added to the guns already defending the anchorages, these
increases would give naval targets nearly two fifths of all the HAA
weapons due to be available in early summer 1940. The first of
these layouts – Rosyth – was due for completion, with 96 HAA
guns, in January 1940.[22] Under these plans, ADGB was rapidly
becoming an air defence arm of the Royal Navy.

It was at this point that Dowding felt it necessary to intervene.
Writing to the Air Ministry on 5 November, two days after these
orders had been issued, he reported that 24 mobile 3.7in guns had
duly been moved to Rosyth to protect the Fleet when it moved
south; but beyond that, Dowding warned that for several reasons
they 'should not be too precipitate' in marshalling further AA
guns at the anchorages. For one thing, Dowding queried whether
the scheme hurried out by the Air Ministry really amounted to a

settled policy. 'The plan does not quite accord with the views of the Commander-in-Chief of the Home Fleet as I understood them during my discussion with him on 1 November,' he explained, adding with a not untypically acerbic touch that 'if he objects to it on his return from his present cruise, he may very possibly induce yet another change of policy.' And even if this was a settled plan, was it wise? The huge allocation of guns to Rosyth and Glasgow/Greenock seemed wildly out of proportion to the value of these targets, especially since the Fleet would often be away at sea. In any case, Dowding argued, Glasgow was an 'extremely unsuitable place' even for a spasmodic Fleet anchorage: hard to defend with guns and balloons, and thanks to the volume of commercial traffic, wide open to submarine penetration through the shipping 'gate' being so frequently thrown wide.

Pile, as may be imagined, shared these views. If the new plan was examined in detail, he argued on 10 November, 'it is clear that many of the Fleet Anchorages are to be defended by HAA guns to a standard out of proportion to the ships that will be at anchor and immensely out of proportion to the defence of other Vital Points in England' (meaning Britain; even the Irishman Pile, like many others, instinctively wrote one for the other). In Pile's view, the plans moreover were tactically misconceived, since ships at anchor were almost certain to be attacked by dive-bombing, against which heavy artillery was not the best defence. Committing such a weight of guns to guard a handful of ships would be wasteful under any circumstances, and was doubly so now that some of the precious new weapons previously earmarked for AA Command had been diverted elsewhere, particularly to the Expeditionary Force (who would ultimately abandon many on the beaches at Dunkirk) and to bolster allies abroad – notably Finland, whose war with the Soviet Union would begin with the bombing of Helsinki on 30 November.

When war broke out [continued Pile] the Anti-Aircraft situation in England, if not rosy, looked promising because production was beginning to assume a fair proportion and there were not any extraneous demands for equipment which would inevitably reduce the number of guns available for ADGB. Unfortunately, as time has passed, the improvement in the Anti-Aircraft situation of this country has not been realised. Many guns have had to be sent to defend the Field Force and others sold to our Allies or allocated to purposes outside the control of ADGB.

Two months ago we expected a deluge of bombs on London. Today there are about the same number of guns defending London as are proposed for four capital ships at Rosyth. The Germans are at least as capable of making heavy air attacks on our civilian population as they were two months ago. It is unlikely that they have become suddenly humane for, in the last war, on every suitable opportunity they bombed non-military objectives in England, either from Zeppelins or from aeroplanes. We must, therefore, never lose sight of this menace.[23]

Nor did they, and ten months later the wisdom of Pile's counsel was proved. Nonetheless, additional guns were provided for many of the Fleet's anchorages, if not everywhere in the numbers which the Admiralty had requested. By the third week in November the defences of the Forth had thickened to 48 guns from the 29 in place at the start of the war, while Dover's HAA weapons had been more than doubled (to fourteen) and modest increases were arranged for the Clyde, the Humber, the Tees and the Tyne.[24] In only one area, however, did the Admiralty get all that they wanted. The vast increase in Scapa's guns was carried through in full, but since this was eventually achieved by trimming back the allocations to other ports to Scapa's advantage,[25] the new defences represented a large drain on resources which were keenly needed elsewhere. By the end of May 1940 a fierce array of 88 HAA weapons clustered around the anchorage. Since 80 of these were static guns (32 of 4.5in calibre and the rest 3.7in) the project called for a mass of new building. This project gave Scapa the largest volume of new anti-aircraft fabric laid down anywhere in Britain during the first six months of war, and marked the largest departure from pre-war plans.

Apart from the drain of new weapons to the Expeditionary Force, the anchorages and the Finns, the pattern of AA defences early in the war was also influenced by evolving ideas on the Luftwaffe's likely target priorities. As Pile argued in November, the knock-out blow against the cities remained a constant threat, but as early as September the pattern of German operations in Poland had begun to suggest other scenarios. On the model of the Polish campaign, Dowding was warned in mid September that the Luftwaffe's first strike against Britain might well be directed not at the cities, but instead at the infrastructure supporting the aircraft industry. Bristol, Coventry, Derby and Sheffield would all occupy the front line in this battle. As far as HAA guns were concerned the threat was met only at Derby, home of the Rolls-Royce engine works, where adding sixteen 3.7in mobiles to the 3in weapons already in place nearly quadrupled the gun defences in the first two months of the war. More could be done with LAA, however, and in early November the supply of these guns was hastened by the decision to accept a proportion of Bofors on fixed mountings, in substitute for the mobile types previously ordered. The first consignment, of 40 weapons, was assigned to nine aircraft factories, some additional to the VP list current at the start of the war.[26] Added to the anchorages, this new commitment took the national pattern of AA defences, and the character of their fabric, a further step away from that anticipated only a few months before.

By the time the war was two months old these new and competing claims for AA resources had exposed a weakness at the heart of Britain's air defence planning. The old Reorientation Committee which had met under a succession of chairmen since October 1934 had been wound up at the beginning of the war, when responsibility for the allocation of guns and the deployment of defences in the field suddenly became somewhat blurred. At first, the job of allocating guns between different types of targets, and even between specific GDAs, devolved upon the Deputy Chiefs of Staff Committee, who issued instructions to Dowding and Pile but heard no direct representation from either in reaching their decisions. The two commanders naturally resented this arrangement, which robbed them of the influence in policy which both had enjoyed through sitting on the Reorientation Committee. Evidently in recognition of this, at one point in autumn 1939 Dowding was told that he might assign guns where he liked, though in Pile's later recollection this arrangement for a time ran in parallel with allocations being made simultaneously by the Deputy Chiefs of Staff, with the result that everything became 'rather confusing'.[27] Confusion was heightened by the sheer volume of work involved in juggling the stocks of guns – new and existing – in the light of the competing claims of different targets, the drain of equipment to third parties (the BEF, the Finns), and the changing intelligence picture. So the weakness which had emerged by early November 1939 lay in co-ordination; and the solution was another committee.

Known formally as the Deputy Chiefs of Staff Sub-Committee's Sub-Committee on the Allocation of Active Air Defences (and invariably called the AA Committee), the new body was formed to meet a request from the three services that the deployment of 'active air defences' – in practice, guns largely – should be referred to a joint-service study group which would advise the Deputy Chiefs of Staff, who approved the idea on 7 November.[28] The committee was at first small: no more than one member from each service, together with a pair of secretaries, and no representative from Fighter or AA Commands. It met first in this form on 4 December,[29] by which time both Pile and Dowding had already staked a claim to be represented. Both became fixtures from the committee's fourth meeting on 2 January 1940,[30] when the new group became truly the successor of the Reorientation Committee of 1934–39. Later assisted by a sub-committee, this body continued to direct the allocation of AA weapons at home until 1945.

As these machinations were in progress among the higher commanders, gunners on their sites were entering what was would later be remembered as the bleakest period of the war. After the bustle of the August mobilisation and the tense days of early September, the autumn dragged out with little sign of action. Sporadic raid alerts came to nothing and the continuing Luftwaffe reconnaissance sorties in the last two months of the year generally remained too far offshore to put targets within range of the guns, which dispatched just three rounds of HAA and ten of small arms ammunition in the whole of December.[31] At the same time the gunners were distracted by occasional alarmist noises emanating from Stanmore. Early in November AA

Command sent word to be alert for a sudden attempt at invasion.[32] Everyone was warned to be watchful for parachutists, the forerunners of an invading force which would follow in transport aircraft. These operations, warned Stanmore solemnly, would probably be accompanied by fierce air attacks on aerodromes and communications targets.

Though accurately foreshadowing the real threat which did emerge six months later, these dire warnings were difficult to credit in the quiet of November 1939, as the days shortened and site crews scanned the skies in the ambivalent hope of seeing an enemy aircraft. A few thought they did. Two months into the war most gunners could probably recognise common RAF aircraft such as Wellingtons or Hurricanes, but few were on certain ground with the Walrus amphibian, let alone the Spartan Cruiser – a commandeered civil trimotor – both of which were confidently identified as hostile on 17 November by gunners at Manchester and Liverpool. The Spartan's crew found themselves the target of only two rounds of 4.5in ammunition before the Manchester gunners realised their mistake, but the lumbering Walrus, taken for a Dornier 18 flying boat, attracted five HAA shells and a hail of Lewis gun rounds from five searchlight sites before the engagement was broken off. The Liverpool incident was partly explained by errors at the GOR – enemy aircraft had been reported in the area – but neither mistake was excused. In his report to Dowding Pile emphasised the need for better recognition training, though another obvious failing was left unremarked: both aircraft had escaped unscathed.[33]

As autumn turned to winter incidents of this kind looked set to increase, as the steady expansion of AA Command meant that gun and searchlight sites were populated by a growing proportion of novices. Pile's organisation expanded prodigiously in the first eighteen months of war, almost tripling from the 106,690 men on strength in September 1939 to pass 300,000 in May 1941, chiefly through the inflow of conscripts. In the first months of war many of these men – and Pile himself was quite frank about this were barely worth having. The first conscripts to arrive under the Militia Act of 1939 reached their operational gunsites just before Christmas, when battery commanders were perturbed to discover that AA Command had generally been allotted the weakest recruits from the rapidly-growing army intake. 'Out of 1,000 recruits in one of my Brigades,' Pile later recorded, '5% had immediately to be discharged, 2% were considered mentally deficient and 18% were of a medical category too low for anti-aircraft work [. . .].'[34] That was Pile's account in his official dispatch; post-war readers of his book *Ack-Ack* enjoyed a more vivid picture, in which of every 25 conscripts arriving at a given battery 'one had a withered arm, one was mentally deficient, one had no thumbs, one had a glass-eye which fell out whenever he doubled to the guns, and two were in the advanced and more obvious stages of venereal disease.'[35] Today we might be less inclined to find comedy in these infirmities, but the fact remains that, on average, one potential gunner in four was unfit for service in any army, of any era, let alone in a specialism demanding physical and mental agility. No one resented this more than the volunteer Territorials, who now found their pre-war regiments and batteries invaded by what Angus Calder termed a 'plague of dimwits'.[36]

Physical hardiness was never more vital among AA gunners than in the winter of 1939–40, when freezing temperatures and liberal snowfalls severed some sites from their supply-lines for days on end. Deliveries of iron rations to many isolated batteries ensured that no one starved, but here and there gunners and searchlight crews suffered some danger from exposure. Chiefly this was because so many sites lacked basic amenities. Some men endured this winter, the hardest for many years, under canvas, while washing and cooking in flimsy 'camp structures' was the norm almost everywhere. Camp structures were the War Office's standard range of type-designs for buildings to house the basic functions of life, and reached the soldiers in the form of manuals illustrating how such things as kitchens, showers and latrines should be locally made using light timbers and corrugated iron. As the examples illustrated show (Fig 8), they were pretty bleak (lavatories, for example, did not necessarily have doors). In a gesture towards comfort and serviceability, in mid September the War Office ordered that concrete floors should be laid in camp structure cookhouses and ablution sheds, while duckboards were issued to combat the rain – meagre improvements whose parsimony reflected not official indifference, but the inability to

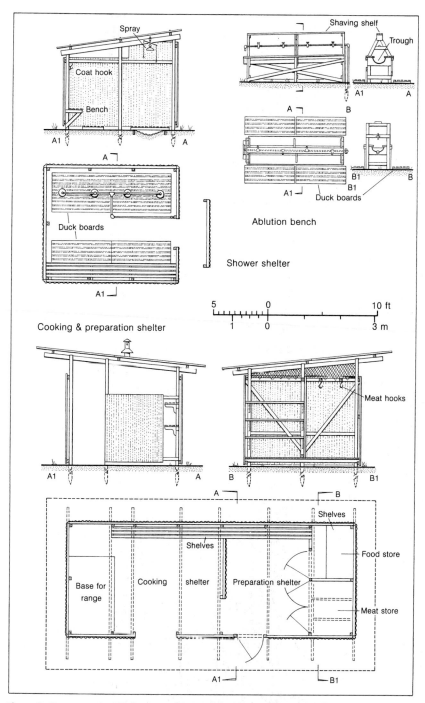

Figure 8 Camp structures: three specimens of the types of improvised domestic buildings used on AA sites (and army camps generally) throughout the war, and especially in the early years when permanent equivalents were rare.

do much more.[37] So serious did these domestic matters become that Pile was eventually obliged to give the War Office an ultimatum. His threat to withdraw troops from any site where proper accommodation was lacking produced a 'most satisfactory burst of energy',[38] though as much seems to have been achieved through the ministrations of kindly volunteers – particularly the Women's Voluntary Service (later the WRVS) – as through official channels. More than three years would pass before AA troops were everywhere decently housed.

What kind of place, then, was an AA battery in the first six months of war? In February 1940 AA Command drew up a definitive list of its HAA positions, which on the date of compilation stood at 449 individual sites (Fig 9).[39] In a sense this figure is artificially precise, since the national layout of heavy gun positions continued to change throughout the war and there were probably no two consecutive weeks in which the tally of sites on AA Command's books was exactly similar. (In February 1940, for example, the number of sites required for the 'Q' Plan was yet undecided, while new defences were authorised for Aberdeen, Dundee and Barrow.[40]) The oldest sites were those selected under the orders of late 1937, some of which had been developed in 1938–39 while others remained only partially complete. These batteries obeyed the neat textbook template cut in the spring of 1938, though not always without adaptation. In mid February, for example, Stanmore issued design drawings showing how standard pre-war permanent HAA emplacements should be modified with sandbags and planking to provide better protection and extra capacity for the ammunition (Fig 10).[41] At the same time work began on permanent sunken magazines – 'substitute EAMs' – at selected sites to take the place of the more remote facilities provided before the war (a project discussed later). The emplacement modifications provide one example of how formal designs produced in the drawing office could contrast with their adaptation in the field (often in ways which would be undetectable from surviving examples) and in turn could influence subsequent formal designs – the next type of permanent emplacement, as we shall see, drew upon the adapted form of its predecessor.

These rather makeshift modifications applied to permanent sites, and appeared at a time when a good many improvised

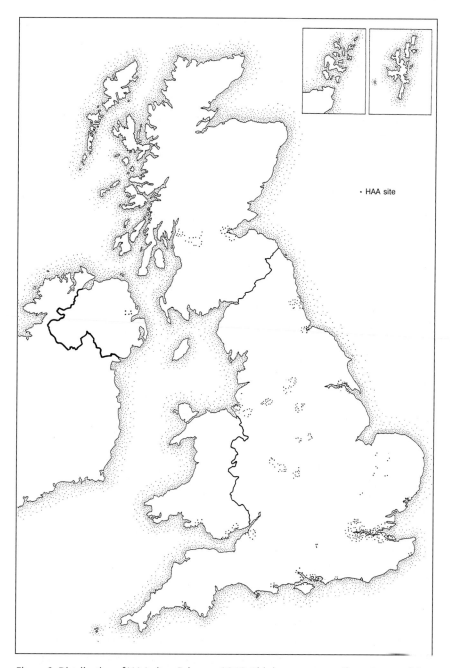

Figure 9 Distribution of HAA sites, February 1940. This in essence was the outcome of the proposed pattern of GDAs enshrined in the Ideal Scheme (Fig 5), though with a few additions resulting from later amendments. Not all of these sites were fully built, many stood unoccupied at this date, and the still undecided layout at Scapa being provided under the 'Q' Plan is omitted.

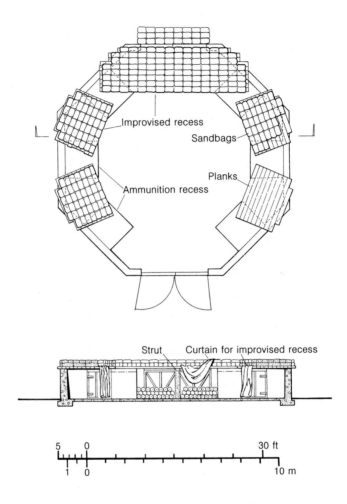

Improvised recess

Sandbags

Planks

Ammunition recess

Strut   Curtain for improvised recess

5   0   30 ft

1   0   10 m

Figure 10 HAA emplacement modified for use, February 1940. Early wartime experience pointed to a need for greater ammunition storage capacity, resulting in the improvised recesses made from planks and sandbags shown here.

positions were also appearing in established GDAs. Newly-developed sites for static HAA guns continued to use holdfasts set in concrete, but the surrounding gunpits tended to be more irregular in form and were built from whatever could be obtained locally – typically brick or breeze blocks banked externally with earth. Mobile 3.7s often made use of gunpits formed from nothing more than a ring of sandbags stacked a few courses high.

The result was that the best-favoured sites were fully furnished with concrete emplacements, tidy ammunition lockers and a well-defined command post, and offered their men a reasonably welcoming cluster of domestic huts, the whole linked up by well-made roads. At the other end of the scale, some of the mobile weapons sat in muddy fields, offering the crews little more than wilting tents and damp sandbags among which to live and work. Since batteries were periodically moved between sites, and across different AA divisions, a unit might find itself rudely shunted from tolerable comfort to squalor at short notice. Pre-war gunsites were described as 'palatial' compared to their successors of a year or so later.

In one respect, however, these older positions were rather too well-built. AA Command had become anxious about the conspicuousness of its gunsites as early as September 1939, but it was early 1940 before detailed instructions on camouflage reached the divisions. Policy on concealment changed several times in the course of the war, and throughout was shaped by the need to manipulate the appearance of sites as seen, on the one hand, by attacking pilots, and on the other by analysts of aerial reconnaissance photographs. As far as the former were concerned it was prudent as far as possible to conceal positions and falsify their patterning, such that pilots approaching low to bomb and strafe would fail to acquire their targets in the few frantic seconds available to look, aim and attack. Early gunsite camouflage was designed with this function in mind, and by late 1940, as we shall see, plans were in hand to supplement concealment of the real sites with dummy HAA positions, in the hope of deflecting attack from the real to the false. Yet the picture of the defences presented for the benefit of high-altitude reconnaissance was shaped by very different considerations, since it was often wise to plant the impression that the weapon strength of any GDA was at least as strong as it actually was, if not more so. Plainly, an inherent tension lay between these objectives. For tactical purposes sites needed to be hidden, while strategically there were advantages in showing them off. Since it was scarcely feasible to do both simultaneously, the extent of camouflage was dictated by the relative importance of concealment or display at particular stages of the war.

In 1940 the fear of attack outweighed other considerations, and camouflage was applied accordingly. But it was also done cheaply, with an emphasis on colour blending and disrupting shadows rather than more subtle techniques which came to be used later (Fig 11). An assessment issued in January 1940 identified four main characteristics of HAA sites which tended to advertise their positions, specifically the regular form of the emplacements, the shadows cast by their walls, the tell-tale routes of tracks threading between the components, and the gun itself. The footprint of the emplacements was hidden largely by colouration, which was applied differently according to whether tree cover lay nearby.[42] Those in wooded areas were given by bold, two-tone disruptive camouflage in green and dark brown paint (creosote could be substituted for the latter), with the floor of the gunpit strewn with ashes or coke breeze to absorb the shadows cast by the wall. Similar techniques were used for sites in more open country, except that two tones of green paint were substituted, the depth of colour shading from lighter to darker between the north-east and south-west sides. This tonal variation did something to absorb the shadows of the gunpits, an effect completed by earth mounding or piling gorse and heather outside the north-easterly quadrant of each. At the same time, the characteristic track 'signature' linking the site's components was made less distinctive by extending tracks beyond their true destinations and out to the edge of the field. All of this work lay in the hands of the troops themselves, and in general it was easier at more recently built positions than among the pre-war permanent sites, whose comprehensive camouflage, it was conceded in April, was 'probably beyond the scope of units' to contrive.[43] 'Mounding' of emplacements and scattering foliage was possible at these sites, and was widely done, together with disruptive camouflage painting of huts (where there were any huts) and other features, but units could do little to hide the gleaming concrete roadways threading between the components of permanent sites, which as much as the emplacements gave them firm visual definition.

Similar camouflage techniques were applied to LAA and searchlight sites in the early months of 1940, when these positions, too, were steadily multiplying. By the third week in

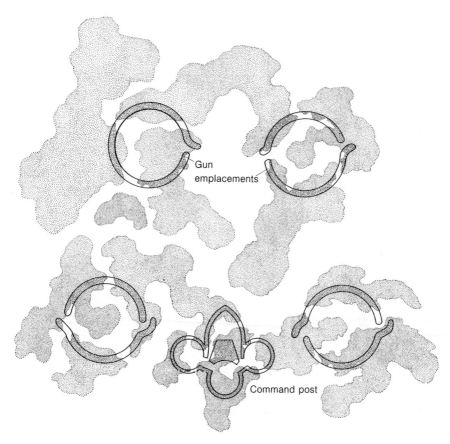

Figure 11 Camouflage arrangements for an HAA site, summer 1940. Based upon a scheme issued by AA Command headquarters, this plan called for colouration to be applied in order to break up the outlines of gunsite features. The plan also illustrates the general arrangement of gunpits and command post used on early wartime mobile HAA sites, in which these features were built in earthwork or sandbags. Plate 10 shows a site laid out on these lines, though with somewhat wider spacings between features.

February the number of permanent VPs authorised in AA Command had risen to 281,[44] up from 156 at the start of the war five months previously. In large part this increase was accounted for by the addition of 95 RAF airfields to Pile's ambit, following the decision of October 1939, but the expansion also reflected many commitments newly emerged since September. It was a diverse list, extending to 25 radar stations, 22 aircraft manufacturers' works, fourteen power stations, ten Royal Ordnance factories, most of the major ports in the south and east, several key railway junctions, three waterworks and a miscellaneous collection of industrial targets. In many respects it was also still very much a wish-list, since many of these targets lacked weapons and others were equipped only with Lewis guns. Nonetheless, papers recommending still more candidates for LAA protection continued to mount on the AA Committee's table – reams of potential factory VPs on 15 March alone, ten of which were approved.[45] Bar a few supplementary shadow factories yet to be selected in March 1940, this completed the review of industrial targets in the highest bracket, known as Category I, though full rosters of vital points in the electrical system, together with the GPO's wireless stations, were still to come. Potential claimants for light AA defences were practically limitless.

The greatest change in the structural character of the LAA layout in the first six months of war was a range of works supporting the new 40mm Bofors gun. November's decision to accept a proportion of these weapons on static mountings echoed that made for the 3.7in weapon under Inskip two years earlier, and brought with it a similar requirement for fixed emplacements. It also heralded a similar tactical compromise. Just as HAA defences had originally been conceived as mobile, but were now increasingly dominated by static guns, so LAA defences would henceforth become more firmly tied to established sites. Light AA guns in general were sited to command a good all-round field of fire and to allow a few degrees' depression from the horizontal – in built-up areas rooftops often gave the best positions. The articulation of the guns with the VPs they were installed to protect varied from place to place, but while no two layouts were quite the same, new orders issued in early November 1939 were to occupy three separate sites, each around 400 yards clear of the VP.[46] When mobile guns – of whatever type – were used at ground level a simple emplacement was generally built around them (Fig 12). The static Bofors introduced in the winter of 1939–40, however, were mounted either on concrete-set holdfasts (Fig 13) or on cruciform baulk platforms – interlocking beams of heavy timber – which stabilised the gun while still allowing mobility. Again, an emplacement of earth or another improvised medium surrounded the gun and its fixture. Baulk platforms were especially useful when there was a possibility that the weapon might be moved, and for the first issue of static Bofors the orders were explicit: settled sites would use concrete, more temporary positions would rely on baulks. This ruling applied to the first ten VPs to receive static Bofors (most of them aircraft factories), and while three of these projects had been cancelled by late March, a second allocation extended the distribution of statics to a further 33 VPs, including nine further aircraft works, 21 radar stations and three dockyards, bringing the full set in this first group to 40 VPs.[47]

As early as November 1939 it was obvious that a proportion of the VPs allocated Bofors offered no sufficiently high sites nearby, and that some other means would be needed to achieve a clear view and an open field of fire. In the first allocation of static weapons divisions were authorised to seek sites on rooftops, but the longer-term solution was a special elevated platform – the Bofors tower – the first variants of which were under design in the War Office in mid December 1939.[48] The earliest towers comprised a family of reinforced concrete structures rising in five-foot intervals from ten to 30 feet, the variant used in any particular case depending upon the needs of the site. The first examples were probably in place by the spring of 1940, though by late summer this rather elaborate design was already being supplanted by a simpler steel-framed type. Concrete Bofors towers of War Office pattern do not appear to have been numerous. Records maintained by DFW show that 53 existed in February 1941 (fewer than half of which actually had guns), from a total requirement then put at 61. A year later this target figure had risen only to 81 structures, all of which were either complete or under construction.[49]

Bofors, however mounted, would constitute only a minor proportion of AA Command's light gun armoury until the middle years of the war, and apart from a few 2pdrs and 20mm guns, VPs with AA defence in 1939–40 mostly used Lewis guns. Since the weapon needed little more than a vertical post mounting on which to rest, a wide variety of simple emplacements was contrived for them, including some which were built into the fabric of other defensive works (some designs of pillboxes from summer of 1940 had them, for example, when the Lewis guns were manned by Home Forces troops). A common and substantial type consisted

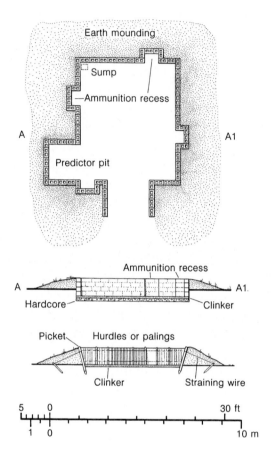

Figure 12 Standard emplacement design for the 40mm Bofors LAA gun, with alternative construction methods, shown in section, for semi-sunken (upper) and surface-built (lower) types.

Figure 13 (right) Bofors holdfast assembly. These concrete and steel structures were built to mount Bofors guns supplied for static use, and were generally confined to the most important, permanently-defended VPs.

Plate 7 The Bofors gun. The weapon occupies an emplacement of the type shown in Figure 12.

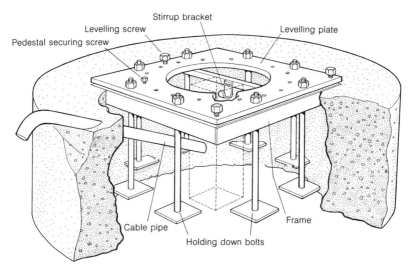

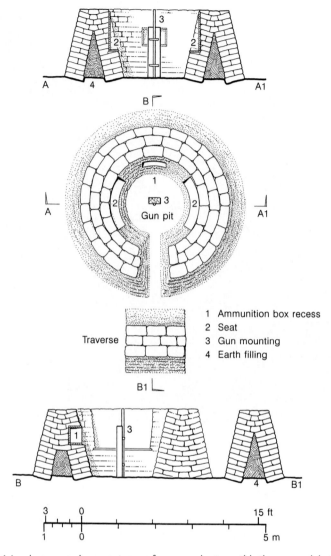

Gun pit

Traverse

1 Ammunition box recess
2 Seat
3 Gun mounting
4 Earth filling

Figure 14 A Lewis gun emplacement, one of many variants on this theme used during the war. This example was designed by Mortimer Wheeler in September 1939.

of a revetted pit with the post mounted centrally and an encircling parapet of earth or sandbags, though others could be entirely surface-built. One such, designed by the officer commanding 42 LAA Regiment in September 1939, was a simple annulus of stacked sandbags with the mounting post set up in the centre (Fig 14), and could obviously be used for gun positions on

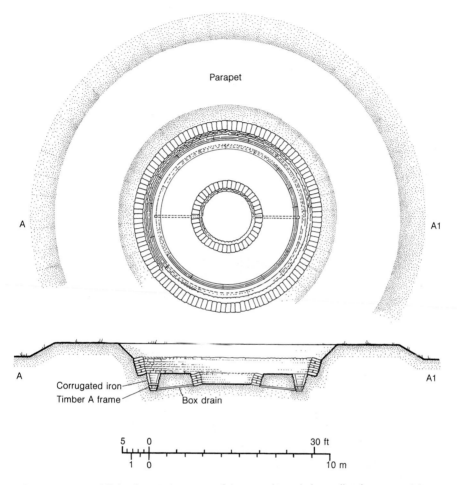

Parapet

A   A1

Corrugated iron
Timber A frame   Box drain

A   A1

5   0   30 ft

1   0   10 m

Figure 15 A searchlight site emplacement of the type shown in immediately pre-war AA manuals. The projector occupied the central circle, which was surrounded by an annular walkway, a drain and a parapet (shown only partially in the plan view).

the roofs of buildings as well as those at ground level. This example also illustrates how numerous works associated with AA defence need leave little or no surface trace once the gunners evacuated the site and moved on, a point we shall revisit in Chapter 12. And an irony here is that the sandbag emplacement illustrated in Figure 12 was designed by an archaeologist, namely Lieutenant Colonel R E M Wheeler, commander of 42 LAA Regiment, later widely known to the British public as Sir Mortimer Wheeler.

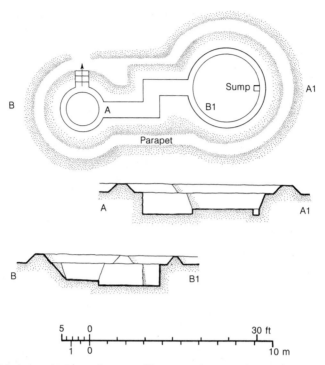

Figure 16 An emplacement for a sound locator and LAA Lewis gun of the type specified for searchlight positions.

Lewis guns were also widely provided for the local AA defence of searchlight positions, which collectively represented one of the most numerous types of defence site constructed in Britain during the Second World War. The broad principles of searchlight site design did not alter much over the duration, though periodic changes to their deployment patterns meant that the number built in the six years from the ordering of the Couverture markedly exceeded those in occupation at any one time. The official pattern for a searchlight site, enshrined in specifications laid down in pre-war manuals,[50] consisted of a broad, flat-topped earthwork parapet thrown up to encircle the light projector, which stood at the centre of a revetted emplace-ment containing a slightly raised operating platform (Fig 15). Variants on this theme were certainly used, however, many including the excavation of an annular ditch around the parapet. Standard designs were also produced for earthwork emplace-ments to accommodate the sound locators and LAA weapons on searchlight sites, and while many local improvisations were doubtless resorted to, the official pre-war pattern called for a combined emplacement for these two pieces of equipment (Fig 16), the two operating pits being linked by a revetted walkway.

By autumn 1939 some of Pile's HAA gunsites were also equipped with GL Mk I gun-laying radars, the fruit of the work begun at Bawdsey three years before. At the end of the year just 59 of these instruments seem to have been in service, though a further 344 were supplied in 1940 and the total manufactured reached 425 before the set was superseded by the GL Mk II in spring 1941. Based entirely upon transportable cabins, these sets made little structural impact upon gunsite design until the introduction of supplementary structures over the winter of 1940–41, which were hurriedly improvised to improve the radar's performance during the London Blitz. It is telling of course that mass raiding against London should have provided the stimulus for intensive work on the GL, a reflection of the capital's abiding

Plate 8 The early dugout command post at Hayes Common (ZS10 in the IAZ) typifies the conditions in which AA gunners worked in the London Blitz, before a concrete version was introduced in 1941.

Plate 9 Gunners at of 303 HAA Battery at Hayes Common (ZS10 in the IAZ) with a 3in static of Great War vintage.

dominance in the priorities of air defence; and it was London alone which, in the early months of the war, was provided with a fully-developed alternative to gunsite radar. This was the 'Fixed Azimuth' system, which consisted of an array of mobile sound-locators positioned out to the east of the capital which by passing plots to the main London GOR in Brompton Road would enable the guns to engage using barrage techniques similar to those developed by Ashmore in 1917. As its name implies, the Fixed Azimuth system relied on the guns holding a constant bearing but varying their elevations such that the barrage produced over the eastern approaches could be matched to the raiders' height. It was a hazardous procedure, since neither sound locator nor gun crews could distinguish hostile bombers from friendly fighters, and also something of a policy of despair, as the barrage would never be more than a deterrent – Heinkels and Dorniers would thus be engaged in much the same way as Gothas and Giants. To limit the danger to fighters the Fixed Azimuth system was supposed to be used only with direct clearance from 11 Group, the Fighter Command formation in the south-east, who were supposed to know when their pilots were flying, and at clearly set times.[51] It was prepared for whatever the Luftwaffe might throw at it in the first weeks of war, and by October was ready for use.[52]

As the New Year of 1940 began the debut of London's Fixed Azimuth system still lay more than nine months in the future, but elsewhere gunners left to fire on more conventional methods began to find themselves a little more actively employed. In January 1940 the Luftwaffe stepped up its activities in coastal waters, with more reconnaissance and attacks on shipping. For the first time some of these sorties strayed fleetingly within reach of the HAA at coastal GDAs. On 11 January the guns opened up in the Tyne, Humber and Thames & Medway areas to meet anti-shipping operations, firing again in similar circumstances next day. The Shetland Isles were the focus of attack on 24 January, when the guns there fired their opening wartime salvoes, and before the end of the month two further incidents had been recorded here and on the Tyne.[53] February brought a similar pattern of events – shipping attacks, reconnaissance, mine-laying – though once again the opportunities to engage were tantalisingly few. Some of the intruders fell to fighters, but even a series of raids on the night of the 22nd/23rd denied the gunners any trade as the Luftwaffe seemed to be avoiding the gun-defended areas.[54]

By early March inactivity seems to have bred laxity, since gunners in two separate GDAs engaged RAF aircraft on consecutive days, though a few days later HAA sites at Aberdeen were in action against a correctly identified Heinkel, which was subsequently shot down by a fighter. The largest incident in March was at Scapa, where a sharp raid was delivered against the Flow and Hatston airfield on the 16th. The additional weapons under installation for the 'Q' Plan doubtless contributed to the gunners' claimed score of two aircraft damaged, though the Luftwaffe's dive-bombing tactics again demonstrated that the challenge to come might not be best met with HAA.[55]

By March 1940 the cumulative result of adjustments since the outbreak of war meant that the strategic balance of Britain's HAA guns bore only an approximate resemblance to plans drafted in peacetime. The first departure, of course, lay in the number of guns in place among the pre-war GDAs, whose armament everywhere fell short of the scales authorised in May 1939, when the 2232-gun plan had been approved. On 20 March 1940, to take a sample date, most defended areas had fewer than half the guns authorised under this plan, and were significantly deficient even by the earlier 1584-gun allotment. Of the larger pre-war GDAs, the Thames & Medway was the healthiest, with 130 guns against an approved strength of 192, while Portsmouth and Southampton both stood at about three-quarters of their authorised scales. London, on the other hand, had about half the weapons allowed by the ultimate peacetime plan (the 130 in place were in fact nine fewer than on the first day of war), while the corresponding proportion at GDAs such as the Mersey, Manchester and Leeds was about one third. The poorest relations among the big city targets included Bristol and Plymouth, where HAA densities reached only a quarter of those authorised. Only one GDA had guns in excess of the share awarded in May 1939. That, of course, was Scapa, whose guns had reached 70 HAA weapons by late March. Scapa's full complement of 88 guns was reached a few weeks later.

Although there was never any expectation that the defence scales authorised in May 1939 could be attained less than a year later, it is true that expansion among the pre-war GDAs had been slower than expected. One reason for this is found in the second large departure from the defence framework planned in the spring of 1939, namely the addition and partial gunning of several GDAs freshly defined since the outbreak of war. Apart from the increases at Scapa – whose additional weapons equalled the number allocated to Leeds or Manchester in May 1939 – guns were absorbed by new GDAs at Bramley, the Shetlands, Newhaven, Dundee, Aberdeen, Scunthorpe, Barrow, the Kyle of Lochalsh, and Brockworth, and while not all of these places yet had guns installed by late March, the need to cater to them formed part of AA Command's overall planning in the allocation of weapons. Together with the HAA allocated to aerodromes (largely 3in guns), these new commitments had already overstepped the 168 guns allocated in May 1939 to the 'new requirements reserve'. By late March, in fact, new requirements approved by the AA Committee had already reached 216 guns; and further recommendations were coming forward all the time.

March 20th 1940 is a useful date on which to survey the overall state of Britain's HAA defences, since it was on this day that Pile wrote to Dowding asking whether the whole tenor of pre-war AA planning might have been misconceived. In short, Pile argued, they might have been preparing for the wrong type of war. Though Britain had for years anticipated high-level bombing attacks, with the assumption of a steady run-up to the target and all the opportunities for HAA fire which accompanied that, the Luftwaffe had disobligingly eschewed these tactics, both in Poland and in the limited raiding so far seen at home. Instead, they had generally used dive bombing, the most difficult of all modes of attack for HAA to engage. Pile of course had made this point before, when in November 1939 he queried whether HAA guns were really the best defence for the Fleet anchorages. Four months later the point was even clearer, the deficiencies in equipment more obvious, and the difficulty of engaging dive-bombers still more sharply defined.

> Fire control instruments for AA guns [wrote Pile] are designed to engage an aircraft in level flight. I have made repeated efforts and have obtained the advice of all available experts to produce a system by which the dive bomber can be engaged by HAA guns with their existing equipment. So far, no solution is apparent, but

I earnestly request that this matter be once more examined. The only defence at present is the light AA gun, of which 1847 barrels are allocated [in the May 1939 plan]. A comprehensive review of all Light [sic] AA requirements has recently been undertaken on this basis. But new requirements are continually coming forward, and in view of use by the Germans of dive bombing, I am already clear that that number will not be adequate. [. . .] the number of modern Light AA guns actually available in AA Command is pitiably few, less than 150 including the defences of Scapa.[56]

Pile's solution to the problem, apart from the continued study of HAA techniques against diving targets, was to adjust the relative priority given to the manufacture and supply of heavy and light guns. The scale of HAA defence in May 1939, Pile argued, was 'an over insurance and [. . .] unnecessarily high, while the scale of Light AA defence is inadequate'.

The GOC's proposal in detail was to cut the target for HAA guns back to 1808 weapons, a saving of 640 (80 batteries of eight weapons each) from the *de facto* strength anticipated under the current plan. It made sense on several grounds, not the least of which was the speedier supply of the light guns needed to deal with the reality of Luftwaffe tactics, in contrast to the much longer timetable anticipated for the full HAA programme, which was not due for completion until 1942. In settling upon the new HAA target figure Pile did his homework carefully, picking over the gun allocations to each defended area, trimming where required and generally reordering priorities to eliminate waste. The result was a redrawn map of projected HAA deployment, in which some areas would retain the higher densities given them in the plan of May 1939, and others would be cut back to between half and two-thirds of existing target strengths. In these days before the fall of France and the Germans' acquisition of bases along the entire Channel seaboard, the western targets were downgraded furthest. Cardiff, Newport and the Mersey, for example, would lose guns in plenty.

Whatever the merits of these arguments, Pile's paper of 20 March embodied two points which could not be gainsaid. First, in concentrating so fixedly upon HAA planning in the first years of rearmament the various committees studying the matter had too long neglected the dangers from low and diving attack. Secondly, if implicitly, Pile's paper illustrated how far HAA defence itself had become statically conceived: after all, there would be no need to assign such precisely-defined gun strengths to each vulnerable area if most guns were mobile, as had been expected five years before. In the old days HAA weapons had been con ceived as a national pool, to be deployed flexibly as circumstances required. Now it was the other way about. The national figure had become the sum of local requirements; and, as events would prove, those requirements were never easy to predict.

Less than a fortnight after the meeting at which Pile's paper was discussed there began a sequence of events which ensured that any new long-term plan would be condemned to obsolescence as soon as it was drafted. On 10 April the Germans invaded Norway, and just a month later opened their operations in the west by advancing across Holland and Belgium towards France. Both campaigns cost AA Command dear. For the Expeditionary Force sent to Norway Pile was asked to sacrifice two HAA regiments and five of LAA from a gun layout already gravely under strength, albeit little taxed by enemy activity in that month;[57] and to make matters worse the Admiralty added to a recent series of claims upon Pile's stocks of Lewis guns by requesting 800 more to defend the Norwegian and Danish merchant ships which had suddenly fallen into their hands.[58] In France, where the BEF already held AA weapons for its own use, stocks of domestic AA guns were drained to bolster the defence of ports. Eventually, thanks to Dowding, the squandering of AA guns, no less than fighters, on France was stopped; but shortly afterwards huge numbers of these weapons were abandoned on the beaches of Dunkirk. What Pile termed the 'merciful respite' of the phoney war was drawing to a close.

In the weeks that followed many officers and men stationed at home listened intently to the stories brought back by survivors from the BEF. One such was Lieutenant Colonel Kennedy, CRE of 23 Division, who was invited to a conference of staff officers of 2 AA Division on 1 June. Kennedy told the whole sorry story: how German armour had broken through in the Ardennes forest – assumed to be tank proof – and run riot behind British lines; how light tanks had outflanked the British positions to enter the town of Albert; and how 70 Infantry Brigade had been 'knocked to bits' at Arras. After that, Kennedy explained, the retreat to the coast had been dogged by refugees and abandoned transport crowding the roads, and by repeated blows from German tanks and aircraft – not in great numbers, but working closely and skilfully together. The Luftwaffe, said Kennedy, had been impressive throughout the BEF's time in France. The usual tactics were dive-bombing and low attack, which proved 'very terrifying' as fast fighter-bombers skimmed through the trees and men found themselves momentarily seized by the instinct to stand and watch. There was a 'great necessity,' warned Kennedy, 'for educating men to take cover at once and to fire back at the planes as quickly as possible'. Fierce attacks on gun and searchlight sites showed that the work done on camouflage at home would not be wasted. There was a curious regularity to these incidents. AA gun positions had been raided in a regular cycle: generally at five and eight in the morning, at noon, and especially at eight PM – nearly always in daylight. And how did the AA guns perform, in Kennedy's experience? Most memorable was an incident in which a 3.7in gun, its muzzle lowered, had blown two tanks 'to smithereens. Used as such', reported Kennedy, 'it was undoubtedly a magnificent weapon.' (Indeed it was: the 3.7in's anti-tank potential would come to be widely remarked, and Pile, drawing upon his earlier expertise, later reflected that it was a pity it was never installed in tanks.) But as an AA weapon the 3.7in was at best unproven – high-level attacks had been few – and in Kennedy's judgement 'nowhere near the Bofors', which was 'very good indeed'. So there was little comfort from the voice of experience, and even less in Kennedy's parting remark. 'Finally,' the record shows, 'Colonel Kennedy declared' that fighter aircraft were the 'only answer' to the Luftwaffe.

CHAPTER 5
Fighter days
JUNE – SEPTEMBER 1940

Events over the following weeks largely vindicated what Colonel Kennedy averred at that rather gloomy meeting on the first day of June. Fighters, not AA guns, were indeed the principal answer to the Luftwaffe in the critical weeks when Britain, finally, faced concerted attack. This is not in doubt, though the unquestionable point that Britain was saved from defeat by Dowding's pilots (and the ground infrastructure supporting them) has given Fighter Command a dominance in historical narratives of summer 1940 which has tended to marginalise other arms. 'Their main contribution came later' was practically all that Churchill, writing of the Battle of Britain, said of Pile's men.[1] That is certainly true; but AA Command's contribution has never been explored in much depth, and nor is it clear how the lessons of the campaign – the AA gunners' first over British soil since 1918 – helped produce the techniques which enabled their 'main contribution' of the later war years to be made.

It was a slow start. For the first few days of June Luftwaffe operations followed the pattern seen in May, with minelayers operating in darkness and occasional reconnaissance flights. Sporadic AA engagements took place at coastal GDAs – Dover, Harwich, Plymouth, Scapa, the Solent – though no claims were made at night. Shooting was better during the day, though the lone aircraft downed by the Solent guns in the early morning of 3 June was soon discovered to be a Fairey Battle. Though its three-man crew managed to abandon the aircraft before it crashed on the Isle of Wight, only the pilot was saved.[2]

The Luftwaffe's first inland penetrations in these overtures to the Battle of Britain came on the night of 5/6 June, when aircraft operated in numbers against scattered targets in north-east England and East Anglia. Repeating the performance on the following night – when Yorkshire, Lincolnshire and Norfolk became the focus of attention – these sorties were chiefly aimed at airfields, and were flown in part to familiarise Göring's crews with night operations over Britain. Though some of the raiders were engaged as they crossed the coast at Dover, the Solent and the Humber, the only local defences to open fire were the LAA at RAF Mildenhall, in Suffolk, which managed to dispatch a few rounds during the second night's raiding.[3] That little damage was done owed less to the airfields' guns – none of which were equipped to engage unseen targets at night – than the embryonic layout of decoy airfields which had been hurried into place in the previous two months.[4] Many of the bombs meant for airfields fell harmlessly amid the twinkling lights of these dummy targets, as they would continue to do for the rest of the war.

The inland night attacks at the end of the first week of June were a temporary diversion for the Luftwaffe, which in the following fortnight reverted to coastal operations, again chiefly minelaying, until the Battle of France was won. And with the strategic geography of Europe daily changing, the members of the AA Committee were now confronted with difficult decisions over how guns should be redeployed to meet the Germans' seemingly inevitable dominance of the northern French coast. In the first week of June, true to the plans of the previous five years, dense concentrations of guns ceased at the Solent, where 77 HAA were in place at Portsmouth and Southampton. The western Channel ports beyond were only lightly gunned and a few were actually defenceless.[5] Studying this problem on 11 June, the AA Committee considered representations from the Admiralty and the War Office, both of whom pressed for substantial gun increases in western coastal districts.[6] The War Office argued that, for their purposes, Southampton was likely to diminish in importance in the near future, as routes for military supplies were pushed further west; but while no guns could be removed here, alternative anchorages at Weymouth, Fowey, Poole and, to a lesser extent, Falmouth all demanded heavier protection for their enlarged roles in shipping vehicles, ammunition and petrol. Of these, only Falmouth was formally listed as a GDA, and the port's first guns – eight 3in HAA – had arrived in the previous week.[7] Further afield, Newport and Swansea among the existing GDAs were set to assume greater importance in landing army supplies together, probably, with Port Talbot, Llanelli and Barry; of these only Newport was actually gunned, and with just four 3in weapons.[8] Taken together with the navy's claims – larger roles for the Fleet were proposed at Plymouth, Dover and Falmouth – it was clear that AA Command faced deepening commitments at coastal targets from Kent to South Wales.

Dowding was present at this meeting, Pile not. And Dowding, while emphasising 'the difficulty finding additional guns for the ports with so many competing requirements',[9] promised to do what he could. Two days later orders were issued.[10] Falmouth had to make do with its eight 3in guns and nothing could yet be found for Fowey, but Plymouth's defences were thickened by ordering-in sixteen 3.7in statics, ten of which would replace existing mobiles; the result would be a 24-gun layout for what was now set to operate as a major Fleet anchorage. Poole was defended for the first time under these orders with four 3in guns robbed from Coventry, while the opportunity was also taken to bolster the

Plate 10 Summer 1940: 3.7in mobiles at Sandgate, Kent. The guns obey the layout shown in Fig 11, and are served by a sandbagged command post with the predictor to the rear in its 'wigwam'. Encircling the guns are the beginnings of sandbag emplacements.

Kyle of Lochalsh – listed as a GDA but as yet unarmed – and Ardeer, where guns were to be doubled by the addition of four 3.7in statics. The orders of 13 June also provided HAA weapons for the Rotol Airscrews works at Cheltenham and industry at Grantham. So began the first rearrangement of guns in preparation for the Battle of Britain.

On the day after these orders Paris fell to the Wehrmacht, practically undefended; just eight days now remained before the Battle of France ended in armistice on 22 June. In the week to the 15 June the Luftwaffe visited Britain only fleetingly, but they returned in force on the night of the 15th/16th and for the two nights following, again laying mines in the Channel. Then the night hours of 18/19 June brought the first intensive overland activity for almost a fortnight, when forces estimated at 50–60 aircraft ranged widely across eastern England, bombing the Northumberland coast, the Humber area, and airfields and other inland targets from the East Riding to Kent. Many of the airfield raids were again drawn off by decoys and none of the LAA detachments at RAF stations seems to have fired a shot, though the HAA guns on the Humber, at Harwich, and in the Thames & Medway GDA were all in action against raiders crossing the coast – together claiming three kills – while the Bofors at Bawdsey radar station claimed a He 111 destroyed. No claims were made on the next night, when raiding was concentrated around the Humber and Tees but extended more widely to Newcastle, Leeds, Southampton and Cardiff. The night of 21/22 June was quiet, but the next brought raids evidently aimed at the oil refineries at Thameshaven and Killingworth, several targets on Wearside and a scatter of coastal objectives from the Humber to the Isle of Wight. Though airfields were emerging as a regular group of targets, by now it was clear that there was little pattern to these raids, which were falling widely and resembled one another chiefly in being light, and difficult to engage. It was a similar story during the last week in June, when in five consecutive nights of activity RAF stations were consistently attacked but small forces also visited targets as diverse as the Forth Bridge, the city of Birmingham, Cardiff docks, shipping in the Humber, and the Lincolnshire towns of Spilsby and Boston.[11] Few claims were made by the gunners. Three raiders were reckoned to have been destroyed by HAA on the Forth and Humber during the night of the 25th/26th, but for the most part the light guns at airfields and other VPs were silent.

The Luftwaffe's targeting of scattered and localised objectives in this phase of raiding emphasised the impoverished state of LAA defences almost everywhere. In the third week of June, the 271 armed VPs on AA Command's books shared 3538 LAA guns in seven types.[12] One hundred and fourteen of these weapons were 2pdrs of one kind or another, 132 were 3in guns prepared for LAA work, and 37 Hispano-Suiza 20mms were also in place. But there were no fewer than 3028 Lewis guns – 86 per cent of the total – in contrast to just 227 Bofors. Guns were routinely deployed in mixed groups at the more heavily armed VPs, so those fielding the better weapons were generally provided with Lewis guns too; but at the same time 141 VPs were defended *solely* by Lewis guns, which were also standard equipment on searchlight sites. In result, a few weeks before the Battle of Britain began, fractionally more than half the listed VPs with LAA defence relied upon a weapon of Great War vintage which, in 1940, was never intended to be more than a stop-gap. And even the better guns were not always equipped with suitable ancillaries. Many Bofors lacked predictors, and relied instead on 'forward area sights' – visual shooting – while the 3in guns prepared for LAA work used deflection sights and were mostly provided with shrapnel shells to engage low-flying targets. The 20mm Hispano-Suizas suffered from a general shortage of ammunition, and particularly of the tracer which glowed hot on firing and allowed visual correction of aim.[13]

This very mixed portfolio of weapons was carefully invested. Bofors of course went to the most vital of all VPs, and by June 1940 the orders of the previous November to equip radar stations and aircraft factories with the static type had been carried through. Each radar station had three statics, while the eleven aircraft factories so armed fielded numbers proportional to their size and vulnerability – generally four or so but, exceptionally, rising to fourteen guns at the Vickers works at Weybridge, the largest number given to a VP of any kind at this date. A few more Bofors had gone to industrial and military targets – among them the Royal Ordnance Factory at Nottingham, the Billingham ICI works, Southampton docks and the Tyne shipyards, where eight statics made the second strongest concentration – but by now many from the remaining stock had been shared among the RAF's airfields, another new group of targets which had been added to AA Command's list of VPs in October of the previous year.

Like the western Channel ports, the defence of aerodromes was a rising commitment in the early summer of 1940. By late June each fielded a range of weapons proportional to its role and position. Fighter airfields were the best defended, particularly those in 11 Group, whose area at that date covered much of southern England but, from early July, would be narrowed down to the main front in south-eastern England from Norfolk to Dorset, loosely corresponding to the territories of 1 and 6 AA Divisions. By 19 June all but four of the airfields in 6 AA Division had Bofors, which were in place at Manston, Biggin Hill, North Weald, Hawkinge, Hornchurch, Kenley, Gravesend, West Malling, Ipswich (formerly the airport) and Martlesham Heath – all fighter stations – while Northolt in 1 AA Division was also so equipped. Reaching further to the west and north, Bofors were also sited at the fighter aerodromes at Debden, Tangmere, Coltishall, Duxford, Digby and Wittering, together with the Bomber and Coastal Command stations at Mildenhall, Waddington, Scampton, Bircham Newton, and North Coates. Bofors sited at airfields were exclusively mobiles. Two or four was the usual allotment, though Debden uniquely had six.

With one or two exceptions the VPs with Bofors in mid June 1940 were mutually exclusive with those guarded by 3in LAA guns, which were generally given to the less exposed fighter airfields in the Midlands and the north, and the more southerly bomber stations. Besides Lewis guns, which protected nearly all the remaining airfields and much else besides, the remaining LAA weapons were scattered across a wide range of targets. The 2pdr Mk VIII singles had a particular concentration in the Orkneys, where 40 were in place at various sites, though a few were also used at RAF support stations in the west and north, such as Ternhill, Cosford, Shawbury and Kirkbride.

By the last week in June many of the airfields which would enter the front line in the weeks to come also fielded HAA weapons, though apart from Ringway, the former Manchester airport whose 3.7s were reckoned as part of the defence of that city, all were 3in guns equipped with Case III sights. Most airfield HAA was in 2 and 6 AA Divisions, covering the area from the Humber southwards to Worthing: thus Grantham, Duxford, Watton, Marham, Feltwell and Wattisham were all protected in this way, along with North Weald, Biggin Hill, Manston, Martlesham Heath, Rochford, Hawkinge, Tangmere, Brooklands, West Malling and Ipswich further south. Since some of these stations also had Bofors by late June, it is true that a proportion of the southern airfields were reasonably well defended against visual engagements by day. Bristling with four Bofors, six Lewis guns and eight 3in HAA weapons, RAF Manston, on the eastern tip of Kent, was the most strongly defended airfield in Britain.

One of the striking features of the Battle of Britain from AA Command's point of view is how little these deployments really changed while the fighting was in progress (a point revealed by Appendix II, which shows the changing monthly distribution of HAA, and the totals of LAA held by AA Command, in the year from May 1940). Heavy AA cover for airfields was extended modestly, as we shall see, while the western Channel ports were reinforced in line with the decisions of early June; at the same time some inland cities with aircraft factories on their margins were also more heavily gunned. Most of the expansions were achieved at the expense of the major urban GDAs, which did not enter the firing line until later in the year and typically lost many of their 3.7in mobiles during the fighting of July and August. AA Command's overall stock of guns, however, would not grow markedly during the Battle of Britain. By early September, when raiding switched to London, 3.7in mobile and static weapons had risen in number by rather less than a fifth of their June figures. The greatest proportional increase was in Bofors, whose numbers rose by 70 per cent between the last week in June and the first week in September; but even that was 70 per cent of rather little. Just 466 Bofors were on AA Command's books by the time the Battle of Britain began to evolve into the Blitz.

To set against these weaknesses Britain did at least enter the Battle of Britain with an efficient system for raid reporting. In the front line of this system was the radar chain, fruit of the work begun at Bawdsey in 1935, and behind that, for aircraft spotting over land, the Observer Corps.[14] Information from both and from other sources such as gun and searchlight sites was passed up the line to Fighter Command headquarters at Bentley Priory, where it was 'filtered' – evaluated to eliminate duplication and assessed against the movements of friendly aircraft – before retransmission back to the periphery in a digested form. In practical terms this meant that raid warnings would be passed to the controllers of the RAF's fighter groups and thence to their counterparts in the air defence sector level, and also at this stage to the gun operations rooms, who would then pass details to the sites. It was a reliable, durable and flexible system, prone to failure chiefly when the front-line reporting information broke down, links were severed, or when events began to overtake it. But this rarely happened, and by the end of the battle one AA formation at least believed it to have been the gunners' saving grace.

As June wore on it was clear that Pile must plan to fight the coming battle using largely what he had, rather than what he might expect to get. Strenuous efforts were made to coax the most from the guns and men. One worry was the continuing call upon 3.7in mobiles, both to reinforce established GDAs and to create new defences unanticipated when the war began, a trend which was steadily sapping AA Command's tactical flexibility. The danger of tying up so many 3.7in mobiles in what were, in effect, permanent deployments led to an important policy decision early in the month, when Pile ruled that many more sites must in future be built for 3.7in statics, allowing any commitment which seemed likely to last to be met with fixed weapons, leaving the mobiles free for emergencies. As insurance, Pile also tried to anticipate new commitments by building fixed gunsites in areas where weapons would probably be sent in future, so allowing statics to be used if guns were subsequently requested. Henceforth this would be normal practice: for the remainder of the war AA Command furnished as many sites as possible to permanent standard. Though it embodied another uncomfortable compromise for a defensive arm which, only a few years earlier, was expected to be largely mobile, this wise policy would pay dividends. It was, perhaps, the inevitable outcome of the trend begun in late 1937, when the Reorientation Committee had first advised Inskip that a quota of 3.7in statics could be accepted. And from a structural point of view it was, obviously, one of the most influential decisions of the war.

To begin this new round of construction on 7 June Pile asked the War Office to supply 200 holdfast assemblies, enough to build another 50 four-gun fixed HAA sites.[15] And the policy that these would be *four*-gun sites was also settled in June, when Pile came to examine the rate at which equipment was coming from production. By the end of the month it was clear that the supply of new HAA weapons was outrunning the manufacture of fire-control instruments (particularly heightfinders) to the point where there would soon be not enough to go around. To make the most of the available instruments, Pile decided to abolish most of the existing two-gun HAA sites and to concentrate practically all of his HAA weapons in fours (in manning terms as half-batteries), at a stroke giving every site a full set of instruments and leaving a surplus in reserve.[16] This entailed a good deal of shuffling. Two-gun sites were still common in summer 1940, with about 50 occupied by static weapons and as many as 125 by mobiles, most of which needed to be concentrated down to four-gun positions. But once the policy was accepted the four-gun HAA battery, permanently built for static weapons, became the 'standard' HAA site of the war. The technique of concentrating guns to optimise the ratio of fire-control instruments also drew precedent from this decision, and would reach its height six months later, when a few sixteen-gun sites were marshalled together to meet the London Blitz.

Sharpening the readiness of his gunners was also much on Pile's mind as invasion fears deepened. In the last week of June a party of officers was sent out from Stanmore to inspect the AA defences at every fighter airfield in the country.[17] Much advice was given. LAA detachments were encouraged to practice aiming at friendly aircraft, with the result that keener-eyed flyers were routinely treated to the sight of LAA barrels beadily tracking their take-offs and landings. When the crunch came, however, gunners were exhorted to withhold fire until the last moment, so luring hostile aircraft into LAA range when there would be a chance of shooting them down; possibly the RAF might have disagreed, but Pile's orders were that one aircraft destroyed 'is worth 10 driven away'. But how to tell when the target entered lethal range? The answer was worthy of Dad's Army. 'A piece of wood,' advised the experts at Stanmore, 'with a hole in it, held at arm's length, will meet the case.' Every LAA crew was encouraged to avail itself of this elementary piece of carpentry.

Dad's Army – the Home Guard – had itself been formed by the time this advice was given, and as their neighbouring villagers began to enlist in this unlikely people's militia, so the AA gunners at sites all over the country were readying themselves to meet the promised invasion. Britain's first structural preparations against a landing began in mid May, shortly after the Germans began their advance in the west, when ports were given all-round defences, potential landing-grounds for troop carrying aircraft were obstructed, and the first steps were taken to fortify London. But the main thrust began in the weeks after Dunkirk, as France was collapsing across the Channel, when the vast programme of anti-invasion defences planned by General Edmund Ironside was put in train. By the end of June orders were out for the main 'stop-lines' which would parcel-up the British Isles into tank-proof zones; and in the first weeks of July the work was underway.

Plate 11 Gunners: Green Street Green (TS18 in the Thames & Medway GDA), probably summer 1940.

Britain now became a fortress, her shores hardened by anti-tank blocks, guarded by pillboxes and weapon emplacements, and sealed from civilians. Inland, the major defensive positions grew, sprouted subsidiary lines, and encircled towns and villages with gun emplacements, roadblocks, and an improvised range of fearsome devices designed to thwart the advance of the Panzers. Everyone would have a part in this battle: the troops of Home Forces chiefly, but also the Home Guard (among them General Ashmore, in the summer of 1940 a Home Guard commander on the south coast) and of course the gunners of AA Command.

Pile's men had two main roles. Air defence, naturally, was the first, and especially the defence of the RAF's airfields, whose destruction or capture would be high on the Germans' scale of priorities. But in common with all troops in Britain, the gunners and searchlight crews also had a role in ground defence – infantry work, in essence, to tackle the invading army, should it come. At airfields these jobs would merge into one another, the gunners first engaging the aircraft fighting for dominance in the skies and delivering troops, and finally coming to terms with any parachutists who had gained a foothold, or ground forces attempting to disembark from transport aircraft. On the model of recent German operations on the continent, the Air Ministry Weekly Intelligence Summary for 20 June painted a vivid picture of how all this would probably happen.

At dawn [explained the summary], enemy fighters would appear over the aerodrome at medium height and draw off fighter opposition. They would be followed almost immediately by very low flying bombers which would cross the aerodrome at about 25–50 feet dropping sticks of light bombs round the perimeter of the aerodrome and on the aerodrome defences. They would be followed by heavy fighters which would attack the aerodrome defences with their front cannons and machine guns. At the same time three or four companies of parachute troops would be dropped (as companies) at three or four points round the aerodrome and about 1,000 to 1,500 yards from it. These parachute troops would form up in their companies again in about 12–15 minutes and would storm the aerodrome from all sides with the intention of capturing it. Their approach to the aerodrome would take perhaps 5 minutes, and they would attack the defences remaining on the aerodrome with heavy and light machine-gun fire, with sub-machine-gun and rifle fire, with hand grenades or, in the case of stubborn resistance, with 2″ mortars. Probably about ten minutes after the beginning of their attack large numbers of Ju 52 and larger troop transports would begin to land on the aerodrome at the rate of about six a minute. These troop transports would disgorge on landing troops armed with heavy and light machine guns with 2″ and 3″ mortars and possibly with 3″ mountain guns. In addition they would carry motor cycles and side-car combinations and possibly a few light tanks. Light anti-aircraft guns (2cm automatics with an effective range of about 4,500 feet and capable of use as anti-tank weapons) would also be landed and set up round the aerodrome. One or two squadrons of single engined fighters would also land. In the meantime, a fighter 'umbrella' at some strength (at least 27 aircraft) would be maintained over each of the [. . .] aerodromes attacked.[18]

To meet these eventualities, in later June Bofors crews were issued with anti-tank ammunition. Instructions were also given to reduce the parapets of LAA emplacements, so enabling the guns to fire on tanks and other ground forces (even rifle fire, gunners were confidently assured, would do something to annoy a tank).[19] HAA weapons, too, would have an important field artillery role against the Panzers – particularly the 3.7s, which had already demonstrated their anti-tank value in France – while instructions were issued on how GL sets might detect the approach of parachute attacks.[20] More generally, the invasion threat prompted a mass of work to prepare each AA artillery and searchlight site as a defended enclave, locally resistant to enemy ground troops and readied to assist in the invasion battle. Field defence works were improvised everywhere, using barbed wire cordons, infantry slit trenches, and sometimes concrete pillboxes to turn each site into a self-contained strong point (Fig 17). Camouflage, too, came under renewed scrutiny in these weeks, and could now benefit from direct experience gained in France and elsewhere. France had shown the importance of concealing even minor features of HAA sites – the predictor, heightfinder, ammunition boxes – and of tidying away such oddmenta as greatcoats and field cookers.[21] Even Finland's 'Winter War' against the Soviets yielded useful experience: word from the Military Attaché in Helsinki was that a 'very roughly dug pit, which avoids any suggestion of regularity, revetment etc' made the best form of emplacement. 'From the air,' explained the attaché, 'this looks like any other shell crater. Digging in was the key to the complete success of Finnish AA weapons in avoiding casualties from air attack.'[22] There was urgency to all of this work. 'Much is being

Figure 17 Ground defence arrangements for an HAA site. Though based upon a specification issued in summer 1941, this layout captures the general principles of ground defence used during the Battle of Britain in the previous summer. Here the gunsite is protected by infantry section posts, pillboxes and barbed wire, while a neighbouring farm has been transformed into a strong-point.

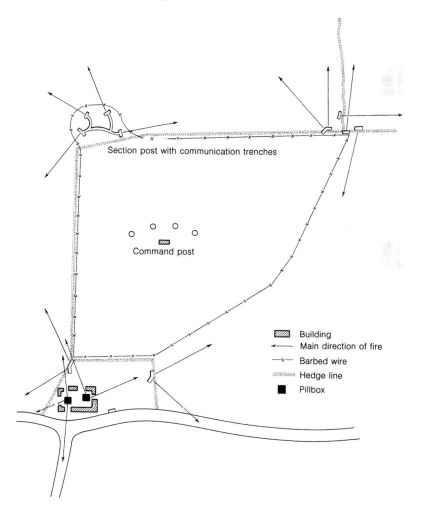

done,' declared Stanmore on 19 June; but 'Still more remains to be done. We have not yet all shaken ourselves out of the rut. In some places excellent results have been achieved by officers of experience, imagination and drive. In others there is an air of complacence [sic], of orthodoxy, and of failure to realise that tomorrow may be too late.' Regimental commanders, ordered Pile, must 'go out continually and see for themselves what is happening, advise the inexperienced, and drive the contented'.[23]

Camouflage and field defences would safeguard the site's AA role once the Germans had landed, but it was accepted that a point might arrive at which batteries soon to be overrun would vacate their permanent sites to move into a mobile AA role, before – in extremis – conceding the air battle and throwing themselves into the final ground war. In that event, AA troops would support the infantry; orders to gunners and searchlight detachments typically assigned units to the local home defence commander. Static HAA positions, of course, could not be moved; and commanders of these sites were given exacting instructions on how, and when, equipment was to be destroyed before the troops took to their heels. The final rounds issuing from fixed HAA gunsites would be spent on their own radar cabin and predictor before vital components were hurriedly stripped from the guns, to be scattered or mutilated. A rifle butt would deal with the heightfinder's optics. Then the site would be abandoned, leaving the Germans nothing more useful than scrap metal, debris and concrete.

In early July the Luftwaffe's operations conformed broadly to the pattern established in June, with the important difference from the gunners' point of view that some of these scattered raids were launched in daylight.[24] But still, the Luftwaffe was hesitant. Though occasionally bold and deep, inland penetrations in daylight were invariably small – single aircraft, sometimes twos and threes – so while many guns fired sporadic rounds at raiders en route to their targets and over them, few claims were made. The greater proportion of the Luftwaffe's effort in these days was instead devoted to attacks on ports, especially in the south, and shipping in the Channel, along with the minelaying and minor nuisance raids which generally continued by night. Day attacks on 1 July saw AA guns in action on the Humber, Mersey and Bramley, on the Tyne the next day, and on 3 July at Bramley, Newport, Bristol, Holton Heath, Dover and Harwich. These were quick engagements of minor raids, but 4 July brought a fiercer battle over Portland harbour, where dive-bombers managed to sink HMS *Foylebank*, as well as harassing the AA gunsites protecting the anchorage. But Portland harbour itself was not seriously damaged by these efforts, and no more were Falmouth, Plymouth, Dover, Folkestone, Bristol, the Humber, Aberdeen, and the Forth, all of which returned fire against minor daylight raids in the days that followed. Here and there the Luftwaffe's efforts brought returns – as at Aldershot on 6 July, where casualties were sustained in a barracks, and at Penhale on the following day – but if the attackers' efforts were doing little more than causing disruption through the frequent sounding of raid alarms, they were also costing the Germans very little. AA Command's claims amounted to just one Bf 109 destroyed, this at Dover on 9 July.[25]

By 10 July the geography of Fighter Command was already being reshaped to respect German command of the entire French coast. Building upon the assessments of mid June, on 6 July the AA Committee confirmed that the whole of the British Isles was now within reach of the Luftwaffe's long-range bombers and fighters, that short-range fighters and dive bombers could reach the territory south of a line between the Humber and Pembroke, and that the enemy 'may launch attacks [. . .] from the South and West in greater force and intensity than he was previously able to from further East'.[26] There was also the growing possibility that hostile operations might be mounted from Eire, should the Germans gain a foothold there. Two days later the RAF formed 10 Group, which took over the western fringe of the broad territory originally held exclusively by 11 Group, with squadrons at Pembrey, St Eval and Exeter and a headquarters at Rudloe Manor in Wiltshire. At the same time efforts deepened to extend the early warning system along the west coast, to form more fighter squadrons to cover the west, and to commission new airfields to suit. The meeting of 6 July recognised the need for additional fighter sectors along the entire west coast – from Cornwall to Ayrshire – and, 'as soon as political considerations permit access', in Eire as well.[27] All of this would necessarily be accompanied by thickening the searchlight and AA gun cover in the western regions, to an extent far surpassing that envisaged only a month previously, when supplementary guns were allocated among some of the western ports. On 6 July the AA sub-committee was set to work on the details of this scheme, a job they began formally three days later.[28]

More than a month would pass before the report from these deliberations was issued, a period more or less precisely coterminous with the next phase of the developing campaign. On 10 July the Germans began a heavier and more sustained programme of daylight raids against ports and convoys, chiefly in the Channel but often ranging up the east and west coasts, while continuing with minelaying and limited inland raiding at night. The daylight anti-shipping operations again threw most of the AA duties onto the coastal GDAs, which were sometimes able to reach the raiders operating out at sea and gave much trade to the gunners at Dover, Portland, Portsmouth and the Bristol Channel in particular. July 10th is recognised as the start of this phase – the official British view defines it as the start of the Battle of Britain as such – largely because the anti-shipping operations were so much heavier than previously, even though attacks upon ships had been a feature of Luftwaffe activity since the previous October. Two large maritime raids were flown on 10 July itself, the first with just two Dornier bombers but as many as 30 escorting fighters, which attacked a convoy off Margate, and the second with a much larger force of about two dozen Dorniers escorted by 40 fighters, split equally between Bf 109s and twin-engined Bf 110s, whose prey was a convoy in the Straits of Dover. Neither raid achieved very much and the second, in particular, was satisfyingly cut about by Dowding's pilots, who claimed to have destroyed seven fighters. Just one small ship was sunk by this fleet of more than 60 aircraft; but at the same time another vessel was destroyed and two damaged by a further raid against Falmouth.[29] Other, minor, incursions by the Luftwaffe brought the AA artillery into action at Aberdeen, Portland, Newport and Cardiff (where a Ju 88 bomber fell to the guns), as well as at Dover.[30]

And this pattern of events, with a degree of ebb and flow for the weather, was typical of the period to the end of the first week in August. In the late morning of 11 July raiders again operated over Portland, where the HAA batteries gave them a warm reception and destroyed no fewer than three (eight, additionally, were claimed by fighters). In the early evening a further raid aimed at Portsmouth with a dozen Heinkels and a similarly-sized escort forced another fighter engagement and resulted in the loss of one hostile aircraft to the AA guns. The next day was quieter, though inconclusive AA engagements were recorded at Plymouth, Falmouth, Portland, the Solent and Dover – every major GDA on the south coast – as well as at Aberdeen. Deteriorating weather explained the easing of operations on the 12th, and continued to inhibit the Luftwaffe for the next week, but activity over the south coast brought the gunners sporadic opportunities. On 13 July a Ju 87 dive-bomber was destroyed by LAA at Dover, one of only three GDAs in action on that day, and a few more raiders fell to the guns at the Tyne, Portland and Dover in the following days. On the evening of the 13th Dowding, dining at Chequers, told the Prime Minister that he was worried by little except his dreams – though one of those speaks volumes, perhaps, of what Dowding really thought of AA Command, as well as capturing a sense of what the two men were fighting for. That morning, confessed the air chief marshal, he had woken deeply disturbed by a dream that only one man in England knew how to use a Bofors gun, and that man's name was William Shakespeare.[31]

Dowding's anxieties aside, by mid July there was a general feeling that the AA defences were performing reasonably well in daylight, given their limited opportunities to engage raiders whose locus of activity remained offshore. At night, however, the guns' performance gave cause for concern. Raids in darkness were not heavy in this period. Some nights passed with little or no enemy activity recorded over land, but even when raiders were operating in discernible numbers – minelaying, chiefly, but also raiding airfields – the AA guns were too often silent. The problem, whose import would deepen in the coming months, was largely the continuing absence of reliable fire control, a difficulty compounded by poor weather inhibiting the searchlights supporting both guns and fighters. By July 1940 a reasonable proportion of AA batteries fielded GL Mk I radars, but very few had yet come to terms with their operation and would not do so until the height of the Blitz in the coming winter, when frantic efforts were made to refine the sets and drill the gunners in their use. The result was that only one night raider was definitely claimed as destroyed by the AA guns in the whole of July, this a Do 17 which fell to the Mersey GDA on the night of the 23rd/24th (though another may have been downed by the Plymouth gunners on the 21st/22nd, a kill denied confirmation by the raider seemingly falling into the sea).[32] Some attempt was made to set up geographical barrages and special layouts to engage dive-bombers, but all the gunners could hope to do at night was fire on whatever positional information could be obtained. And that, as the Luftwaffe soon discovered, was precious little.

In the last fortnight of July such AA engagements which did take place were mostly fought by day, and at the end of the month the gunners could take some satisfaction in a score of 20 victims confirmed in those four weeks, half of which were downed by the guns at Dover, where the crews were doubled to keep the sites on continuous alert.[33] Dover's gunners saw some intense action in these days – as on the 19th, when a heavy attack on shipping in the Straits brought a Dornier fatally into their sights, and again on the next day, when the AA claim was at least one and possibly as many as three victims from a raid on shipping and the harbour itself. On that day, 20 July, Dover had borne the brunt of the Luftwaffe's efforts nationally and while many more hostile aircraft were downed by fighters than by AA guns, the weapons exercised their deterrent effect, fractured the formations and helped signal their positions to Dowding's pilots. As the battle developed the Luftwaffe's habits of evasion began to emerge: first a high-flying formation would climb, holding station one with another; next they would widen out, under fire, but hold course; and lastly they would break, splitting into singletons on widely divergent courses.[34] It was then, often, that Dowding's pilots got them.

Operations in the last ten days of the month were again thwarted by the weather, but 24 July brought another sharp exchange at Dover, when the gunners chalked up another bomber, likewise the following day, when the action continued throughout the day and the AA claim rose to three Ju 87s destroyed. Southampton and Portland were also targeted on 25 July, the only occasion in this month on which the Luftwaffe managed to inflict substantial damage on the shipping which this phase of operations made its target. This was achieved largely by an unusual concentration of force: as many as 120 German aircraft seem to have been operating around midday, and some 60–80 in the afternoon and evening, all of them in carefully co-ordinated attacks. It was the first raid in such numbers, but remained for a time uniquely so. In the closing days of July daylight raids continued and Dover's guns, again, were the busiest in Britain (two further Ju 87s were claimed on the 29th), but the height of the battle had yet to be reached.

During the first week of August the Luftwaffe continued to attack shipping and coastal targets, generally with single aircraft, occasionally with small formations, and always in a shifting pattern.[35] In the period remaining before 12 August, when heavy attacks on airfields began, AA guns were in action somewhere during every 24-hour period bar one (the day and night of 6 August), though most of these engagements were brief and on several days were confined to single GDAs. Dover, Portland and the Solent saw much of the action among the heavy weapons, though at one time or another odd rounds were dispatched from practically every coastal GDA from the Orkneys to Cardiff, while LAA found some trade at Bawdsey and Stoke Holy Cross radar stations. The Dover balloon barrage was thrice harried by Bf 109 fighters: first on the afternoon of 9 August, when one aircraft was claimed as damaged, again on the morning and early afternoon of the 11th, when the claim rose to three fighters destroyed and two winged, and again on the following day. But otherwise kills were few. The Harwich guns claimed a Heinkel damaged on the night of 2/3 August, and Portsmouth's HAA downed a Ju 88 on the next night. But by now the Germans' dominance of the Channel in daylight was complete. On 26 July the Admiralty had abandoned daylight movements of merchant ships through the Straits of Dover, and two days later, with evidence available that the Germans were mounting long-range guns near Calais, Dover was vacated as a naval base in favour of Harwich (where 15 HAA were in place) and Sheerness, which lay under cover of the Thames & Medway guns. Daytime naval movements from Dover ceased on 29 July.[36]

The continued coastal raiding during the first half of August meant that few inland GDAs saw an enemy aircraft until the daylight airfield attacks began on the 13th; the city of Norwich alone seems to have fired its guns, when on 10 August a small force operating over East Anglia was engaged without result.[37] In these weeks, as the main battle drew closer, efforts were redoubled to improve the tactical protection of AA gunsites, which Pile's staff expected to come under heavy assault once the air defence system in general was targeted. Apart from improving conventional camouflage – new and detailed advice upon which was circulated on 4 August[38] – AA Command also examined the value of dummy HAA gunsites, both to divert attacks from their genuine sites and to exaggerate the density of AA cover. By July 1940 bombing decoys of various kinds had been multiplying in eastern Britain for some months, in a programme devised by Colonel John Turner at the Air Ministry, who had been appointed to this novel duty in September 1939.[39] Turner's sites had soon shown results; as we have seen, many of the night raids in June and some of those in July had fallen on decoy airfields contrived using systems of lights. But Turner declined to handle AA Command's dummies, pleading that he was sufficiently occupied with decoying Air Ministry targets. Though some technical advice seems to have been obtained from Sound City Films, who handled the design work for Turner's sites, dummy HAA batteries became largely a home-grown enterprise, quite separate from the extensive national decoy layout which, in July, the Chiefs of Staff authorised to be built under Turner's supervision.

In the event, AA Command's dummy gunsites do not seem to have progressed far during the Battle of Britain, arguably the period when they might have been of most use. A prototype was built on 29–30 July, when five men erected a dummy HAA position at Woodham Lodge, near Addlestone in Surrey. Emplacements and a command post, evidently in timber, were erected and roads simulated by unrolling a series of fabric mats, all of which looked structurally 'excellent' (if somewhat lifeless) to the officers who peered down at the site from a borrowed Anson on 31 July.[40] Next day divisional commanders were invited to submit bids for dummy HAA battery kits, comprising static and mobile emplacements, command posts, roads and bogus guns, which would be fitted with electrical flashes to complete the illusion. But little seems to have been done to build the sites for many months; at any rate the divisions' requirements for kits were not settled until much later in the year, and while some examples were certainly standing by mid 1941, silence in AA Command's correspondence points to a hiatus in the project during the summer of 1940.

By mid August the gunners in any case had other business in hand. The fierce airfield attacks which began on the 13th of the month – *Adlertag* or Eagle Day – now restored the fighting to inland Britain, but on a much heavier scale. This phase of the battle would last until early September, when the night bomber became AA Command's abiding concern. And the first stage of this campaign occupied ten days, until 23 August, during which Göring dispatched large fleets of bombers escorted by fighters to attempt to break the RAF on the ground.

For AA Command the daylight attacks on RAF stations offered the first real experience of the problem first clearly identified in the Air Exercises of 1930, that of snap attacks delivered by aircraft flashing across the airfield practically at ground level. In the 1930 exercises those had been Bristol Bulldog fighters; now they were Messerschmitts, Dorniers and Junkers capable of twice the speed and needing to be engaged by rapidly-laid LAA fire in the few seconds available to identify the target and shoot. In addition, many raids on airfields were launched from much higher levels, capable of being met only by HAA guns which, in mid August 1940, were still concentrated in the urban GDAs rather than in the hinterlands of RAF stations. In short this phase of operations posed many problems for the AA gunners, not the least of which was their continuing deficit in the tools of their trade. In the third week of August heavy guns (all 3in) were in place at only 25 airfields in Britain. Typically the forward airfields had four of these guns – this was true of Tangmere, North Weald, Biggin Hill, Martlesham and Rochford in the south – though a few, such as Manston and Hawkinge, had more and some, notably West Malling and Ipswich, were equipped with just two. At this date Bofors were still allocated with the protection of forward airfields and radar stations paramount, along with targets supporting the aircraft industry; but the raw number of Bofors in AA Command on 21 August was just 430. Pile additionally had 135 Case I 3in guns for LAA work, 158 2pdrs of various types and 40 Hispano-Suiza guns of 20mm calibre, but Lewis guns still dominated LAA artillery everywhere. On 21 August AA Command fielded 7364 of these weapons, of which about two-thirds (4473) were deployed at HAA and searchlight sites and the remainder (2891) for the LAA defence of listed VPs.[41] In mid August 1940 the concentration of weapons supporting the air defence system was nowhere stronger than in eastern Kent (Fig 18), home of airfields at Manston, Hawkinge and Lympne, radar stations at Dunkirk and Dover – the latter with seven Bofors a veritable fortress – and a typical pattern of searchlight sites, all of which had Lewis guns of their own.[42] But the very fact that in mid August 1940 the territory of 6 AA Division, stretching from Suffolk to Sussex, commanded fully one quarter of all the Bofors guns in Britain shows how much had to be made of so little.

The first raids on the coastal elements of the air defence system fell on 12 August, when the Luftwaffe flew a series of concentrated sorties heralding the shift in tactics which would be more fully developed on the 13th. No fewer than seven Bf 109s were claimed by the Portsmouth guns on this day – one by Lewis guns at a searchlight site on the Isle of Wight – together with a Ju 88 and a Dornier bomber at Dover. In a sign of things soon to come, 12 August also brought stiff daylight attacks on airfields at Hawkinge, Lympne and Manston, as well as six radar stations in the south-east, among which Ventnor, on the Isle of Wight, was put off the air. Although these five VPs commanded some of the best LAA defences in Britain, only the Manston guns scored, claiming a single Bf 110 fighter damaged. Troubled by the ineffectiveness of the LAA defences, Dowding ordered an urgent investigation of events at Dunkirk, where dive-bombing in the late afternoon had met silence from the guns. The inquiry found that the radar station's three Bofors and eleven Lewis guns had been poorly sited: too remote from the VP at 2000 yards' distance, the static Bofors were installed with dead arcs over their predictors, which had been set up exactly between the weapons and the target they were emplaced to protect. In a hurried reshuffling the guns were drawn further in, the

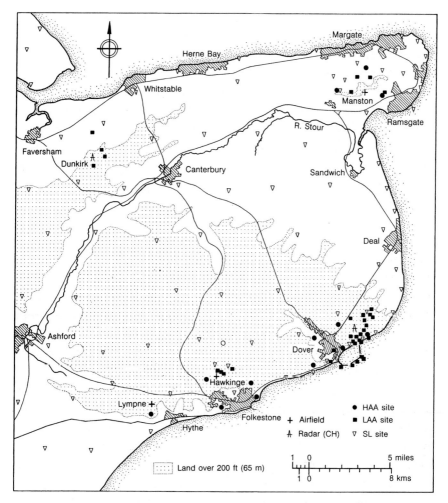

Figure 18 AA defences in east Kent, August 1940. Including some of the most heavily-defended targets during the Battle of Britain, this landscape of HAA, LAA and searchlight positions is based upon 6 AA Division's location statement issued in the middle of the month.

predictors shifted and the defences of radar stations in general urgently reassessed.[43]

The first attack to develop in the early morning of 13 August was at RAF Eastchurch, an airfield of ancient origin occupied in 1940 by Coastal Command but used as a lodger station by 266 Squadron in support of convoy patrols. No AA claims were entered here and the station was badly damaged, though a Ju 88 was downed by the LAA at Poling radar station. Apart from some minor afternoon raids against airfields in central southern England and the south-west, and at Detling, none of which brought the gunners any success, the main action of 13 August was around Portland and the Solent, where three AA claims were made. After the usual nuisance raids overnight, which saw HAA fire over Birmingham, Cardiff and Swansea, the early afternoon of 14 August brought a sharp attack on Manston, where two He 110s fell to the LAA guns but the station sustained heavy damage. Soon after, at about 12.30, a further hostile formation crossed the coast near Folkestone, and while an offshoot from this 100-strong force attacked the Dover balloon barrage – losing two of its number to the gunners – the body of the formation moved inland, though only to mount a passing sweep.[44] Activity such as this, however, shows the tendency of AA guns everywhere to come into action regardless of whether the target they were emplaced to defend was the object of an attack. Thus shortly after one in the afternoon 35 LAA Battery at Hawkinge, where a red air raid warning was in force from 12.15 to 13.30,[45] opened up with five rounds of Bofors fire, scoring two hits on a Ju 88;[46] likewise the LAA at Dunkirk radar station let loose with seven rounds at aircraft, evidently part of this formation, which proved to be out of range.[47] Elsewhere, however, targets purposefully attacked on 14 August were little troubled by the AA defences, notably a scatter of airfields in western Britain, several of which were damaged but not disabled. In all, 14 August was a quieter day than the 12th or 13th, though AA guns were also in action at Cardiff, Bristol, Portland and the Solent, as well as at Pevensey radar station. Among these, guns at Cardiff, Bristol and Pevensey each claimed an aircraft destroyed.[48]

On the night of 14/15 August minor engagements were fought by guns at Cardiff and the Solent, as well as the Tyne HAA, which along with the Lewis guns at a searchlight site near Arbroath claimed one victim.[49] And in contrast to the 14th, the next day was one of furious activity. At 10.40 the satellite airfield at Lympne, already troubled by heavy attacks on the 12th, reeled under sustained blows from dive-bombers, took a direct hit on the sick quarters, and was put out of action for two days.[50] An hour later the performance was repeated at Hawkinge, where Dorniers and Heinkels joined the Stuka dive bombers in a raid delivered at heights ranging from 300 to 2000 feet. At these altitudes the raiders were well within range of the station's four LAA positions, which opened up with a hail of Bofors and Lewis gun fire to claim four hits and one aircraft downed.[51] This same raid also hit Hythe, Folkestone and Dover, where a fierce AA battle developed, the first of what would become a day's total of eleven claims were made by the Dover gunners, and the shell bursts did their work in marking the attacking formations for the RAF's pilots.

The Luftwaffe would return to Kent – and to Hawkinge – later in the day, but at the same time as the early afternoon raids were developing in the south a quite unexpected attack was launched far away, on the north-east coast from Tyneside to Flamborough Head. This famous incident, the only attack to be made in force on northern coastal targets in the whole of the Battle of Britain, came about through the Germans' mistaken assumption that the bulk of the fighter force would have been moved south. In fact it had not, and Dowding's pilots scored a much-needed victory against a force whose members seem to have been taken entirely by surprise when fighter opposition was offered.[52] A fleet estimated at about 130 bombers and fighters operating against Tyneside was severely harassed by Fighter Command; and here the AA gunners on the Tyne claimed six aircraft destroyed and their comrades at the Tees GDA a further one.[53] Further to the south another force crossed the coast near Scarborough and did serious damage to the bomber station at Driffield, which came under heavy attack from around 30 Ju 88s which arrived at about one-thirty in the afternoon. Bombing here was launched from around 500 feet and lasted for three-quarters of an hour, during which the AA defences at Driffield claimed one victim.[54]

At two-thirty in the afternoon, as the last of the raiders were leaving across east Yorkshire, airfields and other targets in east Kent were about to receive their second bout of attacks within three hours. These raids extended from the Suffolk and Essex areas down to eastern Kent, and brought AA guns into action across the whole of the south-eastern coastal region from Harwich, across Thames & Medway down to Dover. One heavy raid fell on Martlesham Heath aerodrome, where dive-bombing from Stukas and Me 110s began exactly half a minute before the siren sounded and thereby caught the station personnel unawares. Beginning at ten minutes past three, the raid was over in five minutes and did substantial damage to buildings, which suffered less from the German bombs than from the consequences of a lucky hit on a parked Fairey Battle, whose full cargo of bombs exploded. No one was killed, but nor were the attackers much troubled by the AA gunners, the Bofors crews claiming that smoke had obscured their targets – a common problem – and those on the Hispano-Suiza 20mms that the raiders were too high to engage.[55] Martlesham was the main airfield victim in this large and sprawling operation, but Hawkinge received a high-level attack which lasted for about ten minutes from 15.25. Ranging from 8000 to 20,000 feet the attackers were again too high for LAA, though the airfield's 3in heavy guns opened up without effect.[56] As this raid was coming to an end, so another began at RAF Eastchurch, where a breakdown in the electricity supply had put the sirens out of action and, at 15.25, the station commander ordered one of the Bofors crews of 34 LAA Battery to fire four rounds across the airfield as a substitute warning. But that was the gunners' only contribution to the proceedings, since the bombs, counted at about 100 in number, which fell across the airfield a quarter of an hour later, came from Dorniers flying at 15,000 feet, again too high for the LAA guns which were this station's only artillery defence.[57]

The afternoon raids across the south-east were the third major German incursion of 15 August, but two more were to follow before darkness fell and the Luftwaffe's night shift made its usual scattered nuisance raids. The next round was on the Portland–Portsmouth front, where hostile formations estimated by the radar operators at 200–300 strong were plotted approaching a little after five o'clock. The fighter force scrambled to meet this attack was the largest yet deployed in the Battle of Britain: fourteen squadrons were thrown into the fight, in all about 150 Hurricanes and Spitfires which forced one of the biggest air engagements of the campaign. German losses were large, the potency of this force was much diminished by its interception before crossing the coast, and those bombers which did press on to their objectives succeeded only in damaging RAF Middle Wallop and making a minor attack on Portsmouth, where one was claimed as destroyed by HAA.[58] And once again, as this raid was coming to an end another developed over to the east, as south-eastern airfields came under attack for the third time in eight hours. The main thrust of this, the Luftwaffe's final daylight incursion of 15 August, was toward RAF West Malling and the aerodrome at Croydon, together with scattered industrial targets. It was the Croydon raid which brought the gunners of 1 AA Division in the IAZ into action for the first time, 319 HAA Battery at ZS13 (Shirley Park) firing fourteen rounds from its 3.7s at a formation of Dorniers and Heinkels which approached the airfield at about 18.50.[59] Though the London gunners believed their fire to have downed two aircraft, appreciable damage was done to Croydon as well as West Malling, where at least 80 bombs were dropped, the LAA crews found themselves outranged and the 3in guns claimed no kills.[60] At that, the daylight operations died away, to be succeeded a few hours later by minelaying and minor night raids aimed at a variety of inland targets. That night Pile's men were at work in Cardiff, Bristol, Brough and in the Humber GDA, where two aircraft were claimed as destroyed.[61]

At close of play on 15 August AA Command could look back on a day of some success. Overshadowed, as always in the Battle of Britain, by the claims of Fighter Command, Pile's men nonetheless reckoned that 30 aircraft had fallen to the guns, eleven at Dover alone. Verifying these claims, of course, brought immense difficulties of its own, none of which directly concerns us here; but in order to standardise and simplify the procedure, 13 August saw the introduction of a new terminology in which aircraft definitely 'destroyed' became Category I claims, aircraft 'probably destroyed', Category II, and those 'damaged', Category III.[62] These terms were used by fighter pilots and gunners alike for the remainder of the war, claims shared between the two being expressed as halves.

Respectable as the AA performance may have been on 15 August, it was put into perspective on the following day with the issue of the AA Committee's definitive report on air defence requirements consequent upon the fall of France, the study begun on 9 July.[63] As a document issued in the heat of battle, this report is of interest equally for its direct tactical consequences, and for its more abstract delineation of what constituted an ideal defence under the circumstances facing Dowding and Pile in mid August 1940. In deciding upon the new ideal scales of AA defence the committee was asked to hold three main considerations in mind: first, the increased risk to western and north-western Britain caused by the new German holdings in France; secondly the danger that the Luftwaffe might acquire bases in Eire; and thirdly the anticipated increases in German air strength over the following months, both through expansion of the Luftwaffe itself, and the likelihood that the Italian air force would join forces with them (Italy had declared war on France and the UK on 10 June). The only possible response to these developments was to ask the Chiefs of Staff to approve huge increases in more or less everything.

Dowding's acute difficulties in mustering sufficient fighter forces as the Battle of Britain rose to its height are well known; the paper of 16 August reflected this in its request for ten additional fighter squadrons, beyond the three which had already formed with foreign aircrew (Poles and Czechs) which were currently working up. But the increases required in ground defences were proportionally greater. Six wholly new balloon barrages were proposed to cover western targets – Falmouth, Pembroke, Ardeer, Yeovil, Newport and Belfast – together with a thickening of ten existing layouts, again chiefly for western ports but also extending to Manchester and Hull to meet the general widening in the Luftwaffe's area of operations. Requirements for searchlights, too, were much increased. With general area defence lights spaced at intervals of 6000 yards and GDA lights at 3500 yards, the number of searchlight projectors needed now rose by 3816. The highest priority here was to complete the layout of lights in the steadily widening AFZ, first in areas already authorised, and then in extensions covering Devon/Cornwall, south Wales, the Edinburgh–Tyne corridor, and finally Northern Ireland. Next would come additional lights for the GDAs, and then a mobile reserve to be used for 'dazzle' lighting at selected targets.

The new plans of August 1940 also called for many more guns, both to thicken existing GDAs and to establish new ones, not simply to shoot down aircraft, but also to deter attacking aircraft and bolster civilian morale. Both of these considerations were made explicit in the AA Committee's report, which cited 'the experience of this campaign' as indicating 'that there is a marked difference between the efficiency of enemy attacks when heavy AA gun defences exist and when there is nothing of this nature to deter him'. And these guns would be widespread.

> It is essential [continued the report] that any enemy, who has penetrated the main defences, should be fired upon. The mere presence of a few AA guns will suffice to avoid considerable loss of industrial output and dislocation of normal life.
>
> Broadly speaking, apart from the obvious necessity of reinforcing certain existing defences, the problem is to provide a measure of defence for all communities of any size engaged on industrial work of national importance and to hold a reserve to meet unforeseen requirements and to cover the operations of land forces at home.[64]

Altogether 1512 additional HAA weapons were requested, among which the largest batch – 672 – was assigned to wholly new GDAs. These were numerous. Covering 'all communities of any size' with a role in war industry suddenly qualified a wide scatter of small towns for HAA defences which had never been thought to warrant them before. Redruth entered the list, for example, where the ICI interest was thought to justify eight HAA guns; so too did Mold, and for the same reason. Other towns promoted to the notional front line included Stafford, Fishguard, Selby and Reading. Not all places on the list were quite so surprising. Doncaster was listed for twelve guns on the grounds of its railway facilities and industry, Hereford for the same number to protect shell-filling works and the Royal Ordnance factory; and a pool of 104 guns was allocated to thirteen Lancashire towns supporting a range of industries. No town was allocated fewer than eight guns, while many would have twelve, a few sixteen, and Chester le Street, exclusively, was allocated 24 to protect its ordnance factories and oxygen plant. Beyond these distributions to new GDAs, 496 guns were proposed for defences already authorised, 272 for aerodromes and 72 to form a mobile reserve. Ideally, however, this last group would not be the only mobile guns. With some optimism the Committee recommended that half the new weapons should be supplied with these mountings, though they conceded that a greater proportion of statics could be accepted if a 'marked increase in the rate of production' would result; in that case additional transport vehicles would be needed, as well as extra holdfasts to build static sites, in line with the policy Pile had formulated in June. LAA weapons, too, were demanded in huge numbers. Currently standing at 1860 barrels to cover about 300 authorised VPs, the requirement was now increased by 2550 guns – Bofors were proposed – to cover a further 425 VPs with six weapons apiece, making 4410 in all. In the week that this study was issued the number of Bofors actually held by AA Command was 430.[65]

To a large extent, of course, these plans were a fantasy. At no stage in the war did AA Command muster the 3744 heavy anti-aircraft guns which the scheme implied, nor the 4410 Bofors. Though these increases were formally approved on 10 October,[66] the target was later trimmed and many of the proposed new GDAs were never formed (though others were created to meet emerging needs). But true to the spirit in which the pre-war Ideal Scheme had been conceived, by 1940 the habit in higher-level AA planning was first to define *desiderata* evolved from logical and explicit principles (partly to stake a claim upon manufacturing resources) and only secondarily to consider their practical attainment. No timetable was proposed for acquiring this huge stock of weapons, though clearly it would take years; the August 1940 plan was a long-term conception, paradoxically born of immediate needs. In formulating it, the AA Committee was working on the (unstated) assumption that the Germans would fail in their current air campaign, but that once they had done so the strategic situation would persist. The plan as drafted was really a blueprint for the AA defences necessary to fight a Battle of Britain in about 1944 or 1945.

But the plan did include one element intended to close the gap in HAA and LAA cover on a rather shorter timetable. This was a newly-defined requirement for large numbers of rocket projectors, the weapons upon which Alwyn Crow had begun work as long ago as 1936. Rocket research had advanced in recent years, and by mid July 1940 the single-barrelled 'UP projector' – the simplest of what would become an increasing complex family of weapons – was poised for production.[67] A month later some

8000 UP projectors of 3in type had already been ordered – 5000 single-barrelled, the remainder twins – in the expectation that they would do something to eke out the stocks of modern LAA. The decision made in August was to supplement these with a number of much larger 24-barrel projectors to act as substitute HAA weapons. Though no one could yet be sure how soon to expect even the simpler single- and double-barrelled LAA surrogates – research on which was yet incomplete – the commitment to UP weapons did something to ease anxieties, since these comparatively simple devices were easily manufactured and, once proven in action, could reach the batteries at a much faster rate than conventional guns. An initial consignment of 160 multiple projectors was recommended for AA Command.

Although the AA requirements now defined would never become a reality, they do illustrate how wide a gap had opened between the actual state of the defences in August 1940 and what the latest thinking suggested those defences should be. Expressed simply in numbers, as the Battle of Britain reached its height, AA Command held about a third of the HAA guns which were now thought necessary, and fractionally over one-tenth of the modern LAA. Measured by the pattern of deployment, it is true that this comparison rather exaggerates the shortfall in Pile's resources, since many of the areas newly-recommended for defences would hardly be crucial in the fighting over the coming weeks. (No one could argue, for example, that the absence of HAA cover at Mold or Fishguard much compromised AA Command's lethality in the Battle of Britain.) Yet the raw numbers of weapons probably counted for more; what Pile needed most of all was a large stock of mobile guns which could be shifted around the board to meet the developing pattern of German operations. What he had was an all-too-static layout of partly obsolete ordnance.

These facts put AA Command's modest performance during the high summer of 1940 into perspective. On 16 August, the day that the new study was issued, the Luftwaffe made heavy and wide-ranging attacks on airfields, striking fighter stations at West Malling and Tangmere – where serious damage resulted – and several aerodromes of Coastal and Bomber Commands.[68] Bombing elsewhere in the south-east reached the fringes of south London, but of approximately 1700 sorties flown by the Luftwaffe, only nine aircraft were claimed destroyed by AA guns (five by the Solent GDA, and two each by Dover and Thames & Medway) from overall German losses for this 24-hour period later confirmed as 45.[69] Despite widespread activity during the night, just one raider was claimed, again by the Solent guns, in a searchlight-illuminated engagement.[70] The next day was quieter. Only the Thames & Medway guns were in action (without result), while on the night of the 17th/18th sporadic AA fire was heard among GDAs covering Cardiff, Bristol, Birmingham and the Mersey. The 18th, however, brought renewed onslaughts against airfields – Kenley was especially hard hit, in a raid which saw the London guns in action for the second time – as well as the balloon barrage at Portsmouth, which was noticeably thinned as a result. This was the gunners' best day of the battle so far. Thirty aircraft were destroyed, some by Lewis guns at scarchlight sites, whose 'hosepipe' fire was beginning to prove deadlier than many had expected. Lewis guns at Cardiff downed another aircraft early in the morning of the 19th, at the end of a night which had also seen AA in action at Portland, Bristol, Sheffield and the Humber.[71] In all, the Germans lost 71 aircraft to the defences in this 24-hour period.[72]

August 19th marked the start of a five-day lull in the Germans' campaign, as Göring took stock and the Luftwaffe prepared for the significant change in tactics which would characterise their offensive's next phase. AA activity in this period was accordingly thin. The guns were in action on every day and every night except 21/22 August, though the Falmouth GDA alone opened up on the preceding night and few engagements anywhere were lengthy or intense. In all, just nine victims were claimed by AA Command before the fight thickened again on 24 August. Airfields continued to be harassed in these days, if less sharply than before – three of the claims were Bf 109s operating against Manston and Hawkinge in the late afternoon of the 22nd – while coastal GDAs were again busier than those inland. It was one such, on the Tyne, where Lewis gunners chalked up another victory on the 22nd, this time against a Ju 88.[73]

The change in German tactics which followed two days later in some ways conspired against AA Command. Now, in order to destroy as many Hurricanes and Spitfires as possible, Göring lowered the proportion of bombers in his own formations – and eased the intensity of ground attacks – in the hope of stage-managing clashes between the fighter arms of the two air forces. Ironically, this tactic on the Germans' part coincided with a directive to Fighter Command's 11 Group that pilots should henceforth concentrate on engaging incoming bombers. At the same time the principal airfields of the RAF's air defence sectors – the sector stations – were to be more vigorously protected by fighters. The result from the fliers' point of view was that Göring was attempting to lure the RAF into the very type of combat which it was explicitly trying to avoid. To the gunners on the ground, the change in tactics simply meant that fewer bombers – better targets than the small, agile fighters – offered themselves to their sights.

Daylight raiding on 24 August saw the Luftwaffe in action chiefly in the Thames Estuary, at Dover, the Solent and over the Bristol Channel. Concentrated attacks were brought to bear at Manston aerodrome (twice) and at North Weald, as a result of which the first was finally evacuated and reduced to an emergency landing ground, to the general relief of all who worked there. Even the stiffest AA defences in the country could not compensate for Manston's innate vulnerability, and on this day the guns of the major GDAs did more damage to the attacking formations than did those protecting the airfields. Dover's gunners downed six aircraft on this day and those of Thames & Medway three, while another was claimed by guns on the Solent, where a major raid fell on Portsmouth dockyard, unfortunately little troubled by Fighter Command. The London guns were also in action again against a raid targeted on Hornchurch, when four IAZ positions at ZS1 (Slade's Green), ZS3 (Plumstead Marshes), ZE2 (Barking Park) and ZE1 (Chadwell Heath) did far more for the protection of the airfield than its own local guns, breaking up a formation of about 40 He 111s escorted by Bf 109s, claiming three destroyed and winning from one of the captured crews the shaken accolade that the AA fire was 'the most accurate they had ever encountered'.[74] The night of the 24th/25th then brought raids as far apart as the Tyneside, the Humber, Cardiff – whose guns fought 'numerous engagements', none of them conclusive – and London, where bombs were scattered widely across the suburbs and also, for the first time, fell in the City itself. Fires were started in London Wall and Fore Street, while around 100 people were made homeless in Bethnal Green.

On the night of 24/25 August London's first heavy night raids lay only a fortnight away, but these first bombs in the heart of the capital were, famously, a mistake on the Luftwaffe's part, and one whose effect on the course of the battle could not at first be foreseen.[75] In fact the crews who had bombed London had become lost; sent to attack industrial targets further down-river, these aircraft had strayed inadvertently over central London, jettisoned their bombs, and turned for home. They were not engaged by the IAZ's guns – which had been rumbling only spasmodically so far – but the raid was answered more fully on the following night, when under War Cabinet authority Bomber Command left its calling card at Berlin. The small force of Hampdens and Wellingtons which made this epic journey deep into Germany did little harm. Few of their bombs struck the city (two people were slightly injured and a suburban Berliner lost his timber summer-house),[76] but Reich pride was outraged, and Göring was personally embarrassed by an intrusion which, by his earlier vows, should never have occurred. Historians today generally agree that the Luftwaffe's deliberate turn upon London a fortnight after this incident was on the cards in any case; but the exchange of explosive between capitals in the last week of August did bring the London Blitz a stage nearer.

The distribution of AA Command's heavy guns in the last week of August, as the new phase began, differed from that of early June only in localised areas. Reinforcements had been given to towns and cities with key industries (especially aircraft factories), with the result that Derby, Birmingham, Langley and Brockworth each fielded respectable numbers of weapons – Birmingham, for example, had 71 guns (half of them 3.7in mobiles), as against the 31 which had been in place ten weeks before (Appendix II). Other beneficiaries included the western ports, among which Cardiff, Newport and Swansea were now heavily gunned, along with Plymouth and, to a lesser extent, Portland and Falmouth (though Weymouth, Fowey and Poole still lacked heavy weapons). Some of these targets had already been in the firing line, as we have seen, and several were so again on

25 August, when AA fire was dispatched from GDAs at Portland, Holton Heath, Plymouth and Pembroke. A major raid on this day was directed at RAF Warmwell, where neither fighters nor AA guns could prevent sharp damage to the station, though seven raiders in total were destroyed by the guns there and at Portland and Holton Heath. Birmingham's heavy reinforcement was justified by the action of the following night, when it and neighbouring Coventry were attacked by a force of around 50 bombers intent on the aircraft factories. That no raiders were destroyed was, perhaps, a worrying portent for the London Blitz, likewise the absence of success elsewhere in another night of scattered raiding in which the Cardiff guns bore the brunt of the action. Low cloud across much of Britain on the night of the 25th/26th certainly hampered the gunners, and equally exposed their abiding weakness against the unseen targets which would soon crowd the night skies over London.

Folkestone and Dymchurch collected some bombs on the morning of 26 August, before a large raid developed against RAF Debden in the afternoon. Here the LAA gunners scored, claiming two aircraft destroyed, while a third was downed by their colleagues at Eastchurch. Gunfire here was directed at a force heading for Hornchurch and North Weald, which was effectively broken up by Fighter Command, whose pilots also managed to neutralise a raid on Portsmouth with some help from the Solent GDA. The Dover guns, as so often in these weeks, dealt with several raiders crossing the coast, downing two Bf 109 fighters and a Dornier with HAA fire. In all, 41 German aircraft were destroyed during this day, on which the Portsmouth raid would be Luftflotte 3's last major daylight operation for some weeks; but of these the gunners could claim just six.

In the last days of August the steady daylight attrition against airfields continued, but a pattern of substantial raiding was also now developing against urban targets at night. Birmingham was hit again on several nights in the last week of August,[77] before a more concerted campaign was launched against Liverpool by crews of Luftflotte 3, who had been briefed to prepare for these operations during the lull in raiding which had ended on the 24th. Lasting for four nights between 28 and 31 August, the Liverpool campaign prefigured the looming London Blitz, and advertised many of the problems which the IAZ would confront in the weeks that followed. For Liverpool's gunners the first raid, on 28/29 August, began at 22.23, when they were ordered to take post, and continued for five hours, during which a two-phase attack developed, first on Warrington and latterly on the Wirral and Liverpool itself. By later standards this high-level raid could not be counted as heavy. Estimates put the number of bombs falling at no more than 50 high explosive (HE), plus incendiaries, which complete cover by low cloud caused to fall more or less indiscriminately. But the cloud cover was one factor which denied the gunners of 33 AA Brigade any purchase on their assailants. Searchlights were exposed but at no stage illuminated an enemy aircraft and probably did more to mark the target than defend it. In these circumstances fire was opened, periodically, on geographic barrages – Ashmore's technique against the Gothas – between one and five sites sporadically launching up to 60 rounds in prearranged concentrations. Subsequent analysis of the raid described the effect of these barrages as 'not known', though it was 'considered that they acted as a deterrent to enemy aircraft'. At the same time, 'numerous targets' were plotted by the gunsites' GL radars;[78] but none of these contacts allowed an aimed engagement against a specific target.

The raid on 28/29 August was typical of what Liverpool faced in the following nights, though the defenders' tactics varied. On this night, when raiders between 10,000 and 20,000 feet arrived as a thin but steady stream for four hours, searchlights were kept dark and the city's defence relied entirely on barrage firing cued by warnings from the GL sets. Again, something was achieved by this, the intermittent bursts of AA fire 'so puzzling the enemy aircraft that bomb dropping became indiscriminate'.[79] But however puzzled they may have been, none of the raiders was shot down. Nor were they on the next night, when the docks again appear to have been the target but only the lock gates at Toxteth were damaged, along with some housing.[80] GL-cued barrages were used again on this occasion, but on the next day, 31 August, the raiders' arrival at dusk caught 33 AA Brigade with its radars switched off, for the sets in Liverpool were not normally manned until half an hour after sunset. So at first this was a visual battle. Warning of the raiders' approach came from site M at Seaforth at 20.14, after which sites J (Bidston) and C (Lower Breck Park) opened up at the small force of six aircraft which approached the docks separately from the north and west between 8000 and 20,000 feet. Unscathed, these aircraft started a fierce blaze which largely consumed the Custom House and – as such fires often would – marked the city for the later waves of raiders which arrived after dark. Despite this vivid visual marker, however, these aircraft delivered a haphazard attack, which was again met with GL-directed barrages. None was shot down, but doubtless their crews were again 'puzzled'.

Liverpool was not the only city to be raided in these weeks. Even as the Merseyside operations were in progress, HAA batteries were in operation at Bristol, Birmingham, Cardiff, Plymouth and other places. And by early September, as the London Blitz drew nearer, AA Command was already able to assess its strengths and weaknesses in a campaign whose character was about to undergo a fundamental change. For the staff of 6 AA Division, who had bore the brunt of the day fighting in the south-east, the 'outstanding lesson' of the Battle of Britain was the vindication of the control and warning organisation, which 'stood the severe test with amazing resilience and adaptability'.[81] Despite the periodic disruption of the radar chain, the system as a whole had held up well and continued to provide GDAs and VPs with the warning they needed to get their guns into action, and to avoid too many engagements of friendly aircraft. When the action was opened, on the other hand, weaknesses were too often evident. The Bofors guns, certainly, had done well and amply justified the decision to order them before the war; but LAA performance overall was weaker than expected, in part though the poor standard of training among the light gun crews, especially in the early stages of the campaign, and partly too because there were simply not enough guns to go around. The crews' inexperience was inevitable, given that LAA defence, if not quite an afterthought in Britain's pre-war preparations, was still very much a latecomer. But while their numbers grew more rapidly than any other weapon type in AA Command's hands during the Battle of Britain, Bofors were still in desperately short supply, reaching only 474 by the last week in September and 535 a month later (Appendix II), a period moreover in which the 3in LAA types and 2pdr naval guns were gradually being withdrawn. In those circumstances it was as well that the stop-gap Lewis guns actually performed much better than anyone expected during the Battle of Britain. Ten aircraft were downed by these weapons on just one day (18 August), though the fact that more than 7300 were deployed puts that achievement in some perspective. And there were other lessons to be digested at Stanmore as the intense day fighting drew to its close. One was the effectiveness of HAA fire against close formations during the day, when accurate engagement of the lead aircraft would often provoke their followers to turn about and flee. Another, as the Great War had led everyone to expect, was the ability of HAA fire to break formations and enable the fighters to tangle with the resultant scatter – fighters which had often been drawn to the formation by the AA shell-bursts – and to force the bombers higher, with a resultant loss in accuracy of aim. All of these achievements were as valuable a contribution to the day fighting of the Battle of Britain as the raw numbers of aircraft downed by the guns. At night, on the other hand, the picture was very different, as the experience over Liverpool in particular was beginning to show. Whatever its contribution to the day fighting, in September 1940 AA Command was still largely foxed by the night raider. That would be the challenge of the months to come.

CHAPTER 6

London nights

SEPTEMBER – NOVEMBER 1940

On the afternoon of Saturday 7 September the Luftwaffe finally turned to London. At six minutes to five batteries across the capital received word of 'many hostiles in SE coming in'.[1] Minutes later they appeared. Shortly after the hour the gunners of 26 AA Brigade in the eastern IAZ began to report heavy formations approaching along the Thames and swinging north up the Lea Valley. Lowest were the bombers, which approached in small 'vics' of three aircraft each, these in turn combining into arrowhead formations of ten to fifty machines. High above was their escort – Bf 110s, and 109s with vivid yellow-painted noses – giving standing cover and periodically orbiting the slower Heinkels, Dorniers and Junkers 88s below. Rising upward from 16,000 feet, the whole stream stood more than a mile high.

At these altitudes the raiders were at least within range of the 3.7in and 4.5in weapons which equipped most of the occupied gunsites in the IAZ. The first London AA battery to claim a victim during this inaugural raid of the Blitz was ZE21 on Hackney Marshes, which engaged for three minutes between 17.01 and 17.04, chalking up an early victory which may have been shared with a fighter. A few minutes later a Ju 88 was winged by the 4.5s of ZE1 at Chadwell Heath.[2] On this fine and reasonably clear day batteries all over east London soon brought their weapons to bear. One by one they opened up, and in the next hour eighteen sites engaged – two thirds of those equipped with guns – including all of those flanking the Thames down-river from docklands, which soon emerged as the target of the attack. At first the gunners had the sky largely to themselves. Most of 11 Group's fighters were late on the scene, partly because on this first day of the Blitz they were still guarding the sector airfields, and in part, too, because the raid came in three waves and its full weight was not immediately clear. When the last hostile aircraft left around six o'clock – by now harried by Fighter Command – huge fires were blazing at Thameshaven, in the dock areas near Tower Bridge, at Woolwich Arsenal, and further down river among the oil depots and factories. A later assessment found that more than 300 bombers had taken part in this opening day raid, escorted by twice as many fighters. The IAZ's gunners were credited with twelve aircraft destroyed for the expenditure of a little over 1000 rounds of HAA ammunition, while their colleagues in the Thames & Medway GDA were awarded seven. But both estimates were probably optimistic.

The fires lit in the late afternoon raid served as aiming marks for London's first heavy night attack, which developed within three hours. Crossing the coast near Beachy Head, the leaders of this 250-strong force reached the capital at around 20.30, when searchlights suddenly found difficulty in holding contact with aircraft which seemed to be working singly and 'flying apparently in all directions'.[3] Fire was opened at 21.06, after which a steady stream of raiders entered the IAZ from the south-east. The first engagements were visual, but at 22.08 permission came from 11 Group to activate the Fixed Azimuth system for the first time. One raider seemed to fall almost immediately, as three sites opened up with nine HAA rounds on the FA lines, but in all only 42 shots were fired by this method before the procedure was suspended a little before two AM. Sites firing on radar and VIE did little better, managing a night's work of only 121 rounds. From these, ZS2 at Dartford Heath claimed an aircraft destroyed at 23.13; this machine hit the Thames in front of the Royal Hotel at Purfleet, near VP139 at Erith, where Mortimer Wheeler's men of 42 LAA Regiment hauled a body from the water three hours later.

Shortly before the raid began troops in London and elsewhere had received the codeword *Cromwell*, advertising the Chiefs of Staffs' belief that invasion might be imminent. Issued at 20.07 on the evening of the 7th, the *Cromwell* signal was prompted less by the Luftwaffe's sudden turn upon London than by reports of intensifying invasion preparations across the Channel, combined with the approach of a moon and tide favourable to a crossing.[4] Despite being carefully briefed on its exact meaning, many troops in Britain misunderstood the *Cromwell* signal as signifying that the invasion had actually begun. The AA gunners in London were no exception, and with their susceptibilities heightened by the raid then in progress, shortly after one in the morning a rumour that the Wehrmacht had landed flashed across the batteries of 1 AA Division, introducing what one regimental commander described as 'unnecessary confusion' at the height of the raid.[5] As this bogus news circulated, the gunners were being reminded that their own sites were as much in the firing line as the tenements of the East End, where the blows were falling hardest. At a quarter to two ZE1 at Chadwell Heath lost its canteen and billets to an incendiary bomb. More serious damage was sustained at ZE8, on the broad loop of the Isle of Dogs, where high explosive blasts ringing the battery severed communications and destroyed the site's access road. Caught in the eye of this particular storm, 154 HAA Battery kept their 4.5s firing throughout the raid, so winning a commendation capped only by that awarded to their GPO, Captain W J S Fletcher. For maintaining fire amid the chaos of the attack, for steadying his men – many of them novices and some arrived at this, their first posting, that very evening – and for venturing into nearby streets to tackle fires and unexploded bombs, Fletcher was awarded the Military Cross.[6]

Individual acts of heroism aside, however, no one could pretend that this overture to the night Blitz was AA Command's finest hour. Most guns had come into action late, radar had proved of little use, and the debut of the Fixed Azimuth network had been a huge disappointment. Of the 185 rounds expended by sites in 26 AA Brigade, for example, only 24 were fired on FA procedures. As early as 7 September it seemed that the Fixed Azimuth system might fail.

Cromwell conditions certainly gave an edge to the fighting in the early part of the Blitz, though when no invasion materialised the alert was relaxed after twelve days. But the concentrated air campaign against London which had now begun was sustained for nine weeks. This was AA Command's first true battle of the war – the long-awaited test of everything done for London's defence since the Reorientation Committee first gathered at Whitehall Gardens in autumn 1934.

On the home front the *de facto* commanders of the AA defences were of course General Pile, and above him Dowding at Fighter Command; and it was Pile in particular who made many of the key tactical decisions on how London's AA defences would work in the following weeks. The field commander of the London guns was the head of 1 AA Division, Major-General F L N Crossman, who at the start of the Blitz commanded seven regiments of HAA, three of light guns and four of searchlights, these to defend the IAZ itself, the separate GDAs at Slough and Stanmore, and a layout of VPs reaching into the fringes of the Home Counties.[7] It was little more than a skeleton force, since by early September 1940 the IAZ contained a mere residue of the armament which had been in place to meet the knock-out blow a year earlier (Fig 19). In those days London had mustered 139 HAA guns – far fewer, certainly, than the approved scale of 288 laid down in May 1939, but a solid basis for growth. But London's guns had soon begun to trickle away, as AA Command was repeatedly obliged to modify pre-war plans to meet extraneous commitments else-where. By early September 1940 the IAZ's defences had slumped to 92 HAA guns, only four more than at Scapa.[8] It was exactly the situation which Pile had feared when, the previous autumn, the Admiralty had made such heavy claims for their anchorages. True, London's remaining guns were good guns – 48 were 4.5in types, while 32 were 3.7in statics and a further six were mobile 3.7s; by early September the IAZ had only six antiquated 3in pieces – but they were still thin on the ground. Simply, London on 7 September had only one third of the HAA due to it under pre-war plans. Only ten sites in the IAZ had GL radars.[9] The sudden turn of events had the makings of a crisis.

Crossman's forces in 1 AA Division were organised into four AA brigades at the start of the Blitz, among which 49 AA Brigade controlled the guns at Slough and Stanmore and 38 AA Brigade took charge of the divisional searchlight layout. The guns in the IAZ itself were shared between 26 and 48 AA Brigades, who now became the front-line artillery formations for the London Blitz. Of the 65 gunsites established in the IAZ by this date, just 27 were actually occupied and gunned in the first week of September

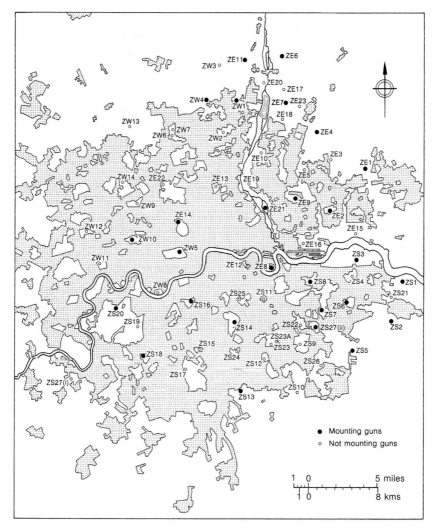

Figure 19 Guns in the London IAZ, Wednesday, 28 August 1940. Pictured ten days before London's first heavy raid on 7 September, the IAZ at this date included many vacant sites in a gun layout whose weight lay firmly toward the south and east. This map and the two succeeding are based upon 1 AA Division's location statements for the dates concerned.

1940 (and some of them only partially), in a layout whose weight showed some bias towards the east and south of the capital at the expense of the north-west. Practically all of these sites were pre-war positions built for the fixed guns which dominated London's weapon stock at this time, though some were structurally unfinished in the first week of September – command posts had

not everywhere been built, many sites lacked domestic accommodation, and by now, many sites were being furnished with
newly-built magazines of concrete[10] – in part because the
engineering staffs in London had for some months been working
on the emergency anti-invasion defences which were turning the
capital into a tank-proof fortress. Those guns which were in place
were shared about equally between the two brigades. North of the
river the seven batteries (in two regiments) of Brigadier R F E
Whittaker's 26 AA Brigade occupied twelve sites from Barking
westward to Primrose Hill, on the northern fringes of Regent's
Park, generally the positions with ZE prefixes but also including
ZW1 at Enfield and ZW4 at Chase Side toward the northern limits
of the layout. The remainder of the IAZ's heavy guns came under
Brigadier H C Murgatroyd's 48 AA Brigade, whose three
regiments manned fifteen sites in the ZW and ZS series.
Murgatroyd's regiments were more widely disposed than Whittaker's,
with positions lying in a broad swathe from north London to the
eastern approaches of the Thames around Dartford. At the start
of the Blitz the sole LAA unit operating within the IAZ was
Wheeler's 42 LAA Regiment, which came under 26 AA Brigade. If
anything these men were more poorly equipped than their
counterparts on heavies. Most of the 36 Bofors in 1 AA Division
were with 49 AA Brigade around Stanmore, and at the start of the
Blitz Wheeler's men were still working largely with Lewis guns.[11]
But the London balloon barrage was expected to deter low-flying
raiders, so the armed VPs were mostly on the margins – armaments factories at Waltham Abbey in Essex, the Brimsdown
power station, the Handley Page works at Hatfield, and Radlett.

The guns of the IAZ were not, of course, the only ground
weapons to play a part in the Blitz. The neighbouring 1 AA
Division GDAs at Slough and Stanmore were often in action, as
too were the guns in positions which intercepted the raiders' lines
of approach – Portsmouth, Southampton, Dover, and particularly
the Thames & Medway, which in early September had 120 HAA
weapons (72 short of the pre-war allotment, a proportionally
smaller deficit than in London itself). But the London guns were
always the front line, in a struggle not simply to destroy enemy
aircraft, but also to loosen formations, to deter attacking crews
and, crucially, to brace the civil population by showing that their

city was actively fighting back. The psychological dimension of this battle would never be far from Pile's thoughts.

For the first few nights none of these objectives was met. Though lighter than their opening salvo on the 7th, the Luftwaffe's operation of 8/9 September put 171 bombers over the capital in a continual stream from eight in the evening until five the following morning. The defences came alive at 20.03, when ZE8 on the Isle of Dogs – still ringed by debris from the previous night – punched twelve rounds at a pair of Do 17s moving south-west at about 19,000 feet. Despite cloud cover, several contacts were made by searchlights early in the raid, enabling sixteen sites to engage visually. Their first victim was claimed to have fallen south-west of Purley at 20.32, just as 11 Group gave permission to engage unseen targets by Fixed Azimuth or radar, but all fire was suspended an hour later when word was received that friendly fighters were entering the IAZ. Clearance to fire was not restored until 01.13, though several further suspensions were imposed later in the night in the northern IAZ, silencing the guns in many areas for long periods. The gunners' frustration was deepened when several of their own batteries suffered near misses from bombs. HEs fell uncomfortably close to ZE21 on Hackney Marshes and at ZE9, a couple of miles to the east at Wanstead, while to the south ZS14 at Dulwich collected a scatter of incendiaries. Fletcher's men at ZE8 on the Isle of Dogs were again in the thick of things, when for a time a fire raging at Millwall threatened to engulf their position. And these gunsite incidents reflected the general pattern of attacks, which by five in the morning had left fires burning from Kensington and Fulham, across the West End and the City into docklands. Long stretches of Southampton Row, Oxford Street and Theobalds Road were cordoned off because of unexploded bombs – each potentially a 'D/A', fused for delayed action – and 'major damage' was reported in Finsbury. Although the gunners believed that some raiders had attempted to target military objectives – railways, docks, factories and power stations – much of the bombing had been through a layer of cloud and was effectively 'indiscriminate'.[12]

Twelve hours later the raiders returned. On 9 September there was a brief flurry of activity in the late afternoon as a force estimated at '60+' bombers and fighters pierced the IAZ from the south-west.[13] At 17.52 the attackers were engaged by ZS27, a long-stop to the London layout at Weston Green, before the formation broke up and its members followed independent courses eastward across the capital. In a few minutes from 17.53 four sites engaged small packets or single aircraft, and it is by their reports that the progress of such raids can be traced. First into action was ZS20 in Richmond Park, which fired on the breaking formation of 30 Ju 88s; next to fire was ZE14 at Primrose Hill; then ZE8 on the Isle of Dogs (where Fletcher's men last saw their damaged prey losing height under the guns of a Spitfire); and finally ZS5 out to the far south-east at St Paul's Cray, which at 17.57 sent a few rounds toward a lame Heinkel exiting the IAZ at 5000 feet. All but the last of these batteries thought they had hit their targets, and the first two went as far as to report that the aircraft had been destroyed by AA fire. Typically, however, these claims were almost certainly exaggerated: fighters were operating in force during the raid and duplicate claims from AA batteries and aircraft were a common – and excusable – source of inflated estimates. Much of the damage had probably been inflicted in the dogfights which the gunners had witnessed over Hayes and Bromley before their batteries opened fire.

The late afternoon raid on 9 September lasted less than fifteen minutes, and was over by six o'clock. The evening's proceedings proper began three hours later, when single aircraft began to penetrate the IAZ from the south. No gun opened up until 22.17, though once the raid was established firing was sporadic until around 04.30 the following morning, latterly to meet raiders approaching across the Essex fringes of the Thames Estuary. Nineteen gunsites were in action on this night, switching frantically between visual, radar-controlled and Fixed Azimuth shooting to discharge 705 rounds in all. Gunners at ZE8 on the Isle of Dogs narrowly escaped injury for the third time when a near miss severed their newly-restored telephone lines and wrecked their transport. Three aircraft were 'confidently claimed' as destroyed in the final two hours of the raid, by ZS2 at Dartford Heath, ZE9 at Wanstead and ZE21 on Hackney Marshes.

Whatever confidence may have attached to those claims, however, in truth the AA defences were turning in a pitiful performance for a system which, more than any other objective, had been planned in the previous five years specifically to defend London. There were many justifications, but none to give Pile comfort. Frequent cease-fires to open the IAZ for fighters was one; another was the limitations of the Fixed Azimuth system, which the Germans seemed to be defeating by throttling back to begin their bombing runs in a mute glide (they were later heard to do so on reaching the locator lines). The capricious jumble of electronics which made up the early GL sets offered little help, and anyway fewer than half the gunsites had them. At the start of the Blitz these factors together probably weakened London's AA defences far more than the simple deficit in guns. No amount of weaponry, after all, would serve when fire was prohibited and the batteries were practically blind.

The gun shortage was, however, the easiest to remedy. Pile had taken steps to reinforce London's guns on the morning of the 8th, when AA Command's national gun stock was scrutinised to see where 3.7in mobiles could be liberated for the deepening battle. Within hours batteries in GDAs throughout the country were receiving orders to up camp and hurry to the capital. Some appeared next day. First on the scene were three batteries of 1 HAA Regiment, who brought their 3.7in mobile guns to occupy six sites in the 26 AA Brigade area and close the gap in the gun layout on the north-west.[14] These were followed during the night of 9/10 September by 12 and 22 HAA Batteries, arriving from Southampton and Birmingham, who were posted in to 48 AA Brigade and set up their 3.7in mobiles on four sites in the south London suburbs, so thickening up the front toward the Luftwaffe's southern approaches.[15] By the late afternoon of Tuesday 10 September the newly-arrived batteries had pushed the occupied gun positions up to 35.

Sporadic activity by enemy aircraft was breaking overhead as the new arrivals were settling in. A few minutes before one in the afternoon a lone Do 215 entered the IAZ from the south-east under partial cloud cover and attempted to machine-gun the barrage balloons over Hyde Park; and shortly before half past five a second solitary intruder came under fire from six batteries in the Dartford–Bexley area.[16] None of the new guns fired in these incidents, however, and nor did they in the night raid which followed a little after eight o'clock.[17] London's fourth consecutive

large underground shelters. Many expressions of bitterness at apparent impossibility of stopping German raiders doing what they like and opinion that Anti-Aircraft gunfire is astonishingly small. This latter point is bewildering and frightening more people than anything else. [. . .][22]

Doubtless some of those elderly women in the East End remembered the Gothas, as perhaps their menfolk – who were elsewhere in 1917–18 – did not. And after the next night of raiding public anxiety as gauged by the ministry deepened further. By the morning of 10 September serious 'trekking' had begun, as the homeless and acutely fearful left for sanctuary in London's rural fringes and further afield. 'Increased tension' was reported everywhere in central London, such that 'when siren goes people run madly for shelter with white faces.' Living conditions in the East End were described as 'almost impossible', with a 'great feeling in dockside areas of living on island surrounded by fire and destruction'. By this time public air-raid shelters in some districts were beginning to be used less as temporary refuges, but as permanent homes, from which shelterers ventured forth only as necessary, inverting the cycle of occupancy for which they had been designed. In a determined but orderly outbreak of civil disobedience, Londoners were also beginning to occupy the Tube stations, substitutes for the deep shelters which government had declined to provide in the years before the war. Inevitably, some people cast about them for scape-goats, found readily in London's Jewish minority – accusations of selfishness were widespread – and bizarrely, if less grotesquely, in the work of the AA searchlights, which some believed to be used by Fifth Columnists to guide the Luftwaffe (a myth which for some reason seized imaginations in Woolwich and Eltham). And again, surveys on 10 September found deepening discontent with AA Command. 'Dismay and wonder at apparent inadequacy of London defences' was reported from 'most districts', especially the East End.[23]

By now Pile, too, was thinking about public opinion, and about the baleful performance of his gunners so far. By his own account he lay awake at night, disturbed less by the noise from his own guns than by their silence, and becoming, as he later wrote, 'both angry and frightened at the same time'.[24] Explaining why his guns were doing so little was simple enough: many technical factors could be adduced to exonerate the gunners from blame. But none counted for anything in the face of widening destruction and growing discontent.

It is a mark of distinction in a military commander to make bold and risky decisions when the occasion demands. Pile made his on 11 September. Crowding his entire London staff together in the Drill Hall at Brompton Road – every GPO, battery commander, and head of brigade – Pile explained that in the coming night's raid the London guns would cease to fret about aiming their rounds accurately, and simply fire. No searchlights would expose, and no fighters would operate in the IAZ. The GOR at Brompton Road would broadcast the incoming raiders' approximate altitude to the batteries, where those equipped with GL sets and VIE equipment would rediffuse the more accurate heights obtained from their instruments to neighbouring sites. But every GPO was instructed 'if in doubt to fire', throwing as many rounds as possible into the sky somewhere near the target to ape Ashmore's 'barrage' technique of September 1917, some 23 years earlier almost to the day. The object, Pile told his men, was less to shoot down aircraft than 'to put up a lot of bursts to worry the enemy and hearten the civil population'.[25] Pile never concealed that this second London 'barrage' was a 'policy of despair' (and neither did he conceal that the tactic, in the technical language of artillery, was no 'barrage' at all).[26] But possibly Pile was too hard on himself. For the first four nights of the Blitz his command had signally failed to do any of the things which AA fire was supposed to; but if this new tactic did succeed in intimidating the Luftwaffe and bracing the Londoner, then two of its goals would be met.

It did both. On the night of 11/12 September the 35 gunsites occupied in the IAZ launched a total of 13,221 rounds of HAA ammunition into the sky above London, the average of 378 rounds per site tending to mask the phenomenal density of fire rising from some – the record went to ZS13 at Shirley Park, which fired 805 rounds of 3.7in on that night, while three sites managed to loose off totals in the 600s: thus ZS3 (Plumstead Marshes), ZS5 (St Paul's Cray) and ZS6 (Welling).[27] This fearsome wall of fire told palpably on the Luftwaffe, whose bombers appeared over the capital at 20.05, pushed their bombing heights steadily higher in the course of the night, and were in many instances deterred from entering the IAZ at all. Only one of the raiders was claimed as destroyed (Category I) from a force of 180 aircraft operating;[28] but that mattered less, for the moment, than the stern deterrent effect which prevented serious damage in London on this first night of the barrage, and the boost which Pile's tactics gave to public morale. As their barrels cooled and their guns were boiled out on the morning of the 12th, gunners across London could read their praises sung in the papers; and the observers of the Home Intelligence Division on that day found a new spirit abroad. 'Morale has jumped to a new level of confidence and cheerfulness since tremendous AA barrage,' they reported. 'This is true of every district contacted, including East End and areas badly hit yesterday such as Woolwich and Lewisham. "We'll give them hell now" is a typical working class comment today.'[29] Not everyone was overjoyed, since some of the outlying districts in south London collected many bombs from crews in the act of turning back; but what we speak of today, however simplistically, as the 'Blitz spirit' – the cheerfulness, resilience and mutual supportiveness of Londoners under fire – began to be felt most clearly on the day after the first night barrage, and in this sense could not have arisen without AA Command. The guns, said one, were 'music'.[30]

On that same day, 12 September, Londoners could also see evidence of their defences growing, as the second contingent of reinforcements arrived from GDAs throughout the country. Some came by rail, batteries from Plymouth, Portland, Falmouth and South Wales unloading their guns at Paddington station. Newcomers from the Midlands and the north travelled by road, making rendezvous with guides from 1 AA Division waiting at junctions in the London suburbs. Roundabouts on the Barnet by-pass and at Esher, road junctions at Epping Forest – refuge for many 'trekkers' who had fled the East End – and on the Cambridge road hosted these meetings with units from Crewe, Coventry, Portsmouth, Derby, the Humber and Harwich.[31] Maps were issued and directions given, guiding the new arrivals to gunsites throughout the IAZ. Sixty-eight 3.7in mobiles came in this consignment, including some provided by Royal Marine AA batteries from Plymouth. The lion's share went to 26 AA Brigade, where 44 guns were set up on eleven sites, ten of them previously vacant.[32] The rest went to Murgatroyd's 48 AA Brigade, whose occupied sites now rose to 24.[33] Less than a week into the Blitz the IAZ was transformed (Fig 20). By 13 September just thirteen of the 65 sites remained empty and the number of guns in the capital had reached 199.

At a second conference on 13 September Pile offered congratulations on the 'excellent' results from the barrage. From now on, he explained, unseen fire at night would be unrestricted, and while the gunners were warned not to waste ammunition, the shotgun approach would continue. Next, he explained, 'we wanted to use scientific means to ensure accuracy.'[34] Exactly what these means were was not yet revealed though, as we shall see, by mid September Pile already had the technical problems of unseen-fire control in hand. For the immediate future, VIE locators were issued more plentifully and intensive training was arranged in their use both with and without GL sets.[35]

The turning point in the Blitz marked by the 'barrage' tactics proved timely. After sending a fairly large force on the night of 11/12 September the Luftwaffe appeared for a few days to be cowed. Only 43 raiders were put over London on the following night,[36] causing 'comparatively little damage', while light day raiding under cloud cover on 13 September cost the Luftwaffe one aircraft downed by the IAZ guns for small result.[37] Heavier raiding resumed on the night of 13/14, when 105 aircraft operating over the capital again met a fearsome canopy of fire. On this occasion the IAZ guns were authorised to engage unseen targets after 19.20 hours, while searchlights remained dark until the last hour of the raid. First reports of raiders entering the IAZ came in at a couple of minutes after nine, when ZS16 on Clapham Common opened up with its 4.5s. Thereafter raiders arrived in a steady stream until well after five in the morning. Every gunsite in the IAZ was in action, and by the early morning the 31 positions which had reported back to 1 AA Division's headquarters sent in a tally of 11,874 rounds fired. So again the music played. Deafened as they were, however, come the morning Londoners found more shrapnel from Pile's guns littering the parks and streets than they did enemy aircraft. No claims were

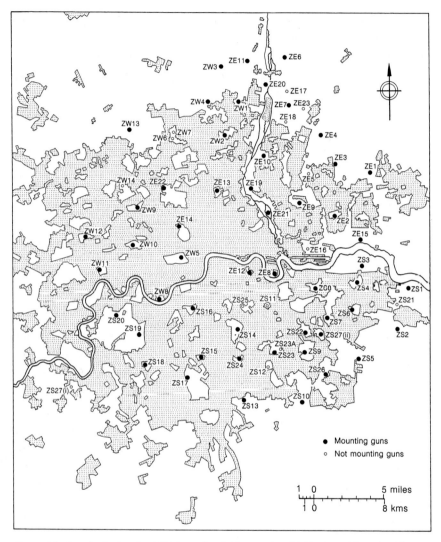

Figure 20 Guns in the London IAZ, Saturday, 14 September 1940. A week into the Blitz many of the IAZ's sites had been hurriedly armed and the gun layout, as well as thickening in the south and east, had been extended in the north and west by gunning many positions in those areas.

confirmed on this night. At around 03.20 one eastbound raider was damaged by ZS3 and ZS4 at Plumstead Marshes and Bostall Heath firing simultaneously, but was last seen by Tilbury police still airborne and struggling homeward. A further Category I claim from ZW11 at Gunnersbury Park could not be confirmed. The intelligence report on this night's events gave almost as much space to suspicious activity on the ground than to AA Command's work in the air.[38] Not for the first time gunsites reported seeing numerous rockets and flares fired during the raid, together with odd flashes of light from buildings. All of these occurrences were confidently attributed to Fifth Columnists and reported, as usual, to the ARP authorities and police. How much credence they deserve is a question. Fires ignited by bombing could themselves yield strange pyrotechnic effects, as volatile substances were consumed by the flames (flares? rockets?), though the 'Very lights' – one green, two red – seen to rise above the Enfield–Waltham area within twenty minutes of the red warning, and again later in the night, sound credible enough.[39] Equally, however, a report from ZW5 in Hyde Park that a light flashed from the Regal Cinema at a quarter to one, 'just before a Molotoff "Breadbasket" was dropped [. . .]', strains circumstantial evidence to its limit.

On 14 September London was again raided during the day, temporarily interrupting supplies from the Battersea power station and leaving the nearby gasworks in flames.[40] That night brought the Luftwaffe's lightest operation of the Blitz so far: just 38 aircraft operated over the capital, one of which fell to ZE20 at Capel House. Bombing was scattered and 'not serious', though 4141 HAA rounds were fired – five or six times as many as on a typical night before the 'barrage' tactics were introduced, at about one-fifth the number of raiders.[41] But the next day, 15 September, the daylight battle reached its peak, when Göring sent massed bomber formations against London, Portland and the Super-marine's Spitfire works near Southampton. That Sunday famously marked the turning point in Fighter Command's fortunes, and insofar as a single episode could do as much, signalled that the Battle of Britain was lost to the Luftwaffe. At the time, it is true, fantastic claims were made by the defenders. Of the 185 aircraft supposedly downed by the fighters and gunners, the Luftwaffe in fact lost only 60. But the combination of efficient early warning and British fighters operating in concentration put the balance sheet more than two to one in the RAF's favour. Just 26 fighters were lost.

This was not an artillery battle. Gunfire in the IAZ was tightly restricted by the presence of friendly fighters, and in all only nine batteries saw sporadic action in two separate raids which succeeded in reaching the capital in the late morning and mid afternoon. All were in the southern IAZ, where much of the action was shared between just three positions on the south-eastern fringe. First to engage was ZS26 at Thornet Wood, one of the sites newly occupied on 12 September by 'B' Battery of the Royal Marines, which fired on a formation of Ju 88s and Bf 109s at 12.00. ZS26's gunners were in action twice more that afternoon, while their neighbours at ZS5 (St Paul's Cray) and ZS13 over at Shirley Park near Croydon also fired on three occasions in the two raids. With so much fighter activity in the IAZ, the few claims made by the London gunners were impossible to disentangle from those of the RAF. At one point ZS5, ZS13 and ZS26 were all firing on a single Dornier, which was also tackled by a Hurricane before coming down somewhere out to the south-east of Orpington. In all, little more than 200 rounds were fired by the London guns in the two main raids, though a few more were loosed off in the early evening when a solitary Heinkel entered the IAZ at about 8000 feet. The Marines at Thornet Wood opened up with their 3.7in mobiles for the fourth time, and in the five minutes from 19.16 five separate batteries aimed 38 rounds at this single aircraft. It was last seen hurrying south with a trio of fighters in pursuit.

AA guns were busier elsewhere in daylight on the 15th when the Thames & Medway GDA claimed eight victims and Dover one, while many less conclusive engagements were entered into elsewhere.[42] But London became the focus of the action again by night, when a raid warning was in force from 20.09 to 05.36, about 9000 rounds were fired by the gunners and three aircraft were claimed as destroyed.[43] And, from now until 13 November, the Battle of London became almost entirely a night battle. Although enemy aircraft operating singly penetrated the IAZ again on the afternoon of 16 September, attacks in darkness by moderate to large formations became the norm for the remainder of the Blitz, as Londoners settled down to face the steady war of attrition waged against their city. The night of 16/17 September saw 170 aircraft over the capital, which was left with fires burning, once again, in the eastern reaches; 24 hours later the number of raiders reached 268, and the night after – 18/19 September – some 300.[44] The barrage boomed on during these nights. Fixed

Azimuth firing was occasionally activated and the gunners did what they could with their GL sets, but unseen shooting of prodigious volumes of ammunition remained the norm. On the night of 18/19 September, when 46 gunsites were in action almost continuously from 20.08 to 05.00, the expenditure reached 13,000 rounds,[45] and while civilian morale was upheld by this and other expedients, Pile and his gunners knew these tactics could not continue indefinitely. Apart from blasting their way through prodigious quantities of expensive ammunition – Churchill would later cavil at AA Command's consumption of 260,000 rounds in September alone[46] – putting so much explosive into the sky vastly accelerated barrel-wear and, of course, peppered London and its citizens with a generous garnish of debris. Occasionally more delicate procedures were tried – as on 20 September, when a true geographic barrage was set up over Hyde Park to concentrate the fire from Primrose Hill (ZE14), Wormwood Scrubbs (ZW10), Hurlingham (ZW8) and Clapham Common (ZS16) in an area regularly circled by enemy aircraft[47] – but for the most part the shotgun technique continued. Figures collected by Pile's staff proved that the barrage worked as a deterrent, a careful survey of events towards the end of the month showing that no fewer than 48 per cent of the aircraft approaching London were turning back once the guns opened up.[48] But as September 1940 drew to a close the desperate need was to find a means of destroying aircraft more regularly, and with fewer rounds.

Pile's underlying problem was that in many respects the IAZ was scarcely ready for night raiding on the scale it was asked to meet. Gun numbers were deficient, of course, and even the 3.7in mobiles rushed to the capital in the reinforcements of September brought problems of their own. It was no easy matter to emplace these guns. Mobile 3.7s had often to be deployed on sites designed for statics, leaving the gunners a choice between interposing mobiles between the fixed emplacements and improvising gunpits from sandbags – a time-consuming job when there was so much else to do – or somehow marrying the mobiles to the fixed structures. Though in many ways preferable the latter was not an easy option. Mobile guns required a level surface, and the holding-down bolts in the emplacement floor were in the way; the floor itself was rather too resilient for mobile mountings, which were designed for grass or earth. Several solutions were tried by the ingenious CRE of London District, among them fitting timber baulks over the obstructing bolts to carry the gun, scattering a clinker layer over the floor of the fixed emplacement, and a combination of these methods; a fourth solution involved laying sandbags and shingle. In the end the timber baulk method performed best in hurried trials, held mainly at ZW11 (Gunnersbury Park) and ZS7 (Eltham), with the result that 3.7in mobiles came to be immured in fixed emplacements using a mounting not dissimilar to that improvised for Bofors guns in the autumn of 1939.[49] The fact that these lash-up arrangements needed to be made in the height of a battle which had been anticipated for more than five years seems little short of tragic.

Installing the new gun platforms was far from the only engineering job in progress among the AA batteries during the Blitz. As late as September 1940 many London gunsites still lacked full domestic accommodation, a problem which would worsen when guns were concentrated in full batteries of eight later in the battle. Added to that, work was proceeding on sunken magazine buildings to provide secure storage for the sites' ammunition reserves – a facility which it would have been useful to have before the barrage began to consume such vast quantities of shell and cartridge. Begun during the summer, this sizeable project seems to have affected all the permanent sites in London and elsewhere and some of those in the IAZ were being surveyed to select positions for their magazines even as 1 AA Division and the Luftwaffe were exchanging barrage and bombs (structural description of the buildings appears in Chapter 8). The result was that 1 AA Division was fighting the Battle of London from positions which were still, to some extent, construction sites rather than fully-developed HAA batteries. Hut components, cement and timber were continuing to arrive alongside the lorries replenishing ammunition.

But even these difficulties seemed minor compared with 1 AA Division's abiding problem with the technicalities of fire control, which in practical terms meant getting to grips with the GL Mk I.

As supplied from September 1939 onwards these sets, as we have seen, could offer reasonably accurate information on the range and azimuth of a target, functions which were refined from August 1940 by a sub-variant with higher transmitter power and other improvements, known as the GL Mk I* (the 'mark one star').[50] But neither the basic Mk I nor its starred offspring could provide the reading of elevation necessary to locate enemy aircraft in three-dimensional space; as such the GL Mk I was useful for local early-warning, but hardly so in the more demanding work of fire control. In an attempt to fill the elevation gap some sites early in the war tried using their GL sets in conjunction with sound locators, feeding the predictor with radar range and azimuth and acoustically-derived elevation data. For the most part it didn't work, chiefly because none of the data were accurate enough for the predictor to digest them without 'severe internal pains'. By 1940 the Vickers predictor, in its most advanced marks, had been joined in AA Command technical armoury by a newer and still better variant made by the Sperry company. But both were mechanical computers packed with moving parts which needed harmonised, non-contradictory data to work their obscure magic: coined for a later generation of computers, the expression 'rubbish in, rubbish out' applied equally to these. As the instrument tried to reconcile vague and inconsistent readings of changing range, azimuth and elevation, the most that could result was a series of disturbing noises emanating from its mechanism. 'The Sperry voiced its indignation audibly,' recalled one expert, while 'the Vickers suffered in silence.'

So other solutions were needed and one was found in the summer of 1940 with the invention of an 'elevation finding' (E/F) attachment for the Mk I set.[51] Developed by L H Bedford of the Cossor company, the E/F was simply an electronic add-on, an adaptation of the elevation-finding component of the GL Mk II, which was under development in 1940 and entered service in the following spring as a replacement for the Mk I and Mk I*. Up to a point it met the case. Able to measure both azimuth and elevation and displaying its readings on a cathode ray tube, the E/F offered a fair degree of accuracy in the eight- to eighteen-degree range of vertical arc, later pushed with difficulty up to 45 degrees. In all,

410 E/F sets were issued, though experience showed that the accessory 'was more in the nature of a scientific laboratory instrument than a piece of service equipment and it had to be run, to make it work well, at the limit of its sensitivity. There was nothing to spare and it had to be handled with care.'[52] Until the GL Mk II became available, however, it was the best thing on offer.

By the second month of the Blitz many London gunsites were fully equipped with GL Mk Is and E/F attachments, but none was performing well and as the night attacks rumbled on it was clear that Pile, once again, must do the best he could with existing equipment, rather than waiting for whatever the new sets might offer in several months' time. And, although the gunners did not yet know as much, Pile had given his attention to improving their existing radars shortly before the Blitz had begun. In August 1940 the GOC had met with Professor A V Hill to discuss a variety of air defence problems, in the course of which Hill suggested that Pile should recruit a scientist to his own staff to have technical advice immediately to hand. Next day, at Hill's invitation, Pile sat in on a meeting of the Royal Society, at which Professor P M S Blackett, a founder member of the original Tizard committee,

Plate 12 Gunners of 208 HAA Battery at Green Street Green (TS18) in the command post with their Sperry predictor (which appears to be new).

who was then engaged in designing bomb sights at the RAE Farnborough, made a contribution to the proceedings. In Blackett Pile thought he had found his man; and despite some resistance from Hill – who in Pile's account had other plans for the young scientist – Patrick Blackett was soon recruited to AA Command as Scientific Adviser.[53] The depth of Pile's difficulties with radar is reflected by the conditions on which Blackett was engaged. Rather than issue explicit terms of reference – to take a defined problem and work to its solution – Pile instead gave the scientist *carte blanche* to do whatever he could to improve fire-control generally. So Pat Blackett's first job was less to find answers to AA Command's problems than to identify what, exactly, those problems were.

To do this he straightaway recruited two colleagues, and it speaks volumes of the informal milieu in which Blackett was working that neither brought experience in radio or electronics: both in fact were physiologists. D M Hill, son of 'A V', had qualified three years previously and in autumn 1940 held a research post at Cambridge, while his close friend Andrew Huxley was a more recent graduate who had since embarked on medical studies. Under Blackett's tutelage, however, Hill and Huxley soon absorbed the basics of radar theory, and before long all three began visiting operational gunsites around London, along with L H Bedford, father of the E/F attachment, to discover what was going on. The start of this work coincided roughly with the first raids of the Blitz.

What they found was salutary. Blackett and his colleagues discovered what might have been guessed all along: that, in the words of a fellow-scientist soon to join them on Pile's staff, the radar equipment 'was of a nature so complicated as to be beyond the powers of the normal individual to understand'. To make matters worse, the high security classification of the GL's technical manuals prohibited their being kept on the gunsites, precisely where they were most needed. The result was widespread incomprehension, less of what radar was supposed to do, than of how on earth it could be made to do it; and even those few who had mastered radar in an empirical sense soon sank into confused frustration when the sets gave trouble which a modicum of theoretical know-how would have enabled them to resolve. The consequences of their incomprehension occasionally bordered the fantastic; never more so, perhaps, than when a regimental commander ordered the aerials to be removed from his GL set on the grounds that they looked untidy.

In fairness to the hapless custodians of this new gadgetry – and the scientists were keen never to be otherwise – the fault in the autumn of 1940 lay as much with the equipment as its operators, if not more so. Formally stated, Blackett's judgement was that 'there was a serious gap between the research stage of GL equipment and the user stage, and that practically no operator of GL was at that time capable of knowing whether it was working correctly or not'. The equipment had simply been issued prematurely, and the addition of the E/F attachment only made matters worse. The GL and E/F together were really no more compatible with the Vickers and Sperry predictors than the radar had been working with sound locators: the 'internal pains' were just as sharp. Another problem lay in the inconsistent performance of the radar gear, which apart from the defects which may have been built into any one set, was liable to be upset by minor variations in siting. Every individual GL set was slightly different, and each demanded fine tuning to match the peculiarities of its site. For a time this is what Blackett and his fellows spent their nights trying to do.

They succeeded, up to a point, and before long it was clear that GL would only function correctly once each set had a scientist on hand to work what the gunners began to term 'ju-ju'. But Blackett and his two assistants could hardly work all the magic themselves, so by the second week in October feelers were out in the scientific community to find additional members for the team. Word circulated, with the result that senior academics engaged in government work either loaned staff, or put Blackett in touch with former pupils. Six were soon enlisted. Dr A Porter, a mathematician and physicist, came from Manchester University; H E Butler, a Cambridge mathematician then beginning research in astronomy, came via Professor Stratton, his chief; the mathematical physicist F R N Nabarro joined the team from Bristol University, while I Evans, a recent physics graduate from Cardiff, was plucked from a central government register. Another recruit came almost by chance. This was Dr L E Bayliss, a physio-

logist with a teaching post in the medical school at Edinburgh
who in autumn 1940 was working at University College London.
Meeting A V Hill in the college's South Quadrangle, Bayliss
mentioned that his teaching commitments had recently been
eased by a parachute mine striking the college buildings. So
Bayliss, too, was roped in. Only one of the new recruits wore
uniform. Visiting sites in the Nottingham and Derby GDAs,
Blackett was introduced to Second Lieutenant G W Raybould, a
surveyor by training, who six months previously had devised an
ingenious barrage procedure based upon slant ranges obtained
from three GL stations working in unison. Since details of his
scheme had been circulated throughout AA Command in early
March, Raybould was one of the few serving officers who could
already claim to have made a solid technical contribution to radar
procedure.[54] Combined with his first-hand experience of gunsite
service – which the scientists lacked – this marked Raybould as
an essential addition to the team.

'Blackett's Circus', they were called. Their first home, in the
very first days, was part of a room in Savoy Hill House, which was
otherwise occupied by the SR1 Branch of the Directorate of
Scientific Research. Finding these cramped quarters 'intolerable'
the team soon decamped to nearby Brettenham House, but when
a week later Savoy Hill House itself was bombed the DSR staff
moved to Great Westminster House in Horseferry Road, where
there was room for all. (The Circus enjoyed 'palatial' accommodation on the sixth floor.) From here, as the Blitz deepened,
the scientists ventured forth daily to the London gunsites.

As Blackett soon discovered, AA Command's overriding
problem was that London's defences had really been designed for
the wrong type of battle: the entire IAZ was essentially a fossil,
ossified in the late 1930s when it had been planned to deal with
fairly slow-moving aircraft, by day, using visual fire control; this
assumption conditioned more or less every characteristic of the
IAZ's layout, and especially the distribution and density of guns.
If every gunsite had been occupied and provided with a radar
giving its best theoretically-attainable performance, this would
hardly have mattered, since unseen fire at night would have been
as effective as visual fire by day. But apart from the shortcomings
of radar performance, as matters stood in October 1940 many

sites were without the equipment at all; and, of course, not all of the sites were gunned. Blackett could do nothing about the shortage of guns, but as far as the radars were concerned there were three problems to overcome: first, how to get the greatest advantage from the limited pool of GL sets; secondly, how to make the output of those sets more accurate; and, thirdly, how to get the radars and predictors working efficiently together so as to aim the guns.

In his thinking on the first of these problems Blackett soon realised that the only way to use the limited supply of radars was to concentrate guns together, such that every weapon was aimed by radar-derived information (however indifferent that may often have been). This meant larger sites, but fewer of them – in rough terms around fifteen eight-gun positions rather than 30 with four weapons apiece, for the number of guns actually present in London. Rearranging the layout on these lines did mean that one of the fundamental ideas behind the original IAZ – to cover the whole of London's airspace with AA fire – would be lost: large chunks of sky would lie beyond the range of any gun. But in fact this was already so simply because London was under-gunned, and in any case Blackett soon discovered that the gaps hardly mattered in technical terms either, since even if every site had been fully armed, blanket coverage would have been lost once night raiding began. At night, Blackett found, the area covered by each site was limited to 'a rather narrow crescent-shaped zone' in front of the battery, its further limit set by the range of the guns and its nearer by the point at which the rate of the target's change of position relative to the guns overtook the radar's ability to follow it. So the notion of complete cover at night was in any case 'illusory'. 'The conception of complete cover,' Blackett later recalled, 'must have originated in the days when slow aircraft were engaged visually in daylight, and just did not apply to the conditions of 1940 when fast aircraft were being engaged at night by means of radar.'[55] Far from commanding the vast dome of the London sky, the gunners, it was realised, were shooting in an irregular scatter of chinks and segments.

Once this finding was accepted the way was clear to concentrate the IAZ's still-growing array of HAA weapons on a select group of sites. For a variety of practical reasons, however, this could not be done exclusively by doubling up guns at existing batteries, so several new sites had to be found. Concentrating guns and sharing radars did something to improve 1 AA Division's tally in late October, as Blackett's scientists concentrated their efforts on improving the GL sets' performance, particularly by testing the E/F attachments against 'control' flights made by friendly aircraft. The E/F equipment had first been installed by the earlier team of calibrators, who had generally tested the sets by taking readings from oscillators dangling from small balloons. The Circus's first job was to check the adjustment of the sets by tracking real aircraft, and to determine – and this was the subtle part – how the instruments' accuracy *varied* with the bearing and elevation being measured at any one time. These fluctuations in performance were then assessed in relation to the ground conditions around the set – the degree of slope in different directions, the surface texture and so on – and with the pattern of obstructions lying around the site, in the expectation that these would probably explain the irregularities in the radar's performance. It was painstaking work, for which the scientists paired up to deal separately with each Brigade's sites. Hill and Huxley – Blackett's first recruits – made their way around the HAA positions in 26 Brigade, in north-east London, while Butler and Evans dealt with 48 Brigade and Porter and Nabarro handled 49 Brigade. At the same time Raybould made theodolite surveys of all the GL-equipped IAZ gunsites, in company with a Major King – otherwise Professor of Geology in the University of Cambridge – who joined the team as soil scientist. This work occupied much of the team's time between October and December, so continued well after the weight of German raiding shifted to the provinces.

Preliminary findings, available by early December, seemed to suggest that the radar's performance was most strongly affected by the slope of the surrounding ground – measured by Raybould's surveys – and by the presence of major surface obstructions nearby; it was also discovered that the E/F attachment was an altogether more exacting piece of equipment than had previously been supposed, and was fatally prone to falling out of adjustment simply by being used. The problem of localised ground effects was cured by the design, towards the end of 1940, of a huge wire mesh mat (described in the following chapter) the first examples of which were constructed on operational sites in December, rather too late to play a part in the full London Blitz but in time to improve radar performance as the weight of raiding moved outward to the provinces over the winter. And by then the original Circus had expanded to include two more mathematicians – A J Skinner and Miss M Keast – and had gained the more formal name of the AA Command Research Group (the first of several titles by which it was known, the more familiar of which was the AA Command Operational Research Group, or ORG).

At the same time, in another part of London, a second cadre of technicians was being trained to play their part in the radar war. These were recruits mustered as the result of another decision made in early October, when Blackett had suggested to Pile and Bedford that AA Command should undertake an extensive 'user study' of gunsite radar performance, ideally by putting a skilled technician permanently onto each site to monitor what was happening in real operations. In order to do this it was necessary to enlist still more men, which Pile arranged by approaching Lord Hankey, the Lord President of the Council, whose direct appeal to electrical engineering firms soon garnered the first twenty recruits. For the future, Hankey also arranged that university science syllabuses would be more closely tailored to the technical requirements of the forces, and in 1941 inaugurated a bursary scheme with a pronounced bias towards subjects useful to radar.[56]

To train this corps of technicians a second new body was established, in the AA Command Wireless School. The first move to found the school was made in the first week of October, when Dr J A Ratcliffe was invited to set up an establishment to train civilian technicians in radar work. An early decision was to look for premises near Richmond Park, where an HAA battery already existed and ground was available for training. A home was found in the hall of All Saints' Church at Petersham, on the western fringes of the park near ZS20, where the school assembled on 24 October with Ratcliffe – Pile called him the 'headmaster' – heading a small staff picked from MAP, ADRDE, AA Command and the RAOC. Like Blackett's Circus, Ratcliffe's academy was at first an improvised affair. Equipment was gathered together as best it could be – Ratcliffe was asked on the spur of the moment what his trainees would need, and reeled off an impromptu list:

fifty Avometers, fifty oscilloscopes, some small hand tools; all duly appeared – and was at first given four GL Mk Is on which to train. Training began on 28 October, when the first intake of civilian Radio Officers settled into their quarters at Grafton House. Especially talented or experienced candidates were selected for this first course, which was completed, in something of a rush, on 11 November. Later courses would take six weeks; these men qualified in just two.

News of their coming was circulated through AA Command a week earlier, on 4 November, when Major-General T C Newton of Pile's General Staff briefed divisional commanders on what the civilians' role would be.

> After completing the course at the School [wrote Newton], Radio Officers will be attached to units. Eventually it is hoped to have one per battery for technical supervision of all GL sets in the battery. In the immediate future each Radio Officer will be posted to a selected gun station, and will confine his work to that station only. He will be in charge of the GL station from the technical point of view and will act as technical advisor to the GPO [Gun Position Officer]. He will be responsible for seeing that the station is working at the highest possible efficiency during all operating hours. To this end he must stay with one station for a period of days long enough to become fully acquainted with the individual peculiarities of the sets and of the site.[57]

Although they were given the status of officers for all domestic purposes – dining and living with the commissioned staff – the civilian technicians who now began to filter out to the gunsites had little real authority over their army colleagues. They could not, for example, take a GL station off the air, regardless of how shakily it might be performing – only the soldiers could do that. Civilians who had earned the rank of Grade I Radio Officer in training could adjust the GL equipment as they thought fit, though the less experienced Grade II men were supposed to seek authority before resetting too many dials and switches. Each officer reported directly to Lennox of the Cossor company, and ultimately to Ratcliffe at Petersham, though as a courtesy they were expected to show written reports to their battery commanders before dispatch. The point is that the new men were eased in, and (officially at least) were restrained from intervening too deeply in the work of the gunners. Later this would change, especially once Radio Officers became 'militarised' (a trend which Ratcliffe tried to block) and were routinely commissioned into the RAOC. But to introduce civilian outsiders on to service gunsites in any capacity was a large innovation, and Pile, wisely, trod with some caution.

Any fears that the men would be treated as interlopers or (worse) as headquarters' snoopers proved groundless. Ratcliffe's belief in what he termed the 'scientific user' was soon vindicated by the results obtained by his radio officers, who found themselves warmly welcomed on gunsites across London, and soon elsewhere, as saviours from the perplexing mysteries of the GL Mk I. Special telephone lines were installed to enable the radio officers to talk freely to Petersham and the GOR in Brompton Road, and in this way was formed a community of experts, men whose knowledge grew daily through dialogue and experience. Soon the radio officers supplanted the team of calibrators whose job it had been to set up the E/F attachments and, as civilians and later uniformed soldiers, became an indispensable component of the AA batteries' personnel.

With the formation of the ORG and Wireless School AA Command was set on its path to become what Pile would later call 'the most highly technical army that ever wore khaki';[58] and certainly these two groups for the remainder of the war did sterling work to bring the gunsites' performance up to the peak which could be wrested from their technical equipment. They were both formed too late, of course, in the sense that the improvements in radar which stemmed from their work were really needed at the start of the Blitz, not towards its end. The London raids of September 1940 began the march of technical progress in AA Command without which the lethally-accurate radar-predicted fire of the later war years would have been impossible; but in the period remaining before the capital gained its reprieve in mid November there were few clear signs of improvement in the London guns' performance.

That was not for want of trying. The policy of greater concen-

tration among the London guns was put into effect in October
and by the middle of the month hurried reconnaissance by
brigades had identified nine new positions, seven of them
capable of accommodating massive double batteries of sixteen
3.7in mobiles.[59] A fortnight later the number of sites prepared to
receive eight-gun batteries had risen to ten, while nine positions
were earmarked for sixteen weapons; together with two additional
sites capable of holding four guns, these new locations brought
the number of IAZ sites on AA Command's books to an all-time
peak of 78 and its theoretical gun capacity to 460 (against 199
weapons actually present).[60] Most of the newly-acquired positions
were to the south, where eight sites, most of them fit for sixteen
guns, took the numbering sequence up to ZS35 and 1 AA Division's
estate as far south as Walton Heath.

Though many eight-gun concentrations came together in
October and November 1940 by concentrating weapons from
former four-gun sites, the number of sixteen-gun sites occupied
was eventually limited both by the practical problems of
operating so many weapons together, and by increased supplies
of GL sets later in the Blitz diminishing the need for them. Some,
however, were certainly occupied and the first such were ZW16 at
Heston, just west of Hounslow, and ZS28 at Nore Hill, a few miles
south-east of Croydon, which AA Command ordered to be
prepared on 15 October.[61] Concentrating weapons together to
form these sites was a trying upheaval for the batteries concerned,
made worse by the need to ensure that their guns were fully
reinstalled by the time darkness fell. On 21 October, for example,
12 HAA Battery began moving from ZS4 at Bostal Heath to a new
sixteen-gun position at four in the morning, to be followed at
intervals to 07.30 by three further batteries from Anerley,
Sundridge Park and Hayes. All were converging on ZS34 at
Addington, where the sixteen weapons were reported ready to
fire, with the GL on the air and calibrated, at seven o'clock that
evening.[62] Here at least the guns remained in this concentration
for at least a month.[63]

Adding the temporary eight- and sixteen-gun sites gave a
rather different look to the geography of the IAZ by mid
November (Fig 21), even if the number of weapons in the capital
was much the same as it had been six weeks before, after the first

waves of reinforcements had settled down. This transformation was achieved so quickly largely because of the great simplicity of the new temporary positions.[64] Intended only for brief occupation, the sixteen-gun sites were structurally among the least substantial that AA Command ever occupied: the general idea was a patch of ground about 300 yards long by 200 wide, within which each clutch of four guns would be laid out in a pattern rather resembling a four-leaf clover with the predictors in the centre (four were needed) and the GL set about 100 yards away down the 'stalk', so to speak. The arrangement of each four-gun group presumably followed the general pattern for mobile 3.7s used elsewhere in 1940 (see Plate 10 and Fig 11, for example), though as the plans of the sites were never committed to paper and no photographs have come to light it is impossible to be certain on this point. Facilities for the men were minimal – cookhouses and latrines in the familiar camp structures alone were authorised – partly on the grounds that the sites were expected to be occupied for periods of not more than 48 hours, though in practice some were certainly used for much longer (such as ZS34 at Addington, just mentioned) and the crews rotated. Even in late November 1940 some permanent sites in London were still deficient in hutting, so even the supernumery personnel sent to double up on eight-gun sites had to be billeted off the site, or bedded down on nearby four-gun positions where vacant hutting was available.

And this is how the IAZ met the relentless night raids of the London Blitz, which continued uninterrupted through October and early November before the Luftwaffe widened its scope to heavy raids on other cities, beginning with Coventry on the 14th. The weightiest blow of the campaign so far fell on 15/16 October, when 235 raiders came over but despite firing more than eight thousand rounds the IAZ's guns shot down just two. In all, the gunners' claim for the month of October as a whole reached 22 aircraft downed from a total number of enemy sorties over the capital later discovered (from German records) to have been 5173,[65] and though nine of these fell in the last four nights of the month in truth there was little to celebrate.[66] However often Pile pointed to the deterrent effect of AA fire – his 48 per cent of bombers turned away – his critics wanted above all to see wreckage on the ground as evidence that the London guns were

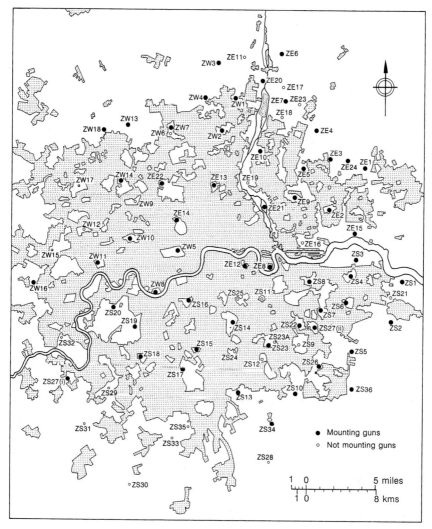

Figure 21 Guns in the London IAZ, Tuesday 19 November 1940. Two months into the Blitz, when the weight of raiding had just shifted to the provinces – beginning with the Coventry operation five days earlier – most of the IAZ's sites were armed and the layout had been pushed southward with new temporary positions designed to accommodate as many as sixteen weapons.

doing their job. There was too little of that.

It told on the gunners. At a conference with his four brigadiers on 15 October the chief of 1 AA Division complained of an 'apparent lack of discipline, organisation and administration on many sites in the Divisional area'. It was not the first time

Crossman had said this, and by mid October there was indeed evidence of faltering morale among his troops. Pile said so in his book,[67] and to judge from Crossman's remarks the problem was caused partly by repeated shifts of position among the gun crews, with the result that officers seldom fully understood their sites, lost track of spares and supplies, neglected paperwork and generally let things slide. For the men on the batteries the deepening squalor of their accommodation did not help, nor the simple deprivation from sleep. Neither were the gunners any longer winning the public admiration which had followed the first barrages in mid September. Pile found critical and sometimes abusive letters in his mail on many mornings – the AA defence of London was 'the biggest scandal since Nero', wrote one historically-minded correspondent – reflecting popular discontent at the tiny number of raiders AA Command was actually managing to shoot down.

Somewhat later in the year, when the pressure on London had eased without being fully lifted, a closer study of morale and performance in 1 AA Division shows how worried senior commanders had become. On 10 December Major-General Whittaker, promoted from 26 AA Brigade to become divisional commander, was forced to admit in a highly classified memorandum that there was 'no doubt whatever that the standard of drill, both on guns and instruments, has deteriorated and now falls far below that required to give even a small chance of good gunnery data bringing effective results'.[68] The limited time for training in months of night operations was one reason, but there were others and among them Whittaker was inclined to censure his officers for allowing 'traces of boredom and tiredness due to avoidable causes' and an 'attitude of complacency and lethargy which is poisonous to efficiency' to take hold. This being the British army, regular PT was seen as one solution: 'I regard twenty minutes per day [. . .] by *all* ranks as essential to their well-being, physical and mental,' wrote Whittaker. 'I want to see Officers, from Battery Commander downwards, taking part [. . .]'. There was doubtless wisdom in that, but the panacea of physical fitness could not answer all the difficulties which 1 AA Division was facing towards the end of 1940.

Quite a lot of our Officers, not only junior, are not, in my opinion, putting forth their full effort [wrote Whittaker]. There is a marked inclination to 'give up the ghost' when all is not going well, to blame RE services (I know full well how irritating this matter is!) and consequently to let things slide. There are many, many occasions when a little energy and initiative can defeat the worst possible conditions. There is a most marked atmosphere, not only in appearance and comfort but in fighting efficiency, at sites where the leaders are really leading and fending for themselves and not merely waiting for services to come somehow, sometime.[69]

There are worse sins for an officer than lassitude and a failure to show initiative in battle, but they are not numerous. Doubtless some of this was explained by the low calibre of AA Command's recruits – or a proportion of them at least – a problem which Pile would tackle vigorously in the spring of 1941. But equally London's gunners in the Blitz were labouring under enormous difficulties, none of their own making and few within their power to resolve. It was Churchill, famously, who said to Roosevelt in February 1941, 'Give us the tools, and we will finish the job;' and anyone in AA Command could have said that to Churchill himself in the autumn of 1940. In fact Pile did, or tried to. When Churchill made a nocturnal tour of London gunsites in October, Pile recalled, he rejoiced to hear the music of the guns, which he called 'cannon'. 'This exhilarates me,' declared the Prime Minister, bouncing on his heels amid the thundering 3.7s at ZS20 in Richmond Park. 'The sound of these cannon gives me a tremendous feeling.' But, Pile added, 'he was always more interested in questioning me as to the number of cannon I had in action in the various areas than in the other equipment so necessary to make those cannon useful.'[70] The labours of Blackett's Circus and Ratcliffe's school notwithstanding, London did not have that equipment in the Blitz. 1 AA Division's GL return for December 1940 shows that 35 sites in the IAZ had radars by that date,[71] but that is not to say that all of those radars were giving of their best. And of course there were never enough guns. In the first week of October HAA stood at 199, of which 113 were 3.7in mobiles.[72] Six weeks later, on 20 November, that figure had risen to 235, the increase supplied chiefly by fifteen more

4.5s and thirteen mobile 3.7s.[73] But by 20 November Coventry had been bombed, the provincial Blitz had started, and London had to sacrifice guns to other cities. So the figure dropped to 200 weapons (exactly) by 11 December, as 3.7 mobiles were carted off to the provinces, the capital fell back on the guns bolted to concrete, and AA Command's problems migrated elsewhere.[74]

CHAPTER 7

After Coventry

NOVEMBER 1940 – MAY 1941

Though London bore the brunt of the Luftwaffe's bombing effort in September and October 1940, it was far from being the only city troubled by night raids in these months. Prominent among the targets for night attack in October were Birmingham, Coventry and, to a lesser extent, Liverpool, Manchester, Hull and Glasgow, at all of which the guns were periodically in action. The AA defence of these targets was, however, weaker than it should have been. Already carrying deficits on their authorised scales, several of these GDAs were further denuded by the first reinforcements sent to London, if not dramatically so – Birmingham's HAA layout was thinned from 71 guns in late August to 64 by mid September, for example, and Coventry's from 32 to 24 (Appendix II). These reductions at first seemed affordable, given the relative lightness of attack on the cities concerned. But by early November it had begun to seem that Coventry, in particular, had been left a little too vulnerable. Though never heavy, by early November sporadic raids here had begun to foster the population's 'trekking' habit already established in London. Less troubling elsewhere, these practices at Coventry were beginning to register effects on production among the city's vital aircraft factories.

So it came about that the AA Committee began to be anxious about Coventry a fortnight before the devastating night raid of 14/15 November. On 30 October Colonel Turner's Department at the Air Ministry was asked to provide decoy fires for the city, arranged somehow to intercept the *X-Gerät* electronic navigation beams which the Germans were using to find cities such as this.[1]

By November 1940 the British had known about the beam technology (both *X-Gerät* and its simpler predecessor, *Knickebein*) for many months and since June 1941 80 Wing of the RAF, based at Radlett, had been working to investigate both techniques and counter them with electronic jamming. Turner undertook to do what he could, though in the event Coventry's decoy fires were arranged only after the raid of the 14th. More conventional measures were, however, put in train a few days after the approach to Turner, when on 3 November the Air Staff urged the AA Committee to review Coventry's defences 'as a matter of urgency', particularly as a means of quelling the trekking habit.[2] Studying the question next day, the committee accepted the point about Coventry's vulnerability, which they knew to be heightened by what the Air Staff described as the 'special methods' used by the Germans, in the recent raids, for 'directing their bombers' to Coventry and Birmingham – a veiled reference to *X-Gerät*. In the light of both factors – the trekking and the beams – the AA Committee recommended that Coventry's guns should be reinforced immediately with eight 3.7in mobiles transferred from Alcester, and that the city's needs should be borne in mind when the November allocations of new HAA weapons became known. They also recommended thickening the balloon barrage.[3]

A few hours later the orders were out. At 20.00 on that same evening Major G S Parkinson of Pile's General Staff at Stanmore sent a signal to divisional headquarters instructing that eight guns currently at Wixford, near Alcester, should be redeployed 'at once' to Coventry.[4] The news reached headquarters 34 AA Brigade later in the evening,[5] and at 23.00 percolated down to 194 HAA Battery at Wixford in the form of a warning order for the move.[6] It is a mark of the urgency surrounding Coventry's reinforcement in this first week of November that the executive order to decamp reached 194 HAA Battery at 03.30 the following morning, the 5th, though with the rider that the guns should stay put until 05.00, probably in recognition of the slight Luftwaffe activity in the area.[7] The gunners spent the morning packing up and left Wixford between one and two o'clock on the afternoon of the 5th. By 20.30 one troop of 194 HAA Battery were in place and ready to fire at site K in the Coventry layout, where orders were to replace 343 HAA Battery.[8] Their companion troop met difficulty, however, when the weight of their first 3.7 mobile collapsed the culvert bridging the entrance to site E, where they had been assigned. With their site entrance blocked the troop spent a sorry night out of action and under canvas – 'stormy night', recorded the War Diary, 'continuous rain' – shifting their stricken gun only at eleven the next morning with the aid of three Matador tractors. By lunchtime everything was more or less straight; but then at two-thirty orders arrived to evacuate site E in favour of a new position (which was given the same code), though the work progressed only as far as towing the weapons into the field before the gunners were bused over to two other Coventry gunsites for an issue of rum and a night's sleep. The troop at K site fired a few rounds on the night of the 7th, but in the event their comrades at the new E site did not come to readiness until the late afternoon of 8 November, and even then were unable to fire thanks to faults with equipment and the absence of the necessary barrage data. Next day this was righted, and on this night both sites received raid alarms but held fire due to bad weather. It was Sunday, 10 November, a week after the AA Committee set the ball rolling, before both troops of 194 HAA Battery fired their guns.[9] On this night the Luftwaffe sent minor forces against Birmingham, West Bromwich and Coventry.[10]

These were not the only gunners sent to Coventry, so to speak, in the week or so before the great raid of the 14th. AA Command's War Diary mentions a further battery dispatched there from Home Forces on 10 November,[11] a unit which appears to equate to the LAA battery which, two days later, 34 AA Brigade ordered to defend nine industrial and railway VPs around the city, a deployment scheduled to last until 3 December.[12] That same afternoon brought minor raiding, while there was further slight activity over Birmingham and Coventry on 13/14 November, a night of gales. These various movements brought the defences of Coventry up to 40 HAA – sixteen 3.7in statics, sixteen 3.7in mobiles and eight 3in[13] – and about a dozen light guns by 14 November, when the great raid took place. Though marginally more HAA (44 guns) had been in place in June, Coventry on 14 November possessed almost the strongest gun defences it had enjoyed since the start of the war.

It is worth picking over the details of these moves to

emphasise how much was done for Coventry at this critical time, and the difficulty with which it was achieved. After the war doubts surfaced about this. It is well known that in mid October 1940 British Air Intelligence predicted that the Luftwaffe would soon turn to heavy night raiding, and that this was followed on 11 November by intelligence pointing to an imminent campaign of attacks on industrial centres using fire-raising pathfinder aircraft, Operation *Moonlight Sonata*.[14] Though some evidence, particularly from ULTRA sources, pointed to Coventry as a likely target for an exceptionally heavy, beam-led, fire-raising raid, its imminent fate did not become certain until three o'clock on the afternoon of the operation, when 80 Wing at Radlett detected an *X-Gerät* beam laid on the city. It has been argued that Coventry might have been evacuated in the days before the operation, or at least that something might have been done to warn the citizenry and the defences in the critical four hours between the detection of the beam alignment at 15.00 and the start of the raid at 19.10.[15] The absence of any evacuation or warning, it has been argued, was the outcome of a personal dilemma for Churchill: save Coventry and compromise ULTRA, or lose Coventry and keep secret the fact that Britain could decrypt the Germans' *Enigma* traffic.[16] Critics have suggested that Churchill resolved this dilemma in favour of ULTRA. But wiser commentators have pointed to the impossibility of evacuating the city at any time in the period before the raid: little imagination is needed to visualise the difficulties of that option. It appears to be true that Coventry's AA batteries received no specific warning, in the late afternoon of the 14th, to expect a heavy raid that night, but this is irrelevant: for Coventry had *already* been reinforced, not as a result of the specific intelligence which began to accumulate from 11 November, but in the general climate of anxiety surrounding the raids earlier in the month and the knowledge of the accuracy which the Germans could achieve with their beams. The result was that the gunners stood ready by their weapons on 14 November just as they did on the previous night, and every night.

It is also true that even a doubling (say) of Coventry's guns immediately before the raid would probably have achieved little more than marginal results, even if such an operation had been feasible. For on the night of 14/15 November everything was in the Luftwaffe's favour. Guided by *X-Gerät*, the specialist target marking force Kampfgruppe 100 opened the bombing at ten past seven, and for the next ten hours central Coventry shook and burned under the bombs from 449 raiders, losing its medieval cathedral, public library, many factories, homes and 568 of its citizens before morning (and nearly losing the city centre GOR). The AA fight was fierce. Coventry's gunners put 6789 HAA rounds into the night sky, managing few aimed engagements but dispatching 128 barrages on GL and VIE. But this huge effort appears to have destroyed just one raider. As ever in the winter of 1940, Coventry's AA defences were weakened more by the vagaries of fire-control than any deficit in guns or will.

The Coventry raid opened a new phase of the Luftwaffe's operations which would last, with varying degrees of intensity, until early in the following summer. Now, instead of pounding London night after night, Göring's forces roamed widely, at first seldom visiting a single city on successive nights but, as the campaign deepened, tending to concentrate their efforts in sequential attacks on selected targets. The German High Command's priorities in the widening Blitz, if not exactly quixotic, saw some change of emphasis. From mid November until the end of January the range of targets included inland industrial cities and ports, together with continuing, if more sporadic raids on London, which remained a target of choice until practically the end of the campaign. With the prospect of invasion in 1940 by now evaporated, these raids were at least a means of sustaining pressure on the British war economy (especially the aircraft industry), and on civilian morale. Then in early February 1941 the weight of attacks shifted to ports, and while the tactics in these raids did not differ from those in the first two and a half months of the provincial campaign, heavier and more sustained onslaughts fell on such places as Plymouth, Portsmouth, Bristol, Liverpool and the Clyde. The result was that AA Command faced continually changing demands for guns at targets as far apart as Portsmouth and Belfast, Plymouth and Glasgow. The claims began within a fortnight of the Coventry raid. Birmingham,

Portsmouth and Southampton were all troubled by heavy raids in late November and early December, and with a weight of attack lingering in the Midlands the Ministry of Aircraft Production began to press for additional defences at aircraft factories there. So Birmingham in particular became the beneficiary of guns stripped from London, as the earlier flow of ordnance from the provinces to the capital came to be reversed.

The result was that the ranking of GDAs by gun strength came to be reordered in the last six weeks of 1940 (Appendix II). In late November Birmingham mustered 64 HAA guns, comprising a fixed core of sixteen 4.5s, a further sixteen 3.7in mobiles and twice that number of statics. By mid December the mobiles had risen to 47, the 21 extra guns bringing the city's HAA defences to 95 weapons and promoting Birmingham to the second most heavily defended GDA in Britain. Third in that ranking was Scapa, splendidly untouched with 88 guns bestowed by the 'Q' Plan of autumn 1939, and after that Thames & Medway (84 HAA weapons) and Liverpool (80). Well below these totals, areas in a secondary tier of gun strengths were led by the Clyde (48 guns), Tyne (46) and Sheffield (44), while Derby, the Forth, Manchester, Coventry and Portsmouth had 40 apiece. With 200 HAA weapons in the IAZ, London still asserted its dominance, and enjoyed further *de facto* protection from the 84 guns in Thames & Medway and 39 elsewhere in 1 AA Division, whose allocations were always made with the needs of the capital in mind. But as 1940 drew to a close the share of heavy guns between other GDAs was assuming a new form, more faithfully reflecting the Luftwaffe's emerging priorities.

Reordering the HAA defences was only one of several new commitments facing AA Command in the autumn of 1940. On 27 October, and again two days later, surprise dusk attacks were launched against Bomber Command airfields by low-flying bombers, who managed to destroy several aircraft on the ground, damage buildings and inflict casualties. It was a troubling development, coming only a day or so after a new directive to Bomber Command's incoming chief, Air Marshal Sir Richard Peirse, to intensify the offensive against a wide range of targets in Germany, Italy and occupied France, as well as the oil installations which had dominated his predecessor's priorities.

The Air Ministry naturally argued that everything possible must be done to prevent Bomber Command's effectiveness being blunted by attrition against its ground organisation. Among the measures proposed was a new allocation of Bofors to thirteen bomber airfields from Wattisham in Suffolk to Dishforth in Yorkshire.[17] These ideas were discussed on 1 November at the inaugural meeting of the 'Shadow Sub-Committee' of the AA Committee (a group formed to relieve the senior body of much of the day-to-day business of studying gun allocations), with the result that 29 Bofors were authorised to be removed from fighter aerodromes and industrial VPs – where attacks had eased in the last two months – in favour of the bomber stations. With these moves complete, 21 operational stations in Bomber Command, all in eastern England, would share 20 HAA guns, eight 3in LAA and 39 Bofors, in addition to Lewis guns manned by the RAF.[18] It was a modest proportion of AA Command's total armament stocks, but one which was palpably set to increase. Beyond its operational bases, Bomber Command in November 1940 consisted of thirteen stations used as operational training units, eighteen satellite airfields, nineteen stations under construction and eight headquarters – 83 potential targets in total.[19] All of these places, and many more, would need AA defences as the bomber offensive mounted in the years to come.

Though the new scales of AA defence devised at the height of the Battle of Britain were formally approved in mid October, as 1940 drew on still more groups of targets began to make demands unanticipated in the new plans. Guns for new RAF airfields in the west had been anticipated, but none had been allocated to the seventeen CH radar stations between Sidmouth and Cape Wrath which came on the air in rudimentary form during the closing months of the year.[20] The stations of the eastern chain had long enjoyed the best guns which AA Command could offer, and on this precedent it seemed that the west coast sites should hardly have less. As late as the first week of January, however, not a single AA barrel defended these sites, which were working either with elementary mobile apparatus or had already reached 'Advance CH' standard, with equipment in timber huts and aerials on transportable masts – a form in which they were both visible and structurally fragile. So the west coast radar stations added another LAA commitment to a wish-list which, by now, bore little relation to what could be achieved with the guns available. In late January 1941 Pile had 627 Bofors in his stocks,[21] against the authorised (October 1940) target of 4410.

Beyond the ever-shifting pattern of priorities which AA Command was obliged to respect in distributing guns, the winter of 1940–41 brought adjustments to some fundamentals of Pile's tactical arrangements. It is no exaggeration to say that many components of Britain's AA defences were remade in these months, some in response to the Luftwaffe's unfolding campaign, but others to realise earlier plans and adapt derelict practices. The period between November 1940 and the following spring saw several things happening more or less at once: the structuring principles of many established GDAs were reassessed; gunsites began to gain GL mats; the first deliveries of the GL Mk II began to reach the batteries, likewise the first searchlight control radars; searchlights themselves were completely repatterned; and a layout of GL sets was installed in southern England to plot enemy aircraft movements over land. Although the new radars were the results of long-term work finally realised, none of the other innovations had even been considered only weeks, or in some cases days, before they were actually put into effect.

Among the first of these steps was a move to improve the layouts of existing GDAs. In autumn 1940 most guns were still deployed within a bone-structure of sites organised on pre-war principles; in general, gun positions were clustered fairly tightly around their urban areas on the assumption that day bombing would be fairly accurate and concentrated, and that night engagements would be aided by searchlights. The increasing availability of GL sets, however, coupled with the bombers' guidance by navigational beams on discoverable alignments, opened the way to pushing weapons further out, to intercept unseen raiders on their approach. On 5 December the southern AA divisions were instructed to reconnoitre for one or more four-gun sites 'on or near the direct line of approach to all gun zones where there is sufficient "land" to enable the guns to bring several bursts of accurate fire to bear before the enemy aircraft reach the line of bomb release'.[22] This could not be done everywhere. It was impossible at targets such as Dover, for example, where the town met the sea, but the divisions were instructed to seek suitable sites at Slough, Weybridge, Sheerness, Chatham, Southampton, Portsmouth and Bristol, in the first instance. 'The first requisite,' explained the orders, 'is that the site should be really good for GL/EF.' The second was for 'space to put another four guns into action temporarily – probably for single nights only – in order to make the best use of the number of GL sets that will be available'. (A stipulation reflecting metropolitan experience filtering out to the provinces, for by now the trend toward eight and sixteen-gun HAA sites in London was entrenched.) The original expectation was that most of these sites would be newly found, but local reconnaissance soon showed that many GDAs already fielded suitable positions.[23] So the next stage was to occupy them, if vacant, and to coax their radars to yield their best. Sites using intercepting fire were given the first allocation of GL mats, while AA Command ran studies to determine the best way of shooting accurately and in concentration on the raiders' lines and heights of approach.

Persuading the radar to give of its best at these and other sites now depended very much on the programme for building GL mats, which got under way towards the end of the year. Divisions were acquainted with these strange contrivances in the first week of December, when Stanmore circulated outline details of the mat's function and construction, and advised battery commanders to examine where they could be fitted in at each site.[24] Many may have been startled to read the full specifications which arrived a few days later.[25] The fruit of the work by Blackett and his team in London was by far the most unlikely device used by AA Command during the war. The mat's purpose was as far as possible to neutralise the vagaries in radar performance (and particularly that of the E/F attachment) by surrounding the set with an uniform area of known electrical properties. And to do that it had to be big: it was, specifically, an octagonal cat's cradle of strained wires, supporting a plateau of two-inch netting 130 yards in diameter, within which the radar cabin stood proudly on a central platform (Fig 22). It was prodigious of materials. Each mat consumed 230 rolls of wire netting, four feet wide and 50 yards in length – six and a half miles of rolled mesh, or an area of more than fifteen thousand square yards – together with more

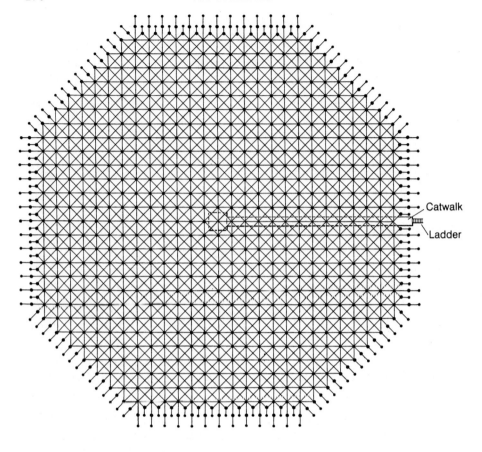

Catwalk

Ladder

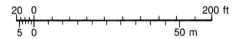

20 0   200 ft

5 0   50 m

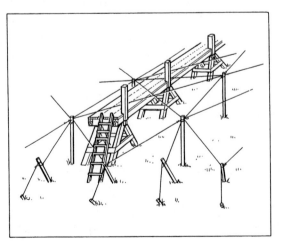

Figure 22 The GL mat.
The radar occupied the
central platform and was
reached when in place
from the catwalk and
ladder (inset).

Plate 13 Eight-gun position at Chadwell Heath (ZE1 in the London IAZ) seen in October 1946. The partial trace of an octagonal pathway to the right of the battery (as shown) defines the position of the GL mat; and note, too, the four on-site concrete magazines inserted between the guns.

than ten miles of galvanised wire. Initial plans called for mats to be installed immediately at 101 sites, so the short-term requirement for galvanised wire alone in December 1940 was something over 1000 miles – the distance from, say, Stanmore to Algeria –

together with 650 miles of wire mesh. In time, as the programme grew, Pile's GL mats absorbed every yard of galvanised wire spooling from British factories. Farmers found that netting for their poultry pens suddenly became scarce.

Erecting this thing was an interesting challenge.[26] The first step was to draw up a ground survey to position the mat and determine its height, which could range from one foot above ground level to nine feet six inches to take account of surface conditions; this work was given to civilian contractors recruited by Home Forces commands.[27] The height determined which of a series of standard 'kits' the site would receive, and with these components delivered and unpacked, erection began by raising the corner angle-iron verticals and bedding them down firmly into brick footings. These uprights were then used as reference points for siting the remaining verticals – first the outer lines, then the inner, which were wedged into place with greenwood pickets – to produce an octagonal forest of metal posts, all at the same height. Next was built the central platform for the radar, along with a sloping ramp up which the set would be towed into place. The supporting wires were installed next. These were threaded through pre-drilled holes at the tops of the uprights, criss-crossing the mat to produce the dense weave shown in Figure 22, and then tensioned by anchoring to further angle-irons used rather like tent pegs at the mat's edge. With these wires pulled taut, this delicately-balanced horizontal cobweb was ready to receive the mesh surface. Each of the 230 rolls was carefully unwound on the ground, persuaded to lie flat, trimmed as necessary and then hoisted up and secured with fine binding wire. And now, if not before, the radar was rolled into place, the avenue closed off, and the timber walkway raised on its supporting trestles.

Although the first 101 GL mats were supposed to be installed within six to eight weeks, this estimate proved wildly optimistic. Winter weather, difficult ground conditions, and numerous snags in executing what was, after all, a tricky piece of civil engineering all hampered the timetable to the point where by late January only one-tenth of the mats were finished.[28] Experience showed that erecting a single mat occupied about 50 men for four weeks, so it was accepted that a much longer timetable was in prospect, both to complete the initial quota and to extend it. By April Pile had come to realise that mats would be necessary for fully 95 per cent of all his GL stations, a total estimated at 600 by about March 1942 when, realistically, it was thought that a couple of hundred might be up.[29] Labour, by then, was the problem: to complete the remaining 400 mats in the year from March 1942 Pile calculated simply that 1600 men would have to be 'permanently employed on this work and nothing else.' AA Command's manpower worries were partially solved later in the year, as we shall see, first by the introduction of ATS women to operational duties on gunsites and then by making use of the Home Guard; but even with these expedients the GL mat programme ran on and on. What was planned as an emergency measure to resolve the shortcomings of the GL Mk I in Blitz conditions became a permanent commitment extending over several years.

Another reason for the extended mat-building programme was that the device was necessary as much for the GL Mk II set as the earlier Mk I with its E/F attachment. As introduced in autumn 1939 the GL Mk I had been less a fully-developed apparatus with certain limitations, than the product of a seam of technical development mined at a rather arbitrary point for a stop-gap operational set. The real advances represented by the GL Mk II – not simply its increased power, sensitivity and practicality, but also its ability to give three-dimensional readings by design – were less the result of building on the Mk I, than of pressing the aims of the original AA radar project to their intended conclusions. And when the first GL Mk IIs began to arrive at Pile's gunsites in the early months of 1941 they did promise much. Less amenable to local experiment than the Mk I (units were warned not to tinker with their Mk IIs, but rather to master the sets' proven capabilities) the new equipment was hailed on its introduction as 'a complete fire-control set',[30] a tight package of electronics able to give the gunners all they needed to fire aimed rounds against unseen targets. Working in the five-metre band, the GL Mk II could sense an incoming aircraft at 50,000 yards or more (approaching 30 miles), follow it continuously at 30,000 yards (seventeen miles) and control HAA fire when the target reached 14,000 yards (eight miles), when range accuracy narrowed to under 50 yards. Fine tolerances were also available on azimuth and elevation, at least between ten and 50 degrees from the horizontal, when true angles to the target would be no more than half a degree from what the radar claimed. In other ways, too, the GL Mk II was an advanced piece of equipment: rugged, easily transported, and designed to cope with conditions ranging from the Arctic to the tropical.

Physically the new set consisted of two trailer-mounted timber cabins for the transmitter and receiver, and a generator, the three together making up a mobile convoy which could be brought in and out of action quickly (though most of those used at home stayed put at settled sites).[31] Once wheeled into position, stabilised with screw jacks and wired up to the generator and to one another, the GL Mk II's two cabins could both be rotated towards the target, the transmitter sending out its beam and the receiver, in the centre of its GL mat, sensing the returned echoes and aligning to get the best response. One of the features of the Mk II was its dual transmitter aerials, one to send out a search beam for early warning and the other a more sharply directional signal to 'hold' the target for fire-control; and another was the three aerials mounted on the receiver cabin (Fig 23), which produced readings respectively for range, azimuth and elevation, displaying these inside the cabin on separate cathode ray screens. As delivered at the command post and predictor the output of the GL Mk II was 'continuous' within the equipment's limits of accuracy, with range measurements between 2000 and 14,000 yards given in 50-yard steps and those beyond in intervals of 250 yards. So in every respect the new equipment was a step up. Though not fully supplied to gunsites until the Blitz had come to an end, it became the standard model in use during 1942–43, before the 'centrimetric' GL Mk III ushered in a revolution in gunsite radar in the later years of the war.

Large as they were, the projects to provide GL mats and the early deliveries of the GL Mk II radars look minor affairs when compared with the great upheaval in the searchlight layout during the winter of 1940–41. At the beginning of the war searchlights for fighter co-operation were sited at 6000-yard intervals, forming a neat grid which, with luck, allowed several sites to illuminate a target simultaneously. Deployed in this way the lights at first gave a good account of themselves, but their

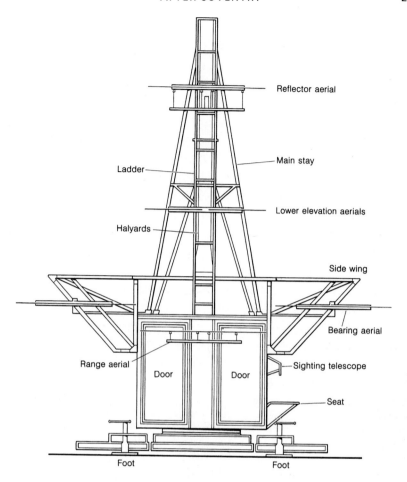

Figure 23 The GL Mk II radar receiver.

early successes were countered by changes in Luftwaffe tactics which, by the autumn of 1940, were beginning to make contacts more elusive. Blacking-out the undersides of aircraft was easily achieved with non-reflective paint, which made engagement more difficult and often allowed the crew to slip the beam by sudden evasive action; and, more generally, bombers were flying higher and faster. Expert searchlight crews could still surmount these difficulties, and on clear nights particularly continued to find their quarries. But a growing scarcity of RAF aircraft for co-operation practice in 1940 slackened the standard of training, at the very time when the searchlight layout was expanding and a flood of novices was reaching the sites. Similar troubles affected the more densely spaced searchlights within the GDAs, which many AA commanders came to see as a liability once the night Blitz opened. The heavy raids on the Midlands towns in particular revived the old suspicion that searchlights in gun zones were doing more to illuminate the target for the enemy than to drive him away. This finding arose less from the beams' tendency to guide the bombers than from the belief that luminosity was reflected back to the ground by cloud cover, bathing the target city in a pool of diffused light. So searchlights, often, were simply switched off. Crews became rusty, rankled at their suspension from the fight and, as Pile put it, sank beneath 'a great depression'.[32]

Trials to find a route out of this impasse began even before the

Plate 14 Elsie: searchlight control radar mounted directly on a 150cm light projector.

provincial Blitz opened in mid November. Experiments with searchlight control (SLC) radar had begun earlier in the year and by the autumn trials were under way in the Tangmere Sector using one of these prototype *Elsie* sets to guide several searchlights drawn together into a cluster.[33] They were not a great success, chiefly through limitations in the early radar's performance, but more was expected from the production models which, in autumn 1940, were expected to begin deliveries at the end of February.[34] In the event, *Elsie* sets did not become numerous until autumn 1941, but the principle that searchlights should operate in clusters rather than singly did win acceptance and on 8 November orders came down from Stanmore that the entire layout would be rearranged.[35]

Though the experiments in October had gone so far as to cluster a full troop of six lights together, the practice introduced in November was the three-light cluster, which was formed by abandoning at least two thirds of the existing sites in each area and drawing three projectors together on sites ideally 10,400 yards apart. Planning this layout was an exercise in applied geometry. Divisions were instructed to develop cluster sites with reference to the 50 degree line of the Cassini grid map, and to work to the 10,400-yard separation uniformly across GDAs and fighter zones, so avoiding discontinuities which might mark the target cities. Coastal searchlights watching for minelaying aircraft alone remained single. Some of the new cluster sites were existing positions enlarged and multiplied, but to approach the theoretical ideal many new positions were found. Some leeway was allowed in siting these, as it always would be in applying abstract templates to the ground, and officers reconnoitring for sites were warned to avoid villages, to respect agricultural interests, and to build the domestic camp for the battery as close as possible to a good road. To complicate matters further, clustering was accompanied by a comprehensive revision of the site notation. Previously numbered according to the AA division in which they lay, searchlight company areas were now brought within a new nomenclature using two-letter codes based upon their RAF air defence sector: searchlights in the Duxford Sector became the DX series, Hornchurch was HC, Tangmere TG, and so on.[36]

In structural terms clustering made searchlight sites larger and more complex. Where possible the three lights comprised one 150cm type and two of 120cm or (more usually) 90cm, often arranged in a triangle with about 50 yards between. Until *Elsie* became widespread sites continued to work with sound locators of various marks, together with VIE equipment. Much hutting and other material was recycled from abandoned positions to build up the accommodation at each cluster site, with the usual attention to camouflage and concealment. (Searchlight crews in 38 AA Brigade based at Harrow, for example, were encouraged to mimic the character of local buildings; huts on suburban sites could be disguised as bungalows, those further out as farm buildings, or so the idea ran. Hardcore for roads at these sites was drawn from air-raid clearance dumps around London.)[37] Many sites split their accommodation into two clutches, with one small group of huts near to the projectors for the operating detachments and a more complete domestic site in a retired position near a road, where the small headquarters staff lived and worked and dining facilities were laid on. Figure 24 shows a typical arrangement, though many sites took time to reach this fully-built stage. Some crews lived under canvas at first.[38]

The searchlights' difficulty in illuminating targets for fighters during the provincial Blitz opened a serious weakness in the air defence system in part because, as yet, no reliable radar cover was in place to guide night interceptions over land. By autumn 1940 the Chain Home system which had been developing since 1935 could provide reliable warning of approaching formations at moderate and high levels out from the coast and by the end of 1940 cover of this type was fast developing in the south-west and west to complete the national cordon. Early in the war CH stations had been joined by Chain Home Low (CHL), which filled the gap in cover against lower-flying targets and was itself steadily expanding westward. But both looked exclusively outward; dedicated to early warning, CH and CHL stations were practically blind against raiders once they had crossed the coast, when by day they were passed to the Observer Corps and, by night, were left to the searchlights and their sound locators. This weakness had always been a worry. As early as June 1939, Winston Churchill had compared the raider's passage across the coast to a transition from 'the middle of the 20th Century to the Early Stone

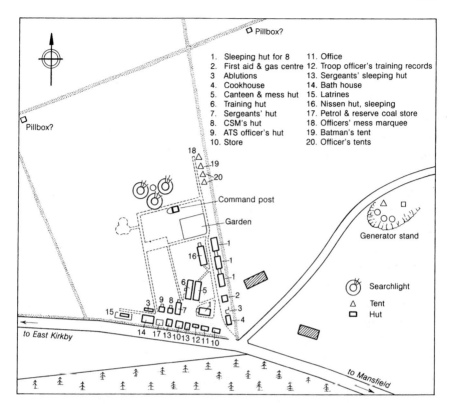

1. Sleeping hut for 8   11. Office
2. First aid & gas centre 12. Troop officer's training records
3 Ablutions   13. Sergeants' sleeping hut
4. Cookhouse   14. Bath house
5. Canteen & mess hut   15. Latrines
6. Training hut   16. Nissen hut, sleeping
7. Sergeants' hut   17. Petrol & reserve coal store
8. CSM's hut   18. Officers' mess marquee
9. ATS officer's hut   19. Batman's tent
10. Store   20. Officer's tents

Figure 24 A searchlight 'cluster' site of 1941, with the three projectors collected together, a remote area for the generators and a well-built domestic camp.

Age', as electronic tracking gave way to fallible human senses.[39] Churchill made this remark when reflecting on a visit to the research station at Bawdsey, where one solution was already in hand. This was airborne interception (AI) radar, equipment carried on board the aircraft to give the night fighter a self-contained means of zeroing-in upon unseen targets from a few miles' range. Rudimentary AI began to appear in the summer of 1939, but it offered only a partial solution to the night raider when the Blitz opened a year or so later. By autumn 1940 few night fighters carried the equipment, and those were Bristol Blenheims, machines originally classified as light bombers and usually outpaced by their quarry in this improvised role. And that was assuming the quarry could be found. Often it was not, for as the night Blitz began there remained no way of vectoring night fighters toward their targets by radar control from the ground.

The first attempts to link the night fighter directly to an earthbound radar controller took place in the summer of 1940, when selected CHL stations on the south coast directed AI fighters operating over the Channel, but it was only during the Battle of Britain that the need for a landward-looking fighter control radar was officially accepted. Preliminary experiments with what would become Ground Controlled Interception (GCI) equipment began in August 1940 at Worth Matravers, near Swanage, where the Bawdsey team had recently come to rest, following a spell in Dundee. The first purpose-built experimental GCI station was commissioned two months later, in October, when a site at Durrington, near Shoreham, came on the air for trials. It worked, more or less, and following the Coventry raid in mid November further sets were hurriedly ordered with the idea that six would be active in southern England by Christmas. But everyone knew that these primitive GCIs, even if they could be built in time, were 'something of a gamble'.[40] An insurance was needed; and the demand for radar cover was in any case urgent.

It was at this point, in late November, that Pile stepped in with a suggestion. Following a discussion with Air Marshal Sir W Sholto Douglas, who had just replaced Dowding at Fighter Command,[41] Pile proposed that GL sets working in isolation – with no guns – could be installed at intervals across southern England and, together with those already operating at gunsites within GDAs, could serve as the missing tool for tracking raiders inland.[42] The resulting 'GL Carpet' was laid by the third week in December. Thirty GL sets were liberated from sites around the country and set up on new, radar-only positions, these forming infill to a grid of 27 positions selected from the existing layout of gunsites with GL sets (Fig 25).[43] Each of these posts was linked to the headquarters of the Fighter Sector in which it lay, with the result that the sectors from Colerne reaching eastwards to Middle Wallop, Tangmere, Kenley, Biggin Hill, Northolt and Hornchurch were all provided with a means of plotting enemy aircraft inland using GL radars many weeks before the first GCI stations came on the air.

In their new study of gun requirements completed in August 1940 the AA Committee had recommended a large structural change in AA Command's organisation to accommodate the

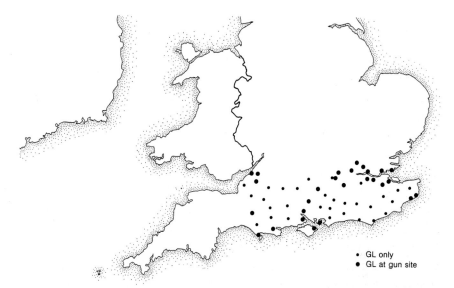

Figure 25 Distribution of sites in the GL carpet, winter 1940–41. GL stations on gunsites and in isolation were linked to Sector operations rooms to provide cover against night raiders before the introduction of GCI radar proper.

gradual increases in weapons and GDAs. Approval of the new scales of defence during mid October coincided with the completion of a report by Pile and others advancing recommendations on what form this should take.[44] The most important proposal in the short term was that five additional AA divisions and six new AA brigades should be formed immediately, and that an intermediate tier of command should for the first time be inserted between Stanmore and the divisions: this was the AA Corps, three of which (the only corps ever formed) were formally constituted on 11 November.[45] From that date, 1 AA Corps headquarters at Hillingdon House in Uxbridge took charge of 1, 5 and 6 AA Divisions in the south-east, along with the soon to be formed 8 and 9 AA Divisions in the south-west and in Wales. From a base at Kimberly in Nottinghamshire, 2 AA Corps handled the Midlands and much of northern England, with the old 2 and 4 AA Divisions now reduced in area and bordered by the new 10 AA Division (broadly, Yorkshire) and 11 AA Division (the West Midlands, Welsh Marches and north Wales). In the far north 3 AA Corps, headquartered at 18 Melville Street, Edinburgh, took charge of 7 AA Division (north-east England), 12 AA Division (the western borders and the Clyde) and 3 AA Division (much of the rest of Scotland, but excluding Orkney and Shetland Defences – OSDEF– which remained a separate formation).[46] Though the gun layout which this reorganisation was designed to accommodate was still a distant hope in November 1940, the need for reorganisation was, in Pile's words, already 'imperative' by the time it was carried out; some formations – notably the old 5 AA Division, stretching from Sussex to mid Wales – had become so large as to be virtually unmanageable. And in a further move towards efficiency, the October report also made a plea that AA Command should itself be promoted to a fully-fledged, independent formation, for the first time handling its own administration rather than working through Home Forces channels.

With a few minor adjustments in boundaries the formation structure defined in autumn 1940 persisted for two years, before another deep restructuring brought the AA organisation more closely into line with Fighter Command's geographical groups. In that time the AA divisions, particularly, developed their own regional traits and strengthened their already firm sense of collective pride. The new corps formations, too, introduced an element of regionalism to AA procedures, if on a broader canvas than that of the divisions, at the same time putting Pile and his staff at Stanmore one further remove from the batteries and sites. This is not to say that Pile ever became personally remote from his gunners – his cheery and businesslike visits of inspection saw to that – but like all senior commanders in WWII, he now headed a weighty and increasingly complex organisation. AA Command was a family firm when Pile took charge in 1939; a year later it was a major national concern.

By the New Year of 1941 the members of this organisation could look back upon three and a half months of continuous night operations in which their performance in action, on the whole, could have been better. Pile later identified the end of 1940 as the point at which his command reached 'about the lowest depths of our discomfiture',[47] chiefly because the technical and tactical refinements initiated in the heat of battle had yet to pay off, and much that was promised had yet to be delivered. Early in December the divisions received the latest in a stream of notes from Stanmore laying down the order of priority in which the first

1600 rocket projectors would be deployed;[48] but these orders, like their forerunners, would soon be overturned and many months would pass before any regular rocket battery was ready to fire. With deliveries of UP weapons continually postponed, the gun deficits which they were supposed to ameliorate were painfully clear. On the first day of the new year AA Command held 1442 HAA guns against an authorised ADGB scale of 3744 – the quota ratified in October – together with just 776 of their entitlement of 4410 modern LAA guns, and a little more than half the 8148 searchlights; there were additionally 245 GL Mk I radars on the air in Britain.[49] To make the most of what he had, in mid January Pile issued orders that 3.7in mobiles meeting long-term commitments in their GDAs should everywhere be replaced by 3.7in statics (which would dominate the new weapons coming from production), so releasing the more flexible weapons to meet emergency commitments;[50] this in essence was a recapitulation of the policy defined in June. Among these items of equipment only the radars had seen a good proportional increase during the Blitz months; up from 164 on the first of September, the radar stock now catered to half as many sites again as it had when the Luftwaffe opened the London campaign (though by now 30 sets had been diverted to the GL Carpet). Heavy guns, by contrast, had grown by only 115 in the period when they were most needed – a rise of just nine per cent on the 1 September figure of 1327 – while the percentage increase in LAA was only marginally greater. And despite their wider availability, GL radars could not give their best until the gunners had more fully penetrated their mysteries, the mats were laid, and the sets had been married to them by recalibration and testing. That work, as we know, was far from complete by the end of January 1941, a month in which the ratio of rounds fired to unseen 'birds' destroyed did show a swing in AA Command's favour, down from more than 6000 to 4087. Pile credited this to Blackett's ju-ju, and to better training all round.[51]

Adjustments to the gun layouts, laying GL mats and carpets, and rearranging the searchlights marched together in the winter of 1940–41 with the continuing night raids on Britain's cities. In

December the Luftwaffe's campaign of attrition was frustrated by
weather and on fifteen nights in the month little enemy activity
was recorded over land, though some of the raids which could be
mounted were severe. Birmingham was bombed on three
occasions during the month and Liverpool, Sheffield and
Manchester twice each, while bombers elsewhere visited Bristol
and the Solent and three penetrated the IAZ – one on 8/9
December, when 413 aircraft made the largest force to operate
since the Coventry raid of 14/15 November, and others on the
27th/28th and 29th/30th. Though smaller than the 8/9 December
operation, the last of these raids gained a lasting notoriety for its
savage incendiary effect: nearly 1500 separate fires were reported
across the capital, St Paul's Cathedral for a time looked set to
follow Coventry's and several historic buildings around the City
perished, along with much else. The London gunners' first
reaction to this incident was puzzlement. Lasting for less than
four hours and ending at ten o'clock, the operation initially
looked like a first-wave incendiary strike designed to mark the
target for a second wave dropping HE; but the second wave never
arrived and it was concluded that on this occasion the Luftwaffe
had been aiming to burn London rather than blow it up.[52] And
this, in London and elsewhere, the Luftwaffe continued to do
freely. In the whole of December the AA guns claimed ten
hostiles destroyed, and fighter aircraft just four.[53]

The Luftwaffe's use of incendiary cargoes delivered by aircraft
using *X-Gerät* opened the way for defensive measures of more
subtle kinds than guns, balloons and fighters. In late November
1940, in the wake of the Coventry raid, Britain's cities began to be
protected with a new form of decoy, known as the Starfish, which
was intended to lure subsequent waves of bombers away from
their intended targets by mimicking the fires started by the
leaders. Starfish decoys won some notable successes in the winter
of 1940–41 and subsequently, but as the national layout grew in
substance even as the Blitz was in progress the tactic as a whole
came too late to achieve the full effect of which it was technically
capable – likewise the urban lighting decoys whose development
largely occupied the second half of 1941.[54]

Despite the frantic work to improve the air defence system
one of Britain's greatest assets in January 1941 as a whole was the

worsening weather, which prevented the Luftwaffe from operating on almost half the nights in the month and obliged them to use smaller forces when they did so.[55] The reprieve lightened further in February, the month which began with Hitler's directive to target ports, when only two raids of any substance were mounted, on consecutive nights (the 19th and 20th) against Swansea. Casualties on the ground fell sharply, likewise AA Command's ratio of rounds to night raiders destroyed, which reached 2963 in February,[56] another encouraging drop in a figure which had fallen to 4087 in the previous month from as many as 20,000 during the London barrage and 11,500 in October.[57] But these statistical improvements were partly explained by the diminished opportunities to fire; the actual number of claims, in any category, which they represented was tiny. As John Ray has pointed out, in the period from November 1940 to February 1941, the Luftwaffe 'lost more aircraft from accidents over Occupied Europe than from British fire'.[58] Fighter Command's claim in November and December was six raiders downed from more than 9000 night sorties. Things looked up a little in January, when three aircraft were destroyed by fighters from 1965 enemy sorties, and in that month AA Command was credited with as many as twelve. But the arguments over the primacy of fighter or gun, which had continued since before the First World War, were not so much resolved by these figures as made to seem irrelevant. Neither fighters nor guns, it seemed, were a true match for the night bomber, which continued to get through.

In the first week of March the Luftwaffe continued to hold back from large raids against industrial centres, instead mounting sporadic minor attacks on bomber stations, launching a large fighter sweep over Kent, and continuing the blockade tactics against maritime supply routes by bombing ports and shipping and laying mines off the coast.[59] By late February the level of minelaying in the Bristol Channel, in particular, was giving cause for concern, not least through the difficulty in bringing fire to bear on aircraft flying over the midwaters of the estuary.

This, in fact, was an historic problem in the defence of the Severn, which in the 1860s gained coast artillery guns on Steepholm and Flatholm islands to form a barrier against hostile warships intent upon targets further upstream (notably Bristol).[60]

These guns, however, had been removed by the beginning of the twentieth century, along with their companions at Brean Down fort and Lavernock, and were not replaced in the Great War, when Bristol's coast defences were sited at Portishead and Avonmouth. After the Armistice these weapons, too, were removed; but the Luftwaffe's minelaying activities in the spring of 1941, coupled with the Admiralty's anxieties about surface craft penetrating the channel, brought the defence of the Severn Estuary under fresh scrutiny.

In the summer of 1940, when the invasion threat had been at its height, Britain had been hurriedly ringed with shore-mounted guns in 'emergency batteries', which for the first time extended the coast artillery cover traditionally provided for the major ports to a near-complete national cordon. The Severn Estuary, however, was omitted from this project until February 1941, when plans were made to reinstate the barrier defence from Brean Down to Lavernock, via Steepholm and Flatholm. The idea that the guns emplaced on one of the mid-estuarine islands should be designed for dual purpose coast artillery/anti-aircraft work originated in the Admiralty, who argued that 4.5in weapons mounted for low angle and skyward fire would provide an economical solution to both surface raiders and the minelayers of the Luftwaffe.[61] In early March, therefore, 1 AA Corps was instructed to reconnoitre both islands with a view to deciding what should be done.[62] The result was that Flatholm was given four 4.5in HAA guns mounted in specially-designed emplacements (Fig 26) to allow dual-role firing, becoming site J16 in the Cardiff GDA. Installed in September 1941,[63] these dual-role 4.5s and their mounting were structurally unique in Britain, and would find a functional parallel only in a single site built for 5.25in guns working in a joint coast artillery and anti-aircraft role at Park Battery at South Shields, a site commissioned in summer 1943 as the sole representative of what had originally been planned as a much larger programme.

The preliminary work on the dual-role project for the Severn Estuary coincided with a wider review of AA dispositions in western Britain which began in mid March to meet the Battle of the Atlantic. Prompted by a prime ministerial directive of 27 February giving 'absolute priority' to defending shipping in the

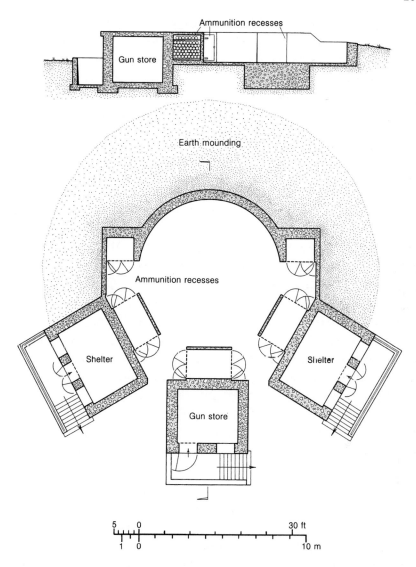

Figure 26 A 4.5in dual role emplacement of the type designed for guns working for joint coast artillery/anti-aircraft defence in the Bristol Channel.

north-western approaches,[64] this project gave rise to a speedy reshuffling of AA guns away from the inland industrial areas towards the west coast ports, as well as further refinements to the radar chain and changes in the dispositions of fighter squadrons. The first new guns were on the move within a few days of the requirement being defined, and by 14 March some 58 additional

HAA weapons had been assigned to the Mersey, the Clyde and the Bristol Channel, together with 23 new guns from the production quota expected in March. At the same time, a plan was thrashed out whereby 150 Bofors guns and crews would be diverted from the factories and ADGB to be made available to the Admiralty; these would be supplemented by returning 106 naval 2pdr Mk VIIIs which the navy had loaned to AA Command earlier in the war.[65] The hurried westerly diversion of HAA weapons, however, was the first stage in what now became a familiar sequence of events. Since the west coast ports were already sharply under-gunned in relation to approved scales, the new weapons merely corrected a deficit, and then only partially so: of the five broad areas reinforced for the Atlantic campaign, only the Mersey was brought up to its approved scale of 96 guns in this first reinforcement, while the Clyde, the Cardiff/Newport/ Barry GDAs, Bristol, and the Swansea/Port Talbot/Llanelli complex retained yawning gaps in their layouts. Then, to compound the problem, the fresh study of AA scales which the original directive had initiated predictably concluded that two of the five areas needed more guns than were scheduled even under the latest plans. So the gap opened still wider, with the result that the Clyde in mid March had 88 HAA guns against a (revised) quota of 144, and the layout of 96 just achieved on the Mersey suddenly became inadequate, as the goal was deftly moved further away (specifically to 112). The cumulative result was that, in all, the Atlantic ports were 104 HAA guns short on 21 March. Reporting to the Air Ministry on that date, Sholto Douglas explained that he planned to deal with the Mersey first, by finding sixteen guns from Slough, Derby and Nottingham, and then with the other areas as far as he could by robbing Peter to pay Paul. And, of course, 58 guns had to be found from somewhere to restore those already stripped from inland cities such as Sheffield and Birmingham. Steps had 'most certainly' to be taken 'to replace these guns at the earliest possible moment', Douglas insisted in a communiqué to the Air Ministry which could not have been more forcefully worded.

I am compelled therefore to request in the strongest possible terms [Douglas concluded] that immediate action may be taken with the Authorities concerned to guarantee without fail that the greatest possible number of HAA guns shall be made available from production for ADGB at the earliest possible moment. All the resources from production, without exception, should in my view be allotted to ADGB until these essential requirements are met. The defence of these vital west coast port areas cannot be regarded as satisfactory until this decision has been taken and fully implemented.[66]

All of this was agreed by the AA Committee, who passed the recommendations on to the Chiefs of Staff.[67] Building on the earlier reinforcements, the cumulative result was that the Mersey's layout reached 109 HAA guns by the last week in April, up from 72 two months earlier, Bristol's rose to 66 from 35 in the same period, the Clyde's from 67 to 101, and smaller increases were seen at Cardiff, Newport, Milford Haven and Swansea.[68] Though lower than recommended, these densities were the highest that the western targets had reached at any stage in the war so far.

The new guns installed at Bristol in March soon proved their worth, when the night of the 29th/30th brought a heavy raid on Avonmouth. But night operations in the last week of this month continued to be dominated by minelaying, chiefly in the Humber Estuary and in coastal waters at Milford Haven, north-east England, East Anglia and, on the night of 1/2 April, in the Thames Estuary; altogether 135 enemy aircraft were engaged in these attacks, though only five were destroyed by the AA guns.[69] By day the Luftwaffe continued to harass shipping in the Channel, while making numerous minor incursions inland and launching occasional fighter sweeps – as on 27 March, when a force assessed as 21 aircraft made two afternoon forays over east Kent.[70] The pattern of light daylight raiding continued during the first week of April, though the 8th of the month brought a more concentrated operation, when 90 enemy aircraft attacked shipping in the outer reaches of the Thames Estuary. Night activity, however, was heavier in this week, when minelaying became rather more intensive and two successive night raids were made on Bristol and Avonmouth. The night of 7/8 April then brought a concentrated attack on the Clyde and supplementary operations

reached as far afield as Belfast, Bristol, Birmingham and the
Thames Estuary, before Coventry was visited the next night and a
smaller force was sent to Portsmouth.[71] And so it continued. The
second week of April produced limited daylight activity and only
one sizeable operation, when 50 aircraft operating at great height
made an inconclusive incursion over the south-east on the 16th;
but the pitch of night raiding was maintained. Birmingham was
hard hit on 9/10 April, when a large volume of incendiaries
raining on the city started many fires; and together with Coventry,
Birmingham was bombed again on the following night. Though
bad weather interrupted the Luftwaffe's work on two nights in
this week, sizeable forces were otherwise busy at targets as
widely spread as Tyneside, Belfast and Portsmouth.[72]

With larger numbers of targets offered to their sights, AA
Command's hit-rate increased to seventeen aircraft in March and
$39^1/_2$ in April,[73] for a slightly increased ammunition expenditure
of 3195 'rounds per bird' at night.[74] These improvements,
however, owed more to the gunners' deepening experience and
the progress of the GL mat programme than to increases in the
number of guns, which were modest and always won in
competition with many other claimants. Between January and
April 1941 AA Command's stock of HAA rose by just 110 guns (to
1552), almost half of which were supplied in March, but in that
same period 42 HAA weapons went to the Middle East, 52 were
sent to ports in the colonies, sixteen went to India and Burma and
an equal number to foreign customers.[75] In all, then, the 126 heavy
weapons diverted to commitments outside ADGB represented a
larger quota than that added to the domestic gun defences. It may
be that Sholto Douglas's blunt missive in March had some effect
in the following months, for the delivery rate of HAA weapons
did rise in April to 72, before falling back to 44 in May and the
same number in June. On 1 July the ADGB total stood at 1712,[76]
but by then the Blitz was over. The LAA position was little better.
Just 88 guns were added to the ADGB stocks between January
and April, compared to 42 for Home Forces (fourteen of which
were on loan to ADGB), 78 for the Middle East, 54 for ports
abroad and sixteen for India and Burma.[77]

One justification for the parsimonious allocations to AA
Command in the early part of 1941 was the expected arrival of

rocket projectors to eke out the conventional guns. In the event these long-awaited devices began to enter service only when the Blitz was nearing its end, and not before numerous changes of plan in how they should be deployed. Divisions received detailed technical briefing notes on the 3in projector in early October 1940, when around 1000 of the single-barrelled version had already been built (by Messrs G A Harvey of Greenwich) and early pilot models of the twin-barrelled variant were in prospect.[78] In October, too, a special trials battery was formed under Duncan Sandys – by now a major, and rising – to complete operational trials at the Aberporth rocket range, standardise drills for the weapon and (no small task) to furnish the basis of the equipment's manuals and other documentation.[79] A month later 2600 projectors were ready and a further 3400 were under construction, but by then the supply of these quickly-built weapons was rapidly outpacing that of ammunition and personnel. So, far from being emplaced as they came from the production lines, most projectors were immediately consigned to store. This was more serious than it sounds, since no proper warehousing was available for such a huge bulk of equipment, nor even tarpaulins to cover them at the ordnance depots and magazines in which they found a damp and uncomfortable home. In mid November Pile sent a testy letter to the War Office warning that these conditions promised rapid deterioration. 'I fully expect,' he declared, 'to discover that when the time comes to emplace these projectors, that a large number are unserviceable.'[80]

The first allocations of UP weapons to sites had been confidently passed down to formations as early as mid August 1940; four months later, after numerous amendments in detail, the plans were revised again, sharing the very first weapons among a number of docks, industrial targets, and highly sensitive VPs, such as the Chain Home station at Dover.[81] At this date UP weapons were conceived chiefly as a tool against dive-bombing, a mode of attack to which their pattern of fire was especially suited, and the initial batch of weapons began to be installed at the first priority VPs for that purpose. But March brought another change of plan. With high-level bombing against ports rumbling on, it was decided to use the next (and much larger) batch of projectors to defend these targets against aircraft flying at up to

Plate 15 A Z battery. Multiple static rocket launchers in action.

20,000 feet. Sandys' men accordingly found themselves dispatched to an operational site in the Cardiff GDA to work out a completely fresh set of drills for high-altitude fire. Happily the 3in projector proved well-adapted to the high-level role – unsurprisingly, perhaps, for it had originally been conceived as just this type of weapon. At the end of March corps headquarters were duly warned that the next batch of projectors would be sited as defence against high flying raiders at nine major ports from Newcastle clockwise to Glasgow.[82] Reconnaissances for these sites were made in April, and in time this second and somewhat larger consignment of weapons came into service. Meanwhile, on 7 April, Sandys' rockets at Cardiff destroyed their first enemy aircraft.[83]

The UP's basic unit of deployment in 1941 was the ZAA battery of 64 projectors, comprising four troops of sixteen weapons each. The first UPs acting in the anti-dive bombing role were allocated either in double-troops or troops, with the former (32 projectors) assigned to Chilwell, Austin's at Longbridge, and docks at Aberdeen, Swansea and Cardiff, and the sixteen-projector troops to the Porthcurno cable station, Dorman Long's

Cleveland works and the radar station at Dover. To simplify control, however, and to concentrate fire, the UPs allocated for high-firing duties during March were used in larger numbers. With the exception of Barrow, the ports to be defended were allocated two 64-projector batteries apiece (Barrow had one), where possible sited not more than two miles apart to enable both to work from a common GL set. In all, the nine ports shared 1088 projectors.

Two common characteristics of wartime ZAA sites – large size, but comparative simplicity – were evident even in these first examples. One of the great virtues of the rocket projector from a tactical point of view (and a characteristic which commended it in the first place) was its elementary engineering. Unlike a conventional gun, which fires a shell by exploding a charge in the breech, a rocket launcher dispatches a projectile whose power is entirely self-contained; the great forces unleashed within a gun when the charge explodes, the sharp recoil of the weapon, and the continuous fire as round succeeds round all require robust engineering of a kind unnecessary in the rocket projector, which is little more than an adjustable launching ramp for a firework. This means that the wartime Z projector required a much lighter emplacement to anchor it to the ground – many indeed were on mobile mountings – and fewer ancillary structures; but at the same time, like all rocket weapons, the blast issuing from the projectile meant that each projector needed plenty of open space around. Hence the simplicity of Z battery sites, and their size.

Sources suggest that the Z projectors assigned to the high-level port defences in March 1941 were equipped with mobile mountings, but fixed emplacements were used both for the earlier group sent to the first priority targets, and for the subsequent issues for which sites were being prepared when the new commitment arose. And these structures were deliberately kept simple. Though AA Command did consider a preliminary design incorporating ammunition recesses and other niceties, this was rejected by the War Office in January 1941 on the grounds that its cost and complexity were unnecessary for a weapon intended to be at least 'transportable', if not fully mobile.[84] The emplacement used for the early projectors, therefore, was simply an eight-foot-square plinth of concrete five inches thick with a series of rag bolts set centrally to accept the weapon's base plate – this essentially was just a concrete mass to anchor the projector to the ground.[85] Early ZAA sites obeyed no standard layout, and ammunition was simply stored at a convenient point not less than fifteen yards from the projector itself, while each projector in a sixteen-weapon group was kept at least 33 yards from any other; the result was often a loosely-arranged grid of weapons, its exact form shaped by local conditions. Each group of sixteen projectors was supervised from a control post, whence the officer or NCO in charge of the troop would issue instructions by Tannoy or field telephone to the two-man crew of each weapon, while a command post equipped similarly to those on HAA sites served the whole 64-projector battery. In early sites both were improvised, making use of whatever was available locally – Nissen huts were sometimes adopted, though other sites made do with simple dugouts. Accommodation, too, was improvised at first, as it was when most conventional AA sites were newly occupied. Some sites were lucky enough to gain their own domestic buildings, while others used requisitioned billets, but some had to make do with tents. There was, in short, little consistency to the pioneering Z battery sites. That came later.

Tactically, the greatest difference between early Z batteries and conventional gunsites was the single-barrel rocket projector's limitation as a 'one-shot' weapon. Where a conventional gun could fire repeatedly, the time taken to reload and re-lay the rocket projector between each firing limited it to just one chance, with one rocket, in the course of a typical engagement; the comparison is not unlike that between a shotgun and a repeating rifle. The shotgun analogy carries a little further, too, in the sense that the UP weapon delivered a cluster of projectiles simultaneously at its target, rather than a rapid stream of rounds. In the Z battery's case those projectiles were the rockets launched separately from each weapon, which against the dive-bomber were fuzed to explode at around 3500 feet and against high-level targets at a suitable altitude, as we have seen, up to 20,000 feet. Alwyn Crow's early work on the rocket projector had anticipated using proximity fuzes to detonate the rocket's warhead, and these did enter service later on; but despite some exploratory discussion in 1940 on the potential of photo-electric fuzes (activated by the shadow of the target), the requirement for all-weather and night firing soon ruled them out. Nonetheless, in the deployment of these first rocket projectors AA Command at last gained a weapon which would do much to offset its shortages of conventional guns as the war progressed.

Although the period from September 1940 to May 1941 is widely recognised as AA Command's stiffest operational test of the early war years, it is less widely appreciated that Pile's men were simultaneously fighting another battle in these months: a battle against the elements and the shortcomings of their living accommodation. Superficially a purely domestic matter, and in this sense tangential to the command's core activity of fighting the Luftwaffe, the battle of the huts was in many ways no less important, and was certainly a pressing concern for the men themselves. Soldiers do not expect to be cosseted, but, to give of their best, in the medium term they need to be properly fed and housed and to find the necessary rest and respite from the rigours of combat, from heavy physical work and from long nights on the guns and instruments. Poor accommodation was a contributor to 1 AA Division's disciplinary and morale troubles in the deepening winter of 1940–41, and was caused in part by the necessary fluidity of London's HAA deployments during the Blitz. Frequent moves to uncertain places were no less common elsewhere, and as the Blitz rumbled on confirmed the need for AA Command to confront its domestic difficulties squarely.

Many problems were the result of the command's rapid expansion in personnel and sites during the first year of the war. A proportion of Pile's permanent gunsites had been moderately well provided with huts in the year after Munich, in a programme which continued into 1940. In July of that year, as the Battle of Britain was beginning, Stanmore had approved a series of 'Emergency Scales' for HAA, LAA and searchlight sites which should, in principle, have ensured that each man slept in a hut rather than a tent, even if camp structures would continue to be used for cookhouses, latrines, ablutions and other ancillaries.[86] But the approval of Emergency Scales during the summer of 1940 was one thing; providing the skilled labour necessary to implement them before the onset of winter was quite another. The summer and autumn of 1940 saw much of the country's labour absorbed by the needs of emergency home defences – pillboxes, anti-tank ditches, concrete obstacles – a task whose demands fell as much upon the civilian contractor as the military, and which continued on a reduced scale into the winter months and beyond. At the same time, the continuing accommodation needs of the BEF, recently evacuated from France, placed additional burdens upon manpower and materials. For AA Command, this was also a period of tactical flux, resulting in many short-term moves of mobile HAA between sites. Not the least of their problems was the tendency of units to vacate sites just as accommodation was nearing completion. Alternatively, cases were known where construction was deferred in the belief that site occupation would be brief, only for men to find themselves camping among unassembled Nissen huts two months later. In the event AA Command was forced to rely upon a large measure of improvisation to accommodate its men during the winter of 1940–41, not always with much success.

During August 1940 Pile had put the view that the shortage of labour and materials could be met in part from AA Command's own resources. It was felt that something could be gained by recycling bricks, sandbags, concrete blocks, corrugated iron and asbestos sheets from any surplus on other projects or from non-essential applications, or through direct purchase on the open market. Equally, the conscript army now deployed on sites throughout the country inevitably contained a proportion of officers and men with building expertise which could be turned to their own needs. It was suggested that units keen to get started on their own accommodation might resort to local purchase of cement and secondhand tools, and that 'with practice' and qualified supervision it was reasonable to expect ten or a dozen unskilled soldiers to erect a Nissen hut in a week. Local supervisory expertise was to be used wherever possible, in consultation with the Royal Engineers.[87]

War Office approval to this 'self-help' scheme was given on 3 September 1940,[88] and troops set to work, as AA Command's historical notes put it, 'in many cases with more will than skill, and in some places with more enthusiasm than others'.[89] Civil engineers now in AA uniform were pressed into service as works supervisors. Others were drafted in from units outside ADGB. Civil contractors continued to be used where available, and a mixed economy based upon outside firms and unit labour developed. To ease the burden on his troops, Pile approved a system in which batteries engaged in building would be retired from the fight, their weapons made temporarily non-operational as lorries laden with Nissen hut kits rolled onto the gunsites. This work was under way as autumn turned to winter, and as the heaviest weight of the German night bombing offensive was brought to bear upon the cities.

In many areas the self-help programme failed outright though inexpert building and operational distractions. Many civilian contractors proved hopeless. Visiting two Leeds sites towards the end of November, the AA Command Welfare Officer discovered disorder at both. His report for one site found that:

There were materials for four huts which had been lying on the site for a period of from 8 to 10 weeks, but there was still no sign of the contractor who was expected to erect them. As a result of this not only was the battery short of hutting but the actual materials which included such things as stoves were deteriorating owing to exposure to the weather.[90]

The second site was found to consist of a brick bath-house, a huddle of requisitioned cottages, and a small, partly complete hutted camp, some of the materials for which had been lying on the site for over two months. Visiting 483 HAA Battery at Combe, the Command Medical Adviser found that:

Conditions were so bad here that I sent a teleprint to Command to try and have something done to improve things. The men were under canvas, at least under such canvas as had not been blown away. All bedding was soaking wet. Heath Robinson cook-houses, water from the farm well, doubtful purity. No cover for latrines, all seats awash. Sections of Nissen huts had been on the site for four weeks. The sergeant in charge told me that on the site they had just left, they had been under canvas two months although Nissen hut material had been on the site all that time.[91]

The position in the south was no better. Toward the end of November, a senior officer's report from Hampshire stated that:

> Owing to a system of contracts, red tape, and egregious folly, many searchlight units are still under canvas in isolated and most unpleasant spots. I have tried all means of getting a move on, and cannot [. . .]. Last year, despite very many difficulties largely due to AA being superimposed on existing areas, ignorant and inexperienced officers putting sites in bogs and other such places, a quarrelsome AA Deputy who infuriated area commanders, etc, etc, things could be done and got righted. Now I see no hope whatever, short of getting to the basis of a bad system. Contracts are given to the lowest bidder. The lowest bidders in two districts I know were men whom I would not dream of employing on private or council work. They have not got the brains, staff, material or, for that matter, honesty. The result is that for months and months wood lies getting warped and rotten, iron rusting, and the result is that men are wet and uncomfortable. In one area they are in luxurious brick erections, the only trouble being there is nearly a hut a man to keep clean – in another they are in sordid discomfort.[92]

Most of these problems were the result of failings by private contractors, but self-help among batteries often brought comparable difficulties. Hutting built by unit labour suffered from poor surveying, which often led to structures being erected on uneven ground. Corrugated iron roof skins buckled, and floors flooded. Sanitation was beyond the expertise of many units, so men were required to wash in their muddy Nissens. The cookhouse at one coastal site was said to consist of driftwood scavenged from the beach. During October, the requisitioning of caravans was authorised;[93] then '4 AA Division proudly announced that they had tried housing 10 men in a double-decker bus and that the experiment had proved successful [. . .]. Command hurried out diagrammatic sketches showing how many men were to sleep upstairs and how many down.'[94] Clearly, permanent solutions were needed.

A War Office meeting on 3 December to assess progress in ADGB accommodation found that Eastern and Southern Commands were faring worst. The situation in 1 AA Division was critical, thanks partly to this area's front-line role in the London Blitz. Pile protested to the War Office on 14 December.

> This is a situation that I cannot possibly accept. If the AA personnel are to live permanently under unsuitable conditions with unsuitable cookhouses, ablution shelters and latrines and without a reasonable standard of comfort when off duty they will not be fit to carry out their arduous day and night duties efficiently. The chief trouble at the moment is in connection with the movement of four-gun detachments to form eight-gun sites. Whilst it is possible for a time to consider bringing up men by bus for night duty from the old site, it cannot continue for long. Whilst I am prepared to accept temporarily some sleeping accommodation in store tents with bell tents inside, a proportion of Nissen huts are [sic] essential at once, and in addition cookhouses, latrines, etc.
>
> What really seems to me outrageous is that our operations of war should be constantly hindered by having recourse to peacetime regulations for our administrative services. This sort of thing would not be tolerated in an overseas theatre of war and I cannot for the life of me see why we should put up with it because our theatre of war is in England.
>
> What I ask then most urgently is this: (a) this hesitation to re-erect huts on the eight-gun sites should be removed; (b) that in view of the urgent importance of their operational role, ADGB units should be given priority at the moment in labour and materials for establishing themselves on their fighting positions; (c) that the same methods employed in rapidly getting on with our defence works last summer should be applicable to the operational necessities of the ADGB units and that regulations for Engineer Services in peace should be put away until the end of the war.
>
> The above is primarily applicable to 1st AA Division requirements. There are, as I have said, scandals in other parts of the country [. . .]. I have heard of a site near Chatham begun in May and still unfinished; this is typical of many similar cases [. . .]. Conditions in the accommodation of ADGB units [. . .] are rapidly, I fear, if not dealt with very soon, going to lead to serious scandals.[95]

These claims are amply borne out by statistical records maintained by the Directorate of Fortifications and Works. The earliest available data belong to mid February 1941, when the situation had begun to improve, but the figures show that of 231 mobile HAA sites on AA Command's books, only four in every five had been hutted to the minimum scale laid down seven months earlier, in July 1940, and that progress in remedying the shortfall was creakingly slow: only four sites of the 186 *with* huts had been so provided in the preceding month.[96] In practice this meant that gunners on the remaining 45 sites were making do, in February, to a greater or lesser extent with tents. Two months later, in mid April 1941, some 2190 mobile HAA troops remained under canvas, together with 252 mobile LAA gunners and 1427 of those on the 1975 searchlight batteries then in place.[97] The situation on static batteries was rather better. In mid February 1941 AA Command nominally had 340 of these sites – though some were still under construction and a few had yet to be started – of which 264 were four-gun positions, twenty were eight-gun and a residue 56 two-gun sites, despite the policy which had made these positions obsolete. Not all of these sites had weapons, of course, though the majority were by now hutted to a reasonable scale. Of the 264 four-gun positions, 209 had all their guns, one had just two, 39 were vacant but ready for guns, one half so, twelve were complete but for holdfasts and three had yet to be started. Of 254 four-gun sites expected to be hutted – ten fewer than the total of sites – progress was put at about 90 per cent of the requirement. The ratios for two-gun sites were similar to this, but the eight-gun sites were far behind. Of the twenty due to be built only four had their full complement of guns, and while domestic accommodation for troops manning the first four guns at each was estimated at 90 per cent complete, that for the men on the second four guns stood at just one-tenth of the required scale. In February 1941 that mattered less than it sounds, since only four of those sites were fully gunned anyway, and by April the requirement for eight-gun sites had itself been shaved down to twelve (it dropped again to ten in September). But the point remains that the eight-gun positions – one of Pile's prime anxieties in December 1940 – were not properly hutted for many months, and that half of the men on those occupied remained under canvas throughout the winter.[98]

If huts and guns were in short supply during the Blitz, so too were men. For much of the war Pile was troubled by deficits in manpower, which began to deepen in late 1940 to reach a shortage of 1114 officers and 17,965 soldiers by the end of the year. As Pile himself recalled, the staff shortage by early 1941 was threatening 'to nullify anything we might do to achieve technical improvement' in gunnery; and nor was this a deficit merely in numbers. At the root of Pile's problem was the steady drain of experienced troops away from AA Command towards other branches of the army, and chiefly to the ill-starred BEF, who had taken a sizeable cadre of his best men before the fall of France. True, when measured in numbers the net exchange of officers between AA Command and the Field Army had worked in Pile's favour; but this statistic, for all that it was parroted to Pile by an Army Council anxious to sidestep the problem, took no account of the flow of *expertise*, which was very much the other way. As Pile put it, with characteristic simplicity, 'we had posted away trained men and we had received in return untrained men.'[99] To make matters worse, far from being dissipated the 'plague of dimwits' which descended on AA Command earlier in the war was still being reinforced.

To test his own judgement on the quality of the new recruits, toward the end of 1940 Pile sought objective advice from Professor F C Bartlett at the Faculty of Psychology at Cambridge, whose 1927 book *Psychology and the Soldier* had early marked him down as an expert in the field.[100] Not altogether to Pile's surprise, Bartlett's clinical opinion was that, while the general conscript intake into the army could 'be regarded as a genuinely unselected group', that proportion allocated to AA Command had 'already, in some way or another, been selected in some negatively useful manner [. . .]'.[101]

Pile's meeting with Bartlett and his assistant, Dr Blackburn, yielded one solution to the problem of quality, if none to that of quantity. Under Bartlett's guidance in early December 1940 Pile decided to run a psychological experiment among his troops in the hope of matching their abilities as individuals to specific gunsite jobs. As Pile explained to the War Office, the thinking behind this trial in what today we should call aptitude testing was simply that 'a man who is to work on a predictor requires a different type of mind from a man who is to handle ammunition at a gun.'[102] To discover what sorts of minds his men had, Pile proposed to begin the experiment simultaneously among the raw recruits and the serving soldiers.

> Intake[s] on their arrival at their training regiments [Pile explained] are put through psychological tests with a view to discovering the duty for which they are most suited. I have decided to carry out similar tests, as an experiment, with selected operational units under my command. On Professor Bartlett's advice, in order to give the experiment a fair trial I am taking approximately five hundred men from each of the HAA, LAA and SL units. The tests will be carried out by Dr Blackburn himself. The men will then be re-trained in the duties for which the tests show them to be suited. At the end of two months the gun units will attend practice camp, we will then decide whether the units have been markedly improved as a result.[103]

Pile's readiness to seek advice from eclectic sources also paid dividends in his attempts to solve AA Command's more basic quantitative personnel problem. As long ago as 1938, shortly after he was appointed to command 1 AA Division, Pile had ruminated on the possibility that women might be brought into anti-aircraft duties – not simply as handmaids to proper soldiers' work but as professionals in the technical trades of fire-control and other ancillaries to gunnery. He decided to find out, and just as he later consulted Professors Blackett and Bartlett for advice in their respective fields, in 1938 Pile approached Caroline Haslett, an electrical engineer who had gained some prominence in inter-war Britain as a champion of women's emancipation. Though her later career took her into many other fields, before the war Haslett had been particularly interested in emancipation of a specific and literal kind: that is in the ability of technology to liberate women from domestic chores. Haslett was thereby some-thing of a specialist in the ergonomic, social and (for want of a better term) cultural relationships between women and machines. Probably no one in Britain was better qualified to judge whether women could operate predictors and heightfinders, and (because 'women' by itself suggests a rather large and heterogeneous category of person), what sorts of women might do it best.

Haslett gave up many of her Sundays in 1938 following Pile and 1 AA Division on their exercises in the Surrey hills, before pronouncing herself satisfied that most women could indeed operate fire-control instruments and searchlights 'and, in fact, do almost everything except fire the guns'. Pile for his part 'saw no logical reason why they should not fire the guns too',[104] but, wary that the notion of employing women on any kind of operational equipment – let alone lethal weapons – was likely to prove anathema to the War Office, he let that idea lie. In the first weeks of the war, however, he did suggest that women might be brought into AA Command to operate searchlights and radars. Nothing came of that; but a year or so later, with the personnel shortage growing, he tried again.

Pile's campaign began in December 1940, when after a series of discussions with interested parties he wrote to the War Office recommending that authority be given to employ ATS in a number of new duties with AA Command. By this date the ATS already had an established role in serving the command through a range of ancillary jobs – chiefly administration, catering and transport – but Pile's idea was to employ them much more widely on fire-control instruments and in operations rooms, forming mixed-sex units in which women would dominate (numerically) and work in most areas of the site except the gunpit itself. Of course there was resistance. Sir James Grigg, Under-Secretary of State for War, found the idea 'breath-taking and revolutionary'; and so too did many senior officers of the ATS itself, particularly when Pile argued that the women should be given ranks, pay scales and other benefits which would bring them fully in line with their male counterparts. (In this 'laudable ambition', wrote Pile, 'I was more of a feminist than the members of the ATS Directorate.'[105]) But in the end, as usual, 'it was pure mathematics that forced everybody's hand,' though it did not do so until the heavy night raids were almost at an end: it was mid May 1941 before War Office sanction to form the first mixed batteries was given. So Pile's campaign to begin his 'great experiment' took six months, and when training for the first batteries was added the delay in getting the first women to the sites extended to the high summer of 1941.

Rocket batteries, ATS soldiers, the Home Guard, better troops, more guns, decent accommodation, efficient radars – all of these were commodities which AA Command needed in the Blitz but acquired, in the event, too late to make a difference in their

stiffest test of the war so far. By the middle of May, when the last
heavy raids struck London and Birmingham, there were definite
signs of improvement in the gunners' performance: fully 31$\frac{1}{2}$
aircraft fell to the guns in the closing fortnight of raiding, of
which six were downed on just one day.[106] Had similar results
been achieved in September, when the first bombers had
appeared over London, the Blitz might well have been shorter
and less bloody than it was. But even at the end the Luftwaffe
were able to send bombers over London in huge numbers, as they
did on 10 May, the second-to-last major raid of the campaign,
when 507 aircraft bombed the capital. Though not the largest
force to hit London in the eight months since the city had entered
the firing line, it was by some margin the most destructive of the
war. On this one night the Luftwaffe poured 711 tons of HE into
the capital, along with 2393 incendiary canisters, less than they
had on London's previous major raid on 16 April, when 712
aircraft had dropped 1026 tons of HE and 4252 fire bombs,[107] but
to greater effect. Some 2154 separate fires were reported on that
night; 1436 people died; 1792 were badly injured, and numerous
others less seriously so; many public buildings and monuments
suffered, among them the Law Courts, the Tower, the War Office,
the Royal Naval College, Westminster School, the Royal Mint, the
Mansion House, St James's Palace, the Houses of Parliament –
this was the night that the Commons was gutted by fire – and
Westminster Abbey, along with several lesser churches. Hit too
were the British Museum and the Public Record Office, not all of
whose precious contents could be evacuated.[108] Firefighting had
been hampered by low water in the Thames and compounded by
ruptured mains, and many firefighters and civil defence workers
were numbered among the dead and maimed. Londoners
emerged from the shelters to fearsome scenes, twelve thousand
finding themselves homeless; and if there was a point in the Blitz
at which public morale began to waver, it has been argued that
this was it. 'It was just one raid too much,' thought one American
journalist.[109] People had suffered enough.

But after this London was spared from sustained attack until the
winter of 1944–45, and when the Blitz is viewed from the perspective of history it is difficult to find any point at which British
public morale even approached the collapse predicted by pre-war

theorists of the bomber doctrine. One reason, certainly, may be the bracing effect of German casualty figures issued for public consumption. Writing of the 10 May London raid, the *Aeroplane* magazine parroted official figures in writing of 33 bombers being destroyed by the air defences on that night, likewise of 114 falling to the guns and fighters in the week of the operation.[110] That, obviously, was ludicrous. The actual claims credited to the gunners in the third week of May 1941 were three and a half in Category I, three in Category II and six in Category III, bringing AA Command's total bag in the war so far, in those three categories, to 578, 192½ and 194.[111] But AA Command had other functions besides shooting down aircraft, and of the many imponderable psychological factors which accounted for the birth and vitality of the 'Blitz spirit', we would be mistaken to forget the roar of the guns. If the Blitz was, in part, a battle of morale, then AA Command may have done more to win it than mere statistics can possibly tell.

CHAPTER 8

Great experiments

JUNE 1941 – FEBRUARY 1942

The weeks following the end of the main air offensive against Britain's cities were a period of change for AA Command. Despite Germany's attack on the Soviet Union in Operation *Barbarossa*, launched in the early morning of 22 June, planning against invasion in the late summer or autumn of 1941 continued, and brought about a substantial rearrangement of gun layouts. At the same time Pile and his staff undertook rigorous analyses of their tactics during the Blitz, an exercise which yielded much new thinking and some material effects upon deployments and procedures. But the greatest change in the character of AA Command as the war approached its third year was social, not tactical, for on 21 August 1941 the first mixed battery became operational, at ZS20 in Richmond Park.

Pile's original plan for the deployment of the mixed batteries had two parts, both intended to introduce huge numbers of ATS to the operational units of AA Command.[1] First, in the thinking of early summer 1941, Pile expected that all new HAA regiments passing through the training mill would in future be exclusively mixed; and secondly that once a contingent of trained women was available the existing single-sex HAA units with static guns (though not mobiles) would be progressively converted to mixed personnel. Though they were termed 'mixed' batteries, they might almost have been designated 'female' units, since women far outnumbered men in their establishments – a typical mixed battery of 388 personnel included 299 women.[2] Overall, by December 1941 Pile expected to have almost 40 mixed batteries fully formed and in action, and to see the jobs of 15,000 men taken by 18,500 women.[3] A year later, it was planned, no fewer than 170,000 of the 220,000 women due by then to be serving with the ATS would be manning (the term persisted) AA Command's gunsites. In fact these totals were not realised. Pile's ATS complement never exceeded 74,000, though thanks to general staffing cuts as the war progressed by the end of 1944 there were more women serving with AA Command than men.[4] But if women eased Pile's personnel shortages in the middle war years to a lesser extent than he had once hoped, this was the only disappointment. It became all the sharper once the professionalism and dedication of the women began to emerge.

As the pioneer ATS volunteers settled into their duties at Richmond Park, Pile reflected proudly that these 'British girls' were 'the first to take their place in a combatant rôle in any army in the world'.[5] In that belief he was wrong. The Soviet Union had mobilised women for combat early in the Second World War, during which some 300,000 served in AA units alone; and unlike their British counterparts – who technically were *not* combatants – the Russians shouldered all the tasks of the battery, firing the guns as well as handling fire-control instruments, telephones and plotting.[6] Meeting these women at Stalingrad a year later, the fliers of Luftflotte 4 found their fire deadly; and no less so the tank commanders of the 16th Panzer Division, who were shocked to discover that the 37mm anti-aircraft fire issuing from the city came from female batteries, their LAA guns desperately engaging ground targets.[7] These contemptuously-dubbed *Flintenweiber* – 'gun women' in a slightly bowdlerised translation – were alien to the Germans' experience and expectations. Women in the confident Reich of 1941–42 were, at most, allowed to serve the military in subordinate, clerical capacities, as an unwelcome diversion from their state-ordained destiny of motherhood. It took the Allied strategic bomber offensive to change that. Pressed for recruits, Hitler eventually allowed women into AA batteries by an order of 17 July 1943, but even then, as in Britain, they were disbarred from the guns. German and British experiences of women in AA work were in fact very similar, except that the Germans hesitated for two years longer than the British.[8]

The duties given to women on British AA batteries were

circumscribed but vital, and since most were highly technical the selection procedures were exacting and the training thorough.[9] A recruit to the ATS who volunteered for AA work took a series of aptitude tests (equivalent to those taken by the men as a result of Pile's consultation with Bartlett in 1940) to assess her 'quickness and keenness of eye, sureness of hand and steadiness of nerve'. On this basis a suitable candidate would be graded to work on radar, predictor, heightfinder, kine-theodolite or as a telephonist or spotter, the main operational duties allowed to her sex. (ATS officers were at first used purely for administration, but eventually served in the command post in parallel duties to their male equivalents.) From there the successful recruit to all but the GL specialisation would pass to one of the AA training regiments and, once assigned to a battery, begin professional instruction alongside the men as a formed unit. The separately-schooled GL operators would then join the battery for the culmination of its training in live firing at the practice camp ('a distinct chapter in the big adventure').[10] With all satisfactory, the battery would disperse, probably for some brief leave, to reunite at an operational gunsite.

Practice in drills continued here, where in common with their all-male equivalents mixed batteries divided their time between general military training, upkeep of their equipment, and recreation. It was entirely coincidental that the first mixed batteries entered the war at the very point when raiding entered a lengthy slump, and in common with gunners everywhere the mixed units at first found themselves occupied far more with practice engagements than live dealings with the Luftwaffe (at least when they were not talking to journalists, who took a keen interest in the whole experiment at first). Perhaps two hours a day were spent running through the fire-control drills, enough to instil the necessary degree of automation without staleness. Much time, too, was given to aircraft recognition, men and women alike studying bakelite models viewed from all angles of presentation. Military training included foot drill ('Men and auxiliaries,' it was found, 'can be taught to march together with great precision'), governed by a voice of command which was soon as likely to be feminine as masculine. Recreation was as diverse as the battery could make it. Lectures were popular, likewise courses in arts and crafts and languages; gardening was both recreational and practical. And the presence of men and women together opened a new world of social possibilities, though not without attendant anxieties. 'Dances and variety shows are the most popular items,' wrote a pair of ATS officers in an anonymous article of autumn 1943; 'darts, table-tennis, "housey-housey," and dramatics find many enthusiasts.'[11]

Was there any foundation for the anxieties of the doubters, which Pile had made so much effort to dispel? Few if any women, it seems, were tempted to smash their instruments in a fit of boredom, as one senior ATS officer had bizarrely warned; on the contrary, many shone their predictors and height-finders to a standard of brilliance rare even in the British army of the 1940s, where buffing was a way of life. The women's turn-out, in fact, usually surpassed that of the men, whose determination not to be outdone lifted standards all round. Many were more adept at close, careful instrument work than their male colleagues. In fact, though few were prepared to say as much at the time, the standard of female recruits into AA Command was on average higher than the male, simply because Pile tended to get the pick of the ATS but the leavings of the Royal Artillery.

If collectively the ATS women did nurse a resentment, it stemmed from the obstacles which the War Office and their own arm put in their way of their recognition as proper soldiers. Despite their integration with the Royal Artillery at work, the women remained members of the separate Auxiliary Territorial Service. Many resented those two qualifying adjectives, which seemed to distance them from the status which their duties clearly warranted. Evidence of this distancing was manifest at first, though it tended to weaken with time. Where ancient artillery tradition designated the junior-ranking men 'gunners' and 'bombardiers', for instance, their women equivalents bore the no less honourable but much less specific appellations of 'private' and 'corporal' (though the men's titles soon came to be used, at first informally, but eventually with a *de facto* authority). Other marks of integration included authority to wear the RA white lanyard and AA Command formation badges on the sleeve. These were more potent symbols than they might seem, for small details of costume and insignia act as fundamental marks of belonging in military units – more is signified by a few square inches of embroidered cloth than an outsider, who just sees uniforms, can possibly grasp. But this tendency to blur the boundaries made the senior figures at the ATS still keener to cling to their charges. Pile, perhaps, was telling only one side of the story when he recalled the trouble which could attend the arrival of senior ATS officers at a mixed site – such as the occasion when one such 'completely upset all the girls by telling them they were not part of the battery – they were ATS and could be moved to any part of England that she chose'.[12] Pile was certainly no sceptic toward the ATS in general (which, interestingly, he termed a 'movement'). He married one of their senior officers in 1951. But his exasperation in such cases is understandable.

Yet the other side of the story is that the senior ATS officers bore a direct responsibility for the welfare, security and discipline of young women suddenly cast into masculine territory. The 'discipline' issues were the most worrisome part of the whole experiment, the word being made to serve here as a delicate catch-all for all manner of anxieties, from unreliability on duty to sexual misconduct. A central problem was that the women had been given pivotal roles in the work of the batteries, but were liable to only light sanctions for misdemeanours. Men, in short, could be hauled over the coals by their officers and NCOs, women not: the sharpest sentence which could be awarded to an ATS miscreant, even in a court martial, was confinement to barracks for fourteen days.[13] Good officers, of course, seldom needed to run their units with a rod of iron. But harsh discipline was necessary at times.

Against that background it came as a relief to all concerned that disciplinary problems proved rare – a relief, but perhaps not altogether a surprise. The women, after all, had volunteered for AA work and were unlikely to undermine their claim for recognition by obliging their sceptics. Officers of mixed batteries usually found the disciplinary issue seldom arose, and when it did a gentler approach rooted in more conventional social dialogue between the sexes usually paid off ('Jones, your hair would be very attractive if you had it tidier or shorter'; 'You just miss being awfully nicely turned out because your trousers are not properly creased', and so on; patronising today, less so in the early 1940s).[14] Most male officers and NCOs, it seems, adapted themselves easily to working with mixed batteries, though a few got around their difficulties by treating the women as honorary men (such as the battery sergeant-major who insisted on addressing ATS officers as 'sir' rather than 'ma'am'; a compliment was intended). Many battery commanders were sceptical about the women recruits at first, and Pile admits that a few simply would not accept them and had to go.[15] But other self-confessed doubters were won round by the performance of their 'gunner-girls'. One told his own story in the summer of 1942.

> I must confess I loathed the idea of commanding this type of battery when I was named for the job [wrote J W Naylor]. I had served only with men, and had actually been in command of a male battery at the loneliest gun site in the British Isles and loved it. I tried hard to get out of the change, but now I have joined this battery, raised it, watched it grow up, and shared in its sorrows and joys, I can say that I have never been happier than I am now. My officers and NCO's are first class. My men and girls are great.[16]

Though a growing proportion of AA Command's permanent gunsites were reasonably well-provided domestic buildings by summer 1941 (at least in line with the rather ungenerous scales laid down earlier in the war), the introduction of mixed batteries brought new requirements, for reasons which were as much political as domestic. Any assumptions in the climate of mid 1941 that women somehow could not cope with the rather spartan accommodation scales stipulated for men were disproved by events, first when the new standards could not actually be realised, and then decisively in the final year of war when the ATS found themselves crewing mobile guns in the flying-bomb campaign and thoroughly roughing it. But in the early days the promise of *de luxe* accommodation was necessary to allay the fears of sceptics. Thus 'the very highest importance was attached to the accommodation being first-class, and nothing was left to chance.'[17] There were other concessions, too, chief among them the rule that the ATS should not be posted to sites in the path of an invading army. That thought was prompted by the fear of atrocities by German soldiers which need not be laboured over; but ironic it is that by the standards of 1941 a good Nazi's first thought on finding women on the gunsites should have been one of fastidious moral distaste.

The women's domestic arrangements were settled between the ATS high command and Pile's staff in April 1941, when it was decided that they would be given the same scales of accommodation as the men – similar unit-space per head for sleeping and so on – but better facilities for dining, cooking, washing and recreation, with huts rather than the terrible camp structures with which many male batteries still had to contend. Importantly, too, these facilities were usually to be separate: the ATS would enjoy their own dining rooms, rest rooms and NAAFI huts, and would also be given 'properly screened' lavatories on a higher scale than the men (enough in fact for fifteen per cent of the female contingent), together of course with their own showers, ablutions and medical rooms. Sleeping huts would in many cases simply be handed over from men to women, with some improvement to their amenities, though any supplementary buildings would be erected in a separate compound. It was also ruled that every woman must have a bed, as some men did not. And beyond that, all sorts of exacting rules governed the siting of latrines in relation to sleeping huts and other niceties.

Though the additional requirements over and above the male allocations were hardly extravagant, the crucial policy difference in the handling of mixed batteries was the stipulation that their accommodation should *actually exist*. This was an sharp departure from established practice, in which War Office scales were treated at best as an abstract ideal, not an absolute right and certainly not one on which the soldiers might insist. Male gunners posted into a new camp were accustomed to making do with whatever they found there – an essential practice if operational movements were not to be dictated by the whereabouts of huts – and making do was in any case a prized soldierly skill. Not so the women. It was AA Command's job to see that accommodation was complete and ready when the ATS arrived, and maintained to the required standard; and it was the duty of senior ATS officers to verify that these undertakings were met. This they most assiduously did, and it was probably this conditionality of their service with AA

Command, and the element of outside scrutiny which accompanied it, which prejudiced some of the more traditionalist male officers against the ATS at first.

So, despite the reasonable progress which had been made in hutting the male permanent batteries by the summer of 1941, the arrival of the ATS brought a large volume of new building. Figures were put to the policy in April. At this date AA Command expected that 181 mixed batteries would be formed, and since batteries of eight guns were commonly deployed in four-gun (half-battery) units, for building purposes it was simplest to think in terms of 362 'half-battery' hutted camps, even if some of these would be paired together as eight-gun sites. On this 'modular' basis work began on converting and upgrading the camps, but it proved enormously difficult. Labour shortages delayed the programme throughout its life, but summer 1941 brought an added complication in a nationwide rearrangement of guns in readiness for the invasion season. In contrast to the preparations of 1940, which had been haphazard at best, AA Command's invasion plans of 1941 were governed by an elaborate scheme designed to reduce the number of gun-moves necessary should the Germans successfully land. In short, this project involved exchanging 244 static guns for mobiles in the forward areas, with the result that many established static sites were switched to mobiles, the overall pattern dissolved into fluidity, and the allocations of sites to mixed batteries had to be changed and changed again; and added to that, many men who might have helped with the building work were tied up in shifting guns. Similar problems troubled the deployment of mixed batteries for the remainder of the war, and eventually the intended correspondence between women and fixed occupancy simply broke down. But in 1941 this supposedly rigid rule was as far as possible observed, with the result that only 57 sites were completed and occupied by the end of the year.[18]

A look at the range of structures used on AA sites in the middle war years, and how they were adapted to accommodate the ATS, shows what was involved in this work at a practical, site-by-site level. During the Second World War a wide and diverse range of prefabricated temporary hutting types was evolved by civilian designers and military works departments to meet the

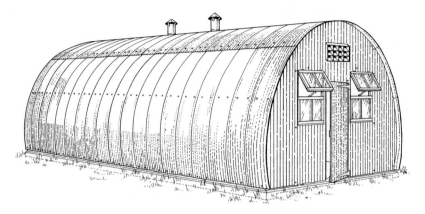

Figure 27 The 16-foot Nissen hut, shown in a variant designed for domestic use.

widespread need for cheap and rapidly-erected accommodation. Some of these are widely familiar, and not just to those who passed a memorable part of their lives in them – the Nissen hut, in particular, so endures as a symbol of temporary wartime accommodation that its name has practically become generic to the type; we speak of Nissens rather as we might of hoovers or biros, or indeed shrapnel. But Nissens were very far from being the whole story of wartime hutting. Many curved-roof buildings with corrugated cladding were not in fact Nissens at all, but Romney, asbestos cement or Gomme huts, among others. Nor were the majority of temporary hutting types used on military camps, strictly speaking, *military* buildings at all. Rather, the armed services were simply the largest consumers of hutting types which were also supplied to farmers, the fire and civil defence services, schools, factories and a host of others in need of temporary accommodation; altogether several dozen types were used during the war.[19] Most of the huts used in all of these contexts were designed by civilian engineers and architects, who offered their designs speculatively for adoption by government, though even those which did originate in military drawing offices often spilled out into civilian contexts, as needs required. Wartime hutting is a large subject, of interest partly for its place within the longer history of prefabrication technology (which found later expression in the 'prefabs' of post-war reconstruction), partly because these buildings collectively represent a huge

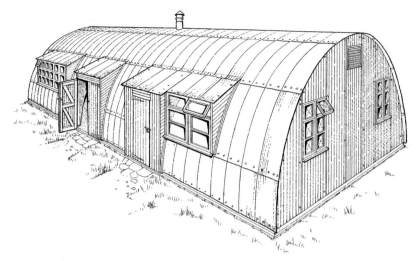

Figure 28 The 24-foot Nissen hut, shown in a domestic variant with two alternative types of dormer window.

episode in the history of British building, and partly because the living conditions of many servicemen and women depended directly upon what prefabrication designers were able to do for them. AA Command's place in this story is a small tile in a large mosaic.

Early in the war, and before it, the huts used on AA batteries and elsewhere were obtained by direct orders placed with suppliers by the relevant department (in our case the War Office). In November 1940, however, as the demand for huts grew on all fronts, the Ministry of Works and Buildings formed a Committee on Prefabricated Huts to act as a central advisory body on design and a clearing-house for allocations to departments; in September 1941 this in turn spawned a second and more specialised committee to deal simply with questions of design.[20] These committees were responsible, among other things, for testing and ratifying external submissions of hut designs and gradually worked towards a definitive register of approved types, which appeared in March 1942.[21] The huts used on AA batteries were drawn from the general range studied by these committees, and while the earliest hutting projects of 1939–40 seem to have used some types which were eventually discontinued (such as the Weblee) by 1941 the main hut used for new construction seems to

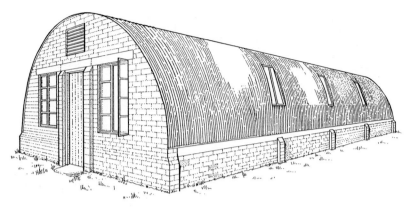

Figure 29 The Curved Asbestos hut. Superficially similar to the Nissen, this building used a rigid asbestos shell resting on a brick or concrete sill.

have been the Nissen. Over the next two years, however, the Nissen was joined by three further types newly introduced in the middle period of the war and in May 1943, when the definitive handbook for AA site fabric was issued in the form of the *Barrack Synopsis (War)*, four types – and only four – were authorised for ADGB use. These were the Nissen, the Curved Asbestos, the MOWP Standard Hut, and the Romney.

Nissens were the commonest prefabricated huts used by the army during the war and were supplied in two main variants, with spans of 16 feet and 24 feet (a third type, of 30 feet span, appears to have been exclusive to the Air Ministry).[22] In its 1940s manifestation the Nissen had not changed much from the original design patented by Colonel Nissen before the Great War. Curved, T-section formers supported a cladding of corrugated iron, while the end walls – usually matchwood or brick – were designed in standard patterns to suit the use to which the building would be put (Figs 27–28). On AA domestic sites those uses were manifold. Nissens were used widely for sleeping, but also served as canteens, rest rooms, offices – their adaptability was the point. And thanks to the Nissen's potential for endless variations on the same basic theme, as dwellings they could be fitted out to offer anything from bleak austerity to tolerable comfort. The most rudimentary Nissen sleeping hut was unlined (just a single skin separating inside from out), concrete-floored, and fitted with end panels containing a single door and one or

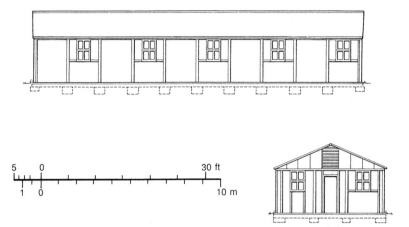

Figure 30 The MOWP Standard hut. Designed by the Ministry of Works and Planning, this building used standard panels made from a wide variety of alternative materials.

two windows. Many male AA gunners lived in such buildings, in which warmth from a central stove might or might not reach the extremities. The rules for ATS Nissens, on the other hand, required timber floorboards, lined and painted interiors, dormer windows, and internal partitions for privacy. Thus accoutred, hung with curtains and personalised, Nissens could be cosy enough. Some ATS women will remember harsher conditions, but these were the results of compromises with the original plans.

Superficially similar to the Nissen, the Curved Asbestos hut (Fig 29) was an example of a common wartime building practice in which existing proprietary products were adapted to new roles. In this case the products were curved asbestos sheets, manufactured by the Everite company, three of which were bolted together to form a self-supporting rigid roof resting on a low brick sill. Like the Nissen, the Curved Asbestos could be fitted with side windows – though in this case simple lights rather than dormers – and was finished by one of a variety of end wall types according to its function. Curved Asbestos huts entered service in early to mid 1942, and like Nissens were expected to be fitted out to a higher standard when occupied by the ATS.[23]

Though efficient enough in their use of space and manu-facturing capacity, like most early wartime prefabricated buildings Nissens and Curved Asbestos huts both required a very specific

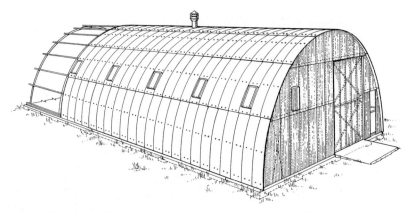

Figure 31 The Romney hut. Another Nissen doppelganger, this building was used for storage and large-capacity functions such as lecture halls and cinemas.

range of materials and components. This was a disadvantage in wartime, when reliance on a narrow range of commodities opened the possibility of supply interruptions through enemy action or the exhaustion of raw materials. To offset this risk the range of approved prefabricated huts was drawn up partly with a view to dispersing sources among many suppliers, and in autumn 1942 this principle was taken a stage further in the MOWP Standard hut, which was designed to exploit a range of alternative materials within the fabric of a single building and to apply them as efficiently as possible (Fig 30).[24] Designed by staff at the Ministry of Works and Planning (MOWP), the hut used a frame of reinforced concrete posts set on a concrete plinth, within which could be set prefabricated walling panels of wood, clay, brick, asbestos or a range of composites including 'wood cement' and 'sawdust concrete'. Roofing panels, similarly, could be made from corrugated asbestos sheets, or from plaster slabs, wool-wood slabs, plasterboard or hardboard clad in roofing felt, while windows, too, were provided in standard prefabricated units. In War Office usage the MOWP Standard hut was designed to be erected as a structure 30 or 60 feet long, in six-foot bays.

The final type of hut authorised in the middle war years differed in its design as a multi-purpose building for storage and other large-space uses. This was the Romney hut, another building easily mistaken for a Nissen and differing, in fact, chiefly in its use of a tubular steel supporting framework (in contrast to

Plate 16 'A welcome cup of tea enjoyed by AA mixed personnel outside the Jamaica hut' ran the official caption to this wartime publicity photograph; 'more self-conscious posing for the cameras' might have been equally apt, especially since the cups look suspiciously empty. Hutting enthusiasts will recognise a 16-foot Nissen.

the Nissen's T-section ribs) and its somewhat larger size (Fig 31). The Romney hut was a home-grown War Office design (its name is taken from DFW's offices at Romney House) and superseded an earlier and less durable variant known as the Iris hut which had a disobliging tendency to collapse under the weight of lying snow.[25] The Romney owed its origin to the availability of the Bessemer steel tubing which forms its ribs, which was strong enough to support a 35-foot-span hut covered, like the Nissen, with corrugated iron sheets. Romneys entered service in 1942 and were authorised on AA batteries for use as cinemas, stores and other large, non-domestic applications.

Although all could be used for a range of purposes, the Nissen, Curved Asbestos and MOWP Standard huts were all well-suited to accommodation blocks, and would be supplied to an AA battery in numbers to give a total floor-area equating to the allotted scale of space per person, multiplied by the establishment of the site.

Plate 17 The pilot's-eye view. One of a series of photographs taken to evaluate the camouflage of HAA sites in the Cardiff and Swansea GDAs, March 1942. This site's combination of two pre-war design emplacements (further from the camera) and two of more recent type suggests wartime extension from a two- to a four-gun position – and note too that only the older emplacements have a concrete magazine. The octagonal GL mat is dimly visible in the foreground.

Which type went where, and in what combination, was largely a matter of availability (and of course chronology). Although DFW did produce standard type-designs for the layouts of HAA domestic camps, these were never much more than guidelines and no two were the same. Camps were placed where the land allowed and could be shared with the troops of adjacent military sites. Some were fairly orderly and regimented, though most were more organic, partly through sporadic growth, partly through adaptation to the available plot, and partly because too much regularity advertised their positions to German pilots and reconnaissance analysts (Plates 17–18). Tactical considerations weakened as the war entered its middle years, however, when the earlier tension between concealment and display (one for protection, the other for deterrence) was resolved in favour of display in most areas of the country. And the forms of AA domestic camps were also conditioned by the numbers they were built to house, a factor modified by the types of weapons emplaced, the presence of a male or a mixed battery, whether the site was home to the battery headquarters (BHQ), and chronology. Though mixed batteries were always larger than male, the populations of both fell somewhat as the war progressed and by spring 1943 the authorised establishment of a mixed four-gun HAA site operating 3.7in statics was 163 (91 of whom were ATS) and that of its male equivalent 133. Two mixed four-gun sites, one with the BHQ attached, gave a full battery population of 375. Larger establishments were authorised for the new types of site

Plate 18 Another from the same series as Plate 17. Again, this site has a combination of emplacement types, but is equipped with two concrete magazines. The GL mat lies to the left, invisible but for its radar platform and walkway.

which appeared later in the war, notably the mixed battery operating 5.25in guns (discussed later), which required 181 personnel; similarly, the relationship between battery establishments and their accommodation was also affected by the introduction of partial Home Guard manning on certain sites (notably Z batteries), in which many personnel lived elsewhere. The Home Guard contingents, however, were the only AA troops who routinely slept away from their sites. Though the possibility of billeting in private dwellings was considered for the ATS, settled War Office policy was to house them at the battery, where supervision could be close.

The middle war years also saw important developments in gunpark layouts, as sites and structures were adapted to new equipment and procedures evolved since 1939. One of the most influential changes had come earlier, of course, with the introduction of the GL mat, but it was the combined effect of advances in radar, target plotting and gun control techniques, together with the arrival of the ATS, which made the greatest impression on operational fabric.

Chief among these developments was the design of a new HAA command post, a building bringing together under a single roof most of the instruments and all of the fire-control functions originally performed in scattered positions behind the guns. The new design (Fig 32) was a semi-roofed concrete structure, designed to accommodate the predictor, heightfinder and telescope in open bays at the front (looking over the guns) with a plotting room, telephonists' posts and offices in covered accommodation behind (Plates 19–22). Though the distribution of some of these functions varied in time – as with all such structures, the original designs say nothing of nuances in usage arising from practical experience – the fixed core of the building remained the plotting room, which provided a comfortable environment in which to receive and process raid data from telephone and radar, and to control the weapons. In 1941 these activities centred around the new semi-automatic plotter (SAP) apparatus, which displayed radar-derived target positions continuously (refreshed every ten seconds) by projecting points of light on a glass screen,[26] though this was later added to by further radar-derived displays – for example the plan position indicator

Figure 32 The HAA command post (1941 pattern) vastly improved the working conditions of plotters and instrument operators, and was a response jointly to the arrival of radar and the ATS. Plotting room fitments changed many times during the war, and here include the new semi-automatic plotter, a plan-position indicator (PPI) tube displaying GCI radar data, and various fire control equipment including a range computer and height meaning board (HMB). The perspective view shows that the gunsite instruments occupied unroofed standings within the overall building line.

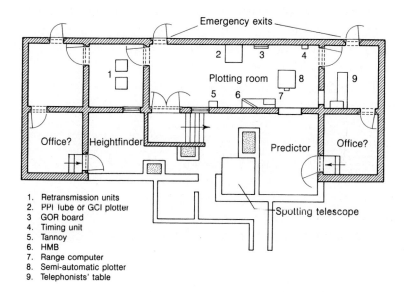

1. Retransmission units
2. PPI tube or GCI plotter
3. GOR board
4. Timing unit
5. Tannoy
6. HMB
7. Range computer
8. Semi-automatic plotter
9. Telephonists' table

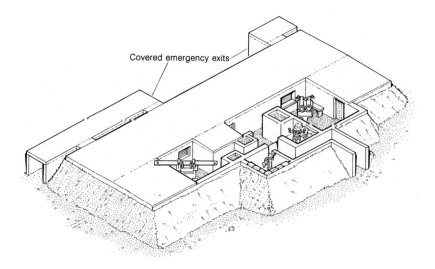

Plate 19 The command post: ATS at work on the predictor, spotting telescope and (in the background) the heightfinder. Easy work on summer days, less so on winter nights.

Plate 20 Richmond Park (ZE20 in the London IAZ) with a new concrete command post, painted for camouflage and roughly banked with bare earth.

Plate 21 ATS at war: a female crew on the heightfinder. The command post is surrounded by camouflage netting and the instrument coloured with disruptive-pattern paint.

Plate 22 The heightfinder team at Primrose Hill (ZE14) one of only three sites to use the 5.25in twin. The ATS much prized the Royal Artillery's white lanyard, likewise the AA Command flash – a drawn bow, raised skyward – visible on the left-hand figure.

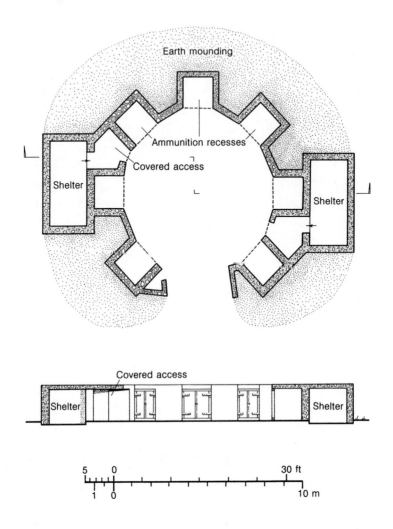

Earth mounding

Ammunition recesses

Covered access

Shelter

Shelter

Covered access

Shelter

Shelter

5   0   30 ft

1   0   10 m

Figure 33 HAA emplacement design (1941 pattern). This type had ammunition recesses opening directly into the gunpit, and welcome shelters for the crew.

tube shown in Figure 32, which displayed the data from a Ground Controlled Interception (GCI) station parked at the gunsite itself. Mobile GCI stations were introduced at certain HAA batteries in summer 1941 – the first, experimentally, at ZW5 in Hyde Park[27] – and these in common with other innovations brought periodic and often locally-decided changes in plotting room layouts and equipment, in some cases involving physical extensions to the structure. Provision for central heating in some of these buildings (evidently a concession to the ATS) together with their comparative comfort and, perhaps, their dominance by women on mixed sites earned them the soldiers' nickname 'gin palaces' – a sobriquet applied by gunners whose working conditions out in the gunpits remained as much at the mercy of weather as ever.

By mid 1941 the 4.5in or 3.7in static gunpit for these men and their weapons had also been redesigned. The standard pattern of emplacement used in the middle war years (Fig 33) differed in several respects from the earlier (1938) type, offering integral shelters for the crew, only one entrance, and seven ammunition recesses which projected outward into the surrounding earth banking rather than into the gunpit from a curtain wall; in these respects it drew upon field adaptations to the earlier type introduced in the spring of 1940. In some cases earth banking was taken up and over the shelter and recesses, producing a much smaller internal area, and with the gunpit floor darkened by camouflage paint these structures were far less conspicuous than their predecessors. A fieldwork equivalent of this gunpit type also was designed, and by spring 1943 these were the sole types authorised for new construction. They were, however, superseded in 1943 by a further variant, discussed later.

The overall layouts of HAA batteries in the first two years or so of war often departed markedly from the ideal template drawn up in the last year of peace. The sunken concrete magazines introduced in spring 1940, many of which were still under construction during the Blitz, were often interposed between two pairs of emplacements, though other positions are certainly known (see Plates 17–18 on pp. 326–7). Another very clear departure from pre-war plans seen by the middle war years was the wide variety of roadway forms linking the emplacements, other site features, and the entrance. Though the guns themselves were laid out in more or less consistent relative positions – which was necessary for technical reasons – the footprints of the metalled surfaces linking them varied to include circular sweeps, geometric forms and a number of irregular layouts. Most of these would clearly allow lorries to manoeuvre more easily –

presumably their purpose – and were in that sense improvements on the standard design. In general, aerial photographs
suggest that the closest conformity to the pre-war site template
shown in Figure 7 (page 147) was among the earliest 'core' sites of
the southern GDAs, notably London and Thames & Medway,
which were of course the first areas to be developed. This seems
to reflect drift from the standard pattern as the construction
programme continued in the early war years, even on sites which
had been selected and begun in peace. Though little more than a
detail in the larger history of wartime AA gunnery, these
variations in site form presumably served a useful subsidiary
purpose in giving German intelligence analysts something
further to mull over: off-the-shelf site designs could be readily
classified and recognised for what they were, less so those
incorporating an element of variety.

The acceptance of women on HAA sites in the summer of 1941
was a sign of an army embracing not so much social progressive-
ness as a compromise forced upon it by the shortage of men. And
it soon became clear that even these steps would be inadequate to
meet Pile's manpower needs, thanks to a sudden restriction on
the anticipated growth of the command which Churchill imposed
in October 1941. AA Command had come through the fighting of
1940 with a total of about 250,000 troops and in autumn 1941
stood at around 280,000, this in progression to a ceiling of 330,000
which Pile needed to operate the full scale of equipment due to
him under current allocations. The shock of 8 October 1941,
however, was the news that 50,000 men needed to reach this
target would instead be diverted to the Field Force, leaving Pile's
command with a strength of just 280,000 men and a ceiling –
which would never be realised – of 170,000 ATS, 'plus any
additional recruitment of women that they can attract'.[28] To make
matters worse, Churchill insisted that as far as possible AA
Command should emphasise mobility in its planning, especially
in developing its capacity to reinforce Home Forces in their anti-
invasion role. For Pile this directive had all the appearances of
another crisis, coming as it did just at a time when long-awaited

equipment – particularly rocket projectors – was at last starting to reach the units, which now looked like exchanging a shortage of *matériel* for one of personnel. 'We had hoped,' he later explained, 'that the employment of ATS would not only make good our deficiencies, but would also, together with our male intake, meet all the requirements of our planned expansion.'[29] But now these hopes were thrown into disarray. Pile was faced with the unwelcome prospect of receiving new equipment and diverting it promptly to store. 'Many more high and low-ceiling guns are coming to hand now,' conceded the Prime Minister's directive. 'Some of these might be mounted in additional batteries, but unless ADGB can contrive by praiseworthy thought and ingenuity to man them within the limits of personnel mentioned they will have to be kept in Care and Maintenance.'[30]

Some hard thinking followed. It resulted in a wide-ranging survey to identify more diverse sources of manpower, and greater flexibility in the way in which troops were employed. Following a conference with his corps commanders on 24 October Pile gave his reply. 'If we are to man more guns without increasing the number of men,' he wrote, 'we must either reduce our establishments, use ATS to an increased extent, or employ Home Guard.'[31] Although these were presented as alternatives, however, Pile's actual solution was to do all three things, first by reducing the establishments of existing batteries, secondly by giving as much as could reasonably be given to the Home Guard, and lastly by bringing the ATS into searchlight work. At the same time a plan was put forward whereby HAA batteries would be reclassified into three groups, embracing fully mobile units, semi-mobile, and static, the last to be staffed by the Home Guard and the ATS with only a small nucleus of Regular personnel.

The first to see material effect was the recruitment of Home Guard. Since its formation in May 1940 some troops from this body had been accustomed to mounting AA Lewis guns on their pillboxes, and in August 1941 they had begun to assume a more formal role in anti-aircraft work when a certain number of factories were given permission to man their local AA defences with Home Guard who happened to be employees.[32] That was easy enough to arrange, but when the idea of their manning permanent defences came under examination the complications soon emerged. For one thing, Home Guard troops were permitted by regulations to serve only 48 hours' duty in any 28-day period, a necessary concession to their civilian employers and to the needs of industry. This implied that fully eight Home Guard would be needed to replace every Regular gunner, so that if they were to serve duty every night, as Pile put it, 'the numbers become astronomic.' Another problem was that so dilute a rota of duty would rule out training for complex jobs. 'It was impracticable,' wrote Pile, 'to permit any of the major defences of the country to be manned on these terms [. . .]'.[33] But quite fortuitously the manpower cuts were imposed at just the time when rocket projectors were at last starting to come forward in plenty, and in this Pile identified a weapon which the Home Guard could realistically operate, thanks to its great simplicity and minimal demands in training. So that was arranged. Early in December Pile recommended to the War Office that all static Z batteries should in future be manned by Home Guard troops,[34] who immediately began training experimentally and by early January had acquitted themselves well. On that basis the plan was developed, with 1400 Home Guard troops assigned to each Z battery, these serving in rotation to provide the 178 men required at any one time. In addition each battery had a tiny complement of 25 regulars to handle maintenance, administration and the GL work. Since these regulars could include ATS, these professional women at last had someone they could feel superior to – and the more so since, as Pile candidly recorded in his official *Dispatch*, the local volunteers did not always come up to the mark. 'Disciplinary control over members of the Home Guard was virtually impossible,' he wrote, 'and it was an easy matter for those who were so inclined to evade all duty. It was due entirely to the service given by the unselfish that the Rocket Batteries became and remained a force which the German aircrews treated with the utmost respect.'[35]

Pile's second initiative to ease the manpower shortage emerging in the winter of 1941–42 was to employ the ATS on searchlight batteries, an idea which once again had a long gestation period before being put into effect. The idea was under test even as the first contingent of women was settling down at ZS20 in Richmond Park. Held from spring to autumn 1941, the ATS searchlight experiment took place first at the Newark militia camp and, from June to October, at a 'cluster' site in the Midlands, where for the first time an exclusively female site crew was left largely to its own devices, though with monitoring, assessment and some supervision, to see how it would perform. The results were good. Just like their counterparts on the HAA instruments, the searchlight ATS found no trouble in operating and maintaining the equipment, nor even in building the necessary fieldworks for light projector, command post and Lewis gun. About the only difficulty discussed in the experiment's long and very detailed report was the unsuitability of some of the women NCOs, who 'tended to be "bossy" and this, with a propensity towards "nagging", as distinct from the male equivalent of cursing which does much less harm, had the effect of putting up the backs of the rank and file [. . .]'.[36]

On the strength of these findings Pile sought formal War Office authority to employ ATS on searchlight batteries in the first week of December 1941.[37] The Army Council greeted this scheme, however, with even more caution than they did the original proposal for mixed HAA batteries. Some of their doubts were reasonable enough – notably that converting the accommodation at searchlight positions to the feminine standard would add hugely to an already overstretched building programme – though in other respects the army's caution owed more to the entrenched attitudes which Pile had met earlier, when trying to get mixed batteries past the authorities. Despite the favourable findings of the experiments in 1941, some in the War Office argued that ATS crews would be insufficiently hardy to perform well in searchlight batteries over a winter, or indeed for any lengthy period of time. Early in 1942 an official appraisal set out the problems thus:

> It is apparent that the proposal [to use ATS crews for searchlight duties] has grave disadvantages from the administrative point of view, and that it is doubtful whether the manning of searchlights over an extended period is within the physical and temperamental capacity of women. Furthermore, it is by no means certain that sufficient volunteers will come forward to justify any addition to the present operational employments for ATS. On the other hand, the manpower situation is so critical

that it may possibly warrant the acceptance of the many disadvantages for the sake of the ultimate economy in men.[38]

The argument from physical hardiness, in retrospect, had little to commend it. But in taking this new step, even Pile confessed to some 'horrid doubts' on quite different grounds.

> For girls to work together in large communal camps was one thing [he explained]. To place a dozen girls in some bleak and desolate spot, five miles or more from the nearest town with night-sentry duties to carry out in a countryside abounding in noises eerie to a townsman was another. How would they deal with possible intruders, with saboteurs, with all the sudden imponderables inherent in the rural life?[39]

Especially since they were prohibited from carrying guns. But in the end, as usual, the logistic arguments carried the day. In mid 1942 AA Command formed its first female searchlight unit – 93 Searchlight Regiment – and eventually the sight of ATS women on the lights became a norm of ADGB life. They had no rifles to protect themselves on guard duty, but instead used pick-helves, beating the bounds on 'stick-picket' and proving themselves 'more horror-inspiring, and more bloodthirsty [. . .] than many a male sentry with his gun, as several luckless and too-presumptuous gentlemen found to their cost before the War was over'.[40] And to begin with, in fact, there *was* one male member of the crew, for only a man was judged strong enough to swing the crank handle of the light's diesel generator. Alone and apart in his tent (the women had huts), this soldier was carefully chosen and, for fear of prurient press interest, remained one of the army's best-kept secrets. But he was eventually made redundant by the self-starter, when the ATS searchlight batteries became exclusively a female domain. 'The girls lived like men,' wrote Pile, 'fought their lights like men, and, alas, some of them died like men.'[41] Or not quite: for male searchlight batteries caught in that terrifying moment when an enemy aircraft began to fire 'down the beam' had a Lewis gun to shoot back. Denied weapons, the women were completely defenceless.[42]

Neither the Home Guard nor the additional duties given to the ATS entirely solved Pile's manpower problems in 1941, problems which would deepen in 1942 when the expected inflow of women recruits proved smaller than expected and the allotment of Regulars was again reduced. But the Luftwaffe, at least, was less troublesome in these months, which emerged as a time of fundamental change in many areas besides personnel.

When the Blitz drew to a close in June 1941 AA Command entered a period of relative quiet which was destined to last for the greater part of a year. German air activity over Britain in the summer and autumn rolled on at a much reduced level, and while there were a few sizeable inland raids much of the Luftwaffe's effort was devoted to minelaying and anti-shipping operations. By August the level of activity had sunk to the point where no enemy aircraft were recorded overland on eleven days in the month, and those which did cross the coast occupied themselves chiefly with nuisance raids on bomber stations in Lincolnshire and East Anglia.[43] September brought a similar pattern, with continuing maritime operations, minor raids against Hull and Tyneside, scattered airfield raids and inconclusive attacks on Portsmouth and Southampton.[44] In these circumstances the gunners' claims plummeted: just three Category I kills were entered in August – one from LAA near Frinton, one from HAA at Plymouth and one attributed to dazzle from a searchlight site in the North Weald sector – followed by a further singleton in September, which fell to HAA at Hull. In a month during which the number of HAA weapons deployed in Britain reached 1784,[45] the availability of targets slumped to the lowest for more than a year.

Though the heavy commitment of German air and land forces to the Russian campaign promised that Britain might be spared a renewed invasion threat in 1941, the planning for this eventuality which had begun before *Barbarossa* was unleashed was continued throughout the summer; indeed, it is a mark of the continuing seriousness accorded to the invasion threat in 1941 that the details of the counter-plan reached finality only in the month *after* Hitler's advance in the east. AA Command's preparations centred around plans for redeploying guns in response to the likely pattern of pre-invasion air attacks and the subsequent progress of a landing, both of which could to some extent be predicted from the events of the previous year. But these were not the only considerations. Coming hard on the heels of the Germans' devastatingly successful capture of Crete during May, anti-invasion thinking of 1941 was also influenced by knowledge of the Wehrmacht's most up-to-date tactics. The 'astounding success' in Crete, wrote Pile in the second week of June, 'makes revision of our methods of defence against air attack a matter of the most urgent importance.'

> The German attack produced the extraordinary phenomenon of completely successful invasion without the use of ships, without the use of tanks, and with guns of the lightest calibre. This success was gained against what are probably the staunchest infantry in the world, equipped to English standards with guns, both field and AA, and often supported by a few tanks.
>
> The astonishing part of the German success was not that they were able to land large numbers of parachutists and glider-borne infantry. This can be achieved by any nation who has the resources and is prepared to face the casualties. It was in the fact that infantry, supported by dive bombers, could drive back first class troops and eventually drive them out of the island.[46]

Germany's decisive weapon in Crete had been the dive-bomber, which Pile described as 'undoubtedly [. . .] the most potent new weapon that has been developed in the war', and one whose efficacy 'lies in the moral effect obtained by the noise created and the feeling that the dive bomber, who appears invulnerable, is aiming at you personally'. If an invasion of Britain in 1941 was not to go the same way as the Cretan campaign, argued Pile, then defence against dive-bombing must be given even higher priority than in 1940, when the technique offered a new challenge which AA Command, as we have seen, was hard pressed to meet. In the light of that experience, Pile was ready to concede that the fighter aircraft rather than the AA gun was the decisive weapon against the Stuka – by mid 1941 about six times as many aircraft overall had been shot down by fighters than by ground defences, and the ratio when dive-bombers were engaged was even more strongly skewed. It followed that the gunners' first role in invasion conditions should

be to support Fighter Command, chiefly by protecting airfields –
especially fighter airfields – with the densest achievable
concentration of fire. Until the aerodromes were 'defended
adequately', argued Pile, 'it is no use thinking of other tasks.' And
there could be no compromise in the allocation of weapons.

> It is quite useless doing as we do now [continued Pile], allotting 3
> or 4 LAA guns to an aerodrome which may cover a square mile
> in area. Nor are LAA guns by themselves adequate. The
> ammunition of these guns self-destroys at 3,500 yards so that the
> guns are only capable of engaging comparatively low flying
> targets. The aerodrome can quite easily be put out of action by
> heavy bombs dropped from heights well above LAA fire. HAA
> defence on the scale of at least one battery per aerodrome is
> essential. The number of LAA guns required should be not less
> than two batteries' worth (24 guns).[47]

After aerodromes, Pile argued, guns should be allocated to the
support of troops in forward areas, in part – again in the light of
Cretan experience – to provide moral support as these men came
under attack from dive bombers; there was 'no use protecting
vital points in the rear,' he argued, 'if the troops in the front are
beginning to get alarmed and to withdraw.' Only then could AA
weapons be given to other sensitive military targets –
headquarters, supply points, defiles and so on.

These recommendations applied in the first instance to the
AA component of the field army, which Pile wished to see
substantially expanded; but their substance was equally pertinent
to home defence, especially in the need to bolster the guns at
airfields. And this is what happened, in the AA anti-invasion plan
of 1941, which awarded first priority to protecting the 'fighter
potential, intelligence system, and communications on which
depend the fight for air superiority' in the south-east.[48] To a large
extent, as ever, the allocations of guns which resulted were
constrained by availability, even the most vulnerable airfields
receiving no more than eight HAA weapons (Pile's recommended
figure) and twelve LAA (half the minimum proposed). The
number of airfields to be gunned on these scales, moreover, was
small: just twelve of the 251 then listed for AA defence were
allocated this number of guns, though many smaller increases

were authorised elsewhere. But however elusive the ideals may
have remained, the promotion of airfields did mark an advance
on the thinking of 1940, when they had taken their place as just
one of a range of target systems drawing from an all too shallow
pool of guns. The invasion never came, of course, but the
preparations for it were careful and widespread. Another practical
element was the herculean interchange of 244 mobile and static
HAA weapons to limit the necessity for moves if an invading
army should land – a project which, as we have seen, badly
disrupted the allocations of mixed batteries in the high summer
of 1941.[49]

The quiet months following the end of heavy night raiding
also gave time to reflect on tactics, and to counterpose pre-war
expectations with the reality of German operations as they had
developed in recent months. The contrast was sometimes sharp,
and no more so than in the tactics which the Germans had
employed in both day and night attacks on cities. Pre-war
thinking had envisaged the Luftwaffe working with a fair degree
of precision; no less so the RAF's own ventures against Germany.
Both expectations had proved false. Far from addressing precise
targets within each GDA, the Luftwaffe's operations had instead
ranged across much wider areas. The deterrent effect of HAA
gunnery itself partly explained this. Early expectations had
visualised German bomber crews closing to their targets at the
constant height, track and speed necessary to sight their bombs
on a given aiming point. On this model HAA sites had been
clustered tightly around the core of each GDA (as shown in
Figure 9, page 173) to exploit the vulnerability of aircraft
behaving thus. In practice, however, the Luftwaffe did things
differently. Though holding a relatively stable course on their
longer 'tactical approach', Göring's crews had proved less resolute
under gunfire and very seldom maintained constant flight in the
target area itself, instead breaking off nervously into irregular
trajectories and often bombing with marked indiscipline and
'indiscriminate' results. In practice the gunners often found their
prey elusive over the target, but easier to tackle further out.

This phenomenon had already been noted as the Blitz was in
progress, when AA Command had begun to extend gun layouts
outwards; many GDAs were already gaining greater depth and

some adjacent layouts were tending to fuze and merge. It seemed to work and at the end of June 1941 Pile put in a paper arguing that the principle should be formalised and extended, to the point where a continuous 'carpet' layout of HAA sites would be created in areas thick with targets – the industrial north, South Wales, the Clyde–Forth area, London and the Home Counties and so on.[50] Pile's idea was to establish his 'carpet' using four-gun sites, each with a GL, such that apart from engaging the Luftwaffe on the tactical approach huge tracts of country miles from any city would also come within range of his barrels. On the face of things the idea had much to commend it. Enemy crews could be harassed by gunfire over large areas of the country, instead of steeling themselves to face the flak as the target approached; shell-bursts would be more widely available to act as visual steers for day fighters; a GL carpet would be available for raid reporting and fire control; many smaller VPs – notably aerodromes – would come within the HAA umbrella; and, not least, many gunners would ply their craft 'under quiet conditions unworried by bombs'. The only disadvantage, as Pile saw it, was the added danger to friendly aircraft from so broad a layout of guns, though this would be offset by the widening availability of the IFF apparatus which identified RAF aircraft to the GL sets. Plainly the whole scheme depended upon the supply of many more guns and radars than had been available a year earlier; but with those coming forward Pile was effectively advancing a new concept of AA deployment. Defence schemes of the 1920s and early '30s had included a barrier element, in the OAZ; by the mid 1930s the fashion was for local or point defence, and the GDA had its day; the rising idea of 1941 was to gun continuous areas.

But it did not rise very fast. A round of discussions extending over some months brought objections on diverse grounds: the complexities of controlling a carpet gun layout; the hazard to fighters; the risks of weakening the GDAs (despite the substitution of rocket projectors for guns); the limitations of IFF; the danger of confusing GCI-led interceptions; and so on. A meeting at the Air Ministry on 27 August produced the general view that extending the GDAs into more discrete 'area carpets' would be a wiser bet,[51] and this in effect is what happened over the following year. But while compromise won the day, the atmosphere of inquiry and revisionism which Pile's paper fostered did stimulate new thinking on HAA tactics in general. It led among other things to the inventive proposal that 240 HAA guns should be stripped from the GDAs to form a barrier defence between Bristol and the north-east, skirting south London on its way (tracing a similar course, indeed, to the main anti-tank position established in summer 1940, Ironside's GHQ Line).[52] That idea was soon quashed, though its tabling illustrates the sleepless worrying at fundamentals which continued at Stanmore as the war entered its third year.

Another instance of innovatory thinking produced a deep restructuring of the national searchlight layout in the autumn of 1941, which resulted in the third system of light deployment to be used since the war began and the second in under a year.[53] When the searchlight crews first occupied their sites in 1939 the lights in the fighter areas outside GDAs were deployed singly at 6000-yard spacings, a pattern which they retained until clustering was introduced in November 1940. Clustering had drawn lights together in threes, on a spacing nominally of 10,400 yards, and this is how they shone in support of night fighters for much of the Blitz. But that campaign exposed weaknesses. With so wide a spacing many contacts were lost in handovers from cluster to cluster, while low-flying raiders frequently wove through the wide, dark passages between the beams. So in September 1941 everything was rearranged again, but this time using principles much more subtle and sophisticated than hitherto.

The autumn 1941 searchlight layout for the fighter areas was based upon a mathematically-derived and empirically-tested concept known as the 'Fighter Box': a block of airspace 44 miles long by fourteen deep, 'within which a night fighter with nothing to aid him except his own eyes and the visual indication of searchlight beams' could locate and intercept a bomber.[54] The territory outside the GDAs was divided up into a patchwork of Fighter Boxes, each with a central single projector whose light rose vertically to form the fixed marker around which a fighter would circle. Once a bomber entered his Box the fighter would break away from this 'orbit beam' and head off in pursuit, when he would find two distinct patterns of lights to help him, both deployed singly. At the edges of each box lights were spaced at wide intervals – at six miles about the same as the old clusters – to form an Indicator Zone, while towards the middle, in the Killer Zone, the spacing dropped to about three and a half miles, similar to that used for all lights at the beginning of the war. In practice adjacent Fighter Boxes created a series of Indicator Belts and Killer Belts, the density of illumination thickening between. Both were separate from the bunches of positions making up the GDA lights, which assisted the guns.

The introduction of the Fighter Box system was made possible in part by the growing availability of *Elsie* searchlight control (SLC) radars. First supplied in autumn 1940, these highly efficient instruments began to reach the light positions in numbers a year later, with priority in allocation given to the Killer zones, followed by a nominated list of half the GDAs (chiefly in coastal areas), the Indicator zones and lastly the remaining GDAs and searchlights deployed for the local defence of airfields.[55] At

Plate 23 High on the hill: 5.25in twin gun at ZE14 (Primrose Hill) looking south toward London, 1943. The tall building beneath the barrage balloon is the University of London Senate House, wartime headquarters of the Ministry of Information, authors of *Roof over Britain*.

the same time as these instruments were coming forward single-barrelled UPs were distributed among selected searchlight sites to engage low-flying targets; at first issued singly, these weapons were later due to be multiplied to make each rocket-equipped searchlight site a small strong point in its own right.[56] In fact by November 1941, when these allocations were made, the rocket weapon had already become a substitute for LAA guns in a variety of roles. In this month the number of Bofors held in AA Command stood at just 1046 against the approved scale of 4410 laid down more than a year previously, and while a new assessment placed the requirement at a more modest 3396, the shortfall of 2350 was still more than double the present holding. To fill the gap, in part, some 78 Bofors positions were being filled by rocket projectors, along with 781 by other types of light guns used in lieu. So again Pile pressed his point. In allocating Bofors, he told the AA Sub-Committee, the priority was to replace the rockets and miscellaneous guns to bring the VPs up to their proper scale of defence.[57] After more than two years of war it was a familiar cry.

Pile's grind to win AA Command's due share of guns and troops would continue for years yet, but in two respects the summer of 1941 brought new stock to the arsenal. In March 1941 Pile had begun negotiations with the Admiralty to obtain some HAA guns able to launch larger shells to greater heights, these to engage the highest-flying bombers tracked during the Blitz. His pitch was unorthodox: first an expensive dinner in a private room at the Dorchester, for more than two dozen senior naval officers and officials; then, over the brandy, down to haggling in which Pile managed to secure a promise of six 5.25in twin guns in exchange for 300 Bofors which, one of his staff assured him in a furtively-passed note, higher authority was probably about to divert to the navy anyway.[58] Pile actually got only half the agreed number, but to his surprise these three turned out to be the first of a consignment of more than 200 weapons of 5.25in calibre which AA Command would receive by late 1945. Originally designed for the decks of cruisers, the early naval guns were the only ones supplied with twin barrels – their successors were singles – and were sent to the IAZ, where test boring at three sites was under way by July 1941.[59] Emplaced at ZE14 (Primrose Hill),

ZS19 (Wimbledon) and ZS27 (Coldharbour Farm), these weapons were proofed and ready to fire by early 1942.

Once in position the new 5.25s found little trade, as London would not be bombed again in earnest until the winter of 1944–45. This was a recurrent feature of AA Command's war – identifying a weakness, struggling to remedy it, finding the pressure eased just as the gap was closed; it was the payoff of pre-war neglect. A kindred case was the commissioning of the first AA sea forts, which were intended to put guns in the remote mid-waters of estuaries as a guard against minelaying. This had been one of the earliest and most consistent Luftwaffe ventures of the war, and one of the most difficult to meet. In the Bristol Channel a solution had been found in mounting the 4.5in guns on Steepholm and Flatholm, while the First World War coast artillery forts in the Humber at Bull Sand and Haile Sand could also accommodate LAA guns, likewise the much older works at Portsmouth and Plymouth. But the more vulnerable estuaries of the Thames and Mersey had no such protection, and it was with their needs particularly in mind that the AA Committee began to consider a special solution.

It was found in the purpose-built forts designed by the engineer G A Maunsell, whose advice on the sea positioning of AA guns had been sought by AA Command as early as the autumn of 1940. At that time Guy Maunsell had been heavily involved in work for the Admiralty, who had commissioned him first to design sea forts for the Thames Estuary and latterly for the waters off Harwich. The first project came to nothing but the second produced the four naval forts which were sited between Harwich and the outer waters of the Thames Estuary between January and August 1942: coded U1 ('Uncle One') to U4, these massive constructions were floated out and sunk at the Roughs, Sunk Head, Knock John and Tongue Sand. With his naval work well advanced in autumn 1941 Maunsell was able to turn his attention to AA Command's problems, rapidly produced designs for specialised AA forts consisting of steel towers resting on legs which would be sunk to the sea-bed, these to be arranged in groups of seven, or in pairs, according to whether heavy and light guns were to be mounted, or LAA alone. The combination groups used one tower each for the four 3.7in guns of a standard battery

Plate 24 One of the Thames Maunsell forts in November 1943, with Bofors gun visible over the parapet and crew practising a casualty-evacuation drill.

– arranged in a rather similar pattern – together with one for the command post, one for a Bofors and one for a searchlight, while the LAA equivalent made do with just the last two.[60] These were the original thoughts, and by March 1942 ambitious plans were in hand to site combinations of these structures in several estuaries and coastal waters, among them the Bristol Channel, the Humber, Mersey, Thames, Harwich and Belfast, to engage both minelayers and conventional bombers approaching over water, distant from shore guns.[61] The Mersey was always intended as the trial area for the towers and was the first to receive them,[62] work on the three Thames groups – U5 to U7 – beginning in summer 1942. Early the following year, however, the project was narrowed to provide combination layouts for the Mersey and Thames alone, and by then the threat they were intended to meet had eased sufficiently for some of the equipment to be put into 'care and maintenance' even as it was installed.[63] So, like the 5.25in twin guns in London, Pile's sea forts were a delayed reaction to a need whose urgency had peaked before the countermeasures were even designed. 'Had we had the Maunsell forts in the winter of 1940,' he later reflected, 'the damage done to Merseyside by the bombing would have been much reduced.'[64]

CHAPTER 9

Passing trade

MARCH 1942 – JUNE 1943

AA Command began the middle year of the Second World War
with expectations that the lull in raiding since the end of the Blitz
might endure. In the spring of 1942 Germany's bomber fleet was
still heavily committed to the Russian campaign, and while a
reasonably strong fighter force remained in France and the Low
Countries to meet the RAF's operations over Europe, there was
little reason to expect a renewal of day raiding or night operations
on the Blitz model for many months at least. Those circumstances alone seemed to justify some relaxation in AA measures;
and, as ever, there were competing claims. Following Japan's
entry into the war, Pile's resources were tapped to supply guns for
the Far East and the Americans, whose embarrassment at Pearl
Harbor had, among other things, exposed their own shortage of
modern LAA. In December 1941 and January 1942 AA Command
sacrificed 214 LAA weapons and 66 heavies to these demands,[1]
whose claim did seem to be the greater. Britain was little troubled
by the Luftwaffe in those weeks, though on a few occasions
fighters in tiny numbers had launched low-level 'tip-and-run'
attacks on eastern and southern coastal towns.[2] Little was
thought of those; but Friday, 27 March brought a rather more
serious incident, when a gaggle of four Bf 109 fighters skimmed
across the Channel to deliver bombs on the coastal resort of
Torquay.

It was not the first occasion on which Torquay had been
attacked, and as recently as 12 February two hotels accommodating
the RAF's 5 Initial Training Wing had collected a few bombs from

a lone, low-level raider.[3] But this rather sharper incident was still something of a puzzle. Despite the RAF training presence the town had little military value. It was undefended. Neither this nor any other seaside resort contributed much to the war effort. For a few days the raid on Torquay, which anyway attracted little attention, was written down as an oddity. But signs that something new might be in the wind came four days later, when a pair of 109s repeated the performance five miles to the south across Torbay at Brixham.[4] And then, on 5 April, Bognor Regis, 120 miles to the east, became the target of six fighters which managed to damage the gas works, amid general alarm. Swanage came next, on 7 April, when just the same type of force – three Bf 109s – delivered a few bombs near Worth Matravers. That might have been a legitimate act of war, since Worth Matravers in April 1942 still accommodated the radar scientists of the Telecommunications Research Establishment who had migrated there from Bawdsey via Dundee; but though Worth was bombed again by the 109s which returned the next day, so too was the innocuous township of Swanage itself. Five days on, Portland received a visit from four 109s skimming the waves at about 50 feet, before Swanage was troubled for the third time on 16 April. On that same day the raiders returned to Devon, attacking a train at Exmouth; and, next day, Budleigh Salterton was bombed. The point at which a series of events forms a pattern, and then solidifies into a phenomenon worthy of a name is often difficult to identify while those events are unfolding. But by mid April it was clear that the vocabulary of 'tip-and-run' raids and 'fringe target' attacks which had entered currency late in 1941 during the skirmishes on the east coast also applied here. No one was sure whether it was yet appropriate to speak of a Fringe Target campaign, for there was no way of telling whether the raids might cease as suddenly as they had begun. In fact they continued for more than a year.

If not exactly blasé about these incidents, Pile at first greeted them in a relaxed frame of mind. The raiding was 'annoying', he wrote, 'but all the same it all seemed a bit pointless. It didn't impede the war effort. The places, generally speaking, had no military significance at all, and, anyway, the size of the raids precluded any serious damage.'[5] Short of rushing Bofors to every resort town on the south coast, there was actually nothing Pile could usefully do; and that was impossible – or so it appeared, with a pool of weapons still deficient and now actually diminishing. Yet, in time, that is what happened. The huge deployment of LAA guns to defend the militarily sterile south coast resorts in 1942–43 was one of the more unlikely episodes in AA Command's war.

Nothing was done for some weeks yet, and in that time the raids continued. On 19 April the 109s made their most easterly attack of the burgeoning campaign when bombs were dropped at Bexhill-on-Sea and Crowhurst, in Sussex. Swanage had its fourth visit on the following day, when the random machine-gunning of streets and houses – soon to be a regular feature of the raids – appears to have added its particular spice for the first time. Then four days passed without incident, before Friday 24 April produced the sharpest raids yet. They started in the early morning with two near-simultaneous strikes at Folkestone (where a gas holder was damaged) and Hastings, 30 miles along the coast in Sussex. Further west, Southwick, near Brighton, collected a few bombs later in the day, together with Bognor Regis, where the municipal gasworks was for the second time singled out.[6] Together with railway stations and trains – one of which had already been hit at Exmouth – gas facilities would be recurrent objectives in these attacks.

This westward-shifting progression of Fringe Target raids was not the only Luftwaffe activity in British skies on 24 April; reconnaissance flights were plotted over the Irish Sea and south-west Scotland, but all of these were overshadowed by a sharp night attack on Exeter, in which a comparatively small force did a disproportionate amount of damage. The Exeter operation was in fact the first of the so-called 'Baedeker' raids – operations against historic cities personally ordered by Hitler in reprisal for Bomber Command's incendiarism against the medieval timbers of Lübeck on 28/29 March. Next morning two reconnaissance aircraft were seen orbiting Exeter at 20–25,000 feet and three or four Bf 109s made landfall over the Isle of Wight in what may have been an abortive fringe attack, but no other hostile activity was recorded in daylight. By night, however, the Luftwaffe was busy. Fierce exchanges developed over Bristol, where 30 raiders attracted more than 4200 rounds of HAA ammunition, together with 100

UP rockets (a ratio of rounds to aircraft resembling that of the London barrage). Elsewhere, too, there were lively engagements. The 370 rounds dispatched from Portland were mostly aimed at the streams heading inland, while several other south coast GDAs came into action briefly against bombers over the Channel. But at the same time a force of 30 aircraft which attacked Bath in the second of the Baedeker raids did so with impunity. There was also a minor raid at Aberdeen, before the night ended with a final flurry on the Kent coast. As 26 April was dawning a pair of 109s appeared over Dungeness, bombed the town and sprayed the lighthouse with cannon fire; at the same time, a few miles along the coast, Focke-Wulf 190 fighter-bombers made their Fringe Target debut by bombing Betteshanger Colliery and a military camp near Lydd.[7] The FW 190 would progressively supplant the Bf 109 in Fringe Target raids during the coming months.

By the morning of 26 April, then, it appeared that two separate campaigns were under way, both distinct from the background of sporadic and generally light raiding which had flickered on since the close of the Blitz. The first thought was to protect the historic towns which were now entering the Baedeker battle, and in the closing days of April arrangements were made to transfer HAA guns accordingly. Selecting the beneficiaries was not easy. A second attack on Bath during the night of 26/27 April – along with operations against scattered targets elsewhere – justified the impression that this would be a southern campaign, so guns were assigned to Canterbury, Maidstone, Ashford, Tunbridge Wells, Aldershot, Guildford, Basingstoke, Salisbury, Winchester, Andover, Taunton, Hayle, Truro and Penzance, as well as Exeter and Bath, victims of the first incidents. But then the Baedeker interest shifted a little further north, when the night of 27/28 April brought an attack on Norwich. In the light of that Group Captain Whitworth Jones, Director of Fighter Operations, was forced to admit that the next targets were 'anybody's guess', but the list of newly-gunned cities was lengthened at the end of the month to include Peterborough, York, Lincoln, Chelmsford, Colchester, Ipswich, Cambridge and Norwich itself, as well as Reigate and Redhill further south, to be followed soon after by Oxford, Brighton and Chichester. In result, the fortnight after the first Exeter raid saw guns provided for 28 previously undefended towns, a total move of 252 HAA weapons, mostly stripped from GDAs in the north and west. In addition, during the first weeks of May Colonel Turner, the Air Ministry's decoy co-ordinator, got to work in improvising temporary Starfish fires for many of the towns on Pile's growing Baedeker list,[8] though few of these were fully operable before the campaign began to tail off at the end of May. Meanwhile public feeling was incensed by what seemed a particularly contemptible turn of events. 'As you can imagine,' wrote Whitworth Jones on 30 April, 'our fanmail from "Indignant Citizen", vox populi etc, has increased enormously since the Bath and Norwich affairs. We are taking a firm line over this. The aim of the Hun is to produce excitement, argument and confusion in our defences. We are refusing to pass on these agitations to the unfortunate Commanders.'[9] The previous night Norwich had been bombed for a second time and, the night before that, York had lost its fifteenth-century guildhall in the fifth and most northerly Baedeker operation yet. The guns had some success. Two Category II 'probables' and two 'damaged' were claimed over Norwich, but the gunners were often forbidden from firing to give the fighters free rein, with the result that AA Command's claim of Category I kills amounted to only three in April – the same number as attributed to miscellaneous 'other causes' – compared to 93 for Fighter Command. Similarly, of the 58 Category II 'probables' chalked up in this month only two and a half were credited to Pile's men, who were also allowed just eleven of the 141 machines written down as 'damaged' in Category III.[10] And while high explosive and incendiaries cascaded on the historic towns, by day there was no let-up in the Fringe attacks. Poling radar station, Littlehampton, Cowes and Newhaven were all raided, though not always with much effect, in the closing days of April. None of the hostiles was shot down.

A few more Baedeker raids followed the main phase in April and early May. Canterbury was hard hit on the last night of May and raided again on the next two nights, while other forces struck Ipswich and Bury St Edmunds. Minor operations against Nuneaton, Great Yarmouth and Weston-super-Mare in June then drew the campaign to an end. A few more bombers were destroyed in these operations but taken overall the AA contribution to the battle was not great. In part this could be explained by the still-parsimonious allocations of guns to ADGB compared to other customers, a state of affairs which prevented massing really strong weapon densities against the raiders. Eight 3.7 mobiles was a typical allocation to one of the newly-gunned cathedral cities, shared between two four-gun sites, and while a few were given twelve weapons one of the three sites so formed was often without a radar (and many were still using GL Mk Is).[11] To limit Pile's options further the Baedeker deployment happened to coincide with the fulfilment of a longer-term plan, known as *Sundry*, to reinforce ten of the southern coastal GDAs to cover the assembly of the fleet for Operation *Torch*, the North African landing scheduled for the late autumn.[12] The 120 HAA guns committed to this reinforcement, which took place at the end of May, would certainly have been useful for Baedeker duties, and to offset the gun shortage ten of the Baedeker targets were given rocket projectors in either full or half batteries. But at the end of May Pile decided that pressures elsewhere had become so great that 160 of the Baedeker weapons must be withdrawn, though some could be replaced by Z batteries.[13]

It was in May, too, that the southern coastal towns received their first reinforcements. For all that they remained light, the continuing Fringe Target raids posed one of the most intractable sets of problems to confront the air defence commanders during the war. Firstly, they were scattered. On the fourteen days in May on which the raids took place, fifteen localities between east Kent and west Devon were targeted in 23 attacks.[14] Several towns suffered more than once – Deal, Eastbourne, Hastings, Bexhill and Brixham were all hit twice, and Folkestone on three occasions – but the operations extended across such a wide front containing so many potential targets that the Luftwaffe was free to switch between them at will, skirting those with guns to exploit the weak points between. Secondly, any targets which were gunned needed a measure of early warning for the weapons to do their work. In late April Pile suggested that three minutes' notice before the raiders attained the LAA range of 3000 yards would be just enough; in other words the gunners needed to know that trouble was developing when its perpetrators were about sixteen miles out. Even if the CHL system could pick up the incoming fighters at all – and events soon proved that this was seldom so –

this was cutting it fine. To speed things up, Pile asked for communications to be laid between the south coast CHL stations and the LAA troops, so bypassing all the usual filtering apparatus and opening a direct channel between the radars and guns.[15] It was many months before this could be done, however; and in any case the low cover chain of spring 1942 was almost useless against small clutches of aircraft closing so low, and so fast.

The third problem was the usual one, with a novel twist. Not only were LAA guns to defend the south coast towns in short supply, the German pilots' tactics in these raids demanded to be met with unusually high concentrations of weapons at each site. Many raids came in directly from the sea, but in some cases it was possible for fighters to flick sideways, make landfall a few miles from their target, and arrive along valleys and other concealed lines of approach at no more than 50 or 100 feet. Adequate defence against these tactics required LAA cover in numerous nooks and crannies which could safely be disregarded when raiders flew just a few hundred feet higher. Usually it couldn't be done.

What could be done, at first, was a fairly circumscribed redistribution of weapons to the most assailable military targets. At the beginning of May 1943 just 43 Bofors guns were in place among the south coast towns, roughly half the authorised scale for those already listed as VPs.[16] At this date ADGB's stock of Bofors amounted to only 884 nationally, thanks to large numbers being diverted from the factories to Home Forces (whose holdings leapt from 98 such weapons at the end of January to 430 at the end of May); and these were the larger proportion of 1019 modern LAA guns held by ADGB overall.[17] In these circumstances weapons could hardly be released purely to defend the coastal resorts, but at the same time 189 LAA guns were requested for the south coast ports under the *Sundry* deployment. Pile simply could not meet that commitment, but scraping around the inland VPs produced 38 Bofors, to which a further 34 were added from production.[18] So these, for the time being, helped to firm up the south coast's general defence against low-flying aircraft.

Despite the thin state of the gun defences in these weeks the raiders did not have things entirely their own way. The first Luftwaffe casualty fell in the early evening of 14 May, when a close formation of four Bf 109Fs attacked Brixham harbour at a height estimated at 300–500 feet. Bombs were scattered and a trawler sunk, but heavy fire from Bofors and Lewis guns swatted one intruder into the sea.[19] Six days later, after further raids on Plymouth, Folkestone, Hastings, Deal, Brighton, Rye and Bexhill, five Bf 109s made shallow penetrations over the coast between Folkestone and Beachy Head, attacking shipping and spraying Folkestone town with machine-gun fire. In the course of these events one of the fighters was downed by the Newhaven HAA, while a second was winged by fire from a warship and came to earth in a crash landing near Eastbourne.[20] Two Category I claims in six days gave some satisfaction, but less comfort could be drawn from the cumulating average; apart from a Category III at Brixham on 7 May, the two aircraft destroyed by 20 May were the total bag from, by now, 158 Fringe Target sorties. By the end of the campaign in June 1943, AA Command had pushed the Category I statistic up to four and a half per cent, and in the final few months were achieving a score sufficient to justify claiming victory in the battle. But this was a world away in early summer 1942, and in these circumstances the temporary easing of the attacks in June was perhaps a more welcome respite than the Luftwaffe knew. Just four raids (comprising ten sorties), took place in this month, during which another Category III claim was made at Brixham and Brighton entered the list of resorts sustaining damage to their gasworks.

Though the Baedeker deployment of May 1942 enlarged the pattern of HAA nationally, it did less to increase the number of gunsites, since several of the towns hurriedly provided with mobile weapons had been identified as future GDAs as early as August 1940, and reconnaissances for their defences had in some cases been completed. Exactly how many HAA gunsites were on AA Command's books at this time is fortunately recorded for us in a national roster compiled in June 1942 – as it happens almost the exact mid-point of the war – setting out the armament and radar equipment (if any) in place at each.[21] The value of this list is heightened by its rarity. Although the position, armament and occupying unit of every site taken for AA use during the war was recorded in the Location Statements routinely filed by units and higher formations (particularly regiments, brigades and divisions), it was seldom necessary to undertake the cumbersome work needed to synthesise these into a master list. At a national level, Stanmore needed accurate and current records of how guns of different types were shared between GDAs and VPs, and these *ADGB Equipment Statements* were compiled throughout the war – daily at first, though soon on a more realistic weekly cycle. But records of exactly *which* sites in each GDA were gunned and which vacant were seldom needed above divisional headquarters level. This national picture can, of course, still be reconstructed for any chosen point, by collating the Location Statements of lower formations spanning the relevant date. The procedure is simple, but prodigious of time.

The master list of 22 June 1942 shows that AA Command had 1014 HAA sites at its disposal on that date, split between 149 separate GDAs. Of these, 494 sites were equipped with guns and most of those with GL sets of Marks I, IA or II. The first point which emerges is, of course, the enormous rise in the number of gunsites in the first half of the war – by the summer of 1942 the total was more than double the 449 which had been in place in February 1940. Geographically, the spread of sites – occupied and vacant – reflects Pile's instinct to establish new sites on a 'carpet' basis, particularly in the Midlands and north; comparison of the tight and orderly GDA layouts of early 1940 (Fig 9) with those of June 1942 (Fig 34) shows many defended areas fusing and merging into near-continuous groups. Leaving aside for a moment the pattern of *guns* in June 1942 – which was sparser and altogether more geographically weighted than that of *sites* – the growth in positions reflected both additions to existing GDAs and the creation of new areas under a succession of policy rulings since the start of the war. Some GDAs grew hugely. The Humber, for example, expanded from fifteen sites to 35 between 1940 and summer 1942, while the Mersey's layout expanded from 24 to 36 sites, Leeds' from 22 to 37 and those around Birmingham/Coventry from 31 to 61 in the same period. These were the largest increases, and were effected in northern and Midland GDAs partly to achieve 'carpet' cover, but some of the southern areas

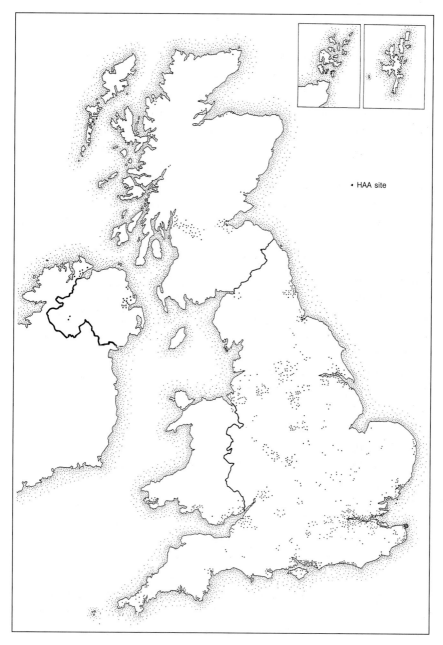

Figure 34 Distribution of HAA sites, June 1942. Comparison with Figure 9 shows the clear tendency of GDAs to spread and merge by the middle years of the war, though as in 1940, not all of these sites were fully constructed and many lay unoccupied at this date.

also grew, if more modestly, either to expand outwards or allow for rising scales of defence. One GDA which initially did both, as we have seen, was London, though by summer 1942 the temporary sites introduced in the Blitz to hold sixteen-gun concentrations had been abandoned and the IAZ had contracted almost to its pre-Blitz density; 67 sites were in place compared to 64 early in 1940. Bristol, on the other hand, showed a straight increase from twelve to nineteen sites in this period, while the Solent GDA expanded from 23 to 36 positions and Dover – always a difficult town for HAA – rose from four sites to seven. Altogether, 565 HAA sites were added between early 1940 and mid 1942.

Wholly new GDAs were also numerous, but many were in areas other than those anticipated by the plans made in the first year or so of the war. Of 111 new GDAs defined since February 1940, only 34 were included in lists authorised down to October 1940; but while several new defended areas anticipated by these plans had not been developed, others had been substituted. The Baedeker targets, of course, accounted for a proportion of these: of the 26 historic towns with guns at the end of May 1942, only eight had been scheduled in the plans of late 1940. Airfields, too, accounted for a good number: of two dozen or so listed in June 1942, only five had been so early in 1940 (since when a few had disappeared from the list). Measured in sites, the largest of the new wartime GDAs extant by summer 1942 were Gloucester/Brockworth (eighteen positions) and Belfast (fourteen), while sizeable layouts were also in place at Swansea (twelve sites), Falmouth, Slough and Scunthorpe (eleven each), Milford Haven (nine sites), Swindon (eight) and Londonderry (seven). Most of the other new defended areas commanded gun positions numbering between two and six. The greatest expansion in sites during the first half of the war was thus in the west, and particularly in Northern Ireland, where the 21 positions in the two major GDAs of Belfast and Londonderry were joined by two sites each at Larne and Loch Erne to give 25 HAA gunsites in the province as a whole.

One striking characteristic of the Northern Irish layout in mid 1942 was that all of these sites bar one (Belfast U12 at Hyde Park) were gunned. Fifteen positions had four 3.7in statics and the remainder the same number of mobiles (the guns at Larne and

Loch Erne were exclusively fixed types). Elsewhere, however, the level of gunning in GDAs was highly varied, and the weight of sites actually occupied by weapons was firmly southern and coastal. Thirty-five of the sites in the IAZ had weapons in June 1942, together with more than half of those in the Thames & Medway GDA; and thanks to the *Sundry* deployment the Solent's three discrete GDAs at Portsmouth, Southampton and the Isle of Wight were all crowded with weapons – just seven of the 36 sites lay vacant – while both Plymouth's and Bristol's site occupancy both exceeded 50 per cent. Given its role in transatlantic shipping it is unsurprising to find the Mersey GDA gunned to around two-thirds of capacity, while the Tyne, Tees, Humber, Clyde and Forth were also occupied to respectable levels. But yawning gaps in cover lay across the inland north and the Midlands, where the demands of the previous two months had reduced several GDAs to just a handful of active sites and left a few with just their 4.5in guns, which for practical purposes could not be moved. Thus the vast Leeds GDA, which also embraced Bradford, Huddersfield, Halifax and their neighbours with 37 sites, was left in June 1942 with only four 4.5in positions occupied; Manchester, too, was deserted apart from these guns, which were emplaced at just six positions. Sheffield was little better served, with four 4.5in batteries occupied, plus two with 3.7in statics, while Coventry and Birmingham were similarly placed. Though the gun distribution of June 1942 is merely a point-in-time snapshot, it does illustrate vividly the large measure of fluidity which remained in the AA deployments, even at this stage of the war, and how major GDAs packed with fully-built gunsites could at times lie vacant and impotent. It is salutary to reflect upon how differently we might interpret the defences of Leeds or Manchester at this date were we obliged to do so merely from the physical evidence of their gunsites, without documentary records of their changing occupancy – as in fact we routinely do when studying the fortifications of earlier eras. Both cities, we would probably conclude, were heavily defended during the Second World War; so indeed they were, but not always, and certainly not during the summer of 1942.

In all probability we should reach a similar conclusion if presented with a dossier of reconnaissance photographs showing the Leeds or Manchester AA defences at this stage of the war. This, at any rate, was how the Germans were intended to interpret the dummy guns which, by now, routinely deputised for the genuine article on vacated HAA sites. AA Command's policy on AA site decoys had evolved significantly since dummies were first considered in the summer of 1940. Then, it may be recalled, the talk was of lifelike tactical decoys, laid out in numbers to exaggerate the gun density and divert attacks from the real thing. Some sites certainly were built on these lines – how many is uncertain – but within a year it was clear that erecting and, no less importantly, maintaining fully-built decoys seldom repaid the effort involved. So in August 1941 it was decided that henceforth dummy AA guns would primarily be used to replace real weapons at vacated sites, to suggest continued occupation.[22] This began a trend, and as the level of Luftwaffe activity over Britain tailed off in the middle war years, AA Command became progressively less concerned to conceal gunsites than to display them. By late 1943 the policy was to camouflage gunsites still liable to attack – largely in coastal districts – but not to do so elsewhere, on the grounds that, among the static AA positions at least, 'it is generally strategically desirable that the enemy should think that these defences are stronger than they really are.'[23]

If the number of HAA weapons deployed in the summer of 1942 still languished far short of theoretical scales, by now the layout was at least dominated by modern guns: just 87 3in HAA guns remained. Apart from at a surviving colony in the Shetlands – whose defence relied exclusively upon twelve of these aged weapons – the 3in HAA guns were dotted fairly randomly around the GDAs, often deployed in pairs, in contrast to the four-gun sites which by now were the norm for more modern equipment. Many were used at airfields, but a few remained even in major layouts such as London, where ZE4 at Buckhurst Hill still used them, and at Thames & Medway, where four armed TS12 at All Hallows. By June 1942 the national layout of sites was dominated by fully-built static positions. The three 5.25in twins in London were the only weapons of this calibre so far emplaced – more would follow in 1943 – but 98 sites were occupied by 4.5in guns, which were present in sixteen GDAs – London, Portsmouth,

Southampton, Thames & Medway, Cardiff, Manchester, Sheffield, Leeds, Birmingham, Scapa, and the Mersey, Humber, Forth, Tyne, Tees and Clyde. Most of these were occupied by four guns, but a few of the London sites accommodated eight. In addition, 226½ sites accommodated 3.7in statics (the fraction reflecting a site which uniquely held two statics and two mobiles), while only 124½ used 3.7in mobile weapons. Although these figures refer only to occupied sites, they do show that approaching three-quarters of the 494 positions with weapons had been fully built to static standard by the middle of the war, a proportion which can probably be read across to the complete complement of 1014 sites listed at that time to suggest that about 700 were structurally complete. This evidence is consistent with the routine progress report on HAA site building issued by DFW in January 1942 (unfortunately the last of the series to have survived) which shows that 601 HAA sites were then scheduled to be fully furnished with emplacements for static guns, of which 517½ had been finished.[24] It is a question, though, how many of the sites not yet built to static standard in June 1942 did eventually reach this form. Some of the those hurriedly occupied for the Baedeker targets certainly came into this category, especially among towns which had not been listed for guns in earlier orders. To these we should probably add some of the sites in smaller and newer GDAs, a few of which may never even have been armed. But the point remains that Pile's policy of building as many sites as possible to static standard continued into the latter war years. To help achieve it, amid deepening manpower worries, in time he was forced to convert some of his operational regiments into construction units, assigned to pouring concrete and erecting Nissens rather than firing guns. In April 1943 men with relevant experience were drawn together into 131 HAA Regiment, the first such unit to be formed, who for a time became AA Command's master builders.[25]

In October 1942 this layout was brought within a new formation layout based upon AA *groups*, which at a stroke replaced the old organisation of corps and divisions and left only one tier of command – the group itself – between the brigades and the command headquarters at Stanmore.[26] There were several reasons for the change: a need to economise in manpower, a drive for greater flexibility and pace in the movement of orders and paperwork, and in particular the benefits which would come from more closely matching the geography of Fighter Command groups, which the original seven AA groups did with some precision. Thus 1 AA Group took charge of London – essentially the old 1 AA Division area – which now became an island within the territory of 2 AA Group, which handled East Anglia and the south-east, shadowing the RAF's 11 Group. At the same time the south-west and south Wales became 3 AA Group, the north-west and north Wales 4 AA Group, and 5, 6 and 7 AA Groups took charge respectively of the Lincolnshire–Yorkshire region, north-east England and Scotland, and Northern Ireland. This arrangement remained in being for well over a year, seeing major changes only during the *Overlord* preparations and the flying-bomb campaign of 1944–45, which brought about such vast transformations in gun layouts that the entire command geography of the air defences needed to be rethought.

The early summer's lull in the Fringe Target attacks ceased abruptly on 9 July, when two Bf 109s bombed Friston in the first such raid since 26 June, and only the fifth since 24 May. Any hopes that June's reprieve signalled the closing of the campaign were banished in the next few days, when raids fell on Great Yarmouth and Brixham (on the 12th), Swanage (on the 13th) and, four days later, on Brixham (again) and Aldeburgh in Suffolk. The inclusion of two East Anglian targets in the renewed raids was a fresh development, though apart from a raid at Felixstowe on 22 July – when seven aircraft bombed the town – this stretch of coast would not be troubled again for almost two months. But these incidents widened the front of a battle which, in the following weeks, brought bombs on many targets which had escaped them in the spring, and saw raids somewhere or other almost daily.

As July turned to August with no sign of the attacks diminishing, Pile was forced to consider how long they could be allowed to continue before heavy reinforcements would have to be sent to the south coast towns at the expense of more conventional targets. Few raiders were troubled by the guns in these weeks. Though a Category III claim was made at Brixham on 17 July, it was 4 August before the gunners downed another raider during a raid on Hove and the nearby Southwick power station (though this claim seems to have taken some time to confirm).[27] Both this and a second victim downed at Brighton four days later were FW 190s, which by early August had virtually supplanted the older Bf 109s in the Fringe Target raids and, with a little help from Dornier and Junkers light bombers, would dominate the remainder of the campaign. In early August, too, the incidents gained intensity. The second anniversary of *Adlertag* on 13 August produced three raids – two quartets visited Eastbourne and Dartmouth, while seven 190s operated against Teignmouth – in the largest number of sorties yet launched in a single day. Those mindful of the date, however, may have reflected on the pitiful contrast with the great events of two years before. Elsewhere on 13 August the Luftwaffe persevered with rather desultory air operations typical of summer 1942 – a few reconnaissance flights, a fifteen-aircraft night raid on Norwich – in a week during which sporadic AA fire was heard across 57 GDAs or VPs, but no major engagements took place.[28]

And so it went on. Between 15 August and 25 September, when the first heavy reinforcements were ordered to the south-coast towns, the Luftwaffe made 47 distinct attacks on Fringe Targets, operating on 24 days and dispatching 135 sorties. For the most part the raiders came in pairs, occasionally rising to threes or fours, though Dungeness was bombed by five FW 190s on 1 September, Torquay by the same number a few days later, and Dartmouth by six aircraft on the 18th. But then on 24 September a much larger force of 20 FW 190s visited Hastings, on a day which also saw the usual small raids at Seaford, Newhaven and Dymchurch. It was now that Pile decided that the attacks, 'however unimportant from a military point of view, must be stopped';[29] and, happily, for the first time, sufficient LAA guns were becoming available to do it. Orders went out on the 25th that LAA would 'be sited to afford maximum protection to the civilian population and to enhance morale'.[30] At first, just 48 additional Bofors were sent south, though some of those already in place among the existing coastal VPs were resited to extend their cover towards the civilian targets. Next day Pile and Sholto Douglas met to examine what else could be done.

Though fully conscious that disarming conventional military VPs to reinforce the seaside resorts might be just what the Germans wanted, the two commanders at last made the bold decision that this, indeed, must be done. Some of the less vital military targets which had earlier sacrificed weapons to the coastal VPs, and had since been rearmed, now lost their guns for the second time. This produced 110 Bofors, but a larger consignment of 142 came direct from the October production batch; adding 24 from reserves, Pile and Sholto Douglas therefore scraped together 276 additional 40mm guns for the Fringe Targets, together with 96 Oerlikon cannons and a few smaller weapons. Added to the 267 already in place, by the end of September the array of Bofors on the south coast was set to reach 543 – plus the other armament – of which no fewer than 360 were assigned to the seaside towns, as distinct from military VPs. (Though the towns were soon brought within AA Command's sequence of VP numbers, gaining designations in the 800s; thus Torquay became 844, Eastbourne 823 and so on.) And new guns were only part of the package. Given the lack of radar warning, standing fighter patrols were instituted by 11 Group, the practicalities of linking CHL stations directly to LAA troop headquarters were examined afresh, and all guns were raised to a higher state of readiness, with a three-man crew constantly standing by. Finally, to eliminate hesitancy on the gunners' part, a free-fire zone was established at certain towns, allowing the artillery to shoot on sight at any aircraft approaching below 500 feet. (To be on the safe side the RAF were told to stay above 1000 feet;[31] pilots with no option but to fly low, because in difficulties, were instructed to lower undercarriage as a sign of peace.) 'These arrangements will simplify the task of the Lt AA units considerably,' advised the command general staff on 2 October. 'The guns have been provided, all possible external help has been given, and the success of our counter measures against this serious threat will now depend on the initiative and resource of the junior Lt AA commanders. They have a magnificent opportunity of defeating a definite challenge.'[32]

By autumn 1942 a 'definite challenge' for LAA had certainly

been wanting for quite a time; but, bracing as these words may
have been, they could not entirely compensate for the inexperience
of many of the junior LAA officers and younger gunners who
were now thrown into their first real clash with the Luftwaffe. No
great surprise, then, that doubling the guns on the south coast did
not at first double the returns. Raiding in October was as frequent
as ever – incidents occurred on sixteen days in the month, sorties
totalled 56, targets eighteen – but only two Category I claims were
returned, and one of those fell to the guns at RAF Manston, which
was hardly a fringe target in the same sense as Teignmouth or
Hove. The other confirmed victim was at Salcombe on 9 October,
the day before the Manston kill, where a pair of FW 190s attacked
barges, among other harmless things. Four Category III claims
were also made during the month and one Category II – a
'probable' – was recorded at Swanage; but that was all. And
October 1942 also saw one of the most tragic incidents in the
entire Fringe Target campaign, when the RAF Officers' Hospital
at Torquay collected a direct hit from a force of four FW 190s
which delivered a snap raid from wave-top height at eleven in the
morning. First put at six dead and twenty injured, the casualty
list steadily rose during the day to twelve killed – ten of them
patients – and several more wounded, among them 22 convalescent
officers.[33] There is of course no suggestion that the Germans
deliberately targeted the hospital, which was accommodated in
one of Torquay's many hotels; incidents such as this were simply
inevitable when bombing was indiscriminate. But local feeling
ran high.

Omitted from the tally of October raids just given is one on
the last day of the month which resembled the fringe attacks in
that fighters flew low in daylight, but differed from them in that
60 machines participated and their target was Canterbury. AA
Command's willingness to include this operation in the 'official'
register of Fringe Target raids shows how loosely some of these
events were classified, a point whose importance begins to
register, perhaps, only when one comes to study the command's
performance statistics – quantification of results, after all, is
credible only when like is compared with like. The two Category
III 'damaged' claims made by the Canterbury guns – which had
not been reinforced in the general expansion earlier in the month

– entered the Fringe Target score when, arguably, they had no place there. But this was the only big daylight fighter raid of the campaign, which in early November resumed its familiar course.

A few more reinforcements had been found during October. On the 5th of the month Home Forces agreed to give up three of their own LAA batteries, and soon after the Canadian forces in Britain offered to lend a third of their light gun troops for duty during the daylight hours. Designed to support a field army, these fully mobile units added a valuable element of flexibility; moving every 48 hours or so to cover obscure and difficult lines of approach, the Canadians likened their job to 'duck shooting'. October also saw study of catenary wires as a means of closing the narrow valleys used by some raiders in the final approach to their targets, though this method was soon judged too elaborate. Guns, the argument ran, were always the best defence.

It was in December 1942, nine months after the first raid on Torquay, that the south coast was finally authorised to receive the guns which would eventually turn the tide in the Fringe Target campaign. By now as many as 400 supplementary Bofors guns had been deployed among the resort targets, in addition to those at established VPs, with the result that many seaside towns were more strongly defended with LAA than the most sensitive military sites had been just a couple of years earlier. Torquay and Brixham were typical (Fig 35). By December 1942 VP844 at Torquay fielded no fewer than twelve Bofors, distributed on single-gun sites to cover the northern sea approaches, the inland attack routes and the town of Paignton, while a further eight clustered around Brixham Harbour (VP809), to the south across Torbay and four protected Brixham town (VP515). Eight or twelve Bofors was the general rule for the Fringe Targets at this time: among 3 AA Group's other fringe VPs on the south-west coast, for example, twelve protected Salcombe and Dartmouth and eight were in place at Teignmouth, Exmouth and Sidmouth.[34]

Although substantial reinforcements were approved for the Fringe Targets during December, the time taken to supply and install the guns meant that little real effect was seen on the score-sheet until March 1943. December brought raids on sixteen of 31 days, aimed at 27 targets with almost 70 individual sorties, and of these the guns claimed eight aircraft damaged, one 'probable' and

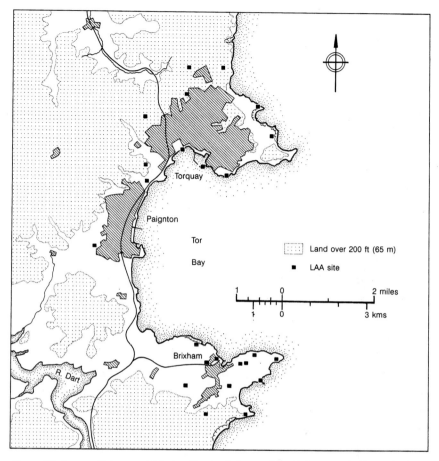

Figure 35 Fortress Paignton: LAA sites for the defence of the Torbay area in December 1942, at the height of the Fringe Target raids. A huge volume of armament was committed to these militarily insignificant resort towns.

three destroyed. (Against this, the RAF's score, thanks to the standing patrols and other measures instituted in the autumn, amounted to eleven destroyed, three 'probables' and four damaged, a score in the first two categories exceeding that for the whole seven-month period from May to November.) As usual, a few of these raids were aimed at more conventional military targets as well as resort towns (Manston and Lympne airfields were both hit); and again, they included occasional departures from the usual 'fringe' pattern, such as the operation on 30 December, when five FW 190s bombed the city of Exeter. But the real diversification came during January, when several fringe attacks were flown by Junkers 88 bombers flying singly and – to complete the inversion of the normal pattern of events – London Docks and inland targets across the Home Counties were attacked on 20 January by a low-flying force of 60 FW 190s and Bf 109 fighters, the latter making a rare reappearance. The twelve aircraft reaching London in particular illustrate, again, that the raids classified as Fringe Target attacks by AA Command were far from consistent in character. (Indeed, this operation might be seen as more closely allied to the isolated night raid against London on 16/17 January – the first since July 1941 and a reprisal for a Bomber Command attack on Berlin the previous night – when 75 enemy operated, about 30 entered the IAZ, and eight were shot down.)[35] In general the fringe operations in January showed a marked upturn in the numbers of raiders taking part in each – six FW 190s attacked Torquay on 8 January, for example, while seven visited Teignmouth on 10 January and eight bombed and machine-gunned Rye a few days later. In all, raids classified as fringe events were more numerous in January. Including the big sweep on the 20th, at least 145 fringe sorties were flown, and even without this unusual operation the number reached 85, spread between 21 days. Despite the multiplicity of targets, however, the gunners' claims in January were proportionally fewer than in the previous month. Three aircraft were destroyed, two 'probable' claims were made and five were listed in Category III as 'damaged'.

From the start of the Fringe Target campaign the ideal weapon to protect against these raids was automatically assumed to be the 40mm Bofors gun, AA Command's most lethal instrument of LAA defence. By late 1942, however, it was emerging that the 40mm weapon by itself was not necessarily the ideal antidote to this particular campaign, chiefly because many gunners found that shooting over open sights was handier against fleeting targets than using the Bofors' predictor. So instead of building up the Bofors front, 200 20mm Hispano cannons were requested, some of them to replace Bofors (whose numbers were set to drop by 60) to produce a more flexible and varied battery of armament. These took time to deliver, however, so the first two months of 1943 saw a veritable armaments fair on the south coast, as gunners set up their stalls with a range of exotic weapons drawn from whatever sources could be tapped. In February the navy supplied 400 rocket projectors of 2in type, 300 of which went to 2 AA Group in the area from the Solent to Norfolk and the rest to 3 AA Group in the south-west, while a few 0.303in twin Vickers 'K' weapons manned by personnel from searchlight batteries were also supplied. A further 120 Vickers 'K's soon arrived in the hands of gunners from the RAF Regiment (soon to be followed by 48 more), together with 70 Hispano 20mm; all of these guns were mounted on the Regiment's Beaverette vehicles. February also saw a huge deployment of multiple LMGs manned by searchlight detachments, 252 of which were in place by the last week of the month. In all, by 22 February there were 472 Bofors guns distributed among the Fringe Targets, 364 Vickers 'K's and – so far – 88 Hispano 20mms, which together with the LMGs brought the artillery defences to a formidable 1176 guns, not counting the naval UP rockets. And by then a further 440 Hispanos were authorised and awaited, 140 of them to be manned by the RAF Regiment and 300 by AA Command.[36]

Siting this vast armoury of new weapons threw considerable strain on local AA staff, whose job it was to assess the tactical characteristics of each target, select and acquire suitable gunsites, and continuously monitor each layout for its performance in action and potential for improvement. This duty was the stock-in-trade of brigade and regimental staff, but evidence that they were not the only ones with such problems on their minds arrived in January, when Miss Camille Lumsden of Torquay wrote to the Air Ministry to air her views on how best her town should be defended from the raids. 'In view of the repeated enemy sneak attacks on Torquay,' asked Miss Lumsden, 'may I as a resident offer a suggestion to help towards our better protection?'

In the months of Aug: Sep: Oct: and Jan: 43 German raiders used the same course and the same tactics to fly in low over the sea. In each case they flew low between the two points locally known as Nolls Hill and Hope's Nose. After the Sep raid AA guns were positioned on high ground between these points, but it would seem because of their altitude they could not bear on the raiders flying in low and in consequence the RAF Officers Hospital was partially demolished with loss of personnel in the Oct raid. On the 8th inst the evacuated Hospital was again hit and further damage done to adjacent residences by the raiders using the identical course they followed in their Oct raid. Anstey Cove which lies mid-way between Nolls Hill and Hope's Nose lies low and just above sea level and it is this route that is used.

The suggestion is that if an AA gun unit is established there it would prevent its future use. At present this low ground has land mines, as a precaution against invasion, but as this danger seems remote at the moment they could be removed with advantage to give place to a protection against a danger that is definitely more in evidence. A further fact that should be mentioned is that if the guns already in position on the high ground can be deflected sufficiently to meet the low flying raiders, it would be of interest to know why they do not go into action before the enemy planes cross the coast.

Residents have seen raiders coming in without action being taken and it is only after bombs have been dropped and damage done that our defences come to life.

I trust you will be kind enough to look into this matter and relieve us of our continued strain, more so as bombs generally drop even before our Alert can give us warning of approaching danger.

Study of army headquarters' files from almost any date during the Second World War shows how frequently private citizens like Miss Lumsden were apt to advance theories of their own on how best the war could be won, especially the war as it affected their own neighbourhoods. On the face of things it may seem surprising that these missives were taken seriously by an overstretched and increasingly formalised service bureaucracy, especially when their authors were civilians with no evident military background; but in fact the unsolicited approaches reaching headquarters at all levels were generally answered, often in detail – as far as the strictures of security allowed – and the exchanges carefully filed away for us to read today. An instinctive respect for English individualism presumably explains this in part; but equally the local amateur was often capable of surprisingly astute tactical judgements. Certainly this was true of Miss Lumsden. Her only mistake, in fact, was to write to the Air Ministry rather than AA Command, since her letter took more than a fortnight to reach the appropriate desk at Stanmore. And when it did, on 4 February, it was discovered that a reinforcement of the Torquay guns ordered a few days after her letter was posted had sited a Bofors precisely in Miss Lumsden's preferred spot, and for precisely her reasons. At that date, of course, Miss Lumsden had yet to receive a reply to her letter, and would simply have seen an LAA crew dutifully setting up where she had suggested. 'No doubt Miss Lumsden will be very pleased,' wrote an officer at Stanmore, 'and will be able to bear full testimony of [sic] the rapid results attainable under our Democratic Government.' But 'Actually,' he conceded, 'I thought her letter was very sensible.'

Torquay itself was attacked on only two occasions between December 1942 and March 1943, first on 8 January – shortly before the additional guns were installed, when two of six 190s were damaged – and again on 26 January, when the newly-reinforced layout proved sufficiently formidable for the two FW 190s which attacked from 100 feet to scoot for home the instant fire was opened. Yet this deterrent effect was not yet possible everywhere, and the Luftwaffe continued to hold the upper hand for some weeks yet. February's raiding was more sporadic than that in January – raiders operated on just thirteen days of 28 – but it was more intensive. Developing the trend newly-emerged in January, the alert now heralded formations seldom numbering fewer than four aircraft, and often eight strong. The 73 individual sorties which made up these raids mostly hit home – in this period the usual scatter of peaceful seaside towns – with only two hostiles destroyed by the guns (in an eight-strong raid on Portsmouth and Brighton on 10 February), one 'probable' and four winged. The RAF's bag, by contrast, amounted to five aircraft downed in each of the months of January and February, and another ten damaged.

The great upswing in AA performance from March onwards was achieved not simply with more guns – early warning arrangements were also steadily improving – but there is no doubt that the switch of fortunes between AA Command and the Luftwaffe was largely due, finally, to saturating the south coast with LAA weapons. Arrangements to thicken the layout still further were made in the middle of the month, when Pile asked that all 20mm guns issuing from the factories over the next three months should be diverted to the fringe campaign, together with additional 2in UPs and the complete production run of 500 rocket projectors of 20-barrelled type, weapons which had originally been earmarked for local AA defences among Home Forces' coast artillery batteries.[37] In fact this last request was turned down, but the coast gunners themselves did enter the campaign thanks to another of Pile's schemes, namely to equip most of their sites on the Fringe Target front with Bofors.[38] By early April some 82 batteries between Yarmouth and the Lizard were listed to receive a total of 133 Bofors,[39] weapons which were generally installed between late April and June.[40] And at the same time the warning system was finally perfected. Communications linking CHL stations directly to LAA troop headquarters, requested as long ago as April 1942, were finally completed in the summer of 1943, together with others between the radar stations and the dispersal points on fighter aerodromes. Both enabled the radar operators to pass their plots directly to the men who were actually engaging the raiders. And, in the summer of 1943, those plots were themselves becoming sharper and more thorough, thanks to technical refinements to the radar equipment among low cover stations on the south coast.

The effect of all this on the guns' performance was profound. March brought raids on just twelve days, but those days saw a total of 116 individual sorties, mostly by FW 190s attacking conventional Fringe Targets in forces now routinely reaching eight or a dozen aircraft. Of these, eight machines were destroyed by the guns, one 'probable' claim was made, and four raiders were damaged. Following these rising losses, the Luftwaffe launched just four raids in early April – the last of them on the 9th – consisting of 30 sorties against five targets, for the loss of three FW 190s and one winged. Possibly cowed by the greater firepower evident among their targets, the Germans then suspended the attacks completely for almost a month, during which time it was unclear from the British side of the Channel whether the campaign had ceased. Any temptation to remove the new guns, however, was firmly resisted – and to have done so would, of course, have played directly into the Luftwaffe's hands. The action which resumed on 7 May brought the Fringe Target campaign to a new pitch of aggression.

On this day Yarmouth was raided by sixteen FW 190s which bombed the town and sprayed the streets with machine-gun fire, and for the next week the renewed onslaught was confined exclusively to targets on the east coast. Yarmouth took more punishment on 11 May, when eighteen FW 190s repeated the performance of four days earlier and bombs fell, among other places, on the AA brigade headquarters. Only one aircraft was destroyed by the guns in the 11 May raid (one more was damaged), but in the three weeks now remaining of the Fringe Target campaign the losses inflicted on the Luftwaffe by guns and fighters became severe. The two waves of raiders which struck Lowestoft on 12 May were not greatly troubled by the guns – one was shot down and two damaged from the 32 which operated – while LAA brought down another of the twenty which attacked Southwold and Felixstowe three days later. But once the operations swung back to the heavily gunned targets on the south coast the score began to run firmly in the defenders' favour. Hastings and Bexhill were visited by a swarm of twenty FW 190s on 23 May, the same day which saw a 22-strong force harry the town centre of Bournemouth; the guns claimed four of these aircraft destroyed and three damaged. Next came Brighton and Folkestone, which were raided by 24 and twelve FW 190s on 25 May, the latter abortively once the guns opened up. Five of these 36 aircraft were downed and three destroyed. Fittingly enough, it was Torquay that saw the climax of the Fringe Target campaign, when a fierce barrage of fire downed no fewer than six of the fifteen FW 190s which attacked on 30 May; and to show that this was no fluke, a twenty-strong force raiding Frinton and Walton on the same day lost four of its number. On this Sunday the Luftwaffe lost ten aircraft to the LAA guns – 40 per cent of the force dispatched – bringing the month's total to 22 FW 190s downed and nine winged by fire from the ground, together with ten fringe raiders destroyed by fighters, one 'probable', and two damaged.

Losses at this level could not continue. Targets on the Isle of Wight, Margate and Broadstairs were raided by 23 aircraft on 1 June – one shot down by LAA, one 'probable' – before Eastbourne was hit for the eleventh time in the penultimate fringe raid, on 4 June. At 11.28 in the morning sixteen FW 190s followed their usual routine – fast approach towards the Beachy Head light-house, flick up over the cliff, steep right bank to swoop down on the target – to release a scatter of HEs across the town. The usual casualties followed.[41] Many shops were destroyed – MacFisheries in Grove Road and the Beach Laundry among them – two hotels suffered hits, and a bomb crashed through the vicarage of St Saviour's before piercing the church roof and coming to rest: alone among the thirteen HEs released, this one was a dud. The only explosive to approach a military target landed near an LAA site in Paradise Drive. Seven died in this raid and 33 were injured, while two fighters were destroyed by the guns and another was damaged. But these victims were not the last. Seven more Eastbourne residents perished in the very last Fringe Target raid, which followed two days later on Sunday, 6 June. Breaking with their usual tactics, on this occasion the fighters approached Eastbourne from the south-east, crossing the coast at about 30 feet in the eastern reaches of the town. Bombs were dropped before the force of fourteen aircraft split into two groups. Eight left the target area to the west, by way of the Downs and Birling Gap, but six remained to finish off the fifteen-month campaign with remarkably accurate cannon and machine-gun fire on the Observer Corps post on Beachy Head – where more than 100 bullet-holes were later counted on the look-out hut – and at LAA sites protecting the town. Whatever those parting shots were intended to achieve, it is tempting to read them as a compliment.

At first, of course, no one in Britain knew that this was the end. It was mid September before the first substantial reductions were ordered among the coastal resorts.[42] But when weeks turned to months and none of the Fringe Targets was further troubled, it seemed safe to make final calculations of profit and loss. When the raids were totted up, Hastings and Swanage emerged as the targets most frequently attacked – both were raided on thirteen occasions – but Eastbourne and Hastings suffered the largest number of sorties, and by some margin. In all, 76 aircraft had bombed and strafed Eastbourne, while 75 had visited Hastings (the total for Swanage, by contrast, was just 34). The only other town to come close to these figures was Canterbury, though here the 60 sorties written down by AA Command as Fringe Target raids have a doubtful place in reckoning, since they simply reflected the unique low-level fighter operation at the end of October 1942. After Eastbourne and Hastings the town suffering the largest number of sorties is better counted as Brighton (52 raiders in ten raids); and after that, Dartmouth (44 sorties, eleven operations), Great Yarmouth (34 of whose 42 raiders came in just two raids in May 1943), and Torquay (40 sorties, eight raids). Next came Deal, Swanage, Lowestoft, Folkestone and Bexhill, all of which received sorties counted in the thirties, before the much larger number of targets which were visited by raiders in the twenties, tens and single figures. Altogether, AA Command reckoned that 1236 separate Fringe Target sorties had been launched between 27 March 1942 and 6 June of the following year, split between 288 discrete operations; and while a few of these events do raise problems of definition, the figures give a valid general picture of a campaign which was very largely directed against coastal resorts and other innocuous targets.

What did the enterprise achieve? Certainly the most important consequence for AA Command was to tie up so many weapons among the south-coast towns, and the drain imposed by the logistical work necessary to put them in place. But the Luftwaffe never really capitalised upon this potential advantage. Having persuaded Pile to commit vast reserves of LAA to the Fringe Targets, the Germans did not then harass the conventional military VPs which they should have supposed to be denuded as a result. Much damage was caused among the target towns, it is true, and many people were killed and injured, but few of those were making a direct contribution to the war. For their efforts the Luftwaffe lost at least 178 aircraft – 127 Category I claims were made by the gunners and 51 by the RAF, plus seventeen 'probables' by the two arms together – and sustained damage to a further 116. In the end it was all rather futile – but look at those casualty figures again. Fifty-one raiders destroyed by fighters and 127 by the guns meant that for every two aircraft shot down by the RAF the gunners had destroyed five. The Fringe Target campaign was the first in which the ratio of kills swung so firmly in the gunners' favour. 'Their main contribution came later,' Churchill wrote. By autumn 1943 'later' was beginning to arrive.

CHAPTER 10

Roof over Britain

JULY 1943 – MAY 1944

On 14 August 1939 the chief of the German army's General Staff, Franz Halder, made a note in his diary recording Hitler's opinions of British war preparations, a subject explored in a conference earlier that day. Though progress had been made 'in bomber and fighter strength', said the Führer, and there were signs of 'improvements in ground organization [. . .] Three years will be needed to build up an adequate anti-aircraft force. Air armament programme,' noted Halder, 'is being pushed in too many directions, with resulting mutual interference.'[1] In fact in the autumn of 1939 German intelligence was underestimating Britain's aircraft production by at least 100 per cent: 300 a month was the German estimate of a figure which, in truth, was at least twice that.[2] But, coming in the wake of the Sandys case and Hore-Belisha's somewhat disingenuous assurances that all would be well, Hitler's remarks reveal a firm grasp of AA Command's unpreparedness as the war approached. Three years to marshal an 'adequate' AA gun defence was not far wide of the mark. As the Fringe Target victory shows, it was in late 1942, or more surely the middle months of 1943, that Britain's AA defences became truly a force to be reckoned with.

It was in 1943, too, that the British public were given their first detailed account of what the domestic AA defences had been up to in the first three years of war. Throughout the Second World War the Ministry of Information, from its headquarters in the tall, tapering Senate House of the University of London, issued a series of paperback booklets on aspects of Britain's war, aimed directly at domestic and service audiences, and obliquely, of course, at German intelligence analysts. Jacketed in A Games's stark modernist montage of searchlight beams, gunfire and a gunner, resolute in silhouette, the AA story – *Roof Over Britain* – offered the British public 88 pages for ninepence. Orwell famously modelled his Ministry of Truth on the MoI, and with some reason. But *Roof Over Britain* is more than propaganda. It contains very few downright lies, and none today seem at all sinister. Much was left unsaid, of course; but if the ministry's narrative fell short of the whole truth, it told the British public little that was not the truth. To describe the gunners' work in the first years of war as, in part, a 'victory over monotony' was certainly true; to claim, on the other hand, that the wartime growth in the AA defences had been 'better than scheduled' was possible only by manipulating the (naturally unquoted) statistics for weapon supply to the point of falsity.[3] But the general tenor of the book was fair. It was true, more or less as Hitler had predicted, that Britain had at least an 'adequate' AA defence by 1943. The title *Roof over Britain*, with its suggestion of a sturdy protective canopy, would not have been apposite only a year earlier.

Many improvements were seen in the AA defence during 1943, not least a useful increase in the number of guns.[4] In the year from January 1943 Pile's arsenal of HAA weapons rose from 2088 to 2729 (31 per cent), meaning that the goal of 2232 HAA decided upon in May 1939 to be reached sometime in 1941 had been attained in the middle months of 1943; by January 1944 Pile was still 1000 guns short of the 3744 target set during the Battle of Britain, though that was no longer current. And by now the dominance of the static 3.7in over its mobile cousin was complete: of the 2284 guns of this calibre serving AA Command only 650 were mobiles, so the weapon intended before the war as the mainstay of the 3.7in arsenal had, after four years of hostilities, shrunk to just 29 per cent of it. On the other hand it was in 1943 that the gunners finally said goodbye to the 3in 20cwt which had served Britain's air defences since 1913: the eighteen of these weapons which remained on the books for HAA work in January (most of them in the Shetlands) had vanished within a few months, likewise the six used for LAA.

By 1943 AA Command's LAA armoury was looking distinctly

modern. Though alternative demands for Bofors often denied AA Command a linear, month-by-month increase, this factor could also be offset by borrowing weapons from Home Forces; in any event the total of Bofors guns defending AA Command targets rose from 1737 to 2223 in 1943, an increase of 28 per cent. AA Command began that year, in fact, with an LAA armoury relying very largely on the Bofors – apart from the six 3in weapons, the mix of 2pdr Mk VIII singles, Hispano Suizas and Oerlikons totalled no more than 94 weapons, and by now Lewis guns numbered just 88. The climax of the Fringe Target campaign had, however, diversified this stock considerably, with the result that 609 guns of types other than Bofors were defending AA Command VPs by the end of December 1943 – a retrograde step perhaps, but one that did at least bring the LAA total to a sturdy 2674. And in 1943 the ever-rising stock of rocket projectors helped to offset deficits in conventional guns. In the year from January 1943 these weapons rose from 5043 to 6265 (24 per cent).

Among Pile's heavy weapon stocks the advances in raw numbers ran in parallel with several qualitative improvements. The first 5.25in singles arrived in the spring, and their sites were begun in the summer; in August work began on a project to convert AA Command's 4.5s to higher-powered versions of the 3.7in, by relining the older weapons' barrels; and a little later in the year the existing stock of 3.7s started to be upgraded with automatic fuze-setting equipment, a device which would bring a radical improvement to the gun's rate of fire. None of these projects was completed quickly – the 5.25in programme, in particular, was a huge and often troubled enterprise, still incomplete at the war's end – but all three contributed to the gradually changing technical character of AA gunnery in the last two years of war.

In the event the introduction of 5.25in singles did not exactly surge ahead in 1943. The first were delivered from the factories in March and assigned to the IAZ, where preliminary site work was under way by the end of June at ZE21 (Hackney Marshes), ZS4 (Bostall Heath), ZS14 (Dulwich) and ZW10 (Wormwood Scrubs), established sites whose conversion would complement the three twins already in place and allow the first sixteen 5.25 singles to command the airspace over central London (the site positions can be identified from the maps at Figs 19–21, pages 235, 246 and 263).[5] These guns were part of an initial allotment of 40 to the south-eastern GDAs, and by the end of July the remaining 24 had been allocated to one battery in the Thames & Medway (TN19 at Ayletts) together with five more sites in the IAZ, at ZE4 (Buckhurst Hill), ZS21 (Crayford), ZS26 (Thornet Wood), ZS17 (Mitcham Common) and ZW13 (Mill Hill). This second group of London sites was chosen as far as possible on tactical criteria – to provide an outer ring of 5.25 singles to complement those already begun – but in practice several compromises were necessary.[6] AA Command policy was that the guns would be operated by mixed batteries, limiting sites to those already hutted on the ATS scale (sites manned by Home Guard were ruled out). Further, since the 5.25s would replace the current guns, it made sense to avoid existing eight-gun batteries to minimise weapon movements and structural redundancy. Another consideration was the need to avoid an excess of new technical buildings – as works projects the new emplacements and ancillaries were already vast – which meant re-using command posts, avoiding too many road extensions, and so on. The bigger guns also required rather wider clearances from housing, roads and railways than the older 3.7s and 4.5s, and these added markedly to the difficulties in siting. In practice the London AA staff got around them in several cases by special pleading, though unwisely, as it turned out, when the guns' first firing alerted people to just how powerful they were. In truth a battery of four 5.25in anti-aircraft guns was a fearsome thing to put in a city.

The first four London sites were the only 5.25in single batteries to be fully commissioned by the end of 1943, though several more positions were selected and begun during the year. By mid August the first 72 guns had been allocated to GDAs, amounting to the 36 already assigned to London and eight (by now) to Thames & Medway, four more to an undecided destination in the south-east, and – the first outside these two areas – sixteen on the Humber and eight for the Mersey. At this time provisional allocations of the remaining 128 weapons were also made between formations, though not to specific cities.[7] Apart from the 5.25in guns in London, the only comparable development elsewhere in 1943 was the completion of a dual-role conversion at Park Battery in the Tyne coast defences, which was commissioned in this form in the summer. Park was one of several coast artillery batteries selected in 1942 as candidates for conversion to joint CA/AA working, though this programme's cancellation towards the end of 1943 (in a general climate of contraction among the coast artillery defences) left this site high and dry as a unique monument to an unfulfilled plan. Park's 5.25in guns, though technically available for AA work, were primarily a coast artillery property and, interestingly, were never included in AA Command's weekly roster of anti-aircraft armaments.

Allocations of the single-role 5.25in were refined in autumn 1943, and by the following spring the overall shape of the intended programme was reasonably clear.[8] By mid April the four original IAZ sites were complete and operational, the second five in London were under construction, together with three in Thames & Medway (TN19, TS2 and TS20), four on the Humber (H2, H4, H20 and H28), two at Portsmouth (P5 and P12), two on the Isle of Wight (IW6 and IW13), and two at Plymouth (H7 and H13). All of these sites were expected to be complete at various dates between May and December 1944, bringing the operational batteries to 22 and weapons to 88. Beyond that, work slated for the future extended to 26 sites for 100 weapons: more in Thames & Medway, Plymouth and the Solent, and others at Dover, Harwich, Yarmouth, Lowestoft, Bristol, Cardiff, the Mersey, Tyne and Tees, at Weybourne practice camp and the Aberporth experimental establishment (the last two with four weapons between them, hence 100 guns and 26 sites). No completion dates were advanced for most of these projects in spring 1944, but the general idea was to commission about half by mid 1945.

That was the plan, but for a number of reasons it was not exactly the reality. One was that the labour shortage, which deepened in 1943, resulted in still more AA Command troops being converted to 'construction units', and inevitably brought knock-on effects to the 5.25in programme. Another was the gradual realisation that the threat which these weapons had been intended to meet was itself easing, and at a time when AA Command had more pressing problems on its hands, notably *Overlord* and the battle against the flying bomb. The result was that some GDAs never got their 5.25in guns, and while London's primacy in claiming the first deliveries did pay benefits when the bombers returned to the capital in the winter of 1943–44, the war was over before the new weapon could claim a wider place in the nation's defence. Only 112 were actually emplaced by VE day (together with the original three London twins), and of those, just 48 were classified as operational.[9] As late as November 1945 the national layout amounted to 31 sites: nine in London, five in Thames & Medway, four each on the Humber, Solent and at Plymouth (where one was unfinished), two on the Mersey, one at Harwich, and two at Dover, neither of which was complete. The programme did continue after the war, but gradually, and in a very different strategic climate; so those 31 sites,[10] begun between the early summer of 1943 and the middle months of 1944, represent the extent of wartime fabric put in place to serve the 5.25in AA gun.

Those sites obeyed consistent principles of design, built around the very distinctive requirements of this formidable weapon. A massive piece of engineering, the fully-enclosed and shielded gun was capable of throwing an 80lb shell to an effective height of 43,000 feet, with a rate of fire (in initial models) of twelve rounds per minute.[11] Fully power-operated, the gun required a gunpit far more elaborate than the simple flat enclosure with ammunition lockers used for the 3.7in and 4.5in. At least two emplacement designs appeared from DFW during the war, both similar in form and differing largely in their means of construction. The early type was made from poured concrete throughout, though the labour difficulties met early in the programme led to the approval, in September 1944 of the 'utility' type – for 'accelerated construction' – which substituted concrete blocks for some of the mass concrete work, and was effectively a blockwork building poised on a concrete raft (Fig 36). In either type the gun was rotated on a heavily-engineered roller race (Fig 37), supporting the weapon over a deep pit which accommodated the 'trunk' for power-turning and was linked, via a cable duct, to the engine room (or 'power house') where the generator was mounted. The ordnance was operated from a circular walkway at the top of the emplacement – the 'ammunition gallery' – which was encircled by lockers for 324 shells and 288 charges. The gun spat its spent cartridges into a channel, for later retrieval.

The requirement for a completely new set of emplacements

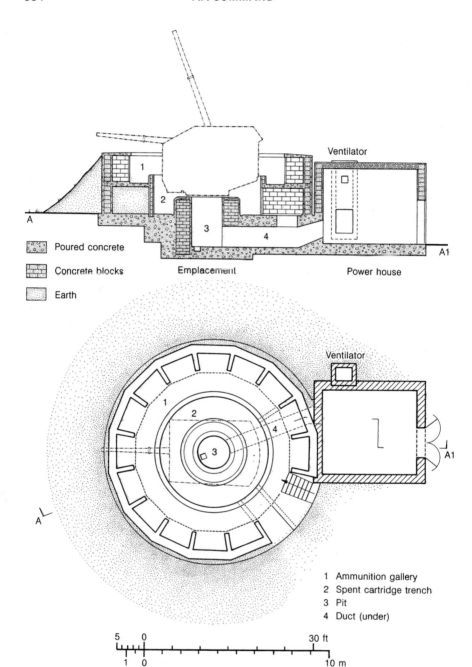

Ventilator

A

Poured concrete

Concrete blocks

Earth

Emplacement

Power house

A1

Ventilator

A1

A

1 Ammunition gallery
2 Spent cartridge trench
3 Pit
4 Duct (under)

5 0   30 ft

1 0   10 m

Figure 36 Emplacement design for the 5.25in gun, this one designed for accelerated construction using concrete blocks rather than poured concrete throughout.

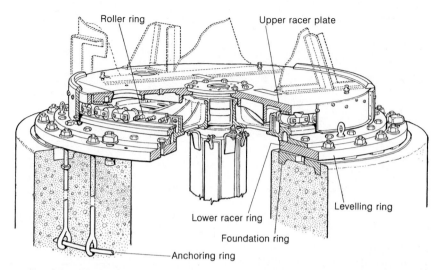

Figure 37 Roller race assembly for the 5.25in gun. Comparison with the 3.7in/4.5in holdfast shown in Figure 6 emphasises the complex engineering necessary for this heavy and sophisticated weapon.

Figure 38 A 5.25in site: Buckland, TN13 in the Thames & Medway GDA. The early HAA position obeys the pre-war design shown in Figure 7, while the new 5.25in fabric has been added to the east. The site was eventually provided with a remote command post which lay outside the limits of this plan.

1. Emplacement for 3.7"/4.5" gun
2. Command post
3. Magazine
4. Emplacement for 5.25" gun

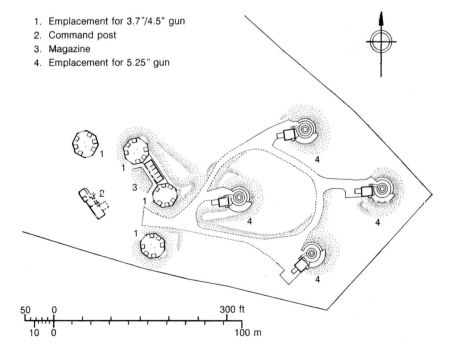

Plate 25 Installing the big guns. Swingate (D2 in the Dover GDA) being rebuilt for 5.25in singles, October 1945. Four new emplacements are visible in differing stages of construction.

meant that installing 5.25in guns was a matter of redesigning the entire battery, rather than simply exchanging one type of weapon for another – and as we have seen, the readiness with which this could be done was as important as any tactical considerations in determining which positions were chosen for conversion. Most 5.25in gunparks, which occupied a rather larger area than their predecessors, were simply erected adjacent to the old 4.5in or 3.7 (static) fabric, which maximised sharing and reuse of the domestic and technical buildings and limited the demand for additional land. Buckland, site TN13 in the Thames & Medway GDA, was typical (Fig 38). Begun in 1944 and approaching completion at the war's end, Buckland was converted by laying out a new set of 5.25in emplacements to the east of the old fabric, whose gunpits were abandoned (though the command post initially remained in use). As 5.25in guns were permanent fixtures, and were never worked simultaneously with 4.5s or 3.7s, the original emplacements invariably became redundant at converted sites. Some were left in situ, but others were demolished and their positions tidily levelled and cleared.

Once installed the 5.25in gun exposed some shortcomings in site design. The most serious was demonstrated by the sheer power of the weapon itself. As soon as the first guns were fired, and command post doors promptly blew from their hinges, stunned crews began to point out that the blast from the new weapons might have been underestimated. Although modifications to the gun itself were considered – including all-round steel plating and curtains to the rear of the turret – it was soon clear that the blast must be avoided rather than damped. In March 1944 AA groups were instructed to reconnoitre their sites to identify those where 'remote' command posts could be built (about 200 yards from the present structure), and where existing buildings would have to be strengthened and provided with blast traverses.[12] Complete by the end of the month, this survey found that remote command posts would be needed at about one-third of the 5.25in sites (including two of the three with twins installed in 1941).[13] The first was built at ZW10 (Wormwood Scrubs), and in time many 5.25in sites in other GDAs gained them, including Buckland, where the building lay outside the area shown in Figure 38.

Even in the optimistic days of summer 1943 no one expected that the 5.25in gun would provide an immediate solution to the high-flying raider, and it was this gap in AA cover which lay behind the second major ordnance project of the middle war period, namely the conversion of the 4.5in gun to accept the 3.7in shell.[14] The possibility of making this (perhaps surprising) adaptation was mooted as early as 1940, when it was examined as one of a range of options to raise the lethal height of HAA fire to meet aircraft whose operating heights were expected to rise appreciably over the next three years – perhaps to the point where heavy and light bombers were touching 45,000 feet, and fighters rather more. One outcome of that study was the 5.25in gun itself; but from an early stage ordnance experts pondered the feasibility of lining the barrels of large guns down to smaller bores, in order to increase the muzzle velocity imparted to the shell and thus raise its ceiling.[15] Three of these ideas envisaged converting 5.25in guns in various ways – including 'lining-down' to 4.5in or 3.7in calibre – but, in the event, the difficulties of producing even the required number of 'standard' 5.25s and mountings militated against these options. The one remaining possibility was lining-down the 4.5 to 3.7 inches, an operation tried experimentally, and with success, at the Shoeburyness range in early autumn 1942. Conscious that the Luftwaffe might soon resume high-level bombing operations – now, perhaps, in imitation of the USAAF's daylight tactics over Germany – in November 1942 Pile asked the War Office for authority to convert a proportion of his 4.5in guns, and for the necessary parts to be put into production. By August 1943 the kits were ready.[16] The first gun to be converted in service was at TS21 (Bell Farm) in the Thames & Medway GDA (which became AA Command's official user trials site in 1943), where firing trials were held during the early autumn. Although these exposed a rather thicker crop of faults than had been suggested by the original Shoeburyness experiments – heavy barrel wear and frequent fuze failure were probably the worst – most were overcome and the full adaptation programme began, rather later than Pile had hoped, in October 1943. London's guns were handled first. Almost 100 4.5s in the IAZ were fully converted by the end of November 1943,[17] when the programme moved outward to other GDAs.

The hybrid weapon which resulted from this technical fix was known as the 3.7in Mk VI (though to confuse the matter, as War Office nomenclature relentlessly did, the mounting was known as the Mk IV; as a result the ordnance was classified as the Mk VI but the whole assemblage the Mk IV). Visually not much different from the standard 4.5in – afficionados would spot a slightly larger barrel and a new breech block – the new gun returned a performance quite distinct from either of its progenitors, sending a 28lb shell to an effective ceiling of 45,000 feet – higher than the 5.25in, though with a shell only one third of the weight – and fully justifying the rather heavy workload involved in conversion. The gun was not without its faults. It disliked the new flashless propellant, which tended to foul the breech after about 50 rounds; from May 1944 spares were issued to enable the mechanism to be regularly changed. Another snag was a tendency for the shells to separate in storage, or for the lip of the cartridge to expand as the projectile worked loose, which deformed and jammed the round. Both defects were cured by more accommodating racking in the ammunition recesses, and by strict orders to handle rounds only when necessary. But for all this the Mk VI (on its Mk IV mounting) was a good gun, and by the end of the war 343 of AA Command's 4.5s had been converted, leaving only 63 weapons in their original form.[18]

The introduction of the 5.25in and the conversion of the 4.5s were the two big ordnance projects of 1943–45, though emphasis upon them should not be allowed to obscure the point that much of AA Command's equipment continued to be modified to a greater or lesser extent throughout the war. Further notable developments in 1943 were the introduction of remote control power-turning for the 3.7in static, together with the No 11 MFS – an automatic fuze-setter, performing mechanically a job previously done by hand and much increasing the gun's rate of fire. It was clear from the start, however, that the improved 3.7in – which became the Mk IIA when fitted with remote control, the IIB when equipped with the No 11 MFS, and the IIc when enjoying both – was beginning to outgrow its emplacement, the standard for which had not been revisited since 1942. In result, the summer of 1943 saw the start of work on a new design, the first stage of which was a user trial of the 3.7in Mk IIc, beginning in June.

Mounted at the School of AA Artillery, Lydstep, the trial was designed to assess the performance of the new MFS equipment and remote control when used with existing emplacement designs and ammunition racks, and to recommend what form any new structure should take. The main finding was that the increased rate of fire brought important implications for the volume of ammunition to be stored in the gunpit, and the amount of space necessary to cope with spent cartridges. A new design was accordingly drafted in July 1943,[19] and in late August a meeting was held at the War Office to settle the final details.[20] This concluded, first, that a square emplacement would best allow space for the spent cartridge cases created by the faster rate of fire, which could simply be accumulated in the corners. The new design was to have four ammunition recesses, ten feet six inches long, with an entrance to one side for the examination of fuzes of ready-for-use rounds. Instead of an on-site magazine, a trench shelter was to be provided for each emplacement, together with a personnel shelter, to which the gunpit should have easy access. The type-design for DFW 55483/1 was duly issued on 30 September 1943, and in the following month was notified as the sole emplacement authorised for the 3.7in Mk II, IIA, IIB and IIc.[21] Sources traced here fall short of the definitive drawing for the structure, but examples can be found in photographs and in the field of a specimen resembling that described (Fig 39). These emplacements are always indicative of late work (post-autumn 1943), and were usually added to existing layouts.

Figure 39 HAA emplacement design (1943 pattern). Designed to cope with the increased rate of fire obtained from the power-driven 3.7in gun with automatic fuze-setting, gunpits of this type were often added to existing layouts.

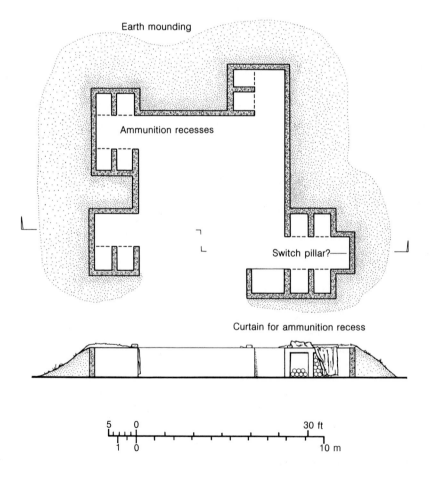

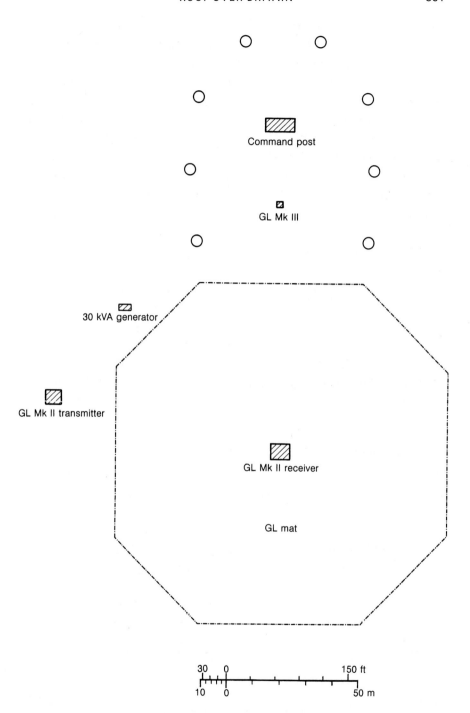

Figure 40 Layout plan for an HAA site, November 1942, showing provision for eight guns, a GL mat and the new GL Mk III equipment.

By the time these new structures entered currency the basic form of the 3.7in/4.5in HAA site had also come under review. Drafted at Stanmore in November 1942 and formalised by DFW in the following February, a revised master plan called for all new HAA sites to be laid out to allow expansion from four to six and then to eight guns, as well as specifying more exacting clearances between weapons and radars (Fig 40). The main practical implication was that space should be left behind the familiar four-gun configuration to add further weapons in a 'horse-shoe' pattern.[22] Though intended primarily for newly-built sites (which by 1943 were actually very rare), this pattern was also used for extending existing positions, and represented a quite different approach to the problem of expansion to eight guns than the side-by-side pairings of four-weapon groups common in 1940–41.

The main reason for that was to allow more efficient working with the combination of HAA radars available in 1943, which in that year began to include the new GL Mk III. A lengthy development period lay behind the ultimate British-designed HAA radar to appear during the war years.[23] The critical difference between the GL Mk III and its two predecessors, in their assorted sub-variants, was the new radar's use of wavelengths measurable in centimetres rather than metres – a development made possible, famously, by British scientists' development of new valve technology in the first two years of war. In its inception this work was designed to overcome the limitations of the GL Mks I and II, many of which resulted from the long wavelengths (in the six metre range) on which these sets operated: it was the wavelength, fundamentally, which limited the early radars' range and accuracy, increased their vulnerability to jamming, and allowed confusion from local ground echoes, so necessitating the GL mat. From an early stage in AA radar research it was realised that the answer would be found in much shorter wavelengths, the search for which began in earnest during the autumn of 1939. By February 1940 this work had produced the first prototype cavity magnetron, or resonator valve, capable on a laboratory bench of producing a power output of one kilowatt on a wavelength of ten centimetres. This valve was the origin of *centimetric* radar; shared with the Americans in the Tizard Mission of spring 1940, it was later described by one US scientist as 'the most valuable cargo ever brought to our shores'.[24]

In the following months this remarkable device was progressively refined. At first it was in competition with a somewhat
older valve type, the klystron, for anti-aircraft applications, but so
rapid was its improvement that in spring 1941, when the power
output had reached 40kW and rising, it was selected to form the
basis of the next generation of AA fire control radars, the GL Mk
III. The first prototype of this new equipment was ready in May
1941, as the Blitz was coming to a close, when it returned azimuth
and elevation readings accurate to ten minutes of arc – a huge
improvement on earlier sets – with a maximum following range
of 18,000 yards, or about ten miles (doubled for the production
version). This early model used separate transmitter and receiver
cabins, on the model of the Mks I and II, but at the same time an
alternative, single-cabin variant was in design by the British
Thomson-Houston Company, in liaison with the scientists at the
Air Defence Experimental Establishment, and it was this type
which was formally adopted in July 1941. Using a single trailer-
mounted cabin with two four-foot paraboloid aerials on the roof,
the first production set was tested in March 1942, though within
that year only eight sets were supplied and full production did
not begin until the spring of 1943, fully three years after the
discoveries underpinning them had been made. In this one,
crucial, respect – the delays in supply – the Radar AA No. 3 Mk II,
as it was alternatively known, was a disappointment: not
untypically in the history of radar the British centimetric set was
already becoming obsolescent as it reached its users. Nonetheless, 876 were supplied worldwide, about two-thirds of them in
1944, and while opportunities to test them against the Luftwaffe
were by then very circumscribed, those which did see action
were widely admired. In the hands of 'average troops', wrote
Brigadier A P Sayer, the War Office's radar historian, centimetric
radar 'brought night, fog and cloud conditions down to the
equivalent of clear daylight'.[25]

Though offered specifically on the GL Mk III, that judgement
applied to centimetric fire-control radar generally, and was equally
true of an imported counterpart to the British equipment, the GL
Mk III(C), whose suffix denoted manufacture in Canada. The
imported equipment arose from an independent strain of
development from the British, but to the same basic specification,

which had been issued to Canadian scientists at the time of the Tizard Mission in 1940. Though in some ways inferior to the British product, the Canadian equipment came with the great advantage of marginally earlier delivery; despite numerous delays in gestation the first sets reached British troops two months earlier than the home-grown version, and for this reason it became the Radar AA No. 3 Mk I, relegating the British to the designation Mk II. One of the Canadian set's manifest disadvantages was its reliance on a small fleet of two lorries and two four-wheeled trailers, where the British equivalent put everything in a single cabin. Another was its rather restricted range, and a third its various inconsistencies with the British set – notably a different type of display – which prevented crews from switching readily between types. But it was still supplied in great numbers. Of the 667 built in Canada, 600 were sent to Britain, the first reaching the units in November 1942, and despite more than half the British quota being shipped abroad many served on AA Command gunsites at home. The GL Mk III(C) formed the mainstay of the London's AA radar cover during the 'Little Blitz' of winter 1943–44 – though not before some teething troubles, as we shall see – and while Pile would look elsewhere for radars to serve the very special needs of the flying bomb campaign, both GL Mk IIIs contributed materially to Britain's orthodox defences in the closing two years of the war. They were often used in conjunction with older sets, but stood apart from them, both technically and physically (as Fig 40, page 391), in that neither had any need of a GL mat. The mat-laying programme was accordingly wound up in March 1943.[26]

If the new 5.25in guns, the converted 4.5s, the upgraded 3.7s and the new British and Canadian radars all played their part in hardening the roof over Britain in 1943, so too did the proliferation of Z batteries. By the end of the year the 6265 3in rocket projectors in service had reached four types – the Nos. 1, 2, 4 and 6 – of which the twin-barrelled No. 2 occupied by far the greatest proportion, 6107 weapons making up 97 per cent of the total in place in the last week of December.[27] By this stage in the war around half the GDAs in Britain were equipped with Z batteries, though to widely differing extents. No fewer than 874 No. 2 projectors were in place in the IAZ, while Birmingham had 346, Liverpool 336, Manchester 275, the Clyde 256, Bristol 254 and the joint Nottingham/Derby GDA 224. The remaining GDAs with these weapons usually fielded numbers ranging from the hundreds down to 64, which remained, in theory, the basic unit of deployment, though several multiples of half and quarter batteries were also used and numerous irregularities in the numbers allocated to specific GDAs betray great flexibility in use.

Flexibility was also seen in the rocket projector's potential for adaptation, particularly by the addition of barrels to increase the density of fire from individual weapons and reduce the number of projectors (and personnel) needed at each site. In addition to the single- and double-barrelled types, by the later war years AA Command was also using a nine-barrelled version (the U9P), conventionally deployed in sets of twelve, and a 20-barrelled variant (the U20P, also known as the No. 6), which was designed for a battery of just six weapons. Like their (much more numerous) counterparts for the No 2 projector, sites for the U9P and U20P were simple. Type-designs for U20P sites issued at the end of 1942 (Fig 41) called for the six launchers to be arranged in a rectangular layout with each anchored to an octagonal or circular concrete apron via the standard holdfast for the type.[28] Structures supporting the battery were rudimentary: each emplacement was served by ammunition and personnel shelters, formed from simple corrugated iron arcs (known as 'trench shelters' from their origin as linings to shelter trenches), banked up with earth to provide stability and act as blast walls. A single command post lay at one end of the layout – typically formed from a standard 16 foot Nissen hut, though brick or concrete buildings could be improvised – and also contained the plotting room, though if the GL set lay more than 500 yards from the battery, orders called for a separate structure (again, a Nissen or similar) near the radar. Nissens or Curved Asbestos huts were recommended for the on-site magazine, likewise for the shelter provided for the radar crew. Each site was also provided with the necessary domestic buildings for its 176 personnel, though by spring 1943 facilities for the site's 54 ATS and 83 Home Guard could be found in requisitioned buildings nearby. Site layouts and structures for the U9P were essentially similar, except that the twelve projectors, producing less blast from their nine barrels, required rather less protection for the intervening shelters.

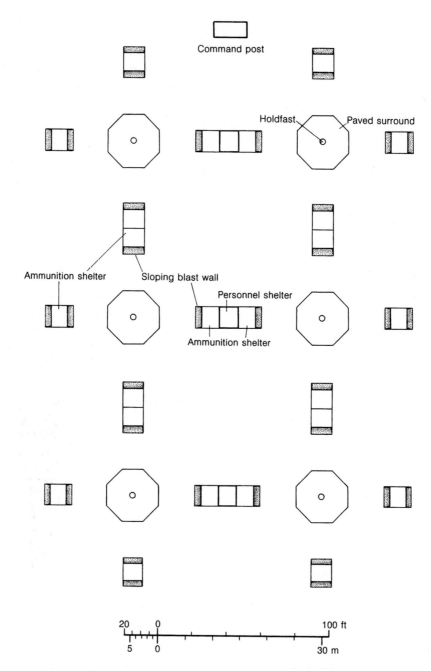

Figure 41 Layout plan for a six-projector U2OP site, with command post, paved surrounds to the projectors, and shelters for ammunition and crew.

Sites for the U9P and U20P were never numerous, and in the last two years of war AA Command's records point to these weapons occurring in only a handful of GDAs: apart from a few at schools and training centres, the 29 U20Ps deployed at the end of the war were at Liverpool, on the Tees, in the Thames & Medway (South) GDA, and at Colchester, while 24 of the 30 U9Ps were in London (equating to two batteries), with half a battery of six projectors, once again, in Thames & Medway (South).[29] The 9-barrelled types were, however, deployed rather more liberally in 1944 – 81 were in use during July of that year – when batteries were shuffled around to crop up at places as widely spread as Plymouth, Leeds, Leicester, Cambridge, the Humber and the Clyde.[30] For the most part, however, it was the U2P – the twin-barrelled No 2 projector – which dominated the Z battery in its maturity, and in general the verdict on the rocket weapon by the later war years was good. Reporting in November 1944, the Army Operational Research Group testified that 'the deterrent effect of rockets is considerable', even if their performance in the destruction of enemy aircraft was less so. Discharge in massive and all too visible salvoes was their main weakness. 'In favourable weather,' reported the AORG, 'and even on nights when there was a fair amount of cloud, enemy aircrews have been able to see the majority of rocket salvoes fired at them in sufficient time for effective avoiding action to be taken.'[31] The characteristic response was a sharp 'jink' from the target as soon as the flash was seen, though that in itself indicated that the Luftwaffe took the fireworks seriously. And, as so often, it was the anti-aircraft weapon's subsidiary functions which revealed its true value. 'Few pilots will fly straight if they believe their aircraft to be the target for a rocket salvo,' concluded the AORG; 'AA Rocket fire, therefore, fulfils the important function of discouraging accurate bombing.'[32]

By the time *Roof over Britain* appeared on the bookstalls in 1943 the contrast between the Luftwaffe's operations over Britain and the RAF's against Germany could hardly have been sharper. As the Fringe Target raids drew to a close in June, Bomber

Command was pushing the Battle of the Ruhr to its climax. Aided by *Oboe* target-marking equipment carried in Mosquito aircraft of the Pathfinder Force, Bomber Command in these months was hitting its city targets with greater reliability, accuracy, and lethal effect. Ruhr cities were not the only victims of the RAF's growing expertise at this time – raids extended widely, to Italy, the Baltic and even Czechoslovakia, as well as elsewhere in Germany – but the sustained campaign against Germany's key industrial conurbations occupied around two-thirds of the offensive effort in the months between March and July.

For all this, the Luftwaffe was sending pitifully little back in return. Apart from a heavyish attack on London on 16/17 January 1943, night raiding was scant during the winter of 1942–43, while daylight operations other than Fringe Target attacks were mostly confined to mine-laying and reconnaissance. In March, however, the Luftwaffe began to operate more frequently in darkness. The night of 3rd/4th saw another attack on London, again answering a Berlin raid by the RAF (though the sixteen aircraft entering the IAZ represented about a twentieth of the force which Bomber Command put over the German capital), while bombers were also in evidence during the month at a scatter of lesser targets, notably Sunderland, Hull, Grimsby and Norwich. But April brought a change of tack. In this month, in addition to their low-level daylight work in the fringe raids, FW 190 fighter-bombers began to operate on moonlit nights, flying high and bombing inland objectives. The first of these outings was something of disaster for the Luftwaffe – of the twelve machines operating most became lost, four attempted to land at RAF West Malling believing Kent to be France and, of those, two crashed on or near the airfield. But the tactics persisted, and became a recurrent theme of the limited but continual German air activity over Britain in the second half of 1943.[33]

Though maddeningly difficult to engage with AA fire, these raids were at first too trivial and intermittent to cause much concern. June brought 71 such sorties spread over eleven nights (during which fifteen aircraft penetrated the IAZ), while the month as a whole also saw six conventional bombing operations, all of them minor, targeted chiefly at Plymouth, Hull, Grimsby and Cleethorpes. But this was light work compared to the Blitz, and by the first week in July AA Command could inform its gunsite officers that 'In a week during which the RAF has despatched 1084 bombers to the RUHR alone the total effort of the GAF against this country has amounted to 13 sorties.'[34] In July the FW 190s operated on only one night, and although this month saw the first recorded appearance of the Bf 410 fighter-bomber over Britain, most of the work on the Luftwaffe's six night operations was given to the more orthodox bomber squadrons. July also brought the first daylight raid (apart from fringe operations) since early May, when a force of ten Dornier 217s roamed over the south-east and skimmed the southern reaches of the IAZ (two were shot down). Rather more determined night raiding was seen in August. Plymouth was raided by 20 aircraft (FW 190s among them) on the night of the 11th/12th, before Portsmouth became the target of a mixed fleet of Ju 88s, Do 217s and He 111s, using both level and power-dive attacks, on the night of the 15th/16th. Of the 25 raiders participating, two were destroyed by AA fire.[35]

The Allies' thickening offensive against Germany, meanwhile, was not without consequences for the domestic AA defences. One was a valuable bounty of intelligence on the tactics and general performance of enemy AA gunnery, as met by Bomber Command's crews operating over Germany and sometimes assessed by AA Command's own observers flying on these most hazardous missions. Evaluated by Pile's intelligence staff and only faintly coloured with a propagandist tinge, these reports were circulated to gunsite officers in AA Command's Intelligence Summaries (later the *Intelligence Review*), weekly digests whose scope and standard of production rose markedly in the latter war years. Another consequence was the ceaseless demand for LAA guns at new airfields, which continued to open in the second half of the war to serve the bomber squadrons of the RAF and USAAF. But this was not Pile's problem. By 1943 the AA guns at RAF stations were crewed by the RAF Regiment and there were, more or less, sufficient barrels to go around.

Beyond these general consequences of the bomber offensive, Pile's staff were occasionally called upon to react to specific incidents which might bring immediate repercussions in Britain. The most striking of these came just as the Fringe Target raids were nearing their end. On 17 May 1943 the British public woke to hear news of an audacious night attack by a small force of Bomber Command Lancasters on the great dams of the Ruhr, an operation which had succeeded in breaching the Möhne and the Eder, damaging the Sorpe, and bringing its leader – a bustling young wing commander named Gibson – an embarrassing excess of national celebrity. 'Gibson VC is Hero No 1 at present,' said one of the MoI's informants in the weekly survey of public opinion, which also discovered a surprising undercurrent of sympathy for the civilians presumed drowned in 617 Squadron's deluge.[36] Guy Gibson was soon off to America, accompanying the Prime Minister to the *Quadrant* conference and winning still greater popularity in a speaking tour before American and Canadian audiences. But one group to whom the 'dam-busters' (as Churchill soon came to call them) may have been rather less popular was the AA Committee, who knew nothing of the raid until, like everyone else, they heard about it on the wireless.

This mattered because of the real risk that the Germans would attempt a reprisal in kind: something they were equipped to do in part through capturing, intact, one of 617 Squadron's *Upkeep* mines (popularly 'bouncing bombs') which had come to earth in occupied territory on a crashed Lancaster. Pile gave this episode some prominence in his book,[37] and understandably so, for thanks to a Chiefs of Staff ruling the security of dams and reservoirs became the AA Committee's abiding preoccupation during the second half of 1943. The first arrangements were made within a couple of days of the RAF raid, and extended to 'frantic' allocations of AA guns and searchlights to London's reservoirs in Middlesex, and similar targets around Birmingham and at Sheffield where, as Pile recalled, 'memories of the Bradfield Reservoir disaster of 1864 were handed down from father to son'[38] – sons who were now admiring the photo-reconnaissance cover of the inundated Möhne and Eder valleys in their daily papers. In the first days of June these precautions were hardened by more searching air and ground reconnaissance of twelve dams and reservoirs around Chingford, Staines, Birmingham, Sheffield, Fort William and Kinlochleven and in Wales.[39] Aircrew from 617 Squadron who had flown to the German dams joined in the aerial dimension to this work – which took them back to at least one stretch of water used in practice –

and pointed on their return to the value of deception in marshalling the AA defence. First, argued the 617 Squadron crews, attack should be deterred by the appearance of strong defence using dummy guns; second, the real guns should be carefully concealed from reconnaissance, to foil the kind of orchestrated approach tactics which they had themselves used on the Ruhr dams. The bomber crews also gave advice on likely routes of approach to each target, and the value of searchlights positioned for dazzle effect – a tactic neglected by the Germans which would have made the RAF raid 'many times more difficult, if not impossible'.[40] None of these points had previously been grasped in defending British dams, in part because low-level attacks of the type used by 617 Squadron had not been expected, but in part, too, because AA Command had never really got to grips with the subtleties of tactical deception. The 617 Squadron crews had commented, in Stanmore's words, 'on the absence of deceptive measures and the obviousness of the real defences, particularly as regards tracks', which showed up the position of the real gun batteries, just as they had in pre-raid reconnaissance of the ill-fated Möhne and Eder.[41]

So all of this was arranged. Formations were advised that stocks of dummy guns could be obtained from AA Command stores, and formidable arrays of real Bofors were put in place around many dams, including four at Caban Coch, eight on other Welsh dams, four at Loch Laggan, eight at Chingford and no fewer than 40 around the Sheffield reservoirs.[42] But the gun defences, at first, were intended to be only transitory, since in July it was decided that the dams would best be guarded by chains slung at 300 feet above the water from masts, a technique soon supplemented by a plan to mask the targets with smoke. The smokescreen equipment proved easy to install and was ready by the autumn of 1943, but the chain defences were postponed and postponed again, before finally being cancelled, incomplete, in the autumn of 1944.[43] In that time Pile was obliged to keep his Bofors and all their crews in place around the dams, so a short-term emergency job dragged out to become a lengthy and rather unwelcome commitment. The Germans, meanwhile, never attacked the dams.

Deception was very much in the air during the summer of 1943. In August Pile was asked to provide AA defences for the pumping stations at Dungeness supporting the *Pluto* project – the pipeline under the ocean (actually the English Channel, though that could hardly have been worked into the acronym) which would supply oil to the troops landed in *Overlord*, now less than a year away. To preserve the secrecy of the installations the pumping equipment was installed in existing buildings, while the established AA guns in the Dungeness area were left alone and supplementary weapons set up in emplacements disguised as refuse dumps, all of this to mask the new activity.[44] The *Pluto* guns appear to have been the first actually deployed in support of *Overlord* preparations, a commitment which would expand hugely in the following months and raise Dungeness, among other places, to a substantial AA fortress. At the same time AA Command was called upon to serve two linked operations which formed the distant background to *Overlord*. These were *Starkey* and *Harlequin*, the first a feint assault on the northern French coast, the second a genuine exercise in troop movements which would provide some practice for the real Normandy landings, as well as lending credence to *Starkey*.[45] AA Command's main contribution lay in the cover given to *Harlequin*, an exercise which threw a large, if temporary, burden upon 2 AA Group to provide additional guns for camps and assembly areas in the Dover, Newhaven and Solent areas (installations which were also protected by tactical decoys).[46] AA Command also furnished a single LAA regiment to sail with the *Starkey* force, which embarked on 9 September 1943 to provoke practically no detectable response from the Germans. *Starkey* was a failure, though *Harlequin* at least gave the staff at Stanmore a taste of what would be involved in the real *Overlord* preparations six months hence.

It was in October that the Luftwaffe's night campaign began to intensify once more. In the first week of the month intruder activity continued 'on a fairly high scale' whenever the weather allowed, and on the night of the 7th/8th a two-pronged attack by 60 aircraft was launched against London and Norwich.[47] Though far from concentrated the London raid did manage to scatter a fair weight of explosive around the suburbs, though their colleagues in the Norwich contingent managed to deliver just one load of bombs on the city. The Norwich incident, in fact, was hardly recognisable as an air raid at all – except perhaps to German propagandists, whose account of the night's action was broadcast on the Reich national radio station in the early evening of 8 October. AA Command's Intelligence Summary for the week gave the gunners a translation.

> When the crews of our heavy bombers assembled for briefing at 1730 last night [declared the broadcast] they were told that another attack on LONDON was planned. Only the night before [6/7 October] they had been over the English capital and had attacked their targets successfully and without loss to themselves.
>
> Now for the second time the target was LONDON, for other formations it was NORWICH. Before dusk the ground staff attached the large, heavy bombs to the fuselage. The engines were revved up. Then everything was quiet again on the airfield, until the crews slowly walked to the machines. Presently the heavy bombers rolled to the runway and punctually to the minute the first Junker thundered across the field. The waxing moon was in the sky and the stars were glittering. Aircraft after aircraft left the runway. On neighbouring airfields as well, bombers were rolling over the runways and taking course towards ENGLAND – towards LONDON and NORWICH. At 2035 the first bombers reached the English coast. They broke through the barrage of night fighters, numbers of which were trying to prevent them flying inland. The nearer they came to LONDON the stronger became the defences. Thousands of searchlights swept excitedly across the clear sky. Heavy AA guns were firing without interruption, but our crews were not to be deterred. At 2045, the first machines were thundering across LONDON and NORWICH.
>
> Underneath the crews saw the big bend of the THAMES by which they could determine their position. After they had located their target areas in the centre of the city, they dropped their bombs. Thousands of shells were bursting close to our machines, but our pilots kept their nerve and dropped their bombs on the selected areas. After the first bombs, large fires began to spread in the centre of LONDON and between them new and heavy explosions occurred continuously. Three huge fires stood out among the smaller ones. They burned fiercely near the THAMES and still the explosions increased.
>
> For almost an hour and a half this concentrated attack by our

bombers went on and long after they had turned for home our pilots saw the spreading fire in the centre of LONDON rise into the night sky. The attack on NORWICH was just as heavy. The second half of the strong German formation had pushed through to the East coast town and, in spite of heavy opposition by AA fire and night fighters, had dropped their bombs right in the centre of the town. Heavy explosions occurred and specially fierce fires could be observed in the centre and the Southern and Northern part of NORWICH. Thick smoke was rolling over the roofs and new fires kept breaking out during this one-and-a-half-hour attack.[48]

Little of this vivid narrative could be recognised by the staff at Stanmore, who peppered the transcript with corrective footnotes. For one thing there had been no raid at all directed towards London on 'the night before' this operation, let alone one in which the Luftwaffe had attacked 'successfully and without loss to themselves' (in fact just nine aircraft had operated on this night, dropping a few bombs in Kent and Essex). On the 7th/8th, no more than fifteen aircraft from the force of 30 directed to London had penetrated the IAZ, and while a number of fires had been started, the largest was at Purfleet in Essex, none was in central London and the closest bombs to the city centre were at Camberwell, Hampstead and Lewisham – the only discernable concentrations were as far out as Bromley and Esher. For their part, Londoners were remarkably blasé about the whole affair. 'The public treated the raid of 7 October as if it were a football match,' complained an official report, 'advice being shouted to both searchlight and gun crews.'[49] And, of course, the heavy explosions and 'specially fierce fires' in Norwich were simply fictitious, likewise the one and a half-hour concentrated attack. (Indeed the broadcast's description of Norwich as an 'east coast' town suggests authorship at some distance from events.) Though the Norwich force was plotted overland for about an hour and twenty minutes, all but one of the aircraft roamed uncertainly over East Anglia without reaching the city, many discharging their bombs over fields and farms. Only the most guileless would admit surprise that German civilians were routinely fed bogus accounts of their air force's operations; but circulating the transcripts to AA gunsites – where readers were well-placed to know the truth – did enable AA Command to turn Reich propaganda to their own advantage.

Minor as it was compared to the version of events recounted in Germany, the London raid did present a difficult challenge to the gunners. In fact this force largely eluded London's HAA batteries, chiefly through flying high and fast, and adopting unusually agile tactics, soaring and swooping in a restless ballet of evasive action. 'Against this attack,' wrote Pile, 'we put up a disappointing show, and the performance of the guns was the worse when it was compared with that of the searchlights, which had consistently improved until they had illuminated enemy aircraft at heights in excess of 25,000 feet – a height that had previously been considered beyond their reach.'[50] That was true of the London searchlights, certainly; but those covering the raiders' approach across East Anglia found themselves badly compromised. For it was on this night – 7/8 October 1943 – that the Luftwaffe made its first use of *Düppel*, a technique known to the British as *Window*, in which bombers scattered bundles of metallised paper strips to muddle defensive radars. By autumn 1943 British scientists had understood the *Window* principle for well over a year, though the RAF had been denied its use for fear of imitation. But the embargo had been lifted on the night of 24 July, when a Bomber Command force *Window*ed their way to a devastating fire attack on Hamburg. AA groups were soon warned that a German version of *Window* might soon be used against Britain; and when it was, on 7/8 October, the effect on radar screens was unmistakable. The GCI station at Neatishead and the Happisburgh CHL were blinded by the echoes, together with the *Elsie*s on eighteen sites in a lane fifteen miles long by ten broad across East Anglia. By 12 October, preliminary analysis of events had suggested that, forewarned as they were, AA Command's site radar crews had been too easily wrong-footed by the shower of *Düppel*; but Stanmore could recommend no countermeasures beyond an entreaty to persevere until the fog began to clear.[51]

The *Düppel* shower justified the limited success of the AA defences in East Anglia on 7/8 October, and in any case this arm of the operation, as we have seen, hardly amounted to much. By this stage of the war the London guns should perhaps have done better, despite a certain rustiness engendered by the inaction of the previous two years. Certainly Pile thought so. Though his own account of the raid in *Ack-Ack* contained an error which rather exaggerated the IAZ's shortcomings – Pile claimed that 60 aircraft had raided London, whereas AA Command's intelligence papers put the number entering the IAZ at fifteen – his memoir and the contemporary record converge on the most important point: none of the raiders was hit. So, just as he had in September 1940, the GOC called a conference at Brompton Road to elicit views from officers on the ground. There was general agreement that the recent introduction of the GL Mk III(C) sets and new electrical predictors had put the gunners in something of a predicament: not yet adept with the new equipment, they had already surrendered the old. The problem recalled that experienced exactly three years previously, when site crews had been forced to master the GL Mk I as bombs exploded around them. And the solution was similar. Just as they did in the Blitz, the recording vans now had a vital part to play in unravelling the peculiarities of radar behaviour at each site. 'What emerged most clearly,' wrote Pile, 'was the need for more and more information about the height, the direction, and the identification of the approaching enemy.'[52] For a time in the autumn of 1943 these basic products of radar were, again, unusually elusive.

To make matters worse the tempo of raiding rose, briefly, in mid October. The week beginning the 17th brought a series of small raids on London and its environs, generally using *Düppel* together with FW 190 aircraft to mark targets with flares. If not exactly heavy – only 56 aircraft penetrated the IAZ in the entire month, over twelve nights[53] – the raids were persistent and randomly destructive. 'What was particularly annoying,' recalled Pile, 'was that the Hun was being allowed to do just what he wanted, although this was no more ambitious a plan than to reach London at a high speed, drop a few anywhere (it didn't matter where), and then get back to his bases before our night fighters caught him.'[54] The sharpness of these incidents gave them a name, coined like so many wartime sobriquets by the press. The phrase 'scalded cat' raids certainly captured their spirit – petulant and faintly desperate replies to the dams, the burning of Hamburg, and Harris's relentless campaign against Germany's cities. But it also dismissed their significance: scalded cats do little harm.

Given Pile's radar troubles it was as well that the raids began to tail off in November. London was visited on eight occasions by just eighteen aircraft (mostly fighter-bombers), light raiding was scattered across Essex and the south-east, and an inconclusive operation by eighteen aircraft was launched against Plymouth. In all, 146 raiders were plotted overland during the month, of which fourteen were destroyed by AA fire. Then early December brought something of a lull, memorable only for an attempted day raid on London by six Ju 188s, of which four aborted before reaching the coast, one was blasted out of the sky by the Dover AA guns, and the last pushed a few miles inland before turning back. Little more was achieved later in the month by the twenty Do 217s sent to bomb targets around Chelmsford; and otherwise Luftwaffe activity in December was confined to minor nuisance raids over Essex and the south-east. Thirty-five sorties were dispatched on five nights, from which ten raiders entered the IAZ.

Those ten, presumably, had been sent specifically to London, ever a conspicuous target; but on many occasions in late 1943 observers found great difficulty in deciphering the raiders' intentions at all. Reviewing the previous twelve months, an AA Command digest of January 1944 recorded that for much of the year 'such specific attacks' as had been made showed 'either a deplorable state of navigational training or a distinct reluctance of crews to press attacks home.'[55] By the end of the year the Luftwaffe in the west seemed firmly on the back foot. And when the score-card was finally closed on 1943 there were grounds for satisfaction at Stanmore. At 2676 overland sorties logged, the scale of Luftwaffe activity had reached barely two-thirds of that seen in the previous year, when the corresponding figure had been 3937. But the bag of Category I claims was much larger and, given the drop in aircraft operating, the proportion was greater still. The 60 Category I claims made in 1942 represented only 1.52 per cent of the Luftwaffe's overland effort – a creditable contribution to the defence, certainly, and one which takes no account of the deterrent and morale effect of AA fire, but hardly a figure to write home about. The 93 Category I claims in 1943, on the other hand, more than doubled the kill-rate, which now reached 3.48 per cent of overland sorties (of these, 37 were downed by HAA fire, 25 by LAA, two by Z batteries, five by Lewis guns and the remaining 24 chiefly by mixed AA fire or jointly with the RAF or navy).[56] As ever, this annual average obscured the highs and masked the lows in the gunners' hit-rate: while some operations had evaded AA fire entirely, others had sustained losses reaching between nine and eleven per cent of the forces dispatched – 'an interesting comparison,' noted AA Command intelligence staff, 'with the considerably smaller losses of Bomber Com[man]d in circumstances which were much more favourable for the defence.'[57] The tally of Category II 'probables' remained more or less stable between 1942–43, at seventeen and a half and fifteen, though the number of Category III 'damaged' claims actually dropped, and sharply, from 100 to 59. Seen together with the rise in Category I claims that of course was good news, for it meant that 'hostiles' engaged by AA fire were now more likely to be destroyed than lamed. By the first week in January 1944 the feeling at Stanmore was that, whatever the reasons for the Luftwaffe's poor performance in 1943, 'these shortcomings augur well for us in 1944'; but at the same time, the command's intelligence digest recognised that 'the GAF is wise in conserving its strength against things to come [. . .].'[58]

To many at Stanmore the renewal of operations against London, together with the introduction of *Düppel* and the new target-marking routine, promised that AA Command would soon be in the thick of things once again. 'We all felt that he ['the Hun'] was preparing for something bigger,' Pile recalled, perhaps 'for big-scale reprisal raids in which his untrained bomber crews would find Pathfinder flares a great help, or [. . .] in preparation for launching glider-bombs.'[59] Recent German tactics could, indeed, point to either of those eventualities, and the first materialised in late January, when the Luftwaffe opened a new campaign of heavy raids against London. But by early 1944 there were other factors to consider. One was *Crossbow*, code-name for the long-awaited bombardment by German V-weapons on which British intelligence had been collating reports since late 1942, and another, of course, was *Overlord*. Together, the *Crossbow* threat and the *Overlord* commitment became the dominant themes of AA planning from the winter of 1943–44. Though no one knew as much at the time, the first would soon gain a hold on AA deployments which was not relaxed until practically the end of the war.

Crossbow, *Overlord*, and the likely renewal of conventional raiding were the three main factors which hardened Pile's resistance to further cuts in AA Command's personnel allocation as the war entered its fifth year. That more cuts were looming was never in doubt. Despite the vital role which AA guns would play in safeguarding the embarkation areas for the cross-Channel landing, Pile had always been aware that *Overlord*, when it came, would impose heavy drains both upon equipment – to be sent abroad in support of the invasion force – and men, especially those in the higher medical categories. In short, wrote Pile, 'we had always known that, whatever promises might be made to the contrary, AA Command was the ultimate reservoir from which the Field Army anti-aircraft requirements would be filled.'[60] Signs that the reservoir would soon be tapped, and deeply, emerged at the end of August 1943, when AA Command was identified as the 'only remaining source' from which Britain 'might still obtain more fit men in any numbers for the build up and maintenance of offensive forces [. . .]'. Already lowered to 177,050 men and 77,000 women, the personnel ceiling was now to be reviewed again: Pile and Leigh-Mallory at Fighter Command were duly invited to examine and report upon the implications of cuts amounting to 20,000 or 50,000 men, on the assumption that no additional Home Guard would be available but that some of the American AA units arriving in Britain would be assigned to support AA Command.[61] In doing so, and in discussing the matter directly with the AA Sub-Committee in late November, Pile pleaded that losing his best men – and it was always the younger and fitter *men* who were at issue here – would cripple his command's mobility, already gravely compromised by the expedients of the previous five years. Ideally, Pile explained, he had always wanted half of his HAA batteries to be fully mobile. As things stood in November 1943, only one-fifth came into that category, and 'many of these were in fact locked up at such places as Dover and the Orkneys', whence they would be unlikely to move.[62] But this case secured only a partial victory. The Sub-Committee recommended a 17,000-man cut in AA Command's personnel, a figure eased from the 20,000 originally proposed to spare a number of HAA batteries.

But that was not the end of the story. On 20 December the JIC issued a report forecasting the likely scale of attack on Britain in the near future; and it was now that the possibility of renewed orthodox bombing, the *Crossbow* threat, and the ever-present (if yet unquantified) AA commitment to *Overlord* began to make themselves felt. 'Each of these three contingencies,' explained Pile and Sir Roderic Hill (since November Leigh-Mallory's successor at ADGB), in a new report to the Chiefs of Staff on 26 December, 'affects AA Command in a different way.'

> As the threat of long range bomber attack increases [they explained], so does a reduction of our Heavy AA defences become more inadvisable. Furthermore, as this threat develops, modern jamming techniques combined with a possibility of high density raids make it necessary for us to place a greater reliance on searchlights than might otherwise be the case.
>
> The CROSSBOW deployment would make very heavy demands on our resources of all three types of AA units, and would require in addition the reinforcement of our defences by a substantial part of the resources of 21 Army Group.
>
> OVERLORD will undoubtedly call for a re-deployment of troops of AA Command and is likely in particular to demand LAA units on a large scale.
>
> Either of the two fresh contingencies mentioned [. . .] above [ie Crossbow and the renewed threat of raiding] might be met while accepting simultaneously a cut of 17,500 men, though it would be necessary to phase the reduction most carefully to suit operational requirements, and some delay in providing the men would have to be accepted.
>
> Each of these contingencies must, however, be considered in conjunction with our commitment for OVERLORD and we cannot exclude the possibility that all three may arise simultaneously.[63]

In the event this last speculation was disproved by events. Heavy orthodox raiding recommenced towards the end of January (three weeks or so after the above was written), and more than four months before *Overlord* was mounted, though the spectre of coeval *Overlord* and *Crossbow* commitments did materialise when the first flying bombs began to land just a week after D-Day. By March 1944 that eventuality was being actively anticipated, but the threat as it appeared to Pile and Hill in late December – everything happening together – did not turn out to be real. In these circumstances, and after further close study, the actual cut in AA Command's establishment was set at 13,700 men,[64] the last such reduction to be implemented before D-Day.

The effect of these cuts was felt chiefly in the less exposed areas of the north and west. London and the south-east were unaffected, and it was London which entered the firing line once again towards the end of January, when the upturn in orthodox bombing predicted by the JIC became a reality. The first raid of what soon came to be known as the 'Little Blitz' fell on the night of 21/22 January, when practically every serviceable Luftwaffe aircraft in the west attempted to deliver the heaviest blow against London since January 1943. It was a long night. The first wave crossed the coast at about 20.25, their approach partly covered by a force of RAF bombers returning from operations against *Crossbow* targets in northern France. *Düppel* was used extensively before the first wave's target indicator flares – reds, whites and yellows – began to cascade across the capital, the first falling at 21.03 in a sequence which lasted for a little under twenty minutes.[65] But only a small proportion of this wave's strength penetrated the IAZ – immediate reports from the batteries put the number at no more than twenty – which entered the IAZ from the south, tracked across the capital and, in general, left rather promptly to the south-east under fire from 49 gunsites in a London layout which, by now, contained 284 HAA weapons.[66] Sixteen of those were 5.25in singles, which by themselves contributed 274 of the 7736 HAA rounds (plus some LAA and rockets) thrown skyward by the IAZ before 21.45, when the last bomber left to meet further heavy fire from the Thames & Medway GDA.[67] But this was not the end of the raid, for in a night of worsening weather – 10/10ths cloud had gathered at 3000 feet over London by the early hours – a second wave of about 50 aircraft began to enter the IAZ at 04.45, operated at high and low levels for about 50 minutes and met over 10,000 rounds of HAA fire from the London guns and, on their way out, nearly 5000 from Thames & Medway and Chelmsford. No fewer than 53 London HAA batteries engaged this wave, together with 34 in the other GDAs, six London Z batteries and one LAA position on the Essex side of the Estuary, which sent three Bofors rounds towards a flare.[68] Seldom had so much anti-aircraft ammunition been expended by so many on so few.

When the gunners' and pilots' reports were collated it emerged that sixteen enemy aircraft could be confirmed as destroyed on this night, eight by AA fire and eight by fighters (four of whose victims were illuminated by searchlights); additionally three 'probables' were allowed and at least three aircraft were written down as Category III, one of each being credited to the gunners. So it had been a good night – as it should have been, perhaps, given an ammunition expenditure which reached 17,128 HAA rounds in the IAZ and a liberal 33,854 in total.[69] The gunners were heartened by Churchill's 'compliments to all ranks' (though the Prime Minister's breezy remark while inspecting bomb damage next day – 'It's quite like old times again' – reportedly went down less well).[70] But in fact the harm done to London was not great, and in that respect these were not quite like old times. 'On the face of it,' reported the *Intelligence Review* a week later, the outcome was:

> [. . .] a substantial victory over the Luftwaffe for the Air Defences of Great Britain, and AA Command may justifiably feel pleased with the part played by gunners and searchlight troops in this result. But the number of aircraft destroyed and damaged is not the only satisfactory feature of the night's activity. No less significant is the relatively small number of casualties and the slight extent of the damage sustained. Of the 29 fatal casualties, 13 were killed in a single incident at a hospital, and only four were killed in LONDON itself. It is instructive to compare these figures with those of the BIRMINGHAM raid of Jul 42, when 95 people were killed. The disproportion between the number of fires and the number of key points affected in each of these raids is equally marked [. . .].[71]

As evidence of the defences' deterrent effect the *Review* reported that only eighteen per cent of the 'incidents' recorded that night – the bombs, fires and so on – had occurred in London itself: 44 in the capital, as against 110 in Kent, 53 in Sussex and a broad scatter elsewhere. In fact of 268 tons of bombs sent to Britain on 447 aircraft, only 32 tons (twelve per cent) had reached the target area.[72] The rest, like the aircraft carrying them, had strayed wide.

This first raid of the new campaign acquainted the London gunners with a Luftwaffe whose composition, tactics and weapons had moved on since the great battles of 1940–41. The force used against London on 21/22 January was a mixed batch, mostly of newer types – Dornier 217s, high-flying Junkers 188s (as well as the older 88s), Bf 410s, FW 190s and, making their first appearance in force over Britain, sub-stratospheric Heinkel 177 bombers, at least fifteen of which were recorded in the course of the night (two were shot down). And these machines together had carried an exotic cocktail of new weapons – SB1000 parachute bombs, SD1 anti-personnel bombs, B2 EZ incendiaries with explosive noses, and a new variant of the 50-kilogram phosphorous bomb (along with 250-kilogram types). Overall, the proportion of incendiaries was high – the highest, in fact, since records began in October 1941 – at about 37 per cent of the 268 tons dropped. And much of the high-explosive was delivered in bulk, especially in 2500-kilogram *Max* and 1800-kilogram *Satan* bombs. (More *Max* types fell in this one night than in the entire German bombing effort to date.) Much of this ordnance, of course, had missed London; but had it not (came the sobering news from AWAS) the raid would have been the capital's fourth heaviest of the war so far.[73]

Why did the Luftwaffe return to London at all? On the previous night Berlin had been raided by 769 Bomber Command aircraft, which delivered the city's eleventh major attack since the opening of Harris's main offensive against the Reich capital in mid November.[74] So in its timing, at any rate, the London raid at first looked like an answer in kind. AA Command's *Intelligence Review* for that week presented it in this light, suggesting that Allied operations against Berlin were proving so successful 'as to necessitate some serious form of reprisal, if only for propaganda purposes'.[75] But in fact this was wrong, as higher-level intelligence analysts in Britain already knew. The force which had visited

Britain on 21/22 January was under command of an officer named Dietrich Peltz, who had been preparing for this new offensive almost since his appointment as Angriffsführer ('attack-leader') England in March 1943, as well as overseeing the rather indifferent operations which the Luftwaffe had mounted in the second half of the preceding year. Luftwaffe plans had slated the new offensive for the end of December, but bad weather had delayed it.[76] And Reich domestic propaganda actually made little capital from this raid, at least and first, confining itself to official announcements and radio features described as 'moderate, unenterprising, and indeed somewhat uninteresting. No figures [. . .] were given,' reported AA Command's *Intelligence Review*, 'the Führer's communique speaking merely of "strong Luftwaffe formations in several waves".[77]

The place of this new campaign in the propaganda war, however, began to emerge after its second instalment, which was delivered on the night of 29/30 January. This raid was practically a re-run of its predecessor, using a similar variety of aircraft in comparable numbers, following much the same tactics (including liberal quantities of *Düppel* and TI flares). Once again, incendiaries were used in high proportion, surpassing that of the earlier raid to reach 51 per cent of all bombs dropped over land. But only 36.5 tonnes of bombs in all categories hit the capital, just 23 per cent of the 158 tonnes dropped by the 285 of Peltz's aircraft operating that night.[78]

Once the dust had settled after this second raid the parallel war of propaganda and misinformation surrounding the Luftwaffe's work over Britain began to take a curious turn. On the day following the operation the Germans issued a communiqué very similar to that which had appeared after the first raid; the news release spoke again of 'strong Luftwaffe formations' and made much of the strength of the British defences – fighters, balloons and AA batteries. But 24 hours later the official line from Berlin suddenly changed. AA Command's *Intelligence Review* takes up the story.

> On the next day (31 Jan) the German Propaganda Bureau seems to have come to a sudden and belated decision to make a big splash with the two LONDON raids which they had previously

dismissed so briefly. On that day a report was circulated by the various European and overseas agencies, which stated that 'both on the 21st and 29th January, when London was raided at night, more than 600 German aircraft dropped bombs of all types on the targets in London allotted to them.' The report also claimed that the 'British defences were completely taken by surprise by the strength of the attacking formations,' and that 'this explains why German losses were so small; 25 aircraft, which is not even four per cent of the heavy bombers employed'. It is noteworthy that not a word of this went out to German Home listeners.

Two days later however the German High Command in their desire for Bigger and Better Raids, threw caution to the winds, and made the following startling announcement (in the Führer's Headquarters communique):

'The British are attempting to minimise the effect of the German air raids on London during the nights of 21–22nd and 29th–30th January by false statements about the number of attacking German aircraft and the damage caused. In face of these statements it is pointed out: More than 900 aircraft were employed. Of these, 750 aircraft attacked London with more than 1000 tons of high explosives and incendiary bombs. The other aircraft carried out diversionary attacks over south-east England. Thirty-four aircraft are missing from all these operations. According to reports from the crews, large fires and destruction in the urban area of London were observed in low-level flights during both attacks.'[79]

To buttress this version of events, continued the *Review*, 'Dr Goebbels also got busy' on a series of fictitious items for radio broadcasts – front line 'atmosphere' pieces, supposedly from bomber airfields, interviews with crews (one of whom claimed that 'AA fire was not as intense as he expected,' except from 'the Hyde Park batteries, which were trying to put up a wild performance'), and even reports, for the benefit of a Portugese audience, of civil indiscipline in London under the bombs and 'ransacking of the great stores by young women and soldiers'. All of these contributed to a completely revised picture of the raids from that given from the same sources immediately after the events.

Apart from its curiosity value this series of contradictory announcements must, it was thought, contain some intelligence content useful to the British cause. But exactly what that might be was far from clear.

> The entire handling of these two raids [continued the *Review*] is one of the most curious episodes in the history of German propaganda. Innumerable questions arise to which it is difficult to find an answer. If the raids were to be played up as propaganda in a big way, then why wait till they were stale before releasing the news? Why break the news of the startling numbers involved first to the outside world only? Why, having decided to let Germany into the secret, further increase the total by the considerable number of 300? Why increase the number admitted as missing from 25 to 34 between 31 Jan and 2 Feb? Is it to be supposed that, so long after the second raid, the assessment of losses has still not been made? If so, it is much more natural to expect a reduction in the number missing, due to late information regarding pilots who have landed far from their bases, than the reverse. In any event it is obvious that a great many people inside Germany must be aware of the contents of overseas programmes; they would surely be surprised that so long after the event the German High Command had not made up their mind within 300 of the number of bombers employed.[80]

Three answers to these questions were suggested. One was that the contradictions and uncertainty of message indicated a weakness in the 'German propaganda machine', which was either 'in very bad repair' or had come under the control of more than one set of persons, who were following independent and contradictory policies. Another possibility was that the 'fantastically high claims' reflected an attempt (perhaps as an afterthought) to probe how far Britain had been misled by *Düppel*. And a third was that Germany had begun the new campaign intending to mount a long series of raids for which propaganda was to have been withheld until the operations entered their stride, but that losses in the first two had proved so serious as to curtail the plan, making it 'necessary to make the most retrospectively of the past'. Ingenious as they were, these interpretations could be no more than speculative; but their justifiably triumphalist tones made a vivid contrast with the equivalent material issuing from Stanmore in the main Blitz, three years before.

That the raids had not been suspended after the losses in the first two became clear when Peltz's forces visited London again on 3/4 February, and on eight further occasions before mid March. This was the main phase of the Little Blitz, which subsequently widened to include attacks on Hull, Bristol, Portsmouth, Plymouth and other southern coastal targets before dwindling to a close in May, the third anniversary of its predecessor's climax. Some of these raids were defeated by the Luftwaffe's extraordinary incompetence – notably the London raid on 13/14 February, which put just four tons of bombs on the target from the 161 tons carried by 230 aircraft – but while others made rather more impression, the performance of the defences was good, despite the London AA guns gaining no significant reinforcement (numbers remained in the 280s throughout). By the week ending 17 March, when the pressure on London was eased, AA Command's running total of kills since 1 January 1944 had reached 49$\frac{1}{2}$ Category I, plus two probables and ten damaged, bringing the overall war achievement in these categories to 810$\frac{1}{2}$, 235 and 408.[81] Not all of the 1944 claims were Little Blitz victims, of course, since odd engagements against minor incursions added hits in ones and twos, and on some of the Blitz nights all the claims went to fighters, aided by GCI, searchlights and their own increasingly sophisticated airborne radars (by now themselves benefiting from the magnetron electronics which had produced the GL Mk III). But AA Command made a substantial contribution to the Germans' steadily rising monthly loss-rates in the Little Blitz, which rose from 5.2 per cent of forces dispatched in February to 8.7 per cent in April, and finally to about one in ten during May 1944,[82] the last month of the campaign, in which some of the raids were directed to south coast ports where the *Overlord* fleets were assembling.

The defences did not have things entirely their own way. Some of the raids did substantial damage, especially two directed at London in mid February, when the percentage of bombs carried to hit the capital reached into the seventies, London receiving more than 250 tons in two nights (the 18th and 20th). In the wake of these attacks Pile called another of his Brompton Road seminars on 14 April, reminding his officers that this was the third such since the great barrage of the first London Blitz. On this occasion, however, Pile 'stressed that the situation was very different: the equipment had changed considerably and LONDON had all the newest and best instruments and guns available'.[83] Yet there were still numerous points of procedure which could be refined, their very quantity a reflection of the technical advances since the first seminar in the dark days of September 1940. Battery and site commanders filed out of the Brompton Road GOR with their heads buzzing with the GOC's correctives: don't open fire before the predictor has settled down; remember to make *rapid* appreciations of course change; don't fire until the target lies within range; don't shoot at *Düppel* echoes on the radar and remember too that *Düppel* decreases pick-up and following range on the GL Mk II; be careful to report *all* unusual incidents, since the Luftwaffe seemed to be trying something new every time; do train the gunners hard, but not for too long: intensive bouts of instruction were preferred, and best of all was training in action, even for novice troops. And in return, Pile went away with as much to think about: batteries needed better information from the GOR on the *character* of each raid; more accurate data was needed from the GCI sets; the airblast gear which cleared the fumes in the turrets of 5.25in singles was often defective (Pile had raised this with the Ministry of Supply on the previous day: 'the trouble was that a new valve had to be manufactured'); 3.7in Mk VI rounds had a maddening propensity to jam, while the wear tables for these guns seemed to be largely fictional – the barrels were wearing faster than predicted; Z batteries were frustrated by limitations on their height and fire control; and – from the commander of 28 AA Brigade – there was far too much 'stooging by fighters over GDAs' to the detriment of the AA defences. So some things, at least, never changed. But much of this would soon be overtaken by events. London's final raid by piloted aircraft fell four days later, on the 18/19 April 1944, and when the IAZ's guns did come into action once again their target was something very different.

CHAPTER 11

Last things

JUNE 1944 – MAY 1945

As the Little Blitz with its attendant propaganda war rumbled on over the winter of 1943–44, Britain's air defence authorities were taking a deepening interest in another threat altogether. By the end of 1943 information on Germany's V-weapon programme had been reaching Britain for about a year, in which time intelligence analysts had drawn a progressively detailed and reasonably accurate series of inferences on the two new devices whose attacks would dominate the final eleven months of the domestic war.[1] Derived chiefly from SIS sources, prisoners of war and aerial reconnaissance, from late April 1943 the reports on these weapons had been channelled for study to the Joint Parliamentary Secretary to the Ministry of Supply, who happened to be none other than Duncan Sandys. Early clues on what came to be known as the *Crossbow* threat were difficult to interpret and for a time it was unclear whether Germany was at work on a single weapon or, possibly, two or three distinct systems. But by the end of the year Sandys' investigations, a project codenamed *Bodyline*, had established that two weapons were at issue, correctly identified as a flying bomb and a long-range rocket: the V1 and V2. It was also clear that the V1 was associated with an array of distinctive launching sites in France, and that the V2 rocket, which commanded greater destructive potential, was likely to come into use somewhat later. Allied attacks on targets supporting the V-weapon project had begun in August 1943, when Bomber Command visited the research establishment at Peenemünde on the Baltic coast,[2] and had widened in early

December with the first raids on the launching sites in northern France, a diversion from their deepening night offensive against Berlin. Raids on *Crossbow* targets intensified in the New Year of 1944 and certainly did something to delay the start of the Germans' campaign. But from an early stage in the proceedings some recognised that defeat of the V-weapons must depend as much upon defensive measures at home as offensive operations, a policy formally endorsed by the Chiefs of Staff in early December.[3]

Planning for this defence in its early stages fell to Pile and Air Marshal Sir Roderic Hill, head of ADGB. By mid December an outline scheme was ready, and this in turn spawned the official ADGB *Crossbow* plan issued on 2 January 1944. Pile's and Hill's plan called for fighters, AA guns and balloons to be committed to the battle against the flying bomb, but in weighing the availability and potential dispositions of these resources the two commanders had to be mindful of the requirements of *Overlord*, which was due to be launched in June and imposed competing requirements of its own – chiefly to defend the embarkation points – according to a timetable whose articulation with the looming *Crossbow* threat could only be guessed at. The dedicated air defence plan for *Overlord* was issued on 7 February, but a few days before it appeared the Vice Chiefs of Staff instructed that a third plan must be prepared to meet the range of contingencies surrounding the flying bomb threat and the opening of the second front jointly. This very complex study took another month, and resulted in the 'Concurrent Plan' for defences supporting *Overlord* interleaved with the threat from the V1, lately codenamed *Diver*.[4]

Issued on 4 March 1944, the *Overlord/Diver* Concurrent Plan anticipated a range of strategic scenarios over the following months, among which *Overlord* was a known commitment with a definite time element and *Diver* – the start of the V1 offensive – was an increasing possibility which, if it materialised at all, was likely to appear at a late stage of preparations for the invasion, and certainly after defences for the embarkation points had been put in place. The plan was 'concurrent', therefore, in the sense that it allowed for *Diver* defences to be mobilised after those for *Overlord*, to meet commitments which would then become simultaneous. As such, it superseded the earlier *Crossbow* scheme but not that for *Overlord* issued in early February, much of which remained in force.

Simply stated, the purpose of the Concurrent Plan was to provide a solid air defence for the embarkation areas handling troops for *Overlord* and for any targets troubled by *Diver*, without neglecting continuing threats to the remainder of the UK. It was a tall order, demanding the most careful allocation of guns, in particular, between the three very different commitments, and in this respect the *Overlord/Diver* conundrum became a classic proof of the wisdom of maintaining a high degree of mobility in defence, something which AA Command had been steadily sacrificing since 1938. The mobility problem would eventually be solved in a novel way when, in mid July, the *Diver* deployment jettisoned practically all the principles laid down in the Concurrent Plan and the case was irrevocably altered. But from the perspective of early March 1944, it was necessary to make bulk allocations of guns to the various commitments, using statics and mobiles as wisely as possible and drawing upon additional resources from American units in the UK, and readying all the sites which would be used for the two deployments in plenty of time, to quicken the movement of weapons when they were needed.

The first commitment was for *Overlord*, and to this the Concurrent Plan allocated 1258 HAA guns and 950 LAA. Reduced somewhat from the allocations made under the original *Overlord* plan (which had anticipated 1442 and 1122 guns respectively), these totals reflected the maximum scale of defence which could be allocated to the base areas while still leaving a stock of guns for *Diver*. Though the plan conceded a remote possibility that *Diver* attacks would be made on the *Overlord* base areas themselves, the threat from long-range weapons against the assembling force was not seen as great – '[. . .] the direct effects of "CROSSBOW",' analysis showed, 'are among the smaller hazards of war to which "OVERLORD" is liable.'[5] So these reinforcements were essentially conceived as a normal thickening of artillery to meet conventional bombing, not unlike the Baedeker or Fringe Target deployments of the previous two years. The guns were expected to be in place no later than D-30 (30 days before D-Day), with the first arriving about fifteen days earlier, that is on D-45, or about mid April.

Planning for *Diver* was in every respect more complex. In the state of intelligence obtaining in early March it was believed that the Germans commanded 88 launching sites for V1s in north-eastern France together with nine in the Cherbourg area, of which something over one third remained in commission after three months of Allied bombing. This number in future might rise or fall, depending upon the relative success of German repairs and commissioning and the bomber effort, but the point remained that a solid array of launchers was likely to be available through the spring and summer, and from each of these the Germans were thought capable of dispatching two weapons per hour. London of course would be the main target, while the Cherbourg sites were well-placed to launch a minor subsidiary assault on Bristol, though ADGB was confident that bombers could keep this 'in check' given the small number of launching sites and the greater distance the V1s would have to cover. In essence, then, the *Diver* threat as it appeared in March 1944 bestrode a cross-Channel axis between north-eastern France and London. How could this be met?

The answer was with fighters, searchlights, guns and balloons, which remained the basic mix of *Diver* defences despite several changes in detail between the issue of the Concurrent Plan and the start of the operation. Fighters would form the front line, using searchlight support at night, and behind them would lie a dense array of AA guns, light and heavy, spanning the North Downs. Barrage balloons, more conventionally used to force bombers upward into the sights of AA guns, would in this scheme form a final physical barrier against lower-flying V1s, around nine or ten per cent of which were expected to strike the cables or envelopes before reaching London. This scheme did not differ much in detail from the original *Crossbow* plan drafted in January, except that the number of guns allowed was sharply cut, thanks to the more firmly defined requirements for *Overlord*. That plan had anticipated that the North Downs gun belt would be occupied by 50 sites of eight HAA guns apiece, these 400 weapons to be manned entirely by British units. By early March, however, this allocation had been trimmed and modified in the light of scientific study which showed that equal or better results should be obtained from a mix of weapons using better fire-control instruments. The plan called specifically for 128 American HAA weapons equipped with the US-manufactured SCR 584 centimetric radars and BTL predictors, supported by just 64 British 3.7s with GL Mk IIIs and Vickers predictors, both types using time-fuzed shells. There would in addition be 246 LAA barrels (down from 346 in the former plan) and 216 searchlights. That was the ideal, though its achievement depended on many factors, not least whether the American units would be available and fully equipped with their SCR 584s. In the event that they were not, or that AA Command was unable to protect US installations which mobile American batteries would perform by summer 1944, allowance was made for more British guns to be held in reserve for a *Diver* role. But then again – and the fact that three very different possibilities were mooted shows how complex this plan had become – if *more* American guns were available than expected then the *Diver* defences could be thickened still further with US troops. (Certainty on that last contingency was elusive because supplies of American guns depended upon shipping patterns, the extent of competing claims on US resources, and the needs of training, all of which were unclear.) Lastly, some guns were allocated to Bristol – the only target apart from London specifically to be earmarked *Diver* defences – where 96 HAA and 36 LAA were expected to be deployed against Cherbourg-based attacks, though only if *Diver* materialised before *Overlord*. In fact it did not, and Bristol played no part in the *Diver* battle, but even without the allocation of guns there the claims of *Overlord* and *Diver* would seriously weaken GDAs elsewhere.

The value placed upon the American contribution to *Diver* rested chiefly on the acknowledged superiority of the SCR 584 radar, which Pile knew and respected as a better piece of equipment than any home-grown set yet given to his own troops, even the GL Mk III. Married to the BTL predictor the SCR 584 offered fully automated tracking and aiming, with no need for manual intervention once the target had been locked on, and moreover could feed its information to remotely-controlled guns such that the entire engagement was fought automatically. Pile saw the combination of American radars and predictors with remotely-controlled guns as a 'robot defence' against a 'robot target' and in February had lobbied Churchill to obtain a supply of SCR 584s for AA Command, requesting 134 sets immediately and more than 400 in the long term.[6] Eventually he got them, and in the event it was American radars driving British guns which would defeat the flying bomb in the high summer of 1944.

The Concurrent Plan anticipated that it would take eighteen days to deploy the guns, searchlights and balloons for *Diver* once the orders to move had been given. In March 1944 that was seen as a reasonably brisk timetable, achievable largely because the administrative arrangements would be made long in advance, and indeed had been settled in most details before the Concurrent Plan was issued. These arrangements included acquiring the temporary gun positions on the North Downs, grid references for which were circulated with the warning orders for the operation issued to the batteries in March, and it was the prior reservation of these sites – simply green fields for mobile guns – which enabled the units to get their weapons in position on a much shorter timetable once *Diver* was activated in mid June. Those sites had mostly been identified and reserved in February, and in the following month comparable work got under way in the hinterlands of the *Overlord* base areas. Orders to begin that work were issued on 12 March,[7] though the requirement was modified within a couple of days when a new operation order was issued introducing material changes to the balance of guns to be used for the two operations. Under this amended plan the concurrent *Overlord/Diver* deployment would give the London *Diver* defences 192 HAA guns, as before, but now split 50:50 between AA Command and the American ETOUSA units (making 96 each), while the London *Diver* LAA defences were now to consist of 84 AA Command weapons, 108 from 21 Army Group, and 54 from Home Forces – 246 in all. Bristol *Diver* was left at 96 HAA and 36 LAA, as before, all supplied by 21 Army Group, while the *Overlord* element now amounted to 460 HAA weapons and 600 LAA, again supplied in varying proportions from Pile's resources, the Americans, and Montgomery's invasion force.[8] These were the figures on which site reconnaissance proceeded in March, as the Little Blitz continued on provincial targets.[9] On its completion at the end of the month,[10] AA Command had hundreds of new potential sites on its books, both for *Diver* (on the North Downs) and *Overlord* (among the existing GDAs on the southern coasts of England and Wales), plans had been prepared and the units which would take part in these two operations had their orders, ready for the signal to move.

By the end of March it was clear that several options lay before the Chiefs of Staff in mobilising the *Overlord* and *Diver* defences. Surveying the alternatives on the 29th, the AA Sub-Committee was inclined to play down the *Diver* risk, and at the same time pointed to new demands for *Overlord*-related guns which were beginning to crop up in modification to the early plans – that very week, for example, the Admiralty had requested AA for the *Mulberry* harbour assembly points at Selsey and Dungeness (additional to the *Pluto* guns), two targets omitted from previous plans. In these circumstances the committee advised that any further allocations of guns to *Overlord* targets would need to come from the existing allotment to avoid further weakening of ADGB's established GDAs, and that the *Overlord* element of the Concurrent Plan should be initiated not later than 1 April, three days hence.[11] Next day, an appreciation put together at Stanmore identified four options in handling the general *Overlord/Diver* defences as the Normandy landings loomed and the flying bomb threat continued to exert its definite but ambiguous presence.[12] First, they could activate the entire Concurrent Plan (in its modified form) from 1 April. This would get both the *Diver* and *Overlord* guns out to their stations in ample time, allowing the gunners to settle in and calibrate their equipment and avoid large-scale moves of weapons later, at a time when the south coast would be bustling with other activity. On the minus side, however, this pre-emptive deployment of the *Diver* weapons would be wasted if no flying bomb threat materialised, would negate the value of strategic intelligence on the character of that threat which might emerge after 1 April, and would rob the ETOUSA and 21 Army Group gunners of valuable training by committing them prematurely to a *Diver* role. A second and more radical course was to discount the *Diver* threat altogether and throw everything into defending the *Overlord* base areas at an early date. That brought risks, chief among them the difficulty of redeploying for *Diver* if the flying bombs did arrive, and was clearly less preferable to ordering the *Overlord* guns into position while keeping the *Diver* guns in reserve – the third option. The last possibility, thought Pile's staff, was to deploy the

full *Overlord* defences and the *Diver* guns less the American and
21 Army Group contingents, which could continue to train; this
would leave many moves to be made later, though fewer than if
all the *Diver* guns were kept in reserve. In the event it was the
third option which won the day – deploying for *Overlord* while
putting *Diver* on hold. But the fact that Pile's staff were weighing
so many contradictory contingencies as late as the end of March
is a telling reflection on the uncertainty surrounding the whole
enterprise.

The 1 April landmark came and went before this decision was
taken. It was in the early evening of Thursday, 6 April that the
teleprinters in AA group headquarters up and down the country
began to rattle out their message to deploy for *Overlord*
'forthwith'; 'units earmarked for the DIVER portion of the
concurrent plan will be held in res until further notice,' ran AA
Command's telegraphese, 'less AA Comd and HOFOR units which
will be deployed in rft [reinforcement] of OVERLORD defs [. . .].'[13] If
Diver materialised, the message explained, then these AA Command
and Home Forces units would be withdrawn from *Overlord* base
areas and dispatched to their *Diver* positions; and if the *Diver*
threat seemed nugatory then the 21 Army Group troops held in
reserve for the flying bomb battle would be committed to *Overlord*
instead, though not the ETOUSA units. In essence the plan now
actuated was that defined in the operation order of 14 March.

The following days and weeks saw another huge reshuffling of
weapons throughout southern Britain, as the gunners occupied
their *Overlord* positions in an operation which the formal ADGB
covering order, issued on 12 April, required to be complete 'as far
as possible' by the 28th, and in any event by 1 May.[14] One factor
governing the timetable was the need to have the guns in position
before Exercise *Fabius*, part of the *Overlord* training preparations,
scheduled for 29 April, and by this date much of the work was
indeed complete (though *Fabius* was later brought forward to the
23rd).[15] As Appendix III shows, by 19 April, nine days before the
deadline, many of the areas due additional guns for *Overlord* had
already attained the HAA strengths they would hold on 6 June,
and most of the others were well on the way. One hundred and
eight 3.7in mobiles arrived in Southampton in the fortnight
before 19 April, bringing the city's HAA strength to 160 weapons

(up from 52 in the week before the moves began), all but eight of which were ready to fire. Portsmouth's rose from 30 guns to 60 in the same period, *en route* to the 101 which would be in place on D-Day, while fresh guns arrived on the Isle of Wight, at Newhaven, Shoreham and Brighton, at Yarmouth/Lowestoft, and at North Foreland, Falmouth, Portland, and Plymouth (whose D-Day total of 64 HAA was already in place by 19 April, up from 48 a fortnight before). At the same time GDAs using 3.7in mobiles exclusively were newly created or reactivated at Chichester (with 56 guns on 19 April), Dartmouth (48) and RAF Tarrant Rushdon (sixteen). Some of these totals were later adjusted and Southampton, in particular, lost weapons in favour of some of the other *Overlord* GDAs in the six weeks remaining before the Normandy fleet sailed. But the build-up in the middle fortnight of April was rapid and effective, and extended to light weapons equally.

These guns had to come from somewhere, and while a proportion was provided from non-ADGB sources, many GDAs remote from the *Overlord/Diver* areas now entered a phase of terminal contraction which would accelerate sharply once the flying bombs began to fall two months later. In the first fortnight of April, 3.7in mobiles were liberated by stripping several minor GDAs, some of whose names were abruptly deleted from the weekly returns and none of which, in any case, was ever rearmed. Cambridge went in these weeks, along with its fellow Baedeker targets at Lincoln, Grantham, Bath and Peterborough. So too did Dundee, Barrow and Invergordon, along with Corby, Ramsgate and AA Command's representation at RAF Manston. At the same time many northern and Midland GDAs lost guns in single figures and some were summarily deprived of all their 3.7in mobiles, such as the Humber (28 sacrificed) the Tyne (twelve) and the Forth (four). By the end of April the demands of *Overlord*, the Allies' single most crucial operation of the Second World War, were leaving all other considerations in the shade.

In the light of that it is just as well that the Luftwaffe never exploited the resulting weaknesses in many GDAs. London's guns were never tapped to meet the demands of *Overlord* and actually thickened a little in the six weeks before early June (though, as we have seen, the capital was untroubled by conventional bombing after 18 April). Hull, on the other hand, met an attempted 130-bomber raid on 20 April with only 80 per cent of the weapons in place there at the end of March, a deficit which fortunately lay unexposed because none of the raiders hit the city.[16] Had the Luftwaffe revisited the Baedeker targets in April 1944 they would have met no opposition from AA Command (though their inability to find Hull by itself suggests that Bath or Cambridge would have been safe), but when they turned to raiding against the southern ports in the last phase of the Little Blitz they met defences much strengthened by the *Overlord* plans. Moderate to heavy raids were attempted against shipping at Portsmouth in the last week of April, and on Plymouth, Portsmouth, Weymouth, Torquay and Falmouth during May. But the Luftwaffe's ineptitude, deepening for over a year, reached its lowest point in this sequence of operations, none of which managed any concentration on their targets and sometimes missed them altogether. And those raiders which did get through met the formidable *Overlord* gun layouts which contributed to losses that, as we have seen, reached about ten per cent of the forces dispatched in these last weeks of the campaign.

On the morning of D-Day, Tuesday, 6 June 1944, AA Command's contribution to the *Overlord* ports was formidable.[17] Portsmouth had 101 HAA guns and Southampton 122, between them about the same number as London had fielded at the height of the first Blitz in November 1940, to say nothing of the 171 rocket projectors in place at these two targets. Plymouth had 64 guns and 69 UPs, Portland/Weymouth had 52 guns, the Isle of Wight 66, Newhaven 60, Falmouth 32, Dartmouth and Harwich both 48, and Swansea was equipped with 40 HAA guns and 107 rockets. Together with many LAA, these were the weapons given to the harbours from which the invasion force would sail. But *Overlord* also gave rise to some special deployments, among which the 48 HAA guns and seventeen LAA to support the *Pluto* and *Mulberry* installations was the strongest, a little ahead of the 41 HAA at Selsey, the second *Mulberry* target. On 27 May the headquarters staff in AA formations throughout the country received warning of the special markings to be applied to many types of Allied aircraft in the forthcoming operation, these broad black-and-white stripes being an aid to the gunners in distinguishing friend from foe in the fierce air battle to come.[18] But, over the embarkation ports in Britain, the special installations, the assembly points and transit camps, over the airfields, over the whole vast array of Allied military might spread across southern Britain, that battle never took place. Never had AA Command moved so many guns – more than 1000 HAA and 500 LAA – to so little direct purpose. Cloaked by its elaborate strategic deception plan, Operation *Fortitude*, the invasion force put to sea, landed and was reinforced and supplied while the Germans continued to believe that *Overlord* was not the real thing. As the troops embarking at the south coast ports went on their way untroubled by air attack, it seemed to some that AA Command's war might be coming to an end. On 8 June the Chiefs of Staff examined ways of cutting Pile's personnel allocation still further, this time by 50,000 men and 27,000 women;[19] and on that same day, Pile himself received word from the Chiefs that the flying-bomb threat had 'entirely disappeared'.[20] Operation *Diver* would not take place.

At eighteen minutes past four on the morning of Tuesday, 13 June 1944, the first flying bomb to strike Britain during the Second World War came to earth at Stone, near Dartford, exploding harmlessly on agricultural land bordering the A2 Rochester to Dartford road.[21] It was followed soon after by three more, which struck sequentially in Sussex, at Bethnal Green, and near Sevenoaks in Kent.[22] Casualties were few. Six people died in Bethnal Green, where nine were also seriously injured, but when reports of the four incidents were collated it was obvious that this was not the scale of bombardment predicted by intelligence analysts over the preceding months. 'It was believed that these were only tests,'[23] recalled Pile, whose faith in the Chiefs of Staffs' assurances of five days earlier seems to have survived intact during the first part of this week. In those circumstances there could be no question of ordering the vast redeployment of ground defences implied by the *Diver* plan. All the defenders could do was watch and wait, reassured to some extent by the evidence that the new weapons were at least easily tracked. As AA Command's *Intelligence Review*

noted, the first flying bomb had been reported clearly and accurately by an ROC post at Dymchurch, which it had crossed eleven minutes before impact tracking north at 1000 feet and emitting an 'unusual noise'.[24] At least one other post had logged it crossing the North Downs, when its sound was compared rather precisely to 'a Model-T Ford going up a hill'.[25] In the next eight months the gunners and the public alike would get to know that sound only too well. The danger, as they soon learned, became acute when it ceased.

'The suggestion that the activity of 12/13 Jun[e] was merely experimental,' recorded the *Intelligence Review*, 'is supported by the absence from the German communique of all reference to secret or special weapons.'[26] Reasonable as it seemed on the evidence available, that interpretation was mistaken. The Germans had planned to open their V1 offensive by sending about 500 missiles across the Channel, the first timed to reach London at 23.40 in a bombardment due to last much of the night. But everything had gone wrong, only ten had been launched and, of those, six had been lost to crashes near their launch sites or had otherwise gone astray.[27] But by the time AA Command's weekly *Intelligence Review* appeared on 17 June there had been a second and much more successful bout of raiding. Between ten PM on the evening of Thursday 15 June and midday on the 16th, 244 missiles were dispatched toward London and another 50 or so into the area around Southampton. Again, a proportion never got through. Forty-five crashed soon after launching, but 155 were sighted by the defences, 144 crossed the coast and 73 penetrated to Greater London, where the gunners of the IAZ managed to shoot down eleven. Elsewhere, AA guns accounted for a further fourteen flying-bombs and fighters for seven, while AA and fighters jointly destroyed one more, bringing the total downed to 33, of which no fewer than 25½ were credited to the guns.[28] It was a reasonable start.

It was on the Friday morning, 16 June, that Herbert Morrison told the House of Commons that bombardment with 'pilotless aircraft' had at last begun. Any but the most inattentive Members could probably have grasped that for themselves, but the significance of the Home Secretary's statement lay in its official concession that here was a new phase in the air war, meriting new measures of defence. Within hours German radio broadcasts were gloating: 'he is entirely uncertain about possible countermeasures,' said one, referring to Morrison's announcement, 'and does not know whether or not the use of AA guns as a defensive weapon is appropriate.'[29] But the British did know, and at 13.40 on the afternoon the signal initiating Operation *Diver* was flashed from Stanmore to 1, 2, 3 and 6 AA Groups 'for action' and, for information, to military headquarters throughout London and the south-east.[30]

At varying levels of intensity Operation *Diver* occupied AA Command for the rest of the war. Though the last flying bomb to reach Britain arrived on 29 March 1945, concluding an offensive whose strength had already dwindled many weeks before, a proportion of the anti-aircraft guns deployed to engage the V1 were still in place in their ultimate *Diver* locations on VE Day. In the months following the first *Diver* gun deployment in mid June 1944, the weapons would be moved several times: first, in mid July, from their original positions on the North Downs to the south coast; next, soon after, to form a supplementary cordon closing the Thames Estuary to V1s approaching from the east; then, in mid September, to create a new linear system on the East Anglian coast; and finally, at the end of December 1944, to a further linear layout on the Lincolnshire–Yorkshire coast. Prompted in some cases by tactical second thoughts, these huge upheavals – raising by far the greatest logistic problems which confronted AA Command at any stage in the war – were more usually designed to counter the ever-changing approach tracks of the flying bombs themselves. These, in turn, were directly influenced by the advance of the Allies' second front in Europe, which progressively over-ran the V1 launching sites, obliging the Germans to shift their ground bases and adopt more flexible modes of delivery (notably air-launching from conventional bombers). In the eight months from June 1944, *Diver* forced AA Command to adopt new equipment, tactics and patterns of deployment, and brought Pile's men into communion with AA gunners from several other arms – the RAF Regiment, the Royal Marines, US forces, Montgomery's 21st Army Group, and others. By the end of the operation, which emerged as unquestionably the greatest technical achievement of AA Command's war, the gunners had also occupied more than a thousand wholly new positions, for heavy, light and rocket weapons, from the Kentish Downs to Bridlington. These sites in their turn have left us a distinctive archaeology all of their own. *Diver* was a small war in its own right. And for all these reasons the flying bomb campaign in its many ramifications commands a volume of its own in the present series.[31]

Covering the campaign in detail elsewhere enables us to look more closely at its effects on the AA defences of the remainder of the United Kingdom in the final year of the war. It also opens the way to examining a range of developments entirely unconnected with flying bombs which took place in parallel with the *Diver* struggles and which, understandably, tend to be marginalised in accounts of Britain's AA defences in 1944–45. So great was the volume of weaponry committed to the flying bomb battle, especially in its first two months, that many GDAs and VPs were bled to the point of extinction. And so emphatic was the need for mobility in this ever-shifting deployment, that the habit initiated in the late 1930s to accept ever larger numbers of static weapons reached its true nemesis in the late summer of 1944.

Diver began to make itself felt on Britain's conventional AA layouts almost from the start. The requirement for flying bomb defences in the approaches to Bristol had been formally discounted on 12 June, six days after *Overlord* was launched,[32] so the move ordered in the early afternoon of the 16th called for guns on the North Downs only. The *Diver* element of the original *Overlord/Diver* plan had allocated 192 HAA and 246 LAA weapons for this deployment, of which the HAA would be split equally between AA Command and American units and the LAA would include 108 guns from Home Forces. Eighteen days had been allowed to get these weapons into position, but for a variety of reasons events unfolded rather differently. On 8 June Pile had been warned that the ETOUSA units might not after all be relied upon after D + 10 (in other words after 15 June, since D-Day was then scheduled for the 5th),[33] and in fact the pool of US units was dwindling, as predicted. No extra weapons were gained from cancelling the Bristol defences, since the guns of 21 Army Group allocated to them were already committed elsewhere, so in the event the whole of the HAA requirement – 192 guns – was met by using six AA Command regiments, each equipped with four batteries of eight 3.7in mobiles.[34] Most of these were in position by midday on Saturday, 17 June, less than 24 hours after the orders were issued and only four days after the first flying bombs had reached Britain.

So was born the Kentish Gun Belt, a zone soon to be packed with weapons of all kinds, whose officially delineated boundaries are shown, along with those of its successors, in Figure 42. The guns came into action almost immediately and over the following three weeks, as the V1 onslaught continued, the density of guns on the North Downs was expanded to a point way beyond that envisaged in any pre-operation plans. Further HAA reinforcements

Figure 42 Skeleton plan of successive *Diver* gun zones, June 1944–March 1945, based upon the official deployment boundaries notified in AA Command orders. The point-pattern of sites in each case fitted neatly inside each of these boundaries.

were not long in coming, some from training units, some from the Royal Marines, and others provided by mixed batteries, marking the ATS's entry to a battle they would see through to its end. Light guns, too, were moved up to the North Downs, and by the end of the first week in July there were 373 HAA barrels in operation within the Belt, along with 592 AA Command Bofors. In the next seven days these weapons were supplemented by a forward cordon of more than 500 RAF Regiment guns (mostly 20mm) on the south coast, bringing the total *Diver* arsenal to 373 HAA, 776 LAA (40mm) and 422 LAA (20mm) by 15 July, a month after the operation began.[35]

The huge increase in gun allocations to the *Diver* battle was a response to the intensity of the V1 bombardment. By close of play on 15 July the Germans had dispatched no fewer than 4361 flying bombs against Britain, most from the ramp sites in northern France but, in the latter stages of this phase, including 90 air-launched weapons laid upon Portsmouth or Southampton. All but 50 or so of the 4271 ground-launched bombs were intended for London, and of those, 2934 proved sufficiently viable to be logged by the defences, 1693 escaped destruction and 1270 got through to the capital – or, strictly speaking, landed somewhere in the London Civil Defence Region – with the balance of the survivors falling elsewhere. The defences, by 15 July, managed to destroy 1241 flying bombs, rather more than a quarter of those dispatched and (the more important figure from the contemporary British point of view) about 42 per cent of those seen.[36] But of these, only 261$^{1}/_{3}$ were credited to artillery on the North Downs and elsewhere. Despite the huge efforts to mobilise a force of more than 1400 heavy and light AA guns, by far the greater proportion of the V1s destroyed before 15 July fell to fighter aircraft. By 15 July it was obvious that returns from the guns were less than should be expected.

The reasons became clear at an early stage in the campaign. In conformity with the original plan for the *Diver* operation, the weapons of the Kentish Gun Belt formed one tier in a three-stage defensive layout which allowed fighter aircraft to operate in advance of the artillery and over the sea, and backed the gun cordon with the vast screen of barrage balloons skirting the south of London (by 15 July, when 1247 balloons were bobbing in this pneumatic forest,[37] V1s downed by hitting the cables or envelopes had already reached 55$\frac{1}{3}$). In principle this arrangement should have been preferential to the gunners, but it proved the opposite. In planning the operation Pile had suspected that flying bombs would present very inviting targets to his guns, thanks largely to their 'robotic' character: with no pilot to take evasive action, the V1 would describe a steady track and speed and in this respect oblige all the assumptions on which AA gunnery had been founded. It was to make doubly sure of success that Pile had requested the supply of American SCR 584 radars, which could be meshed with BTL predictors to provide continuous target following and, in turn, drive fully power-operated HAA guns to give a completely automated system. Those sets were not available in any numbers until the second month of the campaign, but given all the necessary equipment, Pile was confident that 'the targets could satisfactorily be dealt with [. . .] provided – and this was especially emphasised – that good results were not to be expected at heights between 2000 and 3000 feet, where the target would be too high for light guns and too low for heavy guns', making the effectiveness of AA fire 'small'.[38] But unfortunately for Pile, that narrow, 1000-foot height band was exactly the level at which the Germans programmed their V1s to fly; and whether or not the guns were equipped with SCR 584s it was obvious that the low approach heights utterly defeated the rate of traverse available from the 3.7in mobile, which was a good deal slower than that available from its static cousin. And these were not the only problems which the gunners discovered in their month on the North Downs. The spheres of operation between guns and fighters overlapped, necessitating a complicated regime of open and closed seasons for AA fire according to weather and other considerations, as well as some danger to the fighters from friendly fire. The existing radar sets, which had mostly been sited in folds and hollows of the Downs to avoid enemy jamming, did more to read the irregular contours of the ground than the approach of V1s, and returned a stream of spurious contacts. Moves were frequent to find better sites, and the gunners' effectiveness generally slumped.

By the time the big decision of mid July was taken, some efforts were already in hand to improve the guns' performance on the Downs. In particular, it was decided that the 3.7in mobiles of the *Diver* deployment must be exchanged for statics, and a means be found of emplacing these guns without recourse to concrete. The solution came in the form of an ingenious portable mattress, designed by Brigadier J A E Burls of Pile's staff, which used interlocking railway sleepers and rails to anchor a standard 3.7in holdfast on an otherwise unprepared site. Named after the GOC-in-C, these 'Pile platforms' had been supplied for just 32 guns on the North Downs when the entire geography of the *Diver* deployment was fundamentally changed.

The big decision of mid July was to abandon the Kentish Gun Belt and move everything down to the coast, where the gunners could have free rein in tackling V1s approaching across the water. Begun on the 14th and completed in four days, this stupendous upheaval created a Coastal Gun Belt from Cuckmere Haven to St Margaret's Bay, as well as a deep supplementary cordon spanning the Thames Estuary, known as the *Diver* Box, to meet air-launched flying bombs approaching London from the east (Fig 42, page 433). This one move involved the migration of 23,000 personnel, 30,000 tons' worth of ammunition and a similar weight of stores, and the laying of 3000 miles of new communications lines,[39] these to operate, supply and integrate a layout of guns which by 22 July amounted to 662 HAA (478 of them operational) and 1326 LAA, including the RAF Regiment weapons which had been in this area from the start.[40] But this was more than simply a move of guns from hills to coast, since enlarging the static element meant numerous exchanges of mobiles for statics, and the construction of hundreds of Pile platforms to take them. In these four days 312 statics were substituted for mobiles in this way.

The full Coastal Gun Belt remained in being until 19 August, when the Allied advance across the water neutralised the westerly V1 launching sites and allowed the portion west of Hastings to be abandoned; the residual Belt on the eastern Sussex and Kent coast thereafter remained in being for a further month, before the move to East Anglia began. In these weeks the number of guns continued to rise, and so did their returns. The peak HAA strength was reached in the first and second weeks of August, when almost a thousand weapons were assigned a *Diver* role in the Belt and Box, though not all of these were specially deployed – the 3.7s on Guy Maunsell's sea forts proved especially fortuitous to close the Box across the Thames Estuary – and around 300 were usually non-operational for various reasons at any one time. LAA numbers hit their peak later in the month, a combination of Bofors and 20mm guns from AA Command, the RAF Regiment and the navy reaching 1938 barrels during the week ending 30 August. It was in the Coastal Belt that Pile also took the opportunity to try out a wide range of experimental armaments: anti-aircraft tanks, various types of Polsten gun, quadruple 20mm weapons designed by the Ministry of Aircraft Production, 9in mortars from the Petroleum Department and 2in naval UPs, as well as novel combinations of standard weapons and predictors. In addition, a searchlight regiment was converted for rocket work, and came into action with four batteries of U2Ps, adding another 512 barrels from 256 launchers. 'More was learned about the potentialities of anti-aircraft work in 80 days,' wrote Pile, 'than had been learned in the previous 30 years.'[41]

Thirty years ago there had been much debate about ammunition and fuzes. Now, for the flying bomb battle, Pile had his first plentiful supply of proximity-fuzed ammunition, which detonated on sensing the target – or, more accurately, sensing almost anything; many seabirds laid down their lives in the defence of London – and could now be brought into use because rounds missing the V1s fell harmlessly into the sea. It was during the spell on the south coast, too, that the American SCR 584s began to reach the batteries in numbers, and with those, the No. 10 Predictors, the new ammunition and the freedom of action granted by their coastal position, the gunners' contribution to the battle soared. Seventeen per cent of all flying bombs entering the Belt were destroyed by the guns in the first week on the coast, rising week-on-week to reach 60 per cent by 23 August and 74 per cent in the last week of the month, when one extraordinary day saw the 24-hour statistic reach 82 per cent of all targets available to the AA barrels.

Pile counted the beginning of September as the end of the campaign's first phase, and reasonably so; for this week saw the final ground-launched V1s dispatched to Britain from French sites, which were now abandoned in the face of the Allied advance. In the period from 13 June to 5 September the Germans had sent 8617 ground-launched missiles toward Britain, together with about 400 delivered by aircraft, the vast majority in both categories toward London. This was by far the greater proportion of all flying bombs directed at Britain during the war (86 per cent of the total, comprising 97 per cent of the ground-launched type, though only a quarter of those dropped by bombers). Of these weapons, say 9017 in all, the guns by 5 September were credited with 1459 (plus the odd fraction) compared with 1771 in whole numbers given to the fighters and 231 (again in whole numbers) which had fallen to the balloon barrage – a total destroyed by all arms of 3463.[42] Since the gunners' main contribution to those totals came in the last five weeks of this phase, it can fairly be said that by the first week in September 1944 AA Command's victory over the flying bomb seemed practically complete. 'The newspapers, the newsreels, and the letters that poured into us,' wrote Pile, 'were full of praise.'[43]

The steady reinforcement of the *Diver* defences and the passing of the threat to *Overlord* targets had meanwhile brought substantial changes in the AA defences elsewhere by early September (Appendix III). In addition to those disarmed earlier in the summer, by the second week in the month AA Command GDAs had become operationally extinct at Ashford, Reading, Littlestone, Brooklands, Dungeness, Chichester, Lyndhurst, Weston-super-Mare, Dartmouth, Exeter, Hayle, Swindon, Salisbury, Oxford, York, Scunthorpe, Crewe, Caerwent, RAF Hawkinge and RAF Tarrant Rushton, as well as at Invergordon and Dundee in Scotland and Belfast, Bangor and Londonderry in Northern Ireland. Disarming these areas released large numbers of 3.7in statics for emplacement on Pile platforms down on the south coast, while at the same time areas still active which had earlier sacrificed their 3.7in mobiles for the first *Diver* deployment were raided for their fixed guns as well. In the six weeks from mid July the IAZ gave up 52 of these guns in favour of *Diver* (the IAZ had early been prohibited from engaging V1s, since hits only brought them down on Londoners' heads) while 56 were lost in Thames &

Medway and many from GDAs outside the south-east such as Bristol (which gave 32), Liverpool (42), Manchester (22), Derby/ Nottingham (25), and Cardiff (24); many more remote targets lost them in smaller numbers, proportional to their already much reduced armament – Leeds, Sheffield, the Tyne, the Tees and Blyth were among the places in this category. The result was that many major GDAs in areas distant from the *Diver* threat were now falling back upon a few 3.7in statics, on 3.7in Mk VIs (or 4.5s where conversion was incomplete) and, for a lucky few, on 5.25s. One of the very few GDAs untouched by these moves was Scapa, which fielded precisely the same 67 HAA guns in September 1944 as it had six months previously.

Although the *Diver* battle was soon reanimated by the onset of a new phase of air-launched attacks, the fight never regained its former pitch and by the autumn it was clear that the suspension in AA Command's contraction could last no longer. The premise for a new round of cuts was a JIC appraisal produced at the end of August, which concluded that the Luftwaffe's capacity for conventional bombing was dwindling fast: for the immediate future the maximum effort on any one night was put at no more than 50–60 bombers, a figure which was confidently expected to 'diminish and be virtually eliminated by the end of the year'.[44] In practical terms this meant that the AA war, apart from any flying-bomb threat, should be over by Christmas. Shortly before this assessment was released Pile and Hill had prepared a joint memorandum advancing ideas on how ADGB should be progressively restructured, first in the period until the Allied armies were in control of the Low Countries, second in the spell between that achievement and the final defeat of Germany, and lastly after the European war was won. The new JIC assessment superseded this report in some respects, but both this and the original Pile–Hill proposals were jointly assessed by the AA Sub-Committee, the Chiefs of Staff, and ultimately by Attlee (as Deputy Prime Minister) in the first three weeks of September. The result was a cut in the AA defences of unprecedented proportions.

In their joint memorandum Pile and Hill, interestingly, had disagreed on how much AA Command could afford to lose in the immediate future, Hill preferring to dispense with anti-aircraft

defences in the west altogether, but with some increase in the
north-east, and Pile advocating a more cautious approach in
which 'the basic organisation and a small scale of defence' was
retained throughout. Pile's preferred option would have left him
with about 7500 more men and women than Hill's, and it was the
issue of personnel which, as much as any purely strategic
consideration, led to the competing proposals being closely
studied over a period of several weeks. Another factor to be
considered in framing the short-term plan was the likely turn of
the *Diver* campaign, and on 5 September the Chiefs of Staff gave
focus to this inquiry by inviting the Air Ministry and other
interested parties to examine the future shape of the flying bomb
defences on the assumption 'that the only remaining threat was
from airborne launchings'. Proposals on this last point were
prepared by Hill on 14 September, and the whole matter studied
by the AA Sub-Committee in a report issued two days later.[45]

The outcome, after further discussion by the Chiefs of Staff,
was that the last week in September saw the approval of
substantial cuts in the ADGB organisation all round. As they
affected the AA guns, these orders required all GDAs in the area
to the south and east of a line from the Humber to the Solent to
revert to approximately their pre-*Overlord* scales, which amounted
to 810 HAA and 356 LAA guns manned by Regular troops, plus
rocket projectors and additional LAA in the hands of the Home
Guard. Defences on the east coast of England north of the
Humber, in Scotland and in the Orkneys and Shetlands were to be
reduced to a ceiling of 200 HAA weapons overall, plus eighteen
Home Guard Z batteries, while the remaining guns in all other
areas – in effect the whole of western Britain and Wales – were to
be withdrawn, though the organisation of GORs and other
support infrastructure was to be retained in 'care and maintenance'. To reoccupy any GDAs whose depletion might turn out to
have been premature, a substantial reserve of mobile guns were
also to be kept active – 24 mobile HAA and the same number of
LAA batteries – but all searchlights except those in the North
Weald, Biggin Hill and Tangmere sectors were to be withdrawn,
together with all the AA smoke companies (units which Pile had
inherited from the Ministry of Home Security in April 1943).[46]
The only flying bomb defences to be retained under these plans

were 136 HAA and 210 Bofors in the *Diver* Box spanning the
Thames Estuary: the orders of 22 September represented formal
authority to abolish what remained of the Coastal Gun Belt. Even
as they were drafted, however, the Air Ministry noted its understanding 'that certain measures are being taken to increase and
extend the AA defences in the Eastern "Diver" gun box and on the
East Coast to the North against the threat of air launched flying
bombs' and trusted that 'details of these measures' would be
forwarded to them in due course.[47]

This opaque and slightly starchy passage was a reference to
the embryonic *Diver* Strip: a new deployment of AA weapons
mobilised four days earlier to meet renewed raiding with air-
launched V1s, the first of which had scudded across the east coast
to the north of the Box two days previously. The first guns in
place to meet attacks on this extended front were shifted on the
18th, when sixteen batteries of HAA and nine of LAA were
deployed between the River Blackwater and Harwich, though
these were immediately outflanked by the Luftwaffe pushing
their approach tracks further north, with the result that Pile on 21
September decided to establish a new coastal belt extending up to
Great Yarmouth. It was on the following day, simultaneously with
the issue of the Air Ministry orders on the latest cuts to ADGB,
that the formal authority to establish this *Diver* Strip was given.[48]

Coincidental as it was, the timing could hardly have been
worse. In forming the new linear system, as Pile recalled, 'we
were not helped by the Cabinet decision that the most recently
proposed man-power cuts should now be brought into effect.'[49]
And for this and other reasons the full occupation of the Strip
took much longer than any previous *Diver* migration; in fact, as
Pile very candidly admitted in his book, this fourth great
upheaval, successor to the Kentish and Coastal Belts and the Box,
was mired in chaos from the start, and a move which over-
confidence suggested could be complete in four days took almost
four weeks. Everything went wrong. Stanmore underestimated
the time necessary to excavate, dismantle, transport and re-lay
the Pile platforms necessary for the power-driven statics. Most of
the lorries turned out to be in the wrong place, substitutes proved
elusive, and even those which could be loaded with guns and sent
on their way from the south to the east coasts were frequently

delayed crossing London or nearer their destinations in Norfolk
and Suffolk. 'On the narrow, twisting roads in that part of East
Anglia where we were redeploying,' recalled Pile, 'convoys of 10-
tonners would suddenly encounter head-on convoys of 3-tonners.
The subsequent delay and confusion were enormous.'[50] Orders
were frequently vague or contradictory, men found themselves
without accommodation, rations, or essential equipment, while
officers already exhausted by the near-continuous duty in the
deployments of the previous three months were often powerless
to remedy the resulting mess. The whole thing was a logistic
calamity, problem rebounding upon problem to produce AA
Command's greatest embarrassment since Munich, whose sixth
anniversary passed as the lorries jostled one another in the East
Anglian lanes. Thunderous teleprints emanating from Pile's office
left no one in doubt of his GOC's displeasure. 'The deployment to
Diver Strip has been deplorable,' ran one, on 2 October, 'and
reflects great discredit on every one of us [. . .] Everywhere there
is some reason for shame [. . .] Everyone is trying to put the
blame on someone else [. . .]. Let us instead get on with the job
and so put matters right.'[51] These were the harshest words which
Pile had addressed to his troops in five years of war.

While these things were happening the flying bombs
continued to fall, though by October 1944 Londoners were less
worried about the comparatively few air-launched V1s which
were reaching their city than by the sinister and much more
deadly V2 rockets, the first salvo of which had struck with terrible
effect on 8 September. AA Command was also doing something to
address those, as we shall see, but in the meantime 13 October
had at last seen the completion of the *Diver* Strip, which bridged
the gap between the Box and the Yarmouth/Lowestoft GDAs with
300 static 3.7s and a variety of LAA guns. These weapons met an
opponent very different from that which they had defeated on
the south coast: now exclusively air-launched from Heinkels
(which had been transferred from bases in Holland to north-west
Germany), the east coast V1s approached usually no higher than
1000 feet, always at night, and on tracks shared more often than
not by Bomber Command aircraft returning from missions over
Germany. Meeting these novel tactics was essentially a technical
job. The SCR 584s were provided with specially-designed wire-

mesh screens to eliminate ground clutter, LAA gunners were given 3.7s and LAA predictors, and again novel combinations of weapons and fire-control instruments were pressed into unlikely forced marriages. More searchlights were necessary, too, to illuminate targets at such low levels – low enough, on some occasions, that V1s ploughed into the coastal sand dunes – and these did much to aid the fighters which, just as they had on the south coast, now roamed wide to meet the approaching targets. And the guns continued to increase, likewise their claims. By the last week in October the Box and Strip combined contained 710 HAA guns from AA Command working in an anti-*Diver* role, together with 401 Bofors, though the 40mm weapons were withdrawn in November, leaving a little under 700 heavies to continue a fight which, in East Anglia, would roll on until January 1945.

And not only there. Wary that the Luftwaffe might again attempt to outflank the gun defences, as early as mid October preparations were under way to install *Diver* defences on the

Plate 26 Night duty for the *Diver* gunners. A 3.7in static resting on an earth-covered Pile platform at one of the *Diver* Strip sites on the east coast, November 1944.

Yorkshire coast, including the Humber GDA, where sites were enlarged with Pile platforms ready for extra guns, and supplementary positions found.[52] This was part of a wider plan to lay the ground for a *Diver* Fringe defence – so called – running from Skegness to Whitby, the rationale for which was discussed, *inter alia*, in a new assessment of the *Diver* threat compiled by Fighter Command in the second week of November.[53] Armed with new intelligence reports suggesting a sharp increase in the scale of air-launched V1 attacks into the winter and spring, Hill argued that London retained a continuing need for *Diver* defences, but that the very success of the Box and Strip increased the likelihood that the Germans would soon turn to attacks on the Midlands, and perhaps work further north to launch V1s on the Tees, Tyne, and the Forth–Clyde area. Preparation was the key, and by mid November reconnaissance for the *Diver* Fringe was well advanced, and sites had been earmarked for a further deployment between the Fringe itself and Newcastle.[54]

It was in November, as this work was in progress, that the manpower cuts agreed earlier in the autumn began to bite. To meet the Chiefs of Staffs' requirements Pile had lost 28 searchlight batteries in September, and two months later was obliged to relinquish a huge legion of men and women: 101 mixed and eleven male HAA batteries were disbanded at a stroke, together with 34 LAA batteries and fourteen more of searchlights. At the same time the Home Guard Z batteries were declared non-operational – units which held almost 120,000 that summer[55] – pending disbandment in January 1945.[56] The overall aim of the cuts decided in September was to release 50,000 men and 23,000 ATS; but to make matters worse Pile was also obliged to cherry-pick his surviving batteries to release younger and fitter men for the infantry, these to be replaced by others in lower medical categories chosen from the disbanding units. All of this happened at a time when AA Command was meeting, in the continuing *Diver* battle, one of its most physically strenuous challenges of the war, and was facing winter with thousands of men – and women – living on temporary sites on the East Anglian coast.

That was the next problem. In the second week of November Labour MP Tom Driberg asked a question in the House of Commons: was the Secretary of State for War aware, queried Mr

Driberg, 'that ATS personnel in anti-aircraft batteries are still sleeping under canvas on marshy ground at a place of which he has been informed; and if he will take immediate steps to transfer them to billets or provide hutments?' To Sir James Grigg's assurance that something was being done, and that meantime the women were under double tentage, Driberg was able to retort that his own visit to the batteries on the previous day had found no such situation; the ATS were 'still sleeping under single canvas – and very leaky canvas at that'.[57] It is not clear whether Driberg realised that such conditions had been endemic on AA Command's mobile gunsites since the beginning of the war, but it remained true, as everyone including Pile agreed, that something ought to be done. Within days the work was begun.[58]

'Winterisation', they called it: a vast building project to supply the more remote *Diver* Box and Strip sites with hutted camps, 3500 huts in total, all but 500 of which had to be scavenged from evacuated batteries scattered all over Britain, concentrated on the east coast and re-erected, together with 60 miles of roadway, 373,000 concrete slabs, half a million concrete blocks, 20,000 panes of glass, 150,000 tons of hardcore (from bombsites in London), and 7500 tons of paving slabs. Pile compared the result to a town the size of Windsor, though it is doubtful that Windsor could be rebuilt for the two million pounds which the venture cost (about 40 million at today's prices). It was complete in ten weeks, in time for the worst of the winter, and proved as smooth an operation as the mobilisation to the Strip had been troubled. 'Now that there was this very big job to be undertaken,' said Pile, 'everyone was working in the way that had made the first Diver deployment along the South Coast such a triumphant occasion.'[59] If only something similar could have been achieved four years earlier, in the London Blitz.

By the time this work was complete the flying bomb campaign had taken its next turn. In the early hours of Christmas Eve about 40 flying bombs were launched for the first time across the Lincolnshire coast towards a northern industrial city: Manchester. Orders to occupy the *Diver* Fringe sites were issued within hours, and in atrocious weather – first fog, then frost, and then snow – several HAA and LAA batteries spent Christmas setting up their stalls on the north-east coast. By the first week in January 56

HAA guns were in place on the Fringe, a number which would rise steadily to reach 152 in the first week of March – despite the fact that no flying bombs ever came that way again.

In the middle of January, in fact, the battle seemed for the second time to be over. Already dwindling by mid November, the pace of attack dropped further in December before, on 14 January 1945, the very last air-launched flying bomb of the war came to earth at Hornsey. In the four months from mid September, when ground-launched bombs had given way exclusively to the air-launched type, about 1200 V1s had been released towards British targets, of which 638 had been observed by the defences. Of these, the gunners were credited with $331^{1}/_{2}$, the fighters $71^{1}/_{2}$ – a ratio of gun to fighter kills of almost five to one – but of the 235 eluding the defences, a mere 66 had gone the whole way to London (one more had hit Manchester in the Christmas Eve raid).[60] By the end of November the gunners' hit-rate in the Box and Strip had reached 82 per cent of all flying bombs coming within AA range and the average number of 'rounds per bird' had plummeted to 156 – this compared to tens of thousands in the London barrage of 1940.[61] Those autumn nights on the East Anglian coast were AA Command's greatest of the war.

The end of the air-launching offensive was not, in fact, the end of Operation *Diver*, but seven weeks were now to pass before the gunners were again troubled by flying bombs. In that time, as the Allied advance in occupied Europe chased the Second World War ever closer to its end, the themes at home were disbandment, dissolution and change. By the New Year of 1945 the 'conventional' AA defences at established GDAs had been chopped to the bone – so much had gone, indeed, that from this point onward it becomes simpler to summarise what remained than to itemise the closures. By the first week in January the only GDAs with guns still operational were, in the south, Yarmouth/Lowestoft, Harwich, Thames & Medway, London, Slough, North Foreland, Dover, Newhaven, Portsmouth, Southampton and the Isle of Wight, creating a cordon from the northern extent of the *Diver* Strip to the Solent, and no further. The north-east coast was also active, with guns on the Humber – flanked by the *Diver* Fringe – the Tees, Blyth, the Tyne and up to the Forth and Aberdeen in Scotland, with weapons also on the Clyde. Scapa remained strongly gunned and a few weapons were also in place in the Shetlands. Apart from London the only inland cities with guns still operational in January 1945 were Liverpool, Manchester and Nottingham/Derby, where the retention of weapons unanticipated by the plans of September 1944 may have been a concession to the continuing danger from air-launched V1s. And that was it; some other GDAs still had guns in place, but these were non-operational, with the result that AA Command's tally of HAA weapons ready to engage the Luftwaffe stood at 1363 in the established GDAs and 370 in the *Diver* deployments, where in the first week of January a further 185 were listed as non-operational – 555 heavy weapons committed to *Diver* in all. Many gunsites were by now serving as holding camps for troops pending re-posting, or ATS awaiting release.

In more than five years of war AA Command had seen and engaged an uninterrupted procession of new aircraft types, from the Heinkels, Dornier, Junkers and Messerschmitts of 1940–41, through the Focke-Wulf 190s of the Fringe Target campaign, the faster and higher-flying bombers of the Little Blitz, and now the flying bomb, which alone among all the machines of this war and the last actually conformed to the assumptions on which AA gunnery had been founded in the years before the First World War: it flew at a steady course and height, and it didn't jink on the flash of the guns. This changing panorama of targets continued until the end of the war. In the closing months of the war Pile became anxious about the threat from jet-propelled aircraft travelling at speeds touching 700 miles per hour – too fast for most of the radars, predictors and guns in AA Command's armoury – and in January 1945 bombarded the War Office with demands for modifications to extend radar reach, hot-up the predictors, accelerate rates of gun traverse, and so on.[62] None of this was necessary during the remaining months of the war, as it happened, but it laid the basis for AA technology in the second half of the 1940s and beyond.

So, too, did one more anti-aircraft problem addressed by Pile's staff as the war in Europe drew to a close. In the V2 long-range

rocket – codenamed *Big Ben* – Britain's air defences faced a
challenge different in every way from the piloted aircraft which
had been operating against Britain throughout the war, and
different again from the *Diver* targets which were regularly being
destroyed by the time the first *Big Ben* arrived. The problem had
two parts, in warning, and interception, and for a time much
headway with either seemed unlikely. Operating at a range of
150–200 miles, the V2 rocket could reach heights of 50 miles and
speeds of 3000 miles per hour, giving an elapsed time from
launch to impact among the streets of London of about five or six
minutes. Even if rockets could be tracked by radar, there would
clearly be no time to issue the usual raid warnings allowing
Londoners to troop to the shelters; and, with the vehicle
travelling at a terminal speed of about 1800 miles per hour, the
chances of interception by AA were fantastically remote and by
fighters, nil. Nonetheless, the radar men and gunners tried. Radar
had first been pointed at the problem in the summer of 1943,
when specially modified Chain Home stations on the south coast
began watching for signs of rocket activity in the hope of
pinpointing the weapons' trials and launching sites. By March
1944, however, with the start of the V-weapon offensive growing
ever more likely, this work was narrowed to more determined
attempts to obtain radar warning of incoming attacks. Among the
ultimate recipients of these warnings were selected HAA and Z
battery sites in the IAZ, which in March were equipped with
pyrotechnic launchers linked up to communications lines which
enabled them to be fired, as a warning, on a remote signal from
the RAF Control Room. HAA sites were also given responsibility
for reporting the fall of missiles.[63] From 1 May 1944 this system
was extended to selected sites at Portsmouth and Southampton,
where signals were sent from the Fareham GOR. In neither these
areas nor in London were the staff at the sites allowed to know
the significance of the pyrotechnics, nor indeed what the system
as a whole was for,[64] though they presumably grasped both soon
enough when the first *Big Ben*s struck on 8 September 1944.

Once the offensive opened, warning cover on the south coast
was soon supplemented by twelve GL Mk II sets strung out in a
chain between Portsmouth and North Foreland, though as the
rockets continued to fall and it became clear that their lines of

approach were more easterly than southern the AA radars were moved to suit. At first the V2 offensive, though alarming, was not especially heavy: 35 were launched in the first ten days at London, of which only sixteen hit the capital and as many as eight never arrived in Britain at all. A second phase followed towards the end of September, in which 44 rockets were sent to Norwich or Ipswich; of these, 37 made it through. But then at the end of October the rockets' rate of fire increased, along with their accuracy, with the result that by November, though the V1 strikes had been reduced to tolerable proportions, London was suffering badly from a weapon against which its citizens had no tangible defence.

Pile first asked for permission to fire on the rockets on 12 December 1944, a proposal which Fighter Command rejected on the grounds that it was supported by no theoretical evidence that such a tactic was even worth trying.[65] But Pile persevered and before long secured agreement that if he could demonstrate, in theory, just a one in 100 chance that a rocket might be struck by an anti-aircraft shell the matter could be taken further. This of course he did, though not without difficulty. After studying the problem and making at least one false start, AA Command's scientific staff recommended that GL sets specially modified for very high-angle working could be sent to the east coast – supplementary to those already there – and so provide more accurate readings on the rockets' tracks for fire control. Orders for this deployment were issued on 28 January, and resulted in a layout of six early-warning stations on four sites at Southwold, Aldeburgh, Felixstowe and Foreness (the last two with a pair of radars), together with three 'experimental fire-control stations' at Aldeburgh (two sets) and Walmer.[66] Success was not exactly quick in coming, for while the radar operators in this most secret venture marvelled at the responses from meteorites – at first mistaken for V2s – the intended targets were at first elusive, and the radars had to be modified many times. Partly for this reason in late February the British stations were supplemented by a further set in Holland, an idea suggested to Pile by his learning of an SCR 584 which had been used by SHAEF to track *Big Ben* launching sites and trajectories on the other side of the North Sea. Since the SHAEF set was due to be withdrawn for other uses, at

the end of February Pile arranged to replace it with an SCR 584 of
his own, again in a much modified form,[67] and it was the
combination of the domestic and Dutch cover which, in March,
finally allowed the AA Command radar operators to refine their
Big Ben plots to the point where aimed fire against incoming
missiles was becoming a practical possibility. The principle of the
system was simple enough. London was divided into a series of
two and a half mile squares, and the radar predictions of which
square each observed rocket would fall into were tested for
accuracy against actual point of impact. The accuracy of these
predictions practically trebled during March, to the point where
almost one-third of the detected rockets were landing where the
radars suggested they would, and another 50 per cent were just
one square out. Since the rocket's incoming flight path could be
read back from the point of impact, fire in geographic barrages
could be brought to bear from the IAZ's guns – given lightning
transmission of the fire data – with a chance of success which
Pile's staff put at about three to ten per cent. Despite numerous
misgivings, and not before the scheme had been subject to
independent scientific audit, Pile's chiefs eventually relented at
the end of March, and on the 28th the IAZ's guns were poised to
fire against the V2 for the first time.[68] But Pile had not made
allowance for Montgomery's 21 Army Group, whose advance
across Holland brought the V2 offensive to a close on that same
day, 28 March 1945.

By then AA Command's war was almost over. The radar
experiments of the spring had coincided with the last flurry of the
flying bomb campaign, which resumed on 3 March using a new
variant of the V1 ground-launched from sites in Holland. But Pile
had been warned to expect those, and had already redeployed
guns from the Strip to meet weapons whose approach tracks were
predicted to lie between the Isle of Sheppey and Orford Ness.
Altogether 275 flying bombs were launched in this phase, of
which the guns destroyed 87 of the 125 seen by the defences and
the fighters just four.[69] No more than thirteen of the bombs
actually reached London and, on 29 March, the day after the last
V2 attack, the final flying bomb to reach Britain during the
Second World War was blasted into the sea by HAA in the *Diver*
Strip near Orford Ness.

The last conventional air attacks on any scale now lay three weeks in the past. Operation *Trigger* was Britain's response to a long-planned Luftwaffe intruder operation against returning bombers and bomber bases, and involved the hurried redeployment of 388 Bofors guns to meet a raid which, in the event, materialised on the night of 3/4 March. About 80 aircraft strong, the Luftwaffe force roamed widely, losing four of its number to fighters but none to the AA guns which were prevented from firing chiefly through the raiders mingling their tracks with those of returning bombers. *Trigger* had been prompted by intelligence, correct as it turned out, from a prisoner of war who had reported that the Luftwaffe had been planning for this operation since 1 December 1944;[70] and it was a similar source which led to AA Command's last major operational plan of the closing war. News that Göring had warned his crews to be prepared for a mission from which they should expect no return led to much lively speculation, eventually narrowed to the supposition that this might imply some kind of suicide raid on central London. At the end of March sites for 412 Bofors and a couple of dozen 0.5in Brownings were reconnoitred on rooftops across central London, with the core of the defences to lie in the Whitehall area – the same rooftops on which London's first AA guns had been emplaced 31 years earlier. This was Operation *Deathride*, as Stanmore dubbed it, a title whose macabre literalism well expressed the Luftwaffe's imagined intent. But neither the deployment nor the operation ever happened, and by the end of March AA Command's war was over.

PART III

Afterlife

CHAPTER 12

Monuments to compromise

1945 – 2001

The end of the European war in May 1945 found most of the elements of Britain's home defences already in contraction. The anti-invasion works so hurriedly improvised in the summer of 1940 (and extended over the next two years) had ceased to be maintained in a state of readiness in 1942, coast artillery guns had been mothballed, and even the radar network had been drawn downward and inward to provide cover largely over the south-east. Britain's layout of bombing decoys, too, had been largely decommissioned by 8 May, VE Day. For AA Command the final ceasefire ended a war which had begun with the Couverture of May 1939. The AA guns had been on alert for practically six years.

On the day of the ceasefire, it is true, no more than a skeleton layout remained. The only GDAs with HAA guns still listed as operational on 9 May 1945 were the IAZ, Thames & Medway and – to support the *Diver* Fringe and the possibility of final air-launched V1s breaching the north-east coast – the Humber, Tees, Tyne, Blyth, and a new area at Louth in Lincolnshire (Appendix III). London still had 284 guns ready to fire and the Thames 98, but the remaining active areas fielded few weapons and elsewhere all guns still in place had been decommissioned pending removal to store, or whatever else post-war planning held for them. On 9 May 1945 the only other GDAs with heavies still bolted to holdfasts were Dover, Folkestone, the Solent, Harwich, Yarmouth/Lowestoft, Bristol, Plymouth, Manchester, Leeds, Sheffield, Birmingham, Derby/Nottingham, the Forth, the

Clyde, Scapa and the Shetlands. Practically all of these weapons were 5.25s, 3.7 Mk VIs, or (occasionally) 4.5s which still awaited conversion at the war's end. And by now AA Command had lost many LAA weapons to other claimants, to the point where, in May 1945, just 493 Bofors were in place together with a mixed bag of 394 other types, this total of 887 standing in sharp contrast to the 4589 guns (including 2681 Bofors) which Pile had mustered in June 1944, at the start of the *Diver* campaign. Stocks of rocket projectors had slumped too, if less so, a loss of about one fifth in numbers bringing the total to a little over five and a half thousand in May 1945. Orders to begin clearing rocket sites had already been issued in April.

How did the end of hostilities look in relation to the numbers game which had dominated much of AA Command's war? No useful comparisons can be made for LAA guns since many had already been given up, but as the redundant heavies still remained on AA Command's books we can point to meaningful contrasts with the scales postulated at various dates since the mid 1930s. At the end of the war AA Command held 2663 HAA guns (2149 of them non-operational), meaning that Britain ended the Second World War in Europe with a little over twice the number of heavies proposed in the Ideal Scheme of February 1937, but only about 70 per cent of the 3744 required by the review of August 1940. But, allied to their fire control instruments and other ancillaries, the guns it did have were much better than either of those studies could have anticipated. The May 1945 figure included more than half the intended total of 5.25s – 114 were in place – and also reflected the near completion of the 3.7in Mk VI conversions; 343 guns had been done, leaving just 63 still to come. For these reasons direct comparisons are difficult, but it may be reasonable to suggest that, had all the non-operational weapons suddenly been re-commissioned, the effective HAA strength of AA Command in May 1945 would have been about equal to that judged necessary as the Battle of Britain neared its height almost five years before.

On 19 May 1945 the 238th edition of AA Command's weekly *Intelligence Review* gave the remaining gunners a summary of their achievement – or that part of it which could be quantified – since the first AA shots of this war had been fired in anger on 16

October 1939 over the Forth.[1] This amounted to 833 enemy aircraft destroyed (Category I), 237 'probables' (Category II) and 422 damaged (Category III). The guns had additionally downed 1972 flying bombs, the greater proportion of them before the target had made landfall.[2] It was a notable achievement, though the figures were given perspective by a further summary, appearing in the very last weekly edition of the *Review*, on 30 June, which set the domestic totals against those reported from other theatres. In the period from the start of the war to 18 June 1940, British troops operating in northern Europe had destroyed 351 enemy aircraft, while in the eleven months from D-Day to the end of the European war Allied forces on the Continent had downed as many as $2663^{1}/_{2}$ (Category I) with their AA guns, of which $522^{1}/_{2}$ fell in the British Sector and 2141 in the American. In addition, AA guns on the Continent had destroyed 2356 of the flying bombs which the Germans had been targeting on Belgium.[3] Those figures, on the face of it, tend to show AA Command's performance in a rather poor light – especially the contrast between 833 Category I victims over Britain in the whole of the war and $2663^{1}/_{2}$ on the Continent since D-Day. But the figures, of course, must be set against the availability of targets in the two theatres, and the steadily improving technical capability of AA gunnery as a whole between the Battle of Britain and the Blitz (when by far the greater proportion of hostile aircraft visited Britain) and the last year of war, when gunners on the Continent had improved weapons and far better fire-control instruments than those available domestically during 1940–41. Nor should we forget that many of the gunners serving on the Continent had actually been trained by AA Command – this is where many of Pile's better men had gone – and that it was the domestic experience in the days when Britain stood alone which fostered many of the improvements in gunnery and equipment which could be exploited in the months following the Normandy landings. To those we should of course add other, familiar considerations in reaching a balanced assessment of AA Command's war: the power of gunnery to deter, to disrupt aim, to sustain civilian morale, to alert day fighters to the whereabouts of enemy formations, and so on. The real measure of AA Command's performance is unquantifiable, like so much else in war and in life, but the hit-rate achieved during the climax of the flying-bomb campaign should be enough to satisfy the most assiduous devotee of the statistical view.

Much of this was to the credit of one man. General Sir Frederick Pile retired from AA Command less than three weeks before victory in Europe, on 15 April 1945, to claim distinction as the war's longest-serving senior commander in a single role. In that period Pile had watched four chiefs come and go at Fighter Command – Dowding, Sholto Douglas, Leigh-Mallory, Hill – and his successor, General Sir W Wyndham Green, would soon work with another, in the person of Air Marshal Sir James Robb, who replaced Roderic Hill a month after Pile's departure. Pile's fixedness against this shifting population testifies to Churchill's abiding faith in his AA commander, who by the end of the war was widely admired as one of the most effective leaders in the British army. It had not always been thus, of course – Pile's critics in the Blitz, particularly, were cruelly pointed – and it is a question for students of generalship how much AA Command's achievements over five and a half years of war owed to one man remaining at the helm throughout. Certainly, the problems which Pile encountered, Pile solved, allowing this one mind to accumulate a fund of expertise which would have been lost if, as so often in like cases, it had been shunted elsewhere at a critical point. Pile the progressive often looked to outside experts for his answers – Haslett, Blackett, Bartlett – and usually found them, fostering as he did so a reputation for humility and a willingness to take advice. He bequeathed his successor a fit, technically-advanced organisation with a record of doing remarkable things with scant resources, albeit one much attentuated since the early years of war. Pile left AA Command with many friends. They were sorry to see him go.

Pile's final duty to his old command was to write a dispatch. At some time in 1945 (evidently) he duly put a few dozen pages of foolscap on the files, omitting little of importance except the date of compilation. But Pile's official *Dispatch* was only one of two accounts which he made available in the first years of peace. The second was his book, *Ack-Ack*, published by Harrap at the end of 1949, and naturally destined to become a fixture in bibliographies of the Home Front in the Second World War. Readers welcomed

Ack-Ack as the first authoritative account of the AA war since *Roof over Britain* in 1943, and as a lively and good-natured tale in itself. Though his war had been more than usually frustrating, Pile did not grumble. One of the few complaints which he aired in his pages was made on behalf of his men, to whom official parsimony had denied the right to wear the 1939–43 campaign star; instead 'AA Command was allowed to share with any civilian who had endured three months of fire-watching the Defence Medal with its "two black stripes representing the black-out".[4] In an ironic way this privation was itself symbolic of AA Command's war.

In the fifty years or so since *Ack-Ack* reached its public access to AA Command's war has also opened through its official documents, a huge collection of which was released for public inspection in the early 1970s. And today, studying those papers, and especially the War Diaries of AA Command's General Staff branch, the researcher is often seized with a curious sense of *déjà vu*. Leafing through the flimsy carbon copies of correspondence, time and again phrases, passages and sometimes whole pages assert an odd familiarity: one has read this somewhere before. But where? The answer tells us much about Pile's working methods in completing his book, and obliquely about Pile himself, since careful comparison reveals that sections of *Ack-Ack*'s narrative are in fact no less than direct transcripts of AA Command papers, rather skilfully assimilated into the text of the book, sometimes with a switch in tense, or light editing. Pile's account of the allocation of HAA to Scapa in autumn 1939, for example, is a more or less faithful replica of the letter he wrote on that subject to the War Office on 10 November 1939, phrases like 'the whole of Derby was defended by no more than 22 guns' departing from the original only in the substitution of 'was' for 'is'.[5] Similarly, his narratives of the Blitz and the Fringe Target campaigns draw heavily, often to the point of transcription, on historical appreciations produced by staff at Stanmore in the latter years of the war. Why does this matter? For two reasons, perhaps. First it emphasises the authority of Pile's account in *Ack-Ack*: there is more solid material than memory here. Secondly it illustrates Sir Frederick's instinct for economy of effort, a skill he brought to generalship as much as writing.

By the late 1940s Pile had more important things to do than write history. He was 61 when he left the army, a greater age then than now, but he still had two careers ahead, and a third marriage. The first career, as director-general of housing in the Ministry of Works, was brief and seems to have interested him less than the opportunities of industry. Pile became a director of the Cementation company in 1945, rising to chairman in 1961, while serving on numerous admirable committees and enjoying the many honours due to a retired officer of distinction. Pile's was a long life. He outlived most of his generation of air defence activists, men who had served on the Reorientation Committee of the '30s – Dowding, Brooke-Popham, Joubert de la Ferté – to die two months after his ninety-second birthday on 14 November 1976.

By then the world of air defence had changed almost beyond recognition. Like Rawlinson and Ashmore before him, Pile concluded his memoir by looking ahead; but unlike them he believed stoutly that his war had seen the end of the fighter aircraft. Fighters, argued Pile, had been defeated by the V-weapons, and would be outpaced by the new generation of supersonic bombers which the new enemy – the Soviet Union – would be capable of sending over Britain. In this Pile was obviously wrong. Though fighters of the late 1940s and early '50s could achieve supersonic speeds only through a rather hair-raising dive, by 1955 the first prototype Lightning aircraft could attain them routinely and in 1958 the developed version became the first British aircraft to reach Mach II – twice the speed of sound.[6] Pile was hardly alone in failing to foresee the Lightning, however, and in other respects his prognosis for the future of air defence was all too accurate. In particular he pointed to the vastly increased lethality of the manned bomber carrying atomic weapons. 'In this last war,' he wrote, 'it did not matter very much if a few bombers got through because their power of destruction was limited. The power of destruction of the bomber of the future,' on the other hand, 'does not appear to be limited, and it is therefore of the greatest importance that none are allowed to come through.'[7] Added to that was the threat from unmanned air vehicles, successors to the V-weapons of the late war, which would entirely defeat the fighter, as Pile believed the V1 had already proved. So in a war to come the stakes would be astronomically higher: the need now was for total air defence, less a roof over Britain than a hardened bunker. But if fighters could not provide it, argued Pile, neither would conventional guns. Air defence of the future must instead rely on the 'controlled projectile' – the rocket-propelled, radar-guided missile, whose development was already under way as his book was completed. Pile's picture of a future air war over Britain showed radar-guided missiles streaking toward supersonic bombers and unmanned rockets, carrying the 'robot' dimension of Operation *Diver* literally and metaphorically to new heights.

Pile's was very far from being the only voice speaking on the future of air defence in the years following the Second World War. In the late 1940s the services' trade papers carried much in the same vein, continuing the themes first defined by Capper and his fellows before the Great War. One question which occupied minds in 1946–47 was the place of anti-aircraft defence within the structure of Britain's armed forces – whether artillery or its successor should remain an army responsibility, or perhaps be transferred to the RAF. Another pressing concern in the climate of post-war retrenchment and worsening east-west relations was the state of readiness in which the AA defences should be maintained, a question with familiar implications for the roles of regular troops and reservists. So some themes, it seemed, were eternal; many arguments over air defence in the late 1940s were strikingly similar to those of a quarter of a century before.

In the decade following the Second World War many of the ideas floated publicly by Pile and others gradually hardened into reality. The fighter survived, but in the mid 1950s and despite continuing technical development the HAA gun in its home defence role was indeed supplanted by the guided missile, and at that point air defence did become exclusively an RAF responsibility. AA Command itself was disbanded in 1955. The decade separating that event from the end of the Second World War is a separate episode in the history of Britain's defence infrastructure, and one to be explored elsewhere;[8] but since our final interest here lies in what has become of England's AA gunsites since 1945, the pattern of events in the late 1940s and early '50s forms a necessary preliminary.

AA Command did not immediately dispose of its enormous range of property holdings at the end of the war. Orders issued even before the end of hostilities required all Z battery sites to be cleared (though a few did escape) while many of the residue of LAA positions were also given up. But the sites of HAA batteries were, in general, retained pending decisions over Britain's postwar air defence layout. In the interim many domestic camps were pressed into service in secondary uses, some as holding points for troops awaiting discharge, others as makeshift colonies for homeless civilians, repatriated servicemen and a miscellaneous band of dispossessed individuals – 'squatters' – desperate for accommodation in a Britain where, for many, privation became acute in the aftermath of war. At the same time the unfinished 5.25in programme was allowed to continue, though not at any great pace; as we have seen, by November 1945 some 31 sites had been established, 28 of which were operational and the remaining three (two at Dover, one at Plymouth) remained under construction. Many years would pass before this huge project was complete.

With the war won the governing principle of Britain's new peacetime AA layout was decided within weeks.[9] This was the 'Nucleus Force': a thin covering of guns, using a proportion of sites in all the major GDAs, designed for speedy occupation and rapid reinforcement in the event of another war. The basic plan for the Nucleus Force called for HAA gunsites to be recast in two categories, comprising battery headquarters (BHQ) sites where guns would be permanently mounted, and 'off' sites, whose ordnance and equipment would be kept in store.[10] Selecting Nucleus sites from the huge number potentially available took time, and even by the autumn of 1945 the land requirements of post-war reconstruction were coming into conflict with those of defence in many instances – a clash of interest which equally hampered the selection of sites for the balance of 5.25in batteries.[11] By November 1945, however, the basic pattern of the Nucleus scheme was clear, if not yet definitively so.[12] In all, 210 sites were listed – half BHQs, half 'off' sites – in 25 GDAs throughout England, Scotland and Wales. At 36 sites London's layout was the largest overall, and included the greatest proportion of wartime positions. Elsewhere, however, the Nucleus scheme was very much what the name implied, a typical GDA holding six to twelve sites picked from a wartime layout of about three times the size. Sites for 5.25in weapons were, of course, always BHQs, since these guns could hardly be kept in store, while the remaining BHQs and the 'off' sites were provided with a mixture of 3.7in Mk IIc and Mk VI weapons (the former 4.5s), along with GL Mk IIs and SCR 584 radars, the guns being deployed in batteries of four, eight, or (exclusively for the Mk IIcs) in groups of six.

Matters stood on this basis until the summer of 1946, when a new air defence plan issued by the Chiefs of Staff defined the 'Full Scale' AA component required in an emergency – that is the second tier to be put in place above the basic 'Nucleus'. This added considerably to the quota of sites required, and while AA groups in the interim had been authorised to release non-Nucleus sites where alternatives could be found,[13] care had been taken to maintain the numbers, so that many remained to be brought within the new classification scheme which appeared in the autumn of 1946.[14] This new set of categories retained the former division between Nucleus BHQ Gun Positions and 'off' sites – now more grandly known as Nucleus Mobilisation Gun Positions – but added two more, in 'Full Scale' Gun Positions with, and without, formally built concrete emplacements.[15] In order to ensure that Britain fielded the requisite number of AA sites for the defence plans of the late 1940s, AA Command staff embarked upon extensive reconnaissance to assess which of its remaining wartime positions fitted into which category, and to ensure that those which would remain were safeguarded from encroachment by building.

This took an immense amount of time and in many cases proved futile. Fully two years later, in autumn 1948, the War Office were still attempting to secure approval for something between 600 and 700 individual sites.[16] The delay came about through deepening competition between the needs of the War Office and those of housing – the problem of 1938–39 in a much enlarged form – which in the event meant that very many wartime sites did have to be relinquished and others found. The result was that the late 1940s saw the local geography of Britain's (still partly abstract) AA defences enter a period of gradual change, as old sites were given up and new positions formally 'safeguarded' under the Town and Country Planning Acts. This work continued into the early 1950s, with the result that many GDAs were transformed by 1952–53, their lists of gun positions bearing only a vague resemblance to wartime predecessors thanks to a process whose dominant characteristic was the outward migration of gunsites to match relentless suburban sprawl.[17] Some of these sites, it appears, were newly built in a programme whose details are not yet fully understood,[18] though its context may have been the *Igloo* plan, a scheme defined in 1950 at the onset of the Korean War, which reportedly marshalled 78 gunsites, 24 of them with weapons held in reserve and the rest manned by Territorials on a 36-hour call out. But whatever the reason for the limited building of the late 1940s or early 1950s, AA Command lost more bricks and mortar in these years than it gained.

And by the end of the Korean War in 1953 AA Command's days were numbered. In this year the Air Ministry embarked upon their first studies of the deployment patterns for surface-to-air guided weapons (SAGWs), the technology which Pile had correctly predicted would supplant the AA gun. British research on these devices had begun as early as 1944, as Pile of course well knew, and by the early 1950s had settled into experiments on two related systems, known as *Red Shoes* and *Red Duster*. Under the terms of a 1953 defence review *Red Duster* was transferred from the army to the RAF as the basis for a domestic air defence system, which under this new management became the radar-guided missile known as Bloodhound.

Early plans for Bloodhound had seen it as a straightforward successor to the HAA gun in conventional GDAs; indeed the weapon's mounting was designed for anchoring to a common holdfast as the 3.7in and 4.5in (as the inset to Fig 6, page 145) to allow missiles to replace artillery on the same sites. But in November 1953, three months after the Soviet Union had detonated its first hydrogen bomb, the Air Staff argued that the 'point defence' principle of guarding separate GDAs was simply obsolete in the face of atomic or nuclear weapons. Just as Pile had done in 1949, the CAS pointed out that future defence must be total, thanks to the catastrophic consequences of just one bomber getting through; the whole of the UK, not simply Birmingham or London or Portsmouth, was now the 'vulnerable area'.[19] The solution to this most critical problem was a linear coastal layout of Bloodhounds poised to intercept the Soviet bombers before they made landfall, with fighters – Javelins and Hunters by the mid 1950s – acting as forward interceptors. These ideas on the Bloodhound layout had something in common with the outer artillery zone of the mid 1930s, but owed more to the coastal *Diver* deployments of 1944–45.

For a variety of reasons, though, it didn't quite happen like that. Detailed planning on a coastal layout of Bloodhound sites began in 1955 and the first, experimental, station was opened early in 1957 at RAF North Coates near the southern bank of the Humber estuary – the North Coates Fittes of 6 Brigade's home defence airfield layout of 1917. But 1958 brought a change of plan, the coastal layout was scrapped, and the Bloodhounds were pulled back to provide point defence for the Bomber Command stations serving the nuclear deterrent: the V-force bases and Thor missile sites in East Anglia, Lincolnshire and Yorkshire. So the Bloodhound squadrons were formed and deployed in 1959–60 not to protect the cities, but instead to ensure that in the event of a nuclear war the British bomber fleet would survive to strike back. But whether the Bloodhounds would lie on the coast, or on inland sites dotted around the eastern counties, from the middle 1950s it was clear that no need remained for gun or missile positions in the hinterlands of cities. It was in that climate that AA Command was finally disbanded in the spring of 1955, and its remaining sites given up.

To advance nearly fifty years from that point is to admit a new perspective on the surviving remains of Britain's wartime AA gunsites. In the late 1940s and early '50s AA Command met immense difficulties, as we have seen, in safeguarding its sites against the claims of post-war housing, which often prevailed and led to many positions being given up, razed and overbuilt. In the late '50s, with the AA defence of cities a thing of the past, it would be surprising indeed to find that anyone argued for a few redundant gunsites to be preserved for posterity. Some service-men and women in the years following the war did feel a nostalgia, never easy to articulate, towards the places where they and their comrades had lived and worked, fought and occasionally died, though it is equally true that many were pleased to see the back of their hutted camps, their guns and instruments, and with them the war which had rudely interrupted their lives. It is a good thing when a nation finds itself able to demolish its gunsites in favour of houses, schools and hospitals. To suggest now that a proportion of AA Command's surviving sites should be preserved as historical monuments is not to imply that anyone should have anticipated this impulse in the 1940s or '50s.

But today that impulse is strong, and growing, and for organisations such as English Heritage it is an article of policy. The rationale for doing so is clear; but before delineating the significance of anti-aircraft batteries as historical sites, we must address the practical issues. What does remain of AA Command's huge volume of pre-war and wartime gunsite fabric? Where is it, and in what condition does it survive?

To answer those questions English Heritage's Monuments Protection Programme has adopted a systematic method, working from AA Command's primary records of site positions, outward to the evidence of survival to be gleaned from maps, aerial photographs and ultimately the fabric to be discovered on the ground. As the preface to this book explains, the task of recovering information on locations was large and time-consuming: site positions are recorded by grid references on an obsolete system, which need to be gathered from a range of sources before 'conversion' to references which will work with modern maps and other research aids, such as the indices to aerial photograph collections. (Methods are explained further in the preamble to Appendix IV.) At an early stage it was decided that a limit must be placed on the amount of information which would be gathered for sites associated with anti-aircraft defence. While as many HAA and LAA positions as possible were to be traced – and certainly all of the permanent sites in the main GDAs – only 'sample' lists would be compiled for Z batteries and searchlight sites, while the survival of the latter would not subsequently be assessed through the next stage of the evaluation programme. It is important to stress, however, that primary sources listing the positions of every Z battery and searchlight site in Britain do survive. This information lies in the War Diaries of AA Command's rocket and searchlight units, safely deposited in the Public Record Office for anyone with the time and inclination to retrieve it and convert the many thousands, perhaps tens of thousands, of grid references involved.

Our work on HAA and LAA positions was complete by early 1996, likewise the comparable recovery and processing work for AA sites built for the *Diver* campaign, whose evaluation forms a separate element of the project (likewise the dissemination of its results).[20] The resulting gazetteer for England alone amounted to 981 HAA and 1238 LAA sites (excluding the *Diver* positions), this total including a small proportion of HAA batteries which may have undergone minor shifts of position while retaining their original site codes. The HAA positions – though not the LAA[21] – together with a handful of additional English sites traced subsequently, appear in the gazetteer which forms Appendix IV to this volume, together with those in the remainder of the United Kingdom recovered in a companion project sponsored by Cadw, the Royal Commission on the Ancient and Historical Monuments of Scotland, and DoE Northern Ireland.[22] The Welsh, Scottish and Northern Irish sites were not, however, included in the survival assessment element of the work, which given its sponsorship by English Heritage was naturally limited to England. Follow-on work for sites in the remainder of the UK is being undertaken by the relevant agencies, who will have their own arrangements for the dissemination of results.

Armed with the gazetteer of site locations, the next step was to ascertain as far as possible which had survived. English Heritage could not claim to be the first to address this issue, since by the mid 1990s several local surveys of Second World War fortifications including AA sites had been undertaken or were actively in progress – in some cases making use of the grid references circulated from the first stage of our own project – yielding results which promised well for the larger, national assessment in prospect.[23] That work was undertaken by Michael Anderton at

Plate 27 Masked survivors. HAA battery at Preston (H4 in the Humber GDA) seen in January 1995. At this site the two sets of emplacements, one for the original 3.7in or 4.5in statics and the other (to the rear) for 5.25in weapons, appear to remain intact beneath an infill of soil.

the National Monuments Record at Swindon, who used a two-stage methodology aimed at identifying where substantial remains could be found: sites were first investigated through large-scale mapping, from which those appearing to show features of interest were isolated for further scrutiny using aerial photographs held in the NMR's collection.[24] As in all such exercises, these methods had their limitations. A few sites could not be examined for want of appropriate aerial cover, while we cannot be sure exactly how many of the HAA sites investigated were originally fully-built with solid command posts and emplacements as 'permanent' batteries (though it would be the

Plate 28 Monument to the Blitz. Slade's Green (ZS1 in the London IAZ) with its gunpark structures surviving largely intact in June 1994. Comparison with Plate 4 shows that the site's access road has been smothered by vegetation and its domestic camp cleared, but the pre-war pattern emplacements and command post survive.

majority) and how many reached only temporary form – factors which would be likely to influence both their survival, and the recognition of that survival. Equally, assessment of surviving wartime fabric could be complicated by post-war additions, even if few sites do seem to have been affected in this way. But research of this type always involves an element of compromise, especially in its scope; and as grid references for England obtained in the original documentary research represented a near-comprehensive population of the original HAA sites and a very large sample of the LAA, the proportion which could be investigated in the follow-on work was more than enough to assess the general level of survival and identify a representative set of examples.

How many AA batteries do survive? The answer depends partly upon how we define 'survival', but of the HAA positions examined, ten were found to have their original structures and layout and most of their camp buildings present, and a further 48 the majority of their features in place – these lying respectively within Classes 1 and 2 of the five-point scale used in classifying the intactness of the site. At the same time no fewer than 828 HAA positions – more than four in every five – revealed no structural evidence discoverable by large-scale map or aerial camera. Some of those sites, no doubt, will retain odd features – a hut base here, a stretch of roadway here – but however valuable those things might be if they were discovered in the excavation of a Roman fort, they hold little historical interest on twentieth-century sites. Some of these positions, no doubt, were originally occupied solely by mobile guns and for this reason would be less likely to present us with substantial remains, but closer study of the land-uses now occupying their positions reveals a useful confirmation of the trends independently documented in the late 1940s and early '50s. More than 40 per cent of the positions lost entirely have been smothered by redevelopment (only slightly fewer than those lost to agriculture, the other major agency of destruction). That statistic reflects the local authorities' post-war housing schemes, which led to the exchanges of established sites for 'safeguarded' fields in the last six or seven years of AA Command's existence.

The 58 sites admitted to Classes 1 and 2 qualify for that designation on the strength of the most up-to-date map and aerial photographic cover available, which in some cases reaches back a decade or more. Happily, though, field visits have since confirmed that the majority remain in more or less the condition in which they were recorded, and it is largely from this group that selections for preservation, for sites within England, will be made. It is a happy chance, too, that most of the major GDAs are represented: the London IAZ, Thames & Medway, Plymouth, Portland, Harwich, Blyth, Leeds, Sheffield, the Mersey, Nottingham and Derby, Birmingham, Bristol, Swindon, Southampton, Portsmouth, the Humber, Yarmouth/Lowestoft, Newhaven and Dover as well as

Plate 29 A few HAA positions made use of earlier fortifications, in part because they could exploit pre-existing War Office estate. Fort Borstal thus became TS7 in the Thames & Medway GDA, and as seen in October 1996 represents a multi-period defence site.

Grantham, Corby, Scunthorpe and the airfield at Predannack. A good range of structural variation is also evident, 5.25in sites appearing in a representative proportion with 3.7s and 4.5s. Occasionally HAA positions represent merely the latest phase in works with a long defensive history, such as Fort Borstal in the Thames & Medway GDA (Plate 29), where the emplacements ride the bastions of a nineteenth-century fort.

Remains of LAA sites are much scarcer than their heavy counterparts. Of nearly 900 examined by the same methods as many as 92 per cent were found to leave no trace and just three sites could safely be brought within the higher survival classes which admitted 58 HAA positions – and even these are subject to review by field visit. A further 42 sites showed evidence of partial remains, though part of an LAA battery seldom amounts to very much. These figures omit more than 200 positions associated with airfields, the subject of a separate assessment,[25] though the level of attrition among these, too, seems to be high. In short then, while a reasonable proportion of HAA batteries survives in a form which can merit preservation, their LAA counterparts are rare indeed.

So, finally, why should we preserve these sites at all?

It is salutary to reflect that in two or three hundred years' time that question will seem strange. By 2200 or 2300, with the Second World War lying several centuries in the past, the remains of its fortifications will appear to contemporaries just as those of the English Civil War do to us today: intriguing monuments of a vanished age, assets to knowledge and education, to be valued for as long as people do value such things. To accept that point is to accept equally the case for preservation today, for of one thing we can be certain: if these sites are allowed to disappear in the next few decades, none will be there in 300 years' time. Historic buildings do not renew themselves, as threatened landscapes sometimes can; and unlike endangered species they have never been known to breed. A long-term view is necessary, far longer indeed than most of us are apt to take in the decisions which affect our everyday lives.

In a more immediate sense, however, the national significance of AA batteries as historical sites rests upon many factors. First, and in general, they are monuments to the achievement of Anti-Aircraft Command, the only branch of the British army at home to be continually in action over five and a half years of war (and at readiness for rather longer). They represent one of the few obvious and tangible facets of Britain's wartime air defence system – airfields, radar sites and decoys are others, and all of these are now subject to similar preservation initiatives – and moreover stand testimony to a specifically twentieth-century form of warfare. Should Britain come under air attack again, we can be confident at least that heavy anti-aircraft batteries and equipment of the type used in 1939–45 will play no part in the nation's defence. So these sites – these few dozen sites from an original population of hundreds – are memorials to a legion of men and women, and monuments to military tactics and technology at a snapshot in time.

But beyond these rather general points the national significance of AA batteries rests also upon three more specific facets of their collective history. The first is their role in the development of radar. From autumn 1939 the HAA batteries, dotted around the suburbs, spread among the fields and farms of rural Britain, were the testing ground for one of the most advanced technologies existing anywhere in the world. Through their successive marks of GL set, Britain's AA gunners, aided by AA Command's scientific staff, played their part in pushing radar technology forward through experience and the supply of endless user-derived data. Every AA site with a radar was a laboratory in the first half of the war, a war in which radar itself was brought to the state of accuracy and reliability which make air travel in its modern form possible, and much else besides.

The second facet is the unique place of these sites in the history of women and warfare. If not quite combatants on the Soviet model, the ATS women who served with AA Command were the first to operate equipment connected with a lethal process, and in this respect were pioneers of a movement which in recent decades has led to women assuming a far greater share of combat responsibilities in the British armed forces. The woman who, today, goes to sea in a warship or flies a jet aircraft is heir to the tradition begun by Pile's 'gunner girls'. The HAA sites where these women served – and particularly the concrete command posts where they worked – are in their small way monuments to one of feminism's more obvious, if contentious, triumphs.

Plate 30 Dereliction. An HAA command post surviving today.

The third consideration lending significance to our surviving
AA batteries is more subtle. Though AA Command used a
proportion of temporary gunsites for its mobile HAA weapons
during the war, all of the batteries surviving today in the standard
GDAs (*Diver* sites aside) were permanent sites, fully built with
concrete structures. The dominance of these sites over their
temporary counterparts in the survival stakes is explained by
several factors: their larger numbers during the war, their
selection for retention afterwards, and their greater inherent
durability. In contemplating the survival of these sites, however,
we should also recall that until late 1937 their numbers were
expected to be tiny: 4.5in weapons would need them, but not
3.7s, which were expected to be mobile. What changed in 1937, of
course, was the acceptance of a proportion of 3.7s on static
mountings, a decision which began a trend leading to the
complete dominance of the static 3.7in over the mobile by the
later war years. That is the sole reason why so many permanent
gunsites were built, and hence existed to survive today. And why
was that decision taken? Why was a defensive arm originally
conceived as mobile eventually to become so wedded to
concrete? The answer was urgency. The 3.7in static mounting
was accepted because it was cheap, and the guns could be
supplied more quickly. And the reason, in turn, why that was
necessary was the neglect of anti-aircraft artillery defence
throughout the 1920s and for much of the 1930s, when the
defence budget went to the air force to spend on bombers. So
HAA sites survive today in the numbers that they do because
they were permanently built for static guns; and the underlying
reason for *that* was the inter-war defence doctrine, only overturned in 1938, which put the bomber first.

Is there a single, overarching theme, then, to which these sites
stand as monuments? The answer is suggested in the title of this
chapter. Our surviving HAA sites are ultimately monuments to
compromise: compromise in the type of gun accepted (and with
it the tactics which AA gunnery would follow) which in turn led
to the proliferation of static gunsites, creating the examples which
survive today. The compromise was necessary from 1938
onwards because people believed for so long in the bomber. But
the bomber did not always get through, as AA Command proved;

and as well as standing testimony to the active air defences which stopped it, in the form they take our AA gunsites also reflect the consequences of the years in which stopping it was believed to be impossible.

Notes

List of abbreviations used in Notes

AA	Anti-aircraft
AA Cmd	Anti-Aircraft Command
AA (S)	Anti-Aircraft Shadow Sub-Committee
ADF TA	Air Defence Formations, Territorial Army
ADGB	Air Defence of Great Britain
AM	Air Ministry
Ann	Annex
AOC-in-C	Air Officer Commanding-in-Chief
AORG	Army Operational Research Group
App	Appendix
Bde	Brigade
Bty	Battery
CAS	Chief of the Air Staff
CID	Committee of Imperial Defence
C-in-C	Commander-in-Chief
Cmd	Command
COS	Chiefs of Staff
CRE	Commander Royal Engineers
DC(S)	Defence Committee (Supply)
DCIGS	Deputy Chief of the Imperial General Staff
DCOS	Deputy Chiefs of Staff
DFW	Directorate of Fortifications and Works
DG TA	Director General, Territorial Army
Det Int Rep	Detailed intelligence report
Div	Division
DMO	Director(ate) of Military Operations
DMOI	Director(ate) of Military Operations and Intelligence
DNB	*Dictionary of National Biography*
DOI	Director(ate) of Intelligence
DW	Director(ate) of Works
ECD	Eastern Coastal District
E Cmd	Eastern Command
FW1(b)	Fortifications and Works Branch 1(b)

G [or GS]	General Staff
G (Int)	General Staff (Intelligence)
GHQ	General Headquarters
GOC	General Officer Commanding
Gp	Group
HAA	Heavy anti-aircraft
HDC	Home Defence Committee
Int Rep	Intelligence Report
Int Sum	Intelligence Summary
ITW	Initial Training Wing
JIC	Joint Intelligence Committee
LAA	Light anti-aircraft
LADA	London Air Defence Area
MO4	Military Operations Branch 4
MoHS	Ministry of Home Security
MoI	Ministry of Information
MoWB	Ministry of Works and Buildings
MOWP	Ministry of Works and Planning
N Cmd	Northern Command
OC	Officer commanding
Op	Operation
ORB	Operations Record Book
Regt	Regiment
RN	Royal Navy
RNVR	Royal Naval Volunteer Reserve
Scot Cmd	Scottish Command
SL	Searchlight
Tp	Troop
TPM	Teleprint message
WO	War Office

Preface

1. See Dobinson 2000, the inaugural volume in the *Monuments of War* series.
2. Until recently it was sometimes claimed otherwise, but wrongly so; on the disposal pattern of army and War Office sources among public records see Roper 1998, 284–91.
3. See further Appendix IV.
4. For an introduction to the English Heritage work see Darvill *et al* 1987, English Heritage 2000.
5. Pile 1949.
6. Historical narratives compiled under official auspices and deposited at the Public Record Office included a series under the general title *HQ AA Command: ADGB, Survey and History of*, at WO 199/2973–2978, a study of London's defences at WO 199/2979c, a narrative of the Fringe Target attacks of 1942–43 filed in WO 166/14235, War Diary AA Cmd G, AA Cmd to Gps, AAC/40512/G/WR, 19 Mar 1944, and a volume compiled by the Historical Section of the Cabinet Office at CAB 44/48. Specialist histories including much AA material compiled by the C3 Branch of the Permanent Under-Secretary's Department at the War Office are WO 277/3, *Army Radar* and WO 277/29, *Works Services and Engineer Stores*.

7.   Hogg 1978; Routledge 1994, and Routledge's contribution to Hughes 1992.
8.   See Dady 1986; Brewer Kerr 1990; Campbell 1993; Robinson 1996; DeGroot 1997A ; *ibid* 1997B.
9.   Churchill 1949, 300.
10.   The original research for the English sites and those in Wales, Scotland and Northern Ireland was commissioned by the bodies concerned through the Council for British Archaeology.

Chapter 1

1   Capper 1910.
2.   CAB 16/7, *Report and Proceedings of a Sub-Committee of the Committee of Imperial Defence on Aerial Navigation*, 29 Jan 1909; also CAB 4/3, CID 106–B, *Aerial Navigation* [. . .], 28 Jan 1909; for a searching analysis of the committee's work see Gollin 1984, 392–432.
3.   CAB 4/3, CID 106–B, *Aerial Navigation* [. . .], 28 Jan 1909.
4.   Paris 1992, 15–64.
5.   Capper 1908, 288–90.
6.   Capper 1910, 440.
7.   Capper 1910, 443.
8.   Hawkins 1910, 254.
9.   Capper 1910, 443.
10.   For contributions and a range of contemporary views see generally Stone 1909; *ibid* 1910; Baden-Powell 1910; Hawkins 1910; *ibid* 1913; Sargeaunt 1910; Burke 1911; Reid 1911; Belcher 1913; Cock 1915; Phillips 1915.
11.   Hogg 1978, 12.
12.   Hogg 1978, 13.
13.   Stone 1910.
14.   Stone 1910, 408–9.
15.   Stone 1945, 98.
16.   Capper 1910, 442.
17.   Eg Baden-Powell 1910, 574; Hawkins 1913, 127; Morgan 1913, 47.
18.   AIR 1/654/17/122/491, Report of a meeting held on 4th Jan 1910 to discuss recent progress made by Foreign Governments in aerial navigation, and any means that may be needed to guard against overhead attack, Naval Intelligence Department, 4 Jan 1910.
19.   AIR 1/654/17/122/491, WO to Admiralty, 12/45 (MT1), 29 Mar 1910.
20.   Jones 1931, 71.
21.   ADM 1/8269/55, Letter to E Cmd, Eastern/276 (MT1), 13 Dec 1912.
22.   ADM 1/8269/55, Letter to E Cmd, Eastern/276 (MT1), 13 Dec 1912.
23.   ADM 1/8369/55, OC ECD to C-in-C Nore, 13 Jan 1913.
24.   Jones 1931, 72.
25.   ADM 1/8369/55, Dawson to Oakley, 3 Jan 1913.
26.   ADM 1/8369/55, DW minute, 25 Feb 1913.
27.   Hogg 1978, 21.
28.   WO 33/683, *Approved Armaments and AA Guns*, 1 Apr 1914, p 32.
29.   See Paris 1992, 95–6.
30.   Jones 1931, 69–70.
31.   *Daily Mail* 11 Sep 1913, quoted in Jackson 1914, 712.
32.   Jackson 1914, 712–3.
33.   See Jones 1931, 107–8, 127.

34.   Jones 1931, 81.
35.   Hogg 1978, 31.
36.   ADM 1/8398/372, *Report on the Subject of the Defence of London Against Aerial Attack*, Admiralty Air Department, 16 Oct 1914, p 2.
37.   See generally Cole & Cheesman 1984.
38.   ADM 1/8398/372, *Report on the Subject of the Defence of London* [. . .], 16 Oct 1914, p 3.
39.   AIR 1/2655, *Report on the work of the Anti-Aircraft Section of the Air Department*, 20 Apr 1915, p 1.
40.   AIR 1/648/17/122/385, RNVR AA Corps, Diaries and Notes compiled by Captain L S Stansfeld, RN, May 1919, p 1.
41.   Ashmore 1929, 4.
42.   AIR 1/648/17/122/385, RNVR AA Corps, Diaries and Notes [. . .], May 1919, p 2; AIR 1/2655, *Report on the work of the Anti-Aircraft Section* [. . .], 20 Apr 1915, p 3.
43.   AIR 1/648/17/122/385, RNVR AA Corps, Diaries and Notes [. . .], May 1919, p 2.
44.   Cole & Cheesman 1984, 448–9.
45.   Jones 1931, 90–1; Cole & Cheesman 1984, 25.
46.   Hogg 1978, 33.
47.   AIR 1/2655, *Report on the work of the Anti-Aircraft Section* [. . .], 20 Apr 1915, p 4.
48.   See Curtois 1940; Stone 1945, 99–101.
49.   AIR 1/648/17/122/385, RNVR AA Corps, Diaries and Notes [. . .], May 1919, p 105.
50.   AIR 1/648/17/122/385, RNVR AA Corps, Diaries and Notes [. . .], May 1919, pp 105, 109.
51.   AIR 1/648/17/122/385, RNVR AA Corps, Diaries and Notes [. . .], May 1919, p 107.
52.   Hogg 1978, 34.
53.   AIR 1/2655, *Report on the work of the Anti-Aircraft Section* [. . .], 20 Apr 1915, App I, p 6.
54.   Hogg 1978, 34.
55.   AIR 1/2655, *Report on the work of the Anti-Aircraft Section* [. . .], 20 Apr 1915, App III, p 8; Jones 1931, 93.
56.   AIR 1/2655, *Report on the work of the Anti-Aircraft Section* [. . .], 20 Apr 1915, p 4.
57.   Ashmore 1929, 5.
58.   Ashmore 1929, 4–5.
59.   Jones 1931, 100.
60.   Cole & Cheesman 1984, 56–9.
61.   Ashmore 1929, 10–11.
62.   Ashmore 1929, 156.
63.   Rawlinson 1923.
64.   Rawlinson 1923, 10–19.
65.   Hogg 1978, 38.
66.   Specifically at Sutton's Farm (later known as Hornchurch), Hainault Farm and Hounslow: Ashmore 1929, 15. For the general scheme see Jones 1931, 123.
67.   Rawlinson 1923, 55.
68.   Jones 1931, 157–8.
69.   Jones 1931, 159.
70.   WO 95/5454, *General Scheme for the Defence of Great Britain against*

attack by aircraft, War Office, 1916, p 4.

71.   Ashmore 1929, 159–60.

72.   Cole & Cheesman 1984, 117–21.

73.   Cole & Cheesman 1984, 448.

74.   Ashmore 1929, 162.

75.   Ashmore 1929, 62.

76.   WO 33/791, *War Establishments Part IIIE, London AA Defences*, War Office (SD2), 11 Nov 1916.

77.   AIR 1/16/15/276, f 21 Report on the air defences of London, RFCR 13788(AA), 17 Jan 1918, p 1.

78.   White 1986, 32–4.

79.   Ashmore 1929, 165–9.

80.   Jones 1935, 36.

81.   Ashmore 1929, 40.

82.   CAB 4/3, CID 106–B, *Aerial Navigation* [. . .], 28 Jan 1909.

83.   Rawlinson 1923, 155–79.

84.   WO 33/828, *Approved Armaments and AA Guns*, War Office, 1 Jun 1917.

85.   AIR 1/16/15/276, f 21 Report on the air defences of London, RFCR 13788(AA), 17 Jan 1918, pp 3–4; Jones 1935, 44–5.

86.   WO 33/828, *Approved Armaments and AA Guns*, War Office, 1 Jun 1917. It should be noted that this source comes attended by the caveat that it shows the 'approximate position as approved to date; in some cases the actual moves of the guns to these stations has not yet taken place.' The source does, however, seem to capture the general share of gun types and strengths of individual commands, even if the details of the weapons at some may be imprecise. In cases where independent verification can be obtained – the London guns, for example – the return seems to hold up well.

87.   Ashmore 1929, 48.

88.   Ashmore 1929, 53.

89.   Ashmore 1929, 49.

90.   Ashmore 1929, 52.

91.   Cole & Cheesman 1984, 302–3.

92.   Ashmore 1929, 171.

93.   Cole & Cheesman 1984, 325.

94.   Rawlinson 1923, 180–90.

95.   Jones 1935, 70–3.

96.   Ashmore 1929, 58–9; Jones 1935, 78; Cole & Cheesman 1984, 326–7.

97.   Ashmore 1929, 59.

98.   Jones 1935, 83–4.

99.   Jones 1935, 84.

100.   Ashmore 1929, 62.

101.   AIR 1/16/15/276, f 21 Report on the air defences of London, RFCR 13788(AA), 17 Jan 1918.

102.   Jones 1935, 113.

103.   Ashmore 1929, 79.

104.   See Collyer 1982; Scarth 1995; *ibid* 1999.

105.   Castle 1982, 218.

106.   Ashmore 1929, 83–4.

107.   Jones 1935, 127.

108.   Jones 1935, 127–34.

109.   Ashmore 1929, 114.

110.   Cole & Cheesman 1984, 448–9.

111. AIR 1/16/15/276, f 21 Report on the air defences of London, RFCR 13788(AA), 17 Jan 1918.
112. Rawlinson 1923, 244.
113. Ashmore to GHQ GB, LADA/22, 22 Nov 1918, quoted in Ashmore 1929, 109.
114. Philips 1940.
115. Philips 1940, 85.
116. Quoted in Jones 1937, 12.

Chapter 2

1. Ashmore 1929.
2. Young 1952, 174.
3. Ashmore 1929, 149.
4. Ashmore 1929, 149–50.
5. Ferris 1999, 879; and see Young 1988 for an earlier treatment of similar themes.
6. Quoted in Ashmore 1929.
7. WO 32/3119, f 17a, DCIGS to CAS et al, 9 Oct 1919.
8. WO 32/3119, Scheme for an interim organisation of the Air Defence of Great Britain, in accordance with the recommendations of a conference held at the War Office on 26th May 1919, GHQ GB (AA), 22 Nov 1919.
9. Hyde 1976, 59.
10. Sturtivant et al 1997, 85.
11. WO 32/3119, f 17a, DCIGS to CAS et al, 9 Oct 1919.
12. WO 32/3119, Proceedings of a conference held at the War Office [. . .] to consider the immediate requirements of AA Defence of Great Britain, War Office, 14 Oct 1919.
13. WO 32/3119, f 28a, GHQ GB to WO, 24042 (AA), 22 Nov 1919.
14. WO 32/3119, f 31a, GHQ GB to WO, 24042 (AA), 1 Dec 1919.
15. WO 32/3121, f 1a, Anti-aircraft policy, [conclusions of conference 23 Feb 1920]; further copy at WO 32/3120, f 6a.
16. WO 32/3121, f 35a, War Office anti-aircraft proposals [conference proceedings 13 Jan 1921].
17. WO 32/3122, MO4 to DMO, Appended statement, 12 Sep 1921.
18. WO 32/3121, Memorandum on air defence policy, Jun – Oct 1920.
19. WO 32/3122, MO4 to DMO, Appended statement, 12 Sep 1921.
20. See Hall 1981; Ferris 1987.
21. Wood 1992, 17–23.
22. See generally Scarth 1995; ibid 1999.
23. Routledge 1992, 217.
24. WO 32/3122, MO4 to DMO, Appended statement, 12 Sep 1921.
25. Routledge 1992, 217
26. WO 32/3121, f 66a, Report of a committee who [sic] visited Biggin Hill on 4 May 1922.
27. Routledge 1992, 217.
28. Routledge 1992, 219.
29. Pile 1949, 53.
30. CAB 16/67, ARC 34, CID AA Research Sub-Committee, AA Gunnery Equipment, Progress Report by the War Office, 26 Apr 1926.
31. Routledge 1992, 220.
32. CAB 16/67, ARC 50, CID AA Research Sub-Committee, AA Gunnery

Equipment, Further Progress Report by the War Office, 24 Feb 1927.
33.   Pile 1949, 54.
34.   AIR 16/313, f 17a, Salmond to AM, AD/5909/Air, 29 Feb 1928.
35.   See generally Young 1988, 502–6.
36.   Stewart 1926.
37.   Stewart 1927, 114.
38.   Stewart 1927, 115.
39.   Williams 1927, 745; Stewart 1927.
40.   AIR 16/313, f 17a, Salmond to AM, AD/5909/Air, 29 Feb 1928.
41.   Stewart 1929, 266–7; Turner 1928.
42.   Stewart 1929; AIR 2/1178, Sector 'C', 6–12 Aug 1928, Final Report [on exercises].
43.   AIR 16/313, f 43a, ADGB to AM, AD/9082/Air OI, 8 Jun 1929.
44.   Stewart 1930, 90.
45.   This is the number of 40mm Bofors guns held by AA Command on 21 August 1940: WO 166/2075, War Diary AA Cmd G, Weekly AA Equipment Statement ADGB, 21 Aug 1940.
46.   Pile 1949, 55.
47.   Ashmore 1927.
48.   WO 32/2607, f 1a, ADF TA to DG TA, ADF/S/5/38, 15 Feb 1933, App A.
49.   CAB 13/5, HDC 103, CID Home Defence Committee, ADGB, Report of Sub-Committee on Air Defence, 25 Feb 1930.
50.   CAB 13/5, HDC 118, CID Home Defence Committee, Defence of Ports at Home, AA Defences, Minute by DMOI (WO), 31 Dec 1930.
51.   CAB 13/5, HDC 121, CID Home Defence Committee, Defence of Ports at Home, AA Defences, Minute by DOI (AM), 10 Jan 1931.
52.   Pile 1949, 57.
53.   Quoted in Hyde 1976, 285.
54.   Smith 1984, 114–5.
55.   WO 32/2687, f 1a, ADF TA to DG TA, ADF/S/5/38, 15 Feb 1933.
56.   WO 32/2687, f 1a, ADF TA to DG TA, ADF/S/5/38, 15 Feb 1933.
57.   CAB 13/5, CID HDC, *Provisional Defence Plan of Territorial Army Air Defence Formations*, Revised Draft, 15 Dec 1933.
58.   WO 32/2687, f 7a, ADF TA to DG TA, 57/2126, 29 Jan 1934.
59.   Ceadel 1980.

Chapter 3

1.   Collier 1957, 25.
2.   CAB 13/18, The Reorientation of the Air Defence System 1934, Memorandum by the Air Staff, S33237/DOI, 30 Jul 1934.
3.   CAB 12/3, HDC, Minutes of 21st Meeting, 4 Aug 1934.
4.   CAB 13/17, Reorientation Committee, Minutes of 1st Meeting, 17 Oct 1934.
5.   CAB 13/18, ADGB 25 (HDC 166), CID HDC, Sub-Committee on the Reorientation of the Air Defence System of Great Britain, *Interim Report*, 31 Jan 1935, p 3.
6.   CAB 13/17, Reorientation Committee, Minutes of 1st Meeting, 17 Oct 1934, p 18.
7.   CAB 13/18, ADGB 25 (HDC 166) [. . .], 31 Jan 1935, p 6.
8.   CAB 13/18, ADGB 25 (HDC 166) [. . .], 31 Jan 1935, p 9.
9.   Pile 1949, 63.
10.   WO 32/2832, f 4a, *Second Interim Report of the Committee on the*

Organisation of the Air Defence Formations, Territorial Army, 6 Feb 1936, refers.

11. Pile 1949, 64.
12. WO 32/2832, f 4a, Second Interim Report of the Committee on the Organisation of the Air Defence Formations, Territorial Army, 6 Feb 1936.
13. CAB 13/19, ADGB 58 (HDC 199), CID HDC, Sub-Committee on the Reorientation of the Air Defence System of Great Britain, Redistribution of the Defences of the Air Defence of Great Britain, Report, 17 Jun 1936.
14. Eg WO 33/1409, Interim Defence Scheme for Newhaven, Aug 1936.
15. Hyde 1976, 517.
16. Collier 1957, 46.
17. Ismay 1960, 73.
18. CAB 21/622, Home Defence, Part 1, H L Ismay, 17 Sep 1936, p 5.
19. Pile 1949, 67, owes this observation to Hart 1939, 165–6.
20. CAB 13/19, HDC 209 (also HDC (AA) 16), CID HDC, Protection of Points of Importance Against Air Attack, First Interim Report of a Sub-Committee, 6 Oct 1936.
21. CAB 13/18, ADGB 25 (HDC 166), CID HDC, Sub-Committee on the Reorientation of the Air Defence System of Great Britain, Interim Report, 31 Jan 1935, p 20.
22. CAB 13/18, HDC 182, CID HDC, Sub-Committee on the Reorientation of the Air Defence System of Great Britain. Anti-Aircraft Defence for Royal Air Force Home Stations, Report, 24 Oct 1935.
23. CAB 13/19, ADGB 70, CID HDC, Sub-Committee on the Reorientation of the Air Defence System of Great Britain, Weapons for Defence against Low-Flying Attack, Memorandum, 7 Nov 1936.
24. WO 32/4624, f 6a, Proceedings of a conference [. . .] to discuss the method of raising Light AA Units for the ADGB, 22 Apr 1937.
25. Pile 1949, 67.
26. Army List, May 1937, cols 312–9. The established core of the force was in London, where the twelve batteries of 51–54 AA Bdes embodied since the early 1920s would take charge of the IAZ's guns. By spring 1937, 55 (Kent) AA Bde was also up to three batteries, based at Rochester, Tunbridge Wells and Chatham, whence it would chiefly man the southern flank of the Thames & Medway layout. Three batteries each were also held by 56 (Cornwall) and 57 (Wessex) AA Bdes, and also by 58 (Kent) and 59 (The Essex Regiment) AA Bdes, the latter one of the converted units which, like all such bodies at this date, remained 'affiliated' to its parent regiment. Other affiliated units properly embodied by spring 1937 were 60 (City of London) AA Bde, which had originated in the Corps of the Royal Fusiliers, and 61 (Finsbury Rifles) AA Bde, whose origin lay in the King's Royal Rifle Corps and which contained the single AAMG battery so far formed. The distribution of the remaining seven brigades reflected the beginnings of inter-war AA cover in the Midlands and north, though they were so embryonic that even their titles remained provisional in the spring of 1937. In numerical order these units were 62 (North and East Riding) AA Bde at the Artillery Barracks in Middlesbrough, 63 (Durham) at Sunderland and Seaham harbour, 64 (Northumbrian) at North Shields and Seaton Delaval, 65 (Manchester Regiment) based at Hulme in Manchester, 66 (West Yorkshire Regiment) at Leeds, 67 (York and Lancaster Regiment) at Rotherham and 69 (Royal Warwickshire Regiment) in Birmingham.

In addition the 'unbrigaded' 409 (Suffolk) AA Battery was based at Lowestoft.

27.   CAB 13/19, ADGB 73 (also HDC 220), CID HDC, Sub-Committee on the Reorientation of the Air Defence System of Great Britain, 'Ideal' Air Defence of Great Britain, *Report*, 9 Feb 1937.

28.   CAB 13/19, ADGB 73 [. . .], *Report*, 9 Feb 1937, pp 4–5.

29.   Eg HO 211/2, *Spain: report on effects of aerial bombardment and emergency measures taken by the municipal authorities in Madrid*, ARP Dept, Mar 1937.

30.   Dobinson 2000.

31.   WO 166/2070, War Diary AA Cmd G, HAA as at 08.00, 3 Sep 1940.

32.   On AA fire-control radar see Postan *et al* 1964, 381–6; Routledge 1994.

33.   Postan *et al* 1964, 281–91; Chamberlain & Gander 1975, 50–2.

34.   CAB 64/7, CID 271-A, *Anti-Aircraft Defences, Note by the Secretary*, 4 Dec 1937.

35.   Pile 1949, 71.

36.   Quoted in Hyde 1976, 409–10.

37.   PREM 1/306, Inskip to Chamberlain, 26 Oct 1937.

38.   CAB 21/623, DPR 220, CID Sub Committee on Defence Policy and Requirements, Peace Establishment of Regular Anti-Aircraft Groups, *Memorandum by the Secretary of State for War*, 7 Oct 1937.

39.   CAB 64/7, 271-A, CID, *Anti-Aircraft Defences, Note by the Secretary*, 4 Dec 1937, citing prime-ministerial decision of 8 Nov 1937.

40.   Hart 1939, 164–5.

41.   CAB 13/17, Reorientation Committee, Minutes of 26th Meeting, 16 Nov 1937.

42.   Hogg 1978, 92.

43.   WO 32/4533, Min 8, DMOI to multiple recipients, 4 Oct 1937.

44.   Forrester 1945.

45.   WO 33/1349, *Interim Defence Scheme for Thames & Medway*, War Office, 1934; WO 33/1343, *Interim Defence Scheme for Harwich*, War Office, 1933; WO 33/1353, *Interim Defence Scheme for Tyne*, War Office, 1934; WO 33/1409, *Interim Defence Scheme for Newhaven*, War Office, 1936.

46.   Pile 1949, 72.

47.   WO 32/4522, f 28a, Fighter Cmd to WO, FCS/15822/AA, 21 Apr 1938.

48.   CAB 13/5, CID HDC, *Provisional Defence Plan of Territorial Army Air Defence Formations* (Revised Draft), 15 Dec 1933.

49.   WO 32/4532, f 46a, GOC N Cmd to WO, CRNC 89086/Q, 23 Mar 1938.

50.   WO 277/29, *Works Services and Engineer Stores*, PUS Dept C3 Branch, 1953, p 62.

51.   WO 32/4623, f 4a, WO to GOCs Cmds, 20/AA/49 (MO2), 31 Dec 1937.

52.   WO 277/29, *Works Services and Engineer Stores*, PUS Dept C3 Branch, 1953, p 62.

53.   See for example 'Four drill halls for the Territorial Army', *Architect & Building News*, **159**, (4 Aug 1939), 127–32.

54.   WO 32/4368, f 15a, WO to AM, 43/AA/598 (MT3), 22 Mar 1938.

55.   Pile 1949, 73.

56.   Pile 1949, 9.

57.   Winton 1985, 61.

58.   Macksey in *DNB* 1971–1980, 670.

59.   Brendon 2000, 359.

60.   WO 199/2979c, History of 1 AA Div, p 8.

61.   WO 199/2979c, History of 1 AA Div, pp 8–9.

62.   WO 199/2979c, History of 1 AA Div, pp 10–11.
63.   Quoted in Pile 1949, 76.
64.   Pile 1949, 76.
65.   Hart 1939, 169.
66.   Pile 1949, 78.
67.   Pile 1949, 80.
68.   Pile 1949, 80.
69.   Richard Lamb in *DNB* 1986–1990, 395–7.
70.   Edward Heath served largely with 107 HAA Regt, initially in the defence of Liverpool but later in France (Campbell 1994, 42–50).
71.   CAB 13/20, ADGB 114 (also HDC 274), CID HDC, Sub-Committee on the Reorientation of the Air Defence System of Great Britain, Revised Lay-Out of Searchlights and Guns for the Air Defence of Great Britain, *Report*, 16 May 1938.
72.   CAB 12/3, CID HDC, Minutes of 40th Meeting, 20 May 1938, p 1.
73.   CAB 13/20, ADGB 114 (also HDC 274) [. . .], 16 May 1938, p 4.
74.   CAB 13/20, ADGB 114 (also HDC 274) [. . .], 16 May 1938, p 5.
75.   Pile 1949, 80.
76.   AIR 2/2994, f 2a, 1 AA Corps to WO, FCS/15423/AA, 8 Sep 1938.
77.   Pile 1949, 81.
78.   Pile 1949, 82.
79.   Pile 1949, 82.
80.   Quoted in Pile 1949, 85.
81.   AIR 20/212, f 6b, Air Staff note on the War Office programme [. . .], 27 Oct 1938.
82.   CAB 13/17, Reorientation Committee, Minutes of 39th Meeting, 15 Dec 1938.
83.   CAB 13/17, Reorientation Committee, Minutes of 40th Meeting, 24 Jan 1939.
84.   See generally WO 199/2976, *HQ AA Cmd, AA Defence of Great Britain, Survey and History of, Part III: Technical History of AA Gunnery*, Vol II, pp 200–208; WO 277/29 *Works Services and Engineer Stores*, PUS Dept C3 Branch, 1953; and for the holdfast and other components of the 3.7in gun, WO 32/11628, *Identification List for Ordnance QF 3.7in Mk 2A* [. . .], War Office, Aug 1945.
85.   WO 199/2973, citing WO letter 118/Gen/1631 (QMG 1), 27 Oct 1938.
86.   WO 199/2973, p 20.
87.   WO 199/2973, p 21, citing WO letter 118/Gen/2271 (QMG 7), 27 Feb 1939.
88.   WO 199/2973, p 22, citing E Cmd letter CREC No C/28152/Q, 25 Apr 1939.
89.   *Army List*, Mar 1939, 60–62.
90.   Pile 1949, 93.
91.   CAB 21/623, HDC, Minutes of 44th Meeting, 20 Dec 1938.
92.   PREM 1/306, f 7, Notes on the emergency deployment of the First and Second Regular Anti-Aircraft Brigades, 23 Mar 1939.
93.   AIR 20/212, f 18, Air Defence of Great Britain, comments on CID 308-A by DD Ops (H), 8 Feb 1939.
94.   CAB 13/12, HDC 311 (also ADGB 170), CID HDC, Future requirements in AA and light AA guns for the Air Defence of Great Britain, 3 May 1939.
95.   Pile 1949, 89–90.
96.   Routledge 1994, 66.

Chapter 4

1. Ziegler 1998, 36–9.
2. WO 166/2070, War Diary AA Cmd G, App 3, HAA at 08.00, 3 Sep 1939.
3. WO 166/2070, War Diary AA Cmd G, App 3, LAA at 08.00, 3 Sep 1939.
4. WO 166/2070, War Diary, AA Cmd G, App 63, AAC/Z/375/G, 21 Oct 1939.
5. Collier 1957, 80–1.
6. Pile 1949, 105.
7. WO 166/2070, War Diary AA Cmd G, App 3, HAA at 08.00, 3 Sep 1939.
8. CAB 21/1134, CID 330-A (also HDC 56-M), *Anti-Aircraft Defence of Scapa, Memorandum by the Home Defence Committee*, 2 Aug 1939.
9. CAB 21/1134, COS (39) 8, Air Defence of Scapa, Memorandum, 6 Sep 1939.
10. ADM 116/4208, Letter to DCNS, 9 Sep 1939.
11. AIR 16/31, f 6c, WO to Scot Cmd and AA Cmd, 79/HD/819(MO3), 16 Sep 1939.
12. AIR 16/31, f 6b, WO to AA Cmd, 79/General/3329(TO1(b)), 21 Sep 1939.
13. Collier 1957, 83.
14. AIR 24/520, ORB Fighter Cmd, narrative of events, 16 Oct 1939; WO 166/2081, War Diary AA Cmd G (Int), App 1, Raids on Forth, 16 Oct 1939; ADM 267/126, f 17, Summary of experience gained in enemy air attacks on HM ships and convoys up to 19 Dec 1939; Pile 1949, 101–2 (Pile wrongly places this incident on 19 October).
15. Jeffrey 1992, 18.
16. AIR 24/520, ORB Fighter Cmd, narrative of events, 16 Oct 1939, p 5.
17. WO 166/2081, War Diary AA Cmd G (Int), Oct 1939.
18. CAB 82/14, DCOS (AA) 10, 5 Dec 1939, Ann I, copying Air Staff to AOC-in-C Fighter Cmd, S2458/DHO, 3 Nov 1939.
19. WO 166/2070, War Diary AA Cmd G, App 6, AA Cmd to 3 AA Div, AAC/Z/583/G, 28 Oct 1939.
20. WO 166/2071, War Diary AA Cmd G, App 34, Pile to WO, 10 Nov 1939.
21. WO 166/2071, War Diary AA Cmd G, App 68, WO to Scot Cmd, 79/HD/819(MO3), 8 Nov 1939.
22. CAB 82/14, DCOS (AA) 10, 5 Dec 1939, Annex I, copying Air Staff to AOC-in-C Fighter Cmd, S2458/DHO, 3 Nov 1939.
23. WO 166/2071, War Diary AA Cmd G, App 34, Pile to WO, 10 Nov 1939.
24. WO 166/2074, War Diary AA Cmd G, Equipment Statement 29 May 1940.
25. WO 166/2072, War Diary AA Cmd G, App 7, Pile to Fighter Cmd, AAC/Z/689/G, 2 Feb 1940.
26. WO 166/2071, War Diary AA Cmd G, App 38, AA Cmd to Divs, AAC/Z/693/G, 11 Nov 1939.
27. Pile 1949, 106.
28. CAB 82/14, DCOS (AA) 1, 21 Nov 1939.
29. CAB 82/13, DCOS (AA), 1st Meeting, 4 Dec 1939.
30. CAB 82/13, DCOS (AA) 4th Meeting, 2 Jan 1940.
31. WO 166/2081, War Diary AA Cmd G (Int), Nov–Dec 1939.
32. WO 166/2071, War Diary AA Cmd G, App 14, AA Cmd to Divs, AAC/Z/581/G, 6 Nov 1939.
33. WO 166/2071, War Diary AA Cmd G, App 73, AA Cmd to Fighter Cmd, AAC/Z/386/G, 22 Nov 1939.

34. WO 106/2796, Pile *Dispatch* I, p 3.
35. Pile 1949, 115.
36. Calder 1992, 249.
37. WO 199/2973, *HQ AA Cmd, Survey and History of, Part II: Branches and Services*, Vol VI, p 25.
38. Pile 1949, 107.
39. WO 166/2072, War Diary, AA Cmd G, Draft list of HAA gunsites and GL frequencies, 32/Wireless/587(SD6(a)), nd Feb 1940.
40. CAB 82/13, DCOS (AA), 7th Meeting, 6 Feb 1940.
41. WO 166/2090, War Diary AA Cmd G, AA Cmd to Divs, AAC/Z/660/39/Ord, 16 Feb 1940.
42. WO 199/1627, f 1a, AA Cmd to Divs, AAC/Z/676/G, 6 Jan 1940.
43. WO 166/2105, War Diary 1 AA Div G, Ann 1, 1 AA Div to Bdes, W/7274/G, 3 Apr 1940.
44. WO 166/2072, War Diary AA Cmd G, App 71, AA Cmd to Divs, AAC/Z/650/G(Ops), 21 Feb 1940.
45. CAB 82/13, DCOS (AA), 10th Meeting, 15 Mar 1940.
46. WO 166/2071, War Diary AA Cmd G, App 9, AA Cmd to Divs, AAC/Z/653/G, 4 Nov 1939.
47. WO 166/2073, War Diary AA Cmd G, App 64, AA Cmd to Divs, AAC/Z/824/G/Ops, 21 Mar 1940.
48. WO 166/2071, War Diary AA Cmd G, App 73, AA Cmd to Divs, AAC/Z/693/G, 13 Dec 1939.
49. WO 165/91, War Diary DFW, ADGB Progress Report (FW1(b)): static LAA gunsites, Feb 1941–Jan 1942.
50. Eg *Manual of Anti-Aircraft Defence (Army Units), Vol I, Part II: Searchlights*, War Office, 1937.
51. WO 166/2070, War Diary AA Cmd G, AA Cmd Op Instruction 20, Engagement of unseen targets by barrage fire by Fixed Azimuth methods, 29 Sep 1939.
52. AIR 16/62, 11 Gp to multiple recipients, 11G/S763, 15 Oct 1939.
53. WO 166/2081, War Diary AA Cmd G (Int), Jan 1940.
54. WO 166/2081, War Diary AA Cmd G (Int), Feb 1940.
55. WO 166/2081, War Diary AA Cmd G (Int), Mar 1940.
56. WO 166/2073, War Diary AA Cmd G, App 62, Pile to Dowding, AAC/Z/961/G(Ops), 20 Mar 1940.
57. WO 166/2081, War Diary AA Cmd G (Int), Apr 1940.
58. Pile 1949, 116–7.

Chapter 5

1. Churchill 1949, 300.
2. WO 166/2081, War Diary AA Cmd G (Int), 1–4 Jun 1940.
3. WO 166/2081, War Diary AA Cmd G (Int), 5/6–6/7 Jun 1940.
4. Dobinson 2000, 54–7.
5. WO 166/2074, War Diary AA Cmd G, Weekly AA Equipment Statement ADGB, 5 Jun 1940.
6. CAB 82/13, DCOS (AA) 15th Meeting, 11 Jun 1940.
7. WO 166/2074, War Diary AA Cmd G, Weekly AA Equipment Statement ADGB, 12 Jun 1940.
8. WO 166/2074, War Diary AA Cmd G, Weekly AA Equipment Statement ADGB, 12 Jun 1940.
9. CAB 82/13, DCOS (AA) 15th Meeting, 11 Jun 1940, p 2.

10. CAB 82/14, DCOS (AA) 122, 17 Jun 1940 refers.
11. WO 166/2081, War Diary AA Cmd G (Int), 25–30 Jun 1940.
12. WO 166/2074, War Diary AA Cmd G, Light AA, 08.00, 19 Jun 1940.
13. Some problems and achievements of anti-aircraft gunnery during the Battle of Britain, 6 AA Div, 2 Aug 1941, reproduced in Collier 1957, 482–90.
14. Bungay 2000, 62–9.
15. WO 166/2074, War Diary AA Cmd G, Pile to WO, AAC/Z/670/G(Ops), 7 Jun 1940.
16. WO 166/2074, War Diary AA Cmd G, App 236, AA Cmd to Divs, AAC/Z/670/G/Ops, 27 Jun 1940.
17. WO 166/2074, War Diary AA Cmd G, App 228, AA Cmd to Divs, AAC/Z/581/21/SD, 26 Jun 1940.
18. AIR 14/195, f 98b, Extract from AM Weekly Intelligence Summary 42, 20 Jun 1940, appended to Bomber Cmd letter BC/S 21728/Org, 24 Jun 1940.
19. WO 166/2244, War Diary 26 AA Bde G, App 9, 26 AA Bde Op Instruction 5, 20 Jun 1940.
20. WO 166/2074, War Diary AA Cmd G, App 232, AA Cmd to GHQ Home Forces, AAC/Z/581/26/G/Ops, 26 Jun 1940.
21. WO 166/2074, War Diary AA Cmd G, App 253, AA Cmd to Divs, AAC/Z/1128/G/Ops, 29 Jun 1940.
22. WO 166/2074, War Diary AA Cmd G, App 176, AA Cmd to Divs, AAC/Z/676/G/Ops, 19 Jun 1940.
23. WO 166/2074, War Diary AA Cmd G, App 174, AA Cmd to Divs, AAC/Z/581/SD, 19 Jun 1940.
24. WO 166/2082, War Diary AA Cmd G (Int), 2–9 Jul 1940.
25. WO 166/2082, War Diary AA Cmd G (Int), 9 Jul 1940.
26. CAB 82/14, DCOS (AA) 130, 6 Jul 1940.
27. CAB 82/14, DCOS (AA) 130, 6 Jul 1940, p 2.
28. CAB 82/13, DCOS (AA) 17th Meeting, 9 Jul 1940.
29. James 2000, 27.
30. WO 166/2082, War Diary AA Cmd G (Int), 10–11 Jul 1940.
31. Quoted in Bungay 2000, 155.
32. WO 166/2081, War Diary AA Cmd G (Int), Jul 1940.
33. Pile 1949, 134.
34. Some problems and achievements of anti-aircraft gunnery [. . .], Collier 1957, 483–4.
35. WO 166/2082, War Diary AA Cmd G (Int), 1–12 Aug 1940.
36. Bungay 2000, 179.
37. WO 166/2082, War Diary AA Cmd G (Int), 10 Aug 1940.
38. WO 166/2075, War Diary AA Cmd G, App 13, AA Cmd to Divs, AAC/Z/1267/SD, 4 Aug 1940.
39. Dobinson 2000.
40. WO 166/2075, War Diary AA Cmd G, App 10, AA Cmd to WO, AAC/Z/1267/1/SD, 2 Aug 1940.
41. WO 166/2075, War Diary AA Cmd G, Weekly AA Equipment Statement ADGB, 21 Aug 1940.
42. WO 166/2169, War Diary 6 AA Div G, Location Statement, 6 AA Div, Aug 1940.
43. WO 166/2075, War Diary AA Cmd G, 60 Gp to Fighter Cmd, 60G/S40/1/Air, 18 Aug 1940.
44. James 2000, 82.

45. AIR 28/345, ORB Hawkinge, 14 Aug 1940.
46. WO 166/2784, War Diary 35 AA Bty, Int Rep for Serial 125A [Hawkinge], 14 Aug 1940.
47. WO 166/2682, War Diary 12 LAA Regt, 14 Aug 1940.
48. WO 166/2081, War Diary AA Cmd G (Int), 14 Aug 1940.
49. WO 166/2081, War Diary AA Cmd G (Int), 14/15 Aug 1940.
50. AIR 28/509, ORB Lympne, 15 Aug 1940.
51. AIR 28/345, ORB Hawkinge, 15 Aug 1940; WO 166/2784, Int Rep, C Tp, 35/12 LAA Regt, 15 Aug 1940.
52. James 2000, 86–91.
53. WO 166/2081, War Diary AA Cmd G (Int), 15 Aug 1940.
54. AIR 28/221, ORB Driffield, 15 Aug 1940.
55. AIR 28/525, ORB Martlesham Heath, 15 Aug 1940.
56. AIR 28/345, ORB Hawkinge, 15 Aug 1940.
57. WO 166/2682, War Diary 12 LAA Regt, Det Int Rep for Serial 603 [Eastchurch], 24 hours ended 08.00, 16 Aug 1940.
58. WO 166/2081, War Diary AA Cmd G (Int), 15 Aug 1940.
59. WO 199/2979C, History of 1 AA Div, p 19.
60. WO 166/2682, War Diary 12 LAA Regt, Det Int Rep for Serial 126A [West Malling], Period ending 08.00 hours, 16 Aug 1940; AIR 28/907, ORB West Malling, 15 Aug 1940.
61. WO 166/2081, War Diary AA Cmd G (Int), 15/16 Aug 1940.
62. James 2000, 394–7.
63. CAB 82/14, DCOS (AA) 150 (also COS (40) 632), 16 Aug 1940.
64. CAB 82/14, DCOS (AA) 150 (also COS (40) 632), 16 Aug 1940.
65. WO 166/2075, War Diary AA Cmd G, Weekly AA Equipment Statement ADGB, 21 Aug 1940.
66. WO 32/9474, f 15a, WO to AA Cmd, 79/HD/1522 (AA4), 10 Oct 1940.
67. CAB 70/2, DC(S) (40) 23, 15 Jul 1940.
68. Collier 1957, 199.
69. Collier 1957, 456.
70. WO 166/2082, War Diary AA Cmd G (Int), 16/17 Aug 1940.
71. WO 166/2082, War Diary AA Cmd G (Int), 17–19 Aug 1940.
72. Collier 1957, 457.
73. WO 166/2082, War Diary AA Cmd G (Int), 19–23 Aug 1940.
74. WO 199/2979C, History of 1 AA Div, p 20.
75. Boog 2000, 44.
76. Middlebrook & Everitt 1990, 85.
77. WO 166/2140, War Diary 4 AA Div G, 4 AA Div Intelligence Summary 9, 12.00 24 Aug–12.00 1 Sep 1940.
78. WO 166/2258, War Diary 33 AA Bde, Det Int Rep for period ending 09.00, 29 Aug 1940.
79. WO 166/2258, War Diary 33 AA Bde, Det Int Rep for period ending 09.00, 30 Aug 1940.
80. WO 166/2258, War Diary 33 AA Bde, Det Int Rep for period ending 09.00, 31 Aug 1940.
81. Some problems and achievements of anti-aircraft gunnery [...], Collier 1957, 482–90.

Chapter 6

1. WO 166/2342, War Diary 52 HAA Regt, 7 Sep 1940.

2.   WO 166/2244, War Diary 26 AA Bde G, Det Int Rep 09.00 7 Sep
        1940–09.00 8 Sep 1940.
3.   WO 166/2244, War Diary 26 AA Bde G, Det Int Rep 09.00 7 Sep
        1940–09.00 8 Sep 1940.
4.   Collier 1957, 223.
5.   WO 166/2375, War Diary 84 HAA Regt, 8 Sep 1940.
6.   WO 199/2979c, History of 1 AA Div, p 25.
7.   WO 166/2106, War Diary 1 AA Div G, Ann 36, Divisional Location
        Statement, 28 Aug 1940.
8.   WO 166/2075, War Diary AA Cmd G, Weekly AA Equipment Statement,
        4 Sep 1940.
9.   WO 166/2106, War Diary 1 AA Div G, Ann 2, GL Return, 1 Sep 1940.
10.   WO 166/1161, War Diary CRE London District, Sep 1940.
11.   WO 166/2715, War Diary 42 LAA Regt, Sep 1940.
12.   WO 166/2106, War Diary 1 AA Div, Ann 20, Int Rep 38, 8/9 Sep 1940;
        WO 166/2244, War Diary 26 AA Bde G: Det Int Rep 09.00 8 Sep
        1940–09.00 9 Sep 1940.
13.   WO 166/2106, War Diary 1 AA Div G, Ann 21, Int Rep 40, 9 Sep 1940;
        WO 166/2244, War Diary 26 AA Bde G, Det Int Rep 09.00 9 Sep
        1940 09.00 10 Sep 1940.
14.   WO 166/2244, War Diary 26 AA Bde G, 9 Sep 1940.
15.   WO 166/2292, War Diary 48 AA Bde G, 9/10 Sep 1940.
16.   WO 166/2106, War Diary 1 AA Div G, Ann 23, Int Rep 42, 10 Sep 1940.
17.   WO 166/2106, War Diary 1 AA Div G, Ann 24, Int Rep 43, 10/11 Sep
        1940.
18.   Collier 1957, 494.
19.   WO 166/2082, War Diary AA Cmd G (Int), 7–10 Sep 1940.
20.   INF 1/264, MoI Home Intelligence Div, daily report on morale 93, 6
        Sep 1940.
21.   INF 1/264, MoI Home Intelligence Div, London, [morale report], 6 Sep
        1940.
22.   INF 1/264, MoI Home Intelligence Div, London, [morale report], 9 Sep
        1940.
23.   INF 1/264, MoI Home Intelligence Div, London, [morale report], 10 Sep
        1940.
24.   Pile 1949, 151.
25.   WO 166/2244, War Diary 26 AA Bde G, 12 Sep 1940.
26.   Pile 1949, 172.
27.   WO 199/2979c, History of 1 AA Div, p 27.
28.   WO 166/2082, War Diary AA Cmd G (Int), 11/12 Sep 1940; Collier 1957,
        494.
29.   INF 1/264, MoI Home Intelligence Div, London, [morale report], 12 Sep
        1940.
30.   Pile 1949, 153.
31.   WO 166/2106, War Diary 1 AA Div G, Ann 26, 1 AA Div to 26 AA Bde,
        W/9447/G, 11 Sep 1940.
32.   WO 166/2244, War Diary 26 AA Bde G, 12 Sep 1940.
33.   WO 166/2292, War Diary 48 AA Bde G, Bde Location Statement, 09.00,
        13 Sep 1940.
34.   WO 166/2244, War Diary 26 AA Bde G, 13 Sep 1940.
35.   WO 166/2292, War Diary 48 AA Bde G, 12 Sep 1940.
36.   Collier 1957, 494.
37.   WO 166/2082, War Diary AA Cmd G (Int), 12–13 Sep 1940.

38. WO 166/2106, War Diary 1 AA Div G, Int Rep 49, 13/14 Sep 1940.
39. WO 166/2244, War Diary 26 AA Bde G, 14 Sep 1940
40. WO 166/2106, War Diary 1 AA Div G, Int Rep 50, 14 Sep 1940.
41. Collier 1957, 494; WO 166/2082, War Diary AA Cmd G (Int), 14–15 Sep 1940; WO 166/2106, War Diary 1 AA Div G, Int Rep 51, 14/15 Sep 1940.
42. WO 166/2082, War Diary AA Cmd G (Int), 15 Sep 1940.
43. WO 166/2106, War Diary 1 AA Div G, Int Rep 56, 15/16 Sep 1940.
44. Collier 1957, 494.
45. WO 166/2016, War Diary 1 AA Div G, Int Rep 62, 18/19 Sep 1940.
46. Pile 1949, 167.
47. WO 166/2106, War Diary 1 AA Div G, Ann 47, 1 AA Div to multiple recipients, 20 Sep 1940.
48. Pile 1949, 167.
49. WO 166/1161, War Diary CRE London District, 18–23 Sep 1940.
50. Sayer 1950 [WO 277/3], 47.
51. Sayer 1950 [WO 277/3], 47.
52. AVIA 22/2308, AA Cmd HQ, 'History of Anti-Aircraft: Scientific Development and Advice', Oct 1943, p 6.
53. Pile 1949; Blackett 1962, 206. Unless indicated otherwise the following account of the origin and early work of the AA Command Operational Research Group and the AA Command Wireless School is derived from three sets of unpublished historical notes made during the war or soon after by those involved, and filed in AVIA 22/2308. The papers are Dr L E Bayliss, 'Army Operational Research Group, History of the origins of Operational Research in AA Command', A50/LEB, 18 May 1945; Dr J A Ratcliffe, 'History of the early days of the AA Radio School at Petersham', nd; and AA Cmd HQ, 'History of Anti-Aircraft: Scientific Development and Advice', Oct 1943.
54. WO 166/2073, War Diary, AA Cmd G, App 11, AA Cmd to Divs, AAC/Z/596/Gt, 2 Mar 1940.
55. Blackett 1962, 209.
56. Calder 1992, 475.
57. WO 166/2076, War Diary AA Cmd G, Newton to Divs, AAC/Z/1410/1/Gt, 4 Nov 1940.
58. Pile 1949, 114.
59. WO 166/2106, War Diary 1 AA Div G, Ann 41, Minutes of Brigadiers' Conference, 14 Oct 1940, W/7853/G, 15 Oct 1940.
60. WO 166/2106, War Diary 1 AA Div G, Ann 79, 1 AA Div to E Cmd, W/7067/G, 29 Oct 1940.
61. WO 166/2106, War Diary 1 AA Div G, Ann 41, Minutes of Brigadiers' Conference, 14 Oct 1940, W/7853/G, 15 Oct 1940.
62. WO 166/2292, War Diary 48 AA Bde, 21 Oct 1940.
63. WO 166/2292, War Diary 48 AA Bde, Location Statement, 09.00 hours, 19 Nov 1940.
64. WO 166/2106, War Diary 1 AA Div G, Ann 41, Minutes of Brigadiers' Conference, 14 Oct 1940, W/7853/G, 15 Oct 1940.
65. Collier 1957, 494–5.
66. Pile 1949, 175.
67. Pile 1949, 172.
68. WO 166/2106, War Diary 1 AA Div G, Ann 18, GOC's Memorandum 3, 10 Dec 1940.
69. WO 166/2106, War Diary 1 AA Div G, Ann 18, GOC's Memorandum 3, 10 Dec 1940, p 2.

70.   Pile 1949, 169.
71.   WO 166/2106, War Diary 1 AA Div G, GL Return, Dec 1940.
72.   WO 166/2075, War Diary AA Cmd G, Weekly AA Equipment Statement, ADGB, 2 Oct 1940.
73.   WO 166/2076, War Diary AA Cmd G, Weekly AA Equipment Statement, ADGB, 20 Nov 1940.
74.   WO 166/2076, War Diary AA Cmd G, Weekly AA Equipment Statement, ADGB, 11 Dec 1940.

Chapter 7

1.   Dobinson 2000, 80.
2.   CAB 82/29, AA (S) 40 4, 3 Nov 1940.
3.   CAB 82/29, AA (S) 40, 2nd Meeting, 4 Nov 1940.
4.   WO 166/2076, War Diary AA Cmd G, Nov 1940, Message Form 13, AA Cmd GS to General Chester, 20.00, 4 Nov 1940.
5.   WO 166/2261, War Diary 34 AA Bde, 4 Nov 1940.
6.   WO 166/2480, War Diary 194 HAA Bty, 4 Nov 1940.
7.   WO 166/2480, War Diary 194 HAA Bty, 5 Nov 1940.
8.   WO 166/2480, War Diary 194 HAA Bty, App A, 194 HAA Bty Op Order 9, 5 Nov 1940.
9.   WO 166/2480, War Diary 194 HAA Bty, 4–10 Nov 1940.
10.   WO 166/2261, War Diary 34 AA Bde, 10 Nov 1940.
11.   WO 166/2076, War Diary AA Cmd G, 10 Nov 1940.
12.   WO 166/2261, War Diary 34 AA Bde, 34 AA Bde Op Order 18, 12 Nov 1940.
13.   WO 166/2076, War Diary AA Cmd G, Weekly AA Equipment Statements ADGB, 6 Nov, 13 Nov and 20 Nov 1940 all give the same figures, though (whatever the other merits of their accounts) several writers have stated that Coventry was defended by only 24 guns on this night (eg Ray 1996, 156 evidently drawing on Longmate 1979, 142).
14.   Hinsley 1979, 316–7, 528–48.
15.   For the case in general see Hinsley op cit; Longmate 1979.
16.   See, recently, Stafford 1997, 227–8.
17.   CAB 82/29, AA(S) (40) 2, 31 Oct 1940.
18.   CAB 82/29, AA(S) (40), 1st Meeting, 1 Nov 1940.
19.   CAB 82/29, AA(S) (40) 2, 31 Oct 1940.
20.   CAB 82/29, AA(S) (41) 1, 2 Jan 1941.
21.   WO 166/2077, War Diary AA Cmd G, Weekly AA Equipment Statement ADGB, 22 Jan 1941.
22.   WO 166/2091, War Diary 1 AA Corps G, 1 AA Corps to 1, 5 and 6 AA Divs, S/1AA/115/G, 5 Dec 1940.
23.   WO 166/2091, War Diary 1 AA Corps G, 1 AA Corps to 1, 5 and 6 AA Divs, S/1AA/115/G, 8 Dec 1940.
24.   WO 166/2076, War Diary AA Cmd G, AA Cmd to Divs, AAC/Z/419/2/G/Ops, 2 Dec 1940.
25.   WO 166/2076, War Diary AA Cmd G, AA Cmd to Corps, AAC/Z/419/2/G/Ops, 7 Dec 1940.
26.   WO 166/2076, War Diary AA Cmd G, Instructions for making wire mat for GL site, appended to AA Cmd letter, 7 Dec 1940.
27.   WO 166/2076, War Diary AA Cmd G, AA Cmd to WO, AAC/Z/1514/G(Tech), 13 Dec 1940.
28.   WO 166/2077, War Diary AA Cmd G, Pile to WO, AAC/Z/1514/G(Tech),

20 Jan 1941.
29. WO 166/2078, War Diary AA Cmd G, Pile to WO, AAC/Z/1514/1/G(Tech), 1 Apr 1941.
30. WO 166/2078, War Diary AA Cmd G, WO letter 57/PF/226 (AA1), 8 Apr 1941.
31. *Directions for the use of AA artillery instruments, Pamphlet 13: GL Station Mk II, War Office, Sep 1941* [WO 287/166].
32. WO 166/2080, War Diary AA Cmd G, Pile to AOC-in-C Fighter Cmd, AAC/Z/681/G, 24 Sep 1941. Pile's reflections on the searchlight experience of 1939–40 are summarised in this letter.
33. WO 166/2076, War Diary AA Cmd G, Night Interception, paper by H C T Dowding, 3 Nov 1940.
34. Pile 1949, 184.
35. WO 166/2076, War Diary AA Cmd G, Pile to Divs, AAC/Z/1409/G/Ops, 8 Nov 1940.
36. WO 166/2076, War Diary AA Cmd G, AA Cmd to Divs, AAC/Z/681/G/Ops, 11 Nov 1940.
37. WO 166/2271, War Diary 38 AA Bde G, 38 AA Bde to Regts, S/G/1, 23 Nov 1940.
38. WO 166/3038, War Diary 2 SL Regt, Op Order 2, S/1/732, 15 Nov 1940.
39. AIR 20/222, f 36, CID Sub-Committee on Air Defence Research, Observations by Mr Churchill on his visit to the Air Ministry Research Station at Bawdsey in June 1939.
40. AIR 10/5520, p 188.
41. Or just possibly with Dowding. Pile's letter of 28 November making the suggestion was addressed to the AOC-in-C Fighter Command, and refers to 'my conversation with you'. Since Dowding was formally replaced by Douglas on 25 November it would appear to be the latter with whom Pile had spoken, though the possibility that the hand-over took place between the letter's drafting and dispatch must remain.
42. WO 166/2076, f 163, War Diary AA Cmd G, Pile to Sholto Douglas, AAC/Z/1490/G/Ops, 28 Nov 1940.
43. WO 166/2076, War Diary AA Cmd G, AA Cmd to Fighter Cmd, AAC/Z/1490/G(Tech), 20 Dec 1940.
44. WO 163/458, 11 Oct 1940.
45. WO 166/2091, War Diary 1 AA Corps G, WO to AA Cmd, 79/HD/1444(AA2), 7 Nov 1940.
46. WO 166/2091, War Diary 1 AA Corps G, WO to AA Cmd, 79/HD/1444(AG1a), 13 Nov 1940.
47. Pile 1949, 183.
48. WO 166/2076, War Diary AA Cmd G, AA Cmd to Divs, AAC/Z/1221/1/G/Ops, 1 Dec 1940.
49. WO 106/2798, AA guns, searchlights and GL stations as issued, 1 Jan 1941.
50. WO 166/2077, War Diary AA Cmd G, AA Cmd to Corps, ZZC/Z/1416/G/Ops, 16 Jan 1941.
51. Pile 1949, 183.
52. WO 166/2107, War Diary 1 AA Div G, Ann 9, 1 AA Div Int Sum 4, 28 Dec 1940–4 Jan 1941.
53. Collier 1957, 273.
54. Dobinson 2000.
55. Ray 1996, 183.
56. Ray 1996, 193.

57.   Ray 1996, 160.
58.   Ray 1996, 190.
59.   WO 166/2084, War Diary AA Cmd G (Int), AA Cmd Int Sum, AAC/Z/334/3/G (Int), 28 Feb–6 Mar 1941.
60.   Pinsent 1983, 66.
61.   WO 166/2077, War Diary AA Cmd G, f 135, AA Cmd to WO, AAC/Z/762/G/Ops, 19 Feb 1941.
62.   WO 166/2078, War Diary AA Cmd G, AA Cmd to 1 AA Corps, AAC/Z/836/23/G/Ops, 5 Mar 1941.
63.   Pinsent 1983, 72.
64.   Ray 1996, 198.
65.   CAB 82/15, COS (AA) 267 (also COS (41) 164), 14 Mar 1941.
66.   CAB 82/15, Annex to COS (AA) 274, 24 Mar 1941, Sholto Douglas to AM, FC/S 23358, 21 Mar 1941.
67.   CAB 82/15, COS (AA) 275 (also COS (41) 216), 2 Apr 1941.
68.   WO 166/2077, War Diary AA Cmd G, Weekly AA Equipment Statement ADGB, 19 Feb 1941; WO 166/2078, War Diary AA Cmd G, Weekly AA Equipment Statement ADGB, 23 Apr 1941.
69.   WO 166/2084, War Diary AA Cmd G (Int), Return of enemy aircraft brought down [. . .], 26 Feb–5 Mar 1941.
70.   WO 166/2084, War Diary AA Cmd G (Int), AA Cmd Int Sum 36, 24 Mar–3 Apr 1941.
71.   WO 166/2084, War Diary AA Cmd G (Int), AA Cmd Int Sum 37, 3–9 Apr 1941.
72.   WO 166/2084, War Diary AA Cmd G (Int), AA Cmd Int Sum 38, 9–16 Apr 1941.
73.   Ray 1996, 237.
74.   WO 166/2084, War Diary AA Cmd G (Int), AA Cmd Int Sum 40, 26 Apr–5 May 1941.
75.   WO 106/2798, AA guns, searchlights and GL stations issued, 1 Apr 1941.
76.   WO 106/2798, AA guns, searchlights and GL stations issued, 1 Sep 1941.
77.   WO 106/2798, AA guns, searchlights and GL stations issued, 1 Apr 1941.
78.   WO 166/2075, War Diary AA Cmd G, AA Cmd to Divs, AAC/Z/1221/14/G/Ops, 9 Oct 1940.
79.   Napier 1946, 14.
80.   WO 166/2076, War Diary AA Cmd G, Pile to WO, AAC/Z/1221/1/G/Ops, 15 Nov 1940.
81.   WO 166/2076, War Diary AA Cmd G, AA Cmd to Divs, AAC/Z/1221/1/G/Ops, 1 Dec 1940.
82.   WO 166/2078, War Diary AA Cmd G, AA Cmd to Corps, AAC/Z/1221/5/G/Ops, 28 Mar 1941.
83.   Napier 1946, 14.
84.   WO 166/2078, War Diary AA Cmd G, AA Cmd to 5 AA Div, AAC/Z/1221/21/G/Ops, 19 Jan 1941.
85.   WO 166/2077, War Diary AA Cmd G, WO to AA Cmd, Notes on projectors AA 3-inch single, 26/General/6839 (AA1), 17 Feb 1941.
86.   WO 199/2973, quoting WO letter 118/Gen/2715, 29 Jul 1940.
87.   WO 199/2973, pp 28–9; cit AA Cmd letter AAC/Z/1277/E, 24 Aug 1940.
88.   WO 199/2973, p 29; cit WO (FW1) letter 118/Gen/2715, 3 Sep 1940.
89.   WO 199/2973, p 29.
90.   WO 199/2973, p 30, cit AA Cmd letter AAC/Z/1277/3, 2 Dec 1940.
91.   Quoted in WO 199/2973, p 30.
92.   WO 199/2973, pp 30–1, cit AA Cmd letter AAC/Z/1277/3, 25 Nov 1940.

93.	WO 199/2973, p 31; quoting WO letter 118/Gen/3471 (Q1), 8 Oct 1940.
94.	WO 199/2973, p 31.
95.	WO 199/2973, pp 31–3; quoting AA Cmd letter AAC/Z/1277/Q, 14 Dec 1940.
96.	WO 165/91, War Diary DFW, ADGB Hutting Report for month ending 15 Feb 1941: mobile sites.
97.	WO 165/91, War Diary DFW, ADGB Hutting Report for month ending 15 Apr 1941: mobile sites.
98.	WO 195/91, War Diary DFW, ADGB Hutting Report for month ending 15 Apr 1941
99.	Pile 1949, 185.
100.	Bartlett 1927.
101.	Quoted in Pile 1949, 185.
102.	WO 166/2076, War Diary AA Cmd G, Pile to WO, AAC/4175/Gt, 5 Dec 1940.
103.	WO 166/2076, War Diary AA Cmd G, Pile to WO, AAC/4175/Gt, 5 Dec 1940.
104.	Pile 1949, 186.
105.	Pile 1949, 189.
106.	Ray 1996, 237.
107.	Collier 1957, 504–5.
108.	Ray 1996, 231–2; Ziegler 1998, 160–1.
109.	Ziegler 1998, 161, quoting journalist Larry Rue.
110.	WO 166/2107, War Diary 1 AA Div, App 43, 1 AA Div Int Sum 24, 18–25 May 1941, quoting the *Aeroplane*.
111.	WO 166/2084, War Diary AA Cmd G (Int), Return of enemy aircraft brought down by AA fire, 09.00 14 May–09.00 21 May 1941.

Chapter 8

1.	WO 106/2796, Pile *Dispatch* II, p 1.
2.	DeGroot 1997B, 74.
3.	Pile 1949, 187.
4.	DeGroot 1997A, 436.
5.	Pile 1949, 194.
6.	Campbell 1993, 318–9.
7.	Beevor 1999, 104–8.
8.	Campbell 1993, 313–7.
9.	Naylor 1942; 'Two ATS Officers' 1943, 81.
10.	Naylor 1942, 200.
11.	'Two ATS Officers' 1943, 82.
12.	Pile 1949, 192.
13.	Pile 1949, 190.
14.	Naylor 1942, 206.
15.	Pile 1949, 191.
16.	Naylor 1942, 206.
17.	WO 199/2973, p 35.
18.	WO 199/2973, p 40.
19.	For a survey of the types used on airfields see Francis 1989; *ibid* 1996, 204–20.
20.	DSIR 4/2616 has the minutes of the first committee; those of the second are in HO 196/46.
21.	HO 192/46, Ministry of Works and Buildings, Committee on the Design

of Prefabricated Huts, *Approved Designs for Prefabricated Huts*, MoWB, Mar 1942.

22. HO 192/46, [. . .], *Approved Designs for Prefabricated Huts*, MoWB, Mar 1942, drawings 2–3; *Handbook of Nissen Huts* [. . .], Engineer-in-Chief (Army), Dec 1944 [RE Library].

23. HO 192/46, Committee on the Design of Prefabricated Huts, Progress Report, Mar 1942, describes them as 'in course of development', though they were included in the *Approved Designs for Prefabricated Huts* issued by the MoWB in the same month.

24. 'The MOWP Standard hut', *Journal of the Royal Institute of British Architects*, 49(11), Sep 1942, 193–4; *MOWP Standard Hut* [. . .], DFW(FW4), Jan 1943 [RE Library].

25. *The Romney Hut* [. . .], DFW(FW4), Aug 1942 [RE Library]; Hopthrow 1988.

26. Routledge 1994, 393.

27. WO 166/2079, War Diary AA Cmd G, AA Cmd to WO, AAC/Z/1762/G(Tech), 2 Aug 1941.

28. CAB 81/63, COS (41) 612, 8 Oct 1941.

29. Pile 1949, 222.

30 CAB 81/63, COS (41) 612, 8 Oct 1941.

31. CAB 81/63, ADGB (41) 4 (Final), 8 Nov 1941, Ann II, Analysis of the Directive by the Prime Minister and Minister of Defence dated 8 Oct 1941, F A Pile, 24 Oct 1941.

32. WO 166/2079, War Diary AA Cmd G, AA Cmd Standing Op Instruction 43, AA defence of commercial establishments by Home Guard, 23 Aug 1941.

33. WO 106/2796, Pile *Dispatch* I, 2–3.

34. WO 166/2080, War Diary AA Cmd G, Pile to WO, AAC/Z/1160/G/SD, 3 Dec 1941.

35. WO 106/2796, Pile *Dispatch* I, 3.

36. WO 32/9752.

37. WO 32/9752, Pile to WO, AAC/Z/1668/Gt, 2 Dec 1941.

38. WO 32/9752, f 16a, Employment of ATS in searchlights, nd [but Jan–Feb 1942].

39. Pile 1949, 226.

40. Pile 1949, 226.

41. Pile 1949, 228.

42. DeGroot 1997A, 445.

43. WO 166/2085, War Diary AA Cmd G (Int), Aug 1941.

44. WO 166/2085, War Diary AA Cmd G (Int), Sep 1941.

45. AIR 16/476, f 30b, Review of policy of deploying AA defences, 12 Sep 1941.

46. WO 166/2079, War Diary AA Cmd G, Pile to WO, AAC/Z/710/3/G, 9 Jun 1941.

47. WO 166/2079, War Diary AA Cmd G, Pile to WO, AAC/Z/710/3/G, 9 Jun 1941, p 2.

48. ADM 199/1190, COS (AA) 330 (Final), 14 Jul 1941.

49. WO 106/2796, Pile *Dispatch* II, p 2.

50. WO 32/9474, f 40a, Pile to Fighter Cmd, AAC/Z/961/[. . .]/G/Ops, 27 Jun 1941.

51. AIR 16/476, Minute 29, 27 Aug 1941.

52. AIR 16/476, f 30b, Review of policy of deploying AA defences, 12 Sep 1941.

53. WO 166/2080, War Diary AA Cmd G, Pile to Fighter Cmd,

AAC/Z/681/G, 24 Sep 1941.
54. WO 106/2796, Pile *Dispatch* II, p 6.
55. WO 166/2080, War Diary AA Cmd G, AA Cmd to Corps, AAC/Z/681/G/Ops, 12 Nov 1941.
56. WO 166/2080, War Diary AA Cmd G, AA Cmd to Corps, AAC/Z/1221/111/G/Ops, 25 Nov 1941.
57. CAB 82/29, AA (S) (41) 52, 30 Nov 1941.
58. Pile 1949, 198–9.
59. WO 32/9475, f 40a, Teleprint signal Jul 1941.
60. WO 166/2080, War Diary AA Cmd G, AA Cmd to Corps, AAC/Z/762/G/Ops, 12 Oct 1940.
61. AIR 16/478, f 44a, AA Cmd to Corps, AAC/Z/762/G/Ops, 16 Mar 1942.
62. CAB 82/13, DCOS (AA) Minutes of 40th Meeting, 18 Nov 1941.
63. AIR 16/478, f 72a, AA Cmd to Gps, AAC/40306/G/Ops, 12 Feb 1943.
64. Pile 1949, 217.

Chapter 9

1. Pile 1949, 229.
2. Collier 1957, 304.
3. AIR 28/866, ORB 5 ITW Torquay, App 15, 6 Mar 1942.
4. Unless indicated otherwise the chronology of the Fringe Target campaign given in this chapter derives from a summary compiled in March 1944 at WO 166/14235, War Diary AA Cmd G, AA Cmd to Gps, AAC/40512/G/WR, 19 Mar 1944. Pile drew heavily on this source in *Ack-Ack* (Pile 1949, 237–44).
5. Pile 1949, 232.
6. WO 166/7281, War Diary AA Cmd G, AA Cmd Int Sum 79, 24 Apr–1 May 1942.
7. WO 166/7281, War Diary AA Cmd G, AA Cmd Int Sum 79, 24 Apr–1 May 1942.
8. Dobinson 2000, 164–70.
9. AIR 2/5182, f 15a, Whitworth Jones to J F Turner, 30 Apr 1942.
10. WO 166/7281, War Diary AA Cmd G, AA Cmd Int Sum 81, 8 May–15 May 1942.
11. WO 166/7281, War Diary AA Cmd G, Pile to Fighter Cmd, AAC/Z/2262/G/Ops, 29 May 1942.
12. WO 106/2796, Pile *Dispatch* II, p 8.
13. WO 166/7281, War Diary AA Cmd G, Pile to Fighter Cmd, AAC/Z/2262/G/Ops, 29 May 1942.
14. Pile's book (or at least the first edition) contains a confusing misprint here (1949, 238) which has him saying 'On May 23 attacks took place.' Details are given. The sentence should have read 'In May, 23 attacks took place.'
15. WO 166/7280, War Diary AA Cmd G, Pile to WO, 27 Apr 1942.
16. WO 166/14235, War Diary AA Cmd G, AA Cmd to Gps, AAC/40512/G/WR, 19 Mar 1944, p 1.
17. WO 106/2798, AA guns, searchlights and GL stations allocated, Dec 1941–May 1942.
18. Pile 1949, 238.
19. WO 166/7281, War Diary AA Cmd G, AA Cmd Int Sum 81, 8–15 May 1942.
20. WO 166/7281, War Diary AA Cmd G, AA Cmd Int Sum 82, 15–22 May 1942.

21.   AIR 2/4768, AA Cmd to multiple recipients, AAC/40265/G/Ops, 23 Jun
        1942.
22.   WO 166/2079, War Diary AA Cmd G, AA Cmd to Corps,
        AAC/Z/1267/1/Gt, 21 Aug 1941.
23.   WO 287/199, *Barrack Synopsis (War)*, Chap V, amendment of Oct 1943,
        p 64.
24.   WO 165/91, War Diary DFW, ADGB Progress Report, static HAA gun
        sites for month ending 15 Jan 1942.
25.   WO 166/11144, War Diary AA Cmd G, Pile to WO,
        AAC/40146/22/G(SD), 7 Apr 1943.
26.   WO 106/2796, Pile *Dispatch* II, p 6–7.
27.   No mention of the claim is made in WO 166/7281, War Diary AA Cmd
        G (Int), AA Cmd Int Sum 93, 31 Jul–7 Aug 1942, though it does appear
        in the diary at WO 166/14235, War Diary AA Cmd G, AA Cmd to Gps,
        AAC/40512/G/WR, 19 Mar 1944.
28.   WO 166/7281, War Diary AA Cmd G, AA Cmd Int Sum 94, 7–14 Aug
        1942.
29.   WO 106/2796, Pile, *Dispatch* II, p 8.
30.   WO 166/14235, War Diary AA Cmd G, AA Cmd to Gps,
        AAC/40512/G/WR, 19 Mar 1944, p 1.
31.   Pile 1949, 241.
32.   WO 166/7282, War Diary AA Cmd G, AA Cmd Op Instruction 1, 2 Oct
        1942.
33.   AIR 49/323, f 10a, Notes on enemy attack on RAF Officers' Hospital,
        Torquay, 25 Oct 1942.
34.   WO 166/7303, War Diary 3 AA Gp G, App 3, 3 AA Gp Gun Deployment
        Statement, 7 Dec 1942.
35.   WO 166/14234, War Diary AA Cmd G, 1943: A Retrospect, Maj C E
        Stones, 7 Jan 1944.
36.   WO 166/14235, War Diary AA Cmd G, AA Cmd to Gps,
        AAC/40512/G/WR, 19 Mar 1944, pp 6–7.
37.   WO 166/11147, War Diary AA Cmd G, Pile to WO,
        AAC/40267/73/G/Ops, 16 Mar 1943.
38.   WO 199/2583, f 95a, AA Cmd to 2, 3 and 5 AA Gps,
        AAC/40223/3/G/Ops, 17 Mar 1943.
39.   WO 199/2583, f 107a, GHQ Home Forces to Eastern, Southern and
        South-Eastern Cmds, HF 757/4/Ops, 2 Apr 1943.
40.   WO 166/11144, AA Cmd Op Instruction 10, 28 May 1943.
41.   Details of these Eastbourne raids are given in Hardy [1947], 32–3.
42.   WO 166/11146, War Diary AA Cmd G, AA Cmd to 1, 2 3 and 5 AA Gps,
        AAC/40217/15/G/Ops, 17 Sep 1943.

Chapter 10

1.   Quoted in Overy 1998, 459–60.
2.   Overy 1998, 459.
3.   MoI 1943, 4.
4.   The figures quoted here are from WO 166/11147, War Diary AA Cmd G,
        Weekly Equipment Statement ADGB, 12 Jan 1943; and WO 166/14234,
        War Diary AA Cmd G, Weekly Equipment Statement ADGB, 29 Dec
        1943.
5.   WO 166/14617, War Diary 1 AA Gp, 1 AA Gp to Bdes, 1Gp/115/21/G, 27
        Jun 1943.

6.   WO 166/14617, War Diary 1 AA Gp, 1 AA Gp to AA Cmd, 1Gp/115/21/G, 25 Jul 1943.

7.   WO 166/11145, War Diary AA Cmd G, AA Cmd to Gps, AAC/40236/2/G/Ops, 16 Aug 1943.

8.   WO 32/9475, f 127b, AA Cmd to Gps, AAC/40339/G/Ops, 23 Apr 1944.

9.   WO 166/16630, War Diary AA Cmd G, Weekly Equipment Statement ADGB, 9 May 1945.

10.   The sites completed or under construction by November 1945, to summarise, were, in the IAZ, ZE21, ZS4, ZS14, ZW10, ZE4, ZS21, ZS26, ZS17 and ZW13; in Thames & Medway, TS2, TS10, TN9, TN13 and TN19; at Plymouth H4, H7, H11 (under construction) and H13; on the Mersey, H4 and 37; at Harwich, H2; on the Solent, P5 and P12 at Portsmouth and IW6 and IW13 on the Isle of Wight; on the Humber, H2, H4, H20 and H28, and at Dover (both under construction), D2 and D3. For locations see Appendix IV.

11.   Postan *et al* 1964, 297.

12.   WO 166/14235, War Diary AA Cmd G, AA Cmd to Gps, AAC/40298/G(Tech), 5 Mar 1944.

13.   WO 166/14235, War Diary AA Cmd G, AA Cmd to 1 AA Gp, AAC/40298/G(Tech), 27 Mar 1944.

14.   WO 199/2975, *AA Defence of Great Britain, Survey and History of*, Part III, Vol I, p 122–8.

15.   Postan *et al* 1964, 294.

16.   WO 166/11145, War Diary AA Cmd G, AA Cmd to Gps, AAC/40236/2/G/Ops, 16 Aug 1943.

17.   WO 166/11147, War Diary AA Cmd G, Weekly AA Equipment Statement ADGB, 24 Nov 1943.

18.   WO 166/16630, War Diary AA Cmd G, Weekly Equipment Statement ADGB, 9 May 1945.

19.   WO 165/91, War Diary, DFW, Jul 1943, Pt II: Designs and Specifications.; WO 287/199, *Barrack Synopsis (War)*, Chap V, undated amendment 1 (post-May 1943), states that the existing emplacement designs DFW 55414 and DFW 55415/1 will shortly be replaced by DFW 55483, 'to be issued shortly'.

20.   WO 166/11145, War Diary AA Cmd G, Meeting at War Office [. . .] to discuss 3.7in gun emplacement design, AAC/40245/G(Tech), 26 Aug 1943.

21.   WO 287/199, *Barrack Synopsis (War)*, Chap V, Appendix A, amendment V/55/2, Oct 1943.

22.   WO 166/7282, War Diary AA Cmd G, AA Cmd to Gps. AAC/40316/G(Tech)/2, 23 Nov 1942.

23.   See Sayer 1950 [WO 277/3], 56–67; Postan *et al* 1964, 384–6.

24.   Baxter 1946, 142.

25.   Sayer 1950, 65.

26.   WO 166/11158, War Diary 2 AA Gp, 2 AA Gp to Ddos, X/13/5/G (Ops), 25 Mar 1943.

27.   WO 166/14234, War Diary AA Cmd G, Weekly Equipment Statement ADGB, 29 Dec 1943.

28.   WO 166/7282, War Diary AA Cmd G, AA Cmd to Gps, AAC/40267/65/G (Tech), 27 Dec 1942; WO 287/199, *Barrack Synopsis (War)*, Schedule 11, Oct 1943.

29.   WO 166/16630, War Diary AA Cmd G, Weekly Equipment Statement ADGB, 9 May 1945.

30.   WO 166/14237, War Diary AA Cmd G, Weekly Equipment Statement
       ADGB, 8 Jul 1944.
31.   AORG Report 226, 2 Nov 1944, quoted in Napier 1946, 14–15.
32.   AORG Report 226, 2 Nov 1944, quoted in Napier 1946, 15.
33.   WO 166/14234, War Diary AA Cmd G, 1943: A Retrospect, Maj C E
       Stones, 7 Jan 1944.
34.   WO 166/11145, War Diary AA Cmd G, AA Cmd *Intelligence Review* 140,
       25 June–2 July 1943.
35.   WO 166/11145, War Diary AA Cmd G, AA Cmd *Intelligence Review* 147,
       13–20 Aug 1943.
36.   INF 1/292, MoI *Home Intelligence Weekly Report*, 139, for 25 May–1 Jun,
       3 Jun 1943, p 2.
37.   Pile 1949, 281–3.
38.   Pile 1949, 281.
39.   WO 166/11145, War Diary AA Cmd G, AA Cmd to Gps,
       AAC/40217/65/G/Ops, 2 Jun 1943.
40.   Pile 1949, 282.
41.   WO 166/11145, War Diary AA Cmd G, AA Cmd to Gps,
       AAC/40217/65/G/Ops, 16 Jun 1943.
42.   WO 166/11145, War Diary AA Cmd G, Monthly LAA Armament Report,
       1 Aug 1943.
43.   Pile 1949, 283.
44.   Pile 1949, 283.
45.   Pile 1949, 285. On *Starkey* see Howard 1990, 233–4.
46.   Dobinson 2000, 186–91.
47.   WO 166/11146, War Diary AA Cmd G, AA Cmd *Intelligence Review* 154,
       1–8 Oct 1943.
48.   WO 166/11146, War Diary AA Cmd G, AA Cmd *Intelligence Review* 154,
       1–8 Oct 1943, p 3–4.
49.   Ziegler 1998, 235.
50.   Pile 1949, 302.
51.   WO 166/11146, War Diary AA Cmd G, AA Cmd to Gps,
       AAC/40172/20/G(Ops) (SL), 12 Oct 1943.
52.   Pile 1949, 303.
53.   WO 166/14234, War Diary AA Cmd G, 1943: A Retrospect, Maj C E
       Stones, 7 Jan 1944.
54.   Pile 1949, 303.
55.   WO 166/14234, War Diary AA Cmd G, 1943: A Retrospect, Maj C E
       Stones, 7 Jan 1944, p 14.
56.   WO 166/14234, War Diary AA Cmd G, 1943: A Retrospect, Maj C E
       Stones, 7 Jan 1944, p 15.
57.   WO 166/11147, War Diary AA Cmd G, f 59d, G(Ops) monthly summary
       for September and October, 12 Nov 1943, p 1.
58.   WO 166/14234, War Diary AA Cmd G, 1943: A Retrospect, Maj C E
       Stones, 7 Jan 1944, p 14.
59.   Pile 1949, 303.
60.   Pile 1949, 288.
61.   AIR 20/2625, COS(43)245, 29 Aug 1943.
62.   CAB 82/13, COS (AA) 61st meeting (29 Nov 1943), 3 Dec 1943.
63.   AIR 20/2625, COS(43)790 (O), 26 Dec 1943.
64.   WO 106/2796, Pile *Dispatch* II, p 4.
65.   WO 166/14617, War Diary 1 AA Gp, raid report teleprint, 1 AA Gp to AA
       Cmd, 12.15, 23 Jan 1944.

66. WO 166/14234, War Diary AA Cmd G, Weekly Equipment Statement ADGB, 29 Dec 1943.
67. WO 166/14617, War Diary 1 AA Gp, raid report teleprint, 1 AA Gp to AA Cmd, 16.00, 22 Jan 1944.
68. WO 166/14617, War Diary 1 AA Gp, raid report teleprint, 1 AA Gp to AA Cmd, 19.10, 22 Jan 1944.
69. WO 166/14234, War Diary AA Cmd G, AA Cmd *Intelligence Review* 170, 21–28 Jan 1944, p 8.
70. Ziegler 1998, 269.
71. WO 166/14234, War Diary AA Cmd G, AA Cmd *Intelligence Review* 170, 21–28 Jan 1944, p 7.
72. Collier 1957, 520. Ziegler, incidentally, says 268 tons, but this is the weight carried by the aircraft, not that reaching the capital (Ziegler 1998, 268).
73. WO 166/14235, War Diary AA Cmd G, AA Cmd *Intelligence Review* 175, 4 Mar 1944, p 7.
74. Middlebrook & Everitt 1990, 446–66.
75. WO 166/14234, War Diary AA Cmd G, AA Cmd *Intelligence Review* 170, 21–28 Jan 1944, p 7.
76. Hinsley *et al* 1984, 324.
77. WO 166/14234, War Diary AA Cmd G, AA Cmd *Intelligence Review* 171, 28 Jan–4 Feb 1944, p 9.
78. Collier 1957, 520.
79. WO 166/14234, War Diary AA Cmd G, AA Cmd *Intelligence Review* 171, 28 Jan–4 Feb 1944, p 9.
80. WO 166/14234, War Diary AA Cmd G, AA Cmd *Intelligence Review* 171, 28 Jan–4 Feb 1944, p 10.
81. WO 166/14235, War Diary AA Cmd G, AA Cmd *Intelligence Review* 177, 10–17 Mar 1944, p 5.
82. Collier 1957, 520.
83. WO 166/14236, War Diary AA Cmd G, Notes on GOC-in-C's meeting of London battery and site commanders held at Brompton Road on 14 Apr 1944, AAC/40295/5/G(Tech), 15 Apr 1944.

Chapter 11

1. Hinsley *et al* 1984, 357–414.
2. See Middlebrook 1988.
3. Collier 1957, 362.
4. AIR 16/451, ADGB Provisional Concurrent Air Defence Plan for Operations 'Overlord' and 'Diver', 4 Mar 1944.
5. AIR 8/1194, COS (44) 290 (O), 28 Mar 1944, p 1.
6. Pile 1949, 314.
7. WO 199/2284, f 54a, 3 AA Gp to Districts, 4090/4/5/Q, 12 Mar 1944.
8. WO 199/2999, f 1a, AA Cmd Op Order 14, 14 Mar 1944.
9. WO 199/2999, f 8a, AA Cmd to Gps, AAC/40217/78/G/Ops, 16 Mar 1944.
10. WO 199/2999, f 36a, 4 AA Gp to AA Cmd, 4AA/2310/1/G(Ops), 27 Mar 1944; f 38a, 3 AA Gp to AA Cmd, 2067/G(Ops), 28 Mar 1944; f 39a, 6 AA Gp to AA Cmd, 6AAG/MS/2020/G(Ops), 28 Mar 1944; f 48a, 2 AA Gp to AA Cmd, X/401/G(Ops), 30 Mar 1944.
11. AIR 8/1194, COS (44) 296 (O), also COS (AA) (44) 13, 29 Mar 1944.

12.   WO 199/2999, f 50a, Air defence plans for Operation OVERLORD and
       DIVER: appreciation, 30 Mar 1944.
13.   WO 199/3000, f 1a, AA Cmd TPM to Gps, 17.00, 6 Apr 1944.
14.   AIR 16/451, f 27a, ADGB to multiple recipients, ADGB/TS37573/Ops
       5B, 12 Apr 1944.
15.   WO 199/3000, f 57a, ADGB Op Order 4/1944, ADGB/TS37570/Ops 1,
       20 Apr 1944.
16.   Collier 1957, 520.
17.   CAB 106/1185, Memorandum on Planning and Defences throughout
       the south of England & Wales including the the 'Overlord' Operation, as
       at 'D' Day (6th June 1944), also Anti 'Diver' Defences throughout the
       periods of attack (June 1944 to March 1945), MoHS, May 1945, App A.
18.   WO 199/3001, f 129a, AA Cmd to Gps, AAC/40217/68/G/Ops, 27 May
       1944.
19.   Pile 1949, 326.
20.   WO 106/2796, Pile *Dispatch* II, p 13.
21.   WO 199/553, f 5a, Report on incident at Stone (nr Dartford), night
       12/13 Jun, nd.
22.   Collier 1957, 370
23.   WO 106/2796, Pile *Dispatch* II, p 13.
24.   WO 166/14237, War Diary AA Cmd G, AA Cmd *Intelligence Review* 190,
       17 Jun 1944, p 4.
25.   Collier 1957, 370.
26.   WO 166/14237, War Diary AA Cmd G, AA Cmd *Intelligence Review* 190,
       17 Jun 1944, p 4.
27.   Collier 1957, 369–70.
28.   Collier 1957, 371.
29.   Quoted in WO 166/14237, War Diary AA Cmd G, AA Cmd *Intelligence
       Review* 190, 17 Jun 1944, p 7.
30.   WO 199/3001, f 217a, AA Cmd TPM, 13.40, 16 Jun 1944.
31.   Publication is expected in the summer of 2004, but for an interim
       analysis of the *Diver* deployments see Dobinson 1996B.
32.   WO 199/3001, f 206a, AA Cmd to 3 AA Gp, AAC/40217/78/G/Ops, 12
       Jun 1944.
33.   WO 199/3001, f 199a, ADGB to AA Cmd, ADGB/S36661/Ops 5B, 8 Jun
       1944.
34.   WO 199/2606, 2 AA Gp Op Order 25, 17 Jun 1944.
35.   CAB 106/1185, Memorandum [. . .], MoHS, May 1945, App C; WO
       106/2796, Pile *Dispatch* II, p 13.
36.   Collier 1957.
37.   CAB 106/1185, Memorandum [. . .], MoHS, May 1945, App C.
38.   WO 106/2796, Pile *Dispatch* II, p 14.
39.   WO 106/2796, Pile *Dispatch* II, p 15.
40.   CAB 106/1185, Memorandum [. . .], MoHS, May 1945, App C.
41.   WO 106/2796, Pile *Dispatch* II, p 16.
42.   Collier 1957, 523. Fractions are ignored in these figures, but the
       officially credited totals were, from 12 June to 15 July, $924^1/_3$ to
       fighters, $261^1/_3$ to guns and $55^1/_3$ to balloons and, from 16 July to 5
       September, 847, $1198^1/_3$ and $176^1/_3$ in those three categories.
43.   Pile 1949, 344.
44.   AIR 20/2627, COS (44) 799 (O) (also COS (AA) (44) 35 (Final)), 2 Sep
       1944, citing JIC (44) 383 (O), 28 Aug 1944.
45.   AIR 20/2627, COS (44) 835 (O) (also COS (AA) 44 39), 16 Sep 1944.

46. AIR 20/2627, AM to ADGB, CMS 622/D Ops (AD), 22 Sep 1944.
47. AIR 20/2627. AM to ADGB, CTS 605/D of Ops (AD), 22 Sep 1944.
48. WO 106/2796, Pile *Dispatch* II, p 17.
49. Pile 1949, 369.
50. Pile 1949, 372.
51. Pile 1949, 373.
52. WO 199/1410, 5 AA Gp to 63 AA Bde, 5AAG/1599/31/G(Ops), 17 Oct 1944.
53. AIR 16/463, f 7a, HQ Fighter Cmd to AM (D Ops (AD)), FC/S 39399/Ops 5B, 9 Nov 1944.
54. WO 166/14631, War Diary 5 AA Gp G, 5 AA Gp to AA Cmd, 5AAG/1599/41/G(Ops), 19 Nov 1944.
55. WO 166/14237, War Diary AA Cmd G, AA Cmd to WO, AAC/40160/6/G(SD), 15 Jul 1944.
56. WO 106/2796, Pile *Dispatch* II, p 4.
57. Quoted in Pile 1949, 379–80.
58. Pile's book (1949, 382) says that the project was ordered on 14 October, but he appears to mean 14 November (the day on which Driberg's question appeared in *Hansard*), which is the date implied by primary sources.
59. Pile 1949, 383.
60. Collier 1957, 523.
61. Pile 1949, 376.
62. WO 166/16629, War Diary AA Cmd G, Pile to WO, AAC/40214/5/G(Tech), 9 Jan 1945.
63. WO 166/14617, War Diary 1 AA Gp, App S to 1 AA Gp Procedure Instruction 9, 1Gp/255/1/G, 21 Mar 1944.
64. WO 166/14236, War Diary AA Cmd G, AA Cmd Op Instruction 13, AAC/40251/1/G/Ops, 26 Apr 1944.
65. WO 106/2796, Pile *Dispatch* II, p 19.
66. WO 166/16629, War Diary AA Cmd G, AA Cmd Op Instruction 15, AAC/40251/3/G/Ops, 28 Jan 1945.
67. WO 166/16629, War Diary AA Cmd G, Pile to WO, AAC/40251/g/G/Ops, 23 Feb 1945.
68. So says Pile in WO 106/2796, *Dispatch* II, p 19, though his book (1949, 388) tells us that War Cabinet authority to fire had still to be given when the V2 attacks ceased.
69. Collier 1957, 523.
70. Pile 1949, 388–90.

Chapter 12

1. They were not, of course, strictly the first shots to be fired 'in anger', though those had been aimed at British aircraft, when the anger soon turned to anguish.
2. WO 166/16630, War Diary AA Cmd G, AA Cmd *Intelligence Review* 238, 19 May 1945, p 2.
3. WO 166/16630, War Diary AA Cmd G, AA Cmd *Intelligence Review* 244, 30 Jun 1945, p 2.
4. Pile 1949, 397.
5. Compare Pile 1949, 105–6 with the letter quoted on pp 165–6 above.
6. Thetford 1995, 53–4.
7. Pile 1949, 391.

8. In a forthcoming English Heritage volume by Roger J C Thomas and Wayne Cocroft provisionally titled *Architecture of Armageddon*.
9. WO 166/16644, War Diary 5 AA Gp, 5 AA Gp to Bdes, 5AAG/497/G(SD), 26 Jul 1945.
10. WO 166/16631, War Diary AA Cmd G, AA Cmd to Gps, AAC/40575/G/Ops, 2 Sep 1945.
11. WO 166/16644, War Diary 5 AA Gp, 5 AA Gp to AA Cmd, 5AAG/6051/G(Ops), 26 Sep 1945.
12. WO 166/16631, War Diary AA Cmd G, AA Cmd letter AAC/40575/G(Ops), 23 Nov 1945.
13. WO 166/17848, War Diary AA Cmd G, AA Cmd to Gps, AAC/40575/4/G(Ops), 28 Mar 1946.
14. HLG 71/1602, WO to AA Cmd, 57/Guns/3229 (RA3), 18 Sep 1946.
15. HLG 71/1602, WO to formations, 118/AA/188 (DQ), 28 Nov 1946.
16. HLG 71/ 1062, Notes of a meeting held at the Ministry of Town and Country Planning [. . .] to discuss the progress of the selection of anti-aircraft gun sites, 95223/20/1, 27 Sep 1948.
17. See the site lists at HLG 71/1603, Min Town and County Planning to CLA Chester, 7 Nov 1953.
18. I am grateful to Roger J C Thomas for information on this point.
19. AIR 8/2016, Note of a meeting held in CAS's room [. . .], 4 Nov 1953, para 3.
20. Dobinson 1996A; *ibid* 1996B.
21. Including the LAA positions proved impossible for practical reasons, though interested researchers can obtain this information from the original Monuments Protection Programme report (Dobinson 1996A), copies of which have been deposited with the Sites and Monuments Records maintained by local authorities throughout England.
22. In the hands of Neil Redfern: Redfern 1998.
23. Examples which have included work on AA batteries are (for the Plymouth area) Pye & Woodward 1996 and (for Essex) Nash 1998.
24. See generally Anderton 1999.
25. Francis 1999.

APPENDIX I

Wish-lists

The following table summarises the allocations of HAA weapons to GDAs and other recipients under the successive air defence schemes of the 1930s: the Brooke-Popham Report (January 1935), the Joubert Report (June 1936), Dowding's Ideal Scheme (February 1937) and the revisions of February and May 1939.* It also shows the number of guns actually in place in the GDAs on 3 September 1939 – the first day of the Second World War – and, in the two final columns, the percentage which this represents of the May 1939 and January 1935 figures. The first of these two columns shows that no GDA had more than 70 per cent of the guns considered necessary in the May 1939 scheme and that most had no more than a third to a half of their entitlements: the national aggregate was just 30 per cent. The second percentage column shows that most GDAs had comfortably exceeded their allocations under the January 1935 plans, but also emphasises that more

---

* CAB 13/18, ADGB 25 (HDC 166), CID Home Defence Committee, Sub-Committee on the Reorientation of the Air Defence System of Great Britain, *Interim Report*, 31 Jan 1935; CAB 13/19, ADGB 58 (HDC 199), CID Home Defence Committee, Sub Committee on the Reorientation of the Air Defence System of Great Britain, Redistribution of the Defences of the Air Defence of Great Britain, *Report*, 17 Jun 1936; CAB 13/19, ADGB 73 (also HDC 220), CID Home Defence Committee, Sub-Committee on the Reorientation of the Air Defence System of Great Britain, 'Ideal' Air Defence of Great Britain, *Report*, 9 Feb 1937; CAB 13/12, HDC 311 (also ADGB 170), CID HDC, Future requirements in AA and light AA guns for the Air Defence of Great Britain, 3 May 1939; WO 166/2070, War Diary AA Cmd G, HAA as at 08.00, 3 Sep 1939.

	01.1935 (Brooke-Popham)	06.1936 (Joubert)	02.1937 (Ideal)
IAZ (London)	96	192	224
OAZ (Huntingdon–Tees)	128	–	–
OAZ (Portsmouth–Huntingdon)	32	–	–
Thames & Medway	40	40	224
Birmingham–Coventry	24	40	80
Leeds	24	40	64
Manchester	24	40	56
Sheffield	16	40	48
Humber	16	16	24
Tees	16	32	44
Tyne	16	32	44
Portsmouth	16	20	36
Harwich	8	8	16
Southampton	–	20	36
Forth (Rosyth)	–	16	48
Mersey	–	24	40
Dover	–	8	8
Plymouth	–	16	24
Scapa	–	8	8
Portland	–	8	16
Milford Haven	–	8	–
Bristol	–	–	56
Glasgow	–	–	56
Cardiff	–	–	24
Newport	–	–	24
Derby–Nottingham	–	–	16
Swansea	–	–	–
Invergordon	–	–	–
Aerodromes	–	–	–
Holton Heath	–	–	–
Belfast	–	–	–
Stanmore	–	–	–
Bramley	–	–	–
Mobile pool	–	–	48
Strategic reserve	–	–	–
TOTAL	**456**	**608**	**1264**

02.1939 (Revision)	05.1939 (Revision)	03.9.1939 (Actual)	% 05.1939 (Actual)	% 01.1935 (Actual)
240	240	136	57	142
–	–	–	–	–
–	–	–	–	–
240	240	133	55	333
88	120	32	27	133
64	64	24	38	100
56	56	12	21	200
48	48	20	42	125
40	80	28	70	175
60	48	14	17	88
60	120	34	41	213
36	56	29	52	181
16	16	6	38	75
36	48	30	63	–
48	96	28	58	–
72	104	19	18	–
16	16	6	38	–
32	48	14	29	–
8	24	8	33	–
16	24	2	8	–
–	–	–	–	–
56	56	14	25	–
64	80	19	24	–
24	24	6	25	–
24	24	4	17	–
32	48	12	25	–
16	32	0	0	–
8	16	2	13	–
128	128	15	12	–
–	16	4	–	–
–	24	–	–	–
–	–	4	–	–
–	–	7	–	–
56	168	–	–	–
–	168	–	–	–
1584	**2232**	**662**	**30**	**145**

than half the areas authorised for defences on the first day of war had not been considered for them when rearmament began.

A few points should be borne in mind when studying the table. The first is that the Brooke-Popham plan of 1935 (uniquely) excluded most of the defended ports, which at this date lay outside the ADGB orbit and formed the subject of separate allocations. The total figure of 456 guns (which in the report was actually expressed as 57 eight-gun batteries) is therefore not precisely comparable with the remaining totals, though the individual GDA allocations are. The second point is that the listing of GDAs in the successive reports was not always consistent: occasionally areas occurring separately in the earlier reports are lumped together as one in the later (the IAZ and Thames & Medway, for instance, were discrete in the January 1935 study but amalgamated from the Ideal Scheme onwards). These cases are rare, but where they do occur the later 'grouped' totals are simply split 50:50 between the two areas. Occasionally, too, the reverse happens, GDAs which were separately listed by September 1939 being earlier bunched together, as Birmingham/Coventry and Nottingham/ Derby. In these two cases the separate totals for September 1939 are summed together.

APPENDIX II

HAA strengths: the Battle of Britain and the Blitz

MAY 1940–MAY 1941

This appendix tabulates the changing distribution of HAA guns and the rise in LAA stocks in the period spanning the Battle of Britain and the Blitz. Heavy weapons are shown by type and GDA, light guns simply by numbers, at approximately monthly intervals from May 1940 to May 1941 as shown in the ADGB Equipment Statements issued every Wednesday and filed in the War Diaries of AA Command's General Staff.* Rather than structure the table in conformity with AA Command's divisional organisation – which changed over this period and saw some exchange of areas between divisions – the GDAs are instead grouped geographically, with airfields appearing in a separate section. This means of presentation reflects areas which, at the time, had some real tactical meaning in apportioning HAA resources. Thus we have *London area and approaches*, the *East coast* (of Britain), the *South coast*, the *Midlands and East Anglia*, the *West coast* (of Britain), *Northern England* and *Northern Ireland*. Apart from this re-ordering, however, the table adheres faithfully to the data as recorded in the Equipment Statements.

Much of the table is self-explanatory, but a few words of amplification are needed here and there. First, it should be

---

* The data in the table are drawn from the ADGB Equipment Statements for the dates given filed in the War Diaries of AA Cmd's G Branch at WO 166/2074 (May–Jun 1940), WO 166/2075 (Jul–Oct 1940), WO 166/2076 (Nov–Dec 1940), WO 166/2077 (Jan–Feb 1941), WO 166/2078 (Mar–Apr 1941) and WO 166/2079 (May–Aug 1941).

obvious that *every* GDA which appeared on *any* Equipment Statement within the span of the table appears in the far left-hand column. On dates when a GDA was listed but unarmed the relevant column shows a zero. On those when the GDA did not appear at all – either because it was not yet established or had been abolished – the column shows an en rule (–). A few GDAs appeared on virtually every Equipment Statement but were not armed with HAA on any of the dates included in the table – such as Folkestone, Newhaven and Littlehampton – and were eventually deleted. In the table, therefore, these areas simply display a row of zeros which collapse eventually into en rules. Second, it will be noted that the rows of figures for each GDA are broken down by gun types (at most, 4.5in, 3.7in static, 3.7in mobile and 3in Case III), though types *not* represented on any of the dates shown are omitted from the second column (which apart from saving space allows the range of weapons present in the GDA over the span of the table to be seen at a glance). Third, the totals (shown in bold) for each date refer to all guns held by the GDA, whether or not they were operational. The Equipment Statements do, regularly, include annotation to indicate the odd gun out of action here and there (usually for want of the dials where the predictor data was read at the gunpit), but these are so few as to be discountable when broad trends are of interest. Last, since these are monthly figures sampled from a weekly cycle of lists, a certain amount of 'smoothing' of the data is inevitable. This has two implications. First, in periods of rapid change, the maximum and minimum strengths of GDAs may not have been captured because they fall on dates between those shown here. Second, it should be borne in mind that precise interpolation from the figures would be unsafe: to give a hypothetical example, if a specific area had 100 guns on a certain date and 200 a month later, it definitely would not follow that it had 150 at the mid-point of those two dates – and it may have hit a peak of 210 a week later. That said, however, change in gun strengths was seldom so rapid as to defeat expression on a monthly cycle. If the strength of each GDA was plotted as a line on a graph, restoring each weekly point would sometimes produce a slightly more jagged trace than the monthly intervals here, but the general trends in the strengths of GDAs reflected in the table are nonetheless meaningful and real. The data for intermediate points – and for any week during the war – are readily found in the War Diaries of AA Command's General Staff, to which researchers should turn when more precise, week-by-week information is required.

LAA weapons are listed much more simply: their table simply shows the numbers held, by type, at each date (excluding Lewis guns). The LAA table and the HAA summary figures also include rows titled *Factor*. These are simply an attempt to show the proportional increase in guns between the first date in the table and those succeeding it, with the totals for 29 May 1940 given a value of 1.0, and the subsequent dates taking their values from this. Referring to the table, it will be seen that on 21 May 1941 AA Command held 1.61 times the number of HAA guns as on 29 May 1940 and 2.13 the number of LAA, but that the multiplication figure for Bofors guns alone reached 4.68 between those two dates.

London area and approaches

		29.05.40	26.06.40	24.07.40	21.08.40	18.09.40
London (IAZ)	4.5	48	48	48	48	48
	3.7(s)	32	32	32	32	32
	3.7(m)	31	30	6	6	113
	3.0	8	6	6	6	6
	Total	**119**	**116**	**92**	**92**	**199**
Thames & Medway (N)	4.5	21	32	32	32	32
	3.7(s)	4	4	8	8	8
	3.7(m)	16	4	0	0	0
	3.0	4	8	8	8	8
	Total	**45**	**48**	**48**	**48**	**48**
Thames & Medway (S)	4.5	24	27	31	32	32
	3.7(s)	16	24	24	24	24
	3.7(m)	20	24	8	8	8
	3.0	10	8	8	8	8
	Total	**70**	**83**	**71**	**72**	**72**
Stanmore	3.0	4	4	4	4	4
	Total	**4**	**4**	**4**	**4**	**4**
Langley/Slough	3.7(s)	0	0	0	0	0
	3.7(m)	0	4	4	4	4
	3.0	8	24	24	24	24
	Total	**8**	**28**	**28**	**28**	**28**
Hounslow	3.7(m)	–	4	4	4	4
	Total	**–**	**4**	**4**	**4**	**4**
Brooklands	3.7(s)	0	0	0	0	0
	3.7(m)	8	8	16	16	16
	Total	**8**	**8**	**16**	**16**	**16**
Hatfield	3.7(m)	–	–	–	–	–
	3.0	–	–	–	–	–
	Total	**–**	**–**	**–**	**–**	**–**

East coast

		29.05.40	26.06.40	24.07.40	21.08.40	18.09.40
Harwich	3.7(s)	0	8	8	8	8
	3.7(m)	4	7	7	7	0
	3.0	4	0	0	0	0
	Total	**8**	**15**	**15**	**15**	**8**
Humber	4.5	24	24	24	24	24
	3.7(s)	0	0	0	0	0
	3.7(m)	8	12	12	12	0
	3.0	2	2	2	2	2
	Total	**34**	**36**	**38**	**38**	**26**

23.10.40	20.11.40	18.12.40	22.01.41	19.02.41	19.03.41	23.04.41	21.05.41
59	63	64	72	72	72	72	72
32	40	44	44	44	41	45	58
125	126	86	83	78	72	74	52
6	6	6	6	6	2	2	2
222	**235**	**200**	**205**	**200**	**187**	**193**	**184**
24	24	24	26	28	28	28	28
8	4	4	4	4	4	4	3
0	0	0	0	0	0	0	4
8	8	4	4	4	4	7	0
40	**36**	**32**	**34**	**36**	**36**	**39**	**35**
32	28	28	28	28	28	28	28
24	20	20	20	20	18	16	12
0	0	0	0	0	2	6	8
8	8	4	8	8	8	4	4
64	**56**	**52**	**56**	**56**	**56**	**54**	**52**
4	4	4	0	0	–	–	–
4	**4**	**4**	**0**	**0**	**–**	**–**	**–**
0	4	6	14	14	16	16	16
4	4	4	4	4	8	6	4
24	24	20	12	12	8	4	4
28	**32**	**30**	**30**	**30**	**32**	**26**	**24**
4	4	4	4	4	–	–	–
4	**4**	**4**	**4**	**4**	**–**	**–**	**–**
0	0	0	3	8	8	8	8
16	16	16	16	8	8	8	10
16	**16**	**16**	**19**	**16**	**16**	**16**	**18**
4	4	0	0	0	0	0	0
0	0	3	3	3	3	3	3
4	**4**	**3**	**3**	**3**	**3**	**3**	**3**

23.10.40	20.11.40	18.12.40	22.01.41	19.02.41	19.03.41	23.04.41	21.05.41
8	8	8	8	8	8	8	8
0	0	0	0	0	0	0	0
0	0	0	0	0	0	0	0
8	**8**	**8**	**8**	**8**	**8**	**8**	**8**
24	24	24	24	24	24	20	20
0	0	0	0	0	2	2	6
0	0	0	0	0	8	8	8
2	2	2	2	2	2	6	6
26	**26**	**26**	**26**	**26**	**34**	**36**	**40**

		29.05.40	26.06.40	24.07.40	21.08.40	18.09.40
Scunthorpe	3.7(m)	0	0	0	24	0
	Total	**0**	**0**	**0**	**24**	**0**
Tees	4.5	16	16	16	16	16
	3.7(s)	8	8	8	8	8
	3.7(m)	4	0	0	0	0
	3.0	2	6	6	6	6
	Total	**30**	**30**	**30**	**30**	**30**
Tyne	4.5	32	32	32	32	32
	3.7(s)	4	8	8	8	8
	3.7(m)	2	6	8	4	4
	3.0	10	6	6	6	6
	Total	**48**	**56**	**54**	**50**	**50**
Blyth	3.7(m)	–	–	–	–	–
	Total	**–**	**–**	**=**	**–**	**–**
Forth	4.5	16	16	16	16	16
	3.7(s)	24	24	24	24	24
	3.7(m)	7	8	0	0	0
	Total	**47**	**48**	**40**	**40**	**40**
Dundee	3.7(m)	4	4	0	0	0
	Total	**4**	**4**	**0**	**0**	**0**
Aberdeen	3.7(m)	4	4	4	4	4
	Total	**4**	**4**	**4**	**4**	**4**
Invergordon	3.0	4	4	0	0	0
	Total	**4**	**4**	**0**	**0**	**0**
Castletown	3.0	–	–	2	2	2
	Total	**–**	**–**	**2**	**2**	**2**
Scapa	4.5	32	32	32	32	32
	3.7(s)	48	48	48	48	48
	3.7(m)	8	8	8	8	8
	Total	**88**	**88**	**88**	**88**	**88**
Shetlands	3.0	12	12	12	12	12
	Total	**12**	**12**	**12**	**12**	**12**

South coast

		29.05.40	26.06.40	24.07.40	21.08.40	18.09.40
Dover	3.7(s)	0	8	8	8	8
	3.7(m)	12	8	8	8	4
	3.0	2	2	2	2	2
	Total	**14**	**18**	**18**	**18**	**14**

23.10.40	20.11.40	18.12.40	22.01.41	19.02.41	19.03.41	23.04.41	21.05.41
0	0	0	0	0	–	–	–
0	**0**	**0**	**0**	**0**	**–**	**–**	**–**
16	16	16	16	16	16	16	16
8	8	8	8	10	10	10	10
0	0	0	0	0	0	3	3
6	6	6	6	4	0	0	0
30	**30**	**30**	**30**	**30**	**26**	**29**	**29**
32	32	32	32	32	32	32	32
8	8	8	10	10	12	12	16
0	0	0	0	0	0	0	0
6	6	6	6	4	4	4	4
46	**46**	**46**	**48**	**46**	**48**	**48**	**52**
–	–	–	–	–	–	–	4
–	**–**	**–**	**–**	**–**	**–**	**–**	**4**
16	16	16	16	16	16	16	16
24	24	24	24	24	24	24	24
0	0	0	0	0	0	0	0
40	**40**	**40**	**40**	**40**	**40**	**40**	**40**
0	0	0	0	4	4	3	3
0	**0**	**0**	**0**	**4**	**4**	**3**	**3**
4	4	0	0	0	0	0	0
4	**4**	**0**	**0**	**0**	**0**	**0**	**0**
0	0	0	0	0	–	–	–
0	**0**	**0**	**0**	**0**	**–**	**–**	**–**
2	2	0	0	0	0	0	0
2	**2**	**0**	**0**	**0**	**0**	**0**	**0**
32	32	32	32	32	32	32	32
48	48	48	48	48	48	48	48
8	8	8	8	8	0	0	0
88	**88**	**88**	**88**	**88**	**80**	**80**	**80**
12	12	12	12	12	12	12	12
12	**12**	**12**	**12**	**12**	**12**	**12**	**12**

23.10.40	20.11.40	18.12.40	22.01.41	19.02.41	19.03.41	23.04.41	21.05.41
8	8	8	8	8	8	8	8
4	4	0	0	0	0	0	0
2	2	2	2	2	2	2	2
14	**14**	**10**	**10**	**10**	**10**	**10**	**10**

		29.05.40	26.06.40	24.07.40	21.08.40	18.09.40
Folkestone	**Total**	**0**	**0**	**0**	**0**	**0**
Newhaven	3.0	8	0	0	0	0
	Total	**8**	**0**	**0**	**0**	**0**
Littlehampton	3.0	8	0	0	0	0
	Total	**8**	**0**	**0**	**0**	**0**
Portsmouth	4.5	16	16	16	16	16
	3.7(s)	8	20	24	24	24
	3.7(m)	16	8	4	4	0
	Total	**40**	**44**	**44**	**44**	**40**
Southampton	4.5	8	8	8	8	8
	3.7(s)	8	8	8	8	8
	3.7(m)	16	16	23	23	15
	Total	**32**	**32**	**39**	**39**	**31**
Bramley	3.0	8	8	8	8	8
	Total	**8**	**8**	**8**	**8**	**8**
Holton Heath	3.0	8	8	8	8	8
	Total	**8**	**8**	**8**	**8**	**8**
Portland	3.7(s)	0	0	0	0	8
	3.7(m)	0	0	8	8	0
	3.0	4	6	6	6	6
	Total	**4**	**6**	**14**	**14**	**14**
Exeter	3.7(m)	–	–	–	–	–
	Total	**–**	**–**	**–**	**–**	**–**
Plymouth	3.7(s)	0	0	8	20	24
	3.7(m)	4	12	20	20	0
	3.0	8	6	6	6	2
	Total	**12**	**18**	**34**	**46**	**26**
Falmouth	3.7(m)	0	0	4	4	0
	3.0	0	8	8	8	8
	Total	**0**	**8**	**12**	**12**	**8**

Midlands and East Anglia

		29.05.40	26.06.40	24.07.40	21.08.40	18.09.40
Leighton Buzzard	3.7(m)	–	4	4	4	4
	3.0	–	0	0	0	0
	Total	**–**	**4**	**4**	**4**	**4**
Daventry	3.0	–	4	4	4	4
	Total	**–**	**4**	**4**	**4**	**4**

23.10.40	20.11.40	18.12.40	22.01.41	19.02.41	19.03.41	23.04.41	21.05.41
0	**0**	**0**	**0**	**0**	–	–	–
0	0	0	0	0	–	–	–
0	**0**	**0**	**0**	**0**	–	–	–
0	0	0	0	0	–	–	–
0	**0**	**0**	**0**	**0**	–	–	–
16	16	16	16	16	16	16	16
24	24	12	12	12	12	12	12
0	0	4	4	4	4	4	4
40	**40**	**32**	**32**	**32**	**32**	**32**	**32**
8	8	8	8	8	7	7	8
8	8	20	20	20	20	20	20
16	16	4	4	8	4	4	4
32	**32**	**32**	**32**	**36**	**31**	**31**	**32**
4	4	4	4	4	4	4	4
4	**4**	**4**	**4**	**4**	**4**	**4**	**4**
8	8	8	8	8	8	8	8
8	**8**	**8**	**8**	**8**	**8**	**8**	**8**
8	8	8	8	8	8	8	8
0	0	0	0	0	0	0	0
4	4	4	4	4	4	4	4
12	**12**	**12**	**12**	**12**	**12**	**12**	**12**
–	–	–	–	–	–	–	4
–	–	–	–	–	–	–	**4**
24	24	24	24	24	24	24	24
0	0	0	0	0	0	0	8
0	0	0	0	0	0	0	0
24	**24**	**24**	**24**	**24**	**24**	**24**	**32**
0	0	0	0	0	0	0	0
8	8	8	8	8	8	8	8
8	**8**	**8**	**8**	**8**	**8**	**8**	**8**

23.10.40	20.11.40	18.12.40	22.01.41	19.02.41	19.03.41	23.04.41	21.05.41
4	4	0	0	0	0	0	0
0	0	4	4	4	0	0	0
4	**4**	**4**	**4**	**4**	**0**	**0**	**0**
4	4	4	4	4	0	0	0
4	**4**	**4**	**4**	**4**	**0**	**0**	**0**

		29.05.40	26.06.40	24.07.40	21.08.40	18.09.40
Leicester	3.7(m)	–	–	–	–	–
	Total	–	–	–	–	–
Birmingham	4.5	16	16	16	16	16
	3.7(s)	4	24	29	31	32
	3.7(m)	11	11	24	24	16
	3.0	0	0	0	0	0
	Total	**31**	**51**	**69**	**71**	**64**
Coventry	3.7(s)	0	16	16	16	16
	3.7(m)	16	28	16	16	8
	3.0	12	0	0	0	0
	Total	**28**	**44**	**32**	**32**	**24**
Donington	3.0	–	–	–	–	–
	Total	–	–	–	–	–
Hawarden	3,7(m)		–	–	–	–
	Total	–	–	–	–	–
Norwich	3.7(m)	–	–	–	–	4
	3.0	–	–	–	–	0
	Total	–	–	–	–	**4**

West coast

		29.05.40	26.06.40	24.07.40	21.08.40	18.09.40
Weston-super-Mare	3.7(m)	–	–	–	–	–
	Total	–	–	–	–	–
Brockworth	3.7(s)	0	0	0	0	0
	3.7(m)	8	12	24	24	24
	3.0	0	0	0	0	0
	Total	**8**	**12**	**24**	**24**	**24**
Bristol	3.7(s)	0	24	24	24	24
	3.7(m)	16	4	0	0	0
	3.0	8	8	8	8	8
	Total	**24**	**36**	**32**	**32**	**32**
Caerwent	3.0	0	0	0	0	0
	Total	**0**	**0**	**0**	**0**	**0**
Newport	3.7(s)	0	0	0	6	12
	3.7(m)	0	0	8	8	8
	3.0	4	4	4	2	2
	Total	**4**	**4**	**12**	**16**	**22**

23.10.40	20.11.40	18.12.40	22.01.41	19.02.41	19.03.41	23.04.41	21.05.41
–	–	–	–	–	8	8	8
–	**–**	**–**	**–**	**–**	**8**	**8**	**8**
16	16	16	16	16	16	16	16
32	32	32	32	32	32	32	32
16	16	47	48	48	16	16	16
0	0	0	4	0	0	0	0
64	**64**	**95**	**100**	**96**	**64**	**64**	**64**
16	16	16	24	24	24	24	24
12	16	16	16	16	8	8	8
8	8	8	0	0	0	0	0
36	**40**	**40**	**40**	**40**	**32**	**32**	**32**
4	4	4	4	4	4	4	4
4	**4**	**4**	**4**	**4**	**4**	**4**	**4**
4	4	4	4	4	4	4	4
4	**4**	**4**	**4**	**4**	**4**	**4**	**4**
4	4	0	0	0	0	0	0
0	0	4	4	4	4	4	4
4	**4**	**4**	**4**	**4**	**4**	**4**	**4**

23.10.40	20.11.40	18.12.40	22.01.41	19.02.41	19.03.41	23.04.41	21.05.41
–	–	–	–	8	4	4	4
–	**–**	**–**	**–**	**8**	**4**	**4**	**4**
0	0	0	0	0	4	9	12
24	24	20	20	16	16	13	4
0	0	4	4	4	0	0	0
24	**24**	**24**	**24**	**20**	**20**	**22**	**16**
24	24	23	23	23	24	24	34
0	0	4	4	12	32	34	38
8	8	4	4	0	8	8	8
32	**32**	**31**	**31**	**35**	**64**	**66**	**80**
0	0	0	0	4	4	4	4
0	**0**	**0**	**0**	**4**	**4**	**4**	**4**
12	12	12	12	12	12	12	12
8	8	4	4	4	4	8	8
2	0	0	0	0	0	0	0
22	**20**	**16**	**16**	**16**	**16**	**20**	**20**

		29.05.40	26.06.40	24.07.40	21.08.40	18.09.40
Cardiff	3.7(s)	0	4	4	4	9
	3.7(m)	4	4	8	16	16
	3.0	4	4	4	6	2
	Total	**8**	**12**	**16**	**26**	**27**
Swansea	3.7(s)	0	0	0	0	0
	3.7(m)	0	0	12	16	20
	3.0	0	0	0	0	4
	Total	**0**	**0**	**12**	**16**	**24**
Milford Haven	3.7(m)	–	–	–	–	4
	Total	**–**	**–**	**–**	**–**	**4**
Liverpool	4.5	16	24	24	28	32
	3.7(s)	4	12	12	12	12
	3.7(m)	20	20	16	16	16
	3.0	0	0	0	0	()
	Total	**40**	**56**	**52**	**56**	**60**
Blackpool	3.7(m)	–	–	–	–	–
	Total	**–**	**–**	**–**	**–**	**–**
Heysham	3.0	–	–	–	–	–
	Total	**–**	**–**	**–**	**–**	**–**
Barrow	3.7(s)	0	0	0	0	0
	3.7(m)	0	0	0	0	8
	Total	**0**	**0**	**0**	**0**	**8**
Ardeer	3.7(s)	–	0	0	0	0
	3.7(m)	–	4	8	8	8
	Total	**–**	**4**	**8**	**8**	**8**
Clyde	4.5	16	16	16	19	22
	3.7(s)	0	5	8	8	14
	3.7(m)	7	4	0	0	0
	Total	**23**	**25**	**24**	**27**	**36**
Oban	3.0	–	–	–	–	–
	Total	**–**	**–**	**–**	**–**	**–**
Fort William	3.0	–	–	–	–	–
	Total	**–**	**–**	**–**	**–**	**–**
Inverary	3.0	–	–	–	–	–
	Total	**–**	**–**	**–**	**–**	**–**
Kyle of Lochalsh (Port 'ZA')	3.0	0	4	4	4	4
	Total	**0**	**4**	**4**	**4**	**4**
Loch Ewe (Port 'A')	3.0	0	0	0	0	0
	Total	**0**	**0**	**0**	**0**	**0**

23.10.40	20.11.40	18.12.40	22.01.41	19.02.41	19.03.41	23.04.41	21.05.41
12	12	12	12	12	12	12	12
11	9	8	8	8	16	12	16
2	4	8	8	8	8	8	8
25	**25**	**28**	**28**	**28**	**36**	**32**	**36**
0	0	0	0	0	0	8	12
16	18	18	18	18	26	26	25
4	4	4	4	0	6	10	9
20	**22**	**22**	**22**	**18**	**32**	**44**	**46**
4	4	4	–	4	4	8	8
4	**4**	**4**	**–**	**4**	**4**	**8**	**8**
32	32	32	31	31	31	31	31
20	24	24	23	23	23	27	30
20	16	16	15	15	35	51	51
8	8	8	3	3	0	0	0
80	**80**	**80**	**72**	**72**	**89**	**109**	**112**
–	–	–	–	–	4	4	4
–	**–**	**–**	**–**	**–**	**4**	**4**	**4**
–	–	–	–	–	3	3	3
–	**–**	**–**	**–**	**–**	**3**	**3**	**3**
0	0	0	0	0	0	8	12
8	8	8	8	8	8	8	4
8	**8**	**8**	**8**	**8**	**8**	**16**	**16**
0	0	0	0	8	8	8	8
8	8	8	8	0	0	0	0
8	**8**	**8**	**8**	**8**	**8**	**8**	**8**
24	24	24	24	25	27	32	32
16	22	24	24	32	32	40	48
0	0	0	0	8	16	29	37
40	**46**	**48**	**48**	**65**	**75**	**101**	**117**
–	–	–	–	4	4	4	4
–	**–**	**–**	**–**	**4**	**4**	**4**	**4**
–	–	–	–	–	–	–	4
–	**–**	**–**	**–**	**–**	**–**	**–**	**4**
–	–	–	–	4	4	4	4
–	**–**	**–**	**–**	**4**	**4**	**4**	**4**
4	4	4	4	4	4	4	4
4	**4**	**4**	**4**	**4**	**4**	**4**	**4**
0	0	0	0	0	4	4	4
0	**0**	**0**	**0**	**0**	**4**	**4**	**4**

Northern England

		29.05.40	26.06.40	24.07.40	21.08.40	18.09.40
Derby	3.7(s)	4	8	8	16	16
	3.7(m)	20	28	24	24	16
	Total	**24**	**36**	**32**	**40**	**32**
Nottingham	3.7(s)	8	8	8	8	8
	3.7(m)	0	0	0	0	0
	3.0	8	8	8	8	8
	Total	**16**	**16**	**16**	**16**	**16**
Crewe	3.7(s)	0	0	6	8	8
	3.7(m)	8	8	8	8	0
	Total	**8**	**8**	**14**	**16**	**8**
Sheffield	4.5	16	16	16	16	16
	3.7(s)	4	4	8	8	8
	3.7(m)	4	4	3	3	3
	Total	**24**	**24**	**27**	**27**	**27**
Manchester*	4.5	16	16	16	16	16
	3.7(s)	4	4	4	4	4
	3.7(m)	0	0	0	0	0
	Total	**20**	**20**	**20**	**20**	**20**
Leeds	4.5	16	16	16	16	16
	3.7(s)	4	4	4	4	4
	3.7(m)	2	2	0	0	0
	Total	**22**	**22**	**20**	**20**	**20**
Accrington	3.7(m)	–	–	–	–	–
	Total	**–**	**–**	**–**	**–**	**–**

* Includes four guns at Ringway from 19.03.41

Northern Ireland

		29.05.40	26.06.40	24.07.40	21.08.40	18.09.40
NID [Belfast]	3.7(s)	4	4	4	4	5
	3.7(m)	3	3	3	3	3
	Total	**7**	**7**	**7**	**7**	**8**
Londonderry	3.7(m)	–	–	–	–	4
	Total	**–**	**–**	**–**	**–**	**4**

23.10.40	20.11.40	18.12.40	22.01.41	19.02.41	19.03.41	23.04.41	21.05.41
16	16	16	16	16	16	16	16
16	16	24	24	24	24	16	16
32	**32**	**40**	**40**	**40**	**40**	**32**	**32**
8	8	8	8	8	8	8	8
8	8	8	8	8	8	8	8
0	0	0	0	0	0	0	0
16	**16**	**16**	**16**	**16**	**16**	**16**	**16**
8	8	8	8	8	8	8	8
0	0	8	8	8	8	7	7
8	**8**	**16**	**16**	**16**	**16**	**15**	**15**
16	16	16	16	16	16	16	16
8	8	8	8	15	16	16	16
4	4	20	20	20	4	2	2
28	**28**	**44**	**44**	**51**	**36**	**34**	**34**
16	16	16	16	16	16	20	20
4	4	4	12	16	20	24	24
4	4	20	20	8	8	8	12
24	**24**	**40**	**48**	**40**	**44**	**52**	**56**
16	16	16	16	16	16	16	16
8	8	8	8	8	8	8	8
0	0	0	0	0	0	0	0
24	**24**	**24**	**24**	**24**	**24**	**24**	**24**
–	–	–	–	4	4	4	4
–	**–**	**–**	**–**	**4**	**4**	**4**	**4**

23.10.40	20.11.40	18.12.40	22.01.41	19.02.41	19.03.41	23.04.41	21.05.41
8	8	16	16	16	16	16	16
4	4	4	4	4	0	0	20
12	**12**	**20**	**20**	**20**	**16**	**16**	**36**
4	4	4	4	4	4	4	4
4	**4**	**4**	**4**	**4**	**4**	**4**	**4**

Airfields

		29.05.40	*26.06.40*	*24.07.40*	*21.08.40*	*18.09.40*
RAF Manston	3.0	8	8	8	8	8
	Total	**8**	**8**	**8**	**8**	**8**
RAF Hawkinge	3.0	7	7	7	7	7
	Total	**7**	**7**	**7**	**7**	**7**
RAF Tangmere	3.0	4	4	4	4	4
	Total	**4**	**4**	**4**	**4**	**4**
RAF Biggin Hill	3.0	4	4	4	4	8
	Total	**4**	**4**	**4**	**4**	**8**
RAF Martlesham	3.0	4	4	4	4	4
	Total	**4**	**4**	**4**	**4**	**4**
RAF North Weald	3.7(m)	0	0	0	0	4
	3.0	4	4	4	4	4
	Total	**4**	**4**	**4**	**4**	**4**
RAF Wattisham	3.0	4	4	4	4	4
	Total	**4**	**4**	**4**	**4**	**4**
RAF Wick	3.0	4	4	2	2	2
	Total	**4**	**4**	**2**	**2**	**2**
RAF Linton on Ouse	3.0	4	4	4	4	4
	Total	**4**	**4**	**4**	**4**	**4**
RAF Thornaby	3.0	4	4	4	4	4
	Total	**4**	**4**	**4**	**4**	**4**
RAF Driffield	3.0	4	4	4	4	0
	Total	**4**	**4**	**4**	**4**	**0**
RAF Rochford	3.0	4	4	4	4	4
	Total	**4**	**4**	**4**	**4**	**4**
RAF Ipswich	3.0	4	4	2	2	2
	Total	**4**	**4**	**2**	**2**	**2**
RAF Duxford	3.0	2	2	2	2	2
	Total	**2**	**2**	**2**	**2**	**2**
RAF Acklington	3.0	2	2	2	2	2
	Total	**2**	**2**	**2**	**2**	**2**
RAF Watton	3.0	2	2	2	2	2
	Total	**2**	**2**	**2**	**2**	**2**

23.10.40	20.11.40	18.12.40	22.01.41	19.02.41	19.03.41	23.04.41	21.05.41
8	8	4	4	4	4	4	4
8	**8**	**4**	**4**	**4**	**4**	**4**	**4**
7	7	4	4	4	4	4	4
7	**7**	**4**	**4**	**4**	**4**	**4**	**4**
4	4	4	4	4	4	4	4
4	**4**	**4**	**4**	**4**	**4**	**4**	**4**
4	4	4	4	4	4	4	4
4	**4**	**4**	**4**	**4**	**4**	**4**	**4**
4	4	4	4	4	4	4	4
4	**4**	**4**	**4**	**4**	**4**	**4**	**4**
0	0	0	0	0	0	0	0
4	4	4	4	4	4	4	4
4	**4**	**4**	**4**	**4**	**4**	**4**	**4**
4	4	4	4	4	4	4	2
4	**4**	**4**	**4**	**4**	**4**	**4**	**2**
2	2	2	2	2	2	2	2
2	**2**	**2**	**2**	**2**	**2**	**2**	**2**
4	4	4	4	4	4	4	2
4	**4**	**4**	**4**	**4**	**4**	**4**	**2**
2	–	–	–	–	0	0	0
2	–	–	–	–	**0**	**0**	**0**
0	0	0	0	0	–	–	4
0	**0**	**0**	**0**	**0**	–	–	**4**
4	4	4	0	0	–	–	–
4	**4**	**4**	**0**	**0**	–	–	–
2	2	0	0	0	–	–	–
2	**2**	**0**	**0**	**0**	–	–	–
2	2	2	2	2	2	2	2
2	**2**	**2**	**2**	**2**	**2**	**2**	**2**
2	2	2	2	2	0	0	0
2	**2**	**2**	**2**	**2**	**0**	**0**	**0**
2	2	2	2	2	2	2	2
2	**2**	**2**	**2**	**2**	**2**	**2**	**2**

		29.05.40	26.06.40	24.07.40	21.08.40	18.09.40
RAF Marham	3.0	2	2	2	2	2
	Total	**2**	**2**	**2**	**2**	**2**
RAF Feltwell	3.0	2	2	2	2	2
	Total	**2**	**2**	**2**	**2**	**2**
RAF Ringway*	3.7(s)	–	4	4	4	4
	Total	**–**	**4**	**4**	**4**	**4**
RAF Grantham	3.0	–	4	4	4	4
	Total	**–**	**4**	**4**	**4**	**4**
RAF West Malling	3.0	–	2	2	2	2
	Total	**–**	**2**	**2**	**2**	**2**
Airfield mobile	3.7(m)	–	–	8	8	–
	Total	**–**	**–**	**8**	**8**	**–**
RNAS Yeovil	3.7(m)	–	–	4	4	4
	3.0	–	–	0	0	0
	Total	**–**	**–**	**4**	**4**	**4**
RAF Kinloss	3.0	0	0	2	2	2
	Total	**0**	**0**	**2**	**2**	**2**
RAF Lossiemouth	3.0	0	0	2	2	2
	Total	**0**	**0**	**2**	**2**	**2**
RAF Horsham St Faith	3.0	–	–	2	2	2
	Total	**–**	**–**	**2**	**2**	**2**
RAE Farnborough	3.7(m)	–	–	–	–	4
	Total	**–**	**–**	**–**	**–**	**4**
RAF Dishforth	3.0	–	–	–	–	2
	Total	**–**	**–**	**–**	**–**	**2**
RAF Topcliffe	3.0	–	–	–	–	2
	Total	**–**	**–**	**–**	**–**	**2**
RAF Kenley	3.0	–	–	–	–	–
	Total	**–**	**–**	**–**	**–**	**–**
RAF Pembrey	3.0	–	–	–	–	–
	Total	**–**	**–**	**–**	**–**	**–**
RAF St Eval	3.0	–	–	–	–	–
	Total	**–**	**–**	**–**	**–**	**–**
RAF Aldergrove	3.7(m)	–	–	–	–	–
	Total	**–**	**–**	**–**	**–**	**–**

23.10.40	20.11.40	18.12.40	22.01.41	19.02.41	19.03.41	23.04.41	21.05.41
2	2	2	2	2	2	2	2
2	2	2	2	2	2	2	2
2	2	2	2	2	2	2	2
2	2	2	2	2	2	2	2
4	4	4	4	4	–	–	–
4	4	4	4	4	–	–	–
4	4	4	4	4	8	8	8
4	4	4	4	4	8	8	8
2	2	2	2	2	2	2	2
2	2	2	2	2	2	2	2
–	–	–	–	–	–	–	–
–	–	–	–	–	–	–	–
4	4	0	0	0	0	0	0
0	0	4	4	4	4	4	4
4	4	4	4	4	4	4	4
2	2	2	2	2	2	2	2
2	2	2	2	2	2	2	2
2	2	2	2	2	2	2	2
2	2	2	2	2	2	2	2
2	2	2	2	2	2	2	2
2	2	2	2	2	2	2	2
4	4	–	4	–	–	–	–
4	4	–	4	–	–	–	–
–	2	2	2	2	2	4	–
–	2	2	2	2	2	4	–
2	2	2	2	2	2	–	–
2	2	2	2	2	2	–	–
4	4	4	3	3	3	4	4
4	4	4	3	3	3	4	4
–	–	–	–	4	4	0	0
–	–	–	–	4	4	0	0
–	–	–	–	–	4	4	4
–	–	–	–	–	4	4	4
–	–	–	–	–	4	4	4
–	–	–	–	–	4	4	4

		29.05.40	26.06.40	24.07.40	21.08.40	18.09.40
RAF Leconfield	3.7(m)	–	–	–	–	–
	Total	–	–	–	–	–
RAF Debden	**Total**	**0**	**0**	**0**	**0**	**0**

* Four guns subsumed within Manchester total from 19.03.41

Miscellaneous

		29.05.40	26.06.40	24.07.40	21.08.40	18.09.40
Training schools etc.	4.5	0	0	0	0	0
	3.7(s)	0	0	0	0	0
	3.7(m)	3	3	5	5	1
	3.0	1	1	1	0	0
	Total	**4**	**4**	**6**	**1**	**1**

HAA summary

		29.05.40	26.06.40	24.07.40	21.08.40	18.09.40
Totals	4.5	333	355	359	367	374
	3.7(s)	188	313	347	377	408
	3.7(m)	286	306	319	351	355
	3.0	220	226	226	225	225
GRAND TOTAL		**1027**	**1200**	**1251**	**1320**	**1362**
Factor		*1.0*	*1.17*	*1.22*	*1.29*	*1.33*

LAA summary

	29.05.40	26.06.40	24.07.40	21.08.40	18.09.40
3.0	133	136	135	135	116
Bofors	155	273	366	430	474
2pdr Mk VIII Single	84	87	98	100	102
2pdr Mk VIII Twin	13	15	18	19	23
2pdr Naval	30	38	38	39	26
Hispano-Suiza	33	38	39	40	61
GRAND TOTAL	**448**	**587**	**694**	**763**	**802**
Factor	*1.0*	*1.31*	*1.55*	*1.70*	*1.79*
Factor (Bofors only)	*1.0*	*1.76*	*2.36*	*2.77*	*3.06*

23.10.40	20.11.40	18.12.40	22.01.41	19.02.41	19.03.41	23.04.41	21.05.41
–	–	–	–	–	–	–	4
–	–	–	–	–	–	–	**4**
0	**0**	**0**	**0**	**0**	–	–	–

23.10.40	20.11.40	18.12.40	22.01.41	19.02.41	19.03.41	23.04.41	21.05.41
0	0	0	0	0	0	0	0
0	1	1	1	1	1	1	1
1	1	1	4	5	6	11	14
0	0	0	1	1	1	1	1
1	**2**	**2**	**6**	**7**	**8**	**13**	**16**

23.10.40	20.11.40	18.12.40	22.01.41	19.02.41	19.03.41	23.04.41	21.05.41
379	379	380	389	392	393	398	399
428	443	458	486	520	527	466	614
373	374	372	372	372	381	413	446
225	225	221	200	200	200	200	192
1405	**1421**	**1431**	**1447**	**1484**	**1501**	**1577**	**1651**
1.37	1.38	1.39	1.41	1.45	1.46	1.44	1.61

23.10.40	20.11.40	18.12.40	22.01.41	19.02.41	19.03.41	23.04.41	21.05.41
102	102	102	92	66	62	49	49
535	556	586	627	630	694	698	726
104	105	106	111	112	75	82	62
29	32	36	37	40	48	50	51
4	4	2	3	4	4	3	3
61	64	66	86	91	85	63	62
835	**863**	**898**	**956**	**943**	**968**	**945**	**953**
1.86	1.93	2.00	2.13	2.11	2.16	2.11	2.13
3.45	3.59	3.78	4.05	4.07	4.48	4.50	4.68

HAA strengths:
Overlord and *Diver*

MARCH 1944–MAY 1945

This appendix tabulates the changing distribution of HAA guns in the period from March 1944 to the end of the war, bracketing the deployments for *Overlord* and *Diver*.* The table is organised on similar principles to Appendix II, though it differs in three respects. First, areas have been rearranged to reflect strategic groupings meaningful in 1944–45. The *Southern ports and coastal GDAs* from Yarmouth/Lowestoft clockwise around the coast to Milford Haven are now collected together, to reflect their reinforcement as a group for *Overlord*, while *Southern inland GDAs* and *Northern England* and *Scotland* also have separate sections, the last two including both inland and coastal targets. The *Diver* deployments, too, appear in a separate section. Second, the gun strengths for each date now distinguish between the Total in place (shown underlined) and the **Total (op)**, or operational, shown in bold. Unnecessary in the 1940–41 tabulation of Appendix II, this distinction becomes important in the last year of the war as so many weapons were taken out of service while remaining on strength. Lastly, unlike Appendix II, the date interval of the table is irregular, showing dates in March, April, June, July and August 1944, and then January and May 1945. These choices allow the table to reflect the start of gun moves for

* The data in the table are drawn from the ADGB Equipment Statements for the dates given filed in the War Diaries of AA Cmd's G Branch at WO 166/14235 (Mar 1944); WO 166/14236 (Apr–May 1944); WO 166/14237 (Jun–Jul 1944); WO 166/14238 (Aug–Sep 1944); WO 166/16629 (Jan–Mar 1945) and WO 166/16630 (Apr–Jul 1945).

Overlord (compare March and April 1944), the state of the AA defences in the week of the Normandy landings (the figure for 10 June shows the position four days after the first troops sailed), the effect of *Diver* (compare June 1944 with July and August), and the gradual decommissioning of the layout in 1945 (seen in the contrast between January and May of that year). The 9 May figure shows AA Command's HAA state on the morning of the final ceasefire.

London area and approaches

		29.03.44	19.04.44
London (IAZ)	5.25	30	34
	3.7 Mk VI	57	59
	3.7(s)	198	198
	3.7(m)	26	16
	Total	311	307
	Non-op	23	22
	Total (op)	**288**	**285**
Thames & Medway (N)	5.25	0	0
	3.7 Mk VI	12	12
	3.7(s)	34	34
	3.7(m)	16	8
	Total	62	54
	Non-op	4	0
	Total (op)	**58**	**54**
Thames & Medway (S)	5.25	9	9
	3.7 Mk VI	26	24
	3.7(s)	46	46
	3.7(m)	4	0
	Total	85	79
	Non-op	15	4
	Total (op)	**70**	**75**
Thames Maunsell	3.7(s)	12	12
	Total	12	12
	Non-op	0	0
	Total (op)	**12**	**12**
Brooklands	3.7(s)	8	8
	Total	8	8
	Non-op	0	4
	Total (op)	**8**	**4**
Slough	3.7(s)	20	20
	Total	20	20
	Non-op	0	0
	Total (op)	**20**	**20**

Southern ports and coastal GDAs

		29.03.44	19.04.44
Yarmouth/Lowestoft	3.7(s)	32	32
	3.7(m)	8	24
	Total	40	56
	Non-op	4	4
	Total (op)	**36**	**52**

10.06.44	08.07.44	30.08.44	03.01.45	09.05.45
38	38	42	42	42
66	66	65	64	56
202	172	110	196	190
14	5	22	13	5
<u>320</u>	<u>281</u>	<u>239</u>	<u>315</u>	<u>293</u>
22	33	21	16	9
298	**248**	**218**	**299**	**284**
4	4	4	4	8
12	12	12	12	12
34	42	90	130	158
10	0	0	0	0
<u>60</u>	<u>58</u>	<u>106</u>	<u>146</u>	<u>178</u>
6	4	8	12	140
54	**54**	**98**	**134**	**38**
8	8	8	8	8
21	21	21	20	20
42	42	50	44	60
0	0	0	0	0
<u>71</u>	<u>71</u>	<u>79</u>	<u>72</u>	<u>88</u>
0	0	6	0	28
71	**71**	**73**	**72**	**60**
12	12	12	12	12
<u>12</u>	<u>12</u>	<u>12</u>	<u>12</u>	<u>12</u>
0	0	0	0	12
12	**12**	**12**	**12**	**0**
8	8	–	–	–
<u>8</u>	<u>8</u>	–	–	–
8	0	–	–	–
0	**8**	**–**	**–**	**–**
20	20	20	4	0
<u>20</u>	<u>20</u>	<u>20</u>	<u>4</u>	<u>0</u>
0	0	0	0	0
20	**20**	**20**	**4**	**0**

10.06.44	08.07.44	30.08.44	03.01.45	09.05.45
32	32	32	48	48
24	24	24	0	0
<u>56</u>	<u>56</u>	<u>56</u>	<u>48</u>	<u>48</u>
0	0	0	0	48
56	**56**	**56**	**48**	**0**

		29.03.44	19.04.44
Harwich	5.25	0	0
	3.7(s)	24	24
	3.7(m)	0	0
	Total	24	24
	Non-op	0	0
	Total (op)	**24**	**24**
Clacton	3.7(s)	0	0
	3.7(m)	9	9
	Total	9	9
	Non-op	0	1
	Total (op)	**9**	**8**
North Foreland	3.7(s)	4	12
	3.7(m)	12	32
	Total	16	44
	Non-op	0	0
	Total (op)	**16**	**44**
Ramsgate	3.7(s)	8	–
	Total	8	–
	Non-op	0	–
	Total (op)	**8**	**–**
Dover	5.25	0	0
	3.7(s)	28	24
	3.7(m)	0	0
	Total	28	24
	Non-op	0	0
	Total (op)	**28**	**24**
Folkestone	3.7(s)	–	–
	3.7(m)	–	–
	Total	–	–
	Non-op	–	–
	Total (op)	**–**	**–**
Littlestone	Total	–	–
	Non-op	–	–
	Total (op)	**–**	**–**
Dungeness	3.7(m)	–	–
	Total	–	–
	Non-op	–	–
	Total (op)	**–**	**–**
Newhaven/Shoreham/ Brighton	3.7(s)	46	46
	3.7(m)	12	20
	Total	58	66
	Non-op	8	8
	Total (op)	**50**	**58**

10.06.44	08.07.44	30.08.44	03.01.45	09.05.45
0	0	0	4	4
24	24	24	20	20
24	0	0	0	0
<u>48</u>	<u>24</u>	<u>24</u>	<u>24</u>	<u>24</u>
0	0	0	4	24
48	**24**	**24**	**20**	**0**
0	8	8	4	–
8	0	0	0	–
<u>8</u>	<u>8</u>	<u>8</u>	<u>4</u>	–
0	0	0	4	–
8	**8**	**8**	**0**	–
12	20	20	16	–
32	0	0	0	–
<u>44</u>	<u>20</u>	<u>20</u>	<u>16</u>	–
0	0	0	4	–
44	**20**	**20**	**12**	–
–	–	–	–	–
–	–	–	–	–
–	–	–	–	–
–	**–**	**–**	**–**	**–**
0	0	0	0	1
24	24	24	24	32
28	8	0	0	0
<u>52</u>	<u>32</u>	<u>24</u>	<u>24</u>	<u>33</u>
24	4	8	0	33
28	**28**	**16**	**24**	**0**
–	–	16	4	8
–	–	8	0	0
–	–	<u>24</u>	<u>4</u>	<u>8</u>
–	–	8	4	8
–	**–**	**16**	**0**	**0**
–	<u>0</u>	<u>0</u>	–	–
–	0	0	–	–
–	**0**	**0**	**–**	**–**
48	48	–	–	–
48	<u>48</u>	–	–	–
0	0	–	–	–
48	**48**	**–**	**–**	**–**
46	46	46	46	0
44	4	4	4	0
<u>90</u>	<u>50</u>	<u>50</u>	<u>50</u>	<u>0</u>
0	0	0	8	0
90	**50**	**50**	**42**	**0**

		29.03.44	*19.04.44*
Chichester	3.7(m)	–	56
	Total	–	<u>56</u>
	Non-op	–	0
	Total (op)	**–**	**56**
Selsey	3.7(m)	–	–
	Total	–	–
	Non-op	–	–
	Total (op)	**–**	**–**
Portsmouth	5.25	0	0
	4.5	16	16
	3.7 Mk VI	0	0
	3.7(s)	20	20
	3.7(m)	0	24
	Total	<u>36</u>	<u>60</u>
	Non-op	0	0
	Total (op)	**36**	**60**
Isle of Wight	5.25	0	0
	3.7(s)	20	26
	3.7(m)	6	22
	Total	<u>26</u>	<u>48</u>
	Non-op	0	22
	Total (op)	**26**	**26**
Southampton	4.5	4	4
	3.7 Mk VI	4	4
	3.7(s)	36	36
	3.7(m)	8	116
	Total	<u>52</u>	<u>160</u>
	Non-op	0	8
	Total (op)	**52**	**152**
Holton Heath/Poole	3.7(s)	20	20
	3.7(m)	0	0
	Total	<u>20</u>	<u>20</u>
	Non-op	0	0
	Total (op)	**20**	**20**
Portland/Weymouth	3.7(s)	24	24
	3.7(m)	0	16
	Total	<u>24</u>	<u>40</u>
	Non-op	0	1
	Total (op)	**24**	**39**
Dartmouth	3.7(m)	–	48
	Total	–	<u>48</u>
	Non-op	–	48
	Total (op)	**–**	**0**

10.06.44	08.07.44	30.08.44	03.01.45	09.05.45
33	24	0	–	–
33	24	0	–	–
0	0	0	–	–
33	**24**	**0**	**–**	**–**
41	–	–	–	–
41	–	–	–	–
1	–	–	–	–
40	**–**	**–**	**–**	**–**
1	1	8	8	8
0	0	0	0	0
16	16	16	16	16
20	20	16	16	0
64	58	8	0	0
101	95	48	40	24
1	3	8	16	24
100	**92**	**40**	**24**	**0**
0	0	2	8	8
26	26	26	26	0
40	16	8	8	0
66	42	36	42	8
0	0	2	34	8
66	**42**	**34**	**8**	**0**
0	0	0	0	0
8	8	8	8	8
30	30	40	40	0
84	24	12	0	0
122	62	60	48	8
4	4	0	22	8
118	**58**	**60**	**26**	**0**
20	20	12	12	–
12	0	0	0	–
32	20	12	12	–
0	0	0	12	–
32	**20**	**12**	**0**	**–**
24	24	24	24	–
28	16	16	0	–
52	40	40	24	–
0	0	0	24	–
52	**40**	**40**	**0**	**–**
48	16	–	–	–
48	16	–	–	–
1	0	–	–	–
47	**16**	**–**	**–**	**–**

		29.03.44	*19.04.44*
Plymouth	5.25	0	0
	3.7(s)	48	64
	Total	<u>48</u>	<u>64</u>
	Non-op	0	0
	Total (op)	**48**	**64**
Falmouth	3.7(s)	16	16
	3.7(m)	0	15
	Total	<u>16</u>	<u>31</u>
	Non-op	0	15
	Total (op)	**16**	**16**
Hayle	3.7(s)	8	8
	Total	<u>8</u>	<u>8</u>
	Non-op	0	0
	Total (op)	**8**	**8**
Weston-super-Mare	3.7(s)	12	12
	Total	<u>12</u>	<u>12</u>
	Non-op	0	0
	Total (op)	**12**	**12**
Bristol/Avonmouth	4.5	16	16
	3.7 Mk VI	0	0
	3.7(s)	62	62
	3.7(m)	13	4
	Total	<u>91</u>	<u>82</u>
	Non-op	8	0
	Total (op)	**83**	**82**
Flatholm	4.5 (CA/AA)	4	4
	Total	<u>4</u>	<u>4</u>
	Non-op	0	0
	Total (op)	**4**	**4**
Newport	4.5	12	12
	3.7 Mk VI	0	0
	3.7(s)	24	24
	Total	<u>36</u>	<u>36</u>
	Non-op	0	0
	Total (op)	**36**	**36**
Cardiff/Barry	4.5	8	8
	3.7(s)	44	44
	Total	<u>52</u>	<u>52</u>
	Non-op	0	0
	Total (op)	**52**	**52**
Swansea/Port Talbot	3.7(s)	40	40
	Total	<u>40</u>	<u>40</u>
	Non-op	0	0
	Total (op)	**40**	**40**

10.06.44	08.07.44	30.08.44	03.01.45	09.05.45
0	6	10	12	12
64	64	50	36	0
<u>64</u>	<u>70</u>	<u>60</u>	<u>48</u>	<u>12</u>
0	6	10	48	12
64	**64**	**50**	**0**	**0**
16	16	16	–	–
16	8	0	–	–
<u>32</u>	<u>24</u>	<u>16</u>	–	–
0	0	0	–	–
32	**24**	**16**	**–**	**–**
8	8	–	–	–
<u>8</u>	<u>8</u>	–	–	–
0	0	–	–	–
8	**8**	**–**	**–**	**–**
12	12	–	–	–
<u>12</u>	<u>12</u>	–	–	–
0	0	–	–	–
12	**12**	**–**	**–**	**–**
0	0	0	0	0
16	16	16	16	16
62	62	30	12	0
4	3	0	0	0
<u>82</u>	<u>81</u>	<u>46</u>	<u>28</u>	<u>16</u>
4	3	0	28	16
78	**78**	**46**	**0**	**0**
4	4	4	–	–
<u>4</u>	<u>4</u>	<u>4</u>	–	–
0	0	0	–	–
4	**4**	**4**	**–**	**–**
12	12	16	9	–
0	0	0	11	–
24	24	16	4	–
<u>36</u>	<u>36</u>	<u>32</u>	<u>24</u>	–
0	0	16	24	–
36	**36**	**16**	**0**	**–**
8	8	4	0	0
44	44	20	0	0
<u>52</u>	<u>52</u>	<u>24</u>	<u>0</u>	<u>0</u>
0	0	0	0	0
52	**52**	**24**	**0**	**0**
40	40	24	8	0
<u>40</u>	<u>40</u>	<u>24</u>	<u>8</u>	<u>0</u>
0	0	0	8	0
40	**40**	**24**	**0**	**0**

Milford Haven		*29.03.44*	*19.04.44*
	3.7(s)	24	24
	3.7(m)	8	0
	Total	<u>32</u>	<u>24</u>
	Non-op	0	0
	Total (op)	**32**	**24**

Southern inland GDAs

RAF Manston		*29.03.44*	*19.04.44*	*10.06.44*
	3.7(m)	8	–	
	Total	<u>8</u>	–	
	Non-op	0	–	
	Total (op)	**8**	–	
Canterbury	3.7(s)	12	12	
	3.7(m)	24	8	
	Total	<u>36</u>	<u>20</u>	
	Non-op	0	0	
	Total (op)	**36**	**20**	
RAF Hawkinge	3.7(s)	0	4	
	3.7(m)	4	5	
	Total	<u>4</u>	<u>9</u>	
	Non-op	0	5	
	Total (op)	**4**	**4**	
Ashford	3.7(s)	8	8	
	3.7(m)	8	0	
	Total	<u>16</u>	<u>8</u>	
	Non-op	0	0	
	Total (op)	**16**	**8**	
Reading	3.7(s)	8	8	
	Total	<u>8</u>	<u>8</u>	
	Non-op	0	8	
	Total (op)	**8**	**0**	
Oxford	3.7(s)	0	0	
	3.7(m)	24	24	
	Total	<u>24</u>	<u>24</u>	
	Non-op	0	0	
	Total (op)	**24**	**24**	
Winchester	3.7(s)	8	8	
	3.7(m)	16	12	
	Total	<u>24</u>	<u>20</u>	
	Non-op	0	4	
	Total (op)	**24**	**16**	

10.06.44	08.07.44	30.08.44	03.01.45	09.05.45
24	24	16	–	–
8	0	0	–	–
32	24	16	–	–
0	0	0	–	–
32	**24**	**16**	**–**	**–**

08.07.44	30.08.44	03.01.45	09.05.45	
–	–	–	–	–
–	–	–	–	–
–	–	–	–	–
–	**–**	**–**	**–**	**–**
12	12	8	–	–
9	9	4	–	–
21	21	12	–	–
1	1	8	–	–
20	**20**	**4**	**–**	**–**
4	4	–	–	–
0	0	–	–	–
4	4	–	–	–
0	0	–	–	–
4	**4**	**–**	**–**	**–**
8	8	–	–	–
0	0	–	–	–
8	8	–	–	–
0	0	–	–	–
8	**8**	**–**	**–**	**–**
8	8	0	0	0
8	8	0	0	0
8	0	0	0	0
0	**8**	**0**	**0**	**0**
0	0	0	0	0
0	0	0	0	0
0	0	0	0	0
0	0	0	0	0
0	**0**	**0**	**0**	**0**
8	8	8	–	–
8	4	4	–	–
16	12	12	–	–
0	0	0	–	–
16	**12**	**12**	**–**	**–**

		29.03.44	*19.04.44*
Lyndhurst	3.7(s)	–	–
	3.7(m)	–	–
	Total	–	–
	Non-op	–	–
	Total (op)	**–**	**–**
Swindon	3.7(m)	8	8
	Total	8	8
	Non-op	0	0
	Total (op)	**8**	**8**
Salisbury	3.7(m)	8	8
	Total	8	8
	Non-op	0	0
	Total (op)	**8**	**8**
Bath	3.7(m)	8	–
	Total	8	
	Non-op	0	–
	Total (op)	**8**	**–**
Gloucester/Brockworth	3.7(s)	18	18
	3.7(m)	4	4
	Total	22	22
	Non-op	0	0
	Total (op)	**22**	**22**
Caerwent	3.7(s)	8	8
	3.7(m)	4	0
	Total	12	8
	Non-op	0	0
	Total (op)	**12**	**8**
Yeovil	3.7(m)	4	4
	Total	4	4
	Non-op	0	0
	Total (op)	**4**	**4**
RAF Tarrant Rushton	3.7(m)	–	16
	Total	–	16
	Non-op	–	0
	Total (op)	**–**	**16**
Exeter	3.7(s)	4	4
	3.7(m)	12	12
	Total	16	16
	Non-op	0	0
	Total (op)	**16**	**16**

10.06.44	08.07.44	30.08.44	03.01.45	09.05.45
6	6	–	–	–
24	32	–	–	–
<u>30</u>	<u>38</u>	–	–	–
0	0	–	–	–
30	**38**	**–**	**–**	**–**
0	0	0	0	0
<u>0</u>	<u>0</u>	<u>0</u>	<u>0</u>	<u>0</u>
0	0	0	0	0
0	**0**	**0**	**0**	**0**
–	–	–	–	–
–	–	–	–	–
–	–	–	–	–
–	**–**	**–**	**–**	**–**
–	–	–	–	–
–	–	–	–	–
–	–	–	–	–
–	**–**	**–**	**–**	**–**
18	18	8	0	0
4	4	0	0	0
<u>22</u>	<u>22</u>	<u>8</u>	<u>0</u>	<u>0</u>
4	4	0	0	0
18	**18**	**8**	**0**	**0**
8	8	–	–	–
0	0	–	–	–
<u>8</u>	<u>8</u>	–	–	–
0	0	–	–	–
8	**8**	**–**	**–**	**–**
4	4	4	–	–
<u>4</u>	<u>4</u>	<u>4</u>	–	–
0	0	0	–	–
4	**4**	**4**	**–**	**–**
16	–	–	–	–
<u>16</u>	–	–	–	–
0	–	–	–	–
16	**–**	**–**	**–**	**–**
4	16	–	–	–
12	0	–	–	–
<u>16</u>	<u>16</u>	–	–	–
0	0	–	–	–
16	**16**	**–**	**–**	**–**

Midlands and East Anglia

		29.03.44	*19.04.44*
Ipswich	3.7(s)	4	8
	3.7(m)	16	8
	Total	20	16
	Non-op	0	0
	Total (op)	**20**	**16**
Chelmsford	3.7(m)	24	24
	Total	24	24
	Non-op	0	0
	Total (op)	**24**	**24**
Colchester	3.7(s)	8	8
	3.7(m)	16	8
	Total	24	16
	Non-op	8	8
	Total (op)	**16**	**8**
Norwich	3.7(s)	8	8
	3.7(m)	16	16
	Total	24	24
	Non-op	0	8
	Total (op)	**24**	**16**
Cambridge	3.7(m)	9	0
	Total	8	0
	Non-op	0	0
	Total (op)	**8**	**0**
Peterborough	3.7(m)	16	0
	Total	16	0
	Non-op	0	0
	Total (op)	**16**	**0**
Louth	3.7 Mk VI	–	–
	3.7(s)	–	–
	Total	–	–
	Non-op	–	–
	Total (op)	**–**	**–**
Lincoln	3.7(m)	8	–
	Total	8	–
	Non-op	0	–
	Total (op)	**8**	**–**
Grantham	3.7(m)	8	–
	Total	8	–
	Non-op	0	–
	Total (op)	**8**	**–**

10.06.44	*08.07.44*	*30.08.44*	*03.01.45*	*09.05.45*
8	8	8	8	–
8	8	8	0	–
<u>16</u>	<u>16</u>	<u>16</u>	<u>8</u>	–
0	0	0	8	–
16	**16**	**16**	**0**	**–**
24	24	24	0	0
<u>24</u>	<u>24</u>	<u>24</u>	<u>0</u>	<u>0</u>
0	0	0	0	0
24	**24**	**24**	**0**	**0**
8	8	8	0	0
0	0	0	0	0
<u>8</u>	<u>8</u>	<u>8</u>	<u>0</u>	<u>0</u>
0	0	0	0	0
8	**8**	**8**	**0**	**0**
8	16	16	4	–
8	0	0	0	–
<u>16</u>	<u>16</u>	<u>16</u>	<u>4</u>	–
0	0	0	4	–
16	**16**	**16**	**0**	**–**
0	0	0	0	–
<u>0</u>	<u>0</u>	<u>0</u>	<u>0</u>	–
0	0	0	0	–
0	**0**	**0**	**0**	**–**
0	0	0	0	0
<u>0</u>	<u>0</u>	<u>0</u>	<u>0</u>	<u>0</u>
0	0	0	0	0
0	**0**	**0**	**0**	**0**
–	–	–	–	4
–	–	–	–	8
–	–	–	–	<u>12</u>
–	–	–	–	0
–	**–**	**–**	**–**	**12**
–	–	–	–	–
–	–	–	–	–
–	–	–	–	–
–	**–**	**–**	**–**	**–**
–	–	–	–	–
–	–	–	–	–
–	–	–	–	–
–	**–**	**–**	**–**	**–**

		29.03.44	*19.04.44*
Corby	3.7(m)	8	–
	Total	8	–
	Non-op	0	–
	Total (op)	**8**	**–**
Leicester	Total	0	0
	Non-op	0	0
	Total (op)	**0**	**0**
Birmingham	4.5	24	24
	3.7 Mk VI	0	0
	3.7(s)	48	48
	Total	72	72
	Non-op	0	0
	Total (op)	**72**	**72**
Coventry	4.5	8	8
	3.7(s)	24	24
	Total	32	32
	Non-op	0	0
	Total (op)	**32**	**32**

Northern England

		29.03.44	*19.04.44*
Derby/Nottingham	4.5	15	16
	3.7 Mk VI	0	0
	3.7(s)	38	38
	Total	53	54
	Non-op	0	0
	Total (op)	**53**	**54**
Crewe	3.7(s)	4	4
	3.7(m)	8	8
	Total	12	12
	Non-op	0	12
	Total (op)	**12**	**0**
Sheffield	4.5	8	8
	3.7 Mk VI	0	0
	3.7(s)	44	44
	3.7(m)	0	0
	Total	52	52
	Non-op	0	9
	Total (op)	**52**	**43**
Manchester	4.5	16	16
	3.7(s)	18	18
	Total	34	34
	Non-op	0	14
	Total (op)	**34**	**20**

10.06.44	08.07.44	30.08.44	03.01.45	09.05.45
–	–	–	–	–
–	–	–	–	–
–	–	–	–	–
–	**–**	**–**	**–**	**–**
<u>0</u>	<u>0</u>	<u>0</u>	–	–
0	0	0	–	–
0	**0**	**0**	**–**	**–**
24	24	24	24	1
0	0	0	0	31
48	36	14	4	0
<u>72</u>	<u>60</u>	<u>38</u>	<u>28</u>	<u>32</u>
20	26	18	28	32
52	**34**	**20**	**0**	**0**
8	8	8	8	0
24	24	8	8	0
<u>32</u>	<u>32</u>	<u>16</u>	<u>16</u>	<u>0</u>
0	0	8	16	0
32	**32**	**8**	**0**	**0**

10.06.44	16.07.44	10.09.44	03.01.45	09.05.45
16	16	16	8	0
0	0	0	8	16
35	25	0	12	0
<u>51</u>	<u>41</u>	<u>16</u>	<u>28</u>	<u>16</u>
11	1	0	12	16
40	**40**	**16**	**16**	**0**
4	4	–	–	–
0	0	–	–	–
<u>4</u>	<u>4</u>	–	–	–
4	4	–	–	–
0	**0**	**–**	**–**	**–**
8	8	8	8	4
0	0	0	0	4
44	30	14	14	0
0	2	2	0	0
<u>52</u>	<u>40</u>	<u>24</u>	<u>22</u>	<u>8</u>
18	4	4	22	8
34	**36**	**20**	**0**	**0**
16	16	16	16	16
18	12	6	6	0
<u>34</u>	<u>28</u>	<u>22</u>	<u>22</u>	<u>16</u>
14	8	12	12	16
20	**20**	**10**	**10**	**0**

		29.03.44	*19.04.44*
Humber	5.25	8	12
	4.5	16	16
	3.7 Mk VI	8	8
	3.7(s)	50	50
	3.7(m)	28	0
	Total	110	96
	Non-op	8	12
	Total (op)	**102**	**84**
Scunthorpe	3.7(s)	10	10
	3.7(m)	0	10
	Total	10	20
	Non-op	0	0
	Total (op)	**10**	**20**
Leeds	4.5	15	14
	3.7 Mk VI	0	0
	3.7(s)	24	24
	Total	39	38
	Non-op	0	10
	Total (op)	**39**	**28**
York	3.7(m)	16	16
	Total	16	16
	Non-op	0	0
	Total (op)	**16**	**16**
Tees	4.5	16	16
	3.7 Mk VI	0	0
	3.7(s)	32	32
	3.7(m)	4	4
	Total	52	52
	Non-op	0	4
	Total (op)	**52**	**48**
Tyne	4.5	24	24
	3.7 Mk VI	0	0
	3.7(s)	62	62
	3.7(m)	12	0
	Total	98	86
	Non-op	4	4
	Total (op)	**94**	**82**
Blyth	3.7(s)	12	12
	3.7(m)	2	2
	Total	14	14
	Non-op	4	2
	Total (op)	**10**	**12**

10.06.44	16.07.44	10.09.44	03.01.45	09.05.45
16	16	16	16	16
8	8	8	4	4
16	16	16	16	12
50	48	42	30	12
0	0	0	0	0
<u>90</u>	<u>88</u>	<u>82</u>	<u>66</u>	<u>44</u>
16	14	12	6	20
74	**74**	**70**	**60**	**24**
10	10	–	–	–
0	0	–	–	–
<u>10</u>	<u>10</u>	–	–	–
0	0	–	–	–
10	**10**	**–**	**–**	**–**
13	13	13	16	10
0	0	0	0	6
24	24	8	8	0
<u>37</u>	<u>37</u>	<u>21</u>	<u>24</u>	<u>16</u>
7	7	13	24	16
30	**30**	**8**	**0**	**0**
0	0	0	0	0
<u>0</u>	<u>0</u>	<u>0</u>	<u>0</u>	<u>0</u>
0	0	0	0	0
0	**0**	**0**	**0**	**0**
16	16	8	8	0
0	0	8	8	16
32	32	24	28	4
0	0	0	0	0
<u>48</u>	<u>48</u>	<u>40</u>	<u>44</u>	<u>20</u>
0	0	0	20	4
48	**48**	**40**	**24**	**16**
24	24	12	8	4
0	0	12	16	20
62	62	44	46	8
0	0	0	1	0
<u>86</u>	<u>86</u>	<u>68</u>	<u>71</u>	<u>32</u>
4	4	4	49	4
82	**82**	**64**	**22**	**28**
12	12	8	12	6
1	0	0	0	0
<u>13</u>	<u>12</u>	<u>8</u>	<u>12</u>	<u>6</u>
1	0	0	4	2
12	**12**	**8**	**8**	**4**

		29.03.44	*19.04.44*
Barrow	3.7(m)	8	8
	<u>Total</u>	<u>8</u>	<u>8</u>
	Non-op	0	8
	Total (op)	**8**	**0**
Heysham	<u>Total</u>	<u>0</u>	<u>0</u>
	Non-op	0	0
	Total (op)	**0**	**0**
Liverpool	5.25	8	8
	4.5	20	20
	3.7 Mk VI	4	4
	3.7(s)	64	64
	<u>Total</u>	<u>96</u>	<u>96</u>
	Non-op	0	34
	Total (op)	**96**	**62**
Mersey (Maunsell)	3.7(s)	12	12
	<u>Total</u>	<u>12</u>	<u>12</u>
	Non-op	0	0
	Total (op)	**12**	**12**
Preston	<u>Total</u>	<u>0</u>	<u>0</u>
	Non-op	0	0
	Total (op)	**0**	**0**

Scotland

		29.03.44	*19.04.44*
Forth	4.5	8	8
	3.7 Mk VI	0	0
	3.7(s)	40	40
	3.7(m)	4	0
	<u>Total</u>	<u>52</u>	<u>48</u>
	Non-op	0	14
	Total (op)	**52**	**34**
Dundee	3.7(s)	6	6
	3.7(m)	4	0
	<u>Total</u>	<u>10</u>	<u>6</u>
	Non-op	0	6
	Total (op)	**10**	**0**
Aberdeen	3.7(s)	16	16
	<u>Total</u>	<u>16</u>	<u>16</u>
	Non-op	0	0
	Total (op)	**16**	**16**

10.06.44	16.07.44	10.09.44	03.01.45	09.05.45
0	0	0	0	0
0	0	0	0	0
0	0	0	0	0
0	**0**	**0**	**0**	**0**
–	–	–	–	–
–	–	–	–	–
0	–	–	–	–
8	8	8	8	8
20	20	20	18	18
4	4	4	6	6
60	54	12	2	0
92	86	44	34	32
34	28	20	16	32
58	**58**	**24**	**18**	**0**
12	12	10	–	–
12	12	10	–	–
12	0	0	–	–
0	**12**	**10**	–	–
0	0	0	0	0
0	0	0	0	0
0	**0**	**0**	**0**	**0**

10.06.44	08.07.44	30.08.44	03.01.45	09.05.45
8	8	8	0	0
0	0	0	8	8
40	28	16	10	8
0	0	0	0	0
48	36	24	18	16
12	0	4	0	16
36	**36**	**20**	**18**	**0**
6	6	0	0	0
0	0	0	0	0
6	6	0	0	0
6	0	0	0	0
0	**6**	**0**	**0**	**0**
16	16	16	8	0
16	16	16	8	0
0	0	0	0	0
16	**16**	**16**	**8**	**0**

		29.03.44	*19.04.44*
Scapa	4.5	31	31
	3.7 Mk VI	0	0
	3.7(s)	48	48
	<u>Total</u>	<u>79</u>	<u>79</u>
	Non-op	12	12
	Total (op)	**67**	**67**
Shetland	3.7(s)	4	4
	3.7(m)	8	8
	<u>Total</u>	<u>12</u>	<u>12</u>
	Non-op	0	0
	Total (op)	**12**	**12**
Clyde	4.5	24	24
	3.7 Mk VI	0	0
	3.7(s)	24	24
	<u>Total</u>	<u>48</u>	<u>48</u>
	Non-op	0	10
	Total (op)	**48**	**38**
Ardeer	4.5	0	0
	3.7(s)	12	12
	<u>Total</u>	<u>12</u>	<u>12</u>
	Non-op	0	12
	Total (op)	**12**	**0**
Invergordon	3.7(s)	4	4
	<u>Total</u>	<u>4</u>	<u>4</u>
	Non-op	0	4
	Total (op)	**4**	**0**
Fort William	<u>Total</u>	<u>0</u>	<u>0</u>
	Non-op	0	0
	Total (op)	**0**	**0**

Northern Ireland

		29.03.44	*19.04.44*
Belfast	3.7(s)	44	38
	<u>Total</u>	<u>44</u>	<u>38</u>
	Non–op	0	0
	Total (op)	**44**	**38**
Bangor	3.7(s)	4	4
	<u>Total</u>	<u>4</u>	<u>4</u>
	Non-op	0	0
	Total (op)	**4**	**4**
Londonderry	<u>Total</u>	<u>0</u>	<u>0</u>
	Non-op	0	0
	Total (op)	**0**	**0**

10.06.44	08.07.44	30.08.44	03.01.45	09.05.45
19	19	15	15	0
12	12	16	16	32
48	48	48	46	40
<u>79</u>	<u>79</u>	<u>79</u>	<u>77</u>	<u>72</u>
12	12	12	25	72
67	**67**	**67**	**52**	**0**
4	4	4	4	4
8	8	8	0	0
<u>12</u>	<u>12</u>	<u>12</u>	<u>4</u>	<u>4</u>
0	0	0	0	4
12	**12**	**12**	**4**	**0**
22	22	16	0	0
0	0	0	12	12
24	18	12	16	12
<u>46</u>	<u>40</u>	<u>28</u>	<u>28</u>	<u>24</u>
6	0	0	0	24
40	**40**	**28**	**28**	**0**
0	–	1	–	–
12	–	1	–	–
<u>12</u>	–	<u>2</u>	–	–
12	–	2	–	–
0	–	**0**	–	–
0	0	–	–	–
<u>0</u>	<u>0</u>	–	–	–
0	0	–	–	–
0	**0**	–	–	–
–	–	–	–	–
–	–	–	–	–
–	**–**	**–**	**–**	**–**

10.06.44	08.07.44	30.08.44	03.01.45	09.05.45
38	40	–	–	–
<u>38</u>	<u>40</u>	–	–	–
0	0	–	–	–
38	**40**	–	–	–
4	–	–	–	–
<u>4</u>	–	–	–	–
4	–	–	–	–
0	–	–	–	–
–	–	–	–	–
–	–	–	–	–
–	**–**	**–**	**–**	**–**

Diver **deployments**

		29.03.44	19.04.44
All areas	3.7(s)	–	–
	3.7(m)	–	–
	Total	–	–
	Non-op	–	–
	Total (op)	**–**	**–**

Miscellaneous

		29.03.44	19.04.44
Training schools etc	5.25	0	0
	4.5	9	10
	3.7 Mk VI	7	7
	3.7(s)	66	70
	3.7(m)	203	156
	Total	285	243
	Non-op	285	243
	Total (op)	**0**	**0**

Summary

		29.03.44	19.04.44
Totals	5.25	55	63
	4.5	290	291
	3.7 Mk VI	118	118
	3.7(s)	1654	1678
	3.7(m)	671	779
	Total	2788	2929
	Non-op	383	580
	Total (op)	**2405**	**2349**

10.06.44	08.07.44	30.08.44	03.01.45	09.05.45
–	30	440	370	376
–	376	277	185	192
–	406	617	555	568
–	33	237	185	520
–	**373**	**480**	**370**	**48**

10.06.44	08.07.44	30.08.44	03.01.45	09.05.45
1	1	1	3	3
12	10	16	17	6
3	3	4	8	48
75	114	176	259	619
76	55	103	298	317
167	183	300	585	993
167	183	300	585	993
0	**0**	**0**	**0**	**0**

10.06.44	08.07.44	30.08.44	03.01.45	09.05.45
76	82	99	113	118
238	236	213	159	63
174	174	198	245	343
1672	1673	1701	1621	1625
812	780	536	509	514
2972	2845	2747	2647	2663
444	420	755	1284	2149
2528	**2525**	**1992**	**1363**	**514**

Gazetteer of HAA batteries

The following table provides a listing of the locations of heavy anti-aircraft batteries throughout the United Kingdom, grouped alphabetically by their parent GDAs and identified by a a six-figure Ordnance Survey grid reference (accurate to 100 metres). More than 1200 sites appear in the listing, a total which is believed to represent practically all of the positions in the major permanent GDAs, along with many others of more transient occupation and lesser importance. The listing has been compiled from numerous sources – too many, indeed, to cite here* – though key items include the rosters of HAA positions issued by AA Command in February 1940 and June 1942,† which include all gunsites acquired (though not necessarily developed) by those dates. These have been supplemented by location statements issued by AA formations, chiefly during the later war years, as far as possible to capture sites added to the layout in 1943–45. Apart from the huge number of *Diver* positions, however (and these will appear in a separate volume on the flying bomb campaign), those sites were not plentiful. Some were acquired for *Overlord*, but their occupation was brief and in general the extent of AA

---

* All sources are, however, given in the original reports from which the listing is reproduced (Dobinson 1996A for England, Redfern 1998 for the remainder of the UK). Researchers wishing to evaluate the list critically can turn to those.

† WO 166/2072, War Diary, AA Cmd G, Draft list of HAA gunsites and GL frequencies, 32/Wireless/587(SD6(a)), nd Feb 1940; AIR 2/4768, AA Cmd to multiple recipients, AAC/40265/G/Ops, 23 Jun 1942.

Command's HAA estate by mid 1942 was not greatly enlarged by the requirements of the succeeding three years. We can be confident of this, in part, because location statements for the permanent HAA gunsites in specific areas show a large measure of continuity from the middle of the war onwards.

The listing is arranged in five columns. The first shows the GDA, and here, because some areas tended to be split and others merged over time, the general approach has been to break down the areas into their smaller components, chiefly because this makes the list easier to use. By mid 1942, to give one example, the sites serving Aldershot, Basingstoke, Guildford and Reading were treated as a single GDA and numbered sequentially with the prefix BY, though in the list these appear as four separate GDAs with a note to indicate that the coding sequence was shared. Likewise, Birmingham and Coventry were, in 1940, two separate GDAs but by 1942 had been amalgamated with a common sequence of (new) numbers. These, too, are shown separately, and here as elsewhere two columns for the site number show the earlier and later codes. This tendency to merge GDAs and renumber their sites makes it difficult to decide in which order the individual sites should be listed – whether by the first (shorter) or second (longer) sequence – and is complicated further by the fact that the number of sites had tended to multiply by the time amalgamation had taken place. The procedure adopted here, therefore, has been to list the *earlier* sites in their correct sequence, showing the numbers allocated to these in the later scheme in the second column, with the *additional* sites in the later number sequence then listed in order. (A moment's study of the Birmingham, Coventry or Humber entries should make this clear.) Happily, however, many GDAs did not re-number their sites, as the '–' entry in many of these columns indicates. This same symbol is used where no information on the site number is available, likewise where the site name is unknown. Many GDAs did not name their sites in any formal sense or, if they did, neglected to use the appellation in their routine location statements. Site names have, in general, been reproduced as found, and only obvious errors corrected.

The final column shows the National Grid Reference of the position. These references have been 'converted' from those found in the sources, where positions are recorded using the wartime 'Cassini' grid, a system differing markedly in orientation, origin and geometry from that applied to modern maps (though the original system survives largely unchanged in Northern Ireland). Conversion has been achieved either visually or photographically (in the second case by plotting the locality and point on acetate film, enlarging to match the scale of the modern map and overlaying), processes which yield a similar level of accuracy to the original references. The converted references have been used to locate the original positions of the sites on the ground today using large-scale maps and aerial photographs (as described in Chapter 12) and appear in most cases to refer to the centre of gravity of the gun emplacements. In processing the original references, however, it was sometimes found that a specific site with a consistent name and code was located by a series of grid references varying over time by a few hundred metres. In some cases these variations may reflect differing choices in the reference point used to identify the site – the command post, perhaps, or the radar, or the centre of the guns – and may imply inconsistent procedures used by the succession of occupying units and their supervisory formations. Equally, some will reflect enlargements in the site over time, which will naturally tend to move the central point. In other cases, however, and especially where mobile guns were used, wandering grid references will reflect weapons shuffled to find marginally better tactical positions (a process clearly documented in some War Diaries) and thus the establishment of new sites. Since the original purpose of the exercise was to provide a means of finding the site from large-scale maps and aerial photographs, a policy was obviously needed in processing the data in order to eliminate a large number of redundant grid references clustering around one point and giving essentially the same information. So the policy adopted was to ignore shifts of 200 metres or less from an original position, but to accept any larger than these as reflecting a potential move of the guns, with the result that some site codes and names in the list which follows show more than one grid reference. Whether these always *genuinely* reflect shifted sites is not clear, but in cases where the references are separated by several hundred metres this does seem practically certain. One point on which we can be confident, however, is the veracity of the original grid references. Map data was a common currency of wartime record keeping, treated with care and respect and protected by sanctions from mishandling (a clerk who mistyped a reference might easily receive a spell in jail). So small variations in these references should always mean something, even if that something, today, is not always easy to identify.

The grid references supplied here are published in the interests of historical research, and to enlarge awareness of the historic environment. They can be used together with those in companion volumes of the *Monuments of War* series to reconstruct the defence geography of local areas and regions, as well as nationally (even if researchers will have to return to primary sources to unpick many details of chronology). It should be stressed, however, that the vast majority of the positions listed are on private land and – as we now know – the number retaining substantial wartime fabric is small.

Aberdeen	AB1	–	Aberdeen	NJ 952072
	AB2	–	Aberdeen	NJ 956034
	AB5	–	–	NJ 952097

Aldershot	BY12	–	Hog Hatch	SU 830483
	BY13	–	Ively Farm	SU 845547
	BY15	–	Whitelane Farm	SU 905489

Coding sequence integral with Basingstoke, Guildford and Reading.

Andover	1	–	Finkley	SU 388482
	2	–	Barrow Hill	SU 351421

Ardeer	IC1	–	Tevenson	NS 279426
	IC2	–	Irvine	NS 318370

Ashford	AD1	–	Mersham	TR 047400
	AD2	–	Kingsland	TQ 996454

Banbury	H1	–	Harwell	SP 469424
	H2	–	Astrop	SP 511386
	H3	–	Bloxham	SP 531371
	H4	–	Wroxham	SP 419426

Barrow	H1	–	North Scale	SD 173701
	H2	–	Biggar	SD 183663
	H3	–	Ramsden	SD 202671
	H4	–	Rakesmoor	SD 206732
	H5	–	Southend Haws	SD 199637
	H6	–	–	SD 210782
	H7	–	Roose	SD 241672

Basingstoke	BY10	–	Basing	SU 663525
	BY11	–	Prewitt	SU 617529
	BY18	–	Cliddesden	SU 635491
	BY19	–	Elm Bottom	SU 639545

Coding sequence integral with Aldershot, Guildford and Reading.

Bath	1	–	Lansdown	ST 729679
	2	–	South Store	ST 747621
	3	–	Claverton	ST 773641

Beaulieu	32	–	Fowey	SZ 381960
	33	–	Bunkers Hill	SU 383017

Coding sequence integral with Isle of Wight, Portsmouth and Southampton.

Bedford	H1	–	–	TL 062520
	H2	–	–	TL 029492
	H3	–	–	TL 097434
	H4	–	–	SP 971557

Belfast	U1	–	–	J 390787
	–	U1	Kinnegar	J 398792

Belfast	U1	–	Kinnegar	J 387784
continued	U2	–	Rosepark	J 406737
	U3	U6	Lisnabreeny	J 366705
	–	U3	Sunningdale	J 390786
	U6	–	Sunningdale	J 318777
	U4	–	–	J 306698
	–	–	Bamoral	J 314697
	U5	–	Woodvale	J 308747
	U7	–	Claneboye	J 463795
	U8	–	–	J 446713
	U9	–	Carryduff	J 374654
	U10	–	Lisburn	J 298654
	U11	–	Sleevenagravery	J 252720
	U12	U13	Silnerstream	J 369845
	OR	–	–	J 375725
Bircham Newton	H1	–	–	TF 767342
Birmingham	A	–	Coven Heath	SJ 903044
		H1	Coven Heath	SJ 902053
	B	H50	Bushberry Hill	SJ 923031
	C	H18	Merry Hill	SO 877971
	D	H51	The Elms	SJ 876013
	E	–	Wednesfield	SO 949996
		H52	Wednesfield	SJ 966000
	F	H3	Stoke Cross	SP 012945
	G	H17	Turners Hill	SO 970891
	H	H53	Mons Hill	SO 933926
	I	H6	Park Hall	SP 159904
	K	H4	Perry Park	SP 066924
	L	H10	Erdington	SP 118913
	M	H55	Sheldon	SP 147848
	N	H56	Castle Bromwich	SP 127894
	O	H9	Olton Hall	SP 152825
	P	H7	Oaklands	SP 126852
	Q	H57	Swainhurst Park	SP 091814
	R	–	Edgbaston	SP 058843
	R	H12	Kingswood Farm	SP 072781
	S	H58	Welsh House Farm	SP 018811
	T	H59	Langley Hall Farm	SP 124810
	U	H60	The Uplands	SP 036913
	–	H2	–	SJ 964078
	–	H5	–	SP 106989
	–	H11	Nuthurst	SP 130719
	–	H13	Rubery	SO 988786
	–	H14	–	*unresolved*
	–	H15	–	*unresolved*
	–	H16	–	SO 895878
	–	H19	–	*unresolved*
	–	H20	–	*unresolved*
	–	H49	Upper Penn	SO 897945
	–	H54	Warmley Ash	SP 429929
	–	H61	Castle Bromwich	SP 155915
	–	H62	Glibe Farm	SP 138883

Birmingham	–	H63	Wylde Green	SP 125935
continued	–	H64	Short Heath	SP 104930
	–	H65	Shard End Farm	SP 152884

Later coding sequence integral with Coventry.

| Blackpool | H1 | – | Waterloo | SD 313338 |
| | H2 | – | St Annes | SD 340285 |

Bletchley	H1	–	–	SP 877363
	H2	–	–	SP 965278
	H3	–	–	SP 855340
	H4	–	–	SP 800399

Blyth	A	–	–	NZ 298851
	B	–	–	NZ 318784
	C	–	–	NZ 282819

Bramley	1	–	–	SU 692594
	2	–	–	SU 690548
	3	–	–	SU 620567
	3	–	–	SU 679595
	4	–	–	SU 634611
	5	–	–	SU 644562
	7	–	–	SU 673558
	10	–	–	SU 649596

Brighton	NH8	H27	Blackrock/Kemp Town	TQ 344032
	NH9	–	Southern Cross	TQ 251057
	NH12	H23	Southwick/Kingston-by-Sea	TQ 235053
	NH13	H25	Hangleton/West Blatchington	TQ 276071
	NH14	H26	Hove	TQ 300057

Coding sequences integral with Newhaven and Shoreham.

Bristol	B1	3	Gordano	ST 525747
	B2	1	Portishead/Portbury	ST 487767
	B3	7	Rockingham Farm	ST 523808
	B4	5	Cribbs	ST 568809
	B5	11	Brickfields	ST 634811
	B6	13	Purdown	ST 613766
	B7	17	Whitchurch	ST 604683
	B8	19	Reservoir	ST 564695
	B9	–	Avonmouth	ST 507778
	B10	–	Almondsbury	ST 606833
	–	9	Almondsbury	ST 611833
	B11	–	Hanbrook	ST 636786
	B12	15	Hanham	ST 636715
	B14	–	Blackboy	ST 636715
	B15	–	–	ST 567642
	B17	14	Rodway	ST 666757
	–	2	Lodge Farm	ST 440750
	–	4	St George's Wharf	ST 501711
	–	6	Westbury	ST 577774

Bristol	–	8	Pilning	ST 550862
continued	–	10	Earthcote	ST 637862
	–	12	Henfield	ST 682790
	–	16	Keynsham	ST 685655
	–	18	Chew	ST 551627
	–	20	Backwell	ST 504677
Brooklands	BM1	–	Fairmile	TQ 112607
	BM2	–	Wisley Common	TQ 077593
	BM3	–	Dunford Farm	TQ 020617
	BM4	–	Woburn Park	TQ 065650
	BM5	–	Old Woking	TQ 021566
	BM6	–	Weston Green	TQ 156664
Caerwent	G1	–	Shirenewton	ST 461938
	G2	–	Mounmon	ST 504932
	G3	–	Portskewet	ST 514895
	G4	–	Caldicott	ST 480873
	G5	–	St Brides	ST 435892
	G6	–	Llanvaches	ST 437916
Cambridge	H1	–	–	TL 526643
	H2	–	–	TL 479588
	H2A	–	–	TL 475588
	H3	–	–	TL 401516
	H4	–	–	TL 402628
Canterbury	CN1	–	Fordwych	TR 182590
	CN2	–	Chartham	TR 128543
	CN3	–	Blean	TR 133611
	CN5	–	–	TR 177551
Cardiff	A	J2	Mardy Farm	ST 230779
	B	–	Prarie	ST 203744
	C	–	Lavernock	ST 186680
	D	J1	Llwyn-y-Grant	ST 195800
	J	J5	Sully	ST 152679
	K	J6	Bulwarks	ST 079662
	L	J7	Waters Farm	ST 102691
	M	J8	Ely Racecourse	ST 146762
	W	J9	Llandaff	ST 158789
	–	J3	Llandough	ST 171729
	–	J4	Lavernock	ST 180678
	–	J13	Llanishen	ST 172822
	–	J16	Flathorn	ST 222649

First coding sequence integral with Newport and Swansea.

Carlisle	A	–	–	NY 447574
	B	–	–	NY 350563
	C	–	–	NY 413529
	D	–	–	NY 419621
Castletown	C1	C2	Castletown	ND 211664

Chelmsford	C8	–	Old Lodge Farm	TL 731096
	C9	–	Great Baddow	TL 722044
	C12	–	Recreation Ground	TL 705068
	C13	–	Broomfield	TL 702105
	C14	–	Rumbolds Farm	TL 746061
	C15	–	Rollestone	TL 677057

Coding sequence integral with Clacton and Colchester.

Chichester	CH7	–	Donnington	SU 858016
	CH8	–	Oldwick Farm	SU 848073
	CH9	–	–	SU 781978
	CH10	–	–	SU 745988

Coding sequence integral with Tangmere, Ford and Thorney Island.

| Chilbolton | – | – | Fullerton | SU 367395 |

Clacton	C1	–	East Mersea	TM 052133
	C2	–	St Osyth	TM 108126
	C3	–	Jaywick	TM 149139
	C4	–	Little Holland	TM 215170

Coding sequence integral with Chelmsford and Colchester.

Clyde	GNG1	N1	Hall Hill	NS 671653
	GNG2	N2	Rusby Hill	NS 636704
	GNG3	N3	Black Hill	NS 580710
	GNG4	N4	Garscadden	NS 529714
	GNG5	–	–	NS 666754
	GNG6	–	–	NS 690800
	–	N5	Duntocher	NS 492732
	–	N6	Kilmalid	NS 399770
	–	N7	Greenland	NS 439753
	–	N8	Blair Quhanan	NS 422830
	–	N9	Mugdock	NS 543773
	–	N11	–	NS 674715
	–	N12	Ryding	NS 750689
	GSG1	S1	Blantyreferme	NS 682598
	GSG2	S2	Rogerton	NS 632570
	GSG3	S3	Carmunnock	NS 582585
	GSG4	S4	Darnley	NS 546594
	GSG5	S5	Dykebarhill	NS 498623
	GSG6	S6	Linwood	NS 453641
	GSG7	S7	Drumcross	NS 452709
	GSG8	S8	Houston	NS 396670
	GSG9	S9	Bogside	NS 376721
	GSG10	AS5	Larkfield	NS 246765
	–	S10	Limekilnburn	NS 695509
	–	S11	–	NS 600615
	–	S12	–	NS 539628
	–	S13	Moorpark	NS 510662
	–	S14	Millthird	NS 451573

Clyde	–	AS1	–	NS 331734
continued	–	AS2	Whinhill	NS 275749
	–	AS3	–	NS 238770
	–	AS4	Flaterton	NS 229747
	–	AS6	Matternock	NS 321706
	–	AS7	Wemyss Bay	NS 194702
	–	AN1	–	NS 335788
	–	AN2	Woodend	NS 292839
	–	AN3	Killgreggan	NS 225813
	–	AN4	Chilston	NS 338774
	–	AN5	Rosneath	NS 263815
	–	AN6	Mamore	NS 225868
	–	AN7	–	NS 194702
	–	AN8	Dunoon	NS 168795
	–	AN9	Strone	NS 261899
	–	AN10	Glenacre	NS 155715
	–	BS2	–	NS 246765
Colchester	C5	–	Crockleford Heath	TM 047263
	C6	–	Fridaywood Farm	TL 986213

Coding sequence integral with Chelmsford and Clacton.

Corby	H1	–	Weldon	SP 932892
	H2	–	Rockingham	SP 882912
Coventry	A	H21	Bedworth	SP 378865
	B	H71	Brookfield Farm	SP 382833
	C	H23	Binley	SP 378779
	D	H30	Ryton on Dunsmore	SP 382741
	E	–	Bubben Hall	SP 356728
	F	H67	Gibbett Hill	SP 304751
	G	H26	Tile Hill	SP 284781
	H	–	Keresley	SP 318801
	K	H68	Exhall	SP 340804
	L	H69	Walsgrove	SP 382801
	–	H22	–	SP 433897
	–	H24	–	SP 406658
	–	H25	Bannerhill	SP 274694
	–	H27	Fillongley	SP 300871
	–	H28	Stoneleigh	SP 330735
	–	H29	–	SP 472785
	–	H66	Bubben Hall	SP 343714
	–	H70	Eastern Green	SP 292798
	–	H72	Keresley	SP 343714

Later coding sequence integral with Birmingham.

Crewe	A	H1	Leighton Grange	SJ 672573
	B	–		SJ 713588
	C	H3	Weston Lane Farm	SJ 721538
	D	–		SJ 675533

Crewe	–	H2	Hassall	SJ 763573
continued	–	H4	Walgherton	SJ 701484
Dartmouth	2	–	Coleton	SX 906508
	3	–	Cotton	SX 861506
	5	–	Lupton	SX 893545
	6	–	Fire Beacon	SX 857339
Daventry	B	–	–	SP 596604
	C	–	–	SP 563634
Dishforth	H1	–	–	SE 381721
Donington	A	H2	–	SJ 716110
	C	–	–	SJ 677168
	–	H1	–	SJ 676170
	–	H3	–	SJ 750107
Dover	D1	–	Farthingloe	TR 297399
	D2	–	Swingate	TR 349433
	D3	–	Frith Farm	TR 319436
	D4	–	St Radigund	TR 289424
	D5	–	–	TR 328426
	D6	–	Dover Harbour	TR 328416
	D7	–	Western Heights	TR 310408
	D8	–	–	TR 329461
	D10	–	–	TR 352477
	D12	–	–	TR 356513
Driffield	H1	–	–	SE 983566
	H2	–	–	TA 011554
Dundee	D1	–	–	NO 425324
	D2	D5	–	NO 386339
	–	D2	–	NO 427281
Duxford	–	H1	–	TL 467469
	B	H2	–	TL 446454
Exeter	1	–	Huxham	SX 956972
	2	–	Jack in the Green	SY 012962
	3	–	Holbrook	SX 990922
	4	–	Kenbury	SX 921876
	5	–	Halsford Wood	SX 882943
	5A	–	Hoopern Farm	SX 922940
	6	–	Faringdon	SY 010920
Falmouth	1	–	Pennance	SW 801307
	2	–	Mylor	SW 812368
	3	–	St Just	SW 852351
	4	–	St Anthony	SW 848318
	5	–	Mawnan	SW 790273
	6	–	Roskrow	SW 757353
	B	–	Buller Down	SW 699397

Falmouth	C	–	Chace Water	SW 745448
continued	D	–	Merry Maidens	SW 432243
	E	–	Trevedra	SW 376274
	F	–	Raginnis	SW 459261
Feltwell	A	H1	–	TL 709909
	–	H2	–	TL 700894
Folkestone	FO1	–	–	TR 211352
	FO2	–	–	TR 214367
	FO2	–	–	TR 234380
	FO3	–	–	TR 215368
	FO3	–	Capel Court	TR 257386
	FO4	–	–	TR 212353
	FO5	–	–	TR 179363
	FO6	–	–	TR 119331
Ford	CH4	–	Ford	TQ 009013

Coding sequence integral with Chichester, Tangmere and Thorney Island.

Forth	RNG1	RN1	Donibristle	NT 154828
	RNG2	RN2	Primrose Park	NT 100840
	RNG3	RN3	Mire End	NT 046858
	RNG4	RN4	Crossgates	NT 134884
	RNG5	–	Ban Hill	NT 180837
	RNG6	RN6	Aberdour	NT 191848
	RNG7	–	Bruce Haven	NT 055834
	RNG8	–	Kinghorn	NT 261866
	RSG1	–	Dalmeny Park	NT 158782
	RSG2	RS2	Totley Wells	NT 102764
	RSG3	RS3	Philipstown	NT 045777
	RSG4	RS4	Dalmerry	NT 139782
	RSG5	–	Barbouge	NT 165786
	RSG6	RS6	Clifton Hill	NT 118705
	RSG7	–	Carriden	NT 031801
	EDG1	E1	Restalrig	NT 289749
	EDG2	E2	Liberton	NT 276691
	EDG3	E3	Sighthill	NT 190707
	EDG4	E4	West Pilton	NT 215758
	EDG5	E5	Broomfield	NT 208770
Fort William	FW1	–	–	NN 129773
	FW2	–	Caol	NN 107761
Foulness	N25	–	Barge Pier	TQ 932844
	N26	–	New Burwood	TQ 999906
	N27	–	Fishermans Head	TR 031931
	N28	–	Ridgemarsh Farm	TR 021943
Gloucester/	A1	–	Fiddington	SO 923319
Brockworth	A2	–	Reddings	SO 901208

Gloucester/	A3	–	Prestbury	SO 968229
Brockworth	A4	–	Foxcote	SP 020182
continued	A5	–	Elkstone	SO 960129
	A6	–	Longbridge	SO 882092
	A7	–	Field Court	SO 806138
	A8	–	Derby Hill	SO 756165
	A9	–	Highnam	SO 788195
	A10	–	Linbury	SO 786250
	A11	–	Tirley	SO 826241
	A12	–	Haydons Elm	SO 901239
	A13	–	Dean Farm	SO 902178
	A14	–	Belmont	SO 857135
	A15	–	Parton	SO 863204
	B1	–	Barnwood	SO 852176
	B3	–	Buckholt	SO 891137
	B5	–	Overtown	SO 919127
Grantham	A	–	–	SK 908332
	–	H1	–	SK 904331
	B	H2	–	SK 944361
	–	H3	–	SK 914386
	–	H4	–	SK 885351
Guildford	BY8	–	Warren Farm	TQ 020497
	BY16	–	Whitemoor Common	SU 987533
	BY17	–	Peasmarsh	SU 984467
	BY20	–	Golf Course	TQ 035498

Coding sequence integral with Aldershot, Basingstoke and Reading.

Harwich	H1	–	Landguard	TM 286325
	H2	–	Searsons Farm	TM 278360
	H3	–	Dovercourt	TM 247304
	H4	–	Shetley Street	TM 239349
	H4	–	–	TM 244341
	H5	–	Little Oakley	TM 217290
	H6	–	–	TM 184359
	H7	K22	Old Felixstowe	TM 317358
	–	K10	–	TM 229289

Coding sequence integral with Ipswich and Martlesham.

Hatfield	HM1	–	Lemsford	TL 214116
Hawarden	VA	H23	–	SJ 343671
	VC	H22	–	SJ 338619
Hawkinge	D11	–	Hope Farm	TR 234380
	D12	–	Hawkinge	TR 207420
	D16	–	Arpinge Farm	TR 191386

Coding sequence integral with Dover.

Hayle	1	–	Praze	SW 580352

Hayle *continued*	2	–	Trevarrack	SW 522374
Heysham	H1	–	St Patricks Chapel	SD 410613
	H2	–	Sunderland Point	SD 423563
Holton Heath/	1	–	Upton	SY 979937
Poole	2	–	Slepe	SY 924922
	3	–	Northport	SY 919887
	4	–	Arne	SY 966874
	–	HH1	–	SY 979938
	–	HH2	–	SY 924922
	4	HH4	Arne	SY 971878
	–	–		SZ 029907
	–	HH5	Parkestone Bay	SZ 031907
	–	HH6	Shell Bay	SZ 031857
Honington	A	–	Honington	TL 882750
	B	–	Honington	TL 903751
Humber	A	H29	Chanterlands Ave, Hull	TA 073311
	A1	H2	Wawne Rd, Sutton	TA 112336
	B	H3	Craven Park, Hull	TA 128307
	C	H4	Preston, Hull	TA 163305
	C1	–	–	TA 193291
	C1	–	Hedon, Hull	TA 196292
	–	H5		TA 196291
	D	–	Paull	TA 173266
	–	H7	–	TA 171265
	E	H25	Goxhill	TA 124248
	F	H26	–	TA 094238
	F1	–	–	TA 059232
	F1	–	Barrow Haven	TA 096231
	G	H28	Boothferry Rd, Hull	TA 050278
	H	–	–	TA 199238
	H	H8	Little Humber	TA 199234
	J	H9	Stone Creek	TA 238188
	J1	H10	Sunk Island	TA 277169
	K	H21	Long Strip	TA 210155
	L	–	Immingham	TA 180155
	M	–	–	TA 155190
	P	H12	Kilnsea	TA 420148
	Q	–	Grimsby Sea Wall	TA 283107
	R	H13	Spurn Point	TA 401109
	S	–	Stallingborough	TA 187120
	T	H24	East Halton	TA 137190
	U	H18	Fulne	TA 249088
	X	H11	Welwich	TA 341195
	Y	–	Cleethorpes	TA 323064
	–	H1	–	TA 096404
	–	H6	–	TA 283271
	–	H14	–	TA 348030
	–	H15	–	TA 323065
	–	H16	–	TA 287104
	–	H17	–	TA 247115

Humber	–	H19	–		TA 220062
continued	–	H20	–		TA 185120
	–	H22	–		TA 192156
	–	H23	–		TA 153173
	–	H27	–		TA 056230
	–	H30	–		SE 964324
	–	H31	–		TA 017371
	–	H32	–		TA 167379
	–	H33	–		TA 249343
	–	H36	–		TA 135122
	–	H37	–		TA 169131
	–	H46	–		TA 275375
	–	H47	–		TA 230438
Invergordon	ING1	–	Saltburn		NH 731704
	ING2	–	Rosskeen		NH 679700
Ipswich	H12	–	Nacton Heath		TM 203417
	H14	–	–		TM 214444
	H16	–	–		TM 141403
	H18	–	Grove Farm		TM 164467

Coding sequence integral with Harwich and Martlesham.

Isle of Wight	IW6	–	Nettlestone		SZ 626908
	IW13	–	Whippingham		SZ 519937
	IW14	–	Rew Street		SZ 465942
	IW35	–	Lynn Farm		SZ 539894
	IW36	–	Porchfield		SZ 445915
	IW36	–	Thorley Street		SZ 374881
	IW37	–	Hamstead		SZ 408907
	IW39	–	Cliff End		SZ 332887
	IW44	–	–		SZ 418822

Coding sequence integral with Portsmouth and Southampton.

Kinloss	K1	–	Kinloss		NJ 055639
	K2	–	–		NJ 103645
Kyle of Lochalsh	B1	–	Kyle of Lochalsh		NG 754274
(Port 'ZA')	B2	–	Balmacara		NG 811274
Larne	LR1	–	Ballysnod		D 391007
	LR2	–	Dundresen		D 444028
Leconfield	H1	–	–		TA 050438
Leeds	A	–	–		SE 312379
	B	H6	–		SE 343369
	C	–	–		SE 322341
	D	–	–		SE 321292
	E	–	–		SE 326321
	F	–	–		SE 301305
	G	H11	–		SE 241331
	H	–	–		SE 300365

Leeds	J	H3	–	SE 258375
continued	K	H4	–	SE 274395
	L	–	–	SE 288270
	M	–	–	SE 206362
	N	–	–	SE 169374
	O	H12	–	SE 252230
	P	–	–	SE 215255
	Q	H13	–	SE 243170
	R	H14	–	SE 195215
	S	–	–	SE 172160
	T	–	–	SE 152206
	U	H16	–	SE 150131
	V	H17	–	SE 109173
	W	–	–	SE 111230
	–	H1	–	SE 162414
	–	H2	–	SE 194157
	–	H5	–	SE 312386
	–	H7	–	SE 330318
	–	H8	–	SE 359272
	–	H9	–	SE 308305
	–	H10	–	SE 254306
	–	H15	–	SE 167428
	–	H18	–	SE 108233
	–	H19	–	SE 069304
	–	H20	–	SE 143481
	–	H21	–	SE 226435
	–	H22	–	SE 285470
	–	H23	–	SE 438441
	–	H24	–	SE 400400
	–	H25	–	SE 421340
	–	H26	–	SE 363266
	–	H27	–	SE 323236
	–	H28	–	SE 366198
	–	H29	–	SE 328149
	–	H30	–	SE 188111
	–	H31	–	SE 117086
	–	H32	–	SE 151251
	–	H33	–	SE 186289
	–	H34	–	SE 098374
	–	H35	–	SE 047371
	–	H36	–	SE 018422
	–	H37	–	SE 097434
Leicester	H1	–	Thurnby	SK 645027
	H3	–	Enderby	SP 552999
	H5	–	Anstey	SK 563068
	H6	–	Syston	SK 625103
Leighton Buzzard	A	–	–	SP 956245
	B	–	–	SP 939224
Lincoln	H1	–	Riseholm	SK 973754
	H2	–	Reepham	TF 020737
	H3	–	Sharps Farm	SK 996683

Linton on Ouse	–	–	–	SE 497611
	H1	–	–	SE 493628
	H2	–	–	SE 505604
Littlehampton	L1	–	Preston	TQ 056014
	L1	–	–	TQ 009013
	L2	–	Toddington	TQ 034040
	L2	–	–	TQ 060022
	L3	–	Ford	SU 998034
	L4	–	Atherington	TQ 008008
Loch Ewe (Port 'A')	E1	–	Rhud 'a' Choin	NG 842911
	E2	–	Aultbea	NG 865893
	E3	–	Tuirnaig	NG 875840
	E4	–	Loch Tollie	NG 848790
	E5	–	Inverasdale	NG 819863
	E6	–	An Sguiteach	NG 820881
London (IAZ)	ZE1	–	Chadwell Heath	TQ 488897
	ZE2	–	Barking Park	TQ 449850
	ZE3	–	Asylum	TQ 447907
	ZE4	–	Buckhurst Hill	TQ 432938
	ZE5	–	Clayhall	TQ 420894
	ZE6	–	Breaches	TL 393021
	ZE7	–	Lippits Hill	TQ 397970
	ZE8	–	Isle of Dogs	TQ 382788
	ZE9	–	Wanstead	TQ 411865
	ZE10	–	Highams	TQ 369913
	ZE11	–	Cheshunt	TL 350017
	ZE12	–	Southwark Park	TQ 350794
	ZE12	–	Southwark Park	TQ 353789
	ZE13	–	Finsbury Park	TQ 317875
	ZE14	–	Primrose Hill	TQ 275860
	ZE15	–	Creek Mouth	TQ 477824
	ZE16	–	Beckton	TQ 417815
	ZE17	–	Bealieu	TQ 394985
	ZE18	–	Chingford	TQ 393951
	ZE19	–	Walthamstow	TQ 356819
	ZE20	–	Capel House	TQ 372992
	ZE21	–	Hackney Marshes	TQ 375853
	ZE21	–	Hackney Marshes	TQ 374859
	ZE22	–	–	TQ 326865
	ZE22	–	Hamsptead	TQ 257878
	ZE23	–	Loughton Hall	TQ 440965
	ZW1	–	Enfield	TQ 341973
	ZW2	–	Edmonton	TQ 325937
	ZW3	–	Burnt Farm	TL 321021
	ZW4	–	Chase Side	TQ 306973
	ZW5	–	Hyde Park	TQ 278806
	ZW6	–	Friern Barnet	TQ 266934
	ZW7	–	Glass House	TQ 267939
	ZW8	–	Hurlingham	TQ 252758
	ZW9	–	Dollis Hill	TQ 228857

London (IAZ)	ZW10	–	Wormwood Scrubs	TQ 223818
continued	ZW11	–	Gunnersbury Park	TQ 185792
	ZW12	–	Brentham	TQ 171828
	ZW13	–	Mill Hill	TQ 218945
	ZW14	–	Brent	TQ 211881
	ZS1	–	Slade's Green	TQ 531775
	ZS2	–	Dartford Heath	TQ 521731
	ZS3	–	Plumstead Marshes	TQ 478799
	ZS4	–	Bostall Heath	TQ 473779
	ZS5	–	St Paul's Cray	TQ 474696
	ZS6	–	Welling	TQ 466752
	ZS7	–	Eltham	TQ 438742
	ZS8	–	Woolwich Common	TQ 427773
	ZS9	–	Sundridge Park	TQ 414703
	ZS10	–	Hayes Common	TQ 412651
	ZS11	–	Brockley	TQ 373754
	ZS12	–	Beckenham	TQ 373686
	ZS13	–	Shirley Park	TQ 347652
	ZS14	–	Dulwich	TQ 341727
	ZS15	–	Norbury	TQ 301696
	ZS16	–	Clapham Common	TQ 289751
	ZS17	–	Mitcham Common	TQ 283675
	ZS18	–	Raynes Park	TQ 236689
	ZS19	–	Wimbledon	TQ 231722
	ZS20	–	Richmond Park	TQ 204743
	ZS21	–	Crayford	TQ 518758
	ZS22	–	Grove Park	TQ 413724
	ZS23	–	Ravensbourne	TQ 387706
	ZS23A	–	Summerhouse	TQ 382702
	ZS24	–	Anerley	TQ 343696
	ZS25	–	Peckham Rye	TQ 346753
	ZS26	–	Thornet Wood	TQ 440681
	ZS27	–	Weston Green	TQ 153661
	ZS27	–	Coldharbour Farm	TQ 435724

Excludes temporary sites established for the Blitz.

Londonderry	LO1	–	Waterside	C 439147
	LO2	–	Brookhall	C 437206
	LO3	–	Ballymagororty	C 397188
	LO4	–	Mobuoy	C 478184
	LO5	–	Culmore	C 439148
	LO6	–	Campsie	C 507290

Lossiemouth	LO1	–	–	NJ 227703
	LO2	–	–	NJ 187706

Lough Erne	LE1	–	Boyaghan	H 220573
	LE2	–	Lovally	H 197490

Lowestoft	LH1	–	Ashby	TM 498996
	LH2	–	Oulton	TM 535946
	LH3	–	Golf Course	TM 542909

Lowestoft	LH4	–	–	TM 514946
continued .	LH5	–	–	TM 482896
Lymington	L1	–	–	SZ 301921
	L2	–	–	SZ 297974
	L3	–	–	SZ 349988
Maidstone	M1	–	–	TQ 786599
	M2	–	Leeds	TQ 798564
	M3	–	Boughton Green	TQ 773507
Manchester	A	H15	Heaton Park	SD 834037
	B	H20	Moston	SD 880024
	C	–	Manchester Cent	SD 848003
	C	H16	–	SD 851006
	C	H25	Guide Bridge	SJ 922964
	D	H24	Little Moss	SD 915001
	E	–	Levenshulme	SJ 885948
	E	H21	Levenshulme	SJ 888948
	F	H14	Hough End Fields	SJ 831934
	G	H10	Chorlton cum Hardy	SJ 806937
	H	H6	Lostock	SJ 772958
	J	H1	Barton	SJ 747979
	K	H7	Ellesmere	SJ 778999
	L	H13	Lower Broughton	SJ 821993
	M	H8	Irlam	SD 801011
	N	H17	Middleton	SD 859055
	O	H22	Brookdale	SD 890015
	O	H22	–	SD 899000
	P	H23	Ashton under Lyne	SJ 913977
	R	–	Fallowfield	SJ 858948
	R	H18	–	SJ 862942
	R	H3	Roe Green	SD 748022
	RR	H26	–	SJ 929921
	S	H5	Ackers Farm	SJ 756927
	T	–	Davyhulme	SJ 761950
	T	H2	Davyhulme	SJ 748954
	U	H4	Eccles	SJ 736984
	U	H4	–	SJ 753993
	V	H9	Besses O'th Barn	SD 817040
	W	H9	–	SD 801053
	X	H12	Ringway	SJ 820826
	Y	H11	Baguley	SJ 808900
	Z	H19	–	SJ 879910
Manston	F5	–	Manston	TR 356656
	F6	–	Cleve Court	TR 312662
	F7	–	Manston	TR 342683

Coding sequence integral with Ramsgate/Richborough.

Marham	B	–	–	TF 714098
Martlesham	H9	–	Martlesham	TM 254481

| Martlesham *cont.* | H10 | – | Brightwell | TM 251427 |

Coding sequence integral with Harwich and Martlesham.

Mersey	A	H4	Litherland	SJ 351990
	B	H5	Walton Hall Park	SJ 369951
	C	–	Lower Breck Park	SJ 373928
	C	H2	Fort Crosby	SD 305024
	D	–	Five Ways	SJ 375902
	D	H9	Childwall	SJ 418895
	E	H6	Tramway Road	SJ 372869
	F	H7	Deysbrook	SJ 407929
	FF	H12	Prescot	SJ 448921
	G	H36	New Ferry/Shore Fields	SJ 342855
	G	H29	Hoylake	SJ 243891
	GG	H28	Thurstaston	SJ 238833
	H	H32	Oxton	SJ 298872
	I	H1	Formby	SD 292046
	J	H31	Bidston	SJ 283906
	K	H33	Red Noses	SJ 299941
	L	H11	Speke	SJ 432827
	LL	H25	Upton Heath	SJ 419701
	M	H3	Seaforth	SJ 324973
	N	H8	Kirkby	SD 407002
	NN	H10	Rainford	SJ 459995
	O	H13	Hale Bank	SJ 463840
	P	H15	Ditton	SJ 503866
	PP	H14	Yew Tree Farm	SJ 469864
	Q	H17	Barrows Green	SJ 542880
	R	H20	Moore	SJ 577853
	S	H19	Red Brow	SJ 570819
	T	H18	Sutton	SJ 548794
	U	H16	Overton	SJ 529777
	V	H27	Alvanley	SJ 501735
	VA	H23	–	SJ 342672
	VC	H22	Lower Kinnerton	SJ 339620
	W	H26	Ince	SJ 451762
	WW	H24	Whitby	SJ 403750
	X	H37	Eastham	SJ 349796
	XX	H35	Raby	SJ 313797
	Y	H34	Storeton	SJ 310840
	YY	H21	Puddington	SJ 334732
	Z	H30	Leasowe	SJ 276924

Methil	M1	–	–	NT 352977
	M3	–	–	NO 389017

Mildenhall	A	–	–	TL 674773
	B	–	–	TL 691779

Milford Haven	P1	–	Dale	SM 804046
	P2	–	St Ishmeal's	SM 847077
	P3	–	Steynton	SM 911072
	P4	–	Rosemarket	SM 967075

Milford Haven	P5	–	Bateman Hill	SM 011049
continued	P6	–	Portclew	SR 011987
	P7	–	Whetstone	SR 977004
	P8	–	Bangeston	SM 871013
	P9	–	West Pennar	SM 931029
Newhaven	E1	–	–	TV 468997
	E2	–	–	TQ 459023
	E3	–	–	TQ 431006
	NH1	–	Earthwork	TV 494978
	NH2	H43	Hoddern Farm	TQ 425025
	NH3	H42	–	TQ 422054
	NH5	H48	–	TV 493985
	NH6	H47	Beacon Road	TQ 480000
	NH7	H44	Friars Bay	TQ 429004
	–	H45	–	TQ 443043

Coding sequences integral with Brighton and Shoreham.

Newport	E	H2	Christchurch	ST 354900
	F	H3	Pye Corner	ST 349849
	G	H5	New House	ST 301824
	H	H7	Great Oak	ST 276891
	N	H4	Nash	ST 331833
	O	H6	Pennsylvania	ST 261852
	P	H1	Lodge Farm	ST 329915

First coding sequence integral with Cardiff and Swansea.

Northallerton	A	–	–	SE 335959
	B	–	–	SE 359916
North Coates	H1	–	–	TA 375012
North Foreland	F1	–	Foreness	TR 379709
	F2	–	–	TR 393707
	F10	–	Sandwich	TR 334561
	F10	–	Sandwich	TR 347584
	FX	–	–	TR 376700
North Weald	A3	–	North Weald	TL 497050
Norwich	H1	–	Mousehold	TM 215131
	H2	–	–	TM 256106
	H3	–	–	TM 206058
Nottingham	A	DNH1	Markeaton	SK 331367
& Derby	B	DNH2	Derby Race Course	SK 363371
	C	DNH3	Spondon	SK 414363
	D	DNH4	Elvaston	SK 414324
	E	DNH5	Boulton	SK 379323
	F	DNH6	Stenson	SK 338315
	H	DNH7	–	SK 398367
	–	DNH8	–	SK 386315
	J	DNH9	Chellaston	SK 368313

Nottingham	K	DNH10	–	SK 359305
& Derby	L	DNH11	–	SK 329333
continued	S	DNH14	Robins Wood	SK 534412
	T	DNH15	Clifton	SK 549353
	U	DNH16	Wilford Cemetery	SK 573355
	V	–	Adbolton	SK 604383
	–	DNH17	Adbolton	SK 605380
	W	–	Colwick Wood	SK 601394
	X	DNH19	Mapperley	SK 584426
	Y	–	Sunrise Hill	SK 565449
	–	DNH20	Sunrise Hill	SK 562447
	Z	DNH21	Bulwell Common	SK 549452
	–	DNH12	–	SK 456435
	–	DNH13	Long Baton	SK 474343
	–	DNH18	–	SK 601298
	–	DNH22	Duffield	SK 344385
	–	DNH23	Bunny Park	SK 600298
	–	DNH25	Smalley	SK 414447
	–	DNH26	–	SK 663409
	–	DNH27	–	SK 301433
	–	DNH28	–	SK 605471
	–	DNH29	Ticknall	SK 339235
Oban	O1	–	Lysmore	NM 862440
	–	O2	–	NM 900421
	O2	O3	Benderloch	NM 874385
Oxford	1	–	Marston	SP 531092
	2	–	Southfield	SP 540057
	3	–	Cumnor Hill	SP 478049
	4	–	Partridge Pit	SP 481132
	5	–	Hinksey Hill	SP 499039
Pembrey	O1	–	Pembrey	SO 419025
	O2	–	Gilian Gwyn	SO 499035
Penzance	1	–	Badgers Cross	SW 486329
	2	–	Bosol Jack	SW 456325
Perranporth	1	–	Wheal Kitty	SW 730509
	2	–	Rose	SW 775544
Perth	P1	–	–	NO 126206
	P3	–	–	NO 094207
Peterborough	H3	–	Whittlesey	TL 223957
	H5	–	Longthorpe	TL 174992
Plymouth	1	–	Rame	SX 436493
	2	–	Down Thomas	SX 506492
	3	–	Torpoint	SX 419557
	4	–	Seaton Barracks	SX 493590
	5	–	Higher Tregantle	SX 405529
	5	–	–	SX 395529
	6	–	Billacombe	SX 525540

Plymouth	7	–	Carkeel	SX 414605
continued	8	–	Staddon Heights	SX 490514
	8	–	–	SX 504516
	9	–	Maker Barracks	SX 438514
	10	–	Home Park	SX 473557
	11	–	Netton	SX 556464
	12	–	Bere Alston	SX 452662
	13	–	St Winnolls	SX 341554
	–	–	Penlee	SX 441489
	–	–	–	SX 435516
	–	–	Picklecombe	SX 449514
	–	–	Rennie	SX 492489
Portland/	1	2	Nothe	SY 685787
Weymouth	2	5	Wyke	SY 658775
	3	3	Verne	SY 696732
	4	–	East Weare	SY 698736
	5	–	Southwell	SY 684697
	–	1	Blackhead	SY 723825
	–	–	–	SY 691729
	–	4	Southwell	SY 680700
	–	–	–	SY 623804
	–	6	Fleet	SY 623804
Portreath	1	–	Northcliffe	SW 645450
	2	–	Porthtowan	SW 704447
Portsmouth	P1	–	Southsea Common	SZ 636989
	P2	–	Sinah	SZ 701997
	P2	–	Sinah	SZ 699994
	P3	–	Gilkicker	SZ 603982
	P4	–	Holbrook	SU 592021
	P5	–	Hayling	SU 722037
	–	–	Binstead	SZ 573915
	P11	–	Moorlands	SU 686070
	P12	–	Nelson	SU 601076
	–	–	New Street	SZ 466940
	P19	–	Greenwich	SU 529033
	P20	–	Prospect Farm	SU 728091
	P21	–	Southwich	SU 640075
	P22	–	–	SU 528081
	P24	–	Highgrove	SU 673022
	P28	–	Binstead	SZ 559923
	P40	–	–	SZ 579995
	P41	–	Fareham	SU 553075
	P42	–	Calshot/Hook Grange	SU 501043
	P43	–	Eastoke Farm	SU 745988

Coding sequence integral with Isle of Wight and Southampton.

Predannack	1	–	Aerodrome	SW 697159
	2	–	Heaver	SW 692188
Preston	H1	–	–	SD 498195

Preston	H1	–	Dunkirk Lane	SD 515223
continued	H2	–	Newton	SD 450309
	H3	–	Halloth Hill	SD 603147
	H4	–	Hoghton	SD 614252
	H5	–	Hesketh Bank	SD 437234
	H6	–	Oswaldtwistle	SD 717279
Ramsgate/	F3	–	Dumpton	TR 390664
Richborough	F4	–	Pegswell	TR 362645
	F5	–	Ozengell	TR 355655
	F8	–	Updown House	TR 362695

Coding sequence integral with Manston.

Reading	BY1	–	Amersham	SU 681693
	BY2	–	Tilehurst	SU 676741
	BY3	–	Tanners Farm	SU 708771
	BY4	–	Sonning	SU 772754
	BY5	–	Toutley	SU 797705
	BY6	–	Crockers Farm	SU 751700

Coding sequence integral with Aldershot, Basingstoke and Guildford.

Redhill	HO1	–	Kenley: Warlingham	TQ 341592
	HO3	–	Biggin Hill: Cudham	TQ 437587
	HO6	–	Redhill	TQ 304461
Rye	R1	–	–	TQ 939200
	R2	–	–	TQ 928238
	R3	–	–	TQ 898193
St Athan	K1	–	Boverton	SS 982681
St Eval	1	–	Kerketh	SW 881732
	2	–	Denzel Downs	SW 901674
	3	–	Deer Park	SW 862654
	4	–	Trenance	SW 857681
	5	–	St Mawgan	SW 882656
Salcombe	–	–	Holset	SX 754380
	–	–	Southdown	SX 706384
Salisbury	1	–	Hurdcott	SU 174331
	2	–	Odstock	SU 151272
	3	–	Nether Hampton	SU 106295
Sandy	H1	–	–	TL 150591
	H2	–	–	TL 167517
	H3	–	–	TL 253525
	H4	–	–	TL 208400
Scapa	M1	–	–	HY 322036
	M2	–	–	HY 324036
	M3	–	–	HY 368060
	M4	–	–	HY 347061

Scapa	M5	–	–	HY 413090
continued	M6	–	–	HY 465083
	M7	–	–	HY 466037
	M8	–	–	HY 461027
	M9	–	–	HY 463028
	M10	–	–	HY 465012
	M11	–	Hatston & Grimsetter	HY 468144
	M12	–	Skeabrae	HY 297215
	M14	–	–	HY 245245
	H1	–	–	ND 337903
	H3	–	–	ND 320899
	H4	–	–	ND 313897
	H5	–	–	ND 305932
	H6	–	–	ND 304961
	H7	–	–	ND 284996
	F1	–	–	ND 350947
	F2	–	–	ND 356941
	R1	–	–	ND 417939
	R2	–	–	ND 414932
	R3	–	–	ND 416915
	B1	–	–	ND 457968
Scunthorpe	E	–	–	SE 867130
	F	H1	–	SE 872168
	–	H2	–	SE 913150
	–	H3	–	SE 942132
	–	H4	–	SE 935071
	–	H5	–	SE 898078
	–	H6	–	SE 868132
	–	H7	–	SE 892208
	–	H8	–	SE 932213
	–	H10	–	SE 944100
	–	H11	–	SE 846087
	–	H12	–	SE 824160
Sheffield	A	H2	Park Gate	SK 431955
	B	H4	–	SK 443923
	C	H5	Brinsworth	SK 419907
	D	H6	Freeton	SK 436873
	E	–	The Manor	SK 378868
	–	H7	–	SK 378868
	F	–	–	SK 375844
	G	H10	–	SK 319846
	I	H11	Stanington	SK 313890
	J	–	–	SK 324936
	K	–	Shirecliff	SK 351897
	–	H12	–	SK 350895
	L	H14	Ecclesfield	SK 352956
	X	H3	Thrybergh	SK 472955
	Y	–	Norton	SK 363815

Sheffield	–	H9	–	SK 360815
continued	Z	–	Stubbin	SK 422975
	–	H1	–	SK 405968
	–	H8	–	SK 376846
	–	H13	–	SK 347931
	–	H15	–	SK 399787
	–	H16	–	*unresolved*
	–	H17	–	SE 464028
	–	H18	–	SE 545077
	–	H19	–	SE 605066
	–	H20	–	SE 657055
	–	H21	–	SK 628996
	–	H22	–	SK 470982
	–	H23	–	SE 524023
	–	H24	–	SK 499977
	–	H25	–	SK 473873
	–	H26	–	SK 443825
	–	H27	–	SK 454765
	–	H28	–	SK 484712
	–	H29	–	SK 418665
	–	H30	–	SK 422719
	–	H31	–	SK 349700
	–	H32	–	SK 321759
	–	H33	–	SK 296832
	–	H34	–	SK 273937
	–	H35	–	SK 321964
Shetlands	L1	–	Lerwick	HU 455401
	L2	–	–	HU 482428
	L3	–	–	HU 502421
	S1	–	Sumburgh	HU 390126
	S2	–	–	HU 390099
	Z1	–	–	HU 442752
	Z2	–	–	HU 389722
Shoreham	NH10	H21	Shoreham	TQ 198046
	NH11	H22	Shoreham: Mill Hill	TQ 214064

Coding sequences integral with Brighton and Newhaven.

Slough	SM1	–	Iver	TQ 042802
	SM2	–	Lintells Bridge	TQ 037755
	SM3	–	Datchet Common	SU 999767
	SM4	–	Windsor Park	SU 983767
	SM5	–	Wexham Street	SU 991822
	SM6	–	Lent Rise	SU 933815
	SM7	–	Dorney Common	SU 940786
	SM7	–	Dorney Common	SU 940792
	SM8	–	Uxbridge	TQ 034833
	SM9	–	West Drayton	TQ 066789
	SM10	–	Windsor Great Park	SU 965746
	SM11	–	Bedfont	TQ 092744

Slough *continued*	SM12	–	Northolt airfield	TQ 106825

Southampton	S7	–	Beaulieu	SU 424044
	S8	–	Marchwood	SU 400101
	S9	–	Hounsdown	SU 358118
	S10	–	Weston	SU 463097
	S15	–	Haxland	SZ 441995
	S16	–	Yew Tree	SU 364063
	S17	–	Stoneham	SU 434185
	S18	–	Winslowe	SU 470155
	S23	–	Nursling	SU 361158
	S26	–	Bishopstoke	SU 474201
	–	–	Bishopstoke	SU 463186
	–	–	Brownwich	SU 522036
	W1	–	–	SU 444282
	W2	–	–	SU 467333
	W3	–	–	SU 522298
	W5	–	–	SU 520265

Coding sequence integral with Isle of Wight and Portsmouth.

Swansea	Q	–	Briton Ferry	SS 712920
	R	–	Port Tenant	SS 685928
	S	–	Mumbles	SS 627873
	T	–	Sketty	SS 622920
	U	–	Morriston	SS 680977
	V	–	Neath	SS 748976
	–	N1	Morriston	SS 695984
	–	N2	Neath	SS 745975
	–	N3	Jersey Marine	SS 712934
	–	N4	Raven Hill	SS 643950
	–	N6	Sketty	SS 625916
	–	N7	Briton Ferry	SS 754927
	–	N8	Margam Park	SS 791961
	–	N9	Bryn	SS 801918
	–	N10	Morfa Mawr	SS 779843
	–	N25	–	SS 718933
	–	N26	Sketty	SS 625916

First coding sequence integral with Cardiff and Newport.

Swindon	1	–	Eastrop	SU 218929
	2	–	Shrivenham	SU 235882
	3	–	Farbridge	SU 205844
	4	–	Burderop	SU 169798
	5	–	Whitehill	SU 119838
	6	–	Restrop	SU 083866
	7	–	Calcutt	SU 117929
	8	–	Burytown	SU 161908

Tangmere	CH1	–	Temple Bar	SU 893066

Coding sequence integral with Chichester, Ford and Thorney Island.

Taunton	1	–	Dodhill	ST 218282
	2	–	Wenlade	ST 256241
Tees	A	–	–	NZ 474243
	B	–	–	NZ 505231
	C	–	–	NZ 525200
	D	–	–	NZ 516176
	D	–	–	NZ 501169
	E	–	–	NZ 448156
	F	–	–	NZ 419179
	G	–	–	NZ 431222
	H	–	–	NZ 469202
	J	–	–	NZ 501262
	J	–	–	NZ 509265
	K	–	–	NZ 537225
	K	–	–	NZ 546228
	M	–	–	NZ 563223
	N	–	–	NZ 604194
	O	–	–	NZ 622235
	P	–	–	NZ 483307
	Q	–	–	NZ 545121
	R	–	–	NZ 494344
Thames & Medway	TN1	–	Thorpe Bay	TQ 919853
	TN2	–	Butlers Farm	TQ 898889
	TN3	–	Hawkwell	TQ 852947
	TN4	–	Rayleigh	TQ 785922
	TN5	–	Belfair Farm	TQ 832872
	TN6	–	North Benfleet	TQ 731899
	TN7	–	Furtherwick	TQ 790835
	TN8	–	Northwick	TQ 755840
	TN9	–	Hadleigh	TQ 800864
	TN10	–	Vange	TQ 719866
	TN11	–	Abbotts Hall	TQ 691827
	TN12	–	Laindon	TQ 661857
	TN13	–	Buckland	TQ 679771
	TN14	–	Orsett	TQ 643828
	TN14	–	Orsett	TQ 637828
	TN15	–	Chadwell	TQ 643796
	TN16	–	Buckles Farm	TQ 599819
	TN17	–	North Ockenden	TQ 599856
	TN18	–	Aveley	TQ 577796
	TN19	–	Ayletts	TQ 550828
	TN20	–	Dagenham	TQ 523848
	TN21	–	Crouchmans	TQ 940869
	TN22	–	Jotmans Hall	TQ 762878
	TN23	–	Belmont Castle	TQ 608796
	TN24	–	Wennington	TQ 542809
	TS1	–	Scrapsgate	TQ 943736
	TS2	–	Iwade	TQ 900690
	TS3	–	Wetham Green	TQ 845684
	TS4	–	Rainham	TQ 812651
	TS5	–	Twydall	TQ 795678

Thames &	TS6	–	Gibraltar Farm	TQ 782631
Medway	TS7	–	Fort Borstal	TQ 736656
continued	TS7	–	Fort Borstal	TQ 733664
	TS8	–	Tower Hill	TQ 754702
	TS9	–	Oak St	TQ 726711
	TS10	–	Fenn Street	TQ 802756
	TS11	–	Grain	TQ 893754
	TS12	–	All Hallows	TQ 849783
	TS12	–	All Hallows	TQ 843780
	TS13	–	Cooling	TQ 765762
	TS13	–	–	TQ 696561
	TS14	–	Lower Hope	TQ 720779
	TS15	–	Cobham	TQ 676683
	TS16	–	Denton	TQ 663740
	TS17	–	Northumberland Bottom	TQ 638711
	TS18	–	Green Street Green	TQ 583708
	TS18	–	Green Street Green	TQ 591708
	TS19	–	Sutton at Hone	TQ 558686
	TS20	–	Littlebrook Farm	TQ 572746
	TS20	–	–	TQ 562733
	TS21	–	Bell Farm	TQ 973727
	TS22	–	Whitehall Farm	TQ 882772
	TS23	–	Decoy Farm	TQ 792772
	TS24	–	Burham	TQ 734625
	TS24	–	Burham	TQ 721616
	TS25	–	–	TQ 765762
	TS26	–	–	TQ 720779

Thorney Island	CH5	–	Thorney Island: Chidham	SU 793035

Coding sequence integral with Ford, Chichester and Tangmere.

Topcliffe	H1	–	–	SE 399773

Truro	1	–	Polwhele	SW 834470
	2	–	Porthkea	SW 831418

Tunbridge Wells	TW1	–	Windmill Farm	TQ 601376
	TW2	–	Skeldhurst	TQ 548412

Tyne	A	–	–	NZ 360703
	B	–	–	NZ 381658
	C	–	–	NZ 368637
	D	–	–	NZ 314620
	E	–	–	NZ 277610
	F	–	–	NZ 233609
	G	–	–	NZ 202609
	H	–	–	NZ 208662
	J	–	–	NZ 246690
	K	–	–	NZ 288692
	K	–	–	NZ 294692
	L	–	–	NZ 320678
	M	–	–	NZ 305667
	N	–	–	NZ 291651

Tyne	O	–	–	NZ 394613
continued	P	–	–	NZ 240571
	Q	–	–	NZ 405540
	R	–	–	NZ 367550
	R	–	–	NZ 357555
	S	–	–	NZ 402637
	T	–	–	NZ 331724
	T	–	–	NZ 343748
	U	–	–	NZ 345710
	V	–	–	NZ 375672
	W	–	–	NZ 352591
	X	–	–	NZ 260549
	Y	–	–	NZ 186666
	MP	–	–	NZ 366679
Wattisham	A	–	–	TM 030522
	B	–	–	TM 038503
Watton	–	H1	–	TF 946006
	B	H2	–	TF 929002
Weston-super-Mare	1	–	Uphill	ST 328592
	1	–	Uphill	ST 315594
	2	–	Worle Hill	ST 348633
	3	–	Woolvers	ST 382608
	4	–	Hutton	ST 351578
Wick	W1	–	Noss Farm	ND 374543
	W2	–	South Head	ND 373497
Winchester	W1	–	Pitt	SU 449283
	W2	–	Down Farm	SU 467335
	W3	–	Magdalen Hill	SU 513291
Wittering	H1	–	–	TF 085030
Yarmouth	YH1	–	West Caistor	TG 505114
	YH2	–	–	TG 525025
	YH3	–	Gorleston	TG 517046
	YH4	–	Race Course	TG 527101
	YH4	–	–	TG 487108
	YH5	–	–	TG 479048
Yeovil	1	–	Barwick	ST 552145
	2	–	Golf Course	ST 531171
York	H1	–	–	SE 563526
	H2	–	–	SE 640528
	H3	–	–	SE 594495
	H4	–	–	SE 601544

Photographic credits

Plates 3, 10, 11 and 12 were kindly supplied by Mr D S Holmes and 30 by Roger Thomas, while the remaining plates derived from the collections of the Imperial War Museum and the National Monuments Record. Reference numbers for the IWM and NMR images are given below (against their plate numbers) among which plates 4, 13 and 25 derive from English Heritage (NMR) RAF Photography. To all four suppliers the publisher and author extend thanks for permission to reproduce images in their copyright.

1	IWM	Q42080
2	IWM	Q52932
4	NMR	106G/UK/1356 FR: 5049
5	IWM	H1259
6	IWM	H28440
7	IWM	H32877
8	IWM	H1395
9	IWM	H1386
13	NMR	CPE/UK/1786 FR: 5131
14	IWM	H35909
15	IWM	H32336
16	IWM	H37518
17	IWM	H18388
18	IWM	H18330
19	IWM	H32337
20	IWM	H1263
21	IWM	H25409
22	IWM	H32361
23	IWM	H32321
24	IWM	H34547
25	NMR	106G/UK/1944 FR: 6109
26	IWM	H40814
27	NMR	12612/12 TA 1630/1
28	NMR	15035/50 TQ 5377/3
29	NMR	15578/20 TQ 7366/11

Sources
and bibliography

References to primary sources are given in full among the Notes on pages 476–504, while secondary sources are cited there using the 'Harvard' (author-date-page) system. The vast majority of primary sources used are held by the Public Record Office at Kew, whose standard group, class/piece referencing system has been followed, with supplementary matter added to identify the item concerned with some precision. This being so, the only further explanation required to enable use of the notes is a key to the group and class numbers which appear at the start of each reference. These are given below, together with a bibliography of published material.

ADM 1	Admiralty and Secretariat Papers
ADM 116	Admiralty Cases
ADM 199	Admiralty War History Cases and Papers
ADM 267	Admiralty: Department of the Director of Naval Construction: Damage Reports and Files
AIR 1	Air Historical Branch Records, Series 1
AIR 2	Air Ministry Registered Files
AIR 8	Chief of the Air Staff Papers
AIR 10	Air Ministry Publications
AIR 14	Bomber Command Files
AIR 16	Fighter Command Files
AIR 20	Air Ministry Unregistered Files
AIR 24	Operations Record Books: RAF Commands
AIR 28	Operations Record Books: RAF Stations
AIR 49	Air Ministry: Reports for Official History of RAF

Medical Services, WWII

AVIA 22	Ministry of Supply Registered Files
CAB 4	Committee of Imperial Defence: Miscellaneous Memoranda (B Series)
CAB 12	Committee of Imperial Defence: Home Defence Committee Minutes
CAB 13	Committee of Imperial Defence: Home Defence Committee Memoranda
CAB 16	Committee of Imperial Defence: Ad-Hoc Sub-Committees: Minutes, Memoranda and Reports
CAB 21	Cabinet Office and Predecessors: Registered Files
CAB 44	Committee of Imperial Defence, Historical Branch and Cabinet Office, Historical Section: War Histories: Draft Chapters and Narratives, Military
CAB 64	Minister for the Co-ordination of Defence: Registered Files (CD Series)
CAB 70	War Cabinet and Cabinet: Defence Committee (Supply): Minutes and Papers (DC(S) and SAA Series)
CAB 81	War Cabinet Chiefs of Staff Committees and Sub-Committees: Minutes and Papers
CAB 82	War Cabinet: Deputy Chiefs of Staff Committee and Sub-Committees Minutes and Papers (DCOS Series)
CAB 106	War Cabinet and Cabinet Office: Historical Section: Archivist and Librarian Files: (AL Series)
DSIR 4	Department of Scientific and Industrial Research: Building Research Station: Correspondence and Papers
HLG 71	Ministry of Town and Country Planning and predecessors and successors: Planning Policy and Statutory Planning Functions, Registered Files
HO 192	Ministry of Home Security: Research and Experiments Department, Registered Papers
HO 196	Ministry of Home Security: Research and Experiments Department, Notes
HO 211	Home Office: Air Raid Precautions Department, Committee on Structural Precautions against Air Attack: Minutes and Papers
INF 1	Ministry of Information Files
PREM 1	Prime Minister's Office, Correspondence and

	Papers, 1916–1940
WO 32	War Office Registered Files (General Series)
WO 33	War Office Memoranda and Papers (O and A Series)
WO 95	War Diaries (1914–18): Home Forces
WO 106	War Office Directorate of Military Operations and Intelligence Correspondence and Papers
WO 163	War Office and Ministry of Defence and predecessors: War Office Council, later War Office Consultative Council, Army Council, Army Board and their various committees: Minutes and Papers
WO 165	War Diaries (1939–45): War Office Directorates
WO 166	War Diaries (1939–45): Home Forces
WO 199	Military Headquarters Papers (1939–45): Home Forces
WO 277	War Office: Department of the Permanent Under Secretary of State, C3 Branch: Historical Monographs
WO 287	War Office: Confidential Printed Papers (B Papers)

Bibliography

Addison, P & Crang, J A (eds), 2000 *The Burning Blue: a new history of the Battle of Britain*. London: Pimlico

Anderton, M, 1999. Twentieth Century Military Recording Project: Anti-aircraft sites. English Heritage (Aerial Survey) unpublished report

Ashmore, E B, 1927. Anti-aircraft defence, *Journal of the Royal United Services Institute*, **62**, 1–15

Ashmore, E B, 1929. *Air Defence*. London: Longmans

Baden-Powell, B, 1910. How airships are likely to affect war, *Journal of the Royal United Services Institute*, **54**, 555–82

Baxter, J, 1946. *Scientists against Time*. Boston.

Bartlett, F C, 1927. *Psychology and the Soldier*. Cambridge: Cambridge University Press

Beevor, A, 1999. *Stalingrad*. Harmondsworth: Penguin

Belcher, H T, 1913. A method of attacking aircraft with shrapnel fire, *Journal of the Royal Artillery*, **39(12)**, 499–505

Blackett, P M S, 1962. *Studies of War: nuclear and conventional.* London: Oliver & Boyd

Boog, H, 2000. The Luftwaffe's assault, in Addison & Crang (eds), 39–54

Brendon, P, 2000. *The Dark Valley: a panorama of the 1930s.* London: Cape

Brewer Kerr, D, 1990. *The Girls Behind the Guns. With the ATS in World War II.* London: Robert Hale

Bungay, S, 2000. *The Most Dangerous Enemy: a history of the Battle of Britain.* London: Aurum Press

Burke, C T, 1911. Aeroplanes of to-day and their use in war, *Journal of the Royal United Services Institute*, **55**, 622–32

Calder, A, 1992. *The People's War. Britain 1939–1945.* London: Pimlico

Campbell, D, 1993. Women in combat: the World War II experience in the United States, Great Britain, Germany and the Soviet Union, *Journal of Military History*, **57**, 301–23

Campbell, J, 1994. *Edward Heath: a biography.* London: Pimlico

Capper, J E, 1908. Dirigible balloons, *Royal Engineers Journal*, **7(5)**, 278–90

Capper, J E, 1910. The military aspect of dirigible balloons and aeroplanes, *Journal of the Royal Artillery*, **36(10)**, 433–56

Castle, H G, 1982. *Fire over England: the German air raids of World War I.* London: Secker & Warburg

Ceadel, M, 1980. *Pacifism in Britain, 1914–1945: the defining of a faith.* Oxford: OUP

Chamberlain, P & Gander, T, 1975 *Anti-Aircraft Guns.* London: MacDonald & Jane's

Churchill, W S, 1949. *The Second World War, Vol II: Their Finest Hour.* London: Cassell

Cock, H C L, 1915. 'Duncan' Commended Essay, 1914: to consider the best methods of attack and defence against hostile aircraft by artillery in the field, and to suggest changes in matériel and tactics necessitated by the advent of flying machines, *Journal of the Royal Artillery*, **41(7)**, 433–41

Cole, C & Cheesman, E F, 1984 *The Air Defence of Britain 1914–1918.* London: Putnam

Collier, B, 1957. *The Defence of the United Kingdom.* London: HMSO

Collyer, D, 1982. *Kent's Listening Ears: Britain's first early-warning system.* Aeromilitaria Special

Curtois, J R W, 1940. Infant Archie in France (1914–1918), *Journal of the Royal Artillery*, **67(1)**, 34–53

Dady, M, 1986. *A Woman's War: life in the ATS.* Lewes: The Book Guild

Darvill, T C, Saunders, A D & Startin, D W, 1987 A question of national importance: . approaches to the evaluation of ancient monuments for the Monuments Protection Programme in England, *Antiquity*, **61**, 393–408

DeGroot, G J, 1997A. Whose finger on the trigger? Mixed anti-aircraft batteries and the female combat taboo, *War in History*, **4(4)**, 434–53

DeGroot, G J, 1997B. 'I love the scent of cordite in your hair': gender dynamics in mixed anti-aircraft batteries during the Second World War, *History*, **82**, 73–92

Dobinson, C S, 1996A. Twentieth Century Fortifications in England, Vol I: Anti-aircraft Artillery. Duplicated report (5 parts)

Dobinson, C S, 1996B. Twentieth Century Fortifications in England, Vol IV: Operation *Diver*. Duplicated report

Dobinson, C S, 1998. Twentieth century fortifications in England: the MPP approach, in English Heritage, 2–6

Dobinson, C S, 2000. *Fields of Deception. Britain's bombing decoys of World War II.* London: Methuen

Dobinson, C S, Lake, J & Schofield, A J, 1997 Monuments of war: defining England's 20th century defence heritage, *Antiquity*, **71**, 288–99.

English Heritage, 1998. *Monuments of War. The evaluation, recording and management of twentieth-century military sites.* London: English Heritage

English Heritage, 2000. *MPP 2000: a review of the Monuments Protection Programme, 1986–2000.* London: English Heritage'

Ferris, J, 1987. The theory of a 'French Air Menace', Anglo-French relations and the British home air force programmes of 1921–25, *Journal of Strategic Studies*, **10(1)**, 62–83

Ferris, J, 1999. Fighter defence before Fighter Command: the rise of strategic air defence in Great Britain, 1917–1934, *Journal of Military History*, **63**, 845–84

Forrester, R D, 1945. Permanent gun sites in mining districts,

Royal Engineers Journal, **64**, 103–9

Francis, P, 1989. Airfield building types No 13 – hutting 1935–1944, *Airfield Review,* **10 (2)**, 17–26

Francis, P, 1996. *British Military Airfield Architecture.* Yeovil: Patrick Stephens

Francis, P, 1999. A survey of WW2 airfield defences in England. Unpublished report

Gollin, A, 1984. *No Longer an Island. Britain and the Wright Brothers, 1902–1909.* London: Heinemann

Hall, H H, 1981. British air defence and Anglo-French relations, 1921–24, *Journal of Strategic Studies,* **4(3)**, 271–84

Hardy, N W (ed), [1947]. *Eastbourne 1939–1945.* Eastbourne: Strange

Hart, L, 1939. *The Defence of Britain.* London: Faber & Faber

Hawkins, H T, 1910. The attack of aeroplanes and dirigibles, *Journal of the Royal Artillery,* **37(6)**, 252–7

Hawkins, H T, 1913. Defence of fortified harbours against dirigibles and aeroplanes, *Journal of the Royal Artillery,* **40(3)**, 126–9

Hinsley, F H, 1979. *British Intelligence in the Second World War. Its influence on strategy and operations,* Vol 1. London: HMSO

Hinsley, F H, with Thomas, E E, Ransom, C F G & Knight, R C, 1984 *British Intelligence in . the Second World War: its influence on strategy and operations,* Vol 3, Part I. London: HMSO

Hogg, I V, 1978. *Anti-Aircraft: a history of air defence.* London: Macdonald & Jane's

Hopthrow, H E, 1988. The Romney hut, *Royal Engineers Journal,* **102**, 290–1

Hornby, A H, 1946. The future of anti-aircraft, *Journal of the Royal Artillery,* **73(4)**, 289–92

Howard, M, 1990. *British Intelligence in the Second World War,* Vol 5. *Strategic Deception.* London: HMSO

Hughes, B P (ed), 1992. *History of the Royal Regiment of Artillery: between the wars, 1919–39.* London: Brasseys

Hyde, H M, 1976. *British Air Policy Between the Wars, 1918–1939.* London: Heinemann

Ismay, H, 1960. *The Memoirs of Lord Ismay.* London: Heinemann

Jackson, L, 1914. Defence of localities against aerial attack, *Journal of the Royal United Services Institute,* **58**, 701–26

James, T C G, 2000. *The Battle of Britain.* London: Frank Cass

Jeffrey, A, 1992. *This Present Emergency. Edinburgh, the River Forth and South-East Scotland and the Second World War*. Edinburgh: Mainstream

Jones, H A, 1928. *The War in the Air. Being the story of the part played in the Great War by the Royal Air Force*, Vol 2. Facsimile edition, London: Hamish Hamilton, 1969

Jones, H A, 1931. *The War in the Air. Being the story of the part played in the Great War by the Royal Air Force*, Vol 3. Facsimile edition, London: IWM and Battery Press, 1998

Jones, H A, 1934. *The War in the Air. Being the story of the part played in the Great War by the Royal Air Force*, Vol 4. Facsimile edition, London: IWM and Battery Press, 1998

Jones, H A, 1935. *The War in the Air. Being the story of the part played in the Great War by the Royal Air Force*, Vol 5. Facsimile edition, London: IWM and Battery Press, 1998

Jones, H A, 1937. *The War in the Air. Being the story of the part played in the Great War by the Royal Air Force*, Vol 6. Facsimile edition, London: IWM and Battery Press, 1998

Kemp, N, 1956. *The Devices of War*. London: Laurie

Longmate, N, 1979. *Air Raid. The bombing of Coventry, 1940*. London: Arrow

May, E R (ed), 1984. *Knowing One's Enemies. Intelligence assessment before the two world wars*. Princeton: Princeton University Press

Meilinger, P S, 1996. Trenchard and 'morale bombing': the evolution of Royal Air Force doctrine before World War II, *Journal of Military History*, **60**, 243–70

Meilinger, P, 1999. Clipping the bomber's wings: the Geneva Disarmament Conference and the Royal Air Force, 1932–1934, *War in History*, **6(3)**, 306–30

Middlebrook, M, 1988. *The Peenemünde Raid: 17/18 August 1943*. London: Penguin

Middlebrook, M & Everitt, C, 1990 *The Bomber Command War Diaries: an operational . reference book, 1939–1945*. London: Penguin

MoI, 1943. *Roof over Britain. The official story of the AA defences, 1939–1942*. London: HMSO

Morgan, F C, 1913. On means of defence against aeroplanes and dirigibles, *Journal of the Royal Artillery*, **40(1)**, 45–8

Napier, A F S, 1946. British rockets in the world war, *Journal of the*

Royal Artillery, **73(1)**, 11–20

Nash, F, 1998. World War Two heavy anti-aircraft gun sites in Essex. Unpublished report, Essex County Council (Planning)

[Naylor, J W], 1942. 'Mixed' batteries, *Journal of the Royal Artillery*, **69(3)**, 199–206

Naylor, J W, 1944. A Polish HAA battery in AA Command, *Journal of the Royal Artillery*, **71(4)**, 261–8

Overy, R, 1998. Strategic intelligence and the outbreak of the Second World War, *War in History*, **5(4)**, 451–80

Pargiter, R B, 1945. The future of anti-aircraft, *Journal of the Royal Artillery*, **77(4)**, 273–8

Paris, M, 1992. *Winged Warfare. The literature and theory of aerial warfare in Britain, 1859–1917*. Manchester University Press

Phillips, H de T, 1915. Attack and defence against hostile aircraft, *Journal of the Royal Artillery*, **41(2)**, 733–45

Philips, T R, 1940. Defence against night bombardment: the problems of yesterday and to-day, *Army Quarterly*, **41**, 84–96

Pile, F, 1949. *Ack-Ack. Britain's defences against air attack during the Second World War.* London: Harrap

Pinsent, M, 1983. The defences of the Bristol Channel in the last two centuries, *Fort*, **11**, 63–76

Postan, M M, Hay, D & Scott, J D, 1964 *Design and Development of Weapons. Studies in government and industrial organisation.* History of the Second World War, United Kingdom Civil Series. London: HMSO and Longmans

Pye, A, & Woodward, F, 1996 *The Historic Defences of Plymouth.* Truro: Cornwall County . Council

Ray, J, 1996. *The Night Blitz, 1940–1941.* London: Cassell

Rawlinson, A, 1923. *The Air Defence of London 1915–1918.* London: Andrew Melrose

Redfern, N, 1998. Twentieth Century Fortifications in the United Kingdom. Unpublished report.

Reid, W F, 1911. The use of explosives in aerial warfare, with some remarks on methods of defence, *Journal of the Royal United Services Institute*, **55**, 735–49

Reynolds, R C, 1946. The future of anti-aircraft, *Journal of the Royal Artillery*, **73(2)**, 97–102

Robertson, F A de V, 1932. Air Exercises, 1932, *Journal of the Royal United Services Institute*, **77**, 808–14

Robinson, V, 1996. *Sisters in Arms: how female gunners defended*

Britain against the Luftwaffe. London: Harper Collins

Roper, M, 1998. *The Records of the War Office and Related Departments.* PRO Handbooks **29**, London: PRO Publications

Roskill, S W, 1969. *Documents Relating to the Naval Air Service, Vol I, 1908-1918. Publications of the Navy Records Society,* **113**. London: Navy Records Society

Routledge, N W, 1992. Anti-aircraft artillery between the wars, in Hughes (ed), 216–30

Routledge, N W, 1994. *History of the Royal Regiment of Artillery: anti-aircraft artillery.* London: Brasseys

Sargeaunt, H G, 1910. The attack of dirigible balloons and aeroplanes, *Journal of the Royal Artillery,* **36(2)**, 493–6

Sayer, A P, 1950. *Army Radar.* London: War Office [also WO 277/3]

Scarth, R N, 1995. *Mirrors by the Sea. An account of the Hythe sound mirror system.* Hythe: Hythe Civic Society

Scarth, R N, 1999. *Echoes from the Sky. A story of acoustic defence.* Hythe: Hythe Civic Society

Shilstone, W R, 1940. Anti-aircraft 'lay-outs' for the defence of vulnerable areas, *Journal of the Royal Artillery,* **66(2)**, 184–204

Smith, M, 1984. *British Air Strategy between the Wars.* Oxford: OUP

Stafford, D, 1997. *Churchill and Secret Service.* London: John Murray

Stewart, O, 1926. Air manoeuvres, *Army Quarterly,* **13**, 42–49

Stewart, O, 1927. The Air Exercises, *Army Quarterly,* **15**, 115–23

Stewart, O, 1929. The Air Exercises, *Army Quarterly,* **17**, 266–74

Stewart, O, 1930. The Air Exercises 1930: balance of air forces, *Army Quarterly,* **21**, 87–93

Stewart, O, 1931. The Royal Air Force Exercises of 1931, *Army Quarterly,* **23**, 109–15

Sturtivant, R, Hamlin, J & Halley, J J, 1997 *Royal Air Force Flying Training and Support Units.* Tonbridge: Air-Britain

Stone, A K, 1945. The evolution of 'AA', *Journal of the Royal Artillery,* **77(2)**, 96–106

Stone, F G, 1909. Defence of harbours against naval airships, *Journal of the Royal United Services Institute,* **53**, 559–77

Stone, F G, 1910. Dirigible balloons and special ordnance for attacking them; exhibited at the Frankfurt International Exhibition, *Journal of the Royal Artillery,* **36(9)**, 393–416

Taylor, E, 1988. *Women who went to War, 1938–46.* London: Robert Hale

Thetford, O, 1995. *Aircraft of the Royal Air Force since 1918.* London:Putnam

Turner, C C, 1928. The aerial defence of cities: some lessons from the Air Exercises, 1928, *Journal of the Royal United Services Institute,* **73**, 697–8

Turner, C C, 1931. British and foreign air exercises of 1931, *Journal of the Royal United Services Institute,* **76**, 731–9

'Two ATS AA officers', 1943. Life in a mixed anti-aircraft battery, *Army Quarterly,* **47**, 80–83

War Office, 1934. *Military Engineering (vol VII). Accommodation and installations.* London: HMSO

Watt, D C, 1984. British intelligence and the coming of the Second World War in Europe, in May (ed), 237–70

Wheeler, R E M, 1958. *Still Digging.* London: Pan

White, C M, 1986. *The Gotha Summer: the German daytime raids on England, May to August 1917.* London: Hale

Williams, W T S, 1927. Air Exercises, 1927, *Journal of the Royal United Services Institute,* **72**, 741

Winton, H R, 1985. The evolution of British mechanised and armoured doctrine 1919–1938, *Journal of the Royal United Services Institute,* **130**, 57–65

Wood, D, 1992. *Attack Warning Red. The Royal Observer Corps and the Defence of Britain, 1925 to 1992.* Portsmouth: Carmichael & Sweet

Yool, W M, 1930. Air Exercises 1930, *Journal of the Royal United Services Institute,* **75**, 755

Young, D, 1943. On behalf of the 3.7, *Journal of the Royal Artillery,* **70(1)**, 8–9

Young, G M, 1952. *Stanley Baldwin.* London: Hart-Davis

Young, N, 1988. British home air defence planning in the 1920s, *Journal of Strategic Studies,* **11**, 492–508

Young, N, 1990. Foundations of victory: the development of Britain's air defences, 1934–1940, *Journal of the Royal United Services Institute,* **135** (Autumn 1990), 62–8

Ziegler, P, 1998. *London at War, 1939–1945.* London: Arrow

Index

Page numbers in italics refer to illustrations and/or their captions.

ARP 140
Arras 192
Ashford 353
Ashmore, Major-General E B:
    and AA personnel 78
    Air Defence 59
    air defence's future 55, 59-62
    air doctrine 60-61, 100, 119
    balloon aprons 46, 61
    in Home Guard 203
    and LADA 37, 39
    on Romer Committee 70
    and TA units 70
    weapon standards 52-53
Athenia 160
Atlee, Clement 439
ATS women: on gunsites 279, 309, 311-
        17, 331, 473
Austria 128
auto-cannon 10, 28, 30
Avonmouth 295
Ayletts 381

Baedeker raids 352, 353-55, 360
Baldwin, Stanley 59, 72, 80, 81, 87, 108,
        118
Balfour, Arthur (First Earl of Balfour)
        28, 66-67
balloon barrages 220
'balloon guns' 8, 10
balloons:
    battlefield use 3
    German lead in 12
    navigable *see* airships
    reconnaissance 8
Banks, Second Lieutenant C C 44
Barking Park 126, 225
Barr and Stroud heightfinder 73
Barrow 15, 25, 31, 41:
    Second World War 172, 189, 427
Barry 195
Bartholomew, Colonel W H 68
Bartlett, Professor F C 307
Barton's Point 47
Basingstoke 353
Bath 353, 354, 427, 428
Battersea 20
Bawdsey 115, 184, 196, 200, 286, 351
Bayliss, Dr L E 254-55
Beachy Head 232, 376
Bedford, L H 251, 253, 258
Belfast 151, 220, 360:
    sea forts 348
Belfield, Major-General H E 3
Belgium 24, 38, 85, 87, 102, 191, 457

Bell Farm 388
Bentley Priory 300
Bethnal Green 429
Betteshanger Colliery 353
Bexhill 355, 357, 375
Bexhill-on-Sea 352
Bf 109s 214, 224, 225, 231
Bf 110s 216, 231
Big Ben 448
Biggin Hill 63, 70, 73, 198, 199, 213
Billericay 33
billeting 144, 328
Billingham ICI factory 104, 197
Bircham Newton 198
Birkenhead, Lord 72
Birmingham:
    First World War 25
    interwar 85, 88, 98, 127
    post-war survival 470
    Second World War 158, 196, 226, 227,
        229, 267, 269, 271, 358
Blackburn, Dr 307-8
Blackett, Professor P M S 252-53, 254,
        255, 258
Blériot, Louis 4
Blitz:
    AA guns 234:
        concentration of 261, 275
        failures 238-39, 240, 260
    balloon barrage 236, 239
    barrage technique 243-44, 245, 248
    beginnings of 199
    campaign 233-66
    civil population 236-37, 240
    concentrating guns 201
    defence command 234
    end of 339
    equipment short-comings 265
    fires 237, 247
    guns, numbers of 239
    HAA gun sites 234, 235-36
    inaugural raid 231
    morale 240-43, 311
    night fighting 248, 249
    reinforcements 244-45
    trekking 242, 267
    VPs 236
    see also Little Blitz
blockade tactics 291
Bloodhound missile 464, 465
Blyth 161:
    post-war survival 470
Bodyline 419
Bofors guns:
    airfields 198, 199, 213-14, 273, 274